THE PUNJAB CHIEFS

HISTORICAL

AND

BIOGRAPHICAL NOTICES

THE PUNJAB CHIEFS

HISTORICAL

AND

BIOGRAPHICAL NOTICES

OF THE

PRINCIPAL FAMILIES

IN THE TERRITORIES

UNDER THE PUNJAB GOVERNMENT

LEPEL H. GRIFFIN

GYAN

Published by

Gyan Publishing House
5, Ansari Road
Daryaganj, New Delhi-110002
Phone: 011-47034999, 9811692060
E-mail: books@gyanbooks.com

Distribution Network
gyanbooks.com
India, USA, Canada, UK, Australia

ISBN: 978-93-7097-101-1 (HB)

First Published, 1865

2nd Impression 2025

Printed at: Gyan Press, Delhi.

THE PUNJAB CHIEFS HISTORICAL AND BIOGRAPHICAL NOTICES

Author: LEPEL H. GRIFFIN

THE PANJAB CHIEFS.

HISTORICAL

AND

BIOGRAPHICAL NOTICES

OF THE

PRINCIPAL FAMILIES

IN THE TERRITORIES

UNDER THE PANJAB GOVERNMENT.

BY

LEPEL H. GRIFFIN,

Bengal Civil Service, Assistant Commissioner, Lahore.

1865.

PREFACE.

THE histories of the Panjab Chiefs have been written by desire of Sir Robert Montgomery, Lieutenant Governor of the Panjab.

The first portion of the work includes all the Chiefs and Sirdars of the plain country of the Panjab proper, from the Beas to the Indus. The second portion, which will be shortly published, treats of the outlying districts and dependencies of the province; the Cis-Sutlej States; the Jalandhar Doab; the Rajput Hill States; the Derajat and Peshawar; Bahawalpur and Kashmir, and the Dehli territory.

The intention of the work has been to give a picture of the Panjab aristocracy as it exists at the present day. No mention has accordingly been made of many families, Hindu and Muhammadan, once powerful and wealthy, which fell before the Sikhs. No mention has been made of many old Sikh families, whose jagirs were seized by Maharaja Ranjit Singh, and whose descendants are now plain husbandmen. A few notices of tribes and families of no present importance, have, for special reasons, been given; but, as a general rule, only the histories of those men have been written who possess, at the present time, rank, wealth, or local influence.

It has not been found practicable to give, in the body of the work, the authorities for every statement advanced; and it may therefore be well to mention here the sources from which the information has been derived.

In the first place each Chief has sent a history of his family, sometimes meagre and fragmentary, sometimes full and connected, in many cases exaggerated and false.

Secondly, the whole records of the Panjab Government from annexation to the present year; the letters of the British Agents at Dehli and Ludiana from 1809 to 1845, and the records of the old Sikh Government, have been largely made use of.

Thirdly, almost all histories, travels and memoirs, relating to the Panjab, in English, Persian and Urdu, have been consulted.

Fourthly, the actors in, and eye-witnesses of the events described have been questioned; a large number of the Chiefs and Sirdars, with their bards and family priests have been examined personally, and from their statements much new and interesting information has been gained.

Among those to whom acknowledgments are due for assistance in the preparation of the work, are Pandit Manphool, Extra Assistant Commissioner, attached to the Secretariat, whose learning and great local knowledge have been invaluable; Syad Hadi Hasain Khan, Extra Assistant Commissioner, Gujrat; and Mulvi Rujjib Ali Khan, Khan Buhadar of Ludianah.

LEPEL H. GRIFFIN.

THE photograph on the opposite page is reduced from the original document signed by the chief Ministers of the Lahore State, on the 16th Maghar 1897, Sambat, (27th November 1840.) It was intended to regulate the succession to the throne, and is interesting as bearing the signatures of the leading men of the day. Raja Dhyan Singh, Raja Gulab Singh, Bhai Ram Singh, Sirdar Attar Singh Sindhanwalia, Sirdar Lehna Singh Majithia, Bhai Gurmukh Singh, Jamadar Khushhal Singh, Sirdar Fatah Singh Man, Sirdar Mangal Singh Sindhu, Sirdar (afterwards Raja) Tej Singh, Sirdar Sham Singh Attariwala, Diwan (afterwards Raja) Dinanath and Ghulam Mohiuddin.

The following is a literal translation.

'At this time we all, with one heart and one tongue, swear 'to abide by the stipulations agreed upon amongst us, viz., 'that Singh Sahib, Sher Singhji, shall remain on his own jagir, 'and that Partab Singhji, son of the Singh Sahib, shall sit for 'eight months in the Council of State. If Singh Sahib Sher 'Singhji shall agree to this, it is well; if not we, taking joint 'action, will compel him to agree. Likewise we will make the 'Bibi Sahib (Rani Chand Kour) consent. What has been 'above arranged will hold good until the birth of a son, or 'otherwise, when we will make other arrangements.'

ERRATA.

Page	Line	For		Read
3	24	1839,	...	1829.
4	6	China Jat,	...	Gil Jat.
6	6	1863,	...	1843.
6	10	Nand Kour,	...	Chand Kour.
8	13	Sindh,	...	Sindhu.
40	16	1864,	...	1844.
42	5	1842,	...	1847.
64	13	search his body,	...	search for his body.
74	24	accounts,	...	account.
82	8	Attar Singh,	...	Utar Singh.
84	3	Dewa Singh,	...	Desa Singh.
178	31	toorder,	...	to order.
213	17	Budh Singh,	...	Sudh Singh.
245	14	threw from,	...	threw him from.
388	3 of the Note.	they best,	...	the best.
410	5 of the Note.	burst,	...	burnt.
536	1	Chattar Singh,	...	Charrat Singh.
536	4	Chattar Singh,	...	Charrat Singh.

Precedence List of the Chiefs and Native Gentlemen of the Punjab and its Dependencies [excepting the Simla Hill States] admitted to the Public Viceregal Durbar held at Lahore on the 18th of October 1864.

Division.	No. of seat of Chief.	No. of dependants.	Names.	Nazr.	Khilat.	Remarks.
A.—1	A		Maharaja Ranbir Singh of Kashmir and Jammu.			
		A. 1	Tikah Partab Singh, heir apparent.			
		A. 2	Raja Moti Singh, cousin of Maharaja.			
B.		A. 3	Diwan Joala Sahai, Prime Minister.			
		4	Wazir Zorawaru Musahib.			
		5	Diwan Nihal Chand Moatmid, confidential agent in attendance on His Honor the Lieutenant Governor.			
		6	Diwan Kirpa Ram, Maharaja's Secretary.			
		7	Wazir Labju, Musahib.			
		8	Sirdar Desa Singh, Musahib.			
		9	Diwan Hemraj, Musahib.			
		10	Mian Anant Singh, ditto.			
		11	Colonel Devi Singh, ditto.			
		12	Hakim Wali Shah, Court Physician.			
		13	Bhagwandas, Maharaja's Vukeel in attendence on His Honor the Lieut. Governor.			
		14	Mian Gulab Singh, relation of Maharaja and Musahib of Raja Moti Singh.			

Division.	No. of seat of Chief.	No. of dependants.	NAMES.	Nazr.	Khilat.	REMARKS.
A.—1. Cis-Sutlej States.	1	...	Maharaja Mohindar Singh of Pattiala.	The presentation of Nazr has been excused for the life of the present Chief.	6 Jewels. 49 Trays. Silver Howdah. Elephant Chhul. 2 Sets Gold Horse Trappings. 1 Karchobi Zinposh. Jhalandar Palki. 2 Horses. 1 Elephant.	Rs. 17,600.
B.		a.	Sirdar Jagdis Singh, Member of Council of Regency.	1 Gold-mohur each, to be touched and remitted.	None.	To be seated behind the Chief.
		b.	Sirdar Rahim Baksh, Ditto.			
		c.	Sirdar Basawa Singh, Ditto.			
		d.	Lala Nihal Chand, "Atalik" or Preceptor to Maharaja.			
		e.	Lala Ramchandar, Preceptor to Maharaja.			
		f.	Diwan Kulwant Rai, Financial Minister.			
		g.	Hakim Abdul Nabi Khan, Mir Munshi.			
		h.	Syad Muhammad Hassan, Judicial Minister.			
		i.	Syad Muhammad Husain, Maharaja's Vakil in attendance on His Honor the Lieutenant Governor			
		j.	Sirdar Atar Singh of Bhadour, Feudatory (Zaildar.)			
		k.	Sirdar Achal Singh, Ditto.			
		l.	Sirdar Ishar Singh, Ditto.			

A.—1.	Ditto.	2	...	Raja Raghbir Singh of Jheend	51 Gold-mohurs = Rs. 765.	3 Jewels. 1 Tass Khilat of 7 pcs. 8 Parchas of Shawls. Sword, Shield, Belt. 1 Silver Horse Trappings. 1 Zinposh. Elephant Chhul. 1 Horse. 1 Elephant.	Rs. 3,800.
			a.	Heir-apparent.	1 Gold-mohur each, to be touched and remitted.	None.	To be seated behind the Chief.
B.	...	...	b.	Diwan Singh of Badrukhah, "Zaildar."			
			c.	Hira Singh, Ditto.			
			d.	Bakshi Harbilas, Pay Master of Troops.			
				Gohar Singh, Mir Munshi.			
			e.	Diwan Kanh Singh, Diwan.			
			f.	Rattan Singh, Adalati (Judge.)			
			g. h.	Jailal, Vakil in attendance on His Honor the Lieutenant Governor.			
A.—1.	Jalandhar.	3.	...	Raja Randhir Singh of Kapurthalla.	51 Gold-mohurs = Rs. 765.	1 Khilat of 7 pieces. 5 Jewels. 24 Trays. Sword, Shield and Belt. 1 Gun. 1 Jhalandhar Palki. 1 Silver Howdah. 1 Gold Horse Trappings. 1 Silver ditto. 1 Karchobi Zinposh. 1 Saddle Cloth. 1 Karchobi Chhul. 2 Horses. 1 Elephant.	Rs. 7,500.

Division.	No. of seat of Chief.	No. of dependants.	NAMES.	Nazr.	Khilat.	REMARKS.
A.—1. Jallandhar.		a.	Sirdar Bikrama Singh, brother of Raja.	1 Gold-mohur each, to be touched and remitted.	... ...	To be seated behind the Chief.
		b.	Konwar Suchet Singh, ditto.			
B.		c.	Mian Ghulam Jilani, Wazir (Prime Minister.)			
		d.	Diwan Ramjas, Financial Minister.			
		e.	Lala Ram Milawa Mal, Vakil.			
		f.	Jodshi Dharm Chand.			
		g.	Mian Karm Baksh.			
		h.	Lala Kirparam.			
		i.	Chowdri Ali Baksh.			
		j.	Bhai Gurbaksh Singh.			
A.—1. Ditto		4	Raja Bejai Sein of Mandi.	72 Gold-mohurs= Rs. 1,080.	1 Tass Khilat of 7 parchas. 3 Jewels. Sword, Shield, Belt. 1 Gold Horse Trappings. 1 Saddle Cloth. 1 Zinposh. 1 Horse.	Rs. 1,550.
		a.	Mian Bhag Singh, uncle of Raja.	1 Gold-mohur each, to be touched and remitted.	None.	To be seated behind the Chief.
		b.	Mian Rugnath Singh, ditto.			
		c.	Mian Pardhan Singh, brother of Raja.			
		d.	Mian Man Singh, ditto.			

B.		Stands.	e.	Wazir Gosaon, Wazir.	1 Gold-mohur each, to be touched and remitted.	None.	To be seated behind Chief.
			f.	Jamadar Kapura, a military officer.			
			g.	Mian Raghbir Chand, brother-in-law of Rajah.			
			h.	Shain Das, Vakil in attendance on Commissioner.			
A.—1.	Cis-Sutlej States.	5	...	Nawab Sikandar Ali Khan of Maler Kotlah.	21 Gold-mohurs= Rs. 315.	3 Jewels. A Tass Khilat of 7 parchas. A pair of Shawls and one Rumal. Sword, Shield and Belt. Silver Trappings. 1 Saddle Cloth. 1 Horse.	Rs. 1,750.
			a.	Ibrahim Ali Khan, cousin of Nawab.	1 Gold-mohur each, to be touched and remitted.	None.	To be seated behind the Chief.
			b.	Inayat Ali Khan, cousin of Nawab.			
			c.	Muhammad Rustam Ali Khan, relation of ditto.			
			d.	Ghulam Muhammad Khan, do.			
B.			e.	Fatah Jang Khan, Mir Munshi of Nawab.			
			f.	Shaikh Karim Baksh, Wazir of ditto.			
			g.	Barkat Ali Khan, Tehsildar.			
			h.	Munshi Kanheya Lal, guardian of the sons of Dilawar Ali Khan.			

Division.	No. of dependants.	No. of seat of Chief.	NAMES.	Nazr.	Khilat.	REMARKS.
A.—1. Lahore	6	...	Raja Wazir Singh of Faridkot.	11 Gold-mohurs= Rs. 165.	3 Jewels. 11 Pieces of Khilat. 1 Sword, 1 Belt, 1 Gold Trappings. 1 Saddle Cloth. 1 Zinposh. 1 Horse.	Rs. 1,850.
		a.	Tika Bikram Singh, Heir apparent.			
B.		b. c. d. e.	Bakshi Mehtab Singh, Prime Minister. Shahbaz Khan, Moatmid. Sirdar Umla Singh, Moatmid. Munshi Saudagar Mal, ditto.	1 Gold-mohur each. to be touched and remitted.	None.	To be seated behind the Chief.
A.—1. Jallandhar.	7	...	Raja Sri Singh of Chamba, ...	91 Gold-mohurs= Rs. 1,365.	3 Jewels. Shawl Khilat of 11 pieces. 1 Sword, 1 Belt. 1 Silver Trappings. 1 Saddle Cloth. 1 Horse.	Rs. 1,500.
B.		a. b. c.	Mian Bir Bhudar, Musahib. Mian Utar Singh, Mukhtar. Mian Ganda Singh, Moatmid.	1 Gold-mohur each, to be touched and remitted.	None.	To be seated behind the Chief.

A.—1.	Ditto	8	...	Raja Uggar Sen of Suket, ...	72 Gold-mohurs= Rs. 1,080.	3 Jewels. 1 Tass Khilat of 7 parchas. Sword, Shield. 1 Belt. 1 Gold Trappings. 1 Saddle Cloth. 1 Horse.	Rs. 1,300.
B.		Stands	a. b.	Mian Kesho. Janki Das, Vakil.	1 Gold-mohur each, to be touched and remitted.	None.	To be seated behind the Chief.
A.—1.	Cis-Sutlej States	9	...	Lehna Singh of Kalsia, ...	21 Gold-mohurs= Rs. 315.	3 Jewels. A Tass Khilat of 7 pieces. 1 Sword with Belt. 1 Silver Trappings. 1 Zinposh. 1 Horse.	Rs. 1,100.
			a. b.	The Heir apparent. Konwar-Man Singh, Brother of Sirdar.	1 Gold-mohur each, to be touched and remitted.	None.	To be seated behind the Chief.
B.			c. d.	Diwan Nao Nihal Singh, Diwan. Shaikh Mohibulla, Mir Munshi.			
	Delhi.	10	...	Nawab Muhammad Mukhtar Hussain Khan of Patoudi.	21 Gold-mohurs= Rs. 315.	3 Jewels. 7 Pieces of Tass Khilat. Sword, Shield and Belt. 1 Silver Trappings. 1 Saddle Cloth. 1 Broad-cloth Chhul. 1 Elephant. 1 Horse.	Rs. 1,950.
			a. b.	Muhammad Usghur Ali Khan Regent—(Relative.) Imdad Ali Khan, relation of Nawab.			

Division.	No. of seat of Chief.	No. of dependants.	NAMES.	Nazr.	Khilat.	REMARKS.
A.—1. B.	Stands	c. d.	Pandit Kishanlal, Vakil. Munshi Ahmad Ali Munshi.	1 Gold-mohur each, to be touched and remitted.	None.	To be seated behind the Chief.
Hissar	11	...	Aminuddin Ahmad Khan, Nawab of Loharu.	21 Gold mohurs = Rs. 315.	3 Jewels. 7 Pieces Tass Khilat. 1 Sword, Shield and Belt.	Rs. 1,250.
A.—1.		a. b. c.	Mirza Ziya-ud-din Ahmad Khan, brother of Chief. Mirza Ala-ud-din Ahmad Khan, heir-apparent of Chief. Mirza Shahabuddin Ahmad Khan, nephew of ditto.	1 Gold-mohur each, to be touched and remitted.	None.	To be seated behind the Chief.
Ditto	12	..	Muhammad Hassan Ali Khan, Nawab of Dojana.	21 Gold Mohurs = Rs. 315.	3 Jewels. 7 Pieces of Tass Khil. 1 Silver Trappings. 1 Saddle Cloth. 1 Broad Cloth Chhul. 1 Elephant. 1 Horse.	Rs. 1,500.
A.—1.		a b. c. d.	Muhammad Saadat Ali Khan, heir apparent. Muhammad Sher Khan, brother of do. Muhammad Shamsher Khan, do. Abdulla Khan, cousin of chief.	1 Gold Mohur each, to be touched and remitted.	None.	To be seated behind the Chief.

A.—1. Jallandhar.	13	...	Raja Shamsher Singh, of Goleria of Haripur, Zilla Kangra.	72 Gold mohurs= Rs. 1,080.	3 Jewels. 1 Tass Khilat of 7 parchas. 1 Sword, Shield and Belt. 1 Set Gold Trappings. 1 Saddle Cloth. 1 Horse.	Rs. 1,500.
A. Amritsar,...	14	...	Sirdar Shamsher Singh, Sindhauwalia.	Rs. 1,400.	3 Jewels. 7 Pieces of Tass Khilats. 1 Sword, Shield and Belt.	Rs. 1,750.
B. ...			To be accompanied by his nephew, Sirdar Randhir Singh, a minor, who will not receive a separate seat, ...	Rs. 300.	Rs. 375.	
A. 1. Lahore,...	15	...	Raja Harbans Singh, ...	Rs. 1,400 cash.	3 Jewels, Tass Khilat of 7 pieces. 1 Sword, 1 Shield and Belt.	Adopted son of Raja Tej Singh, Rs. 1,750.
A. 1. Delhi, ...	16	...	Mirza Hidayat Ufza, *alias* Ilahi Baksh,	25 Gold mohurs= Rs. 375.	Khilat of Rs. 500.	Of the Ex-Royal Family of Delhi.
A. 1. Amritsar,	18	..	Raja Sahib Dyal of Kishankot, Zilla Gurdaspur.	Rs. 1,200.	3 Jewels. Shawl Khilat in 20 trays. 1 Sword and Belt.	Rs. 1,500.
A. 1. Jallandhar,	19	...	Raja Ram Singh of Siba, ...	Rs. 1,500.	3 Jewels. 1 Tass Khilat of 7 pieces. Sword, Shield and Belt. 1 Gold Trappings. 1 Saddle Cloth. 1 Zinposh. 1 Horse.	Jagirdar Magistrate of Hoshiarpur. Rs. 1,675.

Division.	No. of seat of Chief.	No. of dependants.	NAMES.	Nazr.	Khilat.	REMARKS.
Nos. 1-20 *to*	*receive*	*Khi-*	*lats in Durbar. All others to*	*be given out of Durbar.*		
A. Cis-Sutlej States,	21	...	Shahzadah Shahpur, ...	5 Gold mohurs=Rs. 75	1 Binocu'ar Glass.	Sons of Shah Shuja.
	22	...	Ditto. Nadir, ...	5 Gold mohurs=Rs. 75	1 Gold Pencil Case.	
Cis-Sutlej States, ...	23	...	Sultan Sikandar, ...	7 Go'd mohurs= Rs. 105.	1 Tass Khilat of 7 parchas. 1 Jewel, valued Rs. 670	
Ditto, ...	24	...	Sultan Jalaluddin.	5 Gold mohurs= Rs. 75.	1 Gold Watch & Chain Rs. 520.	
Lahore, ...	27	...	Shahzada Ali Ahmad, ...	Rs. 800.	Rs. 1,000.	Son of Ajab Shah.
Delhi, ...	28	...	Mirza Dilawar Shah, ...	Rs. 315.	Rs. 400.	Of the Ex-Royal Family of Delhi.
Derajat, ...	29	...	Nawab Sarfaraz Khan, Saddozai of Dera Ismail Khan,	Rs. 515.	Rs. 1,500.	
Ditto, ...	30	...	Nawab Foujdar Khan, Allizai, of Dera Ismail Khan,	Rs. 515.	Rs. 1,500.	
Ditto, ...	31	...	Muhammad Akbar Khan, son of Nawab Shahnawaz Khan, Kattekhail, of Tonk, ...	Rs. 515.	Rs. 1,500.	

A. Peshawar,	32	...	Syad Aya uddin of Kunar, ..	Rs. 800.	Rs. 1,600.	Jagirdar Magistrate of Morazai.
Ditto,...	33	...	Khwaja Muhammad Khan, Khatak, of Western Khatak,	Rs. 600.	Rs. 1,600.	
Ditto,...	34	...	Ghulam Hassan Khan, Allizai,	Rs. 500.	Rs. 1,000.	Kabul Envoy.
Ditto,...	35	...	Muhammad Akram Khan, ..	Rs. 500.	Rs. 1,200.	"Rais" of Tanoul (and Amb).
Cis-Sutlej States, ...	36	...	Raja Gurbaksh Singh of Manni Mazra.	81 Gold mohurs= Rs. 1,215.	Rs. 2,000.	
Ditto,..	37	...	Konwar Bhagwan Singh of Manni Mazra.	9 Gold mohurs= Rs. 135.	Rs. 170.	
Jallandhar,	38	...	Raja Rampal of Kotlehr, Zila Hoshiarpur.	Rs. 1,100.	Rs. 1,375.	
Ditto,...	39	...	Raja Jaswant Singh of Nurpur, Zila Kangra.	Rs. 1,100.	Rs. 1,375.	
Lahore,	40	...	Julaluddin Khan, of Mamdot, Zilla Firozpur.	Rs. 1,100.	Rs. 1,375.	Created a Nawab, Dec. 1864.
Jallandhar,	41	...	Guru Jowahir Singh of Kurtarpur.	Rs. 1,100,	Rs. 1,375.	
Ditto,...	42	...	Baba Sanpuran Singh, Bedi, ...	Rs. 1,000.	Rs. 1,250.	A grandson of Baba Sahib Singh, Bedi, of Unah.
Ditto,...	43	...	Baba Khem Singh, Bedi, ...	Rs. 1,000.	Rs. 1,250.	A grandson of Baba Sahib Singh, Bedi, of Unah.
Amritsar,	41	...	Raja Raghbhir Deo, ..	Rs. 400.	Rs. 500.	Ex-Raja of Jammu.

Division.	No. of seat of Chief.	No. of dependants.	Names.	Nazr.	Khilat.	Remarks.
A. Jallandhar,	45	...	Raja Hamid Ulla Khan, of Rajouri, Zilla Kangra.	Rs. 1,000	Rs. 1,250.	
Ditto,...	47	...	Raja Alukhdeo of Mankot, Zilla Kangra.	Rs. 400.	Rs. 500.	
Lahore,...	50	...	Sirdar Bhagwan Singh, ...	Rs. 1,100.	Rs. 1,375.	Son of Jamadar Khushhal Singh,
Amritsar,	52	...	Sirdar Dyal Singh, Majithia,	Rs. 1,000.	Rs. 1,250.	Son of late Sirdar Lehna Singh, Majithia.
Ditto,...	54	...	Sirdar Lal Singh, Kalianwala,	Rs. 1,000.	Rs. 1,250.	
Delhi, ...	55	...	Nawab Muhammad Ali Khan, of Kunjpura, ...	Rs. 1,000.	Rs. 1,250.	Jagirdar Magistrate.
Lahore,...	56	...	Khan Ali Raza Khan, Kizilbaksh, ...	Rs. 1,000.	Rs. 1,250.	A Kabul Pensioner and Talukdar of Oudh. Honorary Magistrate, Lahore City. Created a Nawab, Nov. 1864.
Cis-Sutlej States.	58	...	Sirdar Narain Singh, of Sialba,	Rs. 1,000.	Rs. 1,000 and a Horse.	
Ditto,...	59	...	Sirdar Jiwan Singh, of Buria,	Rs. 1,000.	Rs. 1,000 and a Horse.	
Ditto,...	60	...	Sirdar Sheo Kirpal Singh, Shahid of Shahzadpur.	Rs. 1,000.	Rs. 1,000 and a Horse.	

A.	Lahore, ...	61	...	Sirdar Kahn Singh, Nakkai, of Behrwal.	Rs. 600.	Rs. 750.	Jagirdar Magistrate.
	Peshawar,	62	...	Buhadar Sher Khan, " Bangash," Khan Buhadar.	Rs. 500.	Rs. 1,000.	"Rais" of Bangash, in in charge of Kohat Pass.
	Lahore, ...	63	...	Diwan Ajodhia Parshad, ...	Rs. 1,000.	Rs. 1,000.	
	Ditto ...	64	...	Sirdar Nihal Singh Chhachhi,	Rs. 1,000.	Rs. 1,250.	
B.	Rawalpindi,	65	...	Raja Faiz Talab Khan, of Bhimbar.	Rs. 400.	Rs. 500.	
	Lahore, ...	66	...	Diwan Amar Nath, ...	Rs. 1,000.	Rs. 1,000.	Son of Raja Dinanath.
	Ditto ...	67	...	Niranjan Nath, ...	Rs. 1,000.	Rs. 1,000.	Second Son of ditto.
	Ditto ...	68	...	Bhai Charanjit Singh, of Lahore	Rs. 400.	Rs. 410.	Son of late Bhai Ram Singh, a Member of the Lahore Durbar.
	Jallandar,	69	...	Sodhi Brijindar Singh, of Anandpur Makhowal, Zilla Hoshiarpur.	Rs. 1,000.	Rs. 1,000.	
	Ditto ..	70	...	Bedi Sojan Singh, ...	Rs. 1,000.	Rs. 1,000.	Son of late Bedi Bikrama Singh of Unah.
	Ditto ...	71	...	Sodhi Partab Singh, of Anandpur, Zillah Hoshiarpur.	Rs. 1,000.	Rs. 1,000.	
	Delhi, ...	72	...	Bhai Jasmir Singh, of Urnouli, Zilla Karnal.	Rs. 400.	Rs. 410.	
	Ditto ...	73	...	Bhai Anokh Singh of Sidhowal, Zilla Karnal.	Rs. 400.	Rs. 410.	

Division.	No. of seat of Chief.	No. of dependants.	NAMES.	Nazr.	Khilat.	REMARKS.
B. Delhi, ...	74	...	Nawab Ahmad Ali Khan of Karnal.	Rs. 1,250.	Rs. 1,250 and Horse.	Jagirdar Magistrate.
Ditto ...	75	...	Kutbuddin Khan, ...	Rs. 400.	Rs. 500.	An Istamrardar of Karnal.
Ditto ...	76	...	Muhammad Ali Khan, ...	Rs. 400.	Rs. 500.	Ditto ditto.
Cis-Sutlej States.	77	...	Sirdar Uttam Singh, of Rampur	Rs. 800.	Rs. 1,000.	
Ditto ...	78	...	Sirdar Mit Singh, of Malod,	Rs. 500.	Rs. 600.	
Ditto ...	79	...	Sirdar Hakikat Singh, of Chimah.	Rs. 500.	Rs. 600.	
Ditto ...	80	...	Sirdar Jai Singh, of Manouli,	Rs. 800.	Rs. 1,000.	
Ditto ...	81	...	Bakir Ali Khan, of Kotahah,	Rs. 400.	Rs. 400.	
Lahore, ...	82	...	Sirdar Jhanda Singh, of Botala. Zilla Gujranwala.	Rs. 500.	Rs. 625.	Jagirdar Magistrate.
Cis-Sutlej States	83	...	Sirdar Bishan Singh, of Kandoula,	Rs. 500.	Rs. 625.	
Rawalpindi.	84	...	Malik Fatah Sher Khan, Tiwana, Khan Buhadar, Zilla Shahpur.	Rs. 600.	Rs. 750.	

	District	No.		Name					Remarks
	Rawalpindi,	85	...	Malik Sher Muhammad Khan, Tiwana, Khan Buhadar.	Rs.	600.	Rs.	750.	
	Jallandar,	86	...	Sirdar Partab Singh, of Nur Mahal, Zilla Jallandhar.	Rs.	600.	Rs.	750.	
	Lahore, ...	87	...	Shaikh Ghulam Mahbub Sobhani.	Rs.	400.	Rs.	500.	Son of late Nawab Imamuddin Khan.
	Ditto ...	88	...	Guru Gulab Singh, of Kot Har Sahai, Zilla Firozpur.	Rs.	400.	Rs.	400.	Jagirdar Magistrate.
	Ditto ...	89	...	Nand Gopal Bhai,...	Rs.	400.	Rs.	410.	Cousin of No. 68.
	Ditto ...	90	...	Kesra Singh Bhai, ...	Rs.	400.	Rs.	410.	Ditto ditto.
	Ditto ...	91	...	Mihan Singh Bhai,...	Rs.	400.	Rs.	410.	A nephew of No. 68.
	Amritsar,	92	...	Bhai Pardoman Singh, ...	Rs.	400.	Rs.	410.	In charge of the Amritsar Temple (building.)
	Jallandar,	93	...	Mian Jai Singh Goleria, ...	Rs.	400.	Rs.	410.	Relative of No. 13.
	Ditto ..	94	...	Mian Bijai Singh, of Siba, Zilla Hoshiarpur.	Rs.	400.	Rs.	410.	
	Ditto ...	97	...	Mian Amar Singh, ...	Rs.	400.	Rs.	410.	Sons of Raja of Nadoun, No. 20.
B.	Ditto ...	98	...	Mian Prithi Singh, ...	Rs.	400.	Rs.	400.	
	Ditto ...	99	...	Mian Amir Singh,...	Rs.	400.	Rs.	400.	
	Ditto ...	100	...	Mian Kishan Chand, of Rai,...	Rs.	400.	Rs.	400.	A younger branch of the Nurpur Family.
	Amritsar,	101	...	Thakur Bulramdas, ...	Rs.	400.	Rs.	400.	Son of Raja Sahib Dyal.

Division.	No. of seat of Chief.	No. of dependants.	NAMES.	Nuzzer.	Khillat.	REMARKS.
Delhi,...	102	...	Muhammad Azmat Ali Khan.	2 Gold mohurs= Rs. 30.	1 Diamond Ring, value Rs. 180.	Son of Nawab of Karnal, No. 74.
Cis-Sutlej States,...	103	...	Badan Singh, ...	2 Gold mohurs= Rs. 30.	Rs. 100.	Son of Mitt Singh, No. 78.
Amritsar,	101	...	Sirdar Mangal Singh, Ramgarbia,	Rs. 300.	Rs. 375.	Honorary Magistrate, Amritsar City, and in charge of the Amritsar Darbar Sahib Temple.
Ditto,...	105	...	Sirdar Thakar Singh, Sindhanwalia,	Rs. 300.	Rs. 500.	Cousin of No. 13.
Ditto,...	106	...	Mehtab Singh, Majithia, ...	Rs. 300.	Rs. 375.	Honorary Magistrate, City Amritsar.
Ditto,...	107	...	Sirdar Sardul Singh Man, ...	Rs. 400.	Rs. 500.	
Ditto,...	109	...	Sirdar Ranjodh Singh, Majithia,	Rs. 400.	Rs. 400.	Half brother of Sirdar Lehna Singh, Mujithia.
Cis-Sutlej States,...	110	...	Sirdar Uttam Singh, of Ghanouli,	Rs. 400.	Rs. 500.	
Ditto,...	111	...	Sirdar Partab Singh, of Ghanouli,	Rs. 400.	Rs. 500.	
Ditto,...	112	...	Sirdar Ram Narayan Singh, of Bunga,	Rs. 400.	Rs. 500.	

B.	Ditto,...	113	... Sirdar Santokh Singh, of Bunga,	Rs. 200.	Rs. 250.	
	Ditto,...	114	... Sirdar Lehna Singh, of Dhurali,	Rs. 400.	Rs. 500.	
	Ditto,...	115	... Sirdar Bhagwan Singh, of Bhedwan,	Rs. 400.	Rs. 500.	Jagirdar Magistrate.
	Ditto,...	116	... Sirdar Partab Singh, of Bhedwan,	Rs. 200.	Rs. 250.	
	Ditto,...	117	... Sirdar Hari Singh, of Kheri,...	Rs. 400.	Rs. 500.	
	Ditto,..	118	.. Sirdar Ganda Singh, of Khurar,	Rs. 400.	Rs. 500.	
	Ditto,...	119	... Sirdar Ranjit Singh, of Ramgarh,	Rs. 400.	Rs. 500.	
	Cis-Sutlej States,	120	... Mian Gobind Saran Singh, of Ramgarh,	Rs. 200.	Rs. 250.	
	Ditto,...	121	... Mian Sheo Saran Singh, of Ramgarh,	Rs. 200.	Rs. 250.	
	Ditto,...	122	... Mian Dya Singh, of Ramgarh,	Rs. 400.	Rs. 500.	
	Ditto,...	123	... Mian Dalip Singh, of Ramgarh,	Rs. 400.	Rs. 500.	
	Ditto,...	124	... Mian Govardhan Singh, of Ramgarh,	Rs. 400.	Rs. 500.	
	Ditto,...	125	... Mian Sukhdarshan Singh, of Ramgarh,	Rs. 400.	Rs. 500.	
	Ditto,...	126	... Sirdar Dharm Singh of Shahabad	Rs. 250.	Rs. 310.	

	Division.	No. of seat of Chief.	No. of dependants.	Names.	Nazr.	Khilat.	Remarks.
B.	Ditto,...	127	...	Sirdar Kishan Singh, of Shahabad,	Rs. 200.	Rs. 250.	
	Jallandar,	129	...	Sirdar Fatah Singh, of Moron,	Rs. 400.	Rs. 500.	
	Ditto,...	130	...	Sirdar Gurbaksh Singh, of Shahabad.	Rs. 400.	Rs. 500.	
	Ditto,...	131	...	Sirdar Bakshish Singh, of Shahkot,	Rs. 400.	Rs. 500.	
	Rawalpindi,	132	...	Fattah Khan Gheba, of Kotpindi Gheb,	Rs. 500.	Rs. 625.	Jagirdar Magistrate.
	Multan,...	133	...	Makhdum Shah Mahmud Kureshi.	Rs. 600.	Rs. 600.	" Sajjada Nishin" of the Shrine of Buhawal-Hak, in Multan.
	Derajat,	134	...	Hyat Ulla Khan, Saddozai ...	Rs. 500.	Rs. 1,000.	One of the former Khans of Tonk.
	Lahore,...	135	...	Ahmad Ali Khan, Multani, ...	Rs. 300.	Rs. 400.	Son of the late Nawab Sarafraz Khan of Multan.
	Ditto,...	136	...	Abdul Majid Khan, Multani,...	Rs. 300.	Rs. 400.	Son of Shahnawaz Khan, brother of Nawab Sarafraz Khan of Multan, Honorary Magistrate, Lahore City. Created a Nawab Nov. 1864.

Derajat,...	137	...	Abdul Rahim Khan, Saddozai,	Rs. 500.	Rs. 800.	Uncle of No. 29.
Ditto,...	138	...	Abdul Karim Khan, Saddozai,	Rs. 500.	Rs. 800.	Ditto ditto.
Ditto,...	139	...	Ghulam Sarwar Khan, Khakwani,	Rs. 500.	Rs. 1,000.	One of the Khans of Dera Ismael Khan.
Multan,	140	...	Sadik Muhammad Khan, Multani,	Rs. 500.	Rs, 800.	Nephew of late Nawab Abdussamad Khan of Daeridiopanah.
Ditto,...	141	...	Ghulam Kadir Khan, ...	Rs. 400.	Rs. 500.	Son of ditto ditto.
Ditto,...,	142	...	Ghulam Mustafa Khan, Khakwani, Khan Buhadar,... ...	Rs. 500.	Rs. 800.	
Derajat,...	143	...	Hafiz Hakumat Khan, Khakwani, ...	Rs. 500,	Rs. 625.	
Ditto,...	144	...	Hafiz Samundar Khan, "Khwajikzai,"	Rs. 500.	Rs. 800.	Son of Payinda Khan, former Khan of Tonk.
Ditto,...	145	...	Mian Shahnawaz, Sarai, ...	Rs. 500.	Rs. 625.	Descendant of the Kulora Ruler of Sind, Jagirdar of Rajanpur, Jagirdar Magistrate.
Lahore, ...	146	...	Nazir Khair Ulla, of Kabul,	Rs. 400.	Rs. 500.	
Peshawar,	147	...	Fatah Khan, Khan Buhadar, Khattak.	Rs. 500.	Rs. 800.	
Ditto,...	148	...	Mir Jaffir Khan, Khan Buhadur, ...	Rs. 400.	Rs. 600.	Late Commandant, 1st P. I.

B.

Division.	No. of seat of Chief.	No. of dependants.	NAMES.	Nuzar.	Khilat.	REMARKS.
Ditto,...	150	...	Ghulam Muhammad Khan, of Mukhad, Zillah Rawalpindi.	Rs. 400.	Rs. 500.	Jagirdar of Shakardura, Kohat.
Ditto,...	151	...	Raja Firoz Khan, Ghakkar, of Khanpur, Hazara.	Rs. 400.	Rs. 500.	
Derajat,...	152	...	Alahdad Khan, Saddozai, ...	Rs. 300.	Rs. 400.	Son of Nawab Sarafraz Khan of Dera Ismael Khan.
Ditto,...	153	...	Hak Nawaz Khan,...	Rs. 200.	Rs. 300.	Brother of ditto.
Ditto,...	154	...	Dost Muhammad Nawaz Khan,	Rs. 200.	Rs. 300.	Ditto ditto.
Ditto,...	155	...	Muhammad Rab Nawaz Khan, Allizai,...	Rs. 300.	Rs. 400.	Son of No. 30, (Foujdar Khan.)
Ditto,...	157	...	Abdulla Khan, Allizai, ...	Rs. 200.	Rs. 300.	Son of No. 34.
Ditto,...	158	...	Izzatyar Khan, ...	Rs. 200.	Rs. 300.	Uncle of No. 31.
Ditto,...	159	...	Muhammad Guldad Khan, Gandapur, ...	Rs. 400.	Rs. 600.	Races of Kulachi.
B. Ditto,...	161	...	Farrokhsair Khan, Khattekhail,	Rs. 300.	Rs. 400.	
Ditto,...	162	...	Atta Muhammad Khan, Khakwani, ...	Rs. 300.	Rs. 600.	Extra Assistant Commissioner, and son of No. 139.

A.	Rawalpindi.	163	...	Malik Sahib Khan, Tiwana, ...	Rs.	400.	Rs.	500.	
B.	Peshawar,	164	...	Arbab Fatah Khan Muhammad,	Rs.	400.	Rs.	500.	Arbab of Tappa Momand.
	Ditto,...	165	...	Arbab Abdul Majid Khan,...	Rs.	400.	Rs.	500.	Arbab of Tappa Khalil.
	Ditto,...	166	...	Abdulla Khan, ...	Rs.	300.	Rs.	400.	Ditto ditto.
	Ditto,...	169	...	Raja Haidar Baksh Khan, Gakkhar, of Khanpur, Huzara,...	Rs.	200.	Rs.	300.	Hazara.
	Ditto,...	170	...	Muhammad Abbas Khan, ...	Rs.	200.	Rs.	300.	Son of the late Wazir Nizam-ud-Dowla.
	Ditto,...	171	...	Muzaffar Khan, ...	Rs.	300.	Rs.	500.	Rais of Hango Kohat.
	Ditto,...	172	...	Jafir Khan, Khattak, ...	Rs.	200.	Rs.	300.	Chiefs of Eastern Khattak.
	Ditto,...	173	...	Afzul Khan, Khattak, ...	Rs.	200.	Rs.	300.	
	Derajat,...	174	...	Ali Wardi Khan, ...	Rs.	300.	Rs.	500.	Late Commandant, Police Battalion.
	Ditto,...	175	...	Hafiz Misri Khan,...	Rs.	200.	Rs.	300.	Brother of Hafiz Ahmad Khan, late Tehsildar of Bannu.
	Ditto,...	175A	...	Nasir Khan, son of late Ahmad Khan, Jamadar of Bahawalpur,	Rs.	200.	Rs.	300.	
A.	Rawalpindi,	176	...	Malik Oulia Khan,...	Rs.	400.	Rs.	500.	Hereditary Rais of Pindi Gheb.
	Ditto,...	177	...	Malik Fatah Khan, ...	Rs.	400.	Rs.	500.	His brother.

Division.	No. of seat of Chief.	No. of dependants.	Names.	Nazr.	Khilat.	Remarks.
Derajat,	178	...	Alam Khan, ...	Rs. 400.	Rs. 500.	Rais of Isakhail.
Ditto,...	179	...	Muhammad Ayaz Khan, ...	Rs. 400.	Rs. 500.	Do. his brother.
Ditto,...	180	...	Abdul Rahman Khan, ...	Rs. 400.	Rs. 500.	Ditto.
Ditto,...	181	...	Muzaffar Khan, Khan Buhadar,	Rs. 300.	Rs. 400.	"Rais" of Kalabagh, Honorary Police Officer.
Ditto,...	182	...	Kowra Khan, Khosa, ...	Rs. 300.	Rs. 600.	Tumandar of the Khosa Tribe.
Ditto,...	183	...	Jamal Khan, Lughari, ...	Rs. 300.	Rs. 500.	Chief of the Lughari Tribe, Honorary Magistrate.
Ditto,...	184	...	Jalal Khan, Lughari, ...	Rs. 300.	Rs. 500.	Uncle of ditto.
Ditto,...	185	...	Sher Muhammad Khan, Muzari, ...	Rs. 300.	Rs. 500.	Tumandar of the Muzari tribe.
B. Derajat,	187	...	Naorang Khan, Gandapur, Khan Buhadar, ...	Rs. 300.	Rs. 600.	
Ditto,...	189	...	Sher Khan, Isakhail, ...	Rs. 300.	Rs. 400.	
Ditto,...	190	...	Abdulla Khan, Isakhail, Khan Buhadar, ...	Rs. 300.	Rs. 400.	

	District	No.		Name					Remarks
	Ditto,...	191	...	Abdur Rahim Khan, Isakhail,	Rs.	300.	Rs.	400.	
	Cis-Sutlej States,	192	...	Sirdar Salah Muhammad Khan Buhadar, Ludianah, ...	Rs.	300.	Rs.	400.	Kabul pensioner.
	Ditto,...	193	...	Sirdar Muhammad Hassan Khan, Gurdezi, Ludianah, ...	Rs.	300.	Rs.	400.	
	Amritsar,	194	...	Muhant Brahmbuta, ...	Rs.	300.	Rs.	350.	Head of the Monastic Institution, called Derah Santokhdas at Amritsar.
A.	Rawalpindi,	195	...	Sirdar Atar Singh, Lamba, ...	Rs.	300.	Rs.	350.	
B.	Lahore,...	196	...	Sirdar Sarup Singh, Malwai,...	Rs.	300.	Rs.	350.	Son of S. Kirpal Singh, Malwai.
	Ditto,..	197	...	Konwar Dewa Singh, Lahore,	Rs.	300.	Rs.	350.	
	Ditto,...	198	...	Sirdar Gurdit Singh, Chhachhi,	Rs.	300.	Rs.	400.	
	Rawalpindi,	200	...	Mubarik Khan, Sahiwal, ...	Rs.	300.	Rs.	350.	Rais of Sahiwal.
	Jalandhar,	204	...	Mirza Yuhia Khan of Rajouri,	Rs.	250.	Rs.	350.	
	Cis-Sutlej States,	205	...	Mulvi Rajab Ali Khan, Khan Buhadar, ...	Rs.	300.	Rs.	400.	
	Ditto,...	206	...	Rai Kishan Singh of Raipur,	Rs.	300.	Rs.	300.	
	Peshawar,	208	...	Sirdar Ali Buhadar Khan, ...	Rs.	200.	Rs.	400.	Rais of the Karral Tribe.
	Derajat,	210	...	Sirdar Muhammad Osman Khan, Ourakzai, ...	Rs.	200.	Rs.	300.	

	Division.	No. of seat of Chief.	No. of dependants.	NAMES.	Nazr.	Khilat.	REMARKS.
A.	Ditto,...	211	...	Azad Khan, ...	Rs. 150.	Rs. 250.	Rais of Kurral Tribe, Hazara.
	Ditto,...	212	...	Syad Muhammad Amin Khan,	Rs. 150.	Rs. 250.	Brother of Syad Ayauddin.
	Ditto,...	213	...	Aziz Khan of Yusafzai,... ...	Rs. 150.	Rs. 300.	
	Ditto,...	214	...	Ajib Khan of Yusafzai,... ...	Rs. 150.	Rs. 300.	
	Ditto,...	215	...	Khan Zaman Khan, ...	Rs. 200.	Rs. 300.	Rais of Khulabut, Hazara.
	Ditto,...	218	...	Muhabat Khan of Yusafzai, Peshawar.	Rs. 150.	Rs. 300.	
	Ditto,...	219	...	Khoidad Khan of Yusafzai, Peshawar, ...	Rs. 150.	Rs. 300.	
	Ditto,	223	...	Ghulam Haidar Khan, Lund,	Rs. 150.	Rs. 300.	Tumandar of the Lund Tribe.
	Derajat,	224	...	Mir Khan, Dreshak, ...	Rs. 150.	Rs. 300.	Tumandar of the Dreshak Tribe.
	Ditto,...	225	...	Ghulam Sarwar Khan, Saddozai,...	Rs. 150.	Rs. 300.	Son of Hyatulla Khan, No.
	Multan,...	226	...	Muhammad Ismail Khan, Khan Buhadur, Sial, Jhang,... ...	Rs. 300.	Rs. 400.	

Class	District	No.		Name	Amount	Amount	Remarks
A.	Jalandhar,	227	...	Sirdar Rajindar Singh, Kathgarhia, Zilla Hoshiarpur, ...	Rs. 300.	Rs. 325.	
	Ditto,...	228	...	Rana Mehtab Chand of Manaswal, Zilla Hoshiarpur, ...	Rs. 300.	Rs. 325.	
	Ditto,...	229	...	Rai Rattan Chand of Bhabur, Zilla Hoshiarpur, ...	Rs. 300.	Rs. 325.	
	Ditto,...	230	...	Sirdar Bur Singh, of Mokerian, Zilla Hoshiarpur,...	Rs. 300.	Rs. 325.	
	Ditto,...	231	...	Sirdar Dasundha Singh of Dhandowal, ...	Rs. 300.	Rs. 325.	
	Ditto, ..	232	...	Sirdar Sher Singh of Dhandowal, ...	Rs. 300.	Rs. 325.	
	Ditto,...	233	...	Sirdar Partab Singh of Dhandowal, ...	Rs. 300.	Rs. 325.	
	Ditto,...	236	...	Sirdar Nihal Singh, Kakar, ...	Rs. 300.	Rs. 325.	
	Ditto,...	237	...	Sirdar Jaimal Singh, ...	Rs. 300.	Rs. 325.	
	Ditto,...	239	...	Sirdar Narayan Singh, Kung,	Rs. 300.	Rs. 325.	
	Amritsar,	240	...	Sirdar Jiwan Singh of Attari,			
	Ditto,...	241	...	Sirdar Hari Singh of Attari,...	Rs. 300.	Rs. 325.	
	Ditto,...	242	...	Sirdar Ajit Singh of Attari, ...			
	Ditto,...	243	...	Sirdar Jaimal Singh of Khunda,	Rs. 300.	Rs. 325.	
	Ditto,...	244	...	Sirdar Jowahir Singh of Zafarwal, ...	Rs. 300.	Rs. 325.	Brother of No. 243.

	Division.	No. of seat of Chief.	No. of dependants.	Names.	Nazr.	Khilat.	Remarks.
A.	Ditto,...	245	...	Sirdar Raja Singh Man,... ...	Rs. 300.	Rs. 325.	
	Ditto,...	246	...	Sirdar Narayun Singh of Attari, ...	Rs. 300.	Rs. 325.	
	Derajat,...	248	...	Diwan Dowlat Rai,...	Rs. 300.	Rs. 400.	
	Lahore,...	249	...	Sirdar Fatah Singh, Thepuria,	Rs. 300.	Rs. 325.	
	Ditto,...	250	...	Sirdar Sadho Singh, Padhania,	Rs. 300.	Ra. 325.	
	Amritsar,	251	...	Sirdar Jassa Singh of Naoshehr-Nangal, ...	Rs. 300.	Rs. 325.	
	Jalandhar,	252	...	Sirdar Isar Singh, Santokh Garhia, ...	Rs. 300.	Rs. 325.	
	Ditto,...	253	...	Sirdar Mehtab Singh, Thabal,	Rs. 150.	Rs. 175.	
	Ditto,...	254	...	Sirdar Dewa Singh of Bichuri,	Rs. 150.	Rs. 175.	
	Ditto,...	255	...	Sirdar Partab Singh of Ghoriwah, ...	Rs. 150.	Rs. 175.	
	Amritsar,	256	...	Sirdar Sahib Singh of Isapur,	Rs. 300.	Rs. 325.	
	Rawalpindi,	257	...	Colonel Dhunraj, ...	Rs. 300.	Rs. 500.	Extra Assistant Commissioner, adopted son of Diwan Kirparam of Kunjah.

Lahore, ...	258	...	Diwan Baijnath, ...	Rs. 250.	Rs. 300.	Son of Diwan Ajodhiaparsad, No. 63, and Extra Assistant Commissioner, Lahore.
Ditto,...	529	...	Rattan Chand, Darhiwala, ...	Rs. 250.	Rs. 300.	Jagirdar and Honorary Magistrate, City Lahore.
Ditto,...	260	...	Fakir Zahur uddin, ...	Rs. 250.	Rs. 300.	Son of Fakir Nuruddin, member of the Darbar Lahore.
Lahore, ...	261	...	Fakir Shamsh uddin, ...	Rs. 250.	Rs. 300.	Honorary Magistrate and second son of do.
Amritsar,	262	...	Sirdar Richpal Singh, ...	Rs. 250.	Rs. 300.	Son of Sirdar Mangul Sing, Sindhu, brother-in-law of Maharaja Kharak Singh.
Ditto,...	263	...	Misr Gian Chand, ...	Rs. 250.	Rs. 300.	Brother of Raja Sahibdial, No. 18, and Amritsar Honorary Magistrate.
Ditto,...	264	...	Sirdar Har Charn Das,... ...	Rs. 250.	Rs. 300.	Brother of ditto ditto.
Lahore,...	265	...	Pandit Shankar Nath, ...	Rs. 250.	Rs. 300.	Honorary Magistrate, Lahore City.
Ditto,...	266	...	Bakshi Bhagatram of Lahore,	Rs. 250.	Rs. 300.	
Rawalpindi,	267	...	Fatah Khan, Dhrek, ...	Rs. 300.	Rs. 330.	Rais of the Khatar Tribe.

Division.	No. of seat of Chief.	No. of dependants.	NAMES.	Nazr.	Khilat.	REMARKS.
A Ditto,...	268	...	Malik Firoz Khan of Shamshabad, ...	Rs. 300.	Rs. 400.	
Ditto,...	269	...	Kazi Fazl Ahmad of Gondal,	Rs. 300.	Rs. 320.	Chief Kazi in Chhachh.
Ditto....	270	...	Raja Sultan Khan of Pothi,...	Rs. 250.	Rs. 300.	Rais of the Chib Tribe, Gujrat.
Ditto,...	271	..	Raja Hyat Ulla Khan, ...	Rs. 250.	Rs. 300.	Head of the Gakkar Tribe in Rawalpindi,
Ditto,...	272	...	Sodhi Sher Singh of Haranpur, Zilla Jhelam, ...	Rs. 250.	Rs. 300.	
Ditto,...	273	...	Sodhi Amrik Singh of Haranpur, Zilla Jhelam, ...	Rs. 200.	Rs. 200.	
Ditto,...	274	...	Sirdar Mul Singh of Haranpur, Zilla Jhelam, ...	Rs. 250.	Rs. 300.	
Ditto,...	275	...	Sodhi Sanpuran Singh of Haranpur, Zilla Jhelam, ...	Rs. 250.	Rs. 250.	
Jalandhar & Amritsar,	276	...	Sodhi Hira Singh of Anandpur, Zilla Hoshiarpur,...	Rs. 250.	Rs. 250.	
Ditto,...	277	...	Sodhi Nihal Singh of Anandpur, Zilla Hoshiarpur,... ...	Rs. 250.	Rs. 250.	

A.	Lahore, ...	278	...	Sodhi Gulab Singh of Manawab, Firozpur, ...	Rs. 250.	Rs. 250.	
	Cis-Satlej States.	279	...	Bhai Narayan Singh of Bagarian, ...	Rs. 250.	Rs. 250.	
	Ditto,...	280	...	Atta Muhammad Khan (or his son Muhammad Alam Khan,) Chief of Kotla Nihang, ...	Rs. 200.	Rs. 250.	
	Delhi,	281	...	Wilayat Hussain, ...	Rs. 200.	Rs. 250.	Late Deputy Collector, Moradabad.
	Ditto,...	283	...	Sirdar Natha Singh of Dhanoura, ...	Rs. 200.	Rs. 200.	
	Ditto,...	284	...	Sirdar Amar Singh of Dhanoura, ...	Rs. 200.	Rs. 200.	
	Cis-Satlej States.	285	...	Sirdar Budh Singh of Liddhran,	Rs. 200.	Rs. 250.	
	Ditto,...	286	...	Sirdar Chimman Singh of Liddhran, ...	Rs. 100.	Rs. 150.	
	Ditto,...	287	...	Sirdar Sahib Singh of Liddhran,	Rs. 100.	Rs. 150.	
	Ditto,...	288	...	Sirdar Kanh Singh of Liddhran,	Rs. 100.	Rs. 150.	
	Ditto,...	289	...	Sirdar Harnam Singh of do.	Rs. 100.	Rs. 150.	
	Ditto,...	290	...	Sirdar Sham Singh of do.	Rs. 100.	Rs. 150.	
	Ditto,...	291	...	Sirdar Bishan Singh of Thol Thangor, ...	Rs. 100.	Rs. 150.	

Division.	No. of seat of Chief.	No. of dependants.	NAMES.	Nazr.	Khilat.	REMARKS.
Ditto,...	292	...	Sirdar Kishan Singh of Thol Thangor, ...	Rs. 100.	Rs. 150.	
Ditto,...	293	...	Sirdar Jasmir Singh of Thol Thangor, ...	Rs. 100.	Rs. 150.	
Ditto,...	294	...	Sirdar Tilok Singh of Mustafabad, ...	Rs. 100.	Rs. 150.	
Cis-Sutlej States,	295	...	Sirdar Gursaran Singh of Mustafabad, ...	Rs. 100.	Rs. 150.	
Ditto,...	296	...	Muhammad Yar Khan of Bayana, ...	Rs. 100.	Rs. 100.	
Ditto,...	297	...	Muhammad Husain Khan of Kunjpura, ...	Rs. 100.	Rs. 100.	
Ditto,...	298	...	Sirdar Dewa Singh of Ledah,	Rs. 100.	Rs. 150.	
Ditto,...	299	...	Rai Imam Baksh of Rai Kot,	Rs. 100.	Rs. 125.	
Ditto,...	301	...	Hardit Singh, ...	Rs. 100.	Rs. 125.	Nephew of late Rani of Dyalgarh.
Ditto,...	302	...	Sirdar Partab Singh of Mianpur, ...	Rs. 100.	Rs. 150.	
Ditto,...	303	...	Sirdar Ram Singh of Shamkot,	Rs. 100.	Rs. 125.	

A.	Ditto,...	304	...	Sirdar Kahn Singh of Shamkot,	Rs.	100.	Rs.	152.	
	Ditto,...	306	...	Sirdar Bhag Singh of Sikandra,	Rs.	100.	Rs,	125.	
	Ditto,...	307	...	Sirdar Gur Baksh Singh of Rupur, ...	Rs.	100.	Rs.	150.	
	Lahore,...	308	...	Sirdar Dial Singh of Botalah,	Rs.	150.	Rs.	200.	
	Ditto,...	309	...	Fakir Jamaluddin,...	Rs.	150.	Rs.	200.	Son of late Fakir Aziz-uddin, minister of Maharaja Ranjit Singh.
	Ditto,...	310	...	Malik Khairuddin Khan, Kasuria, ...	Rs.	200.	Rs.	250.	
	Ditto,...	311	...	Pandit Radha Kishan, ...	Rs.	200.	Rs.	200.	Darbar Pandit.
	Ditto,...	312	...	Rai Mul Singh, ...	Rs.	200.	Rs.	200.	
	Ditto, ..	313	...	Pundit Deodat Parshad, ...	Rs.	200.	Rs.	200.	Son of Pandit Madhoosudan.
	Ditto,...	314	...	Misr Ramdas,...	Rs.	150.	Rs.	150.	Son of the Maharaja's Toshakhania,
	Ditto,...	315	...	Misr Sheodas,...	Rs.	150.	Rs.	150.	Son of late Misr Meghraj; and Treasurer, Lahore and Amritsar Division.
	Amritsar,	316	...	Sharampat Rai, ...	Rs.	200.	Rs.	200.	Son of Rai Kishan Chand.
	Ditto,...	316A	...	Rai Bhag Singh, ...	Rs.	200.	Rs.	200.	

	Division.	No. of seat of Chief.	No. of dependants.	Names.	Nazr.	Khilat.	Remarks.
A.	Lahore,...	317	...	Hari Singh, ...	Rs. 100.	Rs. 150.	Son of Diwan Mulraj.
	Ditto,...	318	...	Sirdar Partab Singh, Kunjahia,	Rs. 150.	Rs. 200.	
	Ditto,...	319	...	Sirdar Kirpal Singh, Kunjahia,	Rs. 150.	Rs. 200.	
	Ditto, ..	320	...	Jahangir Khan, Multani, ...	Rs. 150.	Rs. 200.	A member of the Multan Nawab's Family at Lahore.
	Ditto,...	321	...	Diwan Hukm Chand, Peshawaria, ...	Rs. 150.	Rs. 200.	
	Derajat,...	322	...	Rai Tehlram of Dera Ismail Khan, ...	Rs. 100.	Rs. 200.	
	Lahore,...	323	...	Diwan Karm Chand of Iminabad, Zilla Gujranwala,... ...	Rs. 200.	Rs. 200.	
	Ditto,...	324	...	Colonel Nur uddin, ...	Rs. 150.	Rs. 200.	
	Amritsar,	325	...	Mihan Singh of Bhagowala,...	Rs. 150.	Rs. 200.	
	Ditto,..	326	...	General Gulab Singh of Bhagowala, ...	Rs. 150.	Rs. 200.	
	Ditto,...	327	...	Sirdar Khan Singh, Majithia,	Rs. 150.	Rs. 200.	

Ditto,...	328	...	Sirdar Bhup Singh, Dabanwala, ...	Rs. 150.	Rs. 200.	Representative of the Baggah Family. Son of late Sirdar Kahn Singh, Koharia.
Rawalpindi,	329	...	Sirdar Ram Singh, Koharia,...	Rs. 150.	Rs. 200.	
Ditto,...	329A	...	Sirdar Jodh Singh, Man, ...	Rs. 150.	Rs. 200.	
Lahore,	330	...	Sirdar Hira Singh, Man, ...	Rs. 150.	Rs. 200.	Son of late Sirdar Budh Singh, Man.
Ditto,...	331	...	Hardit Singh, Rosa, ...	Rs. 150.	Rs. 200.	Son of the late Sirdar Kahn Singh, Rosa.
Lahore,	333	...	Fatah Singh (Atthu,) Sirdar Buhadar, ...	Rs. 100.	Rs. 200.	
Ditto,...	333A	...	Sirdar Sher Singh Buhadar, ..	Rs. 100.	Rs. 200.	
Amritsar,	334	...	Dewa Singh, Sirdar Buhadar,	Rs. 100.	Rs. 200.	Late Commandant.
Lahore,	335	...	Mota Singh, Sirdar Buhadar,	Rs. 100.	Rs. 200.	Late Commandant.
Ditto,...	336	...	Muhammad Shah, Sirdar Buhadar, ...	Rs. 100.	Rs. 200.	Ditto ditto.
Jalandhar.	337	...	Atar Singh, ...	Rs. 100.	Rs. 200.	Ditto ditto.
Lahore,	338	...	Mutsaddi Mal, Sirdar Buhadar, ...	Rs 100.	Rs. 200.	Ditto ditto.
Peshawar,	340	...	Ibrahim Khan, ...	Rs. 150.	Rs. 250.	Arbab of Yusafzai Peshawar.
Ditto,...	341	...	Umar Khan, ...	Rs. 150.	Rs 250.	Ditto ditto,

	Division.	No. of seat of Chief.	No. of dependants.	Names.	Nazr.	Khilat.	Remarks.
A.	Peshawar,	342	...	Amir Khan, ...	Rs. 150.	Rs. 250.	Arbab of Shewa.
	Ditto,...	343	...	Shahdad Khan, ...	Rs. 150.	Rs. 250.	Arbab of Hund.
	Ditto,...	346	...	Kazi Abdul Gaffur of Hazara,	Rs. 150.	Rs. 250.	
	Ditto,...	348A	...	Amir Jan, ...	Rs. 150.	Rs. 250.	
	Ditto,...	348B	...	Nasrulla Jan, ...	Rs. 150.	Rs. 250.	
	Ditto,...	352	...	Sarbuland Khan, ...	Rs. 150.	Rs. 250.	Arbabkhel, Peshawar.
	Ditto,...	353	...	Aslam Khan, ...	Rs. 150.	Rs. 250.	Ditto ditto.
	Ditto,...	354	...	Aslam Khan, ...	Rs. 150.	Rs. 250.	Arbab of Hoti, Peshawar.
	Ditto,...	355	...	Sarbuland Khan, ...	Rs. 150.	Rs. 250.	Arbab of Yusafzai Peshawar.
	Ditto,...	356A	...	Nasrulla Khan, Yusafzai, ...	Rs. 150.	Rs. 250.	
	Ditto,...	357	...	Arbab Sher Dil Khan, ...	Rs. 150,	Rs. 250.	Arbabkhel.
	Ditto,...	359	...	Gul Muhammad Khan,... ...	Rs. 100.	Rs. 200.	Popalzai.
	Ditto,...	360	...	Ahmad Sher Khan, ...	Rs. 100.	Rs. 200.	Alimzai.
	Ditto,...	363	...	Mian Zaid Gul, ...	Rs. 100.	Rs. 200.	Lambardar and religious character of Abazai Peshawar.

A.	Ditto,...	363A	...	Mian Muhammad Shah, Yusafzai, ...	Rs. 100.	Rs. 200.	
	Ditto,...	365	...	Muzaffar Khan, Khattak, Kohat, ...	Rs. 100.	Rs. 200.	
	Derajat,...	367	...	Abdul Rahman Khan, Allizai,	Rs. 100.	Rs. 200.	Late Risaldar.
	Ditto,...	368	...	Ghulam Muhammad Khan, ...	Rs. 100.	Rs. 200.	Brother-in-law of Nawab of Derah.
	Ditto,...	368A	...	Kalli Khan, Allizai, ...	Rs. 100.	Rs. 200.	
	Ditto,...	368B	...	Dur Muhammad Khan, Khakwani, ...	Rs. 100.	Rs. 200.	
	Ditto,...	368C	...	Ghulam Sarwar Khan, Allizai,	Rs. 100.	Rs. 200.	
	Ditto,...	368D	...	Bakhtyar Khan, Gandapur, ...	Rs. 100.	Rs. 200.	
	Ditto,...	369	...	Ghulam Mustafa Khan, Khakwani, ...	Rs. 100.	Rs. 200.	Late Risaldar.
	Ditto,...	370	...	Ghulam Muhammad Khan, Khakwani, ...	Rs. 100.	Rs. 200.	Son of Ghulam Sarwar Khan.
	Ditto,...	371	...	Nasir Khan, Popalzai, ...	Rs. 100.	Rs. 200.	
	Ditto,...	372	...	Muhammad Akram Khan, Khakwani, ...	Rs. 100.	Rs. 200.	
	Multan,	373	...	Ghulam Kadir Khan, Khakwani, ...	Rs. 100.	Rs. 200.	Son of Ghulam Mustafa Khan.

Division.	No. of seat of Chief.	No. of dependants.	NAMES.	Nazr.	Khilat.	REMARKS.
Derajat,...	374	...	Sultan Muhammad Khetran,	Rs. 100.	Rs. 250.	
Ditto,...	375	...	Yar Muhammad Khan, Khwajikzai, ...	Rs. 100.	Rs. 200.	Nephew of Hafiz Samundar Khan.
Ditto,...	376	...	Abdulla Khan, Khwajikzai,...	Rs. 100.	Rs. 200.	
Ditto,...	377	...	Mehrdil Khan, Gandapur, ...	Rs. 100.	Rs. 200.	Son of Naorang Khan.
Ditto,...	378	...	Faizulla Khan, Bamezai, ...	Rs. 100.	Rs. 200.	
Derajat,...	379	...	Abdus Samad Khan, Bamezai,	Rs. 100.	Rs. 200.	
Ditto,...	380	...	Shah Alam Khan, Gandapur,	Rs. 100.	Rs. 200.	
Ditto,...	381	...	Sikander Khan, Kupchani,...	Rs. 100.	Rs. 250.	
Ditto,...	382	..	Khuda Baksh, Khattak, ...	Rs. 100.	Rs, 200.	
Ditto,...	383	...	Haidar Shah Sherazi, ...	Rs. 100.	Rs. 200.	
Ditto,...	384	...	Sikandar Khan, Ismailzai, ...	Rs. 100.	Rs. 200.	Nephew of Nawab Foujdar Khan.
Ditto,...	385	...	Khuda Baksh, Awan, ...	Rs. 100.	Rs. 200.	Brother in-law of ditto.
Ditto, ..	386	...	Abdus Samad Khan, Khaisur,	Rs. 100.	Rs. 250.	

A.	Ditto,...	387	...	Shah Nawaz Khan, Khaisur,	Rs. 100.	Rs. 250.	
	Ditto,...	388	...	Gosaen Hetnandlal of Dera Ismael Khan,...	Rs. 100.	Rs. 150.	
	Ditto....	389	...	Massu Khan, Nutkani, ...	Rs. 100.	Rs. 200.	Rais of the Nutkanis, Sanghar.
	Ditto,...	390	...	Azim Khan, Nutkani, ...	Rs. 100.	Rs. 200.	
	Ditto,...	391	...	Mir Alam Khan, Musazai, ...	Ra. 100.	Rs. 150.	" Rais" of the Musazais
	Ditto,...	392	...	Muhammad Gul, Akhunzadah Babar, ...	Rs. 100.	Rs. 150.	" Rais" of the Choudhwan.
	Ditto,...	393	...	Ghulam Haidar Khan, ...	Rs. 100,	Rs. 250.	" Rais" of the Gurchanis.
	Ditto,...	394	...	Fazl Khan, Kasrani, ...	Rs. 100.	Rs. 200.	
	Ditto,...	395	...	Kaura Khan, Kasrani, ...	Rs. 100.	Rs. 150.	
	Ditto,...	397	...	Naorang Khan, Bozdar,... ...	Rs. 100.	Rs. 250.	
	Ditto,...	398	...	Babal Khan, Khatrani, ...	Rs. 100.	Rs. 250.	
	Ditto,...	399	...	Ramzan Khan, Usturana, ...	Rs. 100.	Rs. 250.	
	Ditto,...	400	...	Fatah Khan, Usturana, ...	Rs. 100.	Rs. 250.	
	Multan,...	402	...	Amir Ali Khan, ...	Rs. 100.	Rs. 200.	Son of Sarafraz Kharral, Rais of the Kharrals.
	Ditto,...	402A	...	Kazi Muhammad Jan, ...	Rs. 100.	Rs. 200.	

	Division.	No. of seat of Chief.	No. of dependants.	NAMES.	Nazr.	Khilat.	REMARKS.
A.	Peshawur,	403	...	Sikandar Khan of Mathah, ...	Rs. 100.	Rs. 250.	Arbab, Peshawar.
	Ditto,...	404	...	Shuja Khan, ...	Rs. 100.	Rs. 200.	Arbab of Khazana Dozai, Peshawar.
	Ditto,...	405	..	Nasir Khan, ...	Rs. 100.	Rs. 200.	Malik of Shahi Kalali, Peshawar.
	Ditto,...	405A	...	Hakim Khan, ...	Rs. 100.	Rs. 200.	
	Ditto,...	406A	...	Mir Hassan of Tungi, ...	Rs. 100.	Rs. 200.	
	Ditto,...	407	...	Ursala Khan of Charpareza,...	Rs. 100.	Rs. 200.	
	Ditto,...	408	...	Amir Ulla Khan, ...	Rs. 100.	Rs. 200.	Arbab of Chamkuni.
	Ditto,...	409	...	Atridi Khan, Khalil, ...	Rs. 100.	Rs. 200.	
	Ditto,...	409A	...	Shah Pasand Khan of Gulbela,	Rs. 100.	Rs. 200.	
	Ditto,...	401	...	Shaikh Salim, Khalil, ...	Rs. 100.	Rs. 200.	
	Derajat,...	412	...	Azim Khan, Miankhel, ...	Rs. 50.	Rs. 100.	Malik of Draband.
	Ditto,...	413	...	Sardod Khan,...	Rs. 100.	Rs. 250.	Rais of Gariwal in Bannu, Honorary Police Officer.
	Ditto,...	414	...	Khan Mir Khan, Begokhel, ...	Rs. 100.	Rs. 200.	"Rais" of Marwat.
	Ditto,...	415	...	Ursala Khan, Isakhel, ...	Rs. 100.	Rs. 200.	Ditto ditto.

A.	Derajat,...	416	...	Faiz Ulla Khan, Bannochi, ...	Rs.	100.	Rs.	250.	Son of Lalbaz Khan, Malik of Bannu.
	Ditto,...	417	...	Durab Khan of Bannu, ...	Rs.	100.	Rs.	200.	
	Ditto,...	418	...	Muhammad Raza Khan, Jaskani, ...	Rs.	100.	Rs.	200.	
	Ditto,...	419	...	Muhammad Khan, Jaskani, ...	Rs.	100.	Rs.	200.	
	Ditto,...	420	...	Raza Muhammad Khan, Korreshi, ...	Rs.	100.	Rs.	200.	
	Ditto,...	421	...	Naorang Khan, Billoch, ...	Rs.	100.	Rs.	200.	
	Ditto,...	422	...	Malik Mir Baz, ...	Rs.	100.	Rs.	200.	Attached to the Kabul Envoy.
	Ditto,...	423	...	Muhammad Khan, Kasuria, ...	Rs.	100.	Rs.	200.	
	Ditto,...	424	...	Husain Baksh Shah, Korreshi,	Rs.	100.	Rs.	200.	
	Ditto,. .	425	...	Abdur Rahim Khan, Tarin, ...	Rs.	100.	Rs.	200.	
	Ditto,...	426	...	Hakim Khan, Sikandarkhel,	Rs.	100.	Rs.	200.	Malik of Marwat.
	Ditto,...	427	...	Sahibdad Khan, ...	Rs.	100.	Rs.	200.	Ditto ditto.
	Ditto,...	428	...	Purdil Khan, Ghaznikhel, ...	Rs.	100.	Rs.	200.	Ditto ditto.
	Ditto,...	429	...	Muhammad Khan, ditto. ...	Rs.	100.	Rs.	200.	Ditto ditto.
	Ditto,...	430	...	Wali Khan, Mahdudkhel, ...	Rs.	100.	Rs.	200.	
	Ditto,...	431	...	Laskari Khan, Shahani, ...	Rs.	100.	Rs.	200.	Malik.

Division.	No. of seat of Chief.	No. of dependants.	NAMES.	Nazr.	Khilat.	REMARKS.
Derajat,	434	...	Ghazi Khan, Musakhel, ...	Rs. 100.	Rs. 200.	
Ditto,...	435	...	Gaman Khan, Runga, ...	Rs. 100.	Rs. 200.	
Ditto,...	436	...	Daraz Khan, Mushani, ...	Rs. 100.	Rs. 150.	
Lahore,	437	...	Fakir Moraj Udin,...	Rs. 100.	Rs. 125.	Members of the Fakir Family at Lahore.
Ditto,...	438	...	Fakir Kamr Uddin, ...	Rs. 100.	Rs. 125.	
Ditto,...	439	...	Fakir Hafiz Udin, ...	Rs. 100.	Rs. 125.	
Ditto,...	440	...	Bakhshi Kanheya Lal, ...	Rs. 200.	Rs. 250.	
Ditto,...	441	...	Konwar Bakshish Singh, ...	Rs. 200.	Rs. 250.	
Ditto,...	442	...	Raja Jaimal Singh, Kishtwaria,	Rs. 100.	Rs. 200.	
Ditto,...	443	...	Konwar Thakur Singh,... ...	Rs. 200.	Rs. 250.	
Ditto,...	444	...	Amrik Singh, Sirdar, ...	Rs. 100.	Rs. 125.	Son of Sirdar Nihal Singh, Tehsildar.
A. Ditto,...	445	...	Konwar Narayan Singh, ...	Rs. 100.	Rs. 125.	Rs. 125.
Amritsar,	446	...	Nar Singh, Aimawala, ...	Rs. 100.	Rs. 125.	Rs. 125.
Ditto,...	449	...	Baba Amar Singh of Batala, ..	Rs. 100.	Rs. 125.	

A.	Lahore,...	450	...	Sodhi Rajindar Singh of Moga, Zilla Firozpur, ...	Rs. 100.	Rs. 125.	
	Ditto,...	451	...	Sodhi Man Singh of Moga, ...	Rs. 100.	Rs. 125.	
	Ditto,...	452	...	Sodhi Fatah Singh of Kot Har-sahai, ...	Rs. 100.	Rs. 125.	Son of Guru Gulab Sing.
	Ditto,...	453	...	Sodhi Bhagwan Singh, ...	Rs. 100.	Rs. 125.	
	Ditto,...	454	...	Sodhi Khushhal Singh,... ...	Rs. 100.	Rs. 125.	
	Amritsar,	455	...	Sirdar Lal Singh of Talwandi,	Rs. 100.	Rs. 125.	
	Lahore,...	456	...	Suchet Singh, Kung, ...	Rs. 100.	Rs. 125.	
	Rawalpindi,	457	...	Himmat Singh, Mirpuria, ...	Rs. 100.	Rs. 125.	
	Lahore,...	458	...	Shamsh Uddin Khan, Kassuria,	Rs. 100.	Rs. 125.	
	Ditto,...	459	...	Syad Raza Shah, ...	Rs. 100.	Rs. 125.	Kabul Pensioner.
	Ditto,...	460	...	Shaikh Sandhi Khan, ...	Rs. 100.	Rs. 150.	Cousin of late Nawab Imam Uddin Khan.
	Ditto,...	461	...	Bhaizabar Jang Singh of Jhamba,	Rs. 100.	Rs. 125.	
	Ditto,...	462	...	Shaikh Firoz Uddin, ...	Rs. 100.	Rs. 150.	Brother of late Nawab Imam Uddin.
	Delhi,...	463	...	Salik Ram, ...	Rs. 150.	Rs. 150.	Banker and Jagirdar of Delhi.
	Ditto,...	464	...	Mir Parwarish Ali, ...	Rs. 150.	Rs. 150.	Jagirdar of Sekri, Gurgaon.

	Division.	No. of seat of Chief.	No. of dependants.	NAMES.	Nazr.	Khilat.	REMARKS.
A.	Delhi,...	466	...	Rai Gangaram of Delhi, ...	Rs. 150.	Rs. 150.	
	Ditto,...	468	...	Rai Ganeshi Lal of Delhi, ...	Rs. 150.	Rs. 150.	
	Amritsar,	469	...	Chanda Singh, Kalalwala, ...	Rs. 100.	Rs. 125.	Cousin of Rani Khem-kour, Kalalwali, widow of Maharajah Kharak Singh.
	Rawalpindi,	470	...	Nawab Khan, Drek, ...	Rs. 100.	Rs. 125.	Brother of Fatah khan Drek, No. 267.
	Ditto,...	471	...	Choudhri Sher Khan, Chakri,	Rs. 100.	Rs. 125.	
	Ditto,...	471A	...	Mansabdar Khan of Phulgrain,	Rs. 100.	Rs. 125.	
	Ditto,...	472	...	Diwan Mulraj, ...	Rs. 100.	Rs. 125.	
	Amritsar,	473	...	Hussain Shah Mian of Batala,	Rs. 100.	Rs. 125.	
	Jalandhar,	474	...	Wazir Suchet Singh of Ladouri,	Rs. 100.	Rs. 125.	
	Ditto,...	475	...	Choudhri Tek Chand of Indouri, Kangra,...	Rs. 100.	Rs. 125.	Wazir of Nurpur Raja.
	R. Pindi,...	476	...	Raja Khuda Baksh, ...	Rs. 100.	Rs. 125.	Khokhar of Pinddadan-Khan.

A. R. Pindi & Jalandhar,	477	...	Rai Radhakishan of Alawalpur.	Rs. 100.	Rs. 125.	Vakil in attendance on Commissioner, Rawalpindi, on the part of the Ruler of Kashmir and Jammu.
Amritsar,	478	...	Rai Hardial, ...	Rs. 100.	Rs. 125.	
R. Pindi ...	479	...	Nand Singh, ...	Rs. 100.	Rs. 125.	
Ditto,...	480	...	Hashim Ali of Nar, ...	Rs. 100.	Rs. 125.	
Ditto,...	481	...	Kehr Singh, Lamba of Gujrat,	Rs. 100.	Rs. 125.	
Ditto,...	482	...	Misr Amir Chand, ...	Rs. 100.	Rs. 125.	Cousin of Raja Lal Singh.
Lahore,...	484	...	Diwan Bishan Singh, ...	Rs. 100.	Rs. 125.	
Ditto,..	485	...	Kishan Singh, Povindia, ...	Rs. 100.	Rs. 125.	Grandson of late General Gulab Singh, Povindia,
Ditto,...	486	..	Pandit Badri Nath, ...	Rs. 100.	Bs. 125.	Nephew of Raja Dina Nath.
Ditto,...	487	...	Mehtab Singh, Rania, Zilla Firozpur,...	Rs. 100.	Rs. 125.	
Ditto,...	488	...	Partab Singh, Rania, Zilla Firozpur, ...	Rs. 100.	Rs. 125.	
Ditto,...	489	...	Fatah Singh, Man, ...	Rs. 100.	Rs. 150.	Honorary Magistrate, City Gujranwala.

	Divisions.	No. of seat of Chief.	No of dependants.	NAMES.	Nazr.	Khilat.	REMARKS.
A.	Lahore,...	490	...	Ram Chand, ...	Rs. 100.	Rs. 125.	Grandson of Diwan Sawanmal.
	Ditto,...	491	...	Devidial, ...	Rs. 100.	Rs. 125.	Nephew of above, Pargannah Magistrate.
	Amritsar,	492	...	Jai Singh, Chhina, ...	Rs. 100.	Rs. 150.	Late Risaldar.
	Ditto,...	493	...	Sewa Singh, ...	Rs. 100.	Rs. 150.	Brother of Dewa Singh, No. 334, late Risaldar.
	Ditto,...	494	...	Harsa Singh, ...	Rs. 100.	Rs. 150.	Sirdar Buhadar, late Risaldar.
	Jallandar	496	...	Nidhan Singh of Mokerian, ...	Rs. 100.	Rs. 150.	Late Risaldar. Brother of S. Bur Singh, No. 230.
	Ditto, ..	495	...	Sudh Singh of Mokerian, ...	Rs. 100.	Rs. 150	Ditto ditto,
	Lahore,...	497	...	Bal Singh, Chuhar, Kania, ..	Rs, 100.	Rs. 150.	Late Risaldar.
	Ditto,...	499	...	Man Singh, ...	Rs. 100.	Rs. 150.	Risaldar Buhadar, brother of late Sirdar Jodh Singh, Extra Assistant Commissioner, Amritsar.

A.	Amritsar,...	501	...	Mathra Das, ...	Rs.	100.	Rs.	150.	Late Commandant.
	Lahore, ..	502	...	Tek Singh, Rosa, ...	Rs.	100.	Rs.	150.	Late Risaldar.
	Ditto,...	503	...	Nihal Singh, Man, ...	Rs.	100.	Rs.	150.	Sons of late Sirdar Jag-
	Ditto,...	504	...	Narain Singh, Man, ...	Rs.	100.	Rs.	150.	gat Singh, Man.
	R. Pindi,...	505	...	Raja Roshan Ali Khan of Do-meli Gakkar, ...	Rs.	100.	Rs.	150.	Late Risaldar.
	Ditto,...	507	..	Sultan Mahmud Khan, Tiwana,	Rs.	100.	Rs.	150.	
	Ditto,...	508	...	Malik Jahan Khan, Tiwana,...	Rs.	100.	Rs.	150.	Ditto.
	Amritsar,...	509	...	Didar Singh, Veglin, ...	Rs.	100.	Rs.	150.	Ditto.
	R. Pindi,...	510	...	Alam Sher, Tiwana, ...	Rs.	100.	Rs.	150.	Brother of No.
	Ditto,...	511	...	Sher Bahadar Khan Tiwana,...	Rs.	100.	Rs.	150.	Ditto.
	Ditto,...	512	...	Fatah Khan Nun, ...	Rs.	100.	Rs.	150.	
	Ditto,...	513	...	Malik Ahmad Khan, Tiwana,...	Rs.	100.	Rs.	150.	
	Ditto,...	514	...	Fatah Khan, Tiwana, ...	Rs.	100.	Rs.	150.	
	Ditto,...	514A	...	Mohr Singh, Dowlatalia ...	Rs.	100.	Rs.	125.	
	Ditto,...	515	...	Raja Sultan Ahmad Khan, Khokar of Pinddadan Khan,	Rs.	100.	Rs.	125.	
	Ditto,...	516	...	Raja Shamsher Ali Khan Khokar of Pinddadan Khan' ...	Rr.	100.	Rs.	125.	
	Ditto,...	517A	...		Rs.	100.	Rs.	125.	

	Division.	No. of seat of Chief.	No. of dependants.	NAMES.	Nazr.	Khillat.	REMARKS.
A.	R. Pindi,...	518	...	Malik Khair Mehdi Khan of Darapur, ...	Rs. 100.	Rs. 125.	
	Amritsar,	520	...	Baba Mohanlal, ...	Rs. 100.	Rs. 125.	Honorary Magistrate, Amritsar.
	Ditto,...	521	...	Mahammad Shah, ...	Rs. 100.	Rs. 125.	Ditto ditto.
	Ditto,...	522	...	Duni Chand, ...	Rs. 100.	Rs. 125.	Ditto ditto.
	Dehli,...	523	...	Munshi Jiwanlal, ...	Rs. 100.	Rs. 125.	Ditto ditto.
	Ditto,...	524	...	Chuna Mal, ...	Rs. 100.	Rs. 125.	Ditto ditto.
	Ditto,...	525	...	Moheshdas, ...	Rs. 100.	Rs. 125.	Ditto ditto.
	Ditto,...	526	..	Sahib Singh, ...	Rs. 100.	Rs. 125.	Ditto ditto.
	Ditto,...	529	...	Mahbub Buksh, ...	Rs. 100.	Rs. 125.	Ditto ditto.
	Lahore, ...	531	...	Deviditta Mal, ...	Rs. 100.	Rs. 125.	
	Ditto,...	532	...	Sohna Mal of Akalgarh, ...	Rs. 100.	Rs. 125.	
	Amballa,...	534	...	Kirpal Singh, Dhin, ...	Rs. 100.	Rs. 150.	Jagirdar.
	Ditto,...	535	...	Dalip Singh, Dhin, ...	Rs. 100.	Rs. 150.	Ditto.
	Ditto, ..	536	...	Bishan Singh of Bheri, ...	Rs. 100.	Rs. 150.	

	District	No.		Name	Rs.		Rs.		Remarks
A	Amballa,...	537	...	Gurmukh Singh of Bheri, ..	Rs.	100.	Rs.	150.	
	Ditto,...	538	...	Khewan Singh of Bheri, ...	Rs.	100.	Rs.	150.	
	Lahore, ...	539	...	Muhammad Sultan, ...	Rs.	100.	Rs.	125.	
	Ditto,...	540	...	Colonel Fatah Khan, ...	Rs.	100.	Rs	125,	Son of late Gial Ilahee Bux.
	Ditto,...	541	...	Colonel Sikandar Khan, ...	Rs.	100.	Rs.	125.	Ditto ditto.
	Ditto,...	542	...	Santram, ...	Rs.	100.	Rs.	125.	Son of Dewan Kurm Chund, late Resaldar.
	Amritsar,...	543	...	Bhagwan Singh of Kalalwalia,	Rs.	100.	Rs,	125.	Son of Chunda Singh, Kulalwalee.
	Lahore, ..	545	...	Nasir Khan, Kassuria, ...	Rs.	100.	Rs.	125.	
	Ditto,...	546	...	Kishan Chand Dhun, ...	Rs.	100.	Rs.	125.	
	Ditto,...	547	...	Amar Singh, Chimni, ...	Rs.	100.	Rs-	125.	
	Amritsar,...	548	...	Din Muhammad of Batala, ...	Rs.	100.	Rs.	125.	
	Multan, ...	549	...	Makhdum Shamsudin, Gilani of Multan, ...	Rs.	100.	Rs.	125.	
	Ditto ...	550	...	Fatah Ulla Shah of Khanka, Dogran, Multan, ...	Rs.	100.	Rs.	125.	
	Ditto,...	552	...	Shah Nawaz Khan of Multan,	Rs.	100.	Rs.	125.	
	Ditto,...	553	...	Rahmat Ullah Shah of Multan,	Rs.	100.	Rs.	125.	

	Division.	No. of seat of Chief.	No. of dependants.	Names.	Nazr.	Khillat.	Remarks.
A.	Amballa,...	554	..	Bansi Lal, ...	Rs. 100.	Rs. 150.	Banker of Jugadhri.
	Delhi, ...	556	..	Girdhar Lal, ...	Rs. 50.	Rs. 75.	Banker of Delhi.
	Ditto,...	557	...	Baldeo Singh, ...	Rs. 50.	Rs. 75.	Ditto ditto.
	Amritsar,...	559	...	Amir Baksh, "Tepi," ...	Rs. 100.	Rs. 125.	Late Commandant.
	Lahore, ...	561	...	Jalal Khan, Bhatti, ...	Rs. 100.	Rs. 125.	
	Ditto,...	563	...	Balram, Prohit, ...	Rs. 100.	Rs. 125.	Family Priest of the Maharajas.
	R. Pindi,...	564	...	Bishan Das, ...	Rs. 100.	Rs. 125.	Son of Rattan Chand of Saidpur.
	Peshawar,	565	...	Kazi Nadir Ali, ...	Rs. 100.	Rs. 125.	Vakil of the Jammu Government, in attendance on the Deputy Commissioner of Hazara.
	Ditto,...	566	...	Said Khan of Kohat, ...	Rs. 100.	Rs 125.	
	Ditto,...	566 A	...	Malik Taus Khan, Yusufzai ...	Rs. 100.	Rs. 125.	
	Ditto,...	567	...	Sadr Khan of Yusafzai, ..	Rs. 100.	Rs. 125.	
	Ditto,...	568	...	Ghulam Khan of Peshawar, ...	Rs. 50.	Rs. 150.	

A.	Ditto,...	569	...	Ata Muhammad Khan of Kohat,	Rs. 50.	Rs. 100	
	Ditto,...	569A	...	Abdul Gafur Khan Khattak, of Kohat, ...	Rs. 50.	Rs. 100.	
	Ditto,...	571	...	Syad Ahmad Shah, ...	Rs. 50.	Rs. 100.	
	Ditto,...	571A	..	Syad Jamma Khan, ...	Rs. 50.	Rs. 100.	
	Ditto,...	573	..	Jamma Khan,...	Rs. 50.	Rs. 100.	Malik of zainkhail Afridi.
	Amritsar,	574	...	Pandit Mathradas of Amritsar,	Rs. 50.	Rs. 75.	
	Ditto,...	575	...	Ghulam Murtaza Khan of Kadian, Gurdaspur, ...	Rs. 50.	Rs. 75.	
	Ditto,...	576	...	Niranjandas of Fatahgarh, Gurdaspur, ...	Rs. 50.	Rs. 75.	
	Lahore,...	577	...	Manoharlal of Wazirabad, Gujranwala,...	Rs. 50.	Rs. 75.	
	Ditto,...	578	...	Jodh Singh, Chhachhi,... ...	Rs. 50.	Rs. 75.	
	Rawalpindi,	579	...	Chowdri Ghulam Ali of Baisa,	Rs. 50.	Rs. 75.	Chowdhri of the Chib Tribe.
	Ditto,...	580	...	Chowdri Sultan Ali of Ajnala, Gujrat, ...	Rs. 50.	Rs. 75.	
	Ditto,...	581	...	Hari Singh, ...	Rs. 50.	Rs. 75.	Grandson of Baba Bishan Bhulla, Jagirdar.
	Lahore,...	582	...	Maddimal, ...	Rs. 50.	Rs. 75.	Panch of Lahore or Municipal Commissioner.

	Division.	No. of seat of Chief.	No. of dependants.	NAMES.	Nazr.		Khilat.		REMARKS.
	Ditto,...	583	...	Harjas Rai, ...	Rs.	50.	Rs.	75.	Ditto ditto.
	Ditto,...	584	...	Bhagumal, ...	Rs.	50.	Rs.	75.	Ditto ditto.
	Ditto,...	585	...	Munshi Harsukh Rai, ...	Rs.	50.	Rs.	75.	Ditto ditto.
	Amritsar,	586	...	Rup Narain of Amritsar, ...	Rs.	50.	Rs.	75.	Municipal Commissioner.
	Ditto,...	587	...	Jowahirmal of Amritsar, ...	Rs.	50.	Rs.	75.	Ditto ditto.
	Ditto,...	588	...	Panna Lal of Amritsar, ...	Rs.	50.	Rs.	75.	Ditto ditto.
	Ditto,...	588A	...	Chela Ram, Panch Peshawar,	Rs.	50.	Rs.	75.	Ditto ditto.
A.	Ditto,...	589	...	Daryanamal of Amritsar, ...	Rs.	50.	Rs.	75.	Ditto ditto.
	Lahore,...	590	...	Mathra Parshad, ...	Rs.	100.	Rs.	100.	Mahajan of Karnal, and Commissariat Agent Lahore.
	Amritsar,	592	...	Jodh Singh, Chappa Amritsar,	Rs.	50.	Rs.	75.	
	Ditto,...	593	...	Jaggot Singh,...	Rs.	50.	Rs.	75.	Son of Peshora Singh.
	Ditto,...	594	...	Fatah Singh, ...	Rs.	50.	Rs.	75.	Son of Kashmira Singh.
	Ditto,...	595	...	Joala Singh, Kallewasia of Amritsar, ...	Rs.	50.	Rs.	75.	

A.	Lahore,	596	...	Moti Singh, ...	Rs.	50.	Rs.	75.	Late Subhadar.
A.	Ditto,...	598	...	Duni Chand, ...	Rs.	50.	Rs.	75.	Formerly Vakil, attached to Sirdar Jowahir Singh's Contingent.
A.	Ditto,...	599	...	Hari Singh, ...	Rs.	50.	Rs.	75.	Formerly Vakil of General Gulab Singh, Povindia.
B.		600	...	Tejo Singh, Panch Peshawar,	Rs.	50.	Rs.	75.	
B.		601	...	Muhammad Azim Do. Do....	Rs.	50.	Rs.	75.	
B.		602	...	Nizamuddin, Do. Do....	Rs.	50.	Rs.	75.	
B.		603	...	Sirdar Ganda Singh, Mattu, ...	Rs.	200.	Rs.	400.	This does not indicate this gentleman's position in Durbar.

RESERVED SEATS FOR GOVERNMENT OFFICIALS.

B.	1 a.	...	Sirdar Jowahir Singh, Nalwa,	Rs.	400.	Rs.	500.	
B.	1 b.	...	Anup Singh, Man,...	Rs.	200.	Rs.	400.	
A.	1 c.	...	Panjab Singh, ...	Rs.	200.	Rs.	400.	Risaldar Buhadar.
B.	1 d.	...	Nizamuddin Khan,...	Rs.	200.	Rs.	400.	Risaldar Buhadar.
B.	1 e.	...	Sawan Mal, ...					
B.	1	...	Pandit Manphul, ...	Rs.	200.	Rs.	400.	E. A. C. and Mir Munshi to Panjab Government.

Division.	No. of seat of Chief.	No. of dependants.	NAMES.	Nazr.	Khilat.	REMARKS.
B.	2	...	Muhammad Sultan, ...			
	3	...	Syad Hadi Hussain Khan, ...			
	4	...	Syad Kaim Ali Khan, ...			Extra Assistant Commissioners 1st Class.
	5	...	Aga Kalb Abid, ...			
	6	...	Pandit Moti Lall, ...	Rs. 200.	Rs. 400.	
	7	...	Syad Fazul Hussain, ...			Extra Assistant Commissioners 2d Class.
	8	...	Munshi Jaishi Ram, ...			
	9	...	Kanheya Lal, ...	... ...	... ...	Special Asst. Engineer.
	10	...	Rai Manna Lal, ...			Extra Assistant Commissioners 2nd Class.
	11	...	Mir Masum Ali, ...			
				Rs. 3,400.	Rs. 6,500.	
			Brought Forward, ...	Rs. 3,400.	Rs. 6,500.	
B.	12	...	Gopal Sahai, ...			Extra Assistant Commr. 2nd class.
	13	...	Munshi Amin Chand, ...			
	14	...	Munshi Gopal Dass, ...			
	15	...	Muhammad Hyat Khan, ...	Rs. 200.	Rs. 400.	Extra Assistant Commissioners 3rd class.
	16	...	Hukm Chand, ...			
	17	...	Shaikh Shahabudin, ...			Late Extra Asst. Comr.
	18	...	Mohanbir, ...			Extra Asst. Comr. 3rd. class.

	No.		Name			Designation
	19	...	Rai Lachman Singh, Bahadar,			Insptr. of Police, Delhi.
	19A	...	Malik Sarafraz Khan, ...			Late Jemadar Cureton's Horse.
	20	...	Pandit Moti Lal, ...			Translator to Panjab Government.
	21	..	Balgobind, ...			Supdt. Persian Office Finl. Commr. Lahore.
	22	...	Lachmi Sahai,...			Tehsildar of Kassur,
	23	...	Gurdit Singh, ...			
	24	...	Thakur Das, ...			
	25	...	Jat Mal, ...			Treasurer of Ludhiana.
B.	26	...	Barkat Ali, ...	Rs. 100.	Rs. 200.	Tehsildar of Lahore.
	27	...	Sohan Lal, ...			Do. of Amritsar.
	28	...	Yar Muhammad Khan, ...			Do. of Gujrat,
	29	...	Muhammad Hyat Khan, ...			Do. of Firozpur.
	30	...	Abdus Samad Khan, ...			Do. of Phillor.
	31	...	Pandit Radha Kishan, ...			
	32	...	Nyamat Rai, ...			Do. of Ismail Khan.
	33	...	Diwan Chand, ...			Do, of Moga.
	34	...	Nur Muhammad, ...			Do. of Ghazi Khan.
	35	.	Shaikh Fazluddin Khan, ...			Do. Do.
	36	...	Hafiz Ghulam Muhammad, ...			
	37	...	Muhammad Aslam Khan, ...			Insptr of Police, Lahore.
	38	...	Rahim Khan, ...			Sub-Asst. Surgeon.
	39	...	Syad Bakar Shah, ...			News-writer of Jammu.
				Total Rs. 7,000.	Rs. 13,700.	

LAHORE AND AMRITSAR DIVISIONS.

THE FAMILY OF MAHARAJA RANJIT SINGH.

MAHARAJA RANJIT SINGH.

- M. R. Kharrak Singh. B. 1802. D. 1840.
  - Nao Nihal Singh. B. 1821. D. 1840.
- Ishar Singh reputed. B. 1804. D. 1805.
- M. R. Sher Singh reputed. B. 1807. D. 1843.
  - Partab Singh. B. 1831. D. 1843.
  - Dewa Singh. B. 1842
  - Shahdev Singh. B. 1843. Living at Benares.
- Tara Singh reputed. B. 1807. D. 1859.
- Peshora Singh reputed. D. 1845.
  - Jagjot Singh. B. 1843.
- Kashmira Singh reputed. D. 1844.
  - Fatah Singh. B. 1844.
- Multana Singh reputed. B. 1819. D. 1846.
  - Kishan Singh. B. 1840.
  - Kesra Singh. B. 1842.
  - Arjan Singh (by a concubine.) B. 1840.
- M. R. Dalip Singh reputed. B. 1837.

THE FAMILIES OF MAHARAJAS RANJIT SINGH, KHARRAK SINGH, SHER SINGH, AND KONWAR NAO NIHAL SINGH.

In the Biographies of the Panjab Chiefs, frequent mention will be made of members, real or reputed, of the royal family of Lahore. A short notice of them is accordingly given here. The history of many of them is the history of the Panjab itself, during many eventful years, and has been already written by various hands; but no work, hitherto published, gives any correct account of the wives and children of the great Maharaja.

Sirdar Mahan Singh, father of Maharaja Ranjit Singh, killed, with his own hands, his mother Mai Desan, who had been detected in an intrigue with a Brahman, Misr Jai Ram. Following his father's example, Ranjit Singh put to death, with his own hands, his mother Mai

Malwai, for adultery with one Laik Misr. Both these ladies, however, had more than one lover, and it is doubtful whether Mahan Singh was the son of Charrat Singh, or Ranjit Singh the son of Mahan Singh. With such antecedents, it is not surprising that Ranjit Singh should have had but vague ideas of chastity, delicacy or honor. Perhaps no court in the world was ever more debauched than that of Maharaja Ranjit Singh, and certainly no one of his courtiers was more immoral or debauched than he. When he had secured the legitimate succession, in the persons of his son Kharrak Singh and his grandson Nao Nihal Singh, the intrigues of his wives afforded him more amusement than disgust. He was not unwilling to be the reputed father of their children, though he was never deceived as to their parentage, and on the birth of another and yet another son, would cry, "Wah Guru ji i ghaibi gola kiton aya?" (Whence this mysterious stroke of fortune?) The secret history of his harem, though both instructive and amusing, is too scandalous to be related here. The adventures of Rani Bhuri, of Rani Chand Kour, and others, were at one time the common talk of the Lahore bazaars. Such was the delicacy of the Maharaja that he sent one of his Ranis, Isar Kour, who had been detected in an intrigue, to his son Kharrak Singh, on whose death she became 'Sati.' To his grandson he also sent several women of indifferent character, from his harem, but Nao Nihal Singh did not appreciate the honor and returned the ladies. Such was Sikh morality and good taste, as displayed at the Court of Maharaja Ranjit Singh.

THE WIVES OF MAHARAJA RANJIT SINGH.

Maharaja Ranjit Singh married sixteen wives, nine with the usual rites and ceremonies of orthodox marriage; (shadi or phera) and seven with the less orthodox of chaddar-dalna, or tir-patka, common enough among the Sikhs. *The following are the nine orthodox wives.*

I.—Mehtab Kour, married in 1796. She was the daughter of Sirdar Gurbaksh Singh, and grand-daughter of Sirdar Jai Sing Kanheya. She was the reputed mother of Maharaja Sher Singh and Tara Singh, but, in reality, never bore any children to the Maharaja. She died in 1813.

II.—Raj Kouran, married in 1798. She was the daughter of Sirdar Ran Singh Nakai, a Sindhu Jat, and was the mother of Maharaja Kharrak Singh. She died in 1818. This lady was commonly known by the name of Mai Nakayan. The Maharaja's aunt, daughter of Sirdar Charrat Singh, was also named Raj Kouran, and to distinguish between them, Mai Nakayan had the name Datar Kour given to her.

III.—Rup Kour was the daughter of Jai Singh, Lumberdar of Kotsaid Mehmud, in the Amritsar district. She was married to the Maharaja in 1815, and is still alive, in receipt of a cash pension of 1980 Rs. per annum.

IV.—Lachmi was married to the Maharaja in 1820. She was the daughter of Desa Singh Vadpagga, a Sindhu Jat of Jogki Khan, in the Goojranwala district. She was presented to the Maharaja on his visit to Khai, by her father.

Rani Lachmi is still living, and is in receipt of a cash pension of 11,200 Rs. per annum.

V., VI.—Mehtab Devi and Rajbanso were illegitimate daughters of Raja Sansar Chand, Katoch, of Kangra. When Anrudh Chand, son of Sansar Chand, refused to give a sister in marriage to Raja Hira Singh and fled across the Sutlej to avoid the proposed alliance, the Maharaja himself, in revenge for the slight to his favourite, married two of the sisters, who had been detained at Lahore. This was in 1839.

Rani Rajbanso died before the Maharaja, about the year 1835. Rani Mehtab Devi became 'Sati,' and was burnt with the Maharaja's body, in 1839.

VII.—Gul Begum was an 'Ahl Nishat' (literally *fille de joie*) in the city of Amritsar. The Maharaja took a fancy to her, and in the year 1833, married her, with great splendour.

She died at Lahore in 1863, and was in receipt of a pension of 12,380 Rs. till her death.

VIII.—Ram Devi was the daughter of Kaur Singh of Chhachriwala in the Gujranwala district. The date of her marriage is not known. Her death took place before that of the Maharaja.

IX.—A daughter of Karam Singh China, a China Jat of the Amritsar district. The date of her marriage is not known.

The seven following Ranis were married by the rites of Chaddar-dalna or Tir-patka.

I.—*Rani Devi,* daughter of Wazir Nakudda of Jaswan, in the Hoshiarpur district.

II., III.—*Ratan Kour* and *Dya Kour,* widows of Sirdar Sahib Singh, Banghi, of Gujrat. These ladies were taken into the Maharaja's harem, in 1811, soon after the death of their husband. Rani Ratan Kour is the reputed mother of Multana Singh. She is still alive, and in receipt of a pension of 1,000 Rs. per annum. Rani Dya Kour was the reputed mother of Kashmira Singh and Peshora Singh. She died in 1843.

IV.—*Chand Kour* was the daughter of Jai Singh, Jat, of Chainpur, in the Amritsar district. She was married to the Maharaja in 1815, and died in the year 1840.

V.—*Mehtab Kour* was the daughter of Chowdri Sujan, an Uthwal Jat of Malla, in the Gurdaspur district. She was married to the Maharaja about the year 1822, and is still alive, in receipt of an annual pension of 1,930 Rs.

VI.—*Saman Kour* was the daughter of Suba Singh, a Jat of Malwa, in the Cis-Sutlej States. She was married to the Maharaja in the year 1832, and is still living, in receipt of an annual pension of 1,440 Rs.

VII.—*Golab Kour* was the daughter of a Jat Zamindar of Jagdeo, in the Amritsar district. She died about the year 1838.

The only one of the Maharaja's wives who became 'Sati' was *Mehtab Devi*, but three other ladies (besides slave girls) of the rank of Rani, were burnt on the Maharaja's funeral pile.

These were : *Har Devi*, daughter of Chowdri Ram, a Saleria Rajput of Atalghar, in the Gurdaspur district.

Raj Devi. Daughter of Padma Rajput.

Devno. Daughter of Sand Bhari, a Bhari Chib of Deva-Vatala, now in the Jammu territory.

THE REAL AND REPUTED CHILDREN OF MAHARAJA RANJIT SINGH.

I.—*Kharrak Singh* was the only child legitimate, or illegitimate, by a wife or a slave girl, ever born to Maharaja Ranjit Singh. He was the son of Rani Raj Kour, and was born in the year 1802. His history is well known. He succeeded his father in 1839, and died on the 5th November 1840, by poison, administered under the orders of his son Nao Nihal Singh and Raja Dhyan Singh.

II.—III.—*Sher Singh* and *Tara Singh*. When Rani Mehtab Kour had been married more than ten years to the Maharaja without bearing him any children, it was given out soon after Ranjit Singh's departure from Lahore, on his Cis-Sutlej Campaign of 1807, that the Rani was pregnant. On the Maharaja's return, his wife presented him with Sher Singh and Tara Singh, as her twin-sons.

Sher Singh was the son of a chintz weaver, named Nihala, native of Mokerian (in the Hoshiarpur district), then in the jagir estates of Mai Sada Kour, mother of Mehtab Kour.

Tara Singh was the son of a Muhammadan woman, daughter of Manki, a slave girl of Mai Sada Kour.

Sada Kour, an able and unscrupulous woman, was aware that should her daughter bear sons to the Maharaja, her influence would be much increased, and accordingly purchased these children of their parents, and proclaimed them as the offspring of Mehtab Kour.

Maharaja Ranjit Singh was not deceived; but he acknowledged the children as his own, and they were always treated as his sons. They bore the title of Shahzadah.

Sher Singh succeeded Maharaja Kharrak Singh in 1841, and was assassinated by Sirdar Ajit Singh Sindhanwalia, on the 15th September 1863.

Tara Singh was an imbecile. He lived, for the most part, with his brother Sher Singh, who supported him and his wives.

He married Dharam Kour Randhavi, daughter of Jodh Singh, a Randhawa Jat of Tara, in the Amritsar district, and Nand Kour, known as Bhittividwali of Bhittivid (in the Amritsar district) where her father Chanda Singh resided.

Tara Singh died in September 1859, at Dasuha, in the Hoshiarpur district.

IV.—*Ishar Singh.* Rani Metab Kour wisely resolved to father twins upon the Maharaja in 1807, as she had already experimented with one son, without success. About the year 1804, she had presented the Maharaja with a son, who was named Ishar Singh, but who died a year and a half after his birth. It is not known from whom this child was procured, but it is certain that his mother was not Mehtab Kour, nor his father Ranjit Singh.

V., VI.—*Peshora Singh, Kashmira Singh.* Rani Dya Kour, seeing the plot of Rani Mehtab Kour so successful, determined to follow her example, and on different occasions procured two boys, whom she gave out to be children of her own. These were Peshora Singh and Kashmira Singh. The first was said to be the son of a shop-keeper in Lahore; and the second, the son of a Jammu Rajput. Both were treated as the sons of the Maharaja, and held the Ilaka of Sialkot, worth 50,000 Rs. in jagir.

Kashmira Singh took refuge with Baba Bir Singh, a famous Sikh Guru, when Raja Hira Singh became minister, and he was killed with the Baba and Attar Singh Sindhanwalia by the Sikh army in July 1843. (Vide Statement Sirdar Shamsher Singh Sindhanwalia.)

Peshora Singh was murdered by Fatah Khan Tiwana and Sirdar Chattar Singh Attariwala, at Attock, in August 1844, by the orders of Sirdar Jowahir Singh, the minister. (Vide Statement of Fatah Sher Khan Tiwana). *Kashmira Singh* left one son, Fatah Singh, now about 20 years of age. *Peshora Singh* left one son, Jagjot Singh, now about 21 years of age.

VII.—*Multana Singh* was the reputed son of Rani Rattan Kour, first the wife of Mul Singh of Duburji; then of Sirdar Sahib Singh of Gujrat, and last of Maharaja Ranjit Singh. She procured Multana Singh from a Muhammadan slave girl in 1819, and declared him her son. He was acknowledged by the Maharaja, who gave him a small jagir at Vanyeki Ajnala Parganah, Amritsar District, worth 2,000 Rs. He died in 1846, leaving three sons, Kishan Singh and Kesra Singh, aged 24 and 22 respectively, by his wife Chand Kour; and Arjan Singh, aged 24, by his concubine Man Kour.

VIII.—DALIP SINGH was born in Feb. 1837. His mother was Jindan, daughter of Manna Singh, an Oulakh Jat, of Char, near Gujranwala, a trooper in the Maharaja's service.

Dalip Singh was proclaimed Maharaja, on the death of Sher Singh, in September 1843, and on the 29th of March 1849, and after the second Sikh war was deposed, and sent to Fatahghar, whence, in 1851, he was sent to England, where he still resides.

He married an Abyssinian lady in 1864. His mother, Rani Jindan, died in England, in 1863, aged 46 years.

WIVES OF MAHARAJA KHARRAK SINGH.

Maharaja Kharrak Singh married four wives.

I.—*Chand Kour*, daughter of Sirdar Jaimal Singh Kanheya, of Fatahghar, near Gurdaspur. The marriage took place in 1812. It was celebrated with great splendour, and Sir David Ochterlony attended from Ludiana. In 1821, the Rani gave birth to a son, Nao Nihal Singh. On the death of her husband and son, on the 5th November 1840, she put in a claim to the Crown. She was supported by the Sindhanwalias, and betrayed by the

Dogras, and was compelled to renounce her claim in favour of Sher Singh. She was murdered in 1842, by the order of Raja Dhyan Singh and Sher Singh, who wished to marry her, but whose proposals she had rejected with disdain.

II. *Khem Kour*, daughter of Sirdar Jodh Singh, Kalalwala, and grand-daughter of Sirdar Sahib Singh of Gujrat, was married in 1816, and is still living, in receipt of a pension of 2,400 Rs. per annum. She had a jagir of 12,000 Rs. per annum, which was confiscated by the Lahore Darbar, in 1848, in consequence of her complicity in the rebellion.

III.—*Kishen Kour*, daughter of Chowdri Raja Singh, Jat of Samra, in the Amritsar district. She was married in 1818, and is still living at Lahore. She receives an annual pension of 2,324, Rs.

IV.—*Isar Kour* was the sister of Sirdar Mangal Singh, Sindh, of Soranwali, in the Sialkot district. She was married by *chaddar-dalna* to Kharrak Singh, in 1815, having been sent to him from his father's zanana. This lady became 'Sati' on the death of Kharrak Singh. It is said that she was unwilling to burn with her husband, and that Raja Dhyan Singh compelled her to do so.

WIVES OF KONWAR NAO NIHAL SINGH.

Like his father, Nao Nihal Singh married four wives.

I.—*Nanki*, daughter of Sirdar Sham Singh Attariwala. To the marriage were invited the Governor General, the Lieutenant Governor of the North West, and other Dignitaries; but Sir Henry Fane alone was able to attend. It took place in March 1837. The Rani died in November 1856, when her cash pension of 4,600 Rs. lapsed to Government.

II.—*Sahib Kour*, a daughter of Sirdar Gurdit Singh, Gilwaliwala in the Amritsar district. She died in 1841.

III.—*Bhadauran*, daughter of a Sirdar of Bhadaur, Cis-Sutlej States. She became 'Sati' on her husband's death.

IV.—*Katochan,* daughter of Rai Singh, illegitimate son of Fatah Singh of Lambagraon, a Katoch Rajput. This lady also became Sati.

THE WIVES AND CHILDREN OF MAHARAJA SHER SINGH.

Maharaja Sher Singh married four wives.

I.—*Desa,* daughter of Sirdar Mohr Singh Nakai. She was married in 1819, and died two years later, leaving no issue.

II.—*Prem Kour,* daughter of Hari Singh, a Varaich Jat, lambardar of Ladhewala in the Gujranwala district. She was married to Sher Singh in 1822. In 1831, she gave birth to Partab Singh, who was brutally murdered by Sirdar Lehna Singh, Sindhanwalia, on the 15th September 1843. *Rani Prem Kour,* now aged fifty-five years, is living at Lahore, and receives an annual pension of 7,200 Rs. She has adopted a son, Narayan Singh, son of Atar Singh, of Bhano Bhindi, in the Sialkot district, from whom she purchased him for fifty rupees.

III.—*Partab Kour,* daughter of Sirdar Jaggat Singh of Kot Kapura, was married to Sher Singh in 1825. She died on the 23rd of August 1857, leaving an adopted son, Thakar Singh, aged 14 years. Thakar Singh was the son of *Rani Partab Kour's* cousin, Gajja Singh. She adopted him in 1847, and, on her death, he was granted a pension of 1,800 Rs. per annum, which he still enjoys.

IV.—*Dukno,* was the daughter of a Chang zamindar of Jhujian, near Lambagraon, in the Kangra district. She was married to Maharaja Sher Singh in 1812, being a present from the Kardar of the Kangra district. In 1843 she gave birth to Shahdeo Singh. Both mother and son accompanied Maharaja Dalip Singh to Fatahghar in November 1849, and are now living at Benares under surveillance. Shahdeo Singh, now twenty-one years of age, is a young man of considerable ability, and of pleasing manners. In April 1860 he married the daughter of Fatah Singh, a small Sirdar and Jagirdar of Suga, in the Thanesar district. He has recently been granted a Talukdari in Oude.

Besides these wives, Maharaja Sher Singh lived with *Dharam Kour* and *Chand Kour*, the wives of his reputed twin-brother Tara Singh. On Sher Singh's accession to the throne, in 1841, Tara Singh went to his new Jagir of Dasuha, in the Hoshiarpur district, and his two wives came to Lahore, and lived with Sher Singh till his death. Previous to 1841, Tara Singh had lived with his brother, and in 1838 *Rani Chand Kour* had given birth to a son, Dewa Singh, of whom Sher Singh was the father.

Both the ladies were called 'Sirkars'; like the other wives of Maharaja Sher Singh; they were considered as his wives, and had separate provisions in cash and land assigned to them.

Rani Chand Kour died in 1843. Dewa Singh was always considered the son of Maharaja Sher Singh, and is still living in receipt of an annual pension of 7,200 Rs. He resides at Lahore. *Rani Dharam Kour* also receives a pension of 7,200 Rs. She adopted in 1838, Karam Singh, son of a Zamindar of Mokerian, in Hoshiarpur, whom Sher Singh had purchased from his parents. This young man, now 26 years of age, was prosecuted in 1859 by *Rani Dharam Kour* for the theft of property worth 40,000 Rs. and was sentenced to nine months' imprisonment.

SIRDAR SHAMSHER SINGH SINDHANWALIA.

BUDHA SINGH.

- **Chanda Singh.**
  - **Sirdar Didar Singh.**
    - **Gurbaksh Singh.**
    - **Sirdar Amir Singh.** D. 1827.
      - **S. Attar Singh.** M. D. S. Jai Singh Man. D. 1844.
        - **S. Kehr Singh.** D. 1863.
      - **S. Jaimal Singh.** D. 1810.
      - **S. Budh Singh.** i. M. D. S. Hukm Singh Attariwala. ii. D. of Asa Singh, Powni Rajput Jasrota. D. 1827.
        - **S. Shamsher Singh.** M. D. S. Sudh Singh Chinah. B. 1816.
          - **Bakshish Singh,** son of Thakar Singh adopted.
      - **S. Wasawa Singh,** M. D. of Raja Sansar Chand Katoch D.
        - **S. Ajit Singh** D. 1843.
        - **S. Ranjodh Singh.** D. 1864.
          - **Randhir Singh.** B. 1856.
      - **S. Lehna Singh.** i M. D. of S. Sodh Singh Chinah, ii. daughter of a Hill Chief.
        - **Partab Singh.** D. 1856.
        - **Thakar Singh.** B. 1837.
          - **Gurbaksh Singh.** B. 1855.
          - **Bakshish Singh.** B. 1862.
          - **Narindar Singh.** B. 1863.
    - **Rattan Singh.**
      - **Nidhan Singh.**
        - **Dasonda Singh.**
      - **Khazan Singh.**
        - **Jaggat Singh.**
        - **Bhaggat Singh.**
        - **Gopal Singh.**
    - **Gurmukh Singh.**
  - **Gulab Singh.**
- **Nodh Singh.**
  - **Sirdar Charrat Singh.**
    - **Sirdar Mahan Singh.**
      - **Maharaja Ranjit Singh.**
        - **Maharaja Kharrak Singh.**
          - **Nao Nihal Singh.**

HISTORY OF THE FAMILY.

The two principal families in the Panjab proper, highest in rank and possessing the widest influence, are the Ahluwalia and the Sindhanwalia. The possessions of the Ahluwalia Chief are almost entirely situated in the Jalandhar Doab; whilst of all Sikh families, between the Beas and the Indus, the Sindhanwalia Chief is the acknowledged head. Nearly related to this family was the great Maharaja himself, and it was in a great measure owing to their connection with him, that the Sindhanwalia Sirdars obtained so large a share of wealth and power.

The Sindhanwalias are of the Jat Sansi tribe, and like most Jats claim a Rajput origin, and state that their ancestor, a Bhatti Rajput, by name Shal, came from Ujain to the Panjab, where he founded Sialkot. The Bhattis do not appear however to have settled so far South as Ujain, and the Shal alluded to is, doubtless, Raja Shal, or Salvahan, son of Raja Gaj of Jassalmir, who, after his father's death in battle with the King of Khorasan, came to the Panjab, where he destroyed Lahore and rebuilt the town of Sialkot, * which place he made his capital.

Salvahan introduced a new era called the 'Shaka,' according to some in memorial of a victory which he gained over Vikramaditya, near Sialkot; but Salvahan was not a contemporary of Vikramaditya, who never came to the Punjab at all. The 'Shaka' era was founded in the 146th year of the era of Vikramaditya.

Raja Salvahan had sixteen sons, all of whom became independent,

* NOTE.—Sialkot is one of the most ancient towns in the Panjab. It is said to have been founded about 3400 B. C., by Raja Shal, maternal uncle of the Pandus, whose descendants reigned there for many hundred years. It then was abandoned, until Salvahan rebuilt it, according to Panjab chroniclers, about 90 A. D., according to the Bhatti chroniclers of Rajputana, 16 A. D., supposing that Sialkot is the original Salvahana, the capital of Salvahan, and the identity of the two places seems probable. Sialkot has been also known as Shalkot, Salkunt, Sakalpur and Risalkot (from Risalu the son of Salvahan.) The Sial Rajputs, who now inhabit the country about Jhang, claim to have founded Sialkot, and to have given to the town their name. That they once settled there and built a fort, seems certain, but the town was founded many years before their arrival in the Panjab.

and from whom many of the hill Princes have descended. The chief of them were Baland, Puran, Risalu, Dharamgadh, Rupa and Sundar.

The houses of Pattiala, Nabha, Jheend, Malod, Bhador, Faridkot, Kythal and Attari have descended from the eldest son of Joudhar, the fifth from Raja Salvahan or Shal, while the Sindhanwalias pretend that they and the Muhammadan Bhattis have descended from the second son.

The origin of the family name of Sansi, is thus related by the Sindhanwalias. Sohanda, sixth in descent from Joudhar, saw all his children die, one after another, within a few days of their birth. He, accordingly, consulted the Brahmans and astrologers, who told him that he must give his next child to the first person who should come to the house after its birth. In due time a son was born, and the first person to stop at Sohanda's house, after the event, was a beggar of the Sansi tribe; and to him, in spite of the mother's entreaties, the new-born child was given. The old beggar would have preferred money or food, but he took the child away with him. However, by the next day, he had had quite enough of it, and brought it back to Sohanda, who, after a second consultation with the Brahmans, took the child, who was from this adventure called Sansarpal or Sainhsarpal (cherished-by-the-Sansi,) and the name has belonged to the family ever since. Another story states that the wife of Sohanda was taken in labour at a considerable distance from her home, and was compelled to take refuge in a Sansi village, where she received every attention and remained till she had recovered. The son born under these circumstances was called Sansi. But from a comparison of the Sindhanwalia genealogy with that of the Bhattis, it appears probable that Sans was the name of a son of Bhoni, fourth in descent from Joudhar, and that from Sansi the Sindhanwalias and the Sansis have a common descent. The Sansis are a thievish and degraded tribe, and the house of Sindhanwala naturally feeling ashamed of its Sansi name has invented a romantic story to account for it; but the relationship between the nobles and the beggars does not seem the less certain, and if the history of Maharaja Ranjit Singh be attentively considered, it will appear that much of his policy, and many of his actions had the true Sansi complexion.

Raja Sansi, the present residence of the Sindhanwalias, was founded about the year 1570, by *Raja* and *Kirtu* ; and *Khokhar* the great grandson of *Kirtu,* settled in the Taran Taran waste, and founded there several villages. From *Wigah,* grandson of *Khokhar,* have descended, on one side the family of Sindhanwala, and on the other that of Ladwa. The grandson of *Wigah,* by name *Takht Mal,* received from the Emperor Alamgir a firman, still in possession of the family, making him Chowdri, with power to collect revenue in the Ilaka of Yusufpur. This firman, however, is unattested and may be a modern forgery. *Bhara Mal,* son of *Takht Mal,* seems to have been a Sikh of the unorthodox sect called 'Sahaj Dhari,' and although he never took the pahal (initiatory rite) he wandered through the villages preaching the doctrines of Govind. His son *Budha Singh,* an orthodox Sikh, was celebrated as a bold and successful robber. In his days cattle-lifting was as honourable a profession as it was on the Scottish border three hundred years ago, and *Budha Singh,* on his famous piebald mare Desi, was the terror of the surrounding country. He was wounded some forty times by spear, matchlock or sword, and died at last in his bed, like an honest man, in the year 1718. His two sons, *Chanda Singh* and *Nodh Singh,* were as enterprizing and successful as their father. About the year 1730 they rebuilt the village of Sukar chak, which had been founded some time previously by the Gil Jats, but had fallen into ruin, and collecting round them a band of hard-riding Sikhs, seized several villages in its neighbourhood, and even made marauding expeditions across the Ravi, into the Gujranwala district. *Nodh Singh* was killed in 1763, in a fight with the Afghans at Majitha, where he had gone to celebrate his marriage in the family of Gulab Singh Gil.

His son *Charrat Singh,* who was only five years old at the time of his father's death, became a very powerful Sirdar, and rose to the command of the Sukarchakia misl. Under him, fought his cousin *Didar Singh*, at Gujranwala, Pind Dadan Khan, and elsewhere. After Sirdar Mahan Singh had succeeded his father, and had taken Rasulnagar and Gujranwala, Sirdar *Didar Singh* obtained, as his share of the spoil, Pind Sawakha, Dallot and Sindhanwala, which last village has given its name to the family. He was killed in a skirmish on the banks of the Chenab, in 1784, and his tomb is still to be seen in the village of Dowlat Nagar.

Sirdar *Amir Singh*, with his brothers, *Gurbuksh Singh* and *Rattan Singh*, succeeded to all the estates of his father, and soon contrived to enlarge them. He continued to follow the fortunes of his cousins, the Sukarchakia chiefs, and as they, Mahan Singh and Ranjit Singh, rose to power he seized, with impunity, Bal Sehchandar and other villages in the neighbourhood of Raja Sansi.

In 1803, however, *Amir Singh* fell into deep disgrace at court. The story is that one morning as Ranjit Singh came out of the Samman Burj, and was preparing to mount his horse, *Amir Singh* was seen to unsling his gun, prime it and blow the match. The bystanders accused him of seeking the life of his Chief, and Ranjit Singh, who believed the charge, dismissed him from court. He took refuge with Baba Sahib Singh Bedi of Unah, at whose intercession, after some time, Ranjit Singh again took him into favour, and placed him specially under the protection and in the force of Sirdar Fatah Singh Kalianwala.

Amir Singh accompanied the Maharaja in the Kassur campaign of 1807, and in the expedition against the Muhammadan tribes between the Chenab and the Indus in 1810. In this expedition *Jaimal Singh*, his second son, was killed in a skirmish before Kila Khairabad. In 1809, when on the death of Raja Jai Singh of Jammu, Ranjit Singh seized that country, he made over to *Amir Singh* the Ilakas of Harniah, Naunar and Ratta Abdal. Two years later *Amir Singh* introduced into the Maharaja's service, his son *Budh Singh*, who soon became a great favourite at court.

The first independent command of *Budh Singh* was at Bahawalpur, whither he had been sent to enforce the payment of the stipulated tribute. In 1821, with his father, and brother *Attar Singh*, he captured the forts of Mojghar and Jamghar. For these services *Amir Singh* received Shakarghar in jagir, and *Budh Singh*, Kalar and Nirali, worth about a lakh of rupees. Previous to this the family jagirs in Chhach and Attock, had been exchanged, at their request, for the Ilakas of Sarroh, Talwan, Khotar and Kathunangal, worth 1,80,000 Rs.

Sirdar *Budh Singh* was, after this, sent to the Jammu hills in command of two regiments of infantry and one of cavalry, and afterwards reduced the Thainawala country. He was in command of a portion of the Sikh army at the battle of Theri in 1823. Two battles were indeed fought at Theri. The Maharaja commanded, in person, on the left bank of the Kabul river, and he defeated the Yusufzye fanatics, losing, however, Phula Singh Akali, and some good officers. On the right bank of the river was the main body of the Sikh army, commanded by Hari Singh Nalwa, Jamadar Khushhal Singh, Sirdar *Budh Singh* and others, and the opposing force of Afghans, commanded by Muhammad Azim Khan, who was defeated with loss, and died within the year, of chagrin.

In 1825 the Maharaja was in the Rambagh at Amritsar, dangerously ill. His life was despaired of, and he had become wholly unconscious. Sirdar *Budh Singh*, who saw that on the death of Ranjit Singh the country would again be divided into separate chiefships, and supposing the Maharaja to be dying, determined to make provision for himself. He went at night with a force to the fort of Govindghar and demanded admittance in the name of the Maharaja. The Jamadar of the gate, Dya Ram, would not admit him without orders. *Budh Singh* accordingly went back and induced by large bribes, the keeper of the seal to draw out an order for the fort to be given up to him, and to this the seal was affixed. *Budh Singh* returned to the fort, but the Jamadar was not to be deceived. He would not look at the order, and declared that so late at night he would not open the gates to the Maharaja himself. The Sirdar had to retire discomfited, and in the morning Imamuddin, the Kiladar, told the Maharaja, who had in some measure recovered, the whole affair. The result was that *Budh Singh* was given the Peshawur command, and sent into the Yusufzai country against Khalifa Syad Ahmad, a fanatic who was preaching a Jihad, or holy war, against the Sikhs, the Maharaja hoping that he would leave his bones in the Yusufzai hills, and never return to disturb him.

Budh Singh crossed the Kabul river in advance of the main body, and encamped at Akora, where he threw up entrenchments; but during the night he was attacked by the enemy, and only succeeded in beating them off with a loss of five hundred killed and wounded. Sirdar *Attar Singh* Sindhanwalia was present on this occasion, and displayed much gallantry. The next day the Sikh army moved on nine miles to Jagirah, where it was joined by the Dogra Chiefs, and the Attari Sirdars, with their troops, which, together with those of Sirdar *Budh Singh*, amounted to some ten thousand men, with twelve guns. Their entrenchments were soon surrounded by the large but undisciplined army of the Syad, composed of Kabulis, Yusufzais, and Afghans. For some days the Sikhs remained in their entrenchments, exposed to the incessant assaults of the enemy, till, at length, the supplies and the patience of *Budh Singh* being exhausted, he led his men against the enemy, and, after a severe fight, defeated them with great slaughter. The Syad took refuge in the Yusufzai hills, and it was two years before he recovered his strength sufficiently to again take the field. After this success Sirdar *Budh Singh* returned to Lahore, where he was received with all honor; but a few months later, at the close of 1827, he died of cholera. The Maharaja wrote a letter to his family, expressing his grief at the Sirdar's death, and his regret that so brave a man should have died in his bed, like common mortals. Sirdar *Budh Singh* was one of the bravest and most skilful of the Sikh Generals. At the time of his death there was a rumour that the Dogras had poisoned him, but there is not the smallest foundation for the story.

Amir Singh died before his son, in the same year, but all the jagirs, amounting to upwards of six lakhs, were continued to Sirdars *Attar Singh, Lehna Singh, Wasawa Singh, and Shamsher Singh. Attar Singh* succeeded his brother in the Durbar, and his strength and courage were so great, that after the death of Sirdar Hari Singh Nalwa, in 1837, he was considered the champion of the Khalsaji.

In the same year, *Attar Singh* was sent to Peshawar, with his Contingent, and *Lehna Singh* to Shabkadr. They did good service, and were engaged in constant warfare with the wild tribes in the neighbourhood. *Attar Singh* obtained the title, as long as complimentary, of "Ujjal didar, Nirmal budh, Sirdar ba wakar, Kasir-ul-iktadar, Sarwar-i-giroh-i-namdar, Ali tabbai Shajaud-dowlah, Sirdar Attar Singh, Shamsher-i-Jang buhadar;" and Sirdar *Lehna Singh,* the title of "Ujjal Didar, Nirmal budh, Sirdar ba wakar, Sirdar Lehna Singh, Sindhanwalia, buhadar." The jagirs and power of the family continually increased till the death of Maharaja Kharrak Singh ; when, though nominally in possession of seven lakhs of country, they really possessed between nine and ten.

At this time *Attar Singh* was the head of the family, both by age and ability ; *Lehna Singh* was a man of energy, but illiterate and debauched ; *Ajit Singh,* his nephew, was brave enough, but headstrong and rash ; whilst *Shamsher Singh* was averse to politics, and was absent at Peshawar, with his troops.

When Prince Nao Nihal Singh was killed, by accident or design, the same day that his father died, two claimants appeared for the vacant throne. The first was Rani Chand Kour, widow of Maharaja Kharrak Singh ; the second, Prince Sher Singh, a reputed son of Maharaja Ranjit Singh, a brave soldier and possessing some influence with the army. The claims of Chand Kour were supported by the Sindhanwalia party, including Bhai Ram Singh, Sirdar Tej Singh, and his uncle Jamadar Khushhal Singh. Sher Singh was favoured by the Dogra party at the head of which was Raja Dhyan Singh, and his brothers, Rajas Gulab Singh and Suchet Singh, with Misr (afterwards Raja) Lal Singh and others. Between the Sindhanwalia and the Dogra parties the greatest enmity existed. Both had possessed great power and influence during the latter years of Ranjit's reign, and each looked with jealousy and suspicion upon its rival. But the ambition of the Sindhanwalias had been united with attachment to the reigning Family, and devotion to the State; that of the Dogra brothers had ever been selfish. There are perhaps no characters in history more repulsive than Rajas Gulab Singh and Dhyan Singh. Their splendid talents and their undoubted bravery count as nothing, in the presence of their atrocious cruelty, their avarice, their treachery, and their unscrupulous ambition.

At the time of Prince Nao Nihal Singh's death, *Attar Singh* was at Hardwar, and *Lehna Singh* and *Ajit Singh* in Kulu. On the news reaching them, *Attar Singh* and *Ajit Singh* both hastened to Lahore.

Rani Sahib Kour, widow of Prince Nao Nihal Singh, was pregnant at the time of her husband's death, and Raja Dhyan Singh, seeing that in the temper of the Sikh people, it would be well to wait, agreed that Sher Singh should retire to his estates, leaving his son Partab Singh in the Darbar, professedly for eight months, till it was seen whether a son would be born to Sahib Kour or to any other of the Ranis; in reality, till he, Dhyan Singh, should gain over the troops to the side of Sher Singh. A fac-simile of a very curious state paper, containing this agreement, and signed by Rajas Gulab Singh and Dhyan Singh; the three Sindhanwalia chiefs; Sirdar Lehna Singh Majithia; Sirdar Tej Singh; Bhai Ram Singh; Bhai Govind Ram; Bhai Nidhan Singh; Bhai Gurmukh Singh, Jamadar Khushhal Singh and Sheikh Mohiuddin,—is given at the commencement of this volume. This deed was executed on the 27th of November, three weeks after the death of Prince Nao Nihal Singh, and in accordance with its provisions, Sher Singh left for Battala, and Raja Dhyan Singh retired to Jammu, leaving his agents, in Lahore, to win over the soldiery. The designs of the Jammu brothers were evidently distrusted by the other Chiefs, who, on the 4th of December, signed another paper, declaring their fidelity to the state and their resolution to stand or fall together.

Early in January, Sher Singh, hearing that the army was well disposed towards him, and hoping to gain Lahore without the aid of Dhyan Singh, whom he both hated and feared, appeared with his troops before the city. Raja Gulab Singh, however, determined that Sher Singh should not succeed without his brother's aid, joined the Sindhanwalias, and prepared to defend the fort. The history of the siege of Lahore is too well known to be repeated here. For seven days the garrison held out, bravely, against the whole Sikh army, which lost in the assault a great nummber of men; and it was not till Raja Dhyan Singh returned from Jammu that negotiations were opened, by which Sher Singh ascended the throne, and Rani Chand Kour resigned her claim. Gulab Singh, laughing in his sleeve at the success of his and his brother's plans, marched off to Jammu, amidst the curses of the Sikh army, carrying with him a great part of the treasure, principally jewels, which Maharaja Ranjit Singh had stored in the fort, and which plunder, five years later, helped to purchase Kashmir.

Sirdar *Attar Singh* then went, as an agent of Rani Chand Kour, to the Governor General's agent at Ludhiana, to try and induce him to support their party, but he was not successful; and *Ajit Singh* then tried his persuasive powers with equal bad success. He then travelled to Calcutta, but was not able to obtain audience of the Governor General. The object of their absence was well understood at Lahore, and Sher Singh confiscated all the jagirs of the family, with the exception of those of Sirdar *Shamsher Singh,* who had not joined in the intrigues of his relatives. He sent Budh Singh Mahrah, and Hukm Singh Malwai, to Kulu, where *Lehna Singh* was in command, to bring him to Lahore, with his nephew *Kehr Singh;* and on their arrival, threw them into prison. The other members of the family, except *Shamsher Singh,* then crossed the Satlej and took refuge at Thanesar, in British territories. But the exile of the Sindhanwalias occasioned Maharaja Sher Singh as much anxiety as their presence. They carried on their intrigues at Lahore, and the army, which they had often led to battle, murmured at the severity with which they were treated. Sher Singh was accordingly ready to listen to the sinister advice of Bhai Ram Singh, who urged their recal, and in October 1842, Sirdars *Ajit Singh* and *Lehna Singh*, who had been, some time before, released from confinement, returned to Lahore, and all their jagirs were restored to them. *Attar Singh* remained at Unah in the Hoshiarpur district, in sanctuary with Bedi Bikrama Singh. He had no faith in Maharaja Sher Singh or in the Jammu Rajas. Nor, to tell the truth, was it any love for these latter that induced *Ajit Singh* and *Lehna Singh* to return. They had, doubtless, a longing for their fat jagirs; but they had heard of the murder of Rani Chand Kour, the head of their party and the reputed mistress of *Ajit Singh*, by Sher Singh and Dhyan Singh; they heard that Rani Sahib Kour had been delivered of a still-born son, and the Lahore bazars were whispering that it was not the interest of Sher Singh and Dhyan Singh that the child should be born alive.

All at first went on smoothly. Vainly did Dhyan Singh try to persuade the Sindhanwalias that his interest had procured their recal; they knew his hatred for them, and determined upon his fall. The plot of the Sindhanwalias was a bold one. They were for no half measures. Maharaja Sher Singh and his minister Dhyan Singh were to fall together, and the Sindhanwalias, having gratified their revenge, would wield the whole power of the state as guardians of the young Dalip Singh. Raja Dhyan Singh had also a policy which was no less energetic. He desired to destroy Sher Singh and the Sindhanwalias, and secure for himself the regency, and in the event of any accident happening Dalip Singh, a probable throne for his son Hira Singh.

The Sindhanwalias persuaded the Maharaja that Dhyan Singh had determined to destroy him, and that his safety could only be secured by the death of the Minister. That they, the Sindhanwalias, his relations and friends, were the only persons he could trust, and that they were ready to make away with the obnoxious Minister. Sher Singh believed this story, which was one half true, and signed a paper exonerating them from the guilt of Dhyan Singh's murder, and arranged the manner of its execution.

Some days later, *Ajit Singh* and *Lehna Singh* were to parade their troops before the Maharaja, for inspection, when Dhyan Singh was to be directed to examine them, and the Sindhanwalias were to take this opportunity of putting him to death. The same night that this arrangement was made with the Maharaja, *Lehna Singh* and *Ajit Singh* paid a visit to Raja Dhyan Singh. They told him that Sher Singh had determined, first on his destruction, and then on theirs, and called on him to assist in his overthrow. When Dhyan Singh saw the paper that Sher Singh had signed, he agreed to the Sindhanwalias' proposal, and it was arranged between them, that on the day of the inspection, the victim to fall should be the Prince and not the Minister.

It thus appears that the Sindhanwalias were the originators of the conspiracy against Sher Singh. They themselves assert that Dhyan Singh visited *Ajit Singh* and *Lehna Singh*, and telling them that the Maharaja had determined to destroy them, urged them to join in a plot against his life ; but this story is in no way probable. Sher Singh desired to conciliate the Sindhanwalias, not to destroy them. He had but recently restored their jagirs and honours, and he looked to them, and to them alone, as his defence against the Jammu Rajas, Dhyan Singh and Gulab Singh, whom he feared as much as he hated. The Sindhanwalias knew this well, and they would never have believed that the Maharaja was plotting against them.

The 15th September, 1843, the day for the inspection of the Sindhanwalia troops, at length arrived. The Maharaja had gone to spend the day at a summer house, at Shah Bilawal, half way between Lahore and Shalimar, and thither Sirdars *Ajit Singh* and *Lehna Singh* proceeded. They entered the presence fully armed, but this was not unusual. Sher Singh was in the small room of the house, with but one or two attendants, and Diwan Dina Nath was reading state papers aloud to him. *Ajit Singh* paid his respects, and, coming forward, presented for the Maharaja's inspection a double-barrelled gun, which, he said, he had just purchased. Sher Singh, who was fond of fire-arms, stretched out his hand to take it, when *Ajit Singh*, who had kept the muzzle directed towards the Prince, fired both barrels, which had been loaded with a double charge, full in his breast.

The Maharaja had only time to cry, "I kya dagga hai ?" (what treachery is this ?) when he fell back and expired. His attendants attacked the assassins, but they were few in number and were soon overpowered. Sirdar Budh Singh, Mokerian, was killed on the spot, his cousin severely wounded, and several others were cut down by the Sindhanwalias.

Not far from Shah Bilawal, was the garden of Sirdar Joala Singh Padhania. Here Prince Partab Singh, eldest son of the Maharaja, a handsome and intelligent boy, was peforming his devotions, and distributing alms to Brahmans, for it was the 1st day of Asoj, and the monthly festival of Shankrant. To this garden *Lehna Singh* hurried, with some troops. The Prince saw him approach with a drawn sword, and cried out "Babaji, I will remain your servant," (tumhara naukar main rahunga). Lehna Singh answered, "Your father is killed," and ran the boy through with his sword. At the same time were killed Attar Singh, Parohit, in attendance on the Prince, and several Brahmans.

* While this tragedy was being enacted in Joala Singh's garden, *Ajit Singh* had cut off the Maharaja's head, and, mounting his horse, had galloped off towards Lahore, with 300 followers. At the spot where is now the Badami Bagh, he met Raja Dhyan Singh, riding slowly towards Shah Bilawal, with Fatah Khan Tiwana, and a few attendants. He told the Raja that all had gone off well, and requested him to ride back with him to Lahore. The Raja may have had suspicions, but it was useless then to show them; so he turned his horse's head towards the

---

* Note.—The story of the assassination of Sher Singh and Partab Singh has been told in various ways. It is believed that the above version is the correct one. Eye-witnesses of the tragedy, who have been questioned, are unanimous as to its truthfulness, and among these may be mentioned Diwan Ajodhia Parshad, who was with Maharaja Sher Singh at the time of his death, and Ram Milawar Mal, wakil of the Raja of Kapurthalla, who was in the garden of Joala Singh when Prince Partab Singh was murdered.

city. By the Roshnai gate they entered the city, and on passing into the fort the gates were shut.

As they rode up the ascent, *Ajit Singh* asked the Minister what arrangements he intended to make. He answered " Dalip Singh shall be Maharaja; I, Wazir; and the Sindhanwalias shall enjoy power." Again Ajit Singh asked the question, but the same answer was returned. In his extremity Dhyan Singh would not promise the 'Wizarat' to one of the hated Sindhanwalias. But he now saw from *Ajit Singh's* demeanour that his death was determined on, and he turned to address the Sirdar, but he cried out, " You are the murderer of the Rani Sahib," and fired at the Raja, with his pistol. The attendants of *Ajit Singh* then cut him down with their swords, and threw his body into the pit of the gun foundery in the fort. Ahmad Khan Gheba, who was in attendance on Dhyan Singh, was killed with him. *Lehna Singh* soon afterwards arrived, and the Sirdars then wrote to Raja Suchet Singh, the brother, and Raja Hira Singh the son of the murdered Minister, requesting their presence at a consultation in the fort. The Rajas however were not to be entrapped, and soon the news of the murder got abroad. Raja Hira Singh, who has been himself accused of conspiracy against his father's life, now determined to avenge his death, and addressed the troops, and by extravagant promises gained them over to his side, and, by evening, the army of forty thousand men had surrounded the fort, which the Sindhanwalias had determined to defend to the last. These Chiefs had proclaimed Dalip Singh king, and *Lehna Singh* wazir, but they felt that their chance was lost, and but feebly defended the fort against the first attack of Hira Singh. When, however, the walls had been breached, and the enemy advanced to the assault, the Sindhanwalias fought with desperation, but they had but a few hundred men, and the works were carried, though with great loss. *Ajit Singh* tried to escape, by letting himself over the walls by a rope, but he was seen by a soldier, and in spite of his lavish promises of reward, if his life was spared, was shot dead. His head was cut off and taken to Hira Singh, who ordered his body to be quartered and exposed in different parts of the city. The soldier who slew him was made a subhadar. *Lehna Singh,* whose thigh had been broken by a shot from a zamburah, early in the day, was discovered hiding in a vault, and was also ruthlessly murdered. Dalip Singh was then proclaimed king, and Hira Singh wazir. Thus ended the tragedy.

Raja Hira Singh, on obtaining power, confiscated all the jagirs of the Sindhanwalia family, except those of Sirdar *Shamsher Singh,* who was at Peshawar, and had not joined in the conspiracy. He destroyed Raja Sansi, the family seat, ploughed up the ground on which their palace had stood, and hunted down all their friends and adherents. The surviving members of the family, with Sirdar *Attar Singh,* fled across the Sutlej. It does not appear that *Attar Singh* was aware of the lengths to which his brother and nephew were prepared to go, yet Hira Singh believed him to be privy to the whole conpiracy and determined on his destruction. With this object he forged letters from many of the chiefs and leaders of the army, and sent them to *Attar Singh,* urging him to return to the Panjab, where he might recover his influence and destroy the Wazir. He also sent forged letters to Baba Vir Singh, a Guru much respected by the Sikhs, begging him to use his influence to induce the Sirdar to return. The Princes Kashmira Singh and Peshora Singh were with Baba Vir Singh, at this time, and Hira Singh hoped to destroy his three enemies at one blow. Both *Attar Singh* and the Baba were deceived ; and the former crossed the Satlej with his followers, and joined the camp of the Baba. The Sikh army would not hear of attacking the holy Guru, and Hira Singh had to use still further deceit. He assured the troops that *Attar Singh* had allied himself with the British, who were even now ready to cross the Satlej and seize the Panjab. That if the army marched against him, he would probably return to the Cis-Sutlej States without offering any resistance. The troops, thus cajoled, marched from Lahore, and all turned out as Hira Singh had hoped. By trickery, a tumult was excited, and before the Sikh soldiers knew what they were about, they were engaged in a regular fight with the Sindhanwalia force ; the camp of the Baba was stormed, and he was killed by a cannon shot in the action. Kashmira Singh was killed, fighting gallantly, and *Attar Singh* was shot by Sirdar Gulab Singh Calcuttia. His death took place in May 1844.

Seven months later, Hira Singh himself was assassinated, and Sirdar Jowahir Singh, the drunken brother of Rani Jindan, who succeeded him, as Wazir, recalled the Sindhanwalias from exile, and promised to restore their jagirs. In March, 1845, they received, out of the old estate, jagirs to the value of 1,76,000 Rs. Sirdar *Shamsher Singh* was recalled from Peshawar, and placed in command of a brigade of regular troops, which he commanded throughout the Satlej campaign of 1845-46. He was appointed a member of the Council of Regency, in December, 1846. In February, 1848, the Resident at Lahore deputed *Shamsher Singh* to the districts about Amritsar, known as the Manjha, placing under him the civil and military establishments. This tract of country was infested by robbers, chiefly disbanded soldiers, and the Sirdar, acting with considerable energy, restored to it some degree of quiet. Previous to this he had served, for a short time, at Bannu, with Lieutenant Edwardes, in command of the Mariwala and Mokal levies. When Diwan Mulraj of Multan tendered his resignation, the post of Nazim, or Governor, was offered to *Shamsher Singh.* He did not, however, seem willing to accept it, and it was finally given to Sirdar Khan Singh Man. *Shamsher Singh* was, on the outbreak of rebellion, sent down to Multan, in command of one division of the Sikh army. He warned Major Edwardes of the disaffected state of the troops, and did his best to keep them faithful. Their mutiny at length took him by surprise, and he was carried off by Raja Sher Singh, Attariwala, into Multan, where, before the whole Darbar, he refused to join the rebel cause, and declared that he only owed obedience to the Maharaja. The next morning, the 15th September, 1848, he succeeded in making his escape, on foot, from Sher Singh's camp, leaving behind him all his tents and elephants; on the road he was intercepted by two of the rebels, but he shot one, and the other took to flight. After his return from Mooltan, he rendered good assistance to General Wheeler, in furnishing information of the movements of Ram Singh, son of Shama, Wazir of Nurpur, who was in open rebellion.

After annexation, the personal jagirs of Sirdar *Shamsher Singh*, amounting to 40,250 Rs. per annum, were upheld for life; one quarter descending to his male issue in perpetuity. His service jagir of 30,250 Rs. was resumed.

In 1857, during the mutiny, *Shamsher Singh* raised a troop of 125 horsemen, which formed part of Hodson's Horse, now the 9th and 10th Bengal Cavalry. In February, 1862, he was made Magistrate, in his own jagir, and, a month later, his jurisdiction was extended to cases of dacoity. About the same time the portion of his jagir to descend, in perpetuity, was raised from one quarter to two thirds. Sirdar *Shamsher Singh* has no children of his own, but has adopted *Bakshish Singh*, the second son of his first cousin *Thakar Singh*.

On the death of Sirdar *Attar Singh*, his son *Kehr Singh* became the head of the family. But this Sirdar was a man of no energy or ability. Most extravagant in his habits, he was surrounded by men who grew rich upon his follies. At Multan, where he served with his cousin, he remained faithful to Government, following his cousin's example, for he had no will of his own. On annexation, his personal jagir of 26,000 Rs. was maintained to him, one-third of it to descend to his male issue. This jagir has now lapsed to Government, on the death of *Kehr Singh*, which took place in February, 1864. His life had been much shortened by his intemperate habits. His jagir had been for some time in the hands of his creditors, and he himself had to pass through the insolvent court.

The two sons of *Lehna Singh*, Sirdars *Partab Singh* and *Thakar Singh*, also were confirmed in their personal jagirs. They were too young to be concerned in the rebellion of 1848-49. *Partab Singh* died in 1856, without issue, and his jagir of 10,565 Rs., has lapsed to Government. *Thakar Singh* possesses an estate of 5,565 Rs., of which one-fourth is in perpetuity. Sirdar *Ranjodh Singh*, son of Sirdar *Wasawa Singh*, was a man of no character. He had a jagir of 15,840 Rs., of which one-third 5,280 Rs. is in perpetuity. He died in June, 1864, leaving one son.

Sirdar *Shamsher Singh* resides at Raja Sansi, about five miles north of Amritsar. The village of Sindhanwala is now held by the descendants of *Gurmukh Singh*, brother of Sirdar *Amir Singh*.

RAJA TEJ SINGH.

JAMADAR KHUSHHAL SINGH.

- HAR GOBIND.
  - Niddha.
    - Raja Tej Singh D. 1862.
      - Narindar Singh B. 1859.
    - Harbans Singh B. 1846.
  - Jamadar Khushhal Singh. D. 1844.
    - S. Ram Singh D. 1839.
    - S. Kishan Singh D. 1846.
    - S. Bhagwan Singh B. 1838.
  - Ram Lal.
    - Devi Singh.
      - Fatah Singh.
    - Shiv Ram.
      - Jowahir Singh.
      - Sham Singh.
      - Brahmanand.

HISTORY OF THE FAMILY.

The father of *Khushhal Singh* was a Brahman shop-keeper of the Gour class, and resided at Ikri, in the Sirdhanah pargannah of the Meerat district. The family was poor, and in the year 1807, *Khushhal*, a young man of seventeen, came to Lahore to seek his fortune, and was taken into the Dhonkal Singhwala Regiment, then newly raised, on five rupees a month. He soon made friends with Jatri and Ganga Singh, the Maharaja's chamberlains, and was placed on the personal guard of Ranjit Singh. Here, by his vigilance, aided by good looks, and soldierly bearing, he attracted the favourable notice of the Maharaja. The story told by the family is that, one night, Ranjit Singh went out, in disguise, and on his return to the palace was stopped by *Khushhal*, who was on guard, and who kept his master in the watch-house till the morning, and that this vigilance pleased the Maharaja so much that he kept *Khushhal* by him, as a personal attendant.* However this may be, it is certain that *Khushhal* rose daily in his master's favour, till in 1811, he was appointed deorhiwala, or chamberlain, with the title of Jamadar. The appointment was one of importance. The chamberlain was master of the ceremonies, regulated processions, and superintended the Darbar. It was through him alone that any individual, however high in rank, could obtain a private interview with the Maharaja, although the daily Darbar was open to all men of family or official importance.

The etiquette at Lahore, when the Maharaja went out, was as follows. First went one hundred troopers, two abreast. Then the Maharaja, with foot orderlies at his stirrups, and an umbrella bearer ; the princes immediately behind ; then the Sirdars and Barons, mounted, each with his umbrella bearer ; and lastly, the elephants and led horses. If the Maharaja rode on an elephant, the Sirdars must do the same ; if he was carried in a palanquin, the Sirdars followed on horseback.

The same year that *Khushhal* obtained the charge of the Deorhi, he summoned from Meerut his nephew *Tej Ram,* then a boy of twelve. In 1812, he took the pahal (the Sikh baptism) and became a Singh. *Tej Ram* did not take the pahal, till 1816, and then only by the Maharaja's express orders. He changed his name to *Tej Singh,* though he was almost as often called *Teja Singh. Tej Singh* is, however, the correct name.

Khushhal Singh soon grew both rich and powerful. Most of the household appointments were given by him, with the Maharaja's sanction ; and persons, wishing a private audience of the Maharaja, would give the chamberlain large sums to admit them. He used to read the daily reports of the army to Ranjit Singh, who soon began to employ him on active ser-

* Note.—The popular story regarding Khushhal Singh's rise to favour, states that Ranjit Singh was first attracted by the singing of the young man, who was keeping guard over the tent at night. In the morning, he called for the singer, and, seeing that his face was as pleasing as his voice, kept him about his person.

vice. The young *Tej Singh* was his deputy during his absence from court. In 1816, the *Jamadar* was sent to occupy the country of certain Ramgharia Sirdars, Bir Singh, Diwan Singh, and Khushhal Singh, and afterwards to seize the Ramghavia estates at and around Amritsar. After this he proceeded to Mandi and Kulu, which States had become tributaries of Lahore, and remained, for four months, in the hills. He accompanied the Maharaja in the first Kashmir campaign, in 1814. Raja Agar Khan of Rajaor proved a very treacherous ally. He misled Ranjit Singh as to the number of the enemy, and advised a division of the army; one detachment to pass into Kashmir by the Bhara Galla route, and the main body to proceed by Punch. This advice was followed, to the ruin of the expedition. Both divisions of the army were surrounded, their supplies cut off, and they finally were compelled to retire, in all haste, to Lahore. The retreat was a disastrous one. The *Jamadar* commanded the advance, to clear the road of the enemy; while Hari Singh Nalwa, Nihal Singh Attariwala, and Mit Singh Padhania, covered the rear. Many men were lost, and Sirdar Mit Singh himself mortally wounded. *Tej Singh*, who had been created a Sirdar, was, in this campaign, in close attendance on the Maharaja. The next military service in which the *Jamadar* was concerned, was the third and last siege of Multan, in 1818. Prince Kharrak Singh, nominally, commanded the army, but it was the military genius of Misr Diwan Chand that secured success. The *Jamadar* was in command at the Tomb of Shamash Tabrez.

Soon after the capture of Multan, the *Jamadar* fell somewhat into disfavour. His brother *Ram Lal* had arrived at Lahore, in 1816, and had received an appointment in the body-guard. The Maharaja wished him to become a Sikh, but to this neither of the brothers would consent; and as the Maharaja became very urgent on the point, *Ram Lal*, with the connivance of the *Jamadar*, left the Panjab and returned to Hindostan. *Ranjit Singh* was much displeased, and Misr Diwan Chand, with whom the *Jamadar* had quarrelled about the Multan booty, advised that he should be removed from the charge of the Deorhi. To this Ranjit Singh consented, for Mian Dhyan Singh, a young Rajput in the Ghorcharhas, was now rising into favour, and on him the office of Deorhiwala was conferred. The *Jamadar* was taken by surprise, but wisely made no opposition, and retained all his jagirs, and was admitted to the Council, obtaining more real power than he had had before. He received command of four thousand irregulars, while *Tej Singh* was made General in the regular force.

Sirdar *Tej Singh* accompanied Misr Diwan Chand to Kashmir, in 1819, and in 1821. Both he and the *Jamadar* commanded divisions in the campaign against Mankerah, Leiah, and Dera Ismail Khan; and also in the Peshawar campaign, of 1823. At the battle of Tehri they were with the Maharaja, opposed to the Yusufzais on the right bank of the Lundah river; while the main body of the army under Sirdars Hari Singh Nalwa, and Budh Singh Sindhanwalia, were engaged with the Barakzai Sirdars on the left bank. After the battle the Sikh army advanced upon Peshawur, after having taken Jahangira from Firoz Khan, Khattak, of Akora. Peshawar was plundered, and the troops pushed on to the Khybar, but little was to be done there; the wild Khybaris cut the embankments of the Bara river, and flooded the Maharaja's camp, carrying off in the confusion horses and other spoil, and, after a short stay, Ranjit Singh returned to Lahore.

In 1828 the *Jamadar* and his nephew, with the Nalwa, Padhania, and Majithia Sirdars, reduced the Katoch country, and the forts of Chowki, Aimahghar, Tira and Riah. The last mentioned place alone offered much resistance; but *Tej Singh* brought up some guns from Sujanpur, on elephants, and, after three days, the garrison surrendered. In 1832, the *Jamadar* was sent to Kashmir to assist prince Sher Singh, the governor, under whose administration the revenue had much fallen, and the people become discontented. The advent of the *Jamadar* did not mend matters. He knew nothing of finance, and only cared about pleasing the Maharaja. The season of 1832 had been a bad one in Kashmir, and the *Jamadar* converted scarcity into famine, by his oppression. The few lakhs which he managed to screw out of the people did not count for much, when the annual revenue was diminished by two-thirds, and the inhabitants forced to leave the country in search of bread; and Ranjit Singh was for a time much displeased, but the *Jamadar* soon recovered his influence. General Mian Singh was sent to succeed him, in Kashmir, with fifty thousand maunds of grain for distribution to the poor, but it was many years before Kashmir recovered its former prosperity. ***Ram Lal***, brother of ***Khushhal Singh***, had returned to the Panjab, and he took command of the *Jamadar's* forces in the Peshawar campaign of 1834 under Sirdar Hari Singh and Prince Nao Nihal Singh. *Jamadar* ***Khushhal Singh*** and Raja Dhyan Singh were in command of the forces, which marched to relieve the Sikh army, blockaded at Jamrud, in April, 1837. Although the *Jamadar* reached Peshawar two days before Dhyan Singh, he made no effort to relieve the Sikh army, which was in the greatest straits, till the arrival of the Raja. After the retreat of the Afghans, the *Jamadar* remained at Peshawar, while ***Tej Singh*** was ordered to the Chaj Doab, to preserve order.

Ram Singh, the eldest son of the *Jamadar*, was, about this time, made a General in the army, although a mere boy. He had, however, the passions of a man, and after having returned, in 1837, to Amritsar, with the Maharaja, murdered brutally, with his own hand, Bishan Singh, brother-in-law of Colonel Chet Singh, a fine young man, who had offended him by a boyish jest. Such was the influence of the *Jamadar*, that ***Ram Singh*** remained unpunished, with the exception of a fine, although his victim had been a favourite at court.

In 1838, ***Tej Singh*** was sent to Hazara, and built there the fort of Manakghar, near Darband. In 1839, he proceeded to Peshawar, with the *Jamadar*, Prince Nao Nihal Singh, Raja Gulab Singh, and other Chiefs, to co-operate with the British army invading Kabal; but the Sikh co-operation, as is notorious, was more damaging than serviceable, as the expedition was regarded by the Sikhs with distrust and dislike.

General *Ram Singh* died in this year. Although of a cruel disposition, he was a good officer, and seems to have been the cleverest of the family. After the accession of Maharaja Kharrak Singh, both the *Jamadar* and *Tej Singh* joined in the conspiracy against Sirdar Chet Singh, favourite of the new Monarch, who had shown ill-feeling towards them, and had deprived the *Jamadar* of a portion of his command. On the night of the murder, Prince Nao Nihal Singh, with *Tej Singh* and *Khushkhal Singh*, remained at the gate of the palace to guard against a rescue; while the other conspirators, the Rajas Gulab Singh and Dhyan Singh, and the Sirdars Fatah Singh Man, Attar Singh Sindhanwalia, and Mian Labh Singh, entered the palace and murdered the favourite, in the very presence of the Maharaja.

While Prince Nao Nihal Singh held power, the family of the *Jamadar* was treated with great favour; and on his death, on the 5th November, 1840, both *Khushkhal Singh* and *Tej Singh* signed, with the other Chiefs, a paper, by which it was agreed that no action should be made in appointing a successor to the throne, till it was seen whether the wives of the Prince or the Maharaja would bear a son. The succeeding events are well known. The Sindhanwalia Sirdars and Raja Gulab Singh defended the fort against Prince Sher Singh; while *Tej Singh* and *Khushkhal Singh* kept wisely at home, joining neither party, but waiting to see what turn affairs would take. Sher Singh was much irritated by their conduct, and, on his accession, had serious intentions of putting them both to death, but they were at length forgiven, on the intercession of Bhai Gurmukh Singh. But Sher Singh entertained a grudge against the *Jamadar*, and is said on one occasion to have tried to make away with him, in a manner that should appear accidental. Certain it is that soon after Sher Singh's accession, he was in a pleasure boat on the Ravi with the *Jamadar* and Amar Singh, Ahluwalia, uncle of the present Raja of Kapurthalla. The boat was overturned; the Maharaja sprang into another boat along side; Amar Singh was drowned, and his body never recovered, while the *Jamadar*, who managed to escape, swallowed more water than he had done for many years. It was generally believed in Lahore that Sher Singh capsized the boat intentionally, but this can never be proved.

The *Jamadar* had been in bad health ever since 1840. In July 1844 he died, having mixed but little in politics during the three last years of his life. In June, 1843, he had, with Rajas Gulab Singh and Suchet Singh, attended Prince Partab Singh in his visit to Lord Ellenborough, at Firozpur.

Jamadar Khushhal Singh was not a man of any particular ability. The Maharaja took him into favour, not so much for his courage, genius or learning, as for his broad shoulders, and good looks; though from the pictures taken of him, late in life, he seems to have been an unusually coarse and vulgar-looking man. He was not, however, inferior to many other Sirdars of the Maharaja's court; and if, in the many campaigns in which he served, he displayed no particular bravery, yet it is not anywhere stated that he ever ran away. Of his severity and oppression in Kashmir, mention has been made; and on all occasions, trusting to the Maharaja's favour, he showed himself something of a tyrant. At Amritsar, to obtain ground for his own houses, he pulled down, without offering any compensation, many dwellings of the poorer classes, but Ranjit Singh would not listen to any complaints against him, and would tell any one who came to appeal against the *Jamadar*, to go and obtain justice from Guru Ram Das.

Sirdar *Tej Singh*, at the time of the *Jamadar's* death, was at Peshawar, of which place he had, in 1843, obtained the command; and Raja Hira Singh, who was then Minister, and who had an old grievance with the *Jamadar* about the Chamberlainship, confiscated 1,60,000 Rs. out of the jagirs of 3,40,000 Rs. which had been all granted in the name of *Khushhal Singh*, the family making the distribution among themselves. *Kishan Singh*, son of the *Jamadar*, a wild young man, spent in the ten days succeeding his father's death, about a lakh of rupees upon the dancing girls of Lahore. Hira Singh made this the excuse for confiscation. "If you have so much cash to throw away," said he, "you can, of course, pay up seven lakhs for the good of the state." He also wanted to get a lakh out of Rai Mul Singh, the confidential agent of the family. *Kishan Singh* declared that he could not pay a rupee, and the jagirs were accordingly confiscated.

Tej Singh wrote from Peshawar to protest against the confiscation, and Pandit Jalla said that when the Sirdar returned to Lahore, the matter should be considered, but before this took place the ministry both of Hira Singh and of Jowahir Singh had fallen, and the Maharani, with her favourite, Lal Singh, had assumed the supreme power.

The government of *Tej Singh* at Peshawar was marked by almost the only piece of energy he ever displayed. When the troops under his command heard of the death of Raja Suchet Singh at Lahore, and of the large sums that had been given to the Lahore army, they rose in mutiny, and threatened that if all the money in the treasury was not given to them, they would treat *Tej Singh* as General Mian Singh had been treated, three years before, in Kashmir. The Sirdar amused the troops by promises of rewards, and called in all the Afghan Chiefs of the valley, to his help ; and the next morning had so strong a force at his command, that the mutinous regiments thought it best to recede from their demands. Raja Lal Singh recalled *Tej Singh* from Peshawar, in October, 1845, appointing Sirdar Sher Singh, Attariwala, to succeed him. On his arrival at Lahore, *Tej Singh* found that war with the English was everywhere talked of as probable, and the project was favoured by the Wazir, Raja Lal Singh, and by the Maharani, who feared and hated the army that had recently murdered her brother Jowahir Singh. *Tej Singh* was wealthy and influential, and although he was looked down upon by the old Sikh Sirdars, yet the position of the *Jamadar* and himself under Ranjit Singh, gave him much power at court, and when war with the English was finally determined, he was appointed Commander-in-Chief of the Khalsa army.

On the 17th of November, the plan of the campaign was decided upon ; and on the 23rd, the army set out, in divisions, for Firozpur. But the Commander-in-Chief had little stomach for the fight, and it was not till the 15th of December, when all excuses for remaining behind were exhausted, that he set out to join the army, which, four days previously, had crossed the Satlej.

After the defeat of Raja Lal Singh at the battle of Mudki, he sent to *Tej Singh* to urge him to advance to his support. Accordingly the Sirdar marched, with his division, and some fifteen thousand irregular cavalry, and reached Firushahr on the morning of the 22nd December, when the force of Lal Singh had been again defeated. *Tej Singh* advanced against the British army, which was completely exhausted, and almost without ammunition. He drove in the British cavalry parties, and endeavoured to regain the lost position of Firushahr. He then attacked the left flank of the British army, and made such a demonstration against the captured village, as compelled the English General to change his whole front to the right, the Sikh guns keeping up an incessant and heavy fire during this manoeuvre. At last, when the English cavalry, advancing, threatened both flanks of the Sikh army, and the infantry prepared to advance in line, for its support, *Tej Singh* ceased his fire, and, retiring from the field, crossed the Satlej and encamped at Sobraon, about twenty-five miles north-east of Firozpur, on the right bank of the river. Here the army was soon joined by Raja Lal Singh, who had fled to Amritsar after the defeat of Firushahr, and the troops demanded to be led across the river against the British. The only two Chiefs who opposed this movement were Sirdars *Tej Singh*, and Sham Singh, Attariwala, who had joined the camp on the 28th December, most unwillingly. Their pacific intentions were, however, ridiculed by the Panchayats of the army, and it was determined to cross the Satlej. A bridge of boats was thrown across the river, and a strong *tete de pont* constructed in front of it, and entrenchments, as strong as the sandy soil would allow, were thrown up. Sirdar *Tej Singh* commanded in this entrenchment, and, for his own personal security, had a small shot proof tower erected, into which he might retire in the hour of danger, and here the Sikh army waited, week after week, while the British army was drawing, from every side, men and guns and material of war. On the right Sirdar Attar Singh, Kalianwala, commanded the irregular troops ; on the left were the gallant Sham Singh of Attari, and the brigade of General Mewa Singh, Majithia, both of whom were killed in the battle of Sobraon. In the centre were the troops of Kahn Singh Man, and the brigades of General Avitable, General Mehtab Singh, Majithia, and General Gulab Singh Povindia. In the centre, too, was the brigade and tower of Sirdar *Tej Singh*.

On the 10th February, 1846, the battle of Sobraon was fought, but *Tej Singh* had so little to do with it, that a description of it would be here out of place. During the early part of the action he remained in his tower, and was only induced to come out by threats of personal violence. But even then, instead of heading the troops, and encouraging them when they began to waver, he crossed the bridge, at which he had stationed a guard of his own men, and was one of the first to fly from the field. After the battle, what remained of the defeated army assembled at Patti, and afterwards marched to Bharranah, where it was ordered to remain till after the treaty of the 9th March, 1846, when it was paid up ; many of the soldiers being re-enlisted, and others being discharged. Before this, however, Sirdar *Tej Singh* had been summoned to Lahore, and, under the new arrangements, he was confirmed in his appointment of Commander-in-Chief of the Sikh army, while Raja Lal Singh was confirmed as Wazir.

The conduct of Sirdar *Tej Singh*, both before and during the Satlej campaign, has been much misrepresented. He has been accused of treason to his country by many writers, and, in all probability, will be so accused by more ; but there is no evidence whatever to support the charge. In the first place, the Sirdar was averse to the war. While the Maharani, Raja Lal Singh, and Diwan Dinanath were urging the troops to invade British territory, in the hope that they would never return to disturb the peace of Lahore, *Tej Singh* spoke so constantly against the war, that his life was in imminent danger, and, in the middle of November, 1845, the troops were debating whether they should put both him and

Lal Singh to death, and insist on Raja Gulab Singh leading them to battle. When he was appointed Commander-in-Chief, much against his will, he delayed joining the army as long as he could ; conduct which may prove cowardice or disinclination for the war, but which certainly did not savour of treason. But it is said that his conduct at Firushahr was inconsistent with any other supposition than that he was a traitor, and desired the success of the British. That had he attacked the British army vigorously, and with all his force, when it was exhausted with its conflict with Raja Lal Singh and almost without ammunition, it must, in all probability, have been annihilated. The result would certainly have been disastrous ; but *Tej Singh* was not aware of the state of extreme exhaustion of the British army. All that he saw were the routed troops of Lal Singh flying to the fords of the Satlej ; a sight from which he might argue the strength, but not the weakness of the British. But he did not retire from the field without making an effort to retrieve the disasters of the preceding day. According to the despatch of Sir Hugh Gough, (though the accuracy of despatches may be fairly questioned), "he made strenuous efforts to regain the position at Firushahr ;" he certainly kept up a heavy and damaging fire of artillery, and only retired when the British army advanced in force against him. But even supposing that he had done less than he certainly did, Sirdar *Tej Singh* cannot be fairly blamed. He had no influence whatever with the army, whose Panches decided when they should fight and when they should retire. It is absurd to assert that, in opposition to the will of the Panches and the army, Tej Singh could have refused to make a general attack on the British. Any negotiations which he may have wished to open with the Governor General, after Firushahr, were only intended to bring about peace, and were of such a character as a Commander-in-Chief would have a discretionary power to carry on.

At Sobraon the voice of *Tej Singh* was again raised for peace, but the troops only threw stones at his tent, pulled it down, and threatened to murder him unless he crossed to the left bank of the river. Who can wonder that with such a savage, unruly army, he should have fled from the field, feeling that there was more danger from his own men than from the enemy.

Tej Singh was a weak, timid, vacillating creature, but he was no traitor. He had neither courage nor ability sufficient to influence an insane Sikh army, but he did not, like Raja Lal Singh, first excite the troops to madness, and then betray them to destruction. The stories of his sinking a boat in the bridge, at Sobraon, to cut off the retreat of the Sikh army, and of his turning a battery of guns upon his own men, have never been supported by a fragment of evidence ; though proof of their truth has been sought in every direction, and are evidently calumnies invented by some of his many enemies.

After the conclusion of peace, Sirdar *Tej Singh* had plenty to do in disbanding the old army and enlisting new troops, and his conduct was approved by the Agent of the British Government at Lahore. In September, 1864, very much to his disgust, he was ordered to proceed to Kashmir, with Sirdars Sher Singh, and Mangal Singh, and Generals Kanh Singh, Man, and Lal Singh, Moraria, to reduce the rebellion of Sheikh Imamuddin Khan. He pleaded illness, but at last set out with the troops. He was not alone in his disinclination for the campaign. With almost all the other Sirdars he was unwilling to act under the orders of Raja Lal Singh, whose rapacity and meanness had disgusted them, and whose honesty they thoroughly doubted. When, however, *Tej Singh* had at last set out on the expedition, he acted with energy and promptitude. His force left Lahore on the 1st of October, and reached Naoshera on the 16th, having, in this time, crossed the Ravi and the Chenab, and marched over one hundred and twenty-five miles of country, the last twenty-five miles being an execrable hill road. Imamuddin Khan did not attempt open resistance, and came in to the camp of the Resident, on the 1st of November, and the Sikh troops, having no more to do, returned to Lahore. The trial and deposition of Raja Lal Singh was the result of thi sexpedition, and, as a temporary arrangement, Sirdars *Tej Singh* and

Sher Singh Attariwala, with Diwan Dina Nath and Fakir Nuruddin, were nominated a council to carry on the business of the Government, pending other arrangements. On the 16th December, a council of Regency was appointed, consisting of Sirdar *Tej Singh* as President; Sirdars Shamsher Singh, Sindhanwalia; Ranjodh Singh, Majithia; Sher Singh, Attariwala; Attar Singh, Kalianwala; Diwan Dina Nath; Fakir Nuruddin, and Bhai Nidhan Singh.

The members of the council had distinct duties assigned to them. Sirdar *Tej Singh* was chief in the council, and held supreme military command; Diwan Dina Nath was finance minister, and Sirdar Sher Singh superintended the royal household. The task both of Sirdar *Tej Singh* and of Diwan Dina Nath was an invidious one. They certainly threw all possible blame on Major Lawrence, the British Resident, and represented that they were but instruments in carrying out his measures; but it was pretty well known that most of the redress that was obtained came, directly or indirectly, from the Residency, and that, but for the Resident, no arrears would be paid up, and consequently the two heads of the council came in for more obloquy than they probably expected.

On the 7th August, 1847, Sirdar *Tej Singh* was created Raja of Sialkot, with its fort and adjacent villages, worth 28,000 Rs. per annum. The Maharani, who entertained a bitter hatred, both against the British Resident who destroyed her influence, and *Tej Singh*, who supported his policy, prepared an insult for the latter, on the day of his installation. The young Maharaja had been schooled by her as to the part he was to play, and when *Tej Singh* came forward for the Maharaja to make the saffron *tika* (a sign of Rajaship) on his forehead, the boy-king drew back, and folded his arms, refusing to perform the ceremony. The Resident then called upon Bhai Nidhan Singh, the head of the Sikh religion; who officiated for the Maharaja; but the insult was much felt by *Tej Singh*, and so strongly showed the resolute hatred of the Maharani to the administration, that it hastened her removal from Lahore to the fort of Sheikhopurah, where she remained, under surveillance, until her final removal from the Panjab. Early in the year, she had been cognizant of, if not the instigator of, a conspiracy to murder the Resident and Raja *Tej Singh*. This design, known as the 'Prema conspiracy,' was not joined in by any Sirdar, and was never attempted to be carried into execution. On the 26th November, 1842, Raja *Tej Singh* received the honorary title of Ujjal didar, Nirmal budh, mubazir, ul-mulk, Samsam ud-doulah, Raja Tej Singh salar safdar jang, Raja Sialkot.

Throughout the rebellion of 1848-49, the Raja remained loyal to Government. That he, as well as Sirdar Lehna Singh, Majithia, knew of or anticipated a revolt, is certain, and shortly before it broke out, he wished to leave the Panjab for a time ; but this idea was given up. The Raja had nothing in common with the rebels. He was not on good terms with Raja Sher Singh, Attariwala, or his father Sirdar Chattar Singh, whose avowed object was to restore to power the Maharani, the deadly enemy of *Tej Singh*. Should the Maharani regain power, the death of the Raja, or the confiscation of his property, was certain. Besides this, *Tej Singh* was almost the only man in the country who was tolerably contented. He was very wealthy ; he had been created Raja and President of the council, and was raised high above the whole Sikh aristocracy, and a revolution could only injure him. He was obnoxious to most of the Sikh Sirdars, who looked upon him as an upstart and an imposter ; feeble in council, and ridiculous in the field ; and his ascendancy in the Darbar irritated them beyond expression. Thus Raja *Tej Singh* is entitled to no credit for loyalty, when disloyalty, whichever side conquered, must have been his ruin. But in times of danger, motives do not count for much, and the Raja's actions were loyal, and his assistance valuable to the Government.

On the annexation of the Panjab, the personal jagirs of Raja *Tej Singh*, and Sirdar *Bhagwan Singh*, the only surviving son of the *Jamadar* (*Kishan Singh* having been drowned at Sobraon, after the battle), amounting to 1,52,779 Rs. were confirmed for life. To the Raja 92,779 Rs.

and to *Bhagwan Singh*, 60,000. Rs. Of their respective shares, 20,000 Rs. were to descend in perpetuity to the heirs of Raja *Tej Singh*, and 7,500 to those of *Bhagwan Singh*. After annexation, the Raja was very useful in the disbandment of the Sikh army, and in the formation of a new native force. In 1857, he was of much assistance in raising horsemen, and for his loyalty at that time, he received a khillat of 1,000 Rs. In 1861, his scattered jagirs were consolidated, and the Ilaka of Battala granted him in exchange for them ; and his title was also changed to Raja of Battala. He was also made a jagirdar magistrate, with the powers of a Deputy Commissioner. In 1862, at the recommendation of the Government of the Panjab, the Supreme Government granted two-thirds of his jagir in perpetuity, and to Bhagwan Singh one-sixth.

A son had been born to the Raja, in 1859, by *Karam Kour*, widow of his cousin *Kishan Singh*, whom he had married by chaddar-dalna, in 1857. Previous to this, however, he had adopted a younger brother, by a different mother, *Harbans Singh*, now about 17 years of age.

Raja *Tej Singh* died, of an affection of the chest, on the 2nd of December, 1862, at Lahore. His character will have been plainly seen from the above sketch of his life. He might have filled a subordinate position with credit, for he had no glaring vices, and perhaps as much virtue as the majority of the world. But he was unfitted for times of revolution. He had neither courage nor ability ; and although he rose to be the first person in the state, next to the Maharaja, it was only because his fortune was greater than his desert.

Harbans Singh is under the protection of the Court of Wards : he is a young man of engaging manners, and is a student in the Government College at Lahore.

The estate of Sirdar *Bhagwan Singh* had never been separated from that of Raja *Tej Singh*, and there had been a long dispute between them regarding it. After the death of the Raja, a committeee, consisting of Raja Sahib Dyal, Sirdar Shamsher Singh, Sindhanwalia, Diwan Ajodhia

Pershad and Diwan Shankar Das, was appointed by Government, and a satisfactory division of the property was effected. Raja *Harbans Singh* lives at Lahore, and Sirdar *Bhagwan Singh* at Amritsar. The Sirdar took great interest in the late Panjab Exhibition, and it was, in a great measure, owing to his energy, that the Amritsar Collection took so high a place.

RAJA SAHIB DYAL.

SUGHIA RAM

Kawal Nain,

Chhaju Mal. D. 1822.

Raja Ralia Ram. D. 1864, at Benares. | Jhanda Mal. — Amin Chand.

Ajodhia Parshad. D. 1832. | Raja Sahib Dyal. B. 1801. | Gyan Chand. B. 1805. | Shankar Nath. B. 1808. | Sirdar Harcharan Das. B. 1815.

Jai Gopal. B. 1822. | Bansi Lal, B. 1833. | Balram. B. 1836. | Madho Ram — Washeshar Dyal. | Thakar Das.

Dina Nath. | Bishambar Nath. | Sant Ram. | Lachmi Sahai. B. 1833. | Bhagat Ram. B. 1839.

Devi Sahai. | Joala Sahai. | Mohkam Chand. B. 1854. | Peshori Chand. B. 1858.

HISTORY OF THE FAMILY.

Raja Sahib Dyal is of a respectable Brahman family, whose ancestors were in the service of the Emperors of Dehli. *Sughia Ram* is said to have defended the life of Muhammad Shah, at the risk of his own, for a Rajput assassin, coming one day into the royal Darbar, was about to attack the Emperor, when *Sughia Ram* threw himself upon him, and despatched him, though not without himself receiving a severe wound. His son *Kawal Nain* emigrated to Lahore, which was, in his time, a no very desirable place of residence, from the invasions of Nadir Shah and Ahmad

Shah, and the ever increasing depredations of the Sikhs, who were rapidly gaining strength and boldness. In a fight with the Afghans no less than 26 of his relatives fell, and *Kawal Nain* himself escaped with difficulty. He died young, leaving an only son, *Chhaju Mal,* then a boy of about ten years of age.

When *Chhaju Mal* grew up, he entered the service of Sirdar Jai Singh Kanheya, chief of the most powerful of the Sikh confederacies. He received a command in the Sirdar's force, and accompanied most of the expeditions against the neighbouring Chiefs. He was present at the battle of Achal, in 1783, when Gurbaksh Singh, son of Sirdar Jai Singh, was killed, fighting against Jassa Singh, Ramgharia, and Mahan Singh, Sukarchakia. After this he was made Chowdri of the Kanheya Katra, or quarter, in the town of Amritsar, then rising into importance; and on the death of Jai Singh, he still held the post under that Chief's daughter-in-law, Mai Sadda Kour. The neighbouring Sirdars thought that the principality, ruled by a woman, must be an easy prey; but the lady, well backed by *Chhaju Mal,* held out bravely. Several times had the latter to defend his Katra against assault, and, on one occasion, in repulsing the Ramgharias he received two spear wounds. He reduced the customs duties by more than a half, and thus attracted many merchants, who settled in the Kanheya Katra. The young Ranjit Singh, who, after his marriage with the daughter of Sadda Kour, used to visit Amritsar cautiously, for fear of his enemies the Bhangis, was accustomed to put up with *Chhaju Mal,* and received much assistance from him in obtaining possession of the city, in 1803. With Ramanand, he directed the collection of the customs at Amritsar, till 1813, when he was sent to Kangra, where he remained three years, and then obtained permission to make a pilgrimage to Hardwar and Benares. On his return, in 1820, he did not again engage in public business, for the Maharaja had confiscated all the possessions of Sadda Kour, on whose account *Chhaju Mal* had first entered Ranjit Singh's service. He died in 1822.

His eldest son *Rallia Ram* had received an unusually good education. He was well acquainted with Sanscrit, Persian, and Hindee; and had besides a fair knowledge of mathematics and physical science. In 1811, he was placed in charge of the Amritsar district, and showed great energy in the suppression of dacoity and highway robbery. Ranjit Singh was so pleased with his zeal, that he made him, in 1812, Chief of the Department of Customs. At this time neither Kashmir, Mooltan, nor the Derajat had been conquered; but as each was acquired, it was placed under the management, as far as referred to the customs, of *Rallia Ram.* Before his appointment there had been no regular system of collecting the customs, but each chief got as much out of merchants passing through his territories as he possibly could. *Rallia Ram* largely increased the revenue from the salt mines of Pind Dadan Khan, and introduced the *rawana* or passport system.

In 1821, when the Sikh army was engaged in the Mankerah campaign, Sirdar Jai Singh, Attariwala, rose in rebellion, and *Misr Rallia Ram* with other Sirdars, was despatched against him. With a considerable force, he attacked Kalar Kahar, the stronghold of the rebel Sirdar, reduced it and forced Jai Singh to fly to Dost Muhammad Khan of Kabul for protection. In 1830, *Rallia Ram,* whose energy and probity had made him enemies at court, fell into disgrace; chiefly, it is said, through the influence of Kirpa Ram, Choprah, and was ordered to pay a fine of a lakh of rupees. He was, in 1833, made keeper of the records. In 1841, he discovered, at Makhad, in the Rawal Pindi district, a sulphur mine, which so pleased Maharaja Sher Singh that he granted him a jagir of 11,000 Rs. in the Jandiala Ilaka, with a Persian title of honour.

Sahib Dyal, the second son of *Misr Rallia Ram,* had first entered the Sikh service as a Munshi in the Customs department, under his father; and, in 1832, he was transferred to the Paymaster's office of the regular army. In 1839, he was made chief of the Customs of Jalandhar, and held this appointment till the close of the Satlej campaign. After the separation of the large district of Jhang from the province of Multan, of which it formed nearly a third, in 1846, *Misr Rallia Ram* was appointed its Kardar, and both he and *Sahib Dyal* were appointed to revise the system of imposts. In August 1847, both father and son received Persian titles of honour, and in September of the same year, the whole customs of the country were placed under their superintendence. They were to render accounts every fifteen days, one copy direct to the Resident and one to the Darbar, and had authority to appoint and remove all subordinate officials. The chief burthen of the new arrangements fell upon *Misr Sahib Dyal*, for his father was now an old man, and the greatest credit is due to him for the zeal and ability with which he carried out a system, which must, in many particulars, have been opposed to his own ideas of finance.

Under the old Sikh administration, duty was levied on almost every article whatever. Little care was taken to discriminate between luxuries and necessaries; or equitably to adjust the burthen of taxation between the rich and the poor. Fuel, vegetables, corn, ghi, and other necessaries to the poorest man, had all to pay duty. The taxation was not only ill adjusted, but was also realized in the most vexatious manner. The country was covered with custom-houses, at which the traveller or merchant was subjected to insolence, extortion, and delay. Every town had its own peculiar dues. An article brought into the town must pay import duty; a second duty was demanded on its transfer to the shop, and a third if it were again exported into the country. Yet the advantage to the Government from the heaviness of the customs duties, was, in no way, proportional to the vexation to the people and hinderance to commerce caused by them. Under forty-eight heads the customs yielded a gross revenue of 16,37,114 Rs., while the expense of collection was 1,10,000 Rs., or nearly seven per cent. The accounts of Diwan Mulraj, who was the manager of the salt mines of Pind Dadan Khan, until they were placed under *Rallia Ram*, showed that out of returns of 8,18,820 Rs., thirty per cent was lost by wastage and expenses of management. Under Major H. Lawrence, the Resident, and his brother Mr. John Lawrence, ably seconded by *Misr Rallia Ram* and *Sahib Dyal*, the whole system was changed. The custom-houses, the transit and town dues were abolished ; three frontier lines were established ; one along the Beas and the Satlej ; one along the Indus ; and the third on the north-east frontier for the commerce of Kashmir. The new customs were limited to twenty-two articles, which were estimated to yield 13,04,822 Rs. at a cost of collection of 37,000 Rs. or less than 3 per cent.

The new revenue was to be raised by Abkari Licenses ; a light toll on ferries, estimated to yield a lakh, and by better and more economical management of the salt mines. This immense relief to commerce was effected at a loss of only one-eighth of the customs revenue. After annexation, the customs duties were abolished throughout the Panjab ; but six years later the excise yielded six lakhs, and the salt revenue 19½ lakhs ; and from the removal of restrictions to commerce, the country had increased in material prosperity to an unprecedented extent.

In November 1847, *Misr Sahib Dyal* received the title of "Muhsin-ud-doulah berber." In June, 1848, three months after the outbreak at Multan, Bhai Maharaj Singh, a disciple of the celebrated Baba Vir Singh, having collected a large number of disaffected men, set out from the Manjha to join the rebel Mulraj, at Multan. None of the Sikh troops would attempt his arrest ; but *Misr Sahib Dyal*, then Kardar of Jhang, where the population is Muhammadan, engaged that if Maharaj Singh could be driven in the Jhang direction, he would answer that he proceeded no further. This was fortunately effected ; some irregulars, with part of the 14th Dragoons, pursued the force of the Bhai : Langar Khan of Sahiwal, Malik Sahib Khan, Tiwana, and other Muhammadan Chiefs hung on its rear ; and by the time that the Bhai reached Jhang, his force had diminished to 1,200 exhausted men, who were attacked vigorously by Baba Mali Singh, Tehsildar, with the forces of *Misr Sahib Dyal*, and driven into the swollen Chenab, where more than half the number were drowned, and those who escaped the sword and the river, were taken as prisoners to Lahore.

Throughout the war the services of *Sahib Dyal* and his father, were important and numerous. They preserved order in the Rechna and in part of the Chhaj Doab, and furnished large supplies of grain to the British army on its march. *Sahib Dyal*, when the rebel Sher Singh was marching up from Multan, seized upwards of 2,000 head of mules, camels, and bullocks belonging to the Raja, and thus materially checked the advance of the rebel army, if it did not alter the direction of its march. In November, *Misr Sahib Dyal* was selected by the Resident, to accompany the head-quarters camp of the British army, on the part of the Darbar. In the performance of this duty the Misr showed the greatest intelligence and zeal. He procured excellent information of the movements of the enemy, and kept the army well supplied with provisions. He afterwards, with Nawab Imamuddin Khan, Sikandar Khan, Banda Khan and others, proceeded to join the force of Colonel Taylor, and on the submission of the principal rebels, was useful in disarming the country.

On annexation, the jagir of 1,100 Rs. of *Rallia Ram*, with a cash allowance of 6,900 Rs., was maintained to him for life ; 3,200 Rs. of the cash to descend to his son *Shankar Nath.*

To *Sahib Dyal* was confirmed his jagir of 5,180 Rs., with a cash allowance of 2,800 Rs. for life. Of the jagir, 985 Rs. was to descend for three generations, and 1,200 Rs. was granted in perpetuity. Both *Rallia Ram* and *Sahib Dyal* were rich men. No one who ever held the farm of the salt mines failed to grow rich ; for the contractor paid a certain sum to Government annually, and might sell as he pleased, at his own place and time. In the hands of so able a man as *Rallia Ram* the salt contract was a great source of wealth ; though he, in no way, forgot his duty to the state, in regard for his personal interest. The Lahore Government had few servants so able as *Rallia Ram* and *Sahib Dyal*, and it had none as honest. They were, in the last corrupt days of the administration, almost the only men who, manfully and faithfully, did their duty, and who had the wisdom to understand and support the enlightened policy of the British Resident, the only policy which could have saved the country from the evils that afterwards cam upon it

In 1849, both *Rallia Ram* and *Sahib Dyal* left the Panjab on a pilgrimage to the holy cities. *Rallia Ram,* who had been made Diwan by the Sikh Government of 1847, was, in 1851, created a Raja ; and *Sahib Dyal* also received the same title. Never were honors better merited. *Raja Rallia Ram* never returned to the Panjab, and died at Benares, in April, 1864. *Raja Sahib Dyal* came back in 1851, and has since resided at Kishankot, in the Amritsar district, a town of which he may be said to be the founder, and where he had, at his own expense, built a serai, three temples, a tank, and five wells. During the mutinies of 1857, *Raja Sahib Dyal,* by his advice and actions showed his loyalty to Government, and received a khillat of 1,000 Rs. In 1860, he received an additional grant, in perpetuity, of a jagir of 2,000 Rs. In February, 1864, he was appointed a member of the Legislative Council of India, and took his seat in Calcutta, returning to the Panjab at the close of the session.

The other sons of *Rallia Ram* may be briefly noticed. *Ajodhia Parshad,* the eldest, was of a retiring disposition, and employed himself in devotion. He died young, and his son was employed under *Rallia Ram* in the Customs department.

Gyan Chand was, in the Maharaja's time, at the head of the office of Salt revenue, at Pind Dadan Khan, under Raja Gulab Singh. Under the British Government he was appointed Tehsildar of Pind Dadan Khan, but retired in 1854, and settled at Amritsar, where he now resides, and where, in 1862, he was appointed an Honorary Magistrate. This office he has filled with credit to himself, and to the satisfaction of the people.

Shankar Nath first received an appointment in the Amritsar mint, and was then made Assistant in the Chhach and Hazarah districts. During the rebellion of 1848-49, he, like all his brothers, did good service, and preserved a semblance of order about Battala, Dinanagar, and Pathankot. He is now living at Benares.

Sirdar *Harcharan Das* began public life, as an Assistant in the Customs department ; but during the *Wizarat* of Raja Hira Singh, he was made Commandant of seven hundred horse in the Mulrajia Derah. In 1848, he was appointed by the Darbar, *Adalati* or Judge of Lahore, with the honorary title of 'Rukn-ud-doulah.' On annexation, he held 10,000 Rs., which was confirmed to him, while holding the office of Extra Assistant Commissioner, which had been conferred on him in place of the judgeship. The Sirdar resigned in 1852, and his jagir was reduced to 3,998 Rs. He resides at Amritsar, between which city and Lahore, he has, at his own expense, built a handsome serai. The family has always been known for benevolence and liberality, which is testified to by the many works of public utility and convenience which have been constructed at its expense in many parts of the Panjab. Besides those already mentioned, the serai near the Rambagh gate of Amritsar was built by Raja *Rallia Ram ;* also a serai and temple by the Nagrahwal Ferry on the Beas, and a masonry tank in the city of Amritsar.

THE NAWAB OF MAMDOT.

SULTAN KHAN.

- Maujuddin Khan.
  - Nizamuddin Khan.
    - Fatahdin Khan.
  - Kutbuddin Khan.
    - Kali Khan,
    - Jamaluddin Khan, D. 1863.
      - Khan Bahadar Khan.
      - Muhammad Khan.
    - Jalaluddin Khan.
      - Nizamuddin Khan. B. 1862.
- Muhammad Khan.

HISTORY OF THE FAMILY.

THE ancient city of Kassur, situated some twenty miles to the south of Lahore, was, in 1570, by permission of the Emperor Akbar, settled by a colony of Pathans, numbering about 3,500 souls. Among these came from Kandahar, the ancestors of the Mamdot Chiefs of the Hassanzye tribe, and till the fall of the Mogal empire, they lived at Kassur, sometimes traders, sometimes soldiers, as suited their inclination or their means. When the Sikhs rose to power, they experienced great opposition from the Pathan colony, but in the end, the Bhangi confederacy overran and subdued the whole of the Kassur territory, under Sirdar Gulab Singh; and the two brothers, *Nizamuddin Khan* and *Kutbuddin Khan* entered the service of the Conqueror. These young men, however, were energetic and brave, and in 1794, with the aid of their Afghan countrymen, expelled the Sikhs entirely from Kassur, and established a chiefship of their own. They were not left unmolested. Sirdar Gulab Singh made frequent attempts to recover his lost territory, and later the young Ranjit Singh attacked the brothers several times without success.

Nizamuddin Khan joined vigorously in the cabal against Ranjit Singh, in 1800, when that Chief obtained possession of Lahore, and the next year Kassur was more vigorously attacked, but *Nizamuddin* held out, though he agreed to pay tribute to Ranjit Singh. In 1802, *Nizamuddin Khan* was assassinated by his three brothers-in-law *Wasil Khan, Haji Khan,* and *Najib Khan,* whom he had ousted from their jagirs. *Kutbuddin Khan* has generally been accused of having been privy to the murder, but he appears to have been absent from Kassur, at the time, and on his return, he stormed and took the fort of Azam Khan, whither the murderers had retired, and put *Wasil Khan* and *Najib Khan* to death, *Haji Khan* escaping to the Deccan.

Ranjit Singh at the close of the year again invaded Kassur, but was not able to make much impression, and, till 1807, *Kutbuddin* held his own, when the Maharaja again appeared with a strong army, and after a month's fighting, Kutbuddin gave in, and agreed to retire to his territory of Mamdot, on the other side of the Satlej, holding it in jagir, subject to the service of 100 horsemen. *Kutbuddin* and his brother had conquered Mamdot from the Rai of Raikot, in the year 1800, with the assistance of the Dogars, a turbulent Muhammadan tribe inhabiting the district. Ranjit Singh gave to *Fatah Din Khan* a jagir at Marup, in the Gogaira district, subject to the supply of the same number of horsemen, as Mamdot. But *Fatah Din Khan* was not satisfied, and was always appealing to the Maharaja for the grant of Mamdot, which he considered his right.

At last, with the connivance of the Maharaja, in 1831, he crossed the river, when his uncle's contingent was absent on service, and attacked him. The Dogars, ready for any change, joined him, and *Kutbuddin* was defeated, severely wounded and driven out of the country, and soon after he died at Amritsar. Ranjit Singh now thought fitto interfere on the other side. He recalled *Fatah Din,* and confirmed *Jamal-*

uddin Khan in his father's possessions. Once again *Fatah Din* tried his fortune, but the British Agent interfered, and the Maharaja ordered him back to Lahore.

The Mamdot Chiefs were, at no time, invested with sovereign power, but were merely Jagirdars; feudatories of the Lahore Government. Lahore was the high court of appeal, and there are many instances on record of fines imposed by the Lahore Government upon these Chiefs. In 1824, *Kutbuddin Khan* was fined 12,567 Rs. for conniving at, and sharing in, the plunder of cattle from the Lahore territories. In 1844, *Jamaluddin Khan* was fined 11,100 Rs. for the murder of Soba Rae, the Lahore news-writer at his court, who had rendered himself obnoxious to the Chief by giving information of the disorders committed in the district.

In 1845, before the Satlej campaign, *Jamaluddin Khan* was told that if he stood on our side, his possessions would be confirmed to him; yet at Mudki and *Firushahr* he fought against us, and in the latter battle his nephew, *Fatah Din Khan,* was killed. Only towards the end of the campaign, when he perceived where the victory would eventually be, did he turn round and render some trifling assistance to Sir John Littler, when that General was threatened by the Sikh army at Firozpur, which induced the Government to grant him sovereign powers and to confirm him in his possessions. In 1848, his contingent, under his brother *Jalaluddin,* behaved well at Multan, and *Jamaluddin* was granted the title of Nawab, and the contingent of 100 horsemen, was reduced to 60 in time of peace, and 70 in war.

Jamaluddin Khan was an example of the danger of entrusting irresponsible power to a wicked and sensual man. During the Sikh times his tyranny had been notorious, but, under the British Rule, his power was increased and his tyranny grew in the same proportion. There was no crime or vice which degrades our nature that this wretched man hesitated to commit. His revenue system was but robbery, extortion and violence. The Dogars were the especial objects of his hatred, for by their aid his father had been driven from the country; but all classes, Hindus and Muhammadans, felt his heavy hand. Robbery flourished under his protection, and even the property of British subjects was not secure from his gangs of thieves, who shared the booty with their master. Nor was this all. The sensuality of the Nawab was still more monstrous than his cruelty and violence. He and his sons appeared to think that women were only created to gratify their unbridled passions. No woman in the territory of Mamdot was secure against their lust. If a man was willing to prostitute his wife or his daughter, he might hope to stand well with the Nawab, but if he opposed or thwarted his desires, he would be thrown into prison, where he would languish perhaps for years. At length all men of consideration or wealth left Mamdot. It had once been fertile and populous, with many wells and irrigation canals, but these were all falling to ruin, the towns were deserted, and the cornfields were again becoming jungle.

Retribution at length came. The British Government had, with its known policy, for long refused to interfere with the internal arrangement of a native state; but affairs at length came to such a pass, and the voice of the people was so unanimous against their oppressor, that an investigation was, in 1855, made into the charges against the Nawab, and on their truth being established, he was deprived of his powers and his territory was annexed to the Firozpur district. The Nawab was pensioned and, till 1861, resided at Lahore. He then settled at Machhewarah, in the Firozpur district, where he died, in March 1863, of apoplexy.

The question of succession is still pending before Government between the sons of *Jamaluddin Khan*, and his brother *Jalaluddin*. The latter was in no way concerned in his brother's misgovernment. He is a brave and intelligent man, who has fought well in many battles. He was against us in 1845, but, at Multan in 1848, he did good service, under Lieutenant Lake, and, later in the war, under Lieutenant Lumsden.

His fidelity was at that time fully proved. He also behaved very well in 1857, and laid a camel dak from Firozpur to Bahawalpur, and his conduct was, at the time, highly spoken of by the authorities.

On his brother's deposition, it was proposed to appoint *Jalaluddin* his successor, but he preferred sharing his brother's exile, and did not even accept the separate maintenance assigned to him.

SIRDAR KAHN SINGH ATTARIWALA.

- KHAN CHAND.
  - Gour Singh.
    - Dal Singh.
    - Dyal Singh.
    - S. Nihal Singh, D. 1819
      - S. Sham Singh, D. 1846, at Sobraon,
        - S. Thakar Singh, D. 1842. M. D. of Sirdar Budh Singh, Baggah.
          - S. Jiun Singh, B. 1835.
            i. M. D. of S. Jai Singh, Chinah.
            ii. M. D. of S. Sardul Singh, Man.
            iii. M. D. of S. F. Lakmir Singh, Padania.
          - S. Hari Singh, B. 1837. M. D. of S. Sant Singh, Dyalghar.
            - Son (infant.)
          - S. Ajit Singh, B. 1842. M. D. of S. Gurmukh Singh, Mokal.
        - S. Kahn Singh, B. 1832.
          - A daughter, B. 1859. Betrothed to Narain Singh, Man, son of Col. Jaggat Singh, Man.
        - Rani Naniki. M. Prince Nao Nihal Singh, D. 1848.
  - Kour Singh.
    - S. Tek Singh, D 1805.
      - S. Hukm Singh, D. 1813.
        - S. Jai Singh. M. Sister of S. Raja Singh, Liddhan, C. S. S. D. 1833.
        - S. Nar Singh, B. 1812.
      - S. Jaggat Singh, D. 1835.
      - S Arjan Singh. D. 1823.
      - S. Mehtab Singh, D. 1843.
        - Hira Singh, D. 1862.
          - Narain Singh, B. 1842.
          - Sundar Singh, B 1859.
    - S. Jodh Singh, D. 1805.
      - S. Partab Singh. D. 1831.
        - Karam Singh, D. 1838.
      - S. Chattar Singh, D. 1858, in Calcutta.
        - Raja Sher Singh, M. D. S. Rattan Singh, Gharjakhia, D. 1858, at Benares.
        - Sirdar Gulab Singh, Captain. M. D. of S. Dip Singh, Kahar. B. 1827.
          - B. Har Kour, M. S. Balwant Singh, Rangar Nangalia.
        - S Utar Singh, M. D. S. Dyal Singh, Konowli. B. 1834.
          - Prem Singh, B. 1862.
        - S. Tej Singh, B. 1836. M. D. S. Chanda Singh, Kalalwalia.
          - Son (infant.) D. 1863.
        - Bibi Tej Kour, Betrothed to M. R. Dalip Singh, M. Janmejah Singh, Gil, son of S. Isher S., Mariwala. D. 1863.
    - S. Wazir Singh, D. 1804.
      - S. Jai Singh, D. 1838.
    - S. Charrat Singh, D. 1838.
      - Amir Singh, D. 1838.
      - Nidhan Singh, D. in infancy.
      - Rattan Singh, D. 1809, at Kangra.
        - Jiun Singh, D. 1841.
        - Partab Singh, B. 1814, M. D. of S. Karam S. Chahal.
        - Gulab Singh, B. 1819.
          - Jowahir Singh.
          - Sher Singh.

HISTORY OF THE FAMILY.

The family of Attari, like that of Sindhanwala, is of Rajput origin, and emigrated to the Panjab from the neighbourhood of Jessalmir. But although of the same tribe of Bhatti Rajputs, the families are not, at this day, of equal rank. Their Rajput characteristics have long been lost, and both are now Jats. The Sindhanwalias, from their near relationship to Maharaja Ranjit Singh, and their large possessions, were most powerful, and possessed greater influence at court, but their caste is Sansi Jat, far inferior to the Attariwalas, who stand at the head of the Sidhu Jats, the best blood of the Manjha. This pride of birth was so strong in the family, that Sirdar *Sham Singh*, Attariwala, with the greatest reluctance and only after numerous delays, allowed his daughter, Naniki, to be betrothed to Konwar Nao Nihal Singh, grandson of Maharaja Ranjit Singh. He considered the alliance as a disgrace.

Dhira, son of *Jagmal*, was the first of the family to leave Jessalmir, for Mehraj Phul, in Pattiala, about the year 1580. *Dhira* was a great musician, and his name is still well known to Indian performers. About 1735, the family broke up, some members settling at Indghar, in Jagraon, and the two brothers Gour and Kour coming to the Manjha, with twenty-five horsemen, to seek their fortune. Soon afterwards they went to Amritsar and took the 'Pahal' becoming Singhs, and entered the service of Gurbaksh Singh, Roranwala, then Chief of the Bhangi misl. The two branches of the family soon quarrelled; and their after history is so distinct, that it will be best to treat of them separately.

THE ELDER BRANCH OF THE ATTARIWALA FAMILY.

Gour Singh became a disciple of Baba Muldas, an ascetic of great sanctity, who directed him to settle at Tiblia, or Karewa, where *Gour Singh* accordingly built an 'Attari,' or thatched house, which gave its name to the family, and to the village, which rose around it. After the death of Gurbaksh Singh, Bhangi, *Gour Singh* served under Sirdar Gujar

Singh and Lehna Singh. In 1737, he took possession of the villages around Attari, to the value of 7,000 Rs. per annum, and, two years afterwards, received from Sirdar Gujar Singh, a jagir worth 18,600 Rs. He died in 1763, and his son *Nihal Singh* continued to hold the jagir, under Sirdar Sahib Singh, Bhangi, son of Sirdar Gujar Singh.

Sahib Singh was chief of Gujrat, and here *Nihal Singh* went with his contingent and several of his cousins, sons of *Kour Singh*. He soon became distinguished for courage and ability, and, in the battle which took place between the Sikh Chiefs and the Afghans, under Shahanchi Bashi, officer of Zaman Shah, in 1798, the exertions of *Nihal Singh* contributed very much to the victory. In 1800, soon after Ranjit Singh had obtained possession of Lahore, the Bhangi Chiefs and their allies met at Bassin, to consider what steps they should take against him. Hither came *Nihal Singh*, with his superior Sahib Singh, and Ranjit Singh, happening to see him, was struck with his bold appearance and his excellent horsemanship. He sent for him, and tried to induce him to change sides and take service with him. Sirdar *Nihal Singh*, however, declined. He was not going to desert his old master and told Sahib Singh of the offer, who was much pleased at his refusal, and increased his jagirs and allowances.

This promotion excited much jealousy in the minds of his cousins, *Tek Singh*, *Jodh Singh* and *Wazir Singh*, who were all in the service of the Bhangi Chief, and it was through their representations that Sahib Singh, who was a weak and changeable man, confiscated 15,000 Rs. of his jagir. *Nihal Singh* threw up the Bhangi service in disgust, and retired to Attari, where he took to cattle-lifting and robbery as a means of livelihood. One day he seized a number of camels belonging to Ranjit Singh, and had sold some of them before Ranjit Singh's messengers arrived to demand restitution. After some time, he consented to give back those which he he still had by him, and Ranjit Singh was so pleased at this concession that he again urged the Sirdar to enter his service, to which *Nihal Singh*, after some hesitation, consented. He was placed in command of 416 horsemen, one gun, and seven camel swivels.

In 1803 he was granted the jagir of Sukhu, worth 54,500 Rs., and three years later, the Ilaka of Pasrur, worth a lakh. In 1807, he accompanied the Maharaja on his Kassur expedition, which ended in the defeat and expulsion of Kutb-ud-din Khan, Kassuria, and Nihal Singh was put in possession of the whole Ilaka of Kassur, worth 1,07,000 Rs. On the south side of the Satlej, the Dogars, a wild and turbulent tribe, who were at enmity with Dhanna Singh, son of Gurbaksh Singh, the ruler of Firozpur, invited Nihal Singh to attack it, and promised their assistance. He was ready enough to comply, and, crossing the river, dislodged the garrison of Dhanna Singh, Firozpurwala, from the fort of Dulchi. At this time, another branch of the Dogar tribe, settled at Baraki, who were also hostile to their chief, Dhanna Singh, sent to Lahore to beg Mora, a celebrated courtezan, then high in favour with the Maharaja, to take their part. She asked for a grant of Firozpur, and obtained it; and sending troops to enforce her claim, seized Baraki. *Nihal Singh* now offered to assist Dhanna Singh, who, in spite of his fears, was too weak to refuse. The two Chiefs then drove Mora's troops out of Baraki, and Nihal Singh attacked Firozpur, without success. The next year, 1808, *Nihal Singh* seized, by stratagem, the fort of Khai, and Dhanna Singh, who saw his dangerous ally growing more and more powerful every day, was glad enough, in 1809, to place himself under British protection.

The territory which Nihal Singh thus seized south of the Satlej was worth 18,000 Rs. per annum; and soon after he obtained the grant of villages round Attari to the value of 3,000 Rs. His jagirs amounted to 3,06,800 Rs., of which 1,50,000 Rs. was personal, and 1,56,800 subject to service.

Excepting the Sindhanwalias, no Sikh Sirdar stood so high in the Maharaja's favour as Nihal Singh. His services were numerous and important, indeed there was hardly any campaign, from 1801 to 1817, in which he did not take a distinguished part. He accompanied the first

Kashmir expedition; he was at the affairs of Pind Dadan Khan, Kask, Dallor, Nila, Hola, Chakwal, Saidpur, Narayanghar and Multan. At this latter place, in 1810, he was severely burnt by the explosion of a mine. Attar Singh, Dhari, who was standing beside him, was killed, and many officers were much hurt. *Nihal Singh* had to be sent to Lahore for treatment.

In 1817 Ranjit Singh fell sick at Waniki, and *Nihal Singh* is said to have given his life for the Maharaja by walking, with certain ceremonies, round his bed, and thus taking upon himself, the disorder. The superstition is not an uncommon one in India, and accident or Nihal Singh's imagination seemed to give it some show of truth, for he retired to Attari, where he fell ill and died a few months afterwards. His son *Sham Singh* he had just before introduced into the Maharaja's service, and his first campaign was against Multan, in 1818, where he commanded a battery to the south of the fort. With him, in command of batteries, were Sirdars Dal Singh, Naharna, Amir Singh, Sindhawalia, and Desa Singh, Majithia. The great Bhangi gun was brought from Lahore and was fired four times, doing considerable damage to the walls. The fort was at length taken, Sirdar *Sham Singh* being one of the first on the breach where he was wounded in the shoulder by a sword cut.

After this he served in many battles, and gained as great a name for courage as his father. He accompanied the successful expedition against Kashmir, in 1819, and fought at Gandghar, Theri, Narri-Nari, Duthair, Jahangirah, and Yusufzai. In 1834, he went to Bannu with Diwan Tara Chand, and, in the campaign, had his horse shot under him.

The marriage of his daughter Naniki, to Prince Nao Nihal Singh, to whom she had been betrothed, in 1831, took place at Amritsar on the 7th March, 1837. Sir Henry Fane, Commander-in-Chief, was present, and the ceremony was conducted with the greatest splendour. The Bride brought a dowry to the Prince, of eleven elephants, one hundred and one horses, one hundred and one camels, with a very large amount both of money and jewels. The wedding is said to have cost the Attari Sirdar fifteen lakhs of rupees. Two months afterwards the news came of Sirdar Hari Singh Nalwa's defeat and death, and *Sham Singh* had to march to Peshawar with his troops, and he remained at that station for two years, till the death of Ranjit Singh. After this event, *Sham Singh*, although constantly engaged in military duties, did not meddle with politics. He was in charge of the troops, which, in May 1841, escorted the family of Shah Shuja to Peshawar; afterwards he was sent to Hazara to collect the revenue. He compelled that turbulent Chief, Payindah Khan, to deliver up his son as a hostage, and brought him to Lahore, where he was soon afterwards honorably dismissed. Throughout the reigns of Kharrak Singh and Sher Singh, Sirdar *Sham Singh* retained his jagirs intact. After the assassination of Jowahir Singh, he crossed the Satlej to Kakralah, with the excuse of celebrating the marriage of his son *Kahn Singh*. When, however, the Sikh army invaded the Cis-Satlej territory, he felt that he could not, in honour, remain out of the Panjab, and returned to Attari, where he lived in retirement. No one could doubt his bravery, but he saw, with disgust and sorrow, the Sikh army bent upon a war of which he entirely disapproved, and marching to destruction, under the guidance of false and incompetent men, and he resolved to stand himself aloof. But on the 25th of December, just after the news of Lal Singh's defeat at Firoshahr had reached Lahore, the Maharani heard that *Sham Singh* was at Attari, and sent there ten horsemen, who were to be quartered on the Sirdar, till he joined the army. *Sham Singh* sent, again and again, to the Maharani, denouncing the war and the policy that was destroying the country, but in vain; and at last, when told he was a coward and afraid to die, he determined to join the camp, but swore not to survive the defeat, which he knew was certain. It is said that the night before Sobraon, Sirdar Tej Singh counselled him to fly, with him, on the first attack of the British. *Sham Singh* refused, with scorn, on which Tej Singh angrily said, "If you are so brave you had better take your oath about it, for I believe you will come with me after all." Sirdar *Sham Singh* called for a Granth (the Sikh scriptures), and solemnly swore that should the Sikhs be defeated, he would never leave the trenches alive. On the morning of the battle, the 10th of February, he dressed himself in white, and having mounted his white mare, addressed his men, begging them, as true sons of the Khalsa, to die rather than turn their backs on the enemy. During the first part of the battle, he was every where present, urging the Sikhs to fight bravely; and it was not till he saw that all was lost, that he spurred forward against the 50th Regiment, waving his sword, and calling on his men to follow him. Some fifty of them obeyed the call, but were driven back into the river, and *Sham Singh* fell dead from his horse, pierced with seven balls. After the battle, his servants swam over the river, and begged permission to search his body. The permission was granted, and the body of the old Sirdar, conspicuous by his white dress and long white beard, was discovered, where the dead lay thickest. His servants placed the body on a raft and swam with it across the river, but it was not till the third day that it reached Attari, and his widow, who knew his resolution not to survive defeat, had already burnt herself with the clothes which the Sirdar had worn on his marriage day. This was the last 'Sati' in the Panjab, and the pillar, which marks the spot where it took place, is still standing, without the walls of Attari.

Sirdar *Sham Singh* was one of the best representatives of the Jat race, which, for manliness, honesty, strength and courage, is second to no race in the world. His death was a great loss, for there was no one to take his place. There were, it is true, many of humble rank, in the villages round Gujranwala, Lahore and Amritsar, of equal courage, simplicity and devotion to the interests of the country; but not among the intriguing Sirdars at the court. Had there been more Chiefs like him, the Satlej campaign would never have been undertaken, and the Sikh nation would have preserved the independence which it madly threw away. *Thakar Singh*, the eldest son of Sirdar *Sham Singh*, died before his father : he was a man of no ability, but served in Bannu and Peshawar as Commandant of artillery under his father. He left three sons, to whom the jagir of Sheikoran, worth 7,500 Rs., was assigned, which they still hold, and which is maintained to their heirs in equal shares, in perpetuity. These three Sirdars, *Jiun Singh*, *Hari Singh*, and *Ajit Singh*, reside at Attari. On the close of the Satlej campaign, Raja Lal Singh confiscated 1,59,300 Rs. of the Jagir. 12,000 Rs. was lost by the abolition of the customs duty, and the balance, 74.000 Rs., was continued to Sirdar *Kahn Singh*, subject to the service of ninety-seven horsemen, twenty-five foot, and ten zamburahs. At Multan, in 1848, the contingent of *Kahn Singh* was in the force of Raja *Sher Singh*. After his rebellion, twenty-five sowars remained with the Raja, the rest came away with Shamsher Singh Sindhanwalia. Narayan Singh also, *Kahn Singh's* Diwan, exerted himself to supply the British army, both at Ganda Singhwala and Kassur, with provisions and carriage. For this loyalty, the personal jagir of *Kahn Singh*, being 32,000 Rs. was maintained at annexation ; 7,500 Rs. to descend in perpetuity.

Sirdar *Kahn Singh* is of weak intellect, and is a confirmed invalid. He has no male issue ; he resides at Attari with his nephews, and Diwan Narayan Singh manages his estates.

THE YOUNGER BRANCH OF THE ATTARI FAMILY.

As has been before stated, it was not till the year 1800, when *Nihal Singh*, Attariwala, left the service of Sirdar Sahib Singh, Bhangi, that a feud arose between the two branches of the family. Up to that time they had lived together, and served the same masters, the Bhangi Chiefs at Lahore and Gujrat.

Of the sons of *Kour Singh*, *Tek Singh* and *Jodh Singh* were the most distinguished, and under Sirdar Sahib Singh enjoyed the greatest power and distinction. It was by their influence that *Nihal Singh* was compelled to leave the Bhangi service, and it was thus that the enmity, still strong at the present day, arose between the Attariwalas. *Wazir Singh* and *Charrat Singh* were not men of any note. After the death of Sirdar

Tek Singh, his son abandoned the service of Sahib Singh, and came over to the Maharaja, who was then carrying on operations against Kot Bari Khan. Without paying their respects to the Prince, they joined the battery of Mian Ghosi Khan, and served throughout the siege, *Hukm Singh* receiving a wound in the forehead. After the capture of the fort, Ranjit Singh, pleased with their bold conduct, gave to the young men jagirs at Awan, Meani, and Bahu Chinah. *Hukm Singh* was present at the attaok on Multan, in 1810, and in 1812, accompanied the Maharaja to Jhelam, where he met Fatah Khan the Kabul Wazir. The next year he died, and his sons being minors, his brother *Jaggat Singh* succeeded to the jagirs; but when *Jai Singh* grew up, he received the Ilakas of Miani and Tehnah.

Another *Jai Singh,* son of Sirdar *Wazir Singh* in the year 1821, rebelled against the Maharaja; the story is, that he, with his cousin *Jaggat Singh* and Sirdar Budh Singh, Sindhanwalia, had conspired against the life of the Prince, and the two Attariwalas had entered the Summan Burj, intending to carry out their design, when the Maharaja suddenly appeared, and on enquiring of *Jai Singh* what was the matter, that Sirdar was so confused and terrified, that he allowed Ranjit Singh to guess at the plot against his life. At any rate, *Jai Singh* thought himself suspected, and retired to his fort of Kalar Kahar, which he hastily strengthened and garrisoned. A force was sent against him under Misr Rallia Ram and other chiefs, and being defeated, *Jai Singh* fled across the Indus and took refuge with Dost Muhammad Khan, who was then rising into notice. *Jai Singh* had been sent a short time before this on a mission to Peshawar, where he had become very intimate with the Barakzai Chief, and many a debauch they had had together in the Bagh Nura Khaka, at Peshawar. Ranjit Singh was very jealous of any intimacy between his Chiefs and persons of another nation, and on *Jai Singh's* return to Lahore treated him with much reserve and suspicion. Now that the Sirdar had fallen into trouble, he naturally fled to his Afghan friend, by whom he was well received.

He accompanied Dost Muhammad and Muhammad Azim Khan, in 1823, to Peshawar, when the Barakzai Chiefs had determined to attack Ranjit Singh, who had taken Attock, and was advancing towards Peshawar. One day, after a skirmish between the armies, the heads of thirty Sikhs were placed on the house of *Jai Singh*, who had excited the enmity of many of the Afghans, and he, taking the hint, left Peshawar, and came in to Ranjit Singh, at Akora, after the battle of Theri. He was not very cordially received, and though nominally forgiven, was never taken back into favour. He was one of the agents employed to bring about the meeting of the Maharaja, with Yar Muhammad Khan, and Dost Muhammad Khan, at Peshawar, after the retreat of Muhammad Azim Khan to Daka, when the Sikh Chief rewarded their treason to their brother by dividing between them the Province of Peshawar, which he was himself unable to hold.

Jai Singh died soon after this. His cousin, *Jai Singh*, son of *Hukm Singh*, was killed at Dilassah, in Bannu, 1834, when Diwan Tara Chand received a severe repulse from the Dilassah Chief; and his brother, *Nar Singh*, succeeded to the Tehna and Awan estates, subject to the service of 70 horsemen. At the time of the Multan rebellion, *Nar Singh* was in the enjoyment of an estate of 26,550 Rs., of which 17,500 was subject to service. On the 17th of September, 1849, after Raja *Sher Singh* had joined the rebels, *Nar Singh* was placed under arrest in the Lahore fort. He does not appear to have been directly concerned in the rebellion, but his 70 Sowars, with the exception of eight or ten, went over to the enemy, and his jagirs were consequently resumed. At the close of the war, an allowance of 3000 Rs., per annum, was granted to him, which he still enjoys. He is a great invalid, and resides at Attari with his cousins.

Sirdar *Jodh Singh* entered the service of Ranjit Singh in 1805, atter a brave but vain attempt to hold the fort of Kalar against that Chief, in the interest of his master, Sahib Singh Bhangi. He was received with great favour, and obtained a grant of a large tract of country valued at two lakhs of rupees, in Pothawar, consisting of the tappas of Barsali, Bishandar, Saidpur, &c. subject to the service of two hundred horsemen. *Jodh Singh* soon after this died, and his two sons, *Partab Singh* and *Chattar Singh*, succeeded to the jagirs. *Partab Singh* fought in the battle of Theri, in 1823, when he was wounded in the hand. In the battle of Balakot, where Khalifa Ahmed Ali was defeated and slain, *Partab Singh* was badly wounded, and, returning to his jagir, died, some months later, from the effects of his wound. His son, *Karam Singh*, died soon after, when still a child, and his share of the jagir fell to his first cousin *Sher Singh*. Sirdar *Chattar Singh* was a good farmer, and his estates were much increased in value by his skill and care. He took no great share in politics during the reign of Ranjit Singh, but the family possessed great influence at court, and, in 1843, his daughter, *Tej Kour*, was betrothed to the young Maharaja Dalip Singh. Sirdar *Chattar Singh* was however entirely in the interests of Raja Gulab Singh of Jummu, and when a dispute, excited by Pandit Jalla, arose between that Prince and his nephew Hira Singh, the minister at Lahore, in December, 1844, *Chattar Singh* took up arms in his own part of the country, which he held in the name of Raja Gulab Singh. Six months later, Gulab Singh, who was afraid of the influence and hostility of Prince Peshora Singh, persuaded Jowahir Singh, who had risen to power in Lahore, to send Sirdar *Chattar Singh* and Fatah Khan Tiwanah against him. This task was not at all liked by *Chattar Singh*, for to a Sikh there was something sacred about even a reputed son of the old Maharaja, but he was unable to refuse, and, with the Tiwanah Chief, proceeded against Attock, whither Peshora Singh had retired with a small force. After some days spent in negotiation, the Prince surrendered; the Sirdars solemnly promising his safety and the full consideration of his claims at Lahore. But the next day, while on the march to the capital, the Prince was taken off his guard, seized, placed in irons, and carried back to Attock, where he is believed to have been murdered the same night, and his body thrown into the Indus, which, dark and swift, flows by the fort. The army of the Khalsa were much incensed against *Chattar Singh* for this cruel and treacherous murder, but he took care to avoid Lahore till the troops, content with the blood of Jowahir Singh, had forgotten his share in the crime. Sirdar *Sher Singh*, the eldest son of *Chattar Singh*, had, in 1844, been appointed Governor of Peshawar, in the room of Sirdar Tej Singh, who had been summoned to Lahore. He was an able and spirited young man, and ruled that difficult district to the satisfaction of the Lahore Government. He successfully put down an insurrection in Yusufzai, in 1846, but his administration, though vigorous, was unusually corrupt. Raja Lal Singh, the Minister at Lahore, was his bitter enemy, and, in August, 1846, *Chattar Singh* was appointed to succeed his son at Peshawar, while *Sher Singh* returned to Lahore. This appointment was held by *Chattar Singh* till April, 1847, but his rule was no purer than that of his son. The corrupt practices, which both indulged in, seem to have astonished even the Lahore officials, and the annual embezzlements from the State revenue were estimated at from one and a half to two lakhs of rupees. It was impossible for this to be allowed; but the family was too powerful to be lightly offended, and too nearly connected with the Maharaja to be passed over, and accordingly *Chattar Singh* was made Governor of the country between the Jhelam and the Indus, where he possessed great authority, and *Sher Singh* received a seat in the council. The latter was, however, by no means satisfied. He thought that on the fall of his enemy, Raja Lal Singh, he had a right to succeed him in his office, as he had succeeded him in the affection of the Maharani, and was angry at the failure of his hopes. *Sher Singh* would, perhaps, have been the best selection for Minister, but his claims were hardly as great as those of his father; and *Chattar Singh* was so completely in the hands of Maharaja Gulab Singh, that he would have been a dangerous Minister at Lahore. But the Attariwalas at length appeared content. It was directed that the numerous claims in Peshawar against *Sher Singh*, amounting to upwards of half a lakh of rupees, should not be taken up, the Sirdar paying 8,000 Rs. to some of the poorest claimants, who seemed to have the best grounds for complaint. This arrangement was considered very satisfactory by *Sher Singh*; and his brothers *Gulab Singh* and *Utar Singh* being provided for, the one in Hazara, theother in Lahore, he forgot his grievance about the '*Wizarat.*'

On the 7th August, 1847, Sirdar *Chattar Singh* received a Persian title of honour, at the recommendation of the Resident, at the same time that Sirdar Tej Singh was created a Raja.

On the 26th November, in the same year, *Sher Singh* received the title of Raja. This honour had been recommended for *Chattar Singh*, but, at the last moment, the Sirdar requested that his son *Sher Singh* might be promoted instead, and the request was accordingly granted.

On the 18th April, 1848, the outbreak occurred at Multan. Two British officers were treacherously attacked and slain, and Diwan Mulraj stood forth as a rebel against the authority of the Lahore Government. The news of this outbreak reached Lahore on the 21st April, and the Resident immediately put in motion, for Multan, seven battalions of infantry, two of regular cavalry, and twelve hundred irregular horse under Sirdar Attar Singh, Kalianwala. This force, which was accompanied by Raja *Sher Singh,* was recalled on the 26th, to Lahore, as the Commander-in-Chief of the British Army was unwilling to send European troops to support it, during the hot season, to a part of the country with so bad a name for unhealthiness as Multan. However it was necessary that something should be done, and the Resident was compelled to send against Multan a Sikh force, under the command of Raja *Sher Singh* and Sirdars Shamsher Singh, Sindhanwalia, and Attar Singh, Kalianwala. The force consisted of one regular regiment and half an irregular infantry regiment, three thousand cavalry, ten guns and two mortars, Raja *Sher Singh* was Commander-in-Chief, but his more special command was the infantry, while the two other Sirdars led the cavalry.

On the 12th of June, the force was at Chichawatni, and ready to proceed, but it was not thought expedient to hasten its march until some decided advantage had been gained over Mulraj, by Lieut. Edwardes and the Bahawalpur troops. *Sher Singh* and his colleagues had no thought of treason, but their troops sympathized with the rebels, and would have been only too glad to have joined them. On the 22nd June, *Sher Singh* reached Tolama. He was ordered to stop here, but either his troops were no longer under command, or, fancying that he could trust to their fidelity, he wished to join in the successes of the British (for the battle of Kineyri had now been fought) he advanced to Gogran, nine miles from the city of Multan. Lieutenant Edwardes then directed *Sher Singh* to join him, which he did, pitching his camp at Suraj Khund, three miles from Tibbi, where Lieutenant Edwardes was encamped. He arrived at this place on the 6th of July.

Although the Sikh army was disposed to mutiny, the principal Sirdars had sufficient influence to keep it tolerably steady, although many men deserted to Mulraj, and, on the 20th of July, *Sher Singh* co-operated with the force under the English officers, with energy and success. Thus matters remained until the arrival of General Whish, before Multan, with a European force, on the 18th of August.

Sirdar *Chattar Singh* was at this time governor of Hazarah. His troops were notoriously mutinous, but he gave no notice to the British authorities of the disaffection, which he shared and which he himself encouraged. Affairs were brought to a crisis, on the 6th August, by the murder of Colonel Canora, an American commandant of artillery, in the Sikh service. He was ordered by *Chattar Singh* to bring the guns out of the fort of Harripur, and to encamp on the open ground outside the city. This, Colonel Canora, who suspected the treasonable intentions of *Chattar Singh*, refused to do, unless with the sanction of Capt. Abbott, Boundary Commissioner and Assistant to the Resident, in Hazara. He placed himself between the guns, which he had loaded with grape, and threatened to fire on the first man who should approach. *Chattar Singh* persisted, and as the Colonel would not surrender his charge, a body of Sikh soldiers crept up behind and shot him dead.

On the news of this murder reaching Lahore, the Resident despatched Sirdar Jhanda Singh, Butalia, with a confidential agent from *Chattar Singh's* son, *Gulab Singh*, to try and induce the Sirdar to surrender himself and permit his conduct to be investigated at Lahore. But *Chattar Singh* had decided on his course. The mission of Jhanda Singh failed, and that of Raja Dina Nath, sent to Hazarah, with a like object, was equally unsuccessful. *Chattar Singh's* force did not, at the time of his rebellion, exceed 2,000 men, but it rapidly increased in numbers. He wrote for aid to his son at Multan, to Maharaja Gulab Singh, and to Dost Muhammad Khan ; raised levies in his own district of Pothawar, and used all means in his power to render his rebellion as formidable as possible.

On the 19th of August, news of the outbreak in Hazarah reached the camp of Raja *Sher Singh*, before Multan. This Chief had, in the midst of mutiny and ill-feeling, striven to do his duty to the Government. By severe punishments and by promises of rewards he had kept his troops firm, and even when his father's letters reached him, in August, he did not waver in his fidelity. He did not believe that his father was deeply compromised in the rebellion, and hoped that, by the mediation of Sirdar Jhanda Singh and Raja Dina Nath, every thing would be satisfactorily arranged. On the first of September, when the force of Lieut. Edwardes had to change ground, and was attacked by the enemy, the Raja voluntarily brought out his guns and aided the movement. Again, on the 3rd of September, he cannonaded and threw into great confusion the troops of Mulraj, at the bridge, chiefly to destroy sympathy between his own men and the rebels. But, early in September, still more urgent letters came from Hazarah, stating that Sirdar *Chattar Singh* had rebelled beyond all forgiveness, and calling on *Sher Singh*, and all true Sikhs, to join him. Messengers from Hazarah, and chief among them, Sirdar Surat Singh, Majithia, excited the soldiery, saying that now was the time to expel the Feringhis from the country, and that any Sirdar who opposed the movement was an enemy to the Khalsa. The Sikh force became so dangerous that, on the 13th of September, it was resolved to remove it from Multan and from temptation. The Attariwala, Kalianwala, and Sindhanwalia divisions were to march in different directions; that of *Sher Singh* to the ferry, nominally to protect the passage of the river. The morning of the 14th was appointed for the march, but the soldiers would not move. The whole camp rose in mutiny, excited by Surat Singh and others; the Sirdars were abused and threatened, till their lives were no longer safe, and, at last, Raja *Sher Singh*, in desperation, went over to the side of the rebels, and with his whole force marched to Multan, where he encamped in the Hazuri Bagh, as the Diwan distrusted him and refused him admittance into the fort.

The defection of the force of *Sher Singh* compelled General Whish to raise the siege of Multan; but he only retired to the suburbs of the city, where he waited for reinforcements and siege guns. *Sher Singh* now did all in his power to extend the rebellion and make it a national one, and distributed inflammatory letters over the whole country, calling on the Sikh nation to rise. But Mulraj still thought him on the side of the British; or if against them, desirous of obtaining the fort of Multan for the Khalsa, and put no trust in his professions. He made *Sher Singh* with all his officers, swear, on the Sikh Scriptures, that they had no evil designs, but in spite of their oaths, no one of them was admitted within the city.

At length *Sher Singh* determined to join his father in Hazarah. Mulraj was delighted at his resolution, and lent him money to hasten his march, and, on the 9th of October, the Raja, with his force of 5,300 men left Multan, en route for Hazarah. On the 11th, he crossed the Ravi, with his whole camp, and marched in the direction of Jhang. Here his troops behaved very ill, defiling the mosques, and plundering the Muhammadan inhabitants. *Sher Singh* was here joned by the Bannu troops, who had mutinied, taken the fort of Dalipghur, and slain the brave Fatah Khan, Tiwana, and continued his march along the Chenab in the direction of Wazirabad, which had been occupied by Lal Singh Moraria, Chief

Justice of the Sind Sagar Doab, who had joined the rebels, with 2,000 irregulars.

Sirdar *Chattar Singh* had, during the month of October, been intriguing on all sides. To the Barakzai Sirdars he promised the Province of Peshawar, in return for their assistance; and he had succeeded in inducing the whole of the Sikh troops at Peshawar to join him. In spite of the efforts of some of their officers, who remained firm to their duty, they revolted on the 24th of August, and marched to join *Chattar Singh*. Captain Abbott held out gallantly, in Hazara; and Lieutenant Herbert defended the fort of Attock till the 2nd of January, when, being without hope of succour, and his troops deserting to the enemy, he was compelled to fly. After the fall of Attock, *Chattar Singh* marched to join his son *Sher Singh*.

The army under the Raja had, on the 2nd November, received a severe check at Ram Nagar from the British. under Lord Gough. The affair was entirely fought by the cavalry and artillery, and can hardly be called a battle. On the 1st of December, Sir Joseph Thackwell, with the advanced part of the army, crossed the Chenab, and advanced against the Raja's position. Some sharp fighting took place, in front of the entrenchment, but no attack was made upon the position, and, on the night of the 3rd December, *Sher Singh* retreated by the Jhelam, Jalalpur, and Pind Dadan Khan roads, and took up a position at Chilianwala, where, on the 13th of January, the British army advanced to attack him. The accounts of this battle, little creditable to the British arms, has been often written. It has been called a victory; but neither the Sikh generals, nor the soldiery, considered that they had been defeated. All fought well, but the hero of the day was Jowahir Singh Nalwa, son of Hari Singh, the great Sikh General, who led the cavalry charge which had so great an influence on the result of the battle.

Two or three days after the battle, Sirdar *Chattar Singh* joined his son's camp, being received with a royal salute, and bringing with him, as prisoners, Major George Lawrence, and Lieutenants Herbert and Bowie. He had been successful in inducing Amir Dost Muhammad Khan to join him, having paid that Prince, as the price of his assistance, 30,000 Rs. in cash, 15,000 Rs. in shawls, and 15,000 Rs. he engaged to pay at Rawal Pindi. For this consideration the Amir seized the Province of Peshawar, cooperated in the siege of Attock, and sent a thousand cavalry, under his son, Akram Khan, to join the army of *Chattar Singh.*

On the 21st of February, the battle of Gujrat was fought, when the united Sikh and Afghan army was completely defeated, with the loss of 53 guns. This was virtually the end of the war. The victory was followed up with vigour, and at Rawal Pindi, on the 14th March, *Chattar Singh* and *Sher Singh*, with what remained together of the Sikh army, some 16,000 men, laid down their arms.

As far as regards the Attariwala Sirdars, these were the chief incidents of the war. A connected history of that war, so important to both England and the Panjab, has yet to be written; but it will not be here out of place to say a few words on the causes that led to it.

At the close of the Satlej campaign, the Sikh army, which had, since the death of Maharaja Ranjit Singh, been ever increasing in numbers, was, in a great measure, disbanded. The Panjab villages were filled with a discontented soldiery, averse to peaceful occupations, and firmly believing that their late reverses were alone owing to the treachery and incapacity of their leaders. These men were anxious to try their fortune once more on the field of battle. At the capital, Raja Lal Singh, the Minister, whom it was necessary for the English Government to support, was highly unpopular. By the troops he was hated for his share in the Satlej disaster, and for his intrigues with the Maharani; by the Sirdars for his avarice, which cost many of them their jagirs. Even after his fall from power, the new administration was hardly more popular. Raja Tej Singh was an incompetent man, and an upstart. His rise had been owing more to his fortune than his abilities, and he was supposed to be entirely under the orders of the British

Resident, Major H. Lawrence. There were many minor causes for discontent. Cow-killing was no longer allowed to be a crime, and the hated Muhammadans, who had always, under Sikh rule, been a persecuted race, were allowed to practise their religious rites, publicly and ostentatiously. The people at large, too, believed that the English never intended to leave the Panjab; although the truth was that the British troops only remained at the earnest request of the principal Sirdars, who dreaded a return of the anarchy which had preceded the Satlej campaign. Thus there was plenty of material for rebellion, ready at hand, but the genius and political sagacity of Major Lawrence, and the confidence which the natives placed in him, might have preserved peace, had he not been compelled, by bad health, to leave the country at a most critical time.

The rebellion of 1848 began with the outbreak at Multan. This was entirely unpremeditated. There is no reason to believe that the attack on the British Officers was made by the orders or with the connivance of Diwan Mulraj; but when he had been compromised by that attack, he remembered that he had at his disposal immense wealth, devoted troops, and the strongest fortress in upper India, while the power which could punish and avenge was far off, and to him almost unknown. Of two evils he considered rebellion the lesser. Had a British force marched against Multan, on the first news of the outbreak reaching Lahore; had the punishment followed the offence, swiftly and decisively, the Sikhs would not have rebelled. But the delay in the punishment of one traitor, allowed them to believe that treason might remain altogether unpunished.

The defection of Raja *Sher Singh* before Multan was also unpremeditated. Till the night of the 13th of September, he remained firmly loyal in the presence of temptation, such as few men have ever been exposed to. His influence over his troops was great, and it is possible that he might have kept them to their duty, till the close of the siege, had not the entreaties of his father induced him, much against his will, to join the rebel side. It was the rebellion of Sirdar *Chattar Singh* which caused that of his son. There had been several insignificant outbreaks in outlying Districts of the Panjab before that of *Chattar Singh*, but it was he who made the rebellion a national one and brought ruin upon the country.

What then were the reasons for *Chattar Singh's* conduct? Why was he thus disaffected while his son was actively loyal? It is difficult to believe that he was ambitious for himself. He was an old, broken-down man, and a confirmed invalid. His intellect, never brilliant, had become weakened by ill health and advancing age. He had long talked of abandoning worldly affairs, and going on a pilgrimage to the Ganges, and he had declined a Rajaship in favor of his son. Nor could he have hoped to benefit his son by the expulsion of the English from the Panjab. *Sher Singh* had been placed at the head of the Sikh Aristocracy by the British, and he might reasonably hope, in time, to obtain the Ministership at Lahore, and the Guardianship of the young Prince to whom his sister was betrothed. This engagement, too, gave the family more importance in the eyes of the English than of the Sikhs, for, as the young Maharaja grew up, he would probably marry many other wives, and in the Panjab the influence of a wife is little felt outside the walls of the Zanana. *Sher Singh* was well content with his own prospects; there was no reason that *Chattar Singh* should be dissatisfied. It was at one time asserted that the suspicions of Captain Abbott drove *Chattar Singh* into treason, but that able Officer only suspected where there was good reason for suspicion, and the correctness of his judgment has been fully proved.

Sirdar *Chattar Singh* was a weak and a timid man, and was ever accustomed to depend upon the advice of men wiser and more determined than himself. There was one man upon whom, more than upon all others, he was accustomed to rely, and this was Maharaja Gulab Singh. There had not been an intrigue in the Panjab, for many years past, in which Gulab Singh had not been engaged, and from which he had not reaped advantage. The most accomplished of courtiers, the most subtle of diplomatists, the most unscrupulous of intriguers, *Chattar Singh* found him the most dangerous of friends. The friendship between these men was of the closest description. When the brother of *Chattar Singh* died, it was the influence of Gulab Singh that procured for the Sirdar the grant of half his estates, to the prejudice of the son of the deceased. In the troubles under Raja Hira Singh, *Chattar Singh* had stood boldly by his friend, and, for his sake, became an accomplice in the murder of Prince Peshora Singh. The Sirdar would never have determined on rebellion without consulting Gulab Singh, but, even had he so determined, Gulab Singh could, without difficulty, have dissuaded him from it.

Although the proofs of Gulab Singh's complicity in the rebellion might fail to satisfy a court of law, yet there is sufficient evidence for history to decide against him. In the first place there is the universal belief, shared by the late Dost Muhammad Khan, that Gulab Singh was the instigator of the rebellion, and that, against his will, *Chattar Singh* would not have raised his hand. The evidence of Hira Nand, the agent sent by *Chattar Singh* to the Maharaja, recorded in October, 1849, though in many parts exaggerated and contradictory, bears the general stamp of truth. If his evidence is received, there can be no doubt of the Maharaja's connection with the rebels. Hira Nand does not appear to have had any reason for accusing the Maharaja unjustly, and his evidence is confirmed, in many important particulars, by other witnesses, whose depositions were subsequently taken. No documentary evidence of any importance was discovered, but the most wily of men was not likely to commit himself by writing what might be verbally explained, or expressed by a sign, or by the pressure of a finger. Thus much at least is certain, that rebels, and the families of rebels, took shelter in the Maharaja's territories ; that rebel troops marched through them unmolested, and drew from thence their supplies ; and that, though his professions were large, the aid he rendered to the Lahore Government, was trifling in the extreme.

But with all this, it is impossible to believe that Maharaja Gulab Singh desired the defeat of the British. Gratitude for the grant of Kashmir any other man than Gulab Singh might be expected to feel; but putting this aside, he was well aware that his existence as a sovereign prince depended upon the presence of British troops in the Panjab. He induced *Chattar Singh* to rebel, because he desired his destruction and that of his son; because he hoped for the subversion of the Lahore monarchy, and the establishment of British supremacy in the Panjab. He perceived that, if the country remained tranquil, the British would, as agreed, leave it, and Raja *Sher Singh* obtain power, and he also knew that, in that case, the Sikh arms would be first turned against him. He had been more surprised than any one else at finding himself sovereign of Kashmir, and he knew that the loss of this Province was looked upon by the whole Sikh nation with shame and rage, for it had been won with difficulty by the old Maharaja, and with the blood of many brave Sirdars. Nor were the Sikhs his only fear. Dost Muhammad Khan remembered that Kashmir had once belonged to Kabul, and was ready to attack it at the first opportunity. It was for this that he made an alliance with the Sikhs whom he hated, and intrigued with the wild Muhammadan tribes of Hazarah. Between the Sikhs and the Afghans, Gulab Singh was well aware, that, without British aid, he must inevitably fall.

His policy being thus in favor of the English, the reasons that caused him to refrain from giving active assistance to them are plain. He could not, being himself the instigator of the rebellion, directly oppose it, without exciting great hatred against himself. Sikhs and Afghans would have united against him, and would have overrun Kashmir, while the British troops were barely able to hold their own in the plains. He waited until some decided success of the British army should enable him to declare himself, heart and soul, on its side; but, after Chilianwala, he began to doubt whether the English could really hold the country. The decisive overthrow of the Sikhs, in 1845, had made him believe that, with a larger force, and with far greater advantages of position, possessing as they did Lahore and Amritsar, the English would again obtain an easy victory. Even their temporary retirement would be fatal to him, and thus, when he saw the first portion of the campaign undecisive and unsatisfactory, he trembled for the result, and did not dare to break with the Sikhs. Had Gulab Singh joined the English openly and boldly, the campaign might have been more quickly decided; but this was not possible to him. His caution and hesitation in deciding on a plan were equal to his boldness and vigour in its execution. Every course presented to his keen intellect so many dangers, that he ever forbore to act until circumstances forced him into action. Though personally · brave and fond of war, it was by fraud, not by force, that his policy was distinguished. Throughout his whole life he had never joined a losing party, or even a winning one until its success was undoubted and assured.

The policy of Maharaja Gulab Singh was thus completely successful. The Sikhs were conquered; the Afghans driven, ignominiously, from the Panjab, and the astute contriver of their downfal ruled, in peace, under the strong protection of the only nation he had ever learnt to trust.

The evidence against Maharaja Gulab Singh, however convincing it may appear to those who have studied the history of the times, must still be admitted to be incomplete and indecisive. No evidence in his favour was ever heard, and if Diwan Joala Sahai, and other of his confidential agents were examined, they might be able to explain many points which now appear most suspicious. Whatever hand Gulab Singh may have had in the rebellion of *Chattar Singh*, he was not the sole cause of the second Sikh war. The old Khalsa army, and the whole Sikh nation, which was, by constitution and creed, military, would never have settled down peaceably under British rule, without another trial of strength;

without a defeat which, like that of Gujrat, left them no option but that of submitting to the stronger. Even the troops of Sirdar *Chattar Singh* were thoroughly disaffected, and without any aid or instigation from Gulab Singh, they would, in all probability, have sooner or later, rebelled.

The Maharaja was, at all events, not hostile to the British. If he desired and plotted for the downfal of the Sikh empire, it is impossible to blame him, for the Sikhs hated him fully as much as he did them, and would have seen his ruin with the utmost satisfaction.

Sirdar *Chatter Singh*, Raja *Sher Singh*, and Sirdar *Utar Singh*, who had also joined the rebels, were placed under surveillance at Attari, but being discovered still carrying on a treasonable correspondence, they were, in January, 1850, sent as prisoners, first to Allahabad and then to Calcutta. Their estates were all confiscated. *Chattar Singh* before the war possessed jagirs of the value of 1,22,000 Rs., 57,000 being personal, and 65,000 Rs. subject to service. Raja *Sher Singh* and his brother, had personal jagirs worth 42,220 Rs. An allowance was granted them of 7,200 Rs., being 2,400 Rs. each to *Chattar Singh*, *Sher Singh* and *Utar Singh*. *Gulab Singh* did not join the rebels, being under suveillance at Lahore. He had been placed, with his brother *Sher Singh*, in charge of the young Maharaja and the household arrangements of the palace; and he was evidently preparing to leave Lahore and join his father, when he was arrested on the 17th September, and detained, in safe custody, till the close of the war. Nothing was, however, proved against him, and his pension of 3,000 Rs. was equal in amount to what he had received, in land, previous to the war.

Bibi *Tej Kour* was never married to Maharaja Dalip Singh. After the war the match was broken off, and she eventually married Janmeja Singh, son of Sirdar Ishar Singh, Gil, Mariwala, by whom she had two sons. She died in 1863. In January, 1854, *Chattar Singh*, *Sher Singh* and *Utar Singh*, whose conduct since annexation had been irreproachable, were released from confinement, and allowed to choose their own place of residence, within certain limits. Their allowances were also raised ; that of *Chattar Singh* to 8,000 Rs., and of *Sher Singh* to 6,000 Rs. During the Burmese, the Persian, and the Sonthal campaigns, Raja *Sher Singh* offered his services to Government, and he even volunteered for service in China, during the late war. When the mutinies broke out Sirdar *Gulab Singh* received a command, and served, throughout the war, with distinguished gallantry. He received the title of Captain, and with his brothers *Tej Singh* and *Attar Singh*, the grant of a zamindari, in Oude, worth 28,800 Rs. per annum. Each of the brothers also hold a life pension of 7,200 Rs. raised to that amount on the death of Raja *Sher Singh* which took place, at Benares, in 1858.

Raja *Sher Singh,* according to Hindu ideas, obliterated all the faults of his life, by the sanctity of his death. When he felt his end approaching, he called the Brahmans to his bed-side, and asked of them how he could escape transmigration, the constant and live-long terror of Hindus. They told him that, for seven days, he must lie, fasting, by the Ganges, listening to the Bhagawat, the most sacred of all the eighteen Puranas. So, morning after morning, the dying Raja was carried to the river-side, and, throughout the day, he listened, as well as his fading sense would allow, to the words of the Puran.

On the evening of the seventh day, he gave 2,000 Rs to the Brahmans, and died.

Thus, an exile, far from his country, in the sacred city of Benares, and by the waters of the holy river, died, before his time, Raja *Sher Singh.* His father, Sirdar *Chattar Singh,* had died early in the same year at Calcutta.

SIRDAR DYAL SINGH MAJITHIA.

NODH SINGH.
D. 1788.

Sirdar Desa Singh.
M. D. of Karam Singh Hanjrah.
D. 1832.

Sirdar Lehna Singh.	Sirdar Gujar Singh.	Sirdar Ranjodh Singh
i. M. D. of S. Tara S. Sultanwind.	M. D. of S. Wazir Singh.	i. M. D. of S. Gulab S., Chamiyari.
ii. M. D. of S. Nar S., Aimchwala.	Rangarnangal,	ii. M. D. of Samant Singh, Sanhiwal.
D. 1854.	D. 1837.	B. 1820.

Sirdar Dyal Singh.
B. 1848.
M. D. of S. Sher Singh, Amballa.

HISTORY OF THE FAMILY.

The village of Majitha, situated ten miles to the north of the city of Amritsar, has given its name to one of the most distinguished families of the Panjab. The great Majithia family is divided into three branches; represented by Sirdars *Dyal Singh, Surat Singh,* and *Mehtab Singh.* The relationship between these Sirdars is distant, and the history of their families is quite distinct. Sirdar *Dyal Singh* and Sirdar *Mehtab Singh* are fifth cousins; but *Surat Singh* is a very remote kinsman, and it is necessary to go back fourteen generations to find a common ancestor for the three Majithia Sirdars.

First in rank and influence is the family of Sirdar *Dyal Singh.* His great grandfather, *Nodh Singh,* was a respectable Zamindar of the Shergil Jat tribe, an account of the origin of which will be found on referring to the History of Commandant Dewa Singh, Sirdar Buhadar. *Nodh Singh* married the sister of Sirdar Amar Singh, Baggah, the powerful Chief of Dharamkot-Baggah, and became 'Zaildar,' or feudal retainer, of his brother-in-law, who was of the Kanheya misl, and possessed a large territory in the Gurdaspur district. *Nodh Singh* acquired a jagir of 2,500 Rs. including two wells, at Majitha, and died in 1788, leaving one son, *Dewa Singh,* then twenty years of age. The young man succeeded to his father's estate, and till the year 1809, remained in the service of the Baggah Sirdars. But when Maharaja Ranjit Singh, in that year, marched to Majitha and Dharamkot, determined to seize the estate of Sirdar Budh Singh, Baggah, who had failed to give the supplies demanded of him for the Kangra expedition, *Desa Singh,* who was very wise in his generation, saw that resistance was hopeless, and having besides no love for Budh Singh, went over to the side of the Maharaja, who received him with open arms, and, when Budh Singh was vanquished, bestowed upon him the jagirs of Sukalghar and Bhagowal, which had, for many years, been a portion of the Baggah estate.

Sirdar *Desa Singh* then accompanied Ranjit Singh in his expedition to Kangra, where Raja Sansar Chand of Katoch had begged his assistance to expel the Gurkhas, under Amar Singh, Thapa. Sansar Chand must have found it difficult to distinguish his friends from his enemies, for Ranjit Singh, driving out the Gurkhas, seized his fort, the key to the Kangra Valley, and appointed *Desa Singh* its Commandant. He was also made Nazim, or Governor, of the Hill States, Kangra, Chamba, Nurpur, Kotlah, Shahpur, Jasrota, Bassowli, Mankot, Jaswan, Sibah, Goler, Kolhor, Mandi, Suket, Kulu, and Datarpur. In 1811, Sirdar *Desa Singh* marched against the fort of Kotlah, half way between Kangra and Nurpur, held by Dhyan Singh, who had been wazir of the Raja Goler, and who, trusting to the strength of his position, had given himself the airs of an independent Chief. The Maharaja promised *Desa Singh* half the Ilaka of Tiloknath, in which the fort was situated, in jagir, if he succeeded in reducing it in a week, and the energetic Sirdar did the work in the appointed time, and obtained the jagir, worth 7,000 Rs. Two years later, he was sent to annex the territory of the Raja of Haripur, who had been shamelessly arrested at Lahore.

Sirdar *Desa Singh* was appointed Governor of the city of Amritsar, and in 1818, he served in the Multan campaign, with distinction, in the force of Prince Kharrak Singh. After this he returned to his Hill Governorship, and collected, as usual, the revenue, and the tribute due from the different states. Bilaspur alone was refractory, and *Desa Singh* marched against the Raja and seized his territory, both on the Sikh side of the river, and that under British protection. This was in violation of the Treaty of the 25th August, 1809, and the British troops were, without delay, put in movement to resist it. Ranjit Singh repudiated the action of his lieutenant, and obliged *Desa Singh* to visit Captain Ross, the officer in charge of the Hill frontier, to offer apologies, which were accepted readily, and indeed the civilities which passed between them roused the Maharaja's jeolousy, and, for some time, he forbade Desa Singh to have any intercourse with any British officer. Mr. Moorcroft, passing through Amritsar, in 1820, found that *Desa Singh* was unable to visit him on account of this prohibition. About this time the Sirdar received a grant of Ilaka Bagguwala, in the Firozpur district, where he built a fort, and seized, by violence, some villages belonging to the Alhuwalia Sirdar, in the Malanwala Ilaka. His jagirs were very extensive. During the reign of Ranjit Singh, he, with his son, *Lehna Singh,* received grants to the value of 1,24,250 Rs. per annum. These included Majitha, Tiloknath, Bagguwala, a large portion of the old Baggah estate, of which he had been made governor, Bhaowal, Harriki, Khudpur, Naoshera-Nangli, and Zamanabad, in the Kangra district.

Sirdar *Desa Singh* died in 1832, and was succeeded, in all his estates and honours, by his eldest son Sirdar *Lehna Singh.* His life had been uniformly prosperous, and the favour of his Sovereign who had given him the title of Kasir-ul-iktidar (chief of exalted dignity) never lessened. He was a brave and successful soldier, and a wise and liberal administrator, and his name is still remembered with affection by the people whom he never oppressed.

Sirdar *Lehna Singh* served, with credit, in the Multan campaign of 1818, and soon became known for ability and learning. When Ranjit Singh determined to seize the possessions of his mother-in-law, Mai Sadda Kour, *Lehna Singh* was selected to superintend the unpleasant work. The intriguing lady was seized and carried prisoner to Amritsar. All her estates were confiscated, and the great Kanheya misl, of which she was head, made no attempt to save her. Ranjit Singh had not expected so easy a success, and said, in full Darbar, "All these Kanheyas are cowards and traitors." Among those who heard this speech was Jodh Singh, Harchandar. He set off at once, threw himself, with a few men, into the Nanga fort, and defended it for some time, bravely. The fort of Atalghar also held out for three weeks, defended by one of Mai Sadda Kour's slave girls, who seemed to have acquired some of the spirit of her mistress.

After the death of *Desa Singh,* his son received charge of the Hill territory between the Ravi and the Satlej, and held the appointment till the beginning of 1844. *Lehna Singh* did not reside in the hills, but at Amritsar or Majitha. At the former place, he was in charge of the Darbar Sahib, the Sikh temple, as his father had been, a post of importance, requiring great tact and judgment. Once a year he made a tour in the hills, to inquire into the state of the country, to redress grievances, and to examine the accounts. He was a mild and benevolent man, and, like *Desa Singh,* bears the character of being one of the best Governors that the Sikh rule (famous for rapacity and corruption) ever produced. *Lehna Singh* possessed the greatest influence with Maharaja Ranjit Singh, and his counsel was always listened to with respect. His title was, "Hasam ud Doulah" (the sword of the state).

In 1834, *Gujar Singh,* Majithia, brother of *Lehna Singh,* was selected to take charge of a mission to Calcutta to convey presents for the King of England, and to endeavour, if possible, to ascertain the intentions of the British Government with regard to Shikarpur. The selection was not a happy one. Sirdar *Gujar Singh* was a young man of ordinary ability, considerable conceit, and debauched habits. He took with him 100 men, splendidly appointed, the finest that could be picked out of the Sikh army. With him, too, to keep him in order, were sent Rai Govind Jas, brother to Rai Kishan Chand, Gulab Singh, commandant, called afterwards Calcuttia, and Dewa Singh commandant; and plenty of difficulty they had with their charge, who fell desperately in love with a European woman, in Calcutta, and wanted to marry her, to the horror of Govind Jas, and the annoyance of Ranjit Singh, who excluded him for some time, after his return, from Darbar. He brought back no information about Shikarpur, but plenty of English airs and graces, which created great amusement at the Lahore court. Among other English tastes acquired by *Gujar Singh*, was a love for champagne, from the effects of which, one evening, about two years after his return from Calcutta, he walked over the parapet of the roof of his house at Amritsar, and, falling some 40 feet, was killed on the spot.

In 1840, after the death of Ranjit, Prince Nao Nihal Singh sent a force under Sirdar Ajit Singh, Sindhanwalia, and General Ventura, against Mandi. Raja Balbir Sen was taken prisoner and brought to Amritsar, imprisoned in Govindghar, and his territory annexed. But *Lehna Singh* interested himself, very warmly, for his old friend, and when Maharaja Sher Singh ascended the throne, procured his release and the restoration of his country. He signed, with the Sindhanwalias and other Chiefs, the agreement which was to exclude Sher Singh from the throne, for at least a time; and when that Prince marched to Lahore and besieged the fort, *Lehna Singh* was in great alarm and hid himself in Jamadar Khushhal Singh's house till the end of the siege.

When Raja Hira Singh rose to power, Sirdar *Lehna Singh*, who was hated by Pandit Jalla, the minister's confidant, fearing to lose his estates or his life, and filled with sudden religious aspirations, left the Panjab on a pilgrimage. He first visited Hardwar, and then proceeded to Benares, Allahabad, Jagganath and Calcutta, where he was residing when the Satlej campaign commenced, in November, 1845. Before leaving the Panjab, he made over the management of his estates to his half-brother *Ranjodh Singh*, the youngest son of Sirdar *Desa Singh*, by a hill woman.

Sirdar *Ranjodh Singh* was, at this time, a general in the Sikh army. He had lately returned from the expedition sent by the Wazir Jowahir Singh against Raja Gulab Singh of Jammu, and was quite ready for a war with the English, for whom he had no great love. He moved his brigade, consisting of 10,000 infantry, 60 guns, and some irregular cavalry to Philor, and on the 17th January, 1846, crossed the Satlej, intending to move on Ludianah, and capture, if possible, the siege train which was on its way to the head-quarters of the army. At Baddowal, on the 21st January, he intercepted the force of Sir Harry Smith, who was marching to Ludianah, and, more from the exhaustion of the British troops, than from any display of generalship on his part, captured almost all the baggage of the army. This affair so much encouraged the troops of *Ranjodh Singh*, who had been joined by Sirdar Ajit Singh of Ladwa, that, at Aliwal, on the 28th January, they left a strong position, contrary to the orders of the General, to attack the British force. The defeat which they experienced is matter of history, and there is no occasion to dwell upon it here. *Ranjodh Singh*, was, if any thing, superior to the other leaders of the Sikh army; if leaders they can be called, who were ever the last to enter the fight and the first to run away. His generalship was as contemptible as that of Raja Lal Singh, and his cowardice as conspicuous as that of Raja Tej Singh, but he was no traitor. He had no confidential agents in the British camp as Raja Lal Singh had, nor did he, like the Raja, pray for and labour for the triumph of the English.

Soon after the close of the campaign, Sirdar *Lehna Singh* returned from Calcutta, at the invitation of the Council and the Resident. He declined to be formally admitted into the Council, but was ready to give, privately, any advice he could, and accepted the charge of Amritsar,

Govindghar, and the Manjha, in its widest acceptation, being the whole tract of country between the Ravi and the Bias, from the Hills to Kassur. A great dispute now arose between *Lehna Singh* and *Ranjodh Singh*. The latter had preserved the estates entrusted to him, for two years and a half, in very difficult times, and claimed, on *Lehna Singh's* return, a half share of them. *Lehna Singh* only wished to allow him a pittance, amounting to about a twentieth of the whole. Both proposals were unjust, and it required all the influence of Sir H. Lawrence to settle the dispute, and to induce *Lehna Singh* to allow his half-brother a jagir of 12,000 Rs. per annum.

In August, 1844, *Lehna Singh* consented to join the Council. His administration of the Manjah had been successful. Although he had an objection to capital punishment, he contrived to free the country of robbers and dacoits, who had overrun it, after the close of the war; and there was no Sirdar whose rule was so generally popular. But his practised eye saw the signs of coming disturbances and he determined to leave the Panjab. In January, 1848, he left for Benares. His personal jagirs, and religious grants amounting to 42,000 Rs., and service jagirs of 15,000 Rs., were continued to him. All the other jagirs were resumed, but the Darbar promised to restore them on his return to the country.

At the close of the Satlej campaign, Sirdar *Ranjodh Singh*, who had been most averse to peace, was sent with an English officer to induce the Governor of the Kangra fort to submit. His exertions to effect this object were not great, and there is every reason to believe that, through his instigation, the garrison held out longer than it would otherwise have done. He was then appointed Judge of Lahore, but in this post he did not give any satisfaction. When the dispute with his brother was finally adjusted, some guns, which should have been returned to *Lehna Singh*, were concealed by *Ranjodh Singh* in a house at Amritsar. He denied their concealment, but a forcible search being made, a large mortar, two 24-pound howitzers and a 6-pounder were found. His conduct on this occasion induced the Darbar, on the recommendation of the

Resident, to remove him from the Judgeship, in which he was succeeded by Sirdar Kanh Singh, Man. The next year, 1848, soon after the outbreak at Multan, he was detected in a treasonable correspondence with Mulraj, and was placed in confinement, only being released at the close of the war.

When *Ranjodh Singh* was arrested and carried prisoner to the fort, 10,000 * budkis, were left in his Lahore house, locked up in a chest. When the Sirdar was released, the money was gone. The theft was attributed to common thieves ; but it is believed that some Sirdars, who are now wealthy and honoured, could tell what became of the money. The Darbar confiscated his jagir, but, after annexation, he was allowed by his brother an annuity of 2,500 Rs. On the death of *Lehna Singh*, the allowance ceased ; and the Government granted him a cash pension of 3,000 Rs. per annum, which he still holds.

Sirdar *Lehna Singh* returned to the Punjab, in 1851, but, after two years, went back to Benares where he died on the 25th July, 1854. He left one son, Sirdar *Dyal Singh*, who is now about 16 years of age, and who is in the Court of Wards. He has received a good education in English, Persian and Hindi. He holds a perpetual jagir, of 6,000 Rs., and owns large landed property at Benares, purchased by his father some years ago.

Sirdar *Lehna Singh* was a man of considerable ability. He was a skilful mechanist, and an original inventor. He much improved the Sikh ordnance, and some very beautiful guns, of his manufacture, were taken at Aliwal and elsewhere. Among other things he invented a clock, which showed the hour, the day of the month and the changes of the moon. He was fond of astronomy and mathematics, and was master of several languages. As an administrator, *Lehna Singh* was very popular. The poor were never oppressed by him ; his assessments were moderate, and his decisions essentially just. As a stateman, he may be said to have been

* Budki, a gold coin, worth 5 Rs.

almost the only honest man in Lahore. Fraud and corruption were supreme, but the hands of *Lehna Singh* were always clean; surrounded by the most greedy and unscrupulous of schemers, he preserved his honesty unsullied. But he had one failing, which made shipwreck of all his virtues. * He was a coward. Timid and superstitious, he was ever ready, at the approach of danger, to run off to Hardwar to bathe, or to Benares to feed a crowd of hungry Brahmans.

Had a man of the reputation, and administrative talent, of *Lehna Singh* taken the lead, in 1845, in the Panjab, the great troubles which came upon the country might have been averted. But he was no true patriot. He did not understand that the religion of a statesman, and indeed of every brave man, is to stand by his country in times of danger, sharing her griefs, and, if need be, falling with her fall.

---

* There is a saying, well known in the country, to the effect that three families in the Panjab, Attariwala, Man, and Majithia, have possessed the greatest number of remarkable men.

The Attariwala Sirdars are brave and faithless. The Man Sirdars, handsome, gallant and true; the Majithias, wise and timid.

SIRDAR SURAT SINGH MAJITHIA.

- **Gujar.**
  - Veghu.
    - Dargah Singh.
      - Sirdar Amar Singh.
        - Sirdar Kahn Singh.
  - Taighu.
    - Izzat Singh.
      - Fatah Singh.
        - Chanda Singh.
        - Wasawa Singh. M. D. S. Gulab S. Povindia.
        - Sirdar Attar S.
          - Sirdar Surat Singh. i. M. D. S. Ran S., Wachohar. ii. M. D. Sahib S. of Attari.
        - Partab S. Zamindar.
        - Hera S. Zamindar.
      - Jaimal Singh. Descendants living engaged in agriculture.
    - Sahaj Singh.
      - Sirdar Uttam Singh.

HISTORY OF THE FAMILY.

Like the rest of the Majithia clan, the brothers, *Izzat Singh* and *Sahaj Singh*, followed the fortunes of the Sukarchakia Sirdars. *Izzat Singh* was able to acquire a strip of the Dhanni country on his own account, and held it, with much difficulty, and by dint of constant fighting, till his death, in 1772. His sons, *Fatah Singh* and *Jaimal Singh*, were mere boys at the time of his death, so his brother *Sahaj Singh* took possession of the estate. In 1781, *Sahaj Singh* died, and *Uttam Singh*, his eldest son, succeeded to the whole property, without any opposition from *Fatah Singh* and *Jaimal Singh*, who might have been reasonably expected to have claimed their father's share. The cousins lived together in harmony, and when Ranjit Singh rose to power, submitted to him, and having paid tribute, were confirmed in the estate. However, soon after this in 1803-4, the Maharaja marched in the

Rawalpindi direction and demanded the surrender of Nila and Rotas, a large and strong fort about six miles from the river Jhelam, which had been captured from the Afghans by Sirdar Charrat Singh. Sirdar *Uttam Singh* refused, but before hostilities commenced thought better of it, and gave up both to the Maharaja, who placed the fort in the charge of Mohr Singh Lamba and Raja Nur Khan, and the Maharaja then took possession of the whole Dhanni country, then famous for its breed of horses. *Attar Singh,* the adopted son of *Uttam Singh,* was, in 1809, made governor of the district about Rawalpindi. *Uttam Singh* died in 1827 and all his jagirs were resumed. But the family were not left destitute. *Attar Singh* received an estate of 28,000 Rs. at Syud Kasra and Ganja Mahal, and *Kahn Singh,* his cousin, whose father Sirdar *Amar Singh* had fallen in Hazara, one of the same value at Kot Bhai and Syadpur. *Amar Singh,* the father of *Kahn Singh,* was a very distinguished soldier. He was known as *Amar Singh, Kalan* (great), while the father of Sirdar *Mehtab Singh,* Majithia, was known as *Amar Singh, Khurd* (small).

When Diwan Ram Dyal was killed in Hazara, *Amar Singh, Kalan,* was appointed governor of that country. At first he held it in tolerable quiet; but finally quarrelled with Muhammad Khan, Tarin, a chief of note, and at Taraghar gave a severe defeat to the tribes Dhund, Tarin, Tanol and Karral, who had taken up arms in his favour. The battle was over; the enemy had taken to flight, and the Sikh force had retired from the field, when *Amar Singh,* thirsty and fatigued, went down to the little stream Samandar to bathe and drink. He had only a few horsemen with him, and a number of the enemy returning and seeing the weakness of the little party, came down, and killed *Amar Singh* and his followers, after a desperate defence. For a month the body of the Sirdar was left on the ground where he fell; but at last the Sikhs recovered it, and it was burnt with due honours.

To this day in Yusafzai the name of *Amar Singh* is well remembered, and the people still show a large tree, pierced through and through with an arrow, which they say was shot from the bow af *Amar Singh.*

Attar Singh was some time after allowed to have the management of the old family Ilaka of Dhanni, though not to hold it in jagir. He was killed in Hazara in 1843, and his only son *Surat Singh* succeeded him. This young man was stationed at Peshawar with his sowars, and during the first Panjab war in 1845-46 had to keep order about Naoshera which was in a very unsettled state. When Raja Lal Singh was minister, he tried to induce *Surat Singh* to exchange his jagir in Jhelam for one in the Bari Doab, and when the Sirdar would not consent, he sent his brother Amir Chand to seize, by force, the jagir and the fort of Syad Kaisra. *Surat Singh* resisted this violence, but he would have been overpowered had not Lal Singh's Kashmir intrigues worked his downfal, at the close of 1846. As it was a large portion of his jagirs were resumed, but were restored early in 1847. When the rebellion of 1848 broke out, Sirdar *Kahn Singh* was at Peshawar, where he was in command of the Orderly regiment. He remained faithful to the last, more from timidity than from loyalty, and, when the Peshawar troops mutinied, did his best to induce them to return to their duty. But when Sirdar Chattar Singh, Attariwala, arrived at Peshawar, *Kahn Singh* joined him, though unwillingly, and served with the rebel army till the end of the campaign.

But Sirdar *Surat Singh* in no way shared his cousin's misgivings or fears. He joined the rebellion from the first, and indeed was one of its exciters. It seems that so early as July, 1847, he had talked treason with Sirdar Chattar Singh, and when he was summoned from Peshawar, in July 1848, to join Raja Sher Singh, with 500 horse, he had another meeting on the road with Chattar Singh, and brought to Raja Sher Singh his father's injunctions to rebel. The defection of Raja Sher Singh appears to have been in a great measure owing to *Surat Singh's* evil influence. The evidence of Sheikh Imamuddin Khan is to the effect that at the meeting of Raja Sher Singh's officers at Multan, on the night of the 14th September, Raja Sher Singh tried to persuade his men to remain faithful, but that *Surat Singh* harangued the soldiery, and by his arguments so inflamed their passions that the Raja could only secure his safety by adopting the popular side and going over to Mulraj. When Sher Singh left Multan, *Surat Singh* was placed in command of one division of his army; 2,000 men and two guns. On the march to Jalalpur in the Gujranwala district, this detachment committed many excesses. At Chuniot, especially, where the population is Muhammadan and at Jhang, the mosques were defiled, and many of the inhabitants shamefully treated. *Surat Singh* also plundered two lakhs of Government money on its way to Multan. After the battle of Gujrat retribution came. The jagirs of *Surat Singh*, worth 22,500 Rs. were confiscated, and he was removed to Benares, where he remained, under surveillance, on a pension of 720 Rs. per annum.

Kahn Singh's conduct was regarded with some pity. He had tried to remain faithful, but had not at last strength to resist the persuasions and example of others, but his criminality did not approach that of *Surat Singh*. His jagirs were confiscated, to the value of 40,000 Rs., but he was allowed a pension of 3,600 Rs. per annum, which he enjoyed till his death, in 1853.

When *Kahn Singh* lost his jagirs, he was the owner of two elephants, which had been used on all occasions of state. But the Sirdar considered that both he and his elephants could not live, in idleness, upon his pension, and determined to make them of use. He accordingly had a frame work constructed, to the under side of which some twenty ploughs were fastened, in a long line. To this he yoked his elephants, and the sagacious animals ploughed the Majitha fields, as if they had been born to the work; and people used to come from all quarters to see the wonderful sight. He also had a very large well and Persian wheel constructed, and made the elephants irrigate the fields which they had ploughed.

The mutiny of 1857 found Sirdar *Surat Singh* still in exile, at Benares. Adversity had taught him wisdom, and he was now as warm in his loyalty as he had before been active in rebellion.

On the 4th June, 1857, the 37th N. I. were broken up at Benares, and some suspicious movement being observed in a corps of Ludianah Sikhs present on the ground, the guns which were being served against the 37th, were turned against the Sikhs. The whole affair seems to have been a miserable mistake, and there is no reason to believe that the corps was any thing but loyal; but it were not prepared for so severe a test of its loyalty ; and accordingly charged the guns, but was repulsed with great loss and driven from the field. It happened that the Benares treasury, which contained several lakhs of rupees and the jewels of the Maharani Jindan, valued at twenty lakhs, was guarded by a detachment of the Sikh regiment which had been cut up. Hard by the treasury was the Collector's court, a strong masonry building, on the roof of which some twelve civilians had taken their stand, to defend the treasure and their own lives in the event of an outbreak. When the Sikh guard heard of the fate of their comrades, their agitation and rage was extreme, and they would certainly have mutinied, seized the treasure, and attacked the Europeans, had not Sirdar *Surat Singh* gone in among them, and by his personal influence and expostulations kept them to a sense of their duty. Through that long June night, the Sirdar, ably seconded by Pandit Gokal Chand, argued and entreated, till towards morning, the little party were escorted to the mint by a European force. At Jaunpur, another detachment of the Ludianah regiment was stationed. When these men heard of the destruction of their regiment, they rose in fury, shot their Commanding officer, murdered the Joint Maigstrate, and marched to Lucknow with the treasure. But for the gallantry and loyalty of *Surat Singh,* the same tragedy might have taken place at Benares. Some time later, the Sirdar commanded the force sent to bring in the Sultanpur fugitives, and on several other occasions showed conspicuous gallantry in the field.

On the 6th July, when engaged with a body of Rajputs, who had attacked Benares, he was severely wounded by a sabre cut on the thigh, which confined him to his bed for some months, and from the effects of which he is still lame.

For his services during 1857, the Supreme Government granted Sirdar *Surat Singh* a pension of 4,800 Rs. per annum, and a valuable jagir, in perpetuity, at Dumri, in the Gorakhpur district, N. W. Provinces. He also received permission to return to the Panjab. In 1861, he came back to his old home, at Majitha, where he now generally resides.

SIRDAR MEHTAB SINGH, MAJITHIA.

- **Manna Singh.** D. 1802.
  - Dassonda Singh. D. 1806.
  - Jajji Singh.
  - Sirdar Amar Singh. D. 1848.
    - *Sirdar Mehtab Singh.* i. M. D. of Bhag S. Kila Chunda. ii. M. D. of Oghar S. Lohianwala. iii. M. D. of Gulab S. Bhangi. B. 1811.
    - S. Gurdit Singh. D. 1853.
    - Mith Singh. D. 1857.
      - Bachattar Singh. D. 1858.
      - Bijja Singh. B. 1844.
      - Bishan Singh. B. 1856.
    - Kahn Singh. B. 1826.
    - Hardit Singh. B. 1836.
      - Partab Singh. B. 1855.
      - Bhup Singh. B. 1858.

HISTORY OF THE FAMILY.

Manna Singh was a follower of Sirdar Charrat Singh, Sukarchakia, grandfather of Maharaja Ranjit Singh. He fought with his lord against the Chattahs, and received a service jagir of 4,000 Rs. Under Sirdar Mahan Singh he also served, and received the jagir of Jadah, in the Jhelam district. When Ranjit Singh took Lahore in 1799, *Manna Singh* was an old man, but he was still active, and fought in the campaign of 1802. He was killed in that year, before the fort of Chuniot, which Ranjit Singh was endeavouring to capture from Jassa Singh, Bhangi. Dassonda Singh, the eldest son, had died in his father's life-time, and the whole jagir was resumed.

As soon as *Amar Singh* was old enough to bear arms, the Maharaja gave him the villages of Thallanwala and Sheikhopur, worth 1,500 Rs., and placed him in the Derah Khas, a regiment of irregular cavalry composed of the sons of the Sikh nobility. At the siege of Multan, in 1818, the young *Amar Singh* displayed great gallantry, and for his services in this campaign received the Ilaka of Majrah. The next year, after the Kashmir campaign, he obtained a grant of Jadah, which had been held by his father, Manna Singh. He was sent to reduce the Rokhri insurgents in the Shahpur district, who had refused to pay the revenue, and his expedition was quite successful. In 1834, he accompanied the army under Prince Nao Nihal Singh, and Sirdar Hari Singh, Nalwa, to Peshawar, when that province was formally annexed to the Sikh empire. He was employed, in this campaign, on outpost duty, and many a severe fight he had with the Afghans. At Shabkadr he was wounded by a musket ball in a night attack made by the Afghans, in force, but although taken by surprise he rallied his men and drove back the enemy.

At the battle of Jamrud, on the 30th April, 1837, Sirdar *Amar Singh* commanded the centre '*miyana*' of the Sikh army, consisting of the Maharaja's Orderly troops, called the Jamadarwala Derah, and a thousand irregular cavalry, and distinguished himself by his conspicuous bravery; but the Afghans were very numerous, and the Sikh army was defeated with the loss of the General. The last expedition of Sirdar *Amar Singh* was, in 1843, in Kachhi, where an insurrection had broken out, which he quickly suppressed. He did not serve in the Satlej campaign, and on its close, being a celebrated marksman, was chosen to instruct the young Maharaja Dalip Singh, in shooting. The next year he left the Panjab on a pilgrimage to Hardwar, where he soon after died.

Mehtab Singh was born in the year 1811, and when quite a boy was placed in the irregular cavalry as Subahdar. In 1831, just before the visit of the Maharaja to Rupar, he was made a Colonel, and stationed at Amritsar in charge of two regiments. In 1834, he accompanied his father *Amar Singh* to Peshawar, and served, with distinction, throughout the campaign. In the same year his second brother *Gurdit Singh* entered the Maharaja's service. In 1839, *Mehtab Singh* served under Sirdar Tej Singh in the Afridi expedition. He was made a General by Maharaja

Sher Singh, in 1841, and was stationed at Peshawar, in command of 4 battalions, and 26 guns, with an Akal regiment. His conduct to the British force, which arrived at Peshawar, early in 1842, on the second Kabul expedition, was most unfriendly and hostile. After the assassination of Maharaja Sher Singh and Raja Dhyan Singh, the General, who had returned to Lahore, gave his assistance to Raja Hira Singh, against the Sindhanwalias, and, after the restoration of peace, his conduct was remembered with gratitude by Hira Singh, who bestowed upon him valuable presents. This did not, however, prevent *Mehtab Singh* from turning against the Minister when he became unpopular. He was privy to the conspiracy against the lives of Raja Hira Singh and Pandit Jalla, and his were among the troops who pursued and put them to death. Concerned with him in this conspiracy was General *Mewa Singh* Majithia, whose real name was Sultan Singh, a distant relative of *Mehtab Singh*, and an implacable enemy of the Wazir.

The conduct of *Mehtab Singh* in thus plotting the destruction of a man for whom he professed devoted friendship, does not seem amiable; but his motives were perfectly clear. He, with the army and the whole Sikh nation, was weary of the rule of the arrogant and debauched youth who owned all the Dogra vices, without their ability, their strength, or their courage. The influence of Pandit Jalla was still more odious; and as Hira Singh would not give him up, it was necessary that they should fall together. There were besides private grounds of hatred, Sirdar *Amar Singh*, father of *Mehtab Singh*, had, in the Kachhi expedition, given some four or five thousand rupees to his soldiers, who had behaved admirably, expecting to be reimbursed by the Government; but Pandit Jalla, knowing that when the treasury was full, there was more for him to plunder, refused to repay any portion of the sum, which so disgusted *Amar Singh* that he resigned the service. Again, *Mehtab Singh* had himself been tricked by Hira Singh in the affair of Baba Bir Singh the great Sikh Guru. By soft words, and presents and promises, he had been induced to lead his troops against Sirdar Attar Singh, Sindhanwalia; by treachery an action had been forced on, and, at its close, the holy Baba was found dying on the ground, and *Mehtab Singh* could not but feel himself, in some measure, the cause of his death. But even if his own conscience was clear, he did not escape the reproaches of the Sikh army and people, and his brigade, with that of General Court, commanded by Gulab Singh, Calcuttia, and the Derah Charyari commanded by Jowahir Mal Datt, was long known by the name of *Gurumar* (slayers of the Guru).

Mehtab Singh served throughout the Satlej campaign. He, like many others of the Sikhs, thought only of victory, and promised the Treasury moonshis to bring them silver pen-holders from the spoil of Delhi.

After the campaign, he was made a Sirdar by Raja Lal Singh, and both he and his brother *Gurdit Singh*, who had risen to the rank of General, were stationed at Peshawar ; but in May, 1847, he was transferred to Pind Dadan Khan. He was, at this time, no favourite in the Darbar, and there was but one man, Sirdar Sher Singh, Attariwala, who had a word to say in his favour ; but the influence of Major Lawrence the Resident prevented his dismissal. When the rebellion broke out, in 1848, in the North of the Panjab, Sirdar *Mehtab Singh* was stationed at Rawal Pindi, with 500 horse, under Major Nicholson. His conduct was spoken of in the highest terms by that officer. His troops with his brother *Mith Singh* remained faithful to the Lahore Government, throughout the war, and fought on the side of the British at the battle of Gujrat. On the annexation of the Panjab, all the personal jagirs of the Sirdar, amounting to 9,485 Rs., were released for two lives, and, in 1862, one half of this jagir was maintained to his lineal descendant, in perpetuity.

In 1857, Sirdar *Mehtab Singh* raised some horsemen for service in Hindostan, where they were sent under the command of his nephew *Buchattar Singh.* This force served with credit in Oude, and was engaged several times with the mutineers. *Buchattar Singh* died of cholera, at Cawnpur in 1858. His brother *Bijja Singh* succeeded him in the force as Jamadar.

General *Gurdit Singh* died in 1853, without issue.

Mith Singh, who was a Colonel in the Sikh army in 1844, died in 1857. *Kahn Singh* and *Hardit Singh* are both living and enjoy jagirs of 1,740 Rs. and 720 Rs., respectively. The former succeeded his father in command of the contingent, in 1843, and the latter was General of Maharaja Dalip Singh's juvenile force.

Sirdar *Mehtab Singh* resides at Majitha; but he has houses both at Lahore and Amritsar, at which latter place, he was, in 1862, created an Honorary Magistrate. He is a great sportsman, and spends a large part of his time at Kapurthalla, with the Alhuwalia Raja, with whom he is very intimate.

SIRDAR LAL SINGH, KALIANWALA.

SALABI.
- Sahib Singh.
  - Hukumat Singh.
    - Kour Singh.
      - Sirdar Dal Singh, Naharna. D. 1823.
        - Sirdar Attar Singh. D. 1851.
          - Sirdar Lal Singh. B. 1822.
        - Chattar Singh. D. 1845.
        - Joala Singh, died young.
        - Chet Singh.
        - Ram Singh, died young.

JAIMAL SINGH.
- Jassa Singh.
  - Sirdar Fatah Singh, Kalianwala. D. 1807.
    - Saddan. M. Sirdar Ranjit Singh, Sowrianwala.
      - Sirdar Isar Singh, Sowrianwala.
        - Ichhar Singh.
        - B. Ichhar Devi.
- Jai Singh.

HISTORY OF THE FAMILY.

Sirdar *Lal Singh* does not belong to the old Kalianwala stock, nor is he related to the great Sirdar *Fatah Singh*, through whom the present family attained wealth and honours. The story of *Fatah Singh's* family must be briefly told. *Jaimal Singh*, grandfather of Sirdar *Fatah Singh*, was a Sindhu Jat, and the first of his family to adopt the Sikh faith. He was a resident of Kali Lakhu, near Amritsar. He was a follower of the Sukarchakia chiefs, Charrat Singh and Mahan Singh, and with them was engaged in constant quarrels with the Chattah tribe, inhabiting the northern part of the Gujranwala district, and in one skirmish with some Chattah marauders, both his sons, *Jai Singh* and *Jassa Singh*, were slain. *Fatah Singh* entered the service of Ranjit Singh about 1798, and very rapidly rose in the favour of his master. He was a brave and skilful soldier, and proved himself as such in almost every campaign undertaken by the Maharaja till 1807. He fought against Ghulam Muhammad Khan, Chattah, against Jodh Singh of Wazirabad, and Nidhan Singh, Attu. He was with the Maharaja when he captured the city of Lahore, and when he took Amritsar from the Bhangis and the Ramgharias with the aid of the Alhuwalia and Kanheya Sirdars. He fought in the Jhang and the Pindi-Bhattian campaigns, and it was in a great measure owing to his advice, that Ranjit Singh did not espouse the cause of Rai Jaswant Rao Holkar against the British Government in 1805. Much assisted by Fatah Singh's good offices, peace was concluded between the English and Holkar, who gave to the Sirdar many valuable gifts in recognition of his services. Fatah Singh distinguished himself at the capture of Chuniot, from Jassa Singh Bhangi, and when Jhang was taken, in 1806, from Ahmad Khan, Sial, the district was leased to *Fatah Singh* for 60,000 rupees per annum. Ahmad Khan, however, soon after made a compromise with *Fatah Singh*, who returned to Lahore.

Towards the close of 1806, the Sirdar was sent against Kassur, where Kutbuddin Khan was giving trouble. The Pathan chief held out bravely, but was glad to buy off the Sikh by the payment of a lakh of rupees. At the beginning of 1807, a Sikh army, under Ranjit Singh in person, again marched against Kassur, and after a long fight reduced it. *Fatah Singh* promised to Kutbuddin the quiet possession of his estate at Mamdot, if he would give up the Kassur fort ; and although Ranjit Singh did not approve of the promise, yet he considered himself bound to confirm it.

Beneath the banner of *Fatah Singh*, many of the chief Sikh barons were proud to fight. Among others was Amir Singh, Sindhanwalia, *Dal Singh*, Naharnah, Dhannah Singh, Malwai, Fatah Singh, Mattu, and Uttam Singh, Chhachhi.

In 1807, Ranjit Singh, returning from Pattiala, besieged the fort of Narayanghar, held by Sirdar Kishan Singh. For fifteen days it held out, and the Maharaja became very impatient at the delay, and told *Fatah Singh,* who was in immediate command, that he was fonder of remaining by him (the Maharaja) than of leading the troops in the field. *Fatah Singh* piqued at this, assaulted the fort; but was repulsed, and mortally wounded. Ranjit Singh came to visit him in his tent, and *Fatah Singh* is said to have advised the Maharaja never to raise another Jat to the highest offices in the state. Whether such advice was ever given is doubtful, but the Maharaja appeared to act upon some such principle for, while his bravest officers and generals were Jat Sikhs, in the council he rather gave his confidence to Brahmans, Rajputs, and even Muhammadans.

Fatah Singh left no son, and Ranjit Singh might have resumed all his jagirs; but feeling some remorse for the Sirdar's death, he sent Mith Singh, Padhania, on his arrival at Amritsar, with a valuable khillat, to Mai Sewan the widow; and bid him tell her that any one whom she should nominate as her husband's heir and successor would be recognized. There were several Chiefs well loved by *Fatah Singh,* and none more so than Dhanna Singh, Malwai, and *Dal Singh,* Naharna. The latter was his 'potrela' (godson) and a great favourite. But for the succession to Fatah Singh's estates, *Dal Singh* is said neither to have trusted to fortune or to favour. On the night of Mith Singh's arrival at Kali, *Dal Singh* paid him a private visit, and for 5,000 Rs. Mith Singh told Mai Sewan, that, although she might nominate whom she pleased, Ranjit Singh would be only pleased with Dal Singh, and he was accordingly selected.

Notwithstanding the generosity of Ranjit Singh on this occasion, there were not wanting many who said that the jagirs had been given to Dal Singh as a thank-offering for the death of Fatah Singh; that Ranjit Singh had long feared the Chief, and that he dared him to assault Narayanghar, through an impracticable breach, in the hope of his death. On one occasion, at Wazirabad, Ranjit Singh had told Fatah Singh to draw his forces on one side that he might see how numerous they were. When the order was given, the whole army went over to the great Kalianwala Chief, and Ranjit Singh, to his rage and chagrin, found himself almost deserted. He never forgot the incident, or forgave the Chief who had too much influence with the army.

Dal Singh Naharna's family originally resided at Karial, in Sheikopurah, and is of the Naharna or barber (or, more properly nail-cutter) caste. It is stated that an ancestor, a Wirk Jat fell in love and eloped with one Rami, the daughter of Duni Chand of the Jandi Naharna tribe, and that the name Naharna has been ever since attached to the family; but this is a fiction, and has only been invented since the family rose to importance. Dal Singh was not of Jat descent. *Sahib Singh*, Naharna, was the associate of Bhagwan Singh, and became known as a bold and successful robber. When Charrat Singh became powerful, both *Sahib Singh* and Bhagwan Singh joined him; and when he had conquered the country about Pind Dadan Khan, Bhagwan Singh claimed a third share. This Charrat Singh did not fancy giving, and believing that he could trust *Sahib Singh* he resolved to get rid of his troublesome ally. Soon after the three men went on a hunting expedition, and a wild boar happening, to run past, Charrat Singh cried aloud, "Don't let the beast escape." *Sahib Singh*, who well understood the meaning of these words, shot Bhagwan Singh dead. For this service he was rewarded with a jagir. Both his son, *Hukumat Singh*, and his grandson, *Kour Singh*, were in the service of the Sukarchakia Chiefs, but they were not men of any note.

Sirdar *Dal Singh* was a bold and able man, and was a great favourite with Sirdar *Fatah Singh*, Kalianwalla, under whose orders he used to fight. At the time of *Fatah Singh's* death *Dal Singh* had a jagir of about 68,000 Rs., but when the Kalianwala jagirs, with the exception of 70,000 Rs., settled on Mai Sewan and the children of Fatah Singh's daughter, were made over to him, his estates were worth about 3,50,000 Rs. Most of the Sirdars who had fought under *Fatah Singh*, now were led by *Dal Singh*; and the barber showed himself as brave in battle as the best of the Jat aristocracy. He served with honour in the Kassur, Multan, Kashmir and Derah Ismail Khan campaigns.

In 1814, he was sent, with Ram Dyal, grandson of Diwan Mokham Chand, in command of a detachment of ten thousand men, to force their way into Kashmir, by way of Nandan Sar, while Ranjit Singh himself proceeded by way of Punch. This detachment was surrounded and outnumbered, and it was only on account of the friendship entertained for Diwan Mokham Chand, by Azim Khan, that he was allowed to return unmolested. In the spring of 1815, again in company with Ram Dyal, he ravaged the Multan and Bhawalpur territories, exacting fines and contributions from every town ; and, later in the year, he was sent against the Bhimbar and Rajaori Chiefs. He reduced them to submission, and burnt a large portion of the city of Rajaor. He died in 1823, according to his family, of cholera ; but the commonly received story is that he took poison, after having been severely rebuked by the Maharaja for the inefficient state of his contingent. He was succeeded in his jagir by his eldest son *Attar Singh.*

In 1834, *Attar Singh* was sent to Peshawar, under the command of Prince Nao Nihal Singh. While there, Diwan Hakim Rai, who was the chamberlain of the Prince and a great favourite, induced some of the Sirdars who had been accustomed to fight under the command of *Attar Singh*, to go over to him, with their troops. On this *Attar Singh* left the army, without leave, and came to Lahore to complain to the Maharaja. He was not well received, and was ordered to rejoin the army, then in Bannu, without delay. *Attar Singh* refused ; and the Maharaja confiscated all his jagirs, with the exception of the family estate of Kalah, worth 3,500 Rs., and Hamidpur, 750 Rs.

Thus it remained till the death of Ranjit Singh. His successor Kharrak Singh restored 12,750 Rs., free of services, and Maharaja Sher Singh, on the return of *Attar Singh* from the Ganges, where he had conveyed the ashes of Maharaja Kharrak Singh, and Prince Nao Nihal

Singh, gave him, at Pindi Gheb and Mirowal, jagirs valued at 1,02,000 Rs., this was subject to the service of two hundred horse, and included a grant of 2,000 Rs. to his son *Lal Singh*. *Attar Singh* was made Adalati (chief justice) of Lahore and the surrounding districts, and received command of the Pindiwala irregular cavalry which had been first raised by Milka Singh, Pindiwala. No change took place in his jagir till Jowahir Singh became Wazir, when *Attar Singh* represented that Pindi Gheb, though nominally worth 65,000 Rs., only yielded 50,000 Rs., and obtained, in exchange, the Ilakas of Chunian, Dhundianwali, and Khudian, worth 60,000 Rs.

After the murder of Prince Peshora Singh by Jowahir Singh's orders, the army, enraged at the conduct of the Wazir, determined upon his death and threw off their allegiance to the Lahore Government. Sirda *Attar Singh* was, on the 19th September, sent by the Rani Jindan, with Diwan Dina Nath and Fakir Nur-ud-din, to the camp at Mian Mir, to induce the mutinous troops to return to their duty. No attention was, however, paid to their advice; the Fakir was dismissed, but the Diwan and *Attar Singh* were insulted, abused and confined in camp till after the murder of the Wazir, on the 22nd September, when the army, always afraid of the Rani, sent them to Lahore to try and make their peace.

Sirdar *Attar Singh* served throughout the Satlej campaign of 1845-46, and at the battle of Firushahr, his brother, *Chattar Singh*, was killed.

In September, 1846, *Attar Singh* was ordered to join the Sikh army proceeding to Kashmir to suppress the rebellion there, but he took no notice of repeated injunctions, remaining at his house, near Amritsar, on pretence of celebrating the marriage of his niece. For this conduct his jagir was confiscated. Shortly afterwards, however, it was restored to him, and made up to 1,11,800 Rs. He received a seat in the council of Regency, appointed in December, 1846, and held this post till the annexation of the Panjab.

On the first news of the outbreak at Multan, in April, 1848, he was ordered to proceed thither, in command of all the available irregular troops. He was recalled, with the other Sirdars, when the Resident at Lahore found that it was considered inexpedient to send a European force to Multan, at that time of year; but later he accompanied Raja Sher Singh to Multan, in command of the cavalry.

The Sirdar had little influence over the troops which he commanded. He was of a weak and vacillating character, and although his own intentions were good, he was quite unable to keep his men to their duty. Day by day they grew more and more mutinous, and deserted in numbers to the rebel Mulraj, in Multan. At length it was agreed by the three Sikh generals Raja Sher Singh, Sirdar Shamsher Singh, and Sirdar *Attar Singh,* in concert with Major Edwardes, and with the concurrence of the English General, that the only thing to do was to move the troops out of temptation, away from Multan. Sirdar Attar Singh's division was to be posted at Tulambah, under pretence of keeping open the road; but before the movement could be executed, the whole Sikh army rebelled, and being joined by Raja Sher Singh, marched to Multan. Sirdar *Attar Singh* mounted his horse and fled to the camp of Major Edwardes, with a few horsemen. His son, *Lal Singh,* was carried off by the troops, but soon afterwards contrived to make his escape and joined Major Edwardes also.

Lal Singh had, in June, 1847, been sent, in command of 500 sowars, to Hassan Abdal, and had remained there till the 3rd of May, 1848, when he received an order to join the force of Raja Sher Singh, on its way to Multan. When Diwan Kishen Kour, Adalati of Battala, joined the rebels, Sirdar *Lal Singh* was appointed to succeed him and held the appointment for about three months, till the close of the Sikh administration.

On annexation, all the personal jagirs of Sirdar *Attar Singh,* amounting to 47,750 Rs. were maintained for life; one quarter to descend to his son *Lal Singh* and his male heirs, in perpetuity. The jagir of Sirdar *Lal Singh,* worth 3,600 Rs. being a recent grant of 1848, was resumed ; but he was assigned a cash allowance of 4,800 Rs. from the jagir of his father, with whom he was at feud.

Sirdar *Attar Singh* died in December, 1851, and three-fourths of his jagir was resumed. The share of his son *Lal Singh* was, in February, 1862, raised to 15,000 Rs., which is continued in perpetuity. *Lal Singh* is forty-two years of age, and resides at Kalah in the Amritsur district. He has been four times married, but has no children.

ALI RAZA KHAN, KIZILBASH.

- Sirdar Nauroz Ali Khan.
  - Sirdar Ali Khan.
    - Sirdar Gul Muhammad Khan.
      - Ali Akbar Khan.
      - Ali Jan Khan.
    - Hidayat Khan.
      - Muhammad Hassain Khan.
      - Muhammad Hassain Khan.
      - Haji Muhammad Khan.
      - Ali Raza Khan.
        - Nawazish Ali Khan.
        - Nasir Ali Khan.
          - Fatah Ali Khan.
        - Nasar Ali Khan.
      - Muhammad Raza Khan.
      - Muhammad Takki Khan.
    - Sirdar Ali Muhammad Khan Sirdar.

HISTORY OF THE FAMILY.

Sirdar *Ali Khan,* the grandfather of *Ali Raza Khan,* was the first to leave the province of Sherwan, on the west coast of the Caspian (now part of the Russian territories) where, for many generations, his family, Turks of the Kizilbash tribe, had resided and exercised authority. When Nadir Shah, having driven out the Ghiljis and taken possession of Khorasan, prepared to march to India, in 1738, he took with him *Ali Khan,* and other Kizilbash nobles, who, he feared, in his absence, might excite disturbances.

Ali Khan served throughout the campaign, and on his return from India, he was appointed, by Nadir Shah, Governor of Kandahar, and other Kizilbash Nobles received commands in Kabul and Peshawar, much to the advantage of the kingdom of Persia, which, freed from these turbulent Chiefs, enjoyed peace for eight years, till the assassination of Nadir Shah, and the rise to power of Ahmad Shah, Durani. The new Prince was crowned at Kandahar, in 1747, and, although he thoroughly distrusted the Kizilbash faction, yet he was not strong enough to oppose it, and was compelled to give, to its principal Chiefs, jagirs and military commands.

Ali Khan obtained the district of Hazarah North of Kandahar, and with a strong force reduced the country around, to the neighbourhood of Hirat itself. He accompanied Ahmad Shah on his last invasion of India, in 1760, and shared in the great victory of Panipat, which broke the Mahratta power. The bravery and influence of *Ali Khan* during this campaign excited the jealousy of Ahmad Shah, who, on his return to Afghanistan, tried to deprive him of his estates and command; but *Ali Khan* held his own successfully against open force, and Ahmad Shah was at length compelled to bribe some of his attendants who assassinated him, in 1770. The eldest of the sons, *Gul Muhammad Khan*, was but six years of age at his father's death, and the district fell into great confusion. The widow of *Ali Khan* contrived to maintain her authority for some years, but at last the district was divided into several independent and hostile Chiefships, only united in their hatred of Timur Shah, who had succeeded Ahmad Shah on the throne of Kabul. When the sons of *Ali Khan* grew up, they recovered, by force of arms, a large portion of their family estate, and Timur Shah, thinking it well to conciliate them, summoned *Gul Muhammad Khan* to Kandahar, where he received him with honor and conferred on him the title of Sirdar.

Hadayat Khan, father of *Ali Raza Khan*, accompanied Shah Zaman to Lahore, in 1797, where he remained for some months. On his return to Kabul he exchanged estates with Asad Khan, brother of Amir Dost Muhammad Khan. In 1813, *Ali Muhammad Khan*, the youngest brother, with 4,000 troops, accompanied Wazir Fatah Khan and his brother Muhammad Azim Khan in their successful expedition against Kashmir, and received there a high military command which he held for about eight years, when, returning to Kabul he obtained joint possession, with *Hidayat Khan*, of the family estate, and died in 1835, leaving two sons, *Ali Akbar Khan* and *Ali Jan Khan*. The elder son soon after died, and *Ali Jan Khan* succeeded to his father's share of the estate, which he still holds in Kabul.

Hidayat Khan died in 1836, leaving six sons, of whom the eldest *Muhammad Hassan Khan* served under the order of Wazir Fatah Muhammad Khan, at Hirat-khan, and when his master's eyes had been put out by Prince Kamran, he escorted Khandal Khan and Sherdil Khan to Kandahar, where he remained for some years, and later went with his uncle to Kashmir. On his return to Kabul he resided with his brother *Ali Raza Khan*, and did good service to the British Government during the Afghanistan campaign. *Muhammad Hassain Khan*, the second brother, was in great favour with Muhammad Azim Khan, and held a high appointment under him in Kashmir. After Azim Khan's death, *Hassain Khan* returned to Kabul, and took service with Dost Muhammad Khan. In 1844 he went on pilgrimage to the holy places in Arabia, where he lived for some years. He is now living in Kabul. The third brother is *Haji Muhammad Khan*, who was Minister of Habib-ullah-Khan the Ruler of Kabul, between the death of Azim Khan and the accession of Dost Muhammad. On the accession of that Prince he retired to Mecca, and on his return took up his abode with *Ali Raza Khan*, with whom he still resides.

Ali Raza Khan had always lived on his hereditary estate, which was of the description called in Afghanistan, '*Zar-kharid*' hereditary, but subject to military service. When the British Army, with Shah Shuja, first entered Kabul in 1839, *Ali Raza Khan*, being possessed of great influence in the city, was appointed Chief Agent of the Commissariat Department. His conduct in this office was unexceptionable, and he never failed in any engagement to supply grain or carriage. When the British Cantonment was besieged by the insurgents, he remained firm to English interests, and kept the troops supplied with food and clothing. When the British Officers and Ladies were taken prisoners, *Ali Raza Khan* made the greatest exertions to alleviate their sufferings and obtain their liberation. He paid to their keeper Muhammad Shah Khan, Ghilzai, five hundred rupees a month, besides bribing the subordinate officers, to induce them to treat the prisoners well, and to allow his servants to convey to them clothes, money and provisions. Nor did his humanity end here. He ransomed and saved from slavery nearly one hunded Hindostani sepoys, and kept them secretly in his own house till the second British Army entered Kabul.

When Muhammad Akbar Khan had sent off the prisoners to Khulum by way of Hazarah and Barmian, *Ali Raza Khan,* who possessed great hereditary influence in that country, persuaded and bribed the Hazarah Chiefs not to allow the captives to be conveyed to the hills, and he also sent his agent Murtaza Shah, with a large sum of money, to attempt to win over Salah Muhammad Khan, who was in command of the escort. It was by his influence, and by a lavish expenditure of his money, that the captives were enabled to make their escape and join the relieving army of General Pollock. When Akbar Khan advanced to attack that General, *Ali Raza Khan* won over the Kizilbash Chiefs to the side of the British, and they accordingly deserted Akbar Khan before the battle, and after his defeat their hostility made him fear to return to Kabul, and accordingly he fled through the hill country to Turkistan. On the retreat of the British forces to India, *Ali Raza Khan* accompanied them. His conduct had excited the bitter hatred of Muhammad Akbar Khan and the Barakzais, and his life was no longer safe in Kabul.

His estates (worth three lakhs of rupees) were confiscated, his houses razed to the ground, and with their materials Akbar Khan built two houses for himself.

Such is the dry detail of services the most disinterested, noble and chivalrous, performed by *Ali Raza Khan.* At the greatest personal risk, with the loss of his wealth, position, and hereditary estates, *Ali Raza*

Khan stood bravely and alone in defence of the side to which he had promised allegiance.

But he and his family have done good service to the English Government, in India, as well as in Afghanistan. During the Satlej campaign he joined the British camp with his brothers, and sixty horsemen of his tribe, many members of which had shared his exile, and fought in the battles of Mudki, Firushahr and Sobraon, where four of his sowars were killed. He accompanied Major H. Lawrence to Kangra and Kashmir in 1846, and during the rebellion of 1848-49 furnished one hundred horsemen under the command of his sister's son, *Sher Muhammad*, for active service. In June, 1857, when our need was greatest, *Ali Raza Khan* volunteered to raise a troop of horse for service before Delhi. This he did, and his own presence being desired at Lahore, he sent them under the command of his brothers *Muhammad Raza Khan* and *Muhammad Takki Khan*. In raising this force he did not, at a time when the Government was in want of every procurable rupee, apply for any pecuniary assistance. At his own expense, and by the mortgage of his house and property in Lahore, he equipped the troop and sent with it, besides his brother, his nephews *Abdulla Khan*, *Muhammad Hassan Khan*, *Muhammad Zaman Khan*, *Ghulam Hassan Khan*, and *Sher Muhammad Khan*. Forming part of the celebrated "Hodson's Horse" the troop raised by *Ali Raza Khan* served throughout the campaign, wherever that gallant corps was sent, and its gallantry was ever conspicuous.

At Khasniganj *Muhammad Takki Khan* was slain, fighting bravely, after several mutineers had fallen by his hand. *Muhammad Raza Khan*, the second brother of *Ali Raza Khan*, was among the bravest in his fearless regiment. He was twice wounded at Mallu and Shamsabad, and had two horses shot under him; and in every place where blows were thickest, there was the gallant *Muhammad Raza Khan* to be found. After the campaign he received the first-class Order of Merit, the title of Sirdar Bahadoor, and the grant of his pension of 200 Rs. in perpetuity. He died at Lucknow, whither he had gone on leave shortly afterwards, and his son *Raza Ali Khan* is now living with his uncle at Lahore.

Ali Raza Khan is an Honorary Magistrate of Lahore, and justly possesses great influence in the city; influence which he has always used for good. After his retirement from Kabul he received a pension of 800 Rs. per mensem, and his brother *Muhammad Raza Khan* 200 Rs. per mensem. After the mutinies he received a grant of a Talukdari of 147 villages in Beraich, in Oude, worth 15,000 Rs. per annum. He has also received the title of Khan Buhadar, and his nephews above mentioned, who served so well during the mutinies, the title of Sirdar Buhadar.

Ali Raza Khan has three sons, the eldest of whom, *Nowazish Ali Khan*, was with Major G. Lawrence, at Peshawar, when the Sikh troops mutinied, in 1848. He remained with that officer to the last, and his fidelity cost him his house and property at Peshawar. The third son, *Nasar Ali Khan*, is in charge of the Oude estate. He has there been created an Honorary Assistant Commissioner, and his conduct has given complete satisfaction to the authorities.

Thus for five-and-twenty years *Ali Raza Khan* and his family have served the British Government with a devotion which has been as perfect as it has been disinterested. He was not by birth a British subject, but it would be difficult, throughout Hindostan, to find a family, however bound to the English Government by gratitude or duty, which has, for its sake, risked so nobly and disinterestedly, life and every thing that can make life desirable. As long as the Kabul campaign, with the greatest disaster that ever befel the British arms, is remembered—as long as the sorrows and the glories of 1857 are household words amongst us; so long should the name of *Ali Raza Khan* and his gallant family, be remembered by all true Englishmen with gratitude and esteem.

NOTE.—The Kizilbashes still possess great influence in Kabul, where they number some 8,000 or 10,000. They inhabit a separate quarter to the south-west of the city, strongly fortified, known by the name of Chandol. The present Minister in Kabul (Mustaufi) is a Kizilbash; the chief offices are filled by members of the tribe, and the mother of Dost Muhammad himself was a lady of this tribe. The Shah of Persia is said to be now intriguing with the Kizilbash faction, to weaken the Kabul Government.

Kizilbash قزلباش or 'red-head' is of Turki derivation, and by some is said to have arisen from the red caps worn by the captives given to Sheikh Haidar by Tamarlane. D'Herbelot, however, in his Bibliotheque Orientale, published in 1777, states that the name originated with Ismail, founder of a line of kings who reigned in Persia from 907 A. H., who commanded his soldiers to wear a red cap, around which a turban of twelve folds was bound in honor and in remembrance of the twelve Imams, the successors of Ali, from whom he professed to have descended.

SIRDAR KANH SINGH, NAKKAI.

- Chowdhri Hemraj.
  - S. Hira Singh.
    - S. Dal Singh.
  - Dasundhi.
  - Natha Singh.
    - S. Nar Singh.
    - Sirdar Ran Singh.
      - S. Bhagwan Singh.
      - S. Gyan Singh.
        - Bibi Ratan Kour, m. Sirdar Ram Singh, Taragharia.
        - Sirdar Khan Singh.
          - Hukm Singh, d.
          - Atar Singh.
            - B. Partab Kour, m. son of Fatah Singh, Taragharia.
            - Labh Singh.
            - B. Mehtab Kour, m. S. Ganda Singh, Kulbajwa.
            - Lehna Singh.
          - Chattar Singh, d.
            - B. Isa Kour, m. Nihal Singh, son of S. Jaggat Singh, Man.
            - B. Thakar Kour, m. Amar Singh, son of Diwan Singh, Commandant.
            - Thakar Singh.
            - Partab Singh.
            - Ranjodh Singh.
              - Udho Singh.
              - Narayan Singh.
          - Isar Singh.
        - B. Dya Kour, m. Sirdar Amar Singh, Veglia.
      - Khazan Singh.
        - Panju Singh.
      - B. Raj Kour, m. M. R. Ranjit Singh.
    - Gurbaksh Singh.
  - Galla.

HISTORY OF THE FAMILY.

About the year 1595, the Sikh Guru Arjan, travelling with a few followers in the Lahore district, reached the little town of Bahrwal, which had been founded some years before by a man of the Arora caste, named Bahr. He was not received with hospitality, and passed on to the neighbouring village of Jambar, where, tired and foot-sore, he begged for the loan of a charpai, (native bedstead), and lying down in the shade of a tree, went to sleep. By this time *Hemraj*, a Sindhu Jat, chowdhri or headman of Bahrwal, who was absent when the Guru passed through his village, heard of what had occurred, and, ashamed of his townsmen's inhospitality, set off to Jambar to try and induce the holy man to return. On his arrival at the village he found the Guru asleep. What was to be done? He dared not wake the saint, for he was uncertain of his temper, nor could he suffer him to remain longer at Jambar; so being a man of resource and some physical strength, he lifted the charpai and the Guru together on his head and carried him away to Bahrwal.

When Arjan woke he was much pleased with *Hemraj's* attention, and called for water to drink. He was told that the water of their only well was brackish. The Guru then directed *Hemraj* to throw some sweet cakes down the well. This being done, the water immediately became sweet and pure. The Guru also blessed *Hemraj*, and prophesied that he would have a son, by name *Hira Singh*, who would be a great and powerful Chief.

So runs the legend, believed to this day at Bahrwal; for, is not the water of the well, known as Buddhewala, still sweet and clear?

The legend would have been told with more propriety, of *Alam* the father, or of *Mahmana* the grandfather of Hemraj, for *Hira Singh* who was certainly the first man of note in the family was not born till nearly a hundred years after the death of Guru Arjan, which took place in 1606.

Hira Singh, at the time that the Sikhs grew powerful, about the middle of the last century, took possession of the Nakka country, lying between Lahore and Gogaira, and which has given its name to the family of *Hira Singh*, and to the misl which he commanded. He took Chunian from the Afghans, and joined the Kanheyas and Bhangis in their attacks upon the falling Mogal power.

When Sirdar *Hira Singh* was killed fighting with Shaikh Sujan Chisti of Pak Pattan, his son *Dal Singh* was a minor, and his nephew *Nar Singh* succeeded to the command of the misl. *Nar Singh* was killed in a fight at Kot Kumaliah, in 1768, and his son *Ran Singh* succeeded him.

Under this Chief the misl rose to some strength and importance. It was never powerful compared with some of the other Sikh confederacies, but it could bring into the field nearly two thousand horsemen, with camel swivels and a few guns. But the Jats of the Nakka country are strong and bold, and the little misl did good battle with the Afghans and other neighbours, till at last a tract of country worth nine lakhs of rupees was in the hands of Sirdar *Ran Singh* and his misldars (feudal retainers). They held Chunian, part of the Kassur, Sharakpur and Gogaira pargannahs, and at one time Kot Kumaliah, the head-quarters of the Kharral tribe.

The Chief of Syadwala, Kamar Singh, was the rival of *Ran Singh*, and they fought with varying success for some years, till at length *Ran Singh* obtained a decided advantage and took possession of Syadwala. Sirdar *Ran Singh* died in 1781, and his eldest son *Bhagwan Singh*, who succeeded to the command of the misl, was not able to hold the territory his father had acquired. Syadwala was recovered by Wazir Singh, brother of Kamar Singh, who also took some of the Nukkai villages, but these he eventually gave up. *Bhagwan Singh* now perceived that unless he made powerful friends, he would probably lose his territory altogether, so he betrothed his sister *Nakayan*, generally known as *Raj Kouran*, to Ranjit Singh, son of Mahan Singh, Sukarchakia, who was then one of the most powerful Chiefs in the Panjab. Wazir Singh tried hard to break off this match, which boded no good to him, but was unable to do so. Shortly after this, in 1785, Maha Singh summoned both *Bhagwan Singh* and Wazir Singh to Amritsar, to aid him in his struggle with Jai Singh, Kanheya. The rival Chiefs went accordingly, but when Jai Singh was defeated, they soon began to quarrel, for Mahan Singh treated Wazir Singh with more consideration than *Bhagwan Singh*, which roused the jealousy of the latter. Mahan Singh, with some difficulty, brought about a reconciliation, but the peace was not of long duration, and the quarrel broke out with greater violence than ever, and in the fight which ensued, *Bhagwan Singh* was slain. His brother *Gyan Singh* succeeded him, in 1789. The old enemy of their family, Wazir Singh, was murdered soon after by *Dal Singh*, son of Sirdar *Hira Singh* who took refuge at Bahrwal, but he was followed and assassinated by a servant of Wazir Singh, who had resolved to avenge his master's death. Mahan Singh died in 1792, and in 1798 *Gyan Singh* married his sister to Ranjit Singh, to whom she had been some time betrothed. In 1802, a son, the issue of this marriage, was born, who afterwards ascended the throne as Maharaja Kharrak Singh. The Nakkai family did not find the alliance with Ranjit Singh productive of much advantage. That ambitious Chief hungered after his kinsman's possessions, and tried hard to induce Sirdar *Kanh Singh*, who became the head of the family on the death of *Gyan Singh*, in 1807, to come and reside at court. This the Sirdar steadily denied to do, and in 1810, the Maharaja seized all the possessions of the family, without any resistance on their part, for resistance was unavailing. He gave to *Kanh Singh* estates in the neighbourhood of Bahrwal of the value of 15,000 Rs., and to *Khazan Singh* he also gave a jagir at Nankot.

Sirdar *Kahn Singh* is still alive, and in 1860 was made a jagirdar Magistrate, which office he now holds. He has always lived at Bahrwal, a little town far away from any high road, and has mixed very little in politics since the death of Maharaja Ranjit Singh. In 1848, his troops and his second son *Attar Singh*, who were with the army at Multan, joined the rebels, but *Kahn Singh*, who was then an old man, was not suspected of being a party to his son's disaffection. His eldest son, *Chattar Singh*, who remained faithful, died in 1857, leaving three sons and two daughters.

DIWAN AJODHIA PARSHAD.

PANDIT KISHAN DAS.

- Pandit Kewal Ram.
  - Thakar Parshad.
    - Bhawani Parshad. B. 1812.
- Diwan Ganga Ram. D. 1826.
  - Diwan Ajodhia Parshad. B. 1799.
    - Baij Nath, B. 1822.
  - A daughter.
    - Uttam Nath. B. 1850.

HISTORY OF THE FAMILY.

The family of Diwan *Ajodhia Parshad* is of the Brahman caste, and originally came from Kashmir. It claims to belong to the family known as 'Swaman Gotam,' descended from the famous 'rikhi' or sage, Gotama, who was born about 620 B. C. on the lower Ganges. It is also known as Chhachballi, from the mohalla, or district, in Kashmir, which was its residence.

The Muhammadan religion was established into Kashmir in the year 1326 A. D., by Shamshuddin Shah. For nearly a hundred years no severe measures were taken against the Hindus, but when Sikandar, named Bhut-shikan or the Iconoclast, became King, the Brahman pandits had much difficulty in preserving their religion and their lives. The ancestors of *Ajodhia Parshad* studied Persian as a sort of compromise, and contrived to live in tolerable security till the conquest of Kashmir by Ahmad Shah, Abdali, in 1752. The Hindus were now exposed to constant persecution, and many emigrated to Hindostan and the Panjab. Among the emigrants was Pandit *Kishan Das,* grandfather of *Ajodhia Parshad.* He was a good scholar, and, without difficulty, obtained a situation under the Delhi Emperors, which he held till his death.

His son *Ganga Ram*, who was born at Rampur, near Benares, entered the service of the Maharaja of Gwalior, and was placed with Colonel Louis Burquien, one of the French officers in Sindia's service, under General Perron. Here the young man distinguished himself by his honesty and ability, and became entrusted with many important political affairs. When the Mahrattas, towards the close of the last century, overran Central India, Malwa, and the Delhi territories, *Ganga Ram* was employed under Colonel Burquien in collecting tribute, and in drawing up treaties with subject or allied states.

After the defeat of Burquien, at Patparganj on the Jamna, by Lord Lake, in September, 1803, *Ganga Ram* retired to Delhi, where he lived for the ten succeeding years. He was of great assistance to General Ochterlony when, in 1809, that officer was arranging the relations between the Cis-Satlej States and the British Government, from his knowledge of their past political history, their treaties and their relations with other States.

In March, 1813, Maharaja Ranjit Singh, who had heard *Ganga Ram* spoken of as a man of ability, invited him to Lahore, on the recommendation of Bhai Lal Singh and Sirdar Himmat Singh, Jallawassia. He accepted the invitation, and taking with him a vessel of Ganges water for presentation to the Maharaja, was well received at Lahore, where he was placed at the head of the military office, and made keeper of the seal. He was made one of the paymasters in chief of the irregular forces; Bhawani Das being the head of the department, and rose rapidly in the favour of the Maharaja, who saw the great improvements made in the system of military account. *Ganga Ram* brought from Hindostan numbers of his relatives and friends, for whom he obtained good places about court. Most of them, however, were not mere adventurers, but men of business and literary attainment. Among them may be noticed,

Raja Dina Nath; Pandit Dya Ram, who administered successively, the Ramgharia country, Jhang, Dingah, &c.; Pandit Hari Ram, father of Shanker Nath, Honorary Magistrate of Lahore; Pandit Gopi Nath; Pandit Ram Kishan; Pandit Ganga Bishan, and Pandit Lachman Parshad.

Diwan *Ganga Ram*, Lachman Parshad's father, and Bakht Mal, had married three sisters. *Ganga Ram* had no son born to him, so he adopted his wife's nephew *Ajodhia Parshad*, brother of Lachman Parshad; Dina Nath (afterwards Raja) was son of Bakht Mal, and consequently first cousin of *Ajodhia Parshad*. *Ganga Ram* had, later, a daughter by a second wife, whose son, *Uttam Nath*, is now a student in Lahore.

Thus by his personal ability, and by the family interest which he established in Lahore, *Ganga Ram* obtained considerable power, and the administration of the country about Gujrat was, in 1821, entrusted to him. In this District, which he held two years, he received a grant of Khemi, Kalaichpur, &c., in the Karriali Ilaka. He first organized the Abkari system, which was afterwards so much improved by Misr Rallia Ram.

Diwan *Ganga Ram* died in 1826. He was succeeded as keeper of the seal, and in the military office of account, by Lala Dina Nath, whom he had brought up most carefully, and whose splendid abilities soon made him distinguished in the political world.

Ajodhia Parshad (or *Ajodhia Nath*) had been summoned to Lahore by his father, in 1814. He was then 15 years of age, but he was not suffered to enter, at once, the Government service. For two years he continued his studies, and was then sent to his native country, Kashmir, where he was placed in the military office, on a salary of 1,000 Rs. per annum. Six months later he was recalled to Lahore. In 1819, Generals Ventura and Allard arrived in the Panjab from Europe, by way of Persia and Khorasan, and entered the Maharaja's service. They received command of the 'Fouj Khas' or special brigade, the first in rank in the Sikh army, and *Ajodhia Parshad* was placed under them, as paymaster of the troops and as the medium of communication between the commanding officers and the Maharaja. The 'Fouj Khas' was at one time raised to five battalions of infantry and three cavalry regiments ; but at the request of General Ventura it was again reduced to four infantry battalions and two regiments of cavalry.

On the death of his father, the Maharaja directed him to assume charge of the office for regular troops and artillery, but he was on the best of terms with the French Generals, and begged to be allowed to keep his own appointment. The vacant post was accordingly given to Tej Singh. *Ajodhia Parshad* received the title of Diwan, and the village of Nain Sukh was continued to him from his father's jagir. He continued to serve with the 'Fouj Khas,' and when General Ventura was absent on leave, he commanded the whole force. So ably did he do this, that General Ventura wrote of him in these terms : "On the two occasions that I have been absent on leave in France, *Ajodhia Parshad* has held the command of the life guards of the Maharaja ; I have never had cause to repent appointing him my Deputy, for on my return from France, I have found the troops in as good a condition as if I had been present myself." In 1831, he was sent to the frontier of the Panjab to meet Lieutenant Burnes, who was on his way from Bombay, by way of Sind, with a present of a team of cart horses, a stallion and four mares, and a carriage, for Maharaja Ranjit Singh, from the King of England. *Ajodhia Parshad* met the mission a little way below Multan, and remained attached to it till its arrival in Lahore on the 17th of July.

At the time of the Maharaja's death, *Ajodhia Parshad* was with the brigade at Peshawar, where it had been stationed for two years, but was now summoned to Lahore by Maharaja Kharrak Singh. The Diwan was, with Sirdar Lehna Singh, Majithia, at the close of 1839, directed to accompany the army of the Indus, under Sir John Keane, from Attock to Ferozpur, which was reached on the 31st of December, 1839, and his attention and anxiety to meet the wishes of the General were warmly acknowledged by that officer.

In April and May, 1840, the brigade, with General Ventura and *Ajodhia Parshad*, was sent against Kahn Singh, Bedi, who had murdered his nephew, seized his fort of Malsian, and imprisoned his family. Nao Nihal Singh did not much care for the sanctity of a Bedi, and, to the indignation of many, sent the troops against his fort of Dakhni, which they captured. Eventually this was given up to him again, on his restoring Malsian to his nephew's family, and paying a fine of 20,000 Rs. to the State.

Later in the year the brigade was sent against the Mandi Chief, who had omitted to pay in his tribute since the death of Ranjit Singh, or to acknowledge, in any way, the new Maharaja. Mandi was covered with little forts, said to be 123 in number, besides the strong fort of Kamlaghar, but the Raja was frightened by the force sent against him, and gave in his submission, and was directed to proceed to Lahore. The town of Mandi was occupied, and most of the forts dismantled. Kamlaghar, however, held out, and while its siege was in progress, news arrived of the death of Maharaja Kharrak Singh and Konwar Nao Nihal Singh. This news in some measure raised the courage of the garrison ; but the siege was vigorously pressed, and, at length, the fort surrendered on the 29th November, and the General, leaving a Sikh garrison in it, marched to repress disturbances which had broken out in Kulu. Sirdar Ajit Singh, Sindhanwalia, who had been sent to Mandi, had left for Lahore before the capture of Kamlaghar. General Ventura left for Lahore on the beginning of January, recalled by Raja Dhyan Singh who wished for his support to the claims of Prince Sher Singh, and *Ajodhia Parshad* was left in charge of the brigade.

Reinforcements had been despatched from Lahore to Kulu, and when these arrived, the 'Fouj Khas' heard that the troops in Lahore had received large gratuities from Sher Singh with four months' pay. Only two months' pay had been brought for them, so they rose in mutiny, seized the treasure in their camp, and killed several of their officers. *Ajodhia Parshad*, who had considerable influence with the men, restored order, and promised to obtain for the men whatever the Lahore troops had received.

General Ventura left the Panjab on leave in March, 1840, and on the arrival of the brigade at Lahore, *Ajodhia Parshad* retained the command, though it was placed nominally under the little Prince Partab Singh. The first business in which it was engaged was against Joala Singh,* the agent of the Maharaja. This man had hoped to be wazir when his master became king; and the office had been promised to him by Sher Singh. Raja Dhyan Singh had, however, no intention of vacating the post; to the Maharaja he insinuated suspicions of Joala Singh's loyalty; and he warned Joala Singh of the Maharaja's intentions against him; till, at last, the wretched man was driven into treason, and being encamped with five thousand irregulars at the Dera Charyari near Shalabagh, refused to obey the Maharaja's order to come in to Lahore. Sher Singh moved out against him, and *Ajodhia Parshad* with the 'Fouj Khas,' and supported by artillery, was directed to go in advance. Seeing the approach of this formidable brigade, Joala Singh surrendered,† and he afterwards died in prison in the fort of Shaikhopurah, from ill treatment and starvation, one of Raja Dhyan Singh's many victims.

---

* NOTE.—Joala Singh, though having no designs against Sher Singh, had plotted against the Minister. He had been sent to resume the Sindhanwalia jagirs, and returning from that expedition with the Sindhanwalia Chiefs, they conspired together to eject Dhyan Singh from the ministry, and on the way to Lahore, they visited the sacred shrine at Amritsar, where they swore to persevere till their design was accomplished. Dhyan Singh must have heard of this confederacy, and he never forgot to revenge himself on a rival.

† It is a remarkable proof of the lawlessness and power of the army at this time, that the very Charyari Horse and Akalis, who had, on the 1st of May, supported Joala Singh in mutiny and treason, on the 2nd, demanded and obtained a donation of 30,000 Rs. from Maharaja Sher Singh, for having not *compelled* Joala Singh to fight against him.

The Maharaja paid to the 'Fouj Khas' the gratuity promised to them, in Kulu, by *Ajodhia Parshad*, and to the Diwan himself he made valuable presents. The Raja of Mandi was allowed to return to his hills, taking with him the image of the goddess Devi, in solid silver, of great value and sanctity, which the Sikh soldiers had taken from Kamlaghar. General Ventura returned from Europe in 1840, and took command of the brigade. He, after Sher Singh's assassination, was sent secretly by Raja Hira Singh, the Minister, to Ludhiana to try and strengthen the English alliance, by negotiation with Colonel Richmond, the British Resident; but at the end of 1843, disgusted with the insubordination of the troops, and clearly foreseeing the troubles coming on the country, he finally left the Panjab, where he had served for upwards of twenty-four years. Diwan *Ajodhia Parshad* now took command of the brigade, and held it till the close of the Satlej campaign.

The brigade was composed, in 1845, before the war, of 3,176 regular infantry, 1,667 regular cavalry, and 855 artillery men. Total 5,698 men, and 34 guns.

The infantry force included the Khas battalion, strength 820 men; a Gurkha battalion, 707 men; Dewa Singh's battalion, 839 men; and Sham Singh's battalion, 810 men.

The cavalry force was composed of a grenadier regiment, strength 730 men; a dragoon regiment, 750 men; and a troop of orderly khas, 187 men.

The artillery was the corps known as that of Ilahi Baksh, and was commanded by General Ilahi Baksh, the best artillery officer in the Sikh army. The pay of the whole brigade was 96,067 Rs. per mensem.

The composition of the other brigades may be, in a great measure, seen from this statement regarding the crack brigade of the Sikh army. A great change had taken place since the death of Maharaja Ranjit Singh. His strong hand kept down mutiny and complaint, though even he was once compelled to take refuge in Govindghar from the fury of his Gurkha regiment which could not obtain its arrears of pay; but his successors, fearing for their lives and power, were compelled to increase the numbers and the pay of the army, till it at length became an insupportable burthen to the State, and a standing menace to other powers.

At the time of Maharaja Ranjit Singh's death, the regular army, infantry, cavalry and artillery, was composed of 29,168 men, with 192 guns, at a monthly cost of 3,82,088 Rs.

Under Maharaja Sher Singh, the regular army was composed of 50,065 men, with 232 guns, at a monthly cost of 5,48,603 Rs.

Under Raja Hira Singh, the regular army consisted of 50,805 men, with 282 guns, at a monthly cost of 6,82,984 Rs.

Under Sirdar Jowahir Singh, the regular army consisted of 72,370 men, with 381 guns, at a monthly cost of 8,52,696 Rs.

The increase in the number of guns under Sirdar Jowahir Singh was, in a great measure, nominal. Few new guns were cast, but many old ones were taken out of forts, furbished up, and placed on field carriages.

The irregular cavalry does not appear to have increased in the same proportion as the regular army. At the commencement of hostilities, its numbers were 16,292.

When the Satlej war of 1845 broke out, the Sikh army throughout the whole Panjab was thus composed :—

Regular Infantry, ...	53,756
Regular Cavalry, ...	6,235
Irregular Cavalry, ...	16,292
Artillery, ...	10,968
Camel Swivels,...	584
Miscellaneous, ...	827
Total ...	88,662 men.

Guns. Field : 381. Garrison : 104. Total. 484. Camel Swivels : 308.

The Irregular Levies, and Jagirdari contingents of horse, not included in the above, cannot be accurately determined, but they may be fairly estimated at 30,000 men.

During the troubled administration of Raja Hira Singh, the brigade of *Ajodhia Parshad*, which had been accustomed to discipline under the skilful Ventura, did not become so completely mutinous and disorganized as the rest of the army. When Hira Singh fled from Lahore, and was pursued by Sirdar Jowahir Singh and the Sikh army, the 'Fouj Khas' remained on the plain below the citadel, to guard the person of the young Maharaja. Jowahir Singh added 3,000 Rs., per mensem, to *Ajodhia Parshad's* pay, and gave him the villages of Mouza Khan, Gang, Shadian, Muradi and Kathianwala, in the Hafizabad district.

After the murder of Sirdar Jowahir Singh, Tej Singh, who was hated by the army, was appointed Commander-in-Chief of the regular forces; Raja Lal Singh of the irregular, and when the 'Fouj Khas' was ordered to Peshawar, it distinctly refused to obey.

The Satlej campaign followed. At its close, Diwan *Ajodhia Parshad* tendered his resignation, which was accepted, and he left the corps with which he had served for twenty-six years.

After the treaty of the 16th March, 1856, making over the hill country between the Ravi and the Indus to Maharaja Gulab Singh, *Ajodhia Parshad* was appointed Commissioner, in conjunction with Captain Abbott, to lay down the boundary line of the Lahore and Jammu territories. This work, which was by no means an easy one, occupied two years, and it was not till May, 1848, that the Diwan returned to Lahore. During all this time his conduct had given the greatest satisfaction to the authorities, and without in any way sacrificing the interests of his own Government, he had shown the greatest courtesy and attention to Captain Abbott, the British representative. On November 26th, 1847, he had received the honorary title of "Mumtaz ud dowlah," (eminent in the State), besides substantial addition to his pay.

At annexation, he was in possession of 5,000 Rs. per annum, cash allowance, besides the villages of Nainsukh, Balu Salu, Chhogian, Kot Nao, Khanpur, Khatianwala, Shadman, Gang and Muradi, worth 19,000 Rs. per annum. In April, 1849, immediately after the annexation of the Panjab, the Diwan was appointed to take charge of the young Maharaja Dalip Singh, in conjunction with Dr. Login, and in 1849, he accompanied the Prince to Fatahgarh, where he remained in attendance upon him, until September, 1851. He then, the Maharaja being about to leave for England, returned to the Panjab, and gave up public life. Dr. Login has borne the highest testimony to the Diwan's upright and honourable conduct, while with the Maharaja at Fatahgarh.

The jagirs of the Diwan had lapsed to Government at annexation, but he was granted a pension of 7,500 Rs., and the Supreme Government, in 1862, sanctioned 1,000 Rs. of this pension being upheld in perpetuity.

In 1862, The Diwan was appointed an Honorary Magistrate of the city of Lahore, where he has resided since 1851. In this position he has given satisfaction. His probity is well known ; his learning is considerable, and he has ever been ready to assist in the improvement or embellishment of the city. During the past year he has not been able to give any constant attention to public duties, for his health has been indifferent and his eyesight is failing.

The Diwan has one son, Baijnath, now forty-two years of age. In 1858, he was appointed Tehsildar of Sharakpur, in the Lahore district, and in July, 1859, he was transferred to Lahore. In July, 1862, he was made an Extra Assistant Commissioner, which office he still holds in Lahore. Baijnath is a man of education and ability. So early as 1853 he commenced training for official life in the office of Major Abbott, Deputy Commissioner of Hoshiarpur. He took every advantage of his opportunities, and is now one of the best native officials in the province. His exertions in the cause of education have been great, and, in 1861, he was appointed President of the Committee of Public Instruction of Lahore.

SIRDAR NIHAL SINGH, CHHACHHI.

RAMBAJ.

Sirdar Nihal Singh.

Amrik Singh.	Gopal Singh.	Charrat Singh.	Ram Singh.	Udam Singh
B. 1836.	B. 1850.	B. 1852.	B. 1855.	B. 1853.

HISTORY OF THE FAMILY.

The family of Sirdar *Nihal Singh* is of the Sani Katri caste, and has, for seven generations, been resident at Rawal Pindi. His father was a trader, by name *Rambaj.*

Nihal Singh, in 1830, married the only daughter of Sirdar Gurmukh Singh, Chhachhi. This Chief was the son of Sirdar Fatah Singh, who, with his brother Sher Singh, was killed in the Kashmir campaign. Sirdar Gurmukh Singh succeeded to his father's jagir, but died in 1829, soon after which *Nihal Singh* married his daughter, and was allowed to take the name of Chhachhi and succeed to his father-in-law's jagir at Chakori worth 2,000 Rs.

In 1846, after the Satlej campaign, *Nihal Singh* received the title of Sirdar, and was appointed, on the part of the Darbar, to attend on the Agent of the Governor General at Lahore, as a kind of aide-de-camp, with a contingent of eight sowars. His services in this post were valuable, and, without in any way compromising the interests of his own Government, he rendered prompt and friendly assistance to the English authorities. When the rebellion of 1848 broke out, Sirdar *Nihal Singh* remained loyal, though surrounded by strong temptations. From his close connection with the English Resident, he could have supplied the rebels with information most important to them, but on no occasion did he violate the confidence placed in him. His exertions to complete the supply of carriage for the siege train of Multan were great, and have been acknowledged by Sir Robert Napier. His conduct irritated the rebels, who burnt his house and plundered his property at Rawal Pindi, and treated with severity those members of his family who fell into their hands.

On the annexation of the Panjab, the jagir of 5,978 Rs., which he had received from Raja Lal Singh, in 1846, was maintained to him for life; and the old Chakori jagir of 1,200 Rs. was upheld in perpetuity. Instead of his contingent of eight horsemen being dispensed with, and the jagir which he had held for its maintenance being resumed, it was continued to him as a special favour, with a cash allowance of 2,000 Rs. a year. In 1853 the Sirdar became involved in some pecuniary difficulties, and the Government was pleased to reduce the contingent from eight to four horsemen. In this same year there occurred a petty insurrection in the Rawal Pindi district. Sirdar *Nihal Singh* was at home, at the time, and immediately offered his services to the Commissioner, who sent him to the insurgents to endeavour to induce them to surrender. They, however, seized him, treated him with some indignity, and kept him a prisoner for several days.

During the critical days of 1857, Sirdar *Nihal Singh*, who felt that active and zealous loyalty was better than mere abstinence from rebellion, remained in close attendance on the Chief Commissioner. His advice and the information he at this time supplied were particularly valuable. It was mainly through his assistance that the Chief Commissioner raised the 1st Sikh cavalry, and selected for service so many of the old Sikh officers who had, in former days, fought gallantly against us.

When the wild Muhammadan tribes of Gogaira rebelled, Sirdar *Nihal Singh* was sent to the scene of action. He was engaged in several skirmishes with the insurgents, and in one of them received a severe wound in the knee.

For his services, *Nihal Singh* received in October, 1858, a present of 10,000 Rs., and an additional jagir of 6,000 Rs., to descend to his lineal male heirs in perpetuity, on condition of active loyalty. The remaining four horsemen of his contingent were, also, dispensed with.

In 1862, Sirdar *Nihal Singh* was made a Jagirdar Magistrate, and, in 1862, 10,000 Rs. of his jagir, was, on the recommendation of the Lieutenant Governor, re-leased in perpetuity. At the present time the Sirdar holds,

Jagir in perpetuity,	... ...	10,000
Jagir in life tenure,	... ...	3,175
Cash pension,	... ...	2,000
	Rs. ...	15,175

For eighteen years Sirdar *Nihal Singh* has served the British Government well and faithfully. He has not cared, in times of political difficulty, to count the cost of his loyalty. He has never hesitated or wavered when the sky has been dark, uncertain on which side his personal interests would be most secure, but has ever been most zealous in his loyalty, and most unremitting in his exertions, when men of less courage and honesty have stood aloof.

Amrik Singh, the eldest son of Sirdar *Nihal Singh*, is Tehsildar of Wazirabad. In 1857, he raised a Risala of mounted police in the Panjab, and took them down to Oude, where they did excellent service. He holds a jagir of 650 Rs., for life, left to him, in 1840, by a deed of gift, by his grandmother Mai Devi, widow of Sirdar Gurmukh Singh, Chhachhi.

RAJA DINA NATH.

BAKHT MAL.

- Raja Dina Nath. D. 1857.
  - Diwan Amar Nath. B. 1822.
    - Ram Nath. B. 1844.
  - Narayan Nath.
- Diwan Kidar Nath. D. 1859.
  - Badri Nath.
  - Pran Nath.

HISTORY OF THE FAMILY.

Among the men who rose to power during the latter days of the Sikh empire, the most remarkable was Raja *Dina Nath.* He has been well and happily styled 'The Talleyrand of the Punjab,' and his life and character bear a strong resemblance to those of the European Statesman. Revolutions, in which his friends and patrons perished, passed him by; dynasties rose and fell, but never involved him in their ruin; in the midst of bloodshed and assassination, his life was never endangered; while confiscation and judicial robbery were the rule of the State, his wealth and power continually increased.

His sagacity and far-sightedness were such, that when, to other eyes, the political sky was clear, he could perceive the signs of a coming storm, which warned him to desert a losing party or a falling friend. Honest men do not survive many revolutions, and the Raja's falseness was the measure of his success. He was patriotic, but his love of country was subordinate to his love of self. He hated the English with a bitter hatred, for they were stronger than he, or his country ; but his interests compelled him to serve, like Samson, the Phillistines he hated. He was not without his own notions of fidelity, and would stand by a friend as long as he could do so with safety to himself. Even when he deserted him, it was more from fear of danger to his wealth and influence than from personal fear, for Raja *Dina Nath* was physically brave, and also possessed, in an eminent degree, moral courage, though it did not lead him to do right, regardless of consequences. As a Financier, the policy of the Raja was intelligent and liberal, and he readily appreciated the advantages of the new system of taxation introduced by the English. He possessed immense local knowledge, and as vast a capacity for work ; though, from his desire of keeping power in his own hands, he sometimes retarded instead of advancing business. He was an acccomplished man of the world, courteous and considerate ; well educated, though nothing of a scholar ; and in conversation with Europeans, he would express himself with a boldness and apparent candour, that were as pleasant as they are unusual in Asiatics.

Raja *Dina Nath* should not be judged harshly. His faults would be still considered, in some European countries, as diplomatic virtues, Among the Sikh barons who stood around the throne of the young Maharaja Dalip Singh, there was not one who honestly laboured for his country, or who would have made the smallest sacrifice to save her. If Raja *Dina Nath* was not more honest than his contemporaries, he was, at least, more patriotic.

The family of Raja *Dina Nath* came originally from Kashmir, where, in the reign of Shah Jahan, some members of it held office about the court. It was not till the reign of Muhammad Shah that *Lachhi Ram*, the eldest son of *Bishen Nath*, left Kashmir for Lahore, where he obtained employment. Soon after he went to Delhi, whither he summoned his younger brother *Har Das*, and later to Lucknow, where he chiefly resided. His son *Dilla Ram* entered the service of the Nawab of Oude, but was compelled to leave from some court intrigue. He then went into the English service, and was proceeding with the army to Mysore, in 1791, when he was taken ill and died. Lala *Dina Nath*, whose father *Bakht Mal* had held a subordinate civil appointment at Delhi, was invited to the Panjab in 1815, by Diwan *Ganga Ram*,* a near connection, who was then head of the State office at Lahore. On his arrival he was placed in the same office, and very soon distinguished himself by his intelligence and business-like habits. He first attracted the notice of Ranjit Singh, after the capture of Multan, in 1818, when he made out the lists of those entitled to rewards with great rapidity and clearness. He shortly afterwards adjusted the accounts of the province of Multan, which the first Nazim Sukh Dyal had thrown into great confusion. In 1826, when Ganga Ram died, he received charge of the Royal seal, and in 1834, on the death of Bhawani Das, he was made head of the Civil and Finance office, and in 1838, he received the honorary title of Diwan. Ranjit Singh had the greatest confidence in *Dina Nath's* judgment, and his influence during the latter years of the Maharaja's reign was very great. He was consulted on every occasion of importance, and received jagirs in the Amritsar, Dinanagar, and Kasur districts, to the value of 9,900 Rs. During the time of Maharaja Kharrak Singh and Nao Nihal Singh, Diwan *Dina Nath* retained his office, and received new jagirs, and Maharaja Sher Singh treated him with the same consideration. He was one of those in immediate attendance on the Maharaja, † when he was assassinated by the Sindhanwalias, and when Raja Hira Singh rose to power, he had no more zealous adherent than the Diwan. When Hira Singh had quarrelled, or had pretended to quarrel, with his uncle, Raja Gulab Singh, the Diwan was sent in company with Bhai Ram Singh and

---

* *Vide* Statement Diwan Ajodhia Parshad.

† NOTE—Diwan *Dina Nath* was standing immediately behind Sher Singh when the Sindhanwalias entered the apartment. He would in all probability have been wounded or killed by the shot which killed the Maharaja, had not Mehr Khasitah, a Sindhanwalia Wakil, who was in the plot, drawn him aside, pretending to have something important to communicate to him.

Shaikh Imamuddin, to Jammu to arrange matters with the Raja, and their mission was completely successful. They returned bringing with them as a hostage Mian Sohan Singh, the son of Raja Gulab Singh, who was murdered with his cousin Hira Singh, not long afterwards. On Hira Singh's death, Jowahir Singh, the debauched and contemptible brother of Maharani Jindan, obtained the chief power, but Diwan *Dina Nath* still held office.

After the murder of Prince Peshora Singh, the troops rose in mutiny, and decided to kill Sirdar Jowahir Singh, who had been the instigator of it. The Sirdar was much alarmed, prepared the fort for defence, and on the 19th September, sent Diwan *Dina Nath*, Attar Singh Kalianwala, and Fakir Nuruddin, to conciliate the troops. The mission was only received with scorn, and Attar Singh and Dina Nath were kept prisoners in camp. Here they were detained till the 22nd, the day after the murder of Jowahir Singh, when the soldiery over whom the Rani had still much influence, released them, that they might soothe her violent grief, and they accompanied her back to the fort. Jowahir Singh was burnt with his four wives the same evening, and Diwan *Dina Nath* was present on the part of the Maharani. The unfortunate women who were to burn with the body were shamefully treated by the soldiery, who stripped them of their jewels and tore their nose-rings away. A 'Sati' is a sacred object among Hindus, and her last words are considered prophetic. At the feet of these women, *Dina Nath* and others fell down, asking for their blessings. The 'Satis' blessed him, the Maharani, and her son, but cursed the Sikh army. When asked the fate of the Panjab, they answered that during that year this country would lose its independence, and the Khalsa be overthrown, that the wives of the Sikh soldiers would be widows, but that the Maharaja and his mother would live long and happily. The words were remarkable; though, in truth, it did not require a prophet to tell that the Sikh army was rushing on its destruction.

After this, Diwan *Dina Nath* clearly perceived that while the army remained as powerful and lawless as it then was, there was no safety for him or for any man who filled a conspicuous position, and with Raja Lal Singh, whose motives were similar to his own, and the Maharani who longed to avenge her brother's death, he began to encourage in the army a desire for a war with the English, from which the conspirators hoped it would never return. Reports were industriously circulated tending to inflame the minds of the soldiers. The English, it was said, were determined to take advantage of the disordered state of the Panjab to overrun the country. The red coats were pouring up from Bengal, regiment after regiment, and some were even then preparing to cross the Satlej. When the passions of the troops were sufficiently inflamed, a great council was called at Shalimar, early in November, and here the Diwan made an address so eloquent, artful, and impassioned, that all present unanimously declared for war. The result of that war is well known, and Diwan *Dina Nath* is next seen signing the treaty of the 9th of March, 1846, by which the fairest province of the Panjab was ceded to the English. Although the sentiments of Diwan *Dina Nath* with regard to the presence of the English at Lahore, were well known, he was too wise to show much outward dissatisfaction ; indeed he was anxious for the English to remain till the Government was strong enough to stand without external assistance. When in May, 1846, the fort of Kangra held out, and the Agent of the Governor General had gone there in person to superintend operations, *Dina Nath* was ordered to follow him, to induce the garrison, if possible, to listen to reason. In old days, Ranjit Singh had ordered the garrison never to open the gates to any one except to himself in person, *Dina Nath*, Fakir Azizuddin or Misr Beli Ram ; but on the present occasion the Diwan's influence, or desire to use it, was not very strong, and it was not till a fortnight after he came, that the fort surrendered. The arrival of heavy siege guns from the plains had perhaps more to do with the surrender, than the persuasions of Diwan *Dina Nath*.

When Raja Lal Singh wazir was tried for treason in December, 1846, Diwan *Dina Nath* defended him on the part of the Darbar with skill and energy, though in the face of most criminating facts. On his deposition the powers of Government were vested, as a temporary measure, in Sirdar Tej Singh, Sirdar Sher Singh, Fakir Nuruddin, and Diwan *Dina Nath,* and soon after four other influential Chiefs were added to the number, constituting, under the authority of the Governor General, a Council of Regency. The most able member of the Council was undoubtedly Diwan *Dina Nath,* and although his position as head of the Financial Department gave him great opportunities of enriching himself at the public expense, which there is every reason to believe he availed himself of, he still worked more disinterestedly than others, and was of very great service to the Resident at Lahore. Without his clear head and business-like habits it would have been almost impossible to disentangle the Durbar accounts; and after the annexation of the Panjab the Diwan's aid in Revenue and Jagir matters was almost as valuable as before. The Diwan was not a popular man at this time. The retrenchments which the lavish expenditure of the late ministries had rendered imperative were very distasteful to the Sikh Sirdars and soldiery, and the Diwan with Sirdar Tej Singh, came in for his full share of odium. In November, 1847, the Diwan was raised to the dignity of Raja of Kalanour. The following is the honorary title he received on the occasion: "Imarat wa ayalat, dastgah; Khair andesh-i-daulat-i-alia, dyanatdar, mushir-i-khas, madar ul muham." He received at the same time a jagir of 20,000 Rs. from the Ilaka of Kalanour. In April, 1848, the Multan Nazim, Diwan Mulraj, rebelled. In September, 1846, Diwan *Dina Nath* had been sent by the Durbar to bring Mulraj to Lahore, and it was principally by his means that a satisfactory arrangement was made with the Nazim who did not however cease to intrigue with the Ministry, and especially with Raja Dina Nath for a modification in the terms of his agreement, up to the commencement of 1848. On the first news of the outbreak reaching Lahore, Raja *Dina Nath* was ordered, on the part of the Durbar, with Sirdar Attar Singh, Kalianwala, the commander of the irregular troops, to Multan, but was soon afterwards recalled. When Sirdar Chattar Singh, Atariwala, had turned traitor, and the mission of Sirdar Jhanda Singh, Butalia, to reclaim him had failed, the

Resident sent Raja *Dina Nath* to endeavour to influence him. This mission failed as signally as the former one, for Sirdar Chattar Singh, backed by the Sikh nation, had determined to try once more the fortune of war. Some there were who said that Raja *Dina Nath* was a traitor at heart, that he had himself encouraged the rising, and that had he not been a wealthy man with houses and gardens and many lakhs of rupees in Lahore, convenient for confiscation, he would have joined the rebels without hesitation; but these stories were perhaps invented by his enemies. Certain it is that on his being recalled to Lahore, he zealously carried out the wishes of the authorities, in confiscating the property of the rebels, and in counteracting their schemes.

After the annexation of the Panjab, Raja *Dina Nath* was confirmed in all his jagirs, worth 46,460 Rs., which he held till his death, in 1857. His eldest son, *Amar Nath,* received, during his father's life, a cash pension of 1,200 Rs. On the Raja's death this was raised to 4,000 Rs., and on *Amar Nath's* death his pension will be resumed, and his son will receive a jagir of 4,000 Rs., to descend in perpetuity, according to the rules of primogeniture. *Amar Nath* was not on good terms with his father, who, during the Satlej campaign, had caused him to be removed from the Paymastership of the irregular forces. After the Raja's death *Amar Nath* refused to take any portion of his property, which accordingly went to the younger son, *Narayan Nath.* The Raja had, however, made a will, leaving all his personal property to *Narayan,* his favourite son.

Amar Nath is a man of considerable ability. He is perhaps the most classical poet in the Panjab, and some of his sonnets are of great beauty. In 1858 he published a history of the reign of Ranjit Singh. This work, though too elaborate in style for European taste, is undoubtedly the most valuable and interesting that any native author has produced since the annexation of the Panjab.

Diwan *Kidar Nath,* the Raja's brother, was for many years a servant of the Lahore State. He received the title of Diwan from Maharaja

Dalip Singh, and on annexation received a life pension of 6,000 Rs. He died in 1859, leaving two sons, the elder of whom *Badri Nath*, is Adalati or Judge at Jammu, in the service of Maharaja Ranbir Singh.

Pran Nath, the second son, was Tehsildar of Sowrian, and when the Tehsil establishment was moved to Ajnala, he was transferred there. He was at Ajnala in 1857, and on the 31st of July, about 500 disarmed sepoys of the 26th N. I. which had mutinied at Lahore the day before, and had committed four murders, arrived on the left bank of the Ravi near Balghat, and prepared to cross the river. *Pran Nath* collected the villagers and the police, and attacked the mutineers with vigour, and killed some 150 of them. The Deputy Commissioner of Amritsar, with Sirdar Jodh Singh, arrived soon afterwards, and the remaining mutineers, who had retired to an island in the river, were captured and executed, an act of vigour which saved the country from a great danger.

Pran Nath died in 1860, leaving two sons, who are now under the care of their uncle at Jammu.

Raja *Dina Nath* built, at his own expense, a Shivala (temple to Shiva) near the Police Court in the city of Lahore, and alienated for its support a jagir of 500 Rs., which is still maintained in perpetuity. Another Shivala he built near the Wazir Khan Mosque.

He constructed a large tank at great cost, near the temple of Achint-bhawani Devi, in the Kangra district, and another tank at Devipur, near Shalimar, with a large building for priests and travellers. He also rebuilt and endowed with the two villages Kotla and Chuhanal, worth 2,200 Rs., the shrine of Munsa Ram, Razdan, (knower of secrets) his spiritual teacher, and a great Hindu Saint much venerated by Kashmiris, who died about 40 years ago. The grant is maintained in perpetuity.

BHAI CHARRANJIT SINGH.

- Bhai Bulaka Singh.
  - Bhai Basti Ram.
    - Bhai Harnam.
    - Bhai Harbhaj Rai.
      - Bhai Kahn Sing, D. 1837.
        - Bhai Nidhan Singh, D. 1856.
          - Bhai Mian Singh, B. 1841.
        - Bhai Kesra Singh, B. 1831.
          - Bhai Tara Singh, B. 1855.
          - Bhai Partab Singh, B. 1857.
      - Bhai Ram Singh, D. 1846.
        - Bhai Charranjit Singh, B. 1841.
      - Bhai Govind Ram, D. 1845.
        - Bhai Har Gopal, D. 1849.
        - Bhai Nand Gopal, B. 1841.
  - Bhai Sahai.
  - Bhai Molak Ram.

HISTORY OF THE FAMILY.

In the Sikh polity there is a close union between the Church and the State, and from the time that the Sikh sect grew into a nation, the voice of Fakirs, Babas and Bhais has ever been loud in its councils. One of the most influential of the religious families at the Court of Lahore, was that of Bhai *Charranjit Singh*.

The first of the family to acquire the title of 'Bhai,' was *Bulaka Singh*, a follower of Guru Govind Singh. When the Guru retired to Abchallanagar in the Deccan, in 1707, he directed *Bulaka* to go to Lahore, where he would be married. *Bulaka* was upwards of fifty, and did not consider himself a good match, but he did as he had been ordered; and at Lahore a Sikh offered him his daughter in marriage, saying that the Guru had instructed him to do so in a dream. *Bulaka Singh* could not refuse, and three sons were the issue of the marriage, *Bhai Basti Ram*, *Bhai Sahai*, and *Bhai Molak Ram*.

Basti Ram was born in 1708, and from an early age devoted himself to the study of medicine. He soon became known for his skill, and for the sanctity of his life. He was much consulted by the Bhangi Chiefs, who held Lahore during the latter half of the eighteenth century, and Ranjit Singh, who conquered that city three years before the death of the Bhai, in 1802, had the greatest respect for him. His prophecies were said to be always fulfilled, and his prayers answered, and he was the fortunate possessor of a purse which replenished itself, and which it was impossible to empty. But without crediting the fables * related of the Bhai, he undoubtedly had great influence at Lahore, and, like priests in other countries, probably used his knowledge of natural science to increase his religious reputation. *Bhai Molak Ram*, the youngest brother of *Basti Ram*, died when a child. *Bhai Sahai* lived to a great age, but he was a recluse, entirely devoted to religion, and did not marry. He died in 1793.

Bhai Harbhaj Rai used, during his father's life-time, to come to court, where he was received by the Maharaja with the greatest respect. He had, like his father, studied medicine, and was reputed to be a very skilful doctor. *Basti Ram* had never accepted any jagir, but *Harbhaj* was not so scrupulous, and in 1804, he received the village of Monawan, worth 400 Rs.; and, in 1805, estates in the vicinity of Lahore to the value of 5,740 Rs. Three years later, he received Sundarghar and Rokha; and, at the time of his death, in 1824, he was in possession of jagirs to the value of 9,000 Rs. in the Amritsar and Lahore districts.

---

* NOTE.—*Bhai Basti Ram* lived outside the walls of the city, below the Samman Burj. A large branch of the river Ravi then flowed beneath the walls, and every year did great damage to the city, till the Bhai determined to stop the river, and built his habitation (derah) just outside the walls. From that day the waters never invaded the city or passed the derah of the Bhai. When he died, his tomb was built of white marble on the site of the derah, and the river still respects the spot, though a deep cut to carry off the surplus water, and a considerable change in the course of the Ravi may account for the safety of the city.

These grants were all in perpetuity, and are still in possession of the family.

Harbhaj and his brothers had not become Sikhs, and when *Kahn Singh* took the 'pahal' his father was very angry. *Ram Singh* also allowed his hair to grow, and became a Sikh, though he never took the 'pahal' or became a true Singh.

Bhai Ram Singh, at Ranjit Singh's request, attended Darbar in 1802, and soon gained great influence over the superstitious Maharaja. His opinion was always asked in questions of difficulty, and during a campaign, the tent of the Bhai was pitched next to that of the Maharaja.

During the last years of Ranjit Singh's life, *Bhai Ram Singh's* influence continually increased; and when the Maharaja died, Nao Nihal Singh, who had received the 'pahal' from the Bhai, entrusted him with still greater power, for he was himself very averse to conducting the details of business. He was one of the chief conspirators, with Raja Gulab Singh, Dhyan Singh, and others, in the murder of Sirdar Chet Singh, the minister of Kharrak Singh, and it was at his house that the conspirators assembled before proceeding to the palace to commit the murder. Neither Nao Nihal Singh nor the Bhai were popular with the Chiefs. The former compelled all Sirdars and Jagirdars to fulfil their service, and to keep their contingents in good order, which was most irksome to the men, who, during the last years of Ranjit Singh's life, had done much as they liked, and had been responsible to no one.

* When Nao Nihal Singh died on 5th November, 1840, and his mother Mai Chand Kour claimed the vacant throne, Bhai *Ram Singh* supported her with all his power. His great rival and enemy Bhai Gurmukh Singh as vehemently espoused the cause of Konwar Sher Singh; but they were almost alone in their enthusiasm, and there were none, with the exception of Raja Dhyan Singh, Bhais *Ram Singh* and Gurmukh Singh, Diwan

* *Vide* Statement of Sirdar Jaimal Singh, Kanheya, father of Rani Chand Kour.

Sawan Mal, Attar Singh, Sindhanwalia, and the French Generals, who cared whether the Konwar or the Mai succeeded to the throne. Bhai *Ram Singh* was not altogether averse to a coalition between the two parties, and he foresaw that without the support of Raja Dhyan Singh, the Mai could not possibly stand ; and so convinced was he of the incompetency of her supporters, that he does not appear to have seen the triumph of Sher Singh with any great regret.

The new Prince treated *Ram Singh* with respect, notwithstanding the part the Bhai had taken against him ; and at the investiture, on the 27th January, 1841, he was allowed a chair, the only others who were permitted this honor, being his brother *Govind Ram,* Bhai Gurmukh Singh, Babas Vikrama Singh and Kahn Singh, and the Prince Partab Singh. The Maharaja even began to consult *Ram Singh*, and Raja Dhyan Singh fearing that he might regain his influence, tried to make the Bhai proceed to Multan, on the pretext of recovering arrears of revenue from Diwan Sawan Mal. This project the Bhai vehemently opposed. He did not wish to be banished from court, he was a friend of Sawan Mal, and his religious character should have disqualified him from the duties to which he had been nominated by the minister.

Both Bhai *Ram Singh* and his brother Bhai *Govind Ram* were thoroughly discontented. Although treated with consideration, they were allowed no share of power, and saw their enemy Bhai Gurmukh Singh wealthy and influential. But their turn at length came. Sher Singh and his Minister fell by the hands of the Sindhanwalias, and Bhai Gurmukh Singh, who had been the constant opponent of Raja Dhyan Singh, was imprisoned and murdered.

After the death of Raja Hira Singh, Bhai *Ram Singh* recovered much of his influence with the army. He had ever been associated with Fakir Azizuddin in his English policy ; these two were almost the only men in Lahore who understood the relations of that State to the British Government under the Treaty of 1809, and they were most desirous of keeping on good terms with it. It was on this account that, in March 1845, the Bhai warmly supported Raja Gulab Singh of Jammu as a candidate for the wazirship ; for he knew that he was the only man who could, in any way, restrain the army, and whose vast private means could avert the bankruptcy of the State. The intentions of the Bhai towards the British Government were good, and early in May, 1845, he informed Major Broadfoot, Agent of the Governor General, that Sirdar Jowahir Singh intended, for his own safety, to incite the Sikh army to an invasion of British territory.

Jowahir Singh, though by no means without intellect, was drunken and debauched ; and even in public durbars, he was often seen under the influence of brandy, and he would then abuse *Ram Singh* in the most indecent terms, though in the worst of times the sanctity of the Bhai's character had saved him from insult. On the 12th September, 1845, the Bhai boldly remonstrated in open Darbar against the conduct of the Wazir towards the British Government. He asserted that the conduct of the English authorities had been distinguished by moderation and forbearance, and that the Darbar was entirely in the wrong in the dispute. Jowahir Singh is believed to have promised to retrace his steps, and to write an apology to the British Agent, but on that very night news came of the murder of Prince Peshora Singh, perpetrated by his orders, and he knew that an English war could alone preserve his power: Bhai *Ram Singh* had also heard the fatal news, and had reported it to the troops, and the party hostile to the Minister gained strength every hour. The murder of the obnoxious Minister and the Satlej campaign followed. To the last Bhai *Ram Singh* opposed that insane war, but in vain. To Raja Lal Singh he said, " Beware what you do, and do not march to Hariki with the troops. The English have always behaved as friends and well-wishers, and have never interfered in the affairs of the Khalsa." Raja Lal Singh answered " Bhai Sahib, what can I do ? the soldiers have got me by the throat." However he took the Bhai's advice as far as he could, and, like a coward as he was, made the other Generals go on before him to the scene of danger. After Sobraon, Bhai *Ram Singh* was sent with Raja Gulab Singh, and Diwan Dina Nath, to meet the Governor General at Luliani, on the road to Lahore, to try and obtain favourable terms.

After the treaty of the 9th March, 1816, Bhai *Ram Singh* remained one of the Council; and although, on account of bad health, he was unable to attend the Darbar very regularly, his opinion was always taken before any important measure was adopted. He was opposed generally to Raja Lal Singh, the Minister, and took the part of Mulraj, in the dispute regarding the Governorship of Multan. It was by his advice that Raja Lal Singh called upon all the Sirdars to sign a razinama, a deed expressive of their contentment under the existing Government ; though it was notorious that the majority was opposed to it.

Bhai *Ram Singh* died in November, 1846, and was succeeded in the Council by his nephew Bhai *Nidhan Singh,* son of Bhai *Kahn Singh,* who had died in 1837. Bhai *Govind Ram* did not much meddle with politics after the death of Ranjit Singh. He was for some years a great invalid, and died in 1845.

Nidhan Singh was a very silent member of the Darbar. On the 16th December, 1846, he was appointed a member of the Council of Regency, which office he held till the annexation of the Panjab. In 1848, the Zamindars of Kot-pindi Das, one of the jagirs of the Bhai family, failed to give supplies to the British army when marching through, and the village was consequently confiscated, but was subsequently released, on payment of a fine of 800 Rs. On annexation, however, it was resumed with other personal grants of *Ram Singh.*

The jagirs of the family amounted, at annexation, to 49,000 Rs. Of these, jagirs to the value of 22,447 Rs. were released, 9,729 in perpetuity, in three equal shares to the descendants of the three sons of *Harbhaj Rai,* and 12,718 for the lives of *Nidhan Singh, Kesra Singh, Charranjit Singh,* and *Nand Gopal.* A grant of 3,000 Rs. by Maharaja Ranjit Singh, for the support of the Sikh Temple at Taran Taran was also released during good behaviour, and the administration is in the hands of the three families, who each select one representative. Bhai *Nidhan Singh's* council allowance of 6,000 Rs. was also continued for life. He died in 1856.

The personal property left by Bhai *Ram Singh* was very large, and a suit is at present in progress instituted by *Mian Singh, Kesra Singh,* and *Nand Gopal* against Bhai *Charranjit Singh,* for seven lakhs of rupees, being a moiety of the property.

Charranjit Singh was educated at the Lahore Government College, and is a good English and Persian scholar. The family resides at Lahore.

SIRDAR JHANDA SINGH, BOTALIA.

DHANA SINGH.

Hiba Singh, descendants still living. | Diwan Singh.

(Sons of Diwan Singh:) Bhagwan Singh. D. young. | S. Dharam Singh. | Karam Singh. | S. Sham Singh. D. 1813. | Ram Singh.

(Sons of S. Dharam Singh:) S. Ganda Singh. D. 1845. | Hari Singh.

Hari Singh — Ladha Singh.

(Sons of S. Ganda Singh:) S. Kirpal Singh, Kunjahia. B. 1832. | Dyal Singh. B. 1830. | Partab Singh. B. 1827. | Joala Singh. B. 1822.

(Sons of Dyal Singh:) Wasakha Singh. B. 1849. | Wariam Singh. B. 1860.

(Son of Partab Singh:) Ghodam Singh. B. 1861.

(Sons of Joala Singh:) Sardul Singh. B. 1856. | Gurbaksh Singh. B. 1860.

(Children of S. Sham Singh:) Sirdar Jhanda Singh, M. D. of S. Gurmukh Singh, Lamba. | Daughter M. S. Sher Snigh, Gujranwala.

(Sons of Sirdar Jhanda Singh:) Nihal Singh. D. 1864. M. D. of S. Attar Singh, Dhariwala. | Mehtab Singh. B. 1824. | Mul Singh. B. 1859.

(Son of Nihal Singh:) Balwant Singh. B. 1850.

(Son of Mehtab Singh:) Arjan Singh. B. 1859.

HISTORY OF THE FAMILY.

In the old days of the Muhammadan power, long before the Sikhs obtained possession of the Panjab, an ancestor of Sirdar *Jhanda Singh*, went to Pak Pattan, to visit a celebrated mendicant, probably Baba Farid, who resided there, hoping to obtain an heir by the blessing of the holy man. For long he waited upon him, and prepared his food, and at length obtained the blessing he sought. From this religious service he obtained the name of '*Bhandari*' or steward, which still belongs to the Botalia family.

Dhana Singh was an associate of Sirdar Nodh Singh and after his death served under his son Sirdar Charrat Singh. He died in 1765, leaving two sons, *Diwan Singh* and *Hiba Singh*, who followed the fortunes of the Sukarchakia chief, and when he obtained possession of a great part of the Gujranwala district, they came in for a fair share of the spoil, receiving Botalah, Pahladpur, Kalsian, and other villages. When *Sirdar Mahan Singh* obtained possession of Ramnagar, he assigned to *Diwan Singh* an allowance of 1,000 Rs. per annum, from the salt duties, which was held by him and his descendants till 1848.

Diwan Singh was murdered by his nephew *Rattan Singh*, son of *Hiba Singh*, and his young son *Sham Singh*, (generally called Shamo Singh) was summoned to Court by the Maharaja, and was confirmed in the possession of a part of his father's estates. He rapidly rose to power, and received large jagirs, which at one time amounted to 50,000 Rs. He was called Kunjahia, from Kunjah in the Gujrat district, one of his jagirs, and the name is still held by his cousin *Sirdar Kirpal Singh*, Kunjahia.

Sham Singh was killed at the battle of Baisah, in 1813, being then 27 years of age. The Maharaja treated his young son *Jhanda Singh* with great kindness, but, in 1819, resumed the jagir of Kunjah, giving him in exchange, Sihari in the Sialkot district. *Jhanda Singh's* first military service was in Punch, where Diwan Dhanpat Rai and Mir Baz Khan had been giving trouble, and shortly afterwards he was ordered to Hazara. He accompanied the Maharaja in the campaign of 1821-22, when Mankera and Dera Ismail Khan were taken, and received for his gallantry valuable presents.

About this time, *Jhanda Singh* married his sister to Sher Singh, son of Sirdar Hukm Singh, and a lakh of rupees was spent on the occasion by either party. Never since has so splendid a marriage taken place in the Gujranwala district. Ranjit Singh, who had heard of the festivities, and that the mother of Sirdar *Jhanda Singh* had boasted of possessing two 'parolahs'* of rupees, sent to Hukm Singh and *Jhanda Singh*, saying that as they could afford to spend so much on a marriage, they must each find it convenient to pay 50,000 Rs. for the good of the State.

Sirdar *Jhanda Singh's* chief services were on the frontier, in Chachh, Khattak, Peshawar, Yusafzai, and Hazara. He was a man of energy and ability, and the Maharaja showed his appreciation of his character by giving him charge, under Sirdar Hari Singh, Nalwa, of the most unruly part of the country. His services here were numerous and important, and are detailed in a Sanad of 1834, under the seal of Nao Nihal Singh, by which the villages of Botalah and Pahladpur are granted to *Jhanda Singh*, and his heirs in perpetuity. In 1836, *Jhanda Singh* accompanied Prince Nao Nihal Singh in his Derajat expedition. During part of the Kabul campaign, he was Governor of the fort Attock, and was able to give assistance to the British Army, in the way of supplies and carriage,

The fortunes of Sirdar *Jhanda Singh* were not much disturbed by the many revolutions which occurred after the great Maharaja's death. When Sher Singh ascended the throne, his affection for *Ganda Singh*, cousin of *Jhanda Singh*, caused the latter to become influential at court, though Sher Singh only added 600 Rs., which he soon afterwards resumed, to his jagirs. By Sirdar Jowahir Singh he was made 'Adalati,' or chief justice, of Lahore, in conjunction with Diwan Hakim Rai, and held office till the close of the Satlej campaign.

In 1847, he was sent to Hazara as Naib Nazim, or Deputy Governor under Sirdar Chattar Singh, Attariwala, and Captain Abbott, and in November of the same year, he received, at the suggestion of the Resident, the honorary title of Buhadar, with the affix, "Ujjal Didar, nirmal budh," meaning 'open countenance and pure mind.' In May, 1848, soon after the outbreak at Multan, it was determined

* *Parolah.*—A Panjabi word for a large basket of clay and wicker-work generally used for storing grain.

to send a Sikh force down the Sind Saugar Doab, to aid in drawing a cordon round the city, to prevent the spread of rebellion, and *Jhanda Singh* was selected to command the force. His conduct on this occasion was admirable, and Captain Abbott wrote in high terms of him. Not very long after this, part of the Charranjit regiment of horse under the Sirdar's command joined the rebels, and Captain Abbott began to entertain doubts of his loyalty. He had been, at his urgent desire, sent with his force to Multan, but when within a few miles of the city, he was recalled by the Resident, much to his own disappointment, as his inclination ever carried him where blows were thickest. The influence which *Jhanda Singh* possessed over Sirdar Chattar Singh, Governor of Hazara, was very great; and in August, when that Chief was fast throwing off all pretence of loyalty, *Jhanda Singh* was sent with a confidential Agent from Gulab Singh, son of the Governor, to endeavour to recal him to a sense of his duty. He was totally unsuccessful, and, at the time, most thought that he was willingly so, and that he had done his utmost to widen and not to close the breach; but in those days the best men were suspected, and no one knew whom to trust. The Sirdar was ordered back to Lahore, and placed in arrest; but he was soon after released, and during the last four or five months of the war, he and his sowars kept the road open between Lahore and Ramnagar, and thus performed most valuable service. No proofs of duplicity or disaffection on *Jhanda Singh's* part have ever been forthcoming, and he was unsuccessful with Sirdar Chattar Singh, because another and a stronger influence was urging that Chief to rebel.

On annexation, all the personal estates of Sirdar *Jhanda Singh*, amounting to 15,560 Rs., were confirmed to him for life.

To his eldest son *Nihal Singh*, 3,550 Rs. of the above estate was to descend for life; but *Nihal Singh* died in January, 1864, and his younger brother *Mehtab Singh* will only receive 500 Rs. per annum, with the exception of the jagirs of Botalah and Pahladpur, worth 1,500 Rs. which have been upheld in perpetuity.

Sirdar *Jhanda Singh* resides at Botalah, Gujranwala. He was appointed a Jagirdar Magistrate, in 1862, and possesses considerable influence in the district.

Nihal Singh had been commandant of a thousand horse, under Prince Nao Nihal Singh, in the Charyari Derah, with a jagir of 3,550 Rs., in Chahal and Kot-Shah-Muhammad. This jagir, included in his father's estate, lapsed at his death. He left one son, *Balwant Singh,* a boy of 14 years of age.

SIRDAR KIRPAL SINGH, KUNJAHIA.

Sirdar Kirpal Singh, Kunjahia, is a cousin of Sirdar *Jhanda Singh,* Botalia. His grandfather *Diwan Singh,* with *Karam Singh* and *Ram Singh,* were assassinated by a son of *Hiba Singh,* and the two surviving sons of *Diwan Singh, Dharam Singh* and *Sham Singh,* entered the service of the Maharaja.

After the death of *Sham Singh,* in 1813, *Dharam Singh* received a portion of his jagirs. He served at Multan, Kashmir, Peshawar, and in other campaigns ; and when he grew old, the Maharaja, resuming his jagirs, gave him a cash pension of 2,000 Rs., and placed his son *Ganda Singh* with Prince Sher Singh, who gave him a jagir of 3,000 Rs. from his own estate. He was a great favorite with the Prince, whom he accompanied to Yusafzai, where he was wounded, and afterwards to Kulu. When the Prince was Nazim of Kashmir, *Ganda Singh* held both civil and military appointments under him, and was employed to reduce the Rajas of Bhamba and Khakha to obedience. He afterwards served at Naoshera and Bannu.

When Sher Singh ascended the throne he gave to *Ganda Singh* additional jagirs worth 30,000 Rs. about Battala, and appointed him to the command of the orderly Derah. He was with the Maharaja when he was assassinated, and was severely wounded in the endeavour to defend him. He was killed in December, 1845, at the battle of Firushahr, where *Kirpal Singh* was also wounded. A short time previously he had introduced his sons *Kirpal Singh* and *Dyal Singh* to the young Maharaja Dalip Singh, and had obtained for them a jagir of 1,200 Rs. Shortly afterwards, however, the jagirs were reduced to 6,000 Rs. by Raja Lal Singh.

Sirdar *Kirpal Singh* was in Hazara at the time of the Multan outbreak, and remained faithful to Government ; acting under the orders of Captain Abbott : and *Dyal Singh* was at Lahore, in attendance on the Maharaja.

After annexation, the whole personal jagirs of *Sirdar Kirpal Singh* and his brothers, amounting to 12,000 Rs., were confirmed, and are enjoyed by them at the present day.

Sirdar *Kirpal Singh* resides at Kunjah, about six miles from the town of Gujrat.

NAWAB IMAMUDDIN KHAN.

SHAIKH UJALA.
Shaikh Ghulam Mohiuddin.
D. 1844.

- Nawab Imamuddin Khan.
  D. 1859.
  - Shaikh Ghulam Mahbub Sobhani.
    B. 1842.
    - Saadat Mant Khan.
      B. 1864.
- Shaikh Firozuddin.
  B. 1836.
  - Nasiruddin.
    B. 1853.

HISTORY OF THE FAMILY.

Shaikh Ujala of the Kalal tribe, was a Munshi in the service of Sirdar Bhup Singh, of Hoshiarpur. His son *Ghulam Mohiuddin*, when very young, attracted the attention of Diwan Moti Ram, son of the celebrated general Mohkam Chand, who placed him in attendance on his second son, Shivdyal. Here he soon became a man of importance, and managed all the affairs of Shivdyal, whose two brothers, Ram Dyal and Kirpa Ram, also favoured the young man and advanced his interests.

In 1823, when Muhammad Azim Khan of Kabul had marched to Peshawar to attack the Sikhs, Ranjit Singh wished, if possible, to induce the Afghans to retire without fighting. Kirpa Ram put *Ghulam Mohiuddin* forward as well suited to carry on the negotiation, and he accordingly bought over the 'pir,' or spiritual adviser of Muhammad Azim Khan, who persuaded the Sirdar to retire, to protect his family and treasure at Minchini, which the Sikhs intended to seize.

Yar Muhammad Khan, brother of Muhammad Azim Khan, was also under Sikh influence, and the result was that the Afghan army was hastily broken up, and retired in confusion upon Minchini and Jalalabad. Maharaja Ranjit Singh took possession of Peshawar, and not thinking it wise to remain there long, divided the territory between Muhammad Yar Khan and Dost Muhammad Khan, and returned to Lahore. Before he left, *Ghulam Mohiuddin* was sent on a mission to Muhammad Azim Khan, on the part of the Maharaja. He told the Sirdar of the capture of Peshawar, and its delivery to the brothers who had betrayed him, and the news so affected the Chief with mortification and anger, that he fell ill and died twenty-two days later.

In 1827, Shaikh *Ghulam Mohiuddin* accompanied his patron Kirpa Ram to Kashmir, where the latter had been appointed Governor. The Shaikh became sole agent for Kirpa Ram, and he exercised his power with great cruelty and tyranny. In 1831, when, through the enmity of Raja Dhyan Singh, Kirpa Ram was recalled, *Ghulam Mohiuddin* was also summoned to Lahore, fined and imprisoned. But, later in the same year, he again proceeded to Kashmir as agent and lieutenant of Prince Sher Singh, who had been nominated to succeed Kirpa Ram. The Prince knew little of business, and the Shaikh acquired more power than ever, which he used more ruthlessly than before. The people cried out bitterly against his oppression; and to add to their distress, Kashmir was, in 1832, visited by famine. The Shaikh was again recalled to Lahore and fined. He protested against the amount of the fine, which he said he could never pay, and the Maharaja directed Misr Rup Lal to confiscate his property at Hoshiarpur. There was found concealed no less than nine and a half lakhs of rupees. Vainly the Shaikh swore that this was money accumulated by his father in the service of Sirdar Bhup Singh; but Ranjit Singh well knew that the little Sirdar had never seen a lakh of rupees in his life, and that the treasure had been wrung from the starving Kashmiris. He confiscated the whole, and fined the Shaikh 25,000 Rs. besides.

Ghulam Mohiuddin remained for some time out of employment, till Bhai Ram Singh, wishing to have a friend about the person of Nao Nihal Singh, with ability sufficient to counteract the influence of his enemy, Diwan Hakim Rai, placed him in the service of the Prince. Here he rapidly became a great favourite, and he accompanied the Prince to Peshawar and became his chief fiscal Minister. In 1839, he was made Governor of the Jalandhar Doab, and in the hot season of the next year was sent with General Ventura to subdue the Rajputs of Mandi. The progress of the troops was slow, and in September, 1840, Sirdar Ajit Singh, Sindhanwalia, was sent to their assistance with an additional force.

When Nao Nihal Singh was killed on the 5th November, the Shaikh was still in the hills, but he quickly returned to Lahore, and espoused the cause of Mai Chand Kour, mother of the deceased Prince. When Sher Singh ascended the throne, the Shaikh excused his opposition to him on the ground of fidelity to his late master, and so convinced Sher Singh of his sincerity, that on the arrival of the news of the murder of General Mian Singh, Governor of Kashmir, by his own men, on the 17th April, 1841, the Shaikh was appointed to succeed him. He immediately left for Kashmir, and his son *Imamuddin Khan* was summoned from Mandi to take charge of the Jalandhar Doab.

Raja Gulab Singh was sent with *Ghulam Mohiuddin* to restore order in Kashmir. The former had his hill troops, the latter the Jalandhar levies, chiefly Muhammadan. The Hazara troops and the Afghans of Pakhli and Dhamtour, who had revolted, were after some fighting reduced to submission, and lastly the Kashmir mutineers were defeated and disbanded. The Shaikh, who was Governor more on the part of Raja Gulab Singh than of the Lahore State, raised new regiments, consisting partly of hill Rajputs, subjects of Gulab Singh, and partly of Muhammadans. Being himself a Muhammadan, the Sikh authority in Kashmir depended thenceforward very much on the fidelity of Raja Gulab Singh.

The leading man in the hill country was Sultan Zabardast Khan, Raja of Muzaffarabad. His capital, at which a small Sikh garrison was stationed, was on the road from Hazara into Kashmir. He was a man well disposed to the Lahore Government, in favour with Sher Singh, and had done good service in putting down the mutiny in Kashmir.

This Chief, about two months after Sher Singh's death, was treacherously seized while at prayers in a mosque, by *Ghulam Mohiuddin*, imprisoned and his jagirs confiscated.

At the same time disputes arose between Gulab Singh and his nephew Hira Singh, and the former used every means to attach the people of Kashmir and the hills to himself. In this he partially succeeded, and at all events he showed the hill Chiefs and Muhammadan population their own strength and the Sikh weakness, so clearly, that they determined to make a stand on their own account. Accordingly, in August, 1844, Habibullah Khan of Pakhli attacked the Sikh garrison of Khori, but *Ghulam Mohiuddin* sent 500 men to its relief, who defeated the insurgents, and slew their leader. Soon after this, Raja Sultan Khan of Khori, joined by a son of Habibullah Khan, and other hill Chiefs, attacked and reduced Khori, and, in October, marched to Muzaffarabad and attacked the forts. *Ghulam Mohiuddin* sent nearly all his Sikh troops to the relief of the garrison, but they were attacked and defeated by the insurgents, who burnt the town, and killed such of their Sikh prisoners who would not adopt the Muhammadan faith. The son of Raja Zabardast Khan and the Rajas of Dobheta and Ori now joined the insurgents, who became so strong that, in November, they seized Baramulla, and occupied the Pargannah of Shoupur, within a short march of the capital.

Ghulam Mohiuddin now first informed the court of Lahore of the insurrection. General Gulab Singh, Povindia, then on his way to Peshawar, was ordered to advance into Kashmir, with his troops. Reinforcements were also sent by way of Punch and Jammu, but those sent by Raja Gulab Singh soon halted, the depth of the snow being the excuse;

but the real reason was that the Raja did not wish to co-operate heartily till he had secured some advantages for himself; a retention of the salt mine leases; the repossession of Hazara, and the restoration to favor of Chiefs, like Chattar Singh, Attariwala, who, in the late quarrel, had espoused his cause.

The troops that marched by way of Punch were commanded by *Imamuddin Khan*, son of *Ghulam Mohiuddin*. This young man, though he had served in the Derajat under Prince Nao Nihal Singh, had never been in action, and had no military reputation. He joined the Kashmir expedition with the greatest reluctance, and only consented to go, on the understanding that no Sikh troops were to accompany him, for he was hated by them as the murderer * of Bhai Gurmukh Singh and Misr Beli Ram.

In the meantime Kashmir had been entirely over-run by the insurgents, and *Ghulam Mohiuddin* was shut up in the fort of Hari Parbat. The Muhammadan troops had revolted, the hill Rajas were all up in arms, and the Sikhs found they had their most difficult conquest to make over again.

Among the Yusafzais of Pakhli and Dhamtour, and the tribes of Khakka and Bhamba, the insurrection was a religious one, and a man came

---

* NOTE.—After the destruction of the Sindhanwalias, Raja Hira Singh arrested Bhai Gurmukh Singh, Misr Beli Ram, and his brother Ram Kishan, and made them over to *Imamuddin Khan*, who confined them in the stables adjoining his house, and here a few days later they were all three murdered.

Bhai Gurmukh Singh was an inveterate enemy of Raja Dhyan Singh, and no surpris can be felt at Raja Hira Singh desiring his death; but Misr Beli Ram and his brother, though opposed in policy to Dhyan Singh, were harmless men, and very generally beloved. Their death was barbarous and unnecessary. Misr Rup Lal, who had been employed, in 1832, to confiscate the property of *Ghulam Mohiuddin*, was brother of Misr Beli Ram. By the murder of the latter it was supposed that the revenge of the Shaiks, rather than that of Raja Hira Singh, was satisfied.

forward calling himself the Khalifa or vicar of the Syad,* and was joined by all the fierce population in the attack upon Hazara and Kashmir.

The force of Gulab Singh, Povindia, and Diwan Mulraj,† at length advanced to Muzaffarabad and relieved the garrison. It then marched into the valley, and after some severe fighting the insurgents were defeated. Raja Zabardast Khan was reinstated at Muzuffarabad and the neighbouring Rajas were made subordinate to him. In February, 1845, Shaikh *Ghulam Mohiuddin* tried to open negotiations with the English Government, to which he tendered his allegiance, and that of Raja Rahimulla Khan of Rajaori. His proposals were rejected, and soon afterwards he died, it is believed, from poison, and his son *Imamuddin Khan,* who was in Kashmir at the time, succeeded him as Governor.

The Shaikhs (as the father and son were called) had neither family nor influence, and were useful to the Lahore State chiefly as being unscrupulous collectors of revenue.

Their names are not remembered with any affection, either in Kashmir or in the Jalandhar Doab. They were hated by the Sikhs, and this was considered as a guarantee for their fidelity, but both father and son had a natural genius for treason and intrigue, which no considerations of prudence could overcome.

Imamuddin Khan was Governor of Kashmir when that province was made over to Maharaja Gulab Singh, by the treaty of the 16th March, 1846. This transfer was not popular at Lahore, and to Raja Lal Singh the Minister, it was especially distasteful, for Gulab Singh had always been his rival and enemy. He, accordingly, sent instructions to *Imamuddin Khan* to oppose the Maharaja, and directed the troops to obey the Shaikh implicitly. *Imamuddin Khan* was willing enough to comply. He

* Syad Ahmad, who was defeated and slain by Sher Singh and General Ventura in 1831. His followers (who are numerous all over India) asserted that the river shrank back to aid his escape and closed upon his pursuers, and that he would re-appear and lead them to victory. His last stand was made in Pakhli and Dhamtour.

† Diwan Mulraj was Governor of Hazara, and must not be confounded with Diwan Mulraj, Governor of Multan.

was very rich, and he understood that the success of the Maharaja signified, not only the end of his exactions, but also the rigid scrutiny of his accounts by his declared enemies. It was popularly reported at this time that the family possessed from seventy lakhs to two crores of rupees, and although this was doubtless an exaggeration, yet it is certain that the father and son had amassed an immense fortune during their occupation of Kashmir and Jalandhar.

It is possible that *Imamuddin Khan*, misapprehending the motives of the British Government, imagined that by the payment of a large sum of ready money, he might be allowed to retain Kashmir, as Viceroy, and with this object was ready to carry out the instructions of Raja Lal Singh, and make a prolonged resistance to show his own power and resources. But whatever were the reasons for his conduct, he disregarded the peremptory orders of the Darbar to evacuate the province; he induced, by bribes, many of the Maharaja's troops to join his standard, and with the assistance of Fakir-ullah Khan, son of Raja Rahimullah Khan of Rajaori, and other hill chiefs, he retained possession of the greater part of the country until a large force was sent from Lahore against him.

It was not until the army had reached the border of the Kashmir valley, that the Shaikh, seeing further opposition to be useless, came in to Colonel Lawrence's camp at Thannah and surrendered himself. He then gave up two letters and an address to the troops serving under him, which, he stated, contained the instructions of Raja Lal Singh, and in obedience to which he had acted. Although the sentiments of the Minister towards Gulab Singh were notorious, it was thought hardly conceivable that he should have been foolish enough to put his signature to these treasonable documents; but on the return of the force to Lahore, he was brought to trial. The authenticity of both the letters and the address to the troops was fully proved, and Lal Singh, convicted of deliberate treason, was deposed from the 'Wizarat' and banished to Agra. Shaikh *Imamuddin Khan*, though a willing party to the treason, was pardoned, and his Lahore estates, which, with his other property in that city, had been confiscated, were restored to him.

The generous treatment he received seems to have made a favorable impression upon Imamuddin, and, in 1848, when almost all were traitors to their Government, he remained faithful, though great efforts were made by the leaders of the rebellion to gain him to their side. In June, 1848, with 2,000 newly-raised troops, he marched to Multan, to co-operate with the force of Lieutenant (now Sir Herbert) Edwardes. Both he and his men behaved well, and distinguished themselves in several actions with the rebels.

When peace was restored, he received, as a reward for his services, the title of Nawab, and a life cash pension of 11,600 Rupees, and his jagir of 8,400 Rupees was confirmed to him.

In 1857, he raised, under the orders of Government, two troops of Cavalry for service at Delhi.

He died in March, 1859, aged 40, leaving one son, Shaikh *Ghulam Mahbub Sobhani*, now 22 years of age.

In 1862, at the recommendation of the Panjab Government, the Supreme Government sanctioned 5,600 Rs. of jagirs of *Ghulam Mahbub Sobhani* being upheld in perpetuity; 2,800 Rs. to lapse at his death.

He has one son, an infant of 10 months old.

BHAI PARDOMAN SINGH.

BHAI RAM SINGH.

Bhai Surat Singh.

Bhai Gurdas Singh. | Bhai Sant Singh, D. 1804.

Bhai Sher Singh. | Bhai Jodh Singh. | Bhai Gurmukh Singh, D. 1843. | B. Dewa S.

Bhai Pardoman Singh. | B. Madhsudan S. | B. Lehna S. | B. Arjan S.

B. Jowahir Singh, B. 1859.

Bhai Hardeo Singh, B. 1849. | Bhai Gausham Singh. B. 1863.

HISTORY OF THE FAMILY.

The ancestors of Bhai *Pardoman Singh* resided at Chuniot in the Jhang district, and several of them, at different times, entered the service of the Muhammadan chiefs of Multan, but the early history of the family is in no way important. *Ram Singh* became a Sikh and a follower of Guru Govind Singh. He was a zealous preacher of the Sikh faith, in his own part of the country, so much so that the Multan authorities grew alarmed and ordered his arrest, but he received timely information, and was able to escape to Amritsar. The Multan Governor took *Surat Singh*, the only son of *Ram Singh*, into his service, and the father thinking all danger to be past, returned home, where he died shortly afterwards. *Surat Singh* then left Multan, and wandered about the country, as his father had done, preaching the Sikh faith, and his conduct excited the same suspicions. He contrived to get away to Amritsar, with most of his property, and was soon patronized by the Chiefs who were at that time becoming powerful, and was placed in charge of the building of the Darbar Sahib, the Sikh temple at Amritsar. In the Jalandhar Doab he acquired a small jagir, where he built a fort, and then returned to Amritsar, where he died.

In 1806, Maharaja Ranjit Singh conquered the plain portion of the Jalandhar Doab, but he allowed Sant Singh to retain his jagir, and he appointed him to succeed his father in the superintendence of repairs and decoration of the Darbar Sahib. Bhai *Sant Singh* was no contemptible soldier, and on several occasions he served with credit. During the campaign of 1821 the Maharaja was engaged in the siege of a small fort on the way to Mankerah. Suddenly the sky grew dark and a violent storm came on. Ranjit Singh was caught by a furious blast of wind, and thrown into the ditch, from which the earth for the batteries had been excavated. *Sant Singh* saw his fall, and knowing that it is an ill wind that blows nobody any good, sprang into the ditch, and lifting the Maharaja in his arms carried him in triumph to his tent. For this service he received jagirs in the Amritsar and Sialkot districts to the value of 6,800 Rupees. Whether this story be false or true, it is certain that *Sant Singh's* jagirs were numerous, and that he stood high in the favour of the Maharaja.

About this time Bhai *Gurdas Singh* who had been a reader of the Granth, in the Darbar Sahib, died, and *Sant Singh,* in grief for his loss determined to give up worldly affairs and devote himself to reading and expounding the scriptures. In the room of his father came to court *Gurmukh Singh,* who soon became as great a favourite as Sant Singh had been. Bhai *Sant Singh* was called Gyani (one who meditates on) divine things and was held in much respect till his death. He wrote a commentary on the Ramayana and a treatise on the rite of the Pahal, or Sikh baptism.

When *Pardoman Singh* was thirteen, the Maharaja took him into his service and gave him the jagir of Kaliwal, worth 1100 Rupees. Bhai *Gurmukh Singh* had not enjoyed much influence during the life time of Ranjit Singh, forhis enemy, Bhai Ram Singh, was high in the favour of the Maharaja. With Nao Nihal Singh he had still less influence, and when the prince was killed, he took up the cause of Prince Sher Singh warmly, for the principal reason that Ram Singh was leader of the rival party of Mai Chand Kour.

When Sher Singh became Maharaja, he did not forget the services of *Gurmukh Singh*, whom he treated with great consideration, and to whom he gave large jagirs. But the real power was kept by Raja Dhyan Singh, the minister, in his own hands. The Maharaja, though he hated Dhyan Singh and knew his unpopularity with the nation, could not get rid of him. He, however, played off *Gurmukh Singh* against him, and the Bhai, from his religious character and long friendship with the Maharaja, could not be excluded from the presence. But otherwise the contest between the statesman and the priest was most unequal. *Gurmukh Singh* was supported by no powerful party, he was without character or ability, while Raja Dhyan Singh was the ablest man of his day, subtle, plausible, cautious, though bold even to audacity in attacking and destroying his declared enemies.

Throughout the reign of Sher Singh, the Bhai intrigued against Raja Dhyan Singh, and joined in the Sindhanwalia conspiracy against his life. When Raja Hira Singh, son of the murdered minister, rose to power, he, at the instigation of Bhai Ram Singh and Misr Lal Singh, arrested *Gurmukh Singh* with his friend Misr Beli Ram, the Toshakhania, and made them over for custody to Shaikh Imamuddin Khan, by whom they were put to death. Bhai Ram Singh was a far abler man than his rival *Gurmukh Singh*, but of no higher character. Both were unscrupulous and scheming men, and both made religion a cloak for their ambition and intrigue.

After the death of *Gurmukh Singh*, all the estates of the family were confiscated and their houses and personal property seized. Bhai *Pardaman Singh* and his brothers were imprisoned at Amritsar, placed in irons, and treated with the greatest severity. The religious bodies of the city made great efforts to obtain their release, and, at last, *Pardoman Singh* contrived to escape, and with his youngest brother *Arjan Singh*, fled to Ludianah, where he remained under protection of the British Government, till the murder of Hira Singh allowed him to return to Lahore. The four brothers obtained the release of a portion of their jagirs in the Amritsar District, amounting to Rs. 5488. Bhai *Pardoman Singh* then set out to Hardwar to perform his father's funeral rites, and was promised that on his return the other jagirs of *Gurmukh Singh* should be released. On his return his houses at Amritsar were made over to him, and he would have probably recovered the rest of the property, had not the war with the English commenced, while his case was still pending, followed by the annexation of the country in 1849. The jagir of 5488 Rs. at Mochal and Kuleir Ghuma was released for the lives of the brothers, subject to payment of one quarter revenue. The British Government could do not more for the family. Bhai *Gurmukh Singh* had acquired his large possessions as much by his intrigues as his sanctity. He played for a high stake, wealth and political power, and lost; and although the Sikh Government and especially the army, filled with remorse for the murder of the Bhai, which their own evil passions had allowed, would probably have again placed his family in an influential position, yet the British Government could not be expected to feel either sympathy or remorse.

Bhai *Pardoman Singh* accompanied Sirdar Lehna Singh Majithia to Benares, in 1853. He is now superintendent of the repairs of the Darbar Sahib at Amritsar, and has charge of jagirs to the amount of 4000 Rupees per annum, released in perpetuity for the support of the temple.

Arjan Singh died some years ago, leaving one son *Jowahir Singh*. *Madhsudan Singh* entered the service of Government, in 1857, as Jamadar of ten sowars raised by his brother. He was present at the capture of mutineers at Ajnala in the same year, and having been made a Risaldar, was sent to Thanesar, where he died. His family, and that of *Arjan Singh*, have a pension of 600 Rupees, their share in the jagir having been resumed.

Lehna Singh, the remaining brother, is Naib Tehsildar at Jalandhar.

SIRDAR MANGAL SINGH, RAMGHARIA.

- Har Das.
  - Baghwan Singh. D. 1787.
    - Jai Singh, D. 1756.
    - Jassa Singh, D. 1803.
      - Sirdar Jodh Singh, D. 1816.
      - S. Wir Singh, D. 1828.
        - Jaimal Singh, D. 1848.
          - Utam S. B. 1807.
            - Dharta Singh.
          - Fatah S. B. 1819.
          - Joalla S. B. 1834.
            - Maghar Singh, B. 1859.
        - Sobha S., D. 1845.
          - Achhar Singh, B. 1814.
            - Ganga Singh.
            - Tarkhu Singh.
            - Taringa Singh.
            - Kadar Singh.
    - Khushhal Singh, D. 1812.
      - Mehtab Singh.
      - Sahib Singh.
      - Gulab Singh.
    - Mali Singh, D. 1792.
      - Wariam Singh.
    - Tara Singh, D. 1797.
      - S. Diwan Singh, D. 1834.
        - Sirdar Mangal Singh, B. 1800.
          - Gurdit Singh, B. 1837.
            - Darbara Singh.
          - Mitt Singh, B. 1842.
          - Sher Singh, B. 1846.

HISTORY OF THE FAMILY.

The Ramgharia misl, from which the family of Sirdar *Mangal Singh* takes its name, was one of the most powerful of the Sikh confederacies, and towards the close of the eighteenth century could bring into the field about eight thousand fighting men. Of its leaders, *Jassa Singh* was the most distinguished, although he can hardly be called its founder, for, through many unquiet years it had existed, as an organized body, under Khushhal Singh and Nand Singh. But it was only when *Jassa Singh* succeeded to the command, in 1758, that it became powerful and renowned.

Har Das, the grandfather of *Jassa Singh,* was a Hindu of the Najjar or carpenter caste, resident at Sarsang in the Lahore district. He was content to follow his humble trade in his native village, but his son *Bhagwan*, of a more adventurous disposition, took the 'pahal,' the Sikh baptism, and with the addition of Singh to his name, wandered about the country, making converts to his new faith. He at length settled at Ichugil, where there were born to him five sons, *Jai Singh, Jassa Singh, Khushhal Singh, Mali Singh* and *Tara Singh*, the four last of whom became noted men and leaders of the Ramgharia misl. There was no great difference in the ages of the brothers, and, in 1752, on their reaching manhood, they entered the service of the celebrated Nawab Adina Beg Khan. This able man, then Imperial Governor of the Jalandhar Doab, encouraged the Sikhs in their resistance to Ahmad Shah Durani, hoping to rise, by their assistance, to supreme power in the province; and in this he would probably have been successful, but for his premature death, in 1758.

When Prince Timur, son of Ahmad Shah, marched against him, determined to punish his opposition, Adina Beg retreated to the hills, and *Jassa Singh* and his brothers left him and went to Amritsar, where they joined the force of Nand Singh, Sanghani. *Jai Singh* was about this time killed in action with the Afghans near Majitha.

Amritsar was at this time no more than a large village, and on the retreat of the Afghans, Nand Singh and *Jassa Singh* partially fortified it, surrounding a portion with a high mud wall, which they called Ram Rouni. When Adina Beg returned, thinking the Sikhs were becoming too powerful, he sent Mirza Aziz Bakshi to reduce the new fort, which was, in truth, no difficult matter. *Jassa Singh* and his friends fought gallantly, and made more than one sally from the fort, but they were overmatched and at length abandoned it at night, and, with considerable loss, cut their way through the enemy. The Ram Rouni was dismantled, but Adina Beg died shortly afterwards, and *Jassa Singh*, taking command of the confederacy, named the fort he had defended so bravely, Ramghar; and his misl, the Ramgharia. He seized at this time, aided by the Kanheya misl, Dinanagar, Battala, Kalanur, Sri Hargovindpur, Kadian, Ghumman, and many other towns in the Amritsar and Gurdaspur Districts the revenue of which was estimated at from six to ten lakhs of rupees. Besides this, *Jassa Singh*, who was sole lord of the territory, acquired many villages in the Jalandhar Doab. To his brothers he gave separate jagirs, under him. It was their imprudence which brought great trouble on the family, for as Jassa Singh, Ahluwalia, was passing near Gurdaspur on his way to Achal, a place of pilgrimage, he was attacked by *Khushhal Singh*, *Mali Singh* and *Tara Singh*; his troops were dispersed and himself taken prisoner. *Jassa Singh* Ramgharia, who would have been glad enough had his brothers slain his rival, could only release him with rich gifts, when he was brought in as prisoner, for the old Sikh barons had much of the spirit of chivalry. But the Ahluwalia chieftain was not to be appeased. He was looked up to as the head of the Khalsa, and indeed its founder; his followers and flatterers called him King (Sultan-ul-Kaum) and yet he had been insulted by these Ramgharia youths, whose beards had but just begun to grow, and he swore a mighty oath that he would never loose his turban till he had seized all the Ramgharia estates. Many chiefs came to aid him, thinking not much of the insult, but having an eye to plunder and new jagirs. There was Ganda Singh and Jhanda Singh Bhangi; the Kanheyas, Jai Singh and Hakikat Singh, old friends of the Ramgharias; Charrat Singh Sukarchakia; Nar Singh, Chamyariwala, and many others. They attacked *Jassa Singh* on all sides, and after a severe struggle, took possession of all the Ramgharia territory. *Khushhal Singh* was badly wounded at Wegowal fighting with Jai Singh, Kanheya; *Tara Singh* lost Kalanur, and *Jassa Singh* fled across the Satlej to Sirsa with a large body of irregular horse, having sent his two sons to the Pattiala chief Amar Singh, to beg assistance.

In the Sirsa district he remained till 1783. He overran the country with his horsemen, and plundered up to the walls of Delhi; on one occasion he penetrated into Delhi itself, and carried off four guns from the Mogal quarter. The Nawab of Meerat paid him tribute of 10,000 Rs. a year, to save his district from plunder. One day a Brahman complained to him that the Governor of Hissar had carried off his two daughters by force. *Jassa Singh* collected his forces and marched against Hissar, which he plundered, and restored the girls to their father. Sometimes he was reduced to great straits, and there is a story, which may be true, that at Sirsa, a servant of the Sirdar happening to drop his vessel down a well, a diver was sent to fetch it, who discovered at the bottom four boxes full of gold-mohurs, to the value of five lakhs of rupees, enabling *Jassa Singh* to pay his troops, and enlist new followers.

A great famine desolated Sirsa, in 1783, and the Sirdar returned to the Panjab. At Ludianah he met messengers from Sirdar Mahan Singh, Sukarchakia, and Raja Sansar Chand of Kangra, offering to reinstate him in his possessions if he would join them against Sirdar Jai Singh, Kanheya. *Jassa Singh* consented readily enough, and having joined forces, the allies marched to Battala. Gurbaksh Singh, son of Jai Singh, advanced against them, with 8,000 men, but he was defeated and slain, and the Kanheya chief was compelled to give up the Ramgharia estates to their old owner, and the fort of Kangra, which he had held for four years, to Sansar Chand. But *Jassa Singh* was not destined to enjoy peace, and for many years he was engaged in disputes with the Kanheya misl, in which he was sometimes successful, sometimes defeated.

In 1796, his last and most severe struggle with the Kanheyas took place. Mai Sadda Kour, widow of Sirdar Gurbaksh Singh, was then head of the misl, and with all her own forces and those of her young son-in-law Ranjit Singh, she besieged *Jassa Singh,* in Miani, a fort in the Hoshiarpur district, near the Beas. *Jassa Singh* defended himself for some time, but his provisions ran very low, and he sent a messenger to Sahib Singh, Bedi, at Amritsar, to beg him to interpose between him and his enemies. Jodh Singh, Wazirabadia, and Dal Singh, Gil, were with the Bedi, on the part of Ranjit Singh, when the Ramgharia messenger arrived, and Sahib Singh gave them a message to Sadda Kour and Ranjit Singh, bidding them raise the siege of Miani. But Sadda Kour would not retire without her revenge for her husband's death and her enemy was now in her hands, so no notice was taken of the Bedi's order. Again *Jassa Singh* sent a messenger, and Bedi Sahib Singh said—" They will not mind me ; but God himself will aid you." The messenger returned to Miani, and that very night the river Beas came down in flood, and swept away a large portion of the Kanheya camp, men and horses and camels. Sadda Kour and Ranjit Singh escaped with difficulty, and retired to Gujranwala.

Jassa Singh died in 1803, and was succeeded by his eldest son *Jodh Singh*. The new Sirdar was not a man of any ability, and his cousin *Diwan Singh* seized a large portion of the jagir. At length Ranjit Singh began to lust after the Ramgharia territory, and feigned the greatest affection for Sirdar *Jodh Singh*. He had a contract of eternal friendship between himself and the Ramgharia family drawn out, and before the Granth, in the holy Darbar Sahib at Amritsar, he stamped the paper in his royal and illiterate way, with his open palm, dyed with saffron. The better to cajole *Jodh Singh*, he went over the Ramghar fort almost unattended, and ordered his new fort of Govindghar to be built in the same fashion. Ranjit Singh cared little about keeping oaths, however solemn, but *Jodh Singh* had been won over, and became so devoted a follower, that there was no excuse to annex his territory. He accompanied the Maharaja to Kassur, with all his force, in the last successful expedition against Kutbuddin Khan.

On the death of *Jodh Singh* in 1816, the family began to quarrel ; *Diwan Singh*, *Wir Singh*, and the widow of *Jodh Singh* all claiming the estate. The Maharaja hearing of this, called the three cousins, *Wir Singh*, *Mehtab Singh*, and *Diwan Singh* to him at Nadon, promising to settle the dispute by arbitration. On their arrival they were received with courtesy by the Maharaja, but he soon took occasion to leave the reception tent, which was straightway surrounded with troops, and the three Ramgharias made prisoners. Then Ranjit Singh marched on Amritsar, and after some severe fighting took the fort of Ramghar. Again marching northward, he seized all the vast Ramgharia jagirs, and in a short time reduced all their forts, upwards of a hundred in number. And thus was cancelled the saffron bond.

Wir Singh and *Mehtab Singh* were soon released, and were placed under Sirdar Lehna Singh, Majithia, and at the intercession of Sirdar Nihal Singh, Attariwala, a jagir of 35,000 Rs. was settled on the family. *Diwan Singh* for some time refused to accept his share of 6,000 Rs. at Dharamkot, and remained a prisoner, but at length pretended to acquiese. On regaining his freedom, however, he fled to Pattiala, where he was at first well received, but after a year was compelled to leave, and he then wandered about for some time, till he thought it best to submit, and returning to Lahore, he accepted a command of 700 men, in the expedition then fitting out for Kashmir. After this we hear little of him beyond that he remained in charge of Baramula, a difficult hill post, on the road to Srinagar, till his death, in 1834. *Wir Singh* had died six years before, in 1828, when two-thirds of his Jagir were resumed.

Sirdar *Mangal Singh*, though of the younger branch, is the present representative of the family. He served during his younger days about the person of Maharaja Ranjit Singh, who gave him jagirs in Dharamkot, Kalowala, Tibrah and Kundilah, worth 9,000 Rs. of which 3,600 Rs., were personal, and 5,400 Rs. for service. After his father's death, Sirdar *Mangal Singh* was sent to Peshawar in command of 400 foot and 110 sowars of the old Ramgharia clan. Here, under Sirdar Tej Singh and Sirdar Hari Singh Nalwa, he did good service, and fought in the famous battle of Jamrud, in April, 1837, where the gallant Hari Singh was killed. In 1839, he was recalled, and sent to the hill country between the Beas and the Satlej, under the orders of Sirdar Lehna Singh, Majithia and during the absence of that chief at Peshawar he was placed in charge of the hill forts, and was active in the suppression of the insurrection of 1840.

During the reign of Maharaja Sher Singh he was chiefly employed, under Lehna Singh, in Suket, Mandi and Kulu, and he remained there till the close of the Satlej war in 1846. The Rajput Chiefs, with Raja Balersen of Mandi, at their head, were not slow to take advantage of the war with the English, and gave the Sirdar plenty of work, but he held his ground till the treaty of the 9th March, 1846, enabled him to give up his trust with honor.

During the second Sikh war, Sirdar *Mangal Singh* remained loyal, and did excellent service, in guarding the roads and maintaining order in the Amritsar and Gurdaspur districts. His great exploit however at this time was the capture of the notorious rebel and robber Hari Singh, who had for some time kept the country about Amritsar in a state of alarm. This he effected at Sagarpurah, near Rangar Nangal, a grant of which jagir worth 3,700 was made to him by the Darbar, and confirmed after annexation.

In 1862, on the retirement of Sirdar Jodh Singh, Sirdar *Mangal Singh* was appointed manager of the affairs of the Sikh Temple at Amritsar. This appointment, which is one of some difficulty, has been filled by the Sirdar with tact and ability. In the same year he was appointed Honorary Magistrate of the city of Amritsar.

Sirdar *Mangal Singh* is a man of education and liberal ideas. It has been in a great measure owing to his influence and example, that the cause of female education has been so widely and systematically taken up in the city of Amritsar.

Gurdit Singh, eldest son of the Sirdar *Mangal Singh,* in February, 1858, joined Colonel Abbott, at Hoshiarpur, when that officer was raising a force of cavalry for service in Oude. *Gurdit Singh* was made Resaldar, and served in the Oude Mounted Police to the complete satisfaction of his superior officers, until October, 1859, when, on the reduction of the force, he returned to Amritsar, where he was made 1st class Inspector of Police. He was transferred to Lahore in September, 1864.

Mitt Singh, the second son of Sirdar *Mangal Singh* is in Government civil employ at Amritsar.

SIRDAR SARDUL SINGH MAN, OF MANANWALA.

TARA SINGH.

Sirdar Karam Singh.

Sirdar Ram Singh. — Sirdar Sham Singh. — Daughter, M. S. Lakha Singh, Awan.

(Sirdar Ram Singh:) Bibi Sadda Kour M. S. Sobha Singh, Halluwalla.

(Sirdar Sham Singh:) Sirdar Fatah Singh, M. Sister of S. Nar Singh, Aimahwala, D. 1845.

(Sirdar Fatah Singh:) Bibi Kakoh, M. S. Ajit Singh, Sindhanwalia. D. 1843. — S. Sardul Singh. B. 1810. — S. Jowala Singh. D. 1860.

(S. Sardul Singh:) Bibi Partab Kour, M. S. Isar Singh, Nakkai. — Bibi Nihal Kour, M. S. Kishan Singh, Chinah. — Partab Singh. B. 1834. — Bibi Gulab Kour, M. son of S. Kharrak Singh, Jalandhar. — Jiun Singh. B. 1852.

(S. Jowala Singh:) Raja Singh. B. 1836. — Hira Singh. B. 1838.

(Partab Singh:) Mehtab Singh. B. 1860.

(Raja Singh:) Son, B. 1863.

HISTORY OF THE FAMILY.

Sirdar *Sardul Singh* Man is of the same descent as the Man Sirdars of Mogalchak in the Gujranwala district. Some account of the Man Jat tribe will be found in the history of the Mogalchak family (V. Sirdar Fatah Singh Man).

The branch of the Man tribe to which *Sardul Singh* belongs, had for many generations been resident at Mananwala in the Amritsar district, when, the village having been plundered and destroyed about the year 1720, *Tara Singh* abandoned it, with his whole family, and settled at Narli with his brothers-in-law. The Sikhs were at this time becoming powerful, and *Tara Singh* with a band of horsemen, composed chiefly of members of his own clan, seized and held, till his death, several villages in the Amritsar district.

Karam Singh, his son, was an enterprizing man, and was far more successful than his father in the art of plunder and annexation. He joined the Bhangi confederacy, and acquired jagirs in the Lahore, Sialkot and Amritsar districts. He rebuilt Mananwala and took up his residence there.

Karam Singh was succeeded by his two sons, *Ram Singh* and *Sham Singh*. These young men, about 1780, left the Bhangi misl and went over to Sirdar Mahan Singh, Sukarchakia, by whom they were very well treated, and allowed a share both in his fighting and his plunder. *Ram Singh* does not seem to have had any enmity against his old associates, for he married his only child Bibi *Sadda Kour* to a Bhangi chief, Sirdar Sobha Singh, Halluwalia, builder of Kila Sobha Singh in the Sialkot district, and son of Sirdar Bhag Singh, Halluwalia. In 1788, *Ram Singh* died, and his younger brother *Sham Singh* was allowed to succeed to the whole estate. In 1790, however, Sirdar Mahan Singh confiscated all but Mananwala, and Ralliabadho worth 20,000 Rs. per annum, which Sham Singh enjoyed till his death, giving no service during the life of Mahan Singh, but under Ranjit Singh furnishing a contingent of fifteen horsemen.

Sirdar *Fatah Singh* had been early introduced to Ranjit Singh by his father, and when Prince Kharrak Singh was a few years old, Fatah Singh was appointed especially for his service. The Sirdar served in the Kangra campaign of 1809 ; at Daskah, where he was wounded in the shoulder ; at Chunian, where he was again wounded in his hand, and at Sahiwal, where after the capture of the town from Fatah Khan, he was appointed commandant and where he remained for a year. In 1811, he received from Kharrak Singh, from his personal estates, a jagir worth 1,00,000 Rs. subject to the service of three hundred horse. Other Jagirdars, amounting with their contingents to 700 men, were also placed under his command, and he was sent to Jammu to reduce some insurgents there toorder ; and after this he was sent, with other Sirdars, to Kulu and Kangra. He fought at the battle of Attock, and in the miserable Kashmir expedition of 1814, he, with Dewan Jiwan Mal, accompanied the detachment of Ram Dyal, on the part of Prince Kharrak Singh.

Soon after this Sirdar *Fatah Singh* was again sent to Jammu to put down an insurrection. In this he was successful, and brought in all the ringleaders to Lahore. But Bhaiya Ram Singh, the mukhtar or confidential agent of Prince Kharrak Singh, who hated *Fatah Singh* on account of his power and influence, concocted a plot to destroy his reputation.

He induced Gulab Singh and Dhyan Singh (afterwards Rajas) to murder the two chief ringleaders, by name Trehdu and Suthra, who had been concerned in the murder of their uncle Mian Mota, and to release the other insurgents, who fled to their native hills, and again raised disturbances. At this, as Bhaiya Ram Singh anticipated, the Prince was very angry, and resumed the jagir which he had given to *Fatah Singh*. The Maharaja, however, took pity upon the disgraced favourite, and gave him a jagir of 35,000 Rs. and a cash allowance of 15,000 Rs., subject to the service of 125 horsemen.

At Multan, in 1818, the reduction of the fort of Kot Bajai Khan was entrusted to the Sirdar, and he was successful in taking it. He accompanied the Kashmir expedition of 1819, and the next year crossed the Satlej on a visit to his estate at Mahlan. The Maharaja, who was marching towards Rawal Pindi, summoned him, but he only sent his son *Sardul Singh* with the contingent. This conduct irritated Ranjit Singh, who, suspecting that the Sirdar was intriguing with the English, resumed all his jagirs, with the exception of Mananwala.

It was not till the capture of Mankera, in December, 1821, when *Fatah Singh* behaved gallantly, that he was taken again into favour, received new jagirs, and was made commandant of the captured fort. He went with the Maharaja to Peshawar, in 1823, and afterwards accompanied the two Bannu expeditions of Prince Sher Singh and Kharrak Singh, while his son acted for him at Mankerah.

In 1829, the Sirdar was again placed in the suite of Prince Kharrak Singh, and two years later his son was recalled from Mankerah, and placed in command of a troop of cavalry. In 1831, he accompanied Prince Sher Singh and General Ventura against the celebrated Syad Ahmad, who had lost his influence with the Afghans, Trans-Indus, and had taken up his head-quarters at Balakot in Hazara, where he trusted for support to the tribes of Dhamtour and Pakhli and to his Hindustani followers. Here he was attacked by the Sikhs, the fort of Balakot was taken, and the Syad himself with most of his followers slain, though it was afterwards declared that he escaped, the river opening to receive him. In 1834, the Sirdar went to Peshawar in the suite of Prince Nao Nihal Singh, and afterwards remained on duty at Bannu, Tank and Peshawar, till the death of Maharaja Ranjit Singh. When that event took place, *Fatah Singh* was at Peshawar with Nao Nihal Singh, and *Sardul Singh* was at Tank. From the new Maharaja, the Sirdar received additional jagirs at Kotbari Khan, Gujranwala, worth 30,000 Rs., which made his estates amount to 63,000 Rs. subject to the service of 100 horse.

Sardul Singh served under General Ventura in 1840-41, in the Mandi campaign, and at the siege and capture of Kamlaghar. In April, 1841, *Fatah Singh* with 700 horse was appointed to escort ten lakhs of treasure from Firozpur to Peshawar, en route for Kabul.

In February, 1845, when Raja Lal Singh, after long altercations with his rival Sirdar Jowahir Singh, whom he feared to leave behind at Lahore, consented to head the army proceeding against Raja Gulab Singh at Jammu, *Fatah Singh* Man was one of the Chiefs whom he insisted upon taking with him. Soon after joining the army, Lal Singh sent *Fatah Singh* with some others to negotiate. The envoys were received by Gulab Singh with all honour, and were amused for some days with the alternate promises of submission and threats of defiance which the Raja had always in store for such occasions. At length the envoys returned with the declaration of Gulab Singh that he would abide by the terms of the treaty, concluded by his Agents in Lahore. He denied the amount of the Lahore claims, but said that he would pay them if proved; and for this purpose requested that Wazir Bachna,* Hira Nand and Gunpat Rai, confidential servants of his nephew Hira Singh, and upon whose authority the claims had been made, should be sent to him. The envoys, accordingly, with these three men, returned to Jammu.

Besides *Fatah Singh* Man, the deputation to Jammu consisted of Baba Mian Singh, an old Bedi of great sanctity. Rattan Chand Dogal, one of the most influential of the mutsaddi or munshi party, and Sirdar Sher Singh Attariwala. They remained at Jammu for some days, but could not come to any definite terms, for Gulab Singh was carrying on separate negotiations with the Sikh army, whose panchayats were also in Jammu.

At last on the 28th February, after a violent altercation between Wazir Bachna and the Raja, the latter gave four lakhs of rupees, as an earnest of the full discharge of the just claims against him, and the deputation took its leave. Passing through a hedge of thorns, which had been thrown round the town of Jammu, the envoys were fired at by a body of the Raja's troops. Sirdar *Fatah Singh* and Wazir Bachna were killed on the spot, and Diwan Ganpat Rai, who was on the same elephant with them, was mortally wounded and died the next day. Raja Gulab Singh protested his innocence and his grief, and that the catastrophe had happened contrary to his wishes and his orders. The Baba, Sher Singh, and Rattan Chand he detained at Jammu as hostages, and as negotiators.

* Until the death of Maharaja Sher Singh, Bachna, a Jat of Jandialah in the Shaikhopura Parganah, was Manager of Raja Hira Singh's hill estates under Pandit Jalla. When the Pandit went to Lahore, on Hira Singh becoming Minister, Bachna succeeded him in the hills, with the title of Wazir. When Raja Gulab Singh gave over Jasrota to the Darbar in January, 1845, Bachna remained to give over the treasure, and was then summoned to Lahore. There he took advantage of the discontent excited by the news of Sikh excesses in the hills to get himself reappointed Governor of Jasrota, under the Darbar, and was on his way to take up his Government, when summoned to Jammu. He was an able man, much loved by the hill people for his mildness and honesty.

That this assassination was planned by Gulab Singh there is no shadow of doubt. He had, it is true, no hostile feelings against *Fatah Singh;* but the Sirdar was upon the same elephant with the man he had determined to destroy, and as Mian Uttam Singh died with Nao Nihal Singh, so did *Fatah Singh* with Wazir Bachna.

When Bachna had been reappointed Governor of Jasrota, Gulab Singh thought that it was the same as if he himself had recovered possession of it. But he was disappointed. Pandit Jalla had taught Bachna to hate and distrust Gulab Singh, and when he joined the deputation the Raja saw that his fancied friend was entirely in the interest of the Darbar. He knew that as an enemy Bachna could do him vast injury, for he was so popular in the hills that he could have brought over *Gulab Singh's* Rajput troops to the side of the Sikhs, and the Raja consequently determined on his destruction.

The death of Sirdar *Fatah Singh* was much lamented by the chiefs; but the army, though it was convenient to use his death as a weapon against Gulab Singh, did not at this time care much for Sirdars; certainly not for men of the old school like *Fatah Singh*, who looked upon the regular army as a most dangerous innovation, and whose traditions were all of the days of the Great Maharaja.

Two months later, when Raja Gulab Singh had been brought to Lahore, eleven lakhs of rupees, out of the sixty-eight lakhs which he was compelled to pay, was charged in the account as blood-money for the death of Sirdar *Fatah Singh*.

In May, 1845, Sirdar Jowahir Singh confiscated the 30,000 Rs. jagir given to *Fatah Singh* by Maharaja Kharrak Singh. *Sardul Singh* was at this time at Hassan Abdal, and in August of the same year, he, with the Attariwala and other Sirdars, recovered the fort of Attock from Prince Peshora Singh.

He fought in the Satlej campaign, and in August, 1846, Raja Lal Singh, the Minister, without any apparent cause, confiscated all his remaining jagirs, with the exception of Mananwala, worth 3,000 Rs. *Sardul Singh* went to Simla to appeal to Major H. Lawrence, and accompanied that officer back to Lahore. After Lal Singh's deposition and banishment, the creditors of Sirdar *Fatah Singh* pressed *Sardul Singh* for payment of his father's debts, amounting to 1,25,000 Rs., and Major Lawrence induced the Darbar to allow him jagirs of 21,000 Rs. subject to the service of 30 sowars. Twenty of these sowars, however, were to be excused, for five years; the sum allowed for their service 6,000 Rs. being applied to the liquidation of the debt.

On annexation the personal estates of the family amounting to 10,500, were upheld for life, and 3,000 Rs. in perpetuity; 2,147 Rs. to the male issue of *Sardul Singh*, and 853 Rs. to the male issue of *Jowala Singh.*

Sirdar *Jowala Singh* who was not on good terms with *Sardul Singh*, died in 1860. *Bibi Kakoh*, their sister, who married Sirdar Ajit Singh Sindhanwalia, on hearing the news of the death of her husband in the fort of Lahore, in September, 1843, burnt herself with his clothes, at Naorangabad. During the rebellion of 1848, Sirdar *Sardul Singh* remained faithful to Government; and, in 1857, did as much as his embarrassed circumstances would allow in raising horsemen for service in Hindostan.

He resides at Mananwala, 6 miles from the city of Amritsar.

SIRDAR JOWHAHIR SINGH, NALWA.

HARDAS SINGH,
D. 1752.

Gurdyal Singh,
D. 1798.

Sirdar Hari Singh,
D. 1837.

S. Gurdit Singh, B. 1807. — Fatah Singh, adopted.

S. Jowahir Singh, B. 1809.

S. Panjab Singh, D. 1854.

Daughter, M. Ganda Singh of Fakir Chandkotli.

Daughter, M. S. Kaneya Singh, Garjak.

S. Arjan Singh, D. 1848. — Achhara Singh. (Daughter.) — Sampuran Singh.

HISTORY OF THE FAMILY.

Hardas Singh and his son *Gurdyal Singh* were followers of the Sukarchakia chiefs. The former was killed in action, 1762, and the latter accompained Charrat Singh and Mahan Singh on all their expeditions, and received in jagir the village of Balloke near Shahdera.

Hari Singh, like Ranjit Singh himself, was born at the town of Gujranwala, and was only seven years old, when his father died. He, however, early distinguished himself, and at the seige of Kassur, in 1807, behaved with such gallantry that Ranjit Sing made him a Sirdar and gave him a jagir. During the seige of Multan, in March, 1810, Hari Singh was much burnt by a firepot thrown from the walls of the fort and it was some months before he was again fit for service. He then reduced the Mitha Tiwana country, which he was allowed to hold as a service jagir. In 1818, he accompanied Prince Kharrak Singh in the last and successful expedition against Multan, and the next year commanded one division of the army invading Kashmir. In 1820, he was appointed governor of the conquered province, in the room of Diwan Moti Ram, who was thought too gentle a ruler for the rude and unsettled population. *Hari Singh* did not err on the side of leniency. He ruled with a strong hand, and the Kashmiris hated him so much that the Maharaja was compelled to recal him, in 1821, and reappoint Moti Ram to the governorship.*

Hari Singh was ordered to join the army, then on it way to Mankera, and Misr Diwan Chand, who was a rival of the Sirdar, tried to persuade the Maharaja that he would not obey the order. Obedience was not easy to Hari Singh for the wild mountaineers to the number of 20,000, opposed his passage, and at Pakli he was compelled to halt with his force of 7,000 men. Pakli had long been a spot dreaded by merchants, for the hill men of that place were accustomed to demand a toll on shawl wood and other Kashmir merchandise. *Hari Singh*, after vain efforts to induce the enemy to yield him a passage, attacked them with vigour, and storming their stockades defeated them with great slaughter. After this he imposed a fine of 5½ Rs. on each house in the district, and proceeded southwards to join the Maharaja, who was much pleased with his exploit and forgave him the unpaid balance of the Kashmir revenue.

Hari Singh was now appointed Governor of Hazara, at this time the most turbulent province under Sikh rule. He was not a man suited to conciliate the Hazara tribes, for he hated all Muhammadans fiercely and was never so happy as when fighting against them, but he was brave even to recklessness, fertile in resource and prompt in action. At Theri, in 1823, he was commanding a portion of the Sikh army watching the movements of Muhammad Azim Khan, while the Maharaja was engaged with the Yusafzai Pathans on the other side of the Kabul river. In

* *Hari Singh* Nalwa is well remembered in Kashmir to the present day, and a rupee known as the Hari Singh rupee, which he struck at Srinagar, is still current in all parts of the Panjab.

1824, his harshness excited an insurrection in Draband and he was attacked by the insurgents in great force, and could only maintain his position with difficulty, till the arrival of reinforcements. On another occasion his force, in which were Sirdars Chattar Singh and Sham Singh Attariwala and some of the bravest of the Sikh chiefs, was attacked by a force of Yusafzais five times as numerous. Disdaining flight or surrender, the little band charged the enemy and gallantly cut their way through with but little loss.

In the begining of 1827, Syad Ahmad Shah roused all the fanatic population of Yusafzai for a holy war against Sikhs and infidels, and was joined by the Barakzai chiefs of Peshawar. Sirdar *Hari Singh* with 25,000 men was ordered to prevent the Syad from crossing the Indus till the Maharaja should arrive with reinforcements. But prudence was not part of *Hari Singh's* nature, and half his force, under Sirdar Budh Singh Sindhanwala, crossed the river and entrenched at Saidu, where it was surrounded by overwhelming numbers of the enemy. Budh Singh, however, induced the Peshawar Sirdars to desert the Syad, and sallying from his entrenchments defeated the enemy so completely that it was long before the Syad was able again to appear in the field. When Ranjit Singh and *Hari Singh* arrived the army marched to Peshawar, which was pillaged by the Sikhs. The palace of the Bala Hissar and many of the chief buildings were destroyed ; the mosques were defiled and the trees cut down for fuel. The tribute of Peshawar was increased, and the Maharaja carried away with him, as a hostage, the son of Yar Muhammad Khan.

By the treaty of the 12th March, 1833, with Shah Shuja, the Maharaja obtained a cession of Peshawar, the Derajat and Multan. The Shah's power to bestow anything whatever was purely nominal, but soon afterwards Sirdar *Hari Singh*, with Prince Nao Nihal Singh, was sent to Peshawar, on pretence of demanding an increased tribute, but in reality to seize the city. One morning he sent a polite message to the Barakzai Sirdars informing them that the prince wished to view the city and that it would be well for them to retire to Bagh Ali Mardan Khan, while he went round the walls. Accordingly the whole Sikh force was put in motion, and, accompanied by the young prince mounted on an elephant, moved towards the city. Some of the Afghan troops made a spirited resistance, but the Barakzai Sirdars fled and *Hari Singh* with his small force of 8000 men took possession of Peshawar.

After this success, Sirdar *Hari Singh* remained as Commander in Chief on the frontier. In 1835, Dost Muhammad Khan determined to retake Peshawar, if possible, and sent a force under Muhammad Khan to endeavour to dislodge the Sikhs. No serious attack was, however, then made, although the rival forces were engaged in perpetual skirmishes with varying success.

In 1836, *Hari Singh* was directed to build a fort at Jamrud, at the entrance of the Khaibar Pass, from the walls of which the Maharaja might see Jalalabad. Accordingly the fort was built, of small strength or size, but impregnable to the Khaibar tribes who possessed no artillery. But the suspicions of Amir Dost Muhammad were aroused, and he determined to destroy the fort which commanded the road to Kabul. He collected a force of 7,000 horse, 2,000 matchlock men, and 18 guns; and placed them under his son, Muhammad Akbar Khan, and Mirza Sami Khan, his minister. With the army were three other of the Amir's sons; Muhammad Afzal Khan, Muhammad Azim Khan, and Muhammad Haidar Khan, the last still a boy. The Afghans marched through the pass, and being joined by some 12,000 or 15,000 Khaibaris, encamped before Jamrud. The fort was not, at this time, prepared against attack. It was garrisoned by only 800 Sikhs, and *Hari Singh* was ill with fever in Peshawar. The Afghans surrounded the fort, and commenced a heavy fire on its southern face. On the 6th day the defences were almost entirely destroyed, and so large a breach made in the wall that a troop of cavalry could have charged up it. Mahan Singh Mirpuria, who was in command, sent message after message to *Hari Singh*, and the last was to the effect that the garrison could hold out but one other day. On hearing this, the General, ill as he was, turned out his whole force, 6,000 foot, 1,000 regular cavalry and 3,000 irregular, and marched toward Jamrud ; but the first day he advanced only two miles. But the news of his approach gave fresh life to the garrison, and they repulsed an assault of the Afghans with desperate courage, the assailants losing 300 men. The next day was fortunately a Friday, and the enemy made no attack, being engaged in burying their dead. Early on Saturday morning *Hari Singh* arrived before the fort. For seven days the hostile armies lay opposite each other, neither wishing to commence, till *Hari Singh*, impatient of inaction, gave the signal for battle.

The Sikh attack was directed against that portion of the Afghan position where Zerin Khan and Momind Khan were in command and was completely successful. The Afghan troops were driven back, and both their leaders wounded, and the whole army, seeing the fate of the advanced division, wavered, turned and fled. The Sikhs thought the day was their own, and eagerly pressed on capturing six guns, but their desire for revenge and plunder carried them too far, and at this moment Shamshuddin Khan swept down with a large body of Afghan horse, and driving the Sikhs back in confusion and with great loss, completely changed the aspect of affairs. *Hari Singh* now saw that his presence alone could retrieve the day, and in spite of the entreaties of his officers, Khan Singh Majithia, Sarmukh Singh Botalia, and Diwan Devi Sahai, he rode to the front and urged his men to stand their ground and repulse the enemy. The victory might still have been to the Sikhs, but *Hari Singh* who alone could ensure it, was struck by two balls, one in the side, and the other in the stomach. He knew he was mortally wounded, but fearing to discourage his men, he turned his horse's head, and managed to ride as far as his tent. He swooned as he was taken from his horse, and half an hour later the bravest of the Sikh generals, the man, with the terror of whose name Afghan mothers used to quiet their fretful children, was dead. The army was kept in ignorance of his death, but all knew he was grievously wounded, and fell back beneath the walls of Jamrud, where they threw up entrenchments and waited for reinforcements. For two whole days Mahan Singh Mirpuria and his other officers concealed the death of the general; but at last it could be no longer a secret, and the dismay of the army was extreme. To add to their distress they could obtain no water, and if it had not been for a fall of rain, most unusual at that time of year, the Sikhs would have been compelled to abandon their entrenchments, and cut their way through the enemy to Peshawar. At length help came. Raja Dhyan Singh, Princes Kharrak Singh and Nao Nihal Singh, Jamadar Khushhal Singh, General Ventura and all the flower of the Sikh chivalry, hastened up from Lahore by forced marches, and twelve days after the battle arrived before Jamrud, and the Afghan army broke up their camp and hastily retreated through the Khaibar upon Jalalabad.

The results of this battle were not important. The Sikhs had indeed lost their most dashing General, but the Afghans had retired without attempting to improve the victory. Each army lost three guns, and among those taken from the Afghans, was one of immense size, the fellow of the Zabar Zang of Ghazni.

No sooner was the great Chief dead than his family began to quarrel about his property and jagirs. At the time of his death *Hari Singh* possessed larger estates than any other man in the Panjab proper. He was lord of Gujranwala, Kachhi, Nurpur, Mitha Tiwana, Sheikhowal, Kalarghar, Hazara, Khanpur, Dhanna, Khattak, and other places, worth 8,52,608 Rs. per annum; but with these jagirs he was bound to furnish two regiments of cavalry, a battery of artillery, and a camel swivel battery. His wealth in money and jewels was also very great, and his family thought that its possession was well worth a fight. *Jowahir Singh* and *Gurdit Singh*, were sons of the Sirdar's first wife; *Arjan Singh* and *Panjab Singh* of his second wife; and the half brothers had never been on good terms. *Arjan Singh* and *Panjab Singh* took possession of the late Sirdar's fortified house at Gujranwala (now the residence of the Deputy Commissioner) while *Jowahir Singh* and his brother held the town. So fierce was the dispute between them, that the Maharaja, always glad of an opportunity to fill his own treasury, confiscated all *Hari Singh's* property and estates, with the exception of 19,600 Rs. assigned to the brothers in the following proportion; *Panjab Singh*, 5,400; *Arjan Singh*, 6,500; *Jowahir Singh*, 5,500; *Gurdit Singh*, 2,200 Rs. Gujranwala was given, in jagir, to Misr Beli Ram, and Hazara to Sirdar Tej Singh, in 1838.

Sirdar *Jowahir Singh* had, in 1832, been appointed to command at Jahangira, and two years later he was sent on duty to Peshawar, and was engaged in many of the actions with the Afghans up to the time of his father's death, in April 1837.

In October, 1848, Sirdar *Arjan Singh* joined the rebels. He shut himself up in the fortified house at Gujranwala, with 100 or 150 men, and openly defied the Government. A small detachment sent by the Darbar to bring him in to Lahore, was unsuccessful; but when a body of troops sent by Brigadier Campbell, and a squadron of Skinner's horse marched against him, he fled. The defences of the house were destroyed and the property found in it confiscated.

Sirdar *Jowahir Singh*, whose sympathies were with the rebels, and who was at any rate an enemy of Raja Tej Singh, had been arrested and kept a close prisoner in the house of Golab Singh Kalal, in Lahore. He, however, managed to win over his guards to the popular side, and he and the six soldiers escaped together to Gujranwala. Misr Rallia Ram who was then in authority, at that place, tried to seize him, but *Jowahir Singh* was not to be caught a second time, and escaping from the town he joined the army of Raja Sher Singh. He fought against the British with great gallantry at Chillianwala and Gujrat, and he was the man who led the dashing charge of Irregular Cavalry at Chillianwala, which so nearly ruined the fortune of the day.

Panjab Singh was the only one of the brothers who remained faithful to his government, and his jagir alone was exempted from confiscation. He died in 1854.

Arjan Singh died in 1848, soon after his escape from Gujranwala. His two sons, who are still living, have each a small allowance of 96 Rs.

In 1857, Sirdar *Jowahir Singh* was one of the first of the Panjab Sirdars selected by the Chief Commissioner for service in Hindostan. Proud of the confidence reposed in him, *Jowahir Singh* served throughout the war with a gallantry and devotion which none surpassed. He was Risaldar and Senior Native Officer of the 1st Sikh Cavalry. At Lukhnow, Bithur, Cawnpur, Kalpi, and wherever that noble regiment was engaged, *Jowahir Singh* was present. He was 18 times engaged with the enemy and, at the close of 1859, he received, as a reward for his services, a jagir of 12,000 Rs. per annum. He had previously received the 1st class order of British India, for distinguished services in the field. In 1862, he was made an Honorary Magistrate of Gujranwalla, where both he and his elder brother *Gurdit Singh* reside.

Sirdarni *Desan*, mother of *Panjab Singh* and *Arjan Singh*, and Sirdarni *Rajkouran* mother of *Jowahir Singh* and *Gurdit Singh* are both still living, and hold jagirs of 800 Rs. and 700 Rs. respectively.

The Nalwa family came from Majitha, in the Amritsar district.

The origin of the name Nalwa is uncertain, and several stories are related regarding it, one of them more curious than polite. Most probably it was but an amplification of Nal, a famous Raja and hero of pre-historic times, and was given to *Hari Singh* on account of his unsurpassed bravery.

SIRDAR SARUP SINGH, MALWAI.

MAL SINGH.

Sirdar Dhanna Singh,
D. 1843.

S. Buchattar Singh, D. 1840. M. D. of S. Sher Singh, Jagdeo.	Sirdar Hukm Singh, M. D. S. Fatah Singh, Mattu, D. 1846.	Daughter, M. S. Khazan Singh, Bhadour, C. S. S.	Daughter, M. S. Narayan Singh, Bhakhna, Amritsar.

S. Kirpal Singh,
M. D. of S. Wazir Singh,
Liddhran, C. S. S.,
D. 1859.

S. Sarup Singh,
B. 1850.
M. D. of S. Kehr Singh,
Sindhanwalia.

HISTORY OF THE FAMILY.

Sirdar *Sarup Singh* is descended from a respectable Man Jat family, formerly resident at Mowran Kalan in the Nabha territory. *Mal Singh*, the first of the family to become a Sikh, is stated to have left Nabha, about 1760, for the Panjab, where he entered the service of Sirdar Charrat Singh Sukarchakia, as a sowar, and was killed after some years in the Dhanni campaign. His son *Dhanna Singh*, about the year 1800, enlisted in the force of Sirdar Fatah Singh Kalianwala, as a trooper, and soon rose in the favour of that chief, obtaining an independent command. He fought, in the Kalianwala contingent, in the Bhatti and Kassur campaigns. On the death of Sirdar Fatah Singh, at Narayanghar, in 1807, *Dhanna Singh* entered the service of the Maharaja, who gave him a jagir, at Bilasor, near Taran Taran, worth 2000 Rs. He was one of the agents sent by Ranjit Singh to Wazir Fatah Khan of Kabul, to arrange the interview which took place between them, at Jhelam, on the 1st December, 1812. About this time, *Dhanna Singh* received the jagir of Talah

Gang in the Jhelam District, worth 33,000 Rs. In the campaign of 1810, against Fatah Khan of Sahiwal, he received a wound in the face; and in July, 1813, he fought in the battle of Attock when Fatah Khan Barakzai was defeated by Diwan Mokam Chand. He accompanied the detachment of Ram Dyal and Dal Singh Naharna in the first unsuccessful expedition against Kashmir, and received in a skirmish a sword cut on the arm. The Sirdar fought gallantly at the seige of Multan, in 1818, and was one of the foremost in the assault. The jeweled sword and shield of Nawab Muzaffar Khan fell into his hands, and were brought by him to the Maharaja, who gave him a jagir worth 5,000 Rs., which was, however, soon exchanged for another near Talah Gang.

In 1819, he served in the second Kashmir expedition, and, in 1821, at the siege of Mankerah, where he was again wounded. At this time *Dhanna Singh* was much favoured by the Maharaja, and there were few Sirdars whose influence was greater, or whose advice was more regarded. He was present at the capture of Jahangira, and at the battle of Theri, in 1823, and continued for some time in the Peshawar District, under the command of Sirdar Budh Singh Sindhanwalia and prince Kharrak Singh. *Buchattar Singh*, eldest son of Sirdar *Dhanna Singh,* entered the army about 1827, and his first service was at Bahawalpur where he was sent to receive the tribute. In 1823, *Dhanna Singh* accompanied the force sent to seize Kangra, when Raja Anrudh Chand fled across the Satlej to avoid an alliance with Raja Dhyan Singh, Minister at Lahore. When Peshawar was occupied by the Sikhs in force, *Buchattar Singh* was sent to Shabkadr, where a new cantonment had been laid out and a fort built by Sirdar Chattar Singh Attariwala. He was stationed there when the Afghan army attacked that post and the fort of Jamrud, in April 1837. *Dhanna Singh* heard of the defeat of the Sikh army and the death of Hari Singh Nalwa as he was marching to Peshawar. He was ordered to join the relieving force of Raja Dhyan Singh, which advanced with all haste to the assistance of the army which was surrounded by the Afghans and reduced to the last extremity.

In January, 1839, Sirdars *Buchattar Singh* and *Hukm Singh* were sent with the Sikh force escorting Shahzada Timur, son of Shah Shuja, to Peshawar; and a few months later *Hukm Singh* returned to Lahore with Prince Nao Nihal Singh, who started for the capital immediately he received news of the death of his grand father Ranjit Singh.

In 1841, after Maharaja Sher Singh had ascended the throne, *Hukm Singh* was sent with Budh Singh Mahrah, to Kulu, to bring in to Lahore Sirdars Lehna Singh and Kehr Singh, Sindhanwalia, as prisoners. This duty he performed and received an increase to his jagirs of 8000 Rs. and a grant of 2000 Rs. from the Kashmir customs. *Buchattar Singh* died in 1840, and his father *Dhanna Singh* in May 1843. The death of the latter was the cause of some ill feeling on the part of the Sikh Government towards the British, in the following manner. The native village of *Dhanna Singh* was, as has been already stated, Mowran in the Nabha territory. After the Multan campaign, when he was in high power with Ranjit Singh he begged that Mowran might be obtained for him in jagir. The Maharaja accordingly applied to the Raja ot Nabha, who, in May, 1819, made him a grant of the village, in exchange for certain villages which the Maharaja gave to the sister of the Nabha chief, for her life. Ranjit Singh on obtaining Mowran gave it in jagir to Sirdar *Dhanna Singh*, who held it till his death, and although residing himself at Court, kept there his family and much of his property. The Raja of Nabha had for some time before *Dhanna Singh's* death desired to resume the village, for the Sirdar never obeyed his orders or tendered him any allegiance, but the British authorities, who had a regard for the fine old chief, interposed in his behalf. But when *Dhanna Singh* died, Raja Devindar Singh of Nabha, armed with a letter admitting his right from Sir George Clerk, and a letter from Maharaja Kharrak Singh permitting him to resume the village, marched troops against it, and took possession by force, killing and wounding some of the Malwai retainers and seizing the property of *Hukm Singh*, the son of the deceased Sirdar. *Hukm Singh* loudly protested against this treatment, but before any action had been taken, by either Government, in the matter, Maharaja Sher Singh was assassinated, and every one at Lahore was too busy in looking after his own interests to remember the village of Mowran.

When, however, tranquility had been restored, the Lahore Government made a demand for the restoration of Mowran, an estate given by Raja Jaswant Singh of Nabha to Ranjit Singh. To the British authorities this was a new view of the matter. General Ochterlony, Sir George Clerk and Colonel Richmond had never known that the village had been given to the Maharaja, but imagined that it had been a jagir grant from Nabha to *Dhanna Singh*. The grant to Lahore was in itself invalid, for a dependent state had no power to transfer a village to an independent one without the consent of the paramount power. The letter, too, which the Raja of Nabha stated he had received from Maharaja Kharrak Singh, allowing him to resume the village, turned out to be no more than a copy of a copy. The weak minded Maharaja may have drafted such a letter, and the Raja may have obtained, through secret influence, a copy of it, but Raja Dhyan Singh, the minister at Lahore, had never sanctioned it, and its authenticity was doubtful in the extreme. The result was that Mowran was restored neither to the Lahore State nor to *Hukm Singh*, and the Raja of Nabha received the sharpest reprimand for his unstraightforward conduct. This incident would have been unworthy of so much notice in this place, had not the decision of the British Government irritated, in no small degree, the Sikh nation. There can be no possible doubt but that the conduct of the British Government was just and necessary, but the Sikhs were, at this time in a feverish and excited state. Every precaution which the lawlessness of the Sikh Army forced upon the British, they considered as hostile to themselves, and the refusal to make over the village of Mowran to Lahore, although its first transfer was clandestine and invalid, they considered as a deliberate insult.

To the other jagirs of his father *Hukm Singh* succeeded, and with the grants of Maharaja Sher Singh, personal to himself, his estates amounted to 75,000 Rs. per annum. He was present in the garden of Shah Bilawal when the Maharaja was assassinated by the Sindhanwalias, and in the subsequent struggle was severely wounded in the shoulder.

Little is known of *Hukm Singh* during the two following years when he appears to have lived a retired life. He was killed at the battle of Sobraon, in February, 1846, and soon after his death, Raja Lal Singh reduced the jagirs from 67,000 Rs. to 25,000 Rs. which were continued to Sirdar *Kirpal Singh*, subject to the service of sixty horse.

Kirpal Singh was with Raja Sher Singh at Multan, in 1848. When the Raja's force rebelled, *Kirpal Singh* separated himself from it, and with a few of his sowars came into the camp of Major Edwardes, with whom he had previously served in Bannu. His personal jagir, of 11,000 Rs. was, on annexation, confirmed to him for life ; and a new jagir of 5,000 Rs. for loyalty at Multan, granted in perpetuity.

The jagir was subject to the payment of a pension of 1,500 Rs. per annum, to *Chand Kour*, widow of Sirdar *Hukm Singh*. This lady died in 1863. Sirdar *Kirpal Singh* enlisted sepoys and showed himself well affected to Government in 1857, and received a khillat of 500 Rs. and a sanad of approbation. He died in 1859. His only son, Sirdar *Sarup Singh*, is fourteen years of age, and attends the Government School at Lahore.

Gurdit Singh Malwa ; son of Sirdar Sahib Singh Malwai, and deputy of Sirdar Lal Singh Moraria who was convicted of treasonable correspondence with the rebels in 1848, was not in any way connected with the family of Sirdar *Hukm Singh*.

SIRDAR GURDIT SINGH CHHACHHI.

- SIRDAR TEHIL SINGH, D. 1785.
  - Jassa Singh, D. 1815.
    - Sadhu Singh.
      - Joala Singh.
      - Jowahir Singh.
      - Nihal Singh.
  - S. Fatah Singh, D. 1814.
    - Bhum Singh.
    - S. Gurmukh Singh, D. 1829.
      - Daughter, M. Sirdar Nihal Singh, Chhachhi.
  - Sher Singh, D. 1814.
    - Utam Singh, D. 1826.
      - Jiun Singh, D. 1852.
        - Gurdit Singh, B. 1834.
          - Mehr Singh, B. 1857.
          - Dyal Singh, B. 1858.
          - Jaggat Singh, B. 1860.
          - Son, B. 1863.
        - Ganda Singh.
    - Attar Singh, D. 1837.
      - Dewa Singh.
    - Jit Singh.
      - Gurbuksh Singh, D. 1846, at Sobraon.
      - Mohr Singh, D. 1857.
        - Mit Singh.
      - Mehtab Singh, B. 1810.

HISTORY OF THE FAMILY.

The original home of the Chhachhi family is not certainly known, though being of the Kohli Khatri tribe, its ancestor, in all probability, emigrated from Bhatnir to the Panjab, where he settled at Salargah in Chhachh, whence the title Chhachhi of the family is taken.

Sirdar *Tehil Singh* first entered the service of the Khatar Sirdars, but the later joined Sirdar Charrat Singh, Sukarchakia, when that Chief was becoming powerful, and received from him jagirs to the amount of 36,700 Rs. at Mial Daud Khel, Lawa and Dallur. This was in the year 1741. *Tehil Singh* made conquests on his own account, and captured the fort of Dewar, and Mapal from the Pathans of Makhad, both of which places he held till 1786. On the death of *Tehil Singh* his three sons succeeded to all his jagirs. *Jassa Singh* died soon after his father, but Sirdars *Sher Singh* and *Fatah Singh* throughout the early years of Ranjit Singh's reign, did excellent service, and received large additions to their estates at Bharatpur, Sahiwal, Kunjah and elsewhere to the value of 53,000 Rs. The brothers served at Kask, in the Pind Dadan Khan district, against the Janjuahs; at Pindi Gheb; Jhang, and joined the first unfortunate expedition against Kashmir, in 1814, in which both were slain. On their death the Pind Dadan Khan jagirs and that of Abdal in Gujranwala were resumed. *Gurmukh Singh* and *Sadhu Singh* were taken into the Ghorcharah Kalan, in which the former remained till his death in 1829. He left one daughter who married Nihal Singh, who took the name of Chhachhi, and was allowed to hold his father-in-law's jagir of Chakori in Gujranwala.

Utam Singh eldest son of *Sher Singh* succeeded to the family estate in Gujrat and Gujranwala, and the same year the Maharaja gave to the second son *Attar Singh* the Lawa estate which had formerly been in possession of the family. *Utam Singh* served, with his contingent, at the seige of Multan in 1818, and afterward retired to Lawa, where he was killed, in 1826, in a revenue affray with the zamindars. The Maharaja resumed all his jagirs with the exception of Mial Daud khel and Lawa, worth 21,200, which descended to his son *Jiun Singh.* The new Sirdar was not perhaps so fond of fighting as some of his family, but he had his fair share nevertheless. His contingent consisted of 65 horse, 5 zamburahs, or camel swivels, and a kettle drum, the sound of which was well known all along the frontier. He served at Bannu, Tank, Mitha Tiwana, where he was wounded; and at Peshawar, where in the fatal battle of Jamrud his uncle *Attar Singh* was slain. For some eight years he was stationed at Dera Ismail Khan, and had there plenty of work to do, as the border tribes were fierce haters of the Sikhs and gave him much trouble. After the Satlej war he was posted with his son at Kachhi, under the orders of General Van Cortlandt, but soon after returned home, leaving *Gurdit Singh* with the contingent. He returned to his post, however, soon after Lieutenant H. B. Edwardes arrived in Bannu, and, with his son, who was at this time a mere boy, served under that officer to the close of the second Sikh war. Sirdar *Jiun Singh* was one of the few Sikh chiefs who remained loyal to the end, and of his fifty-five horsemen, only two, during the whole siege of Multan, deserted to the enemy.

On the annexation of the Panjab, his service jagirs were resumed, but his personal jagirs, amounting to 7000 Rs. at Mial, Daudkhel and Salargah, the last of which had been in the family ever since 1741, were released to him for life, one half to descend in perpetuity. Sirdar *Jiun Singh* died on the 22nd September 1852.

Sirdar *Gurdit Singh* did good service in 1857, raising a force of 25 sowars and guarding the ferry at Wazirabad. He also raised 5 sowars for service in Oude, and received in recognition of his loyalty a Khillat of 300 Rs.

Of the three sons of *Jit Singh* Chhachhi, *Gurbaksh Singh* the eldest was killed in 1845, at Firushahr. The second son, *Mohr Singh*, who had served in the same regiment as his brother, was, in 1848, in the Ghorcharah Kalan under Ganpat Rai. He went over with Sirdar Sher Singh to Mulraj at Multan, and obtaining from the Attariwala chief a grant of the whole of the Lawa jagir in which he was legally a third sharer, he went off to take possession; but Amir Devi and Hukm Devi, the widows of *Attar Singh* and *Gurbuksh Singh*, held out gallantly in the Lawa fort, for the Chhachhi women can fight as bravely as the men, and Sher Muhammad Khan Tiwanah coming to the rescue of the ladies, *Mohr Singh* was compelled to return to Sher Singh, completely disappointed, and his rightful share of the jagir was confiscated for his rebellion. He entered the service of the English Government, in 1857, and marching down into Hindostan, died in harness like most of his family.

THE RANDHAWAH FAMILY.

I. SIRDAR JAIMAL SINGH KHUNDAH.

Dyanat Rai

Lachhi Ram.

Majja Singh | Gajja Singh. | Tegh Singh

Panjab Singh
M. D. Sirdar
Nodh Singh.
Majithia.

Sirdar Prem Singh.

Sirdar Jowahir Singh
M. D. Sher Singh Saddorah
B. 1822

Tara Sing.
B. 1860.

Hira Singh
B. 1825.

Sirdar Jaimal Singh
B. .1823.
M. D. Comdt Fatah Singh,
Chabal.

Kirpal Singh.
B. 1850.
M. D. S. Gopal Singh,
Manowli.

Jaswant Singh.
D. 1844.

HISTORY OF THE FAMILY.

The Randhawah tribe is of Rajput origin, and its founder was resident in Bikanir seven hundred years ago. From him have descended seven families more or less distinguished in the history of the Panjab, namely: Dharamkot, Ghanianki, Chamyari, Dodah, Doranghah, or Talwandi, Kathu-Nangal and Khundah. Some account of the five last of these families will be given here. Khunda now takes the highest rank, while Kathu-Naugal, Dharamkot and Ghanianki are of no present consideration whatever.

Little is known of Randhawah, a Jadu Rajput, the ancestor from whem the tribe has derived its name. He was said to have been a great was ior and his name *Ran,* war, and *Dhawa* a local form of *daurna* to run, signifies his prowess, but whether he was wont to run into the battle or away from it is nowhere recorded. Neither he nor his immediate descendants left Bikanir, but Kajjal, fifth in descent from Randhawah, emigrated to the Panjab and settled near Battala,* which had been founded some time before by Ram Deo a Bhatti Rajput.

The brothers took possession of a valuable tract of country in the Gurdaspur district, including Naosherah, Zafarwal, Khundah, Shahpur, and adjacent villages, and the other branches of the Randhawah family, about the some time, rose to importance. The Khundahwalas belonged to the Kanheya misl, and till the death of Sirdar Jai Singh Kanheya, in 1793, they kept possession of all their estates, worth nearly two lakhs of rupees; but Sadda Kour, widow of Jai Singh, and one of the ablest and most unscrupulous of her sex, taking advantage of some dissentions in the family, seized Naosherah and Hyatnagar Kalair. Still later, in the time of Sirdar *Prem Singh,* Maharaja Ranjit Singh seized the whole of the estate, leaving only ten villages to the family, worth 6,000 Rs. *Panjab Singh,* father of *Prem Singh* had married a daughter of Nodh Singh Majithia, whose son Sirdar Desa Singh possessed at this time great influence with the Maharaja. He procured *Prem Singh* to be placed, with his ten sowars, under him, and the young Sirdar accordingly served with the Maharaja's forces in many campaigns, including those of Multan

* Battala is stated to have been founded in 1465. A. D., but in reality its age is far greater. Ram Deo first dug the foundations of the new town about two miles from the present site: but every night the excavation which he had dug during the day was filled up by supernatural agency; and Ram Deo was at last compelled to change the site of the town, which he called *Battala* or change.

Battala was, however, a place of no importance till 1590, when Shamsher Khan, who, from being a eunuch in Akbar's Zanana, rose to the governorship of the Manjha and the Jalandhar Doab, beautified the town with fine buildings and a superb tank. Finding the Hindus averse to bathing in the tank he sent 300 camels to Hardwar to fetch Ganges water with which to purify it, and the story is that from that day the tank has been always full, and the water has been always clear.

and Peshawar. He was drowned on the 2nd November, 1824, when attempting, with the Maharaja's army to ford the Indus, then much swollen by the rains, in pursuit of the Gandghar insurgents who had attacked and defeated Hari Singh Nalwa. The jagir was continued to *Prem Singh's* four sons on the same terms, namely, service of 10 sowars in the Majithia contingent.

In 1836, Sirdar *Jaimal Singh* entered the service of the Maharaja with his brother *Jowahir Singh.* He received a command in the Ramgharia brigade from Sirdar Lehna Singh Majithia, in the place of his father-in-law, Fatah Singh Chahal, who had lately died. The brothers accompanied Lehna Singh to Peshawar, when he marched to relieve the Sikh army after its defeat by the Afghans at Jamrud, in 1837. *Jowahir Singh* served with Lehna Singh in the hill country of Mandi and the Khundah Sirdars were, till the annexation of the Panjab, hereditary jagirdars of the Majithia chiefs. *Jaswant Singh* died in 1844.

Sirdars *Jowahir Singh* and *Hira Singh* are sons of one mother; Sirdars *Jaimal Singh* and *Jaswant Singh* of another, and no love has ever been lost between the half brothers. Sirdar Lehna Singh, their immediate superior, on their disputing about the jagir, divided it between them, thus: *Jaimal Singh* to hold Khundah, Khundi, Sujanpur, Buddhipur, Shahpur, Mali Samrar, and half of Harsian, Jafowal and Bandiwal, value 4000 Rs. with an allowance of 2000 Rs. cash, and to furnish six sowars. *Jowahir Singh* to hold Zafarwal, Mallian and half Harsian, worth 2600 Rs. with a cash allowance of 1200 Rs. and to furnish four sowars. But just before Lehna Singh left the second time for Benares, another dispute arose about the proprietary right of the brothers. A panchayat or committee was appointed by Lehna Singh, which decided that Sirdar *Jaimal Singh* should hold the proprietary rights of Khundah and Shahpur, the ancestral villages, and Sirdar *Jowahir Singh,* the proprietary rights of Naoshera and Jhattupattu. But the proprietors of the last two villages, also of the Randhawah clan, disputed the right, and a decision was given in their favour in the Settlement Court in 1854. *Jowahir Singh* then sued for half of Khundah and Shahpur, but the Settlement Officer decided against him.

Sirdar *Jowahir Singh* has not served under the British Government. In 1850, he visited Sirdar Lehna Singh at Benares, but soon afterwards returned to the Panjab. Sirdar *Jaimal Singh* was, in 1847, appointed Naib Adalati or Deputy Judge of Amritsar, under Sirdar Lehna Singh Majithia. When the rebellion of 1848 broke out, he stood manfully and without hesitation on the side of the Government. He took an active part against the insurgents of the Manjha, whose houses he was directed to confiscate, and by his loyalty, intelligence and zeal won the highest praise from the authorities. After annexation, he accepted service as Tehsildar of Battala, and did his best to render the new administration popular in the country. Although ignorant of the English system of procedure, he conducted his duties with so much ability that he was made an Extra Assistant Commissioner and placed in the Thuggi Department. There Colonel Sleeman, Major McAndrew and Mr. Brereton testified to the value of his services. He was employed in collecting information in the villages, in arresting Thugs, and in conducting prosecutions against them ; and later made himself very useful in taking charge of the Jail and school of Industry. He resigned the office of Extra Assistant in 1860. In 1857 he did excellent service, and received, in acknowledgement of his loyalty, a Khillat of 1000 Rs.

He holds in jagir and cash, 4560 Rs. per annum, of which a jagir of 2000 Rs. descends, on half revenue rates, to his male issue, in perpetuity.

THE RANDHAWAH FAMILY.

II. SIRDAR LAL SINGH TALWANDI.

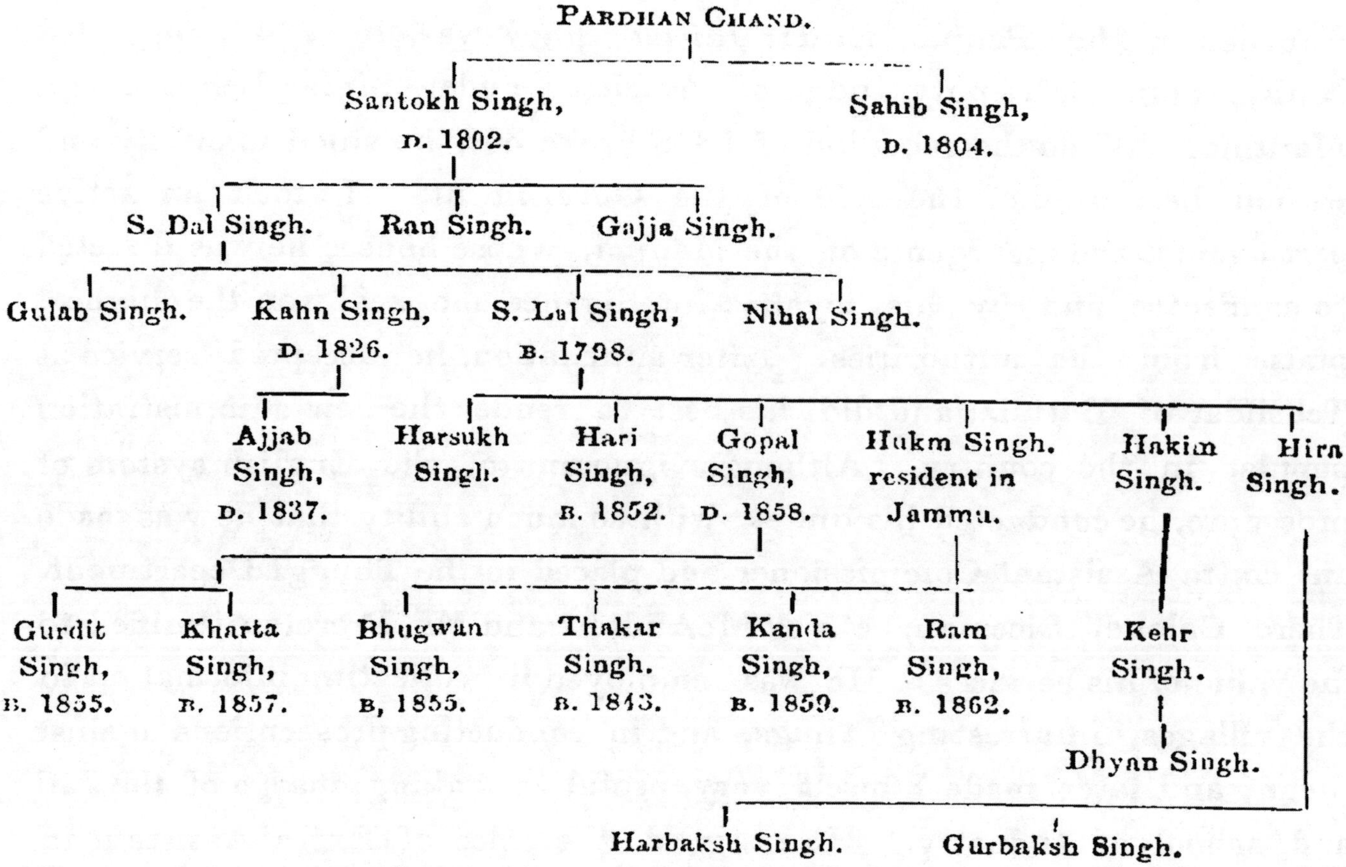

HISTORY OF THE FAMILY

The Talwandi, Khundah and Chamyari houses are all nearly connected, their immediate and common ancestor being Dhir or Randhir Chand, fourteenth in descent from Randhawah the founder of the tribe. He came to the Panjab about the year 1540, and near Battala, where others of his tribe had previously settled, he built a village which he called Jhanda after his eldest son.*

---

* There is a story which, however, the dates will not in any way support, that *Randhir Chand* or *Dhir* was a fellow emigrant of Ram Deo Bhatti, the founder of Battala; and that the name of Battala was given to his new town because he had *exchanged* its original site with *Randhir Chand* for that of Jhanda. Vide ante p. 201.

Turga the grandson of *Randhir Chand* left his father's village and founded Talwandi, the present residence of the family. About 1640, during the reign of Shah Jahan, *Bahar Chand*, the great grandson of *Turga*, received the office of chowdri of Tappa Dabha, which was held in the family until the time of *Pardhan Chand*.

Santokh Singh and *Sahib Singh*, the two sons of *Pardhan Chand* became Sikhs and joining the Kanheya misl, with Sirdar Jai Singh as their chief, they took possession of Talwandi and Dorangla. Little is known of the brothers who were not men of any importance. *Santokh Singh* died in 1802, and *Sahib Singh* two years later. Of the three sons of *Santokh Singh*, *Dal Singh* was the only one to obtain a share of his father's jagir. Talwandi and some neighbouring villages were left him; Dorangla and the Sialkot estate were seized by Ranjit Singh who also took possession of the estate of *Sahib Singh*.

Sirdar *Dal Singh* fought in most of the Maharaja's campaigns. During his life time he divided a portion of his estate between his sons; *Kahn Singh* receiving Rai Chak and Chainiwala, and *Lal Singh*, Talwandi. The Sirdar was killed in the Satlej campaign in 1845, and his jagirs were resumed.

Kahn Singh had died long before his father. He fell in the battle of Saidhu, in March, 1827, fighting against Syad Ahmad Shah. His only son was killed ten years later, in April 1837, in the battle of Jamrud.

Sirdar *Lal Singh* was born in 1798, and has seen a good deal of service. He fought in the Multan and Kashmir expeditions of 1818-19 and at Jamrud, where his nephew was slain.

In 1848, he was appointed to co-operate with Gurmani Lal, the 'adalati' or chief justice of the Manjha, holding the command of fifty horse.

In 1857, at the requisition of Government, he furnished ten horsemen for service in Hindostan and sent with them his two sons

Hira Singh and *Gopal Singh*. Both fought gallantly throughout the campaign: *Hira Singh* was made a Risaldar, and in 1859, on his retirement, received a present of 1800 Rs. and a grant of 50 acres of land, near Nurpur in the Kangra district. *Gopal Singh* was a Daffadar in 'Hodson's Horse.' He was killed in a skirmish with the rebels near Cawnpore, in 1858.

Sirdar *Lal Singh* owns half Talwandi in proprietary right, as also Shaikh Bahlol. The proprietary right of the other half of Talwandi is held by the descendants of *Sahib Singh*

THE RANDHAWAH FAMILY.

III.—SIRDAR GURDIT SINGH CHAMYARI.

- **Nar Singh.** d. 1805.
  - Karam Kour, m. Sirdar Amar Singh, Bhangi.
  - Sada Kour, m. S. Budh Singh.
  - Jai Singh d. 1841.
    - Gurmukh Singh.
    - Ranhai Singh.
  - Hari Singh.
    - Isa Singh.
      - Narayan Singh, b. 1847.
  - Ram Singh, d. 1804,
    - Gurdit Singh.
      - Partab Singh, b. 1823.
      - Nihal Singh, b. 1831.
        - Bhagwan Singh, b. 1857.
        - Sham Singh, b. 1853.
    - Hardit Singh, d. 1834,
      - Rajkour.
      - Jowahir Singh, b. 1823.
        - Gopal Singh, b. 1843.
        - Lehna Singh, b. 1852.
        - Narayan Singh, b. 1838.
          - Suchet Singh, b. 1859.

HISTORY OF THE FAMILY.

The founder of the Chamyari family was not *Nar Singh,* the true ancestor of the family, but Sawal Singh a distant connection, who, about the year 1750, adopted the Sikh faith and became a member of the Bhangi misl. He fought for his chief Hari Singh in many battles but does not appear to have neglected his personal interests as a few years later we find him the possessor of a large tract of country on the left bank of the Ravi, including Ajnala and Chamyari, or Chambyari, from which place the family took its name. Sawal Singh was killed in battle, leaving no issue; but his widow Mai Malkian made over the estate to *Nar Singh,* a cousin of her deceased husband and his devoted follower, a brave and enterprising man. This arrangement was confirmed by the 'Gurmatta' or Sikh National Council and *Nar Singh,* the acknowledged heir of all Sawal Singh's estates, went forth conquering and to conquer. Not content with the Amritsar side of the river, he invaded the Sialkot district and took possession of Pasrur and many villages in its vicinity. He then transferred his services to the rising Kanheya misl and at Nunar in the Sialkot district, had a sharp fight with his old allies. The young Sukarchakia chief, Mahan Singh, was on his side, and opposed to him were Jhanda Singh and all the bravest of the Bhangi Chiefs. The origin of the quarrel was trivial enough. *Nar Singh,* passing through one Jhanda Singh's villages, had turned his horses into a field of young corn to graze. The Bhangi Chief came down in great wrath and insisted on their removal. *Nar Singh* refused to interrupt his horses at their meal. This insult *Jhanda Singh* was unable to endure, and collecting all his men and making as many allies as he was able, he marched against *Nar Singh,* who was prepared to meet him. The fight was not decisive and soon afterwards *Nar Singh* disgusted his Sukarchakia friends by giving his daughter Karam Kour in marriage to Amar Singh, nephew of Sirdar Jhanda Singh. He did not, however, openly break with the Sukar chakias, and, in 1799, we find him assisting the son of Mahan Singh to capture Lahore.

Nar Singh died in 1806. His eldest son *Ram Singh* died some months before him, of cholera, in the camp of Jaswant Rao Holkar the Mahratta Chief. On his death Ranjit Singh took possession of the greater portion of the family estates, including the Sialkot villages and the Talukas of Saddowal, Ghaniwala and Chamyari. The town of Chamyari was left in the possession of the family who still hold it in proprietary right.

Chamyari is a very ancient town and there are several legends regarding its origin which may be given here.

One of these relates that Raja Salvahan of Sialkot, who reigned about 90 A. D., passing with his retinue near the spot where Chamyari now stands saw a young girl drawing water at a well. Struck by her marvellous beauty he enquired her name, and found that it was Chamba, and that she was the daughter of the Rajput Chief of the district. Salvahan asked the girl in marriage, but her father declined as the Raja's name was a terror throughout the Panjab to both parents and daughters, as he was accustomed to take a new wife every day and maidens were becoming scarce in the land. But the Raja was not to be denied. He swore that if Chamba was only given to him, he would not marry again for eight days, and to these reasonable terms the father consented. But by the eighth day, Raja Salvahan had grown so deeply enamoured of the beautiful Chamba, that he was content to divorce all his other wives. and to keep her only for life, and to glorify his love and render it immortal, he built around the well, where he had first seen her drawing water, the town of Chamyari, which he called after her name.

Another story asserts that Chambyari or Chamyari was named after the caste of Raja Salvahan's favourite wife, whose name was Luna, the daughter of Raja Pipa of Papnakhah, a Champal Rajput. She was the mother of Risalu, from whom Sialkot was formerly called Risalkot. Luna was remarkable for her beauty, though not for her virtue, as the following story will show. Ichhran, another of Raja Salvahan's many wives became the mother of a beautiful boy, who was named Puran. The astrologers, who had assembled at the palace to draw the horoscope of the new-born infant, declared that the greatest calamities would befal him should he be seen by his father before his twelfth birthday. In those days astrologers were believed, and a high tower was accordingly built, in which the boy was carefully guarded till the twelve years had come, as the attendants thought, to an end, when they brought him to his delighted father. But one day had been omitted from the calculation; the twelve years had not expired.

When Luna saw the lovely boy she fell in love with him at once. This was less her fault than that of the stars, and at last, unable to control herself she caught Puran in her arms and told him all her love. He had not been taught the art of love in his solitary tower, and only laughed at Luna's distress and ran away, while she, enraged at the repulse, and her love turning to hatred, tore her hair and clothes, and when the Raja came in, told him, with weeping eyes, that Puran had attempted her virtue. The Raja made no enquiries, but straightway ordered that the boy should be taken into the jungle and there put to death. As the poor little fellow was being carried off by the executioners he begged hard for his life ; but for long begged in vain. At length the men promised not to kill him ; but they cut off both his hands and threw him down a well, * where they left him to die. But the life of Puran was miraculously preserved, and about two years afterwards the great magician Ghorakh Nath came to the place with his twelve thousand disciples. One of these, drawing water from the well, saw the boy and having taken him out, carried him to the magician, who by enchantments replaced his hands. Ghorakh Nath then brought Puran to the palace, and restored to sight Ichhran, who had become blind with weeping for the untimely fate of her son. Raja Salvahan, confounded by these prodigies, wished to resign the crown to his son, but Puran would not accept the offer, and renouncing the world became a disciple of Ghorakh Nath with whom he remained until his death. †

Such are the legends regarding the founding of Chamyari, which is undoubtedly of great antiquity. It was almost entirely destroyed in the great inundation, about a thousand years ago, when the five rivers of the Panjab united, but was rebuilt under the Emperors. In 1722, it was burnt down by the Sikhs, and was still in ruins when it came into the possession of *Nar Singh* who restored and enlarged it.

---

* This well is still to be seen near Sialkot.

† Both these legends have somewhat an Arabian Nights' complexion. But they have been current in the Panjab for many hundred years, and it is probable that some of the stories of the Arabian Nights had an Indian derivation.

On the death of the widow of *Nar Singh* and of *Hari Singh* his second son, the little estate left to the family was again reduced, and the whole was resumed by Maharaja Sher Singh, on the death of *Jai Singh*, in 1841.

Sirdar *Gurdit Singh*, who was Commandant of Maharaja Dalip Singh's body guard, holds a jagir at Dhariwal near Ajnala, worth 1200 Rs. per annum, half of which lapses at his death. His two sons *Partab Singh* and *Nihal Singh* joined the rebels in 1848, and lost their jagirs. *Khem Kour*, widow of Sirdar *Jai Singh*, receives a pension of 500 Rs. per annum.

THE RANDHAWA FAMILY.

IV.—Hari Singh, Dodia.

- **Jamal.**
  - Mehr Chand.
    - Nathu.
    - Sirdar Gurbaksh Singh. D. 1795.
      - Sirdar Sudh Singh. D. 1813. M. D. Sirdar Chet Singh Kalianwala.
        - Bibi Rupan M. Fatah Singh of Chittarghar.
      - Dyal Singh.
        - Joala Singh. B. 1834.
  - Sajana.
    - Shian.
    - Sipha.
      - Sirdar Gajja Singh. D. 1822.
        - Hari Singh. B. 1809.
          - Joala Singh. B. 1834. M. D. Sultan Singh Kahlu.
            - Bishan Singh. B. 1856. betrothed to D. of Kesar Singh Chinah.
            - Isar Singh D. 1862.
          - Sant Singh M. D. Sirdar Mehtab Singh Sindhu.
            - Kehr Singh D. 1862.
          - B. Gulab Kour.
          - B. Bishan Kour.
        - Nidhan Singh.
        - Gurdit Singh.
        - B. Chand Kour M. Ram Singh Bheraniah.
      - Dhyan Singh. D. 1837.

HISTORY OF THE FAMILY.

The village of Doda is situated in the Shakarghar Parganah of the Gurdaspur District, and like that of Jhanda was founded by Dhir Randhawa. Jhanda was the original colony, and Doda was populated from it. The Dodia family ploughed and sowed their fields, as simple husbandmen, for some generations, till *Gurbaksh Singh,* in the early days of Sikh power, adopted the new faith, and the profession of arms. He, with his brother joined the Bhangi confederacy, and soon became a chief of some note. He was engaged in perpetual warfare with his neighbours and in one of his expeditions against Imami of the Paddah tribe, his elder brother *Nathu* was slain. *Gurbaksh Singh* acquired a large tract of country in the neighbourhood of Doda, including Sadhanwal, Ranjrur, Jassar and Bhopalwala, and also took possession of part of the Jammu territory, building a fort only a few miles from the city of Jammu itself. He died about 1795, and was succeeded by his son *Sudh Singh*, who also became a man of some importance, and added largely to the family possessions.

Both *Sudh Singh* and his father were bitter enemies of the Jammu Raja, and this enmity nearly cost *Sudh Singh* his life, for on one occasion, as he was riding to Lala Chak, about five miles from Jammu, he fell into an ambush laid for him by Ranjit Deo, and was fired at by a party of the Raja's troops. His horse was wounded in the neck : one ball lodged in *Sudh Singh's* saddle, another struck the handle of his sword, and it was with difficulty that he made his escape. He died in 1813, and his family knowing that they could not successfully oppose Ranjit Singh, sent *Gajja Singh*, cousin of *Budh Singh*, who had left no male issue, to Lahore, with presents of two lakhs of rupees, an elephant and valuable horses and offers of submission. Ranjit Singh, however, hearing of *Sudh Singh's* death, had already sent a force under Ganda Singh, Safi, to seize the fort of Jassar situated about five miles from Doda. The family represented how matters stood and begged for delay, till the pleasure of the Maharaja should be known, but Ganda Singh was not to be stayed and directed an immediate assault upon the fort, from which he was repulsed with loss. When Ranjit Singh heard of this failure he laughed and said that "the 'safi' had lost his 'safa'." The joke requires explanation. Ganda Singh, before he was raised to the command of a regiment was a 'safi' or man employed to brush away flies, and 'safa' is a cloth used as a turban, the loss of which among all orientals is considered disgraceful. Ranjit Singh made but few jokes and the success of this one pleased him so much that *Gajja Singh* was well received, and twenty five villages were released in his favour, subject to the service of eighteen sowars. He accompanied the Maharaja on his expeditions against Multan and Kashmir, and fought under Diwan Mokham Chand in the battle of Attock, in 1813, and was also present at the siege of Mankera. He died the year after this last expedition, in 1822, when all his jagirs were resumed by the Maharaja.

Hari Singh his eldest son was thus almost reduced to poverty, and took service with the Sindhanwalia chiefs, Lehna Singh and Shamsher Singh, from whom he eventually received the command of 50 sowars. He fought gallantly at Jamrud, where Hari Singh Nalwa was slain, and his conduct on this occasion was rewarded by Ranjit Singh.

During the Satlej campaign he served under Sirdar Shamsher Singh Sindhanwalia, and after the occupation of Lahore, he accompanied that chief and Lieut. Edwardes to Bannu, on a Salary of 600 Rs. a year. When the rebellion broke out at Multan, *Hari Singh* marched there with his superior and joined the rebels with Raja Sher Singh. He asserts, indeed, that he attempted, with Commandant Karam Baksh of Batala, to escape from the rebel camp, and that they had even commenced their flight, when they were seen by the enemy: Karam Baksh, who was riding first, was shot dead, and *Hari Singh* himself was taken prisoner. Whatever may be the truth of this story, it is certain that *Hari Singh* fought on the rebel side at Ramnagar and Gujrat, and accordingly his village of Fatowal, worth 600 Rs., and a portion of Doda were resumed. His cash pension of 500 Rs., was also confiscated, but in 1852 he received a cash pension of 100 Rs. which he still enjoys.

The share in the village of Doda possessed by *Ind Kour* the last surviving widow of Sirdar *Sudh Singh*, was not resumed, till the death of that lady some years afterwards.

Joala Singh, son of *Hari Singh*, entered the corps known as the 'Suraj Mukhi' at Amballa. He is now in the Police.

Sant Singh, another son, entered 'Hodson's Horse,' in 1857, and did good service in Hindoostan. In 1860 he was compelled to retire on account of ill health.

THE RANDHAWA FAMILY.

V.—Nand Singh Kathu-Nangal.

Sahib Singh.
D. 1800.

- Jit Singh.
  - Gulab Singh.
    - Nand Singh.
      - Daughter betrothed to Mal Singh, Paralia.
  - Sukha Singh.
    - Budha Singh.
    - Kahn Singh.
- Budh Singh.
  - Partab Singh. D. 1844.

HISTORY OF THE FAMILY.

Chowdhri *Dalah,* tenth in descent from Randhawa, founded the village of Chavinda in the Amritsar district. His four sons, *Gaggu, Jabhu, Ram* and *Lakhan* founded respectively the villages of Kathu-Nangal, Sahniwali, Wariam-Nangal and Rupowali. *Sahib Singh,* who took the ' pahal ' and became a Sikh about the year 1770, was the great grandson of *Gaggu.* He joined Sirdar Jai Singh Kanheya, and took possession of about thirty villages in the neighbourhood of Kathu-Nangal, Dharamkot and Chakowal. *Sahib Singh* was a gallant man and bore the scars of fourteen wounds. He fought on the side of the Kanheyas in all their quarrels, and fell at last before the fort of Atalghar, in a skirmish with the Ramgharia troops. His two sons *Jit Singh* and *Budh Singh* succeeded to his estate, but the elder of these was killed soon afterwards at Lodha-Mandowala, fighting against the Ramgharias who had slain his father.

Budh Singh was one of the last of the Kanheya Sirdars to tender his allegiance to Ranjit Singh, by whom he and the sons of *Jit Singh* were allowed to retain their estates. He served in the army, in Hazara, Yusafzai, and Kashmir, till 1823, when he was obliged to retire through ill health, and the Maharaja resumed all his villages except Ladha-Manda worth 3000 Rs. and a portion of Kathu-Nangal. He died three years later, and his only son *Partab Singh* was placed in the 'Ghorchara Kalan' Regiment, and was afterward transferred as Adjutant to the Pohvindia Regiment, of which he became Commandant, in 1840. In 1842, he was made Colonel and received a grant of the jagir of Khiali, worth 1000 Rs. He died without issue, in 1844.

None others of the family were in any way distinguished. *Nand Singh,* the present representative, resigned the service and lost his jagir in 1848. He resides at Kathu-Nangal where he possesses a well and half the proprietary rights of the village.

THE RANDHAWA FAMILY.

VI.—Sirdar Sahib Singh Isapuria.

Sirdar Dasonda Singh.
|
Sirdar Bhaggat Singh.
|
Sirdar Ram Singh.
D. 1836.
|
Sirdar Sahib Singh.
B. 1805.
|
Akwak Singh.
B. 1834.

HISTORY OF THE FAMILY.

The last family of the Randhawa clan of sufficient importance to be mentioned here is that of Isapur. Its founder *Dasonda Singh* having become a Sikh in 1730, entered the service of Adina Beg with whom he remained till 1758.

He then joined the Bhangi confederacy, and through the influence of Chowdri Raman, a Randhawa Rajput and a distant relative, he obtained a jagir worth about 20,000 Rs. including the village of Isapur, which has ever since remained in the family, and from which *Dasonda Singh* took his family name. His son *Bhaggat Singh* preserved the old estate and acquired new jagirs; and Sirdar *Ram Singh*, about the year 1804, joined Ranjit Singh, who confirmed to him the villages of Isapur, Bolah, Suran, and others in the Amritsar District. He did good service on several occasions, and in 1818, received the grant of jagirs to the value of five lakhs of rupees, subject to the service of 700 horsemen and 2,000 infantry. This was a special grant for the Kashmir campaign, and was resumed in 1821 after the fall of Mankera.

In 1822, *Ram Singh* was placed under the orders of Prince Kharrak Singh, with whom he remained till 1824, he was transferred to Raja

Suchet Singh's division. He served in Kulu, Kangra, and in most of the Maharaja's numerous campaigns, and died in 1836. His son *Sahib Singh* had been for some time in Government employ at the time of his father's death, at which time he was serving with Raja Suchet Singh, on a salary of 2000 Rs. per annum. This was raised to 7,923 Rs. including Isapur and some other villages of the original estate.

Sahib Singh was present at the second seige of Multan in 1818, and in Kashmir, in the following year. He also served under Prince Kharrak Singh and Raja Suchet Singh, at Munkera, Bannu, Yusafzai, Syduki, and the Derajat. After the Satlej campaign his estate was cut down to 5231 Rs. subject to the service of 10 sowars, and also charged with pensions to his father's widows.

In 1847, he was sent in command of 100 horsemen to the Manjha to assist Lala Mangalsen, brother of Diwan Rattan Chand Darhiwala, in the collection of the revenue, and afterwards he proceeded to Hazara under Captain Abbott. He remained faithful to Government during the disturbances of 1848-49, and has been spoken of in the highest terms by many English Officers.

In 1851, a portion of his jagirs, consisting of Isapur, Bolah, Saggal and Suran, worth 2597 Rs., exclusive of some subordinate rent-free holdings in the name of other members of his family, was confirmed to him for life. The villages of Isapur, Saggal, and Suran, worth 1386 Rs. descend to his legitimate male heirs in perpetuity.

His only son *Akwak Singh* was first employed under the English Government as a Jemadar of Police. In 1857, he was made Risaldar and sent to Bannu. He behaved very well during the disturbances and received an extra Buhadari allowance for his gallant conduct. He is now a Risaldar at Kohat in receipt of 280 Rs. a month.

Sirdar Sahib Singh resides at Isapur, in the Amritsar District.

GENERAL HARSUKH RAI.

LACHI RAM.
- Shanat Ram.
  - Jita Mal.
    - Ganda Mal.
      - Sadda Singh.
      - Hoshnak Rai.
      - Gurdit Singh.
        - General Harsukh Rai, B. 1810.
          - Jiun Das, B. 1863.
        - Ram Das.
      - Ram Rakha Mal.
      - Ram Rang.

HISTORY OF THE FAMILY.

Lachi Ram, a respectable Katri of the Kapur tribe, left Lahore about the year 1740 for Hafizabad, where he married and settled, and where his descendants have since resided. The first of the family to take service under the Sikh Government was *Gurdit Singh*, who entered the cavalry, under Prince Kharrak Singh, on a salary of 2000 Rs. per annum. He married a daughter of Lala Nanak Chand, elder brother of Diwan Sawan Mal, Nazim of Multan, and had two sons, one of whom was *Hursukh Rai*. His brothers were not men of any note.

Ram Rang married the daughter of Lala Gurmukh Rai, another brother of Diwan Sawan Mal, and served under his kinsman as Kardar, and afterwards as Commandant at Dera Ghazi Khan, on a salary of 1800 Rs. per annum.

Ram Rakha Mall, who is still living, was also a kardar under Sawan Mall.

Harsukh Rai went to Multan in 1833, and was made 'adalati' or judge by the Diwan, and soon afterwards received a military appointment. But he only remained there for two years, when failing to obtain leave of absence, he threw up his appointment in disgust and came to Lahore, where, in 1836, through the favour of Raja Dhyan Singh, he obtained a lucrative post about court, which he held till 1839, when he was sent to Multan in charge of the Salt customs: but this appointment he only held four months. Maharaja Sher Singh made him Kardar of Sheikhapurah, on a salary of 1800 Rs. per annum; but he fell into disgrace with his patron Raja Dhyan Singh, whose influence was used to procure his dismissal, in 1841. He was then appointed Kardar of Haweli, near Pak Pattan, but his administration was very unpopular. He made Sirdar Jowahir Singh, the minister, his enemy, by his intrigues with Prince Peshora Singh, who after the death of his brother in July, 1843, had fled to Ludhiana; and *Harsukh Rai* was not only dismissed from his employment, but his jagirs and property were confiscated.

When Raja Lal Singh rose to power, *Harsukh Rai* again came into favour; he was created General and received command of the brigade which Lal Singh had begun to form in the hope that it, being his own creation, would stand by him in any new revolution. He was also made Kardar at Patti, at the south western extremity of the Lahore District, in spite of the opposition of his enemies at court, who asserted that if the ruin of any place was desired, it was sufficient to send *Harsukh Rai* there. But the general, though by no means scrupulous, was energetic, and a good officer. His brother *Ram Das* conducted most of the civil work at Patti, while *Harsukh Rai* remained at Lahore, till, at the close of the year, Raja Lal Singh fell from power, and his protege fell with him. The new brigade, of which only one regiment, the Ram Paltan, had been formed, was broken up, and at the same time the General lost the Kardarship of Patti.

Soon after the outbreak at Multan, in 1848, *Harsukh Rai* was again sent, by the desire of Colonel H. Lawrence, to the Manjha, as Kardar, on 4310 Rs. per annum. It was a time when energy, resolution and fidelity were invaluable, and the Resident thought that *Harsukh*

Rai could be depended upon for their exercise. The selection was fully justified by the result. With every temptation to disloyalty, for the rebel governor of Multan was his connection, and his own brother was in the hostile ranks, *Harsukh Rai* performed his duty to the Government faithfully, and through all these troublous days did good and zealous service. On the annexation of the Panjab, his jagir, worth 1790 Rs. was maintained for life, and he was made Tehsildar, receiving an exceptional allowance of 428 Rs.

In 1857, he was stationed at Amritsar, where he was very active, pursuing the mutineers of the 26th Native Infantry and raising the country against them. For this he received from Government a grant of 1000 Rs. and an increase to his allowances. In 1859, *Harsukh Rai* was raised to the rank of Extra Assistant Commissioner, and posted to the Shahpur district. He has been since successively at Mianwali, Gurdaspur and Gujranwala, at which last place he was stationed in 1861. He now fears that he will be compelled to resign the public service, as his sight, which has long been bad, is altogether failing him. His only son living is a boy of two years of age.

SIRDAR FATAH SINGH THEPURIA.

- SIRDAR MILKA SINGH. D. 1804.
  - Sirdar Jiun Singh. D. 1813.
    - Sirdar Anand Singh. D. 1831.
      - Sirdar Fatah Singh. B. 1823.
        - Shamsher Singh. B. 1843.
          - B. Nihal Kour. betrothed to Bhagwan Singh Chabal.
        - B. Attar Kour M. S. Lehna Singh. Povindia.
    - Sirdar Gurmukh Singh. D. 1840
      - B. Mehtab Kour M. Lal Singh Dihlon.
    - Sirdar Ram Singh. D. 1816.

HISTORY OF THE FAMILY.

Sirdar *Milka Singh* was one of the most powerful of the Sikh chiefs who lived during the latter half of the last century. His native place was Kalcki near Kassur, but leaving this he founded the village of Thepur and took possession of Narwar, Jandhir, Dallen and other villages; some in the Lahore district, in the neighbourhood of Thepur; others in the Gujranwala and Gujrat districts. Not content with these possessions, he marched to the northward, and seized Rawalpindi, then an insignificant place inhabited by Rawal mendicants. *Milka Singh* perceived how admirably Rawal pindi was situated and fixed his head quarters there, building new houses and in some measure fortifying the town. Rawalpindi was at this time an undesirable possession. It was on the highway into India, exposed to the attacks of Afghan invaders, and the surrounding country was held by fierce and warlike tribes. But *Milka*

Singh held his own. He conquered a tract of country around Rawalpindi worth three lakhs a year, and even the tribes of Hazara had respect for his name and power. He had adopted the cognomen of Thepuria from the village he had founded; but in the north he was known as *Milka Singh Pindiwala,* and this name still belongs to the family.

He died in 1804. Ranjit Singh, whom *Milka Singh* had joined in several expeditions, did not feel strong enough to seize the estates of his old friend whom he used to call 'Baba' or grandfather, and was compelled to confirm them to *Jiun Singh*, his only son.

Of this Sirdar there is little to record. He fought during the first Kashmir campaign of 1814, and died the next year,

Anand Singh the eldest of *Jiun Singh's* three sons succeeded to a portion of his father's jagirs. The Maharaja resumed 2,92,000 Rs. and left only 8000 Rs. of the old estate, granting new jagirs to the value of 42,000 Rs. in the Firozpur district, near Zafarwal, subject to the service of one hundred horsemen. *Ram Singh*, who survived his father only one year, had a jagir assigned to him in Hazara, and *Gurmukh Singh* received Sultani and Kalri, worth 2,000 Rs. in the Gurdaspur district. The force which Sirdars *Milka Singh* and *Jiun Singh* had kept up, was transferred to the service of the state, and placed under Sirdar Attar Singh Sindhanwalia, bearing the name of the Derah Pindiwala, and *Gurmukh Singh* received an appointment in it. In December, 1840, shortly after General Ventura had taken the fort of Kamlaghar in Mandi, the people of Kulu rose in revolt; cut off and annihilated four companies of the Pindiwala and killed *Gurmukh Singh*, who was in command. *Anand Singh* died in 1831. His only son *Fatah Singh* was then a boy of eight years of age, and in 1836, the Maharaja reduced his jagir to 13,000 Rs. subject to the service of twenty horse. The villages which were left were ten in number: Thepur, Kila Sirdar Dahloki and Kaleki in the Lahore District; Kehli and Raja Tal in Amritsar; Loli, Lohri and Duni in Sialkot, and Kassoki and Samobala in Gujranwala.

On the annexation of the Panjab, the personal jagir of *Fatah Singh*, worth 3000 Rs. was confirmed to him for life, one quarter to descend to his sons.

5,100 Rs. were also confirmed to the two widows of *Anand Singh* and the widows of *Gurmukh Singh* and *Jiun Singh*. *Mai Sadda Kour*, step mother of *Fatah Singh*, has since died, and her pension of 2175 Rs. has lapsed to Government.

Sirdar *Fatah Singh* resides at Thepur, in the Lahore District.

SIRDAR SADHO SINGH PADHANIA.

- HIRA.
  - Talok.
    - Sukha Singh. D. 1803.
      - Chanda Singh.
      - Sirdar Mit Singh. D. 1813.
        - B. Rup Kour. M. Kai Singh. Kahlon.
        - B. Rattan Kour. M. Sirdar Jowahir Singh. Randhawa.
        - S. Joala Singh. D. 1835.
          - S. Hardit Singh. D. 1860.
            - S. Sadho Singh. B. 1851.
      - Sahib Singh.
      - Ganda Singh.
        - Ram Singh.
          - Kahn Singh.
            - Atma Singh. B. 1834.
            - Kirpa Singh. B 1827.
              - Lakha Singh. B. 1851.
            - Badal Singh. B. 1823.
              - Gurbaksh Singh. B. 1850.
            - B. Kishan Kour. M. Sahib Singh. Kulbajwa.
          - B. Anup Kour. M. Dal Singh. Randhawa.

HISTORY OF THE FAMILY.

One of the principal Jat families of the Manjha is the Sindhu, and to this family Sirdar *Sadho Singh* belongs. Its founder Sindhu appears to have been of Rajput origin, but during the 13th century emigrated from Ghazni in Afghanistan to the Manjha where he settled with his family. How his ancestors became first resident in Afghanistan is uncertain, but in all probability they were among the numerous Hindu captives that Sultan Mahmud carried away with him after his Indian expeditions, and a large colony of whom he planted in his new and beautiful capital of Ghazni. Some of the Sindhu Jats assert that it was

Ghazni, in Southern India, from which their ancestor emigrated, but this story is improbable and is entirely unsupported by proof.

Changa, the thirteenth in descent from Sindhu, was an influential Chowdri, and founded, some fifteen miles south east of Lahore, the village of Padhana, where the family still resides. He was the chief of the thirty Jat chowdris and headmen, who went on a mission to the Emperor Akbar, to arrange the marriage of that monarch with a daughter of Mir Mitta Dhariwal, a Zamindar of Dowla Kangra, near Wadni, in the Firozpur district. The Emperor first saw the girl, who was very beautiful, at her village well. She had a pitcher of water on her head, yet contrived to place her foot upon the rope of a refractory and runaway heifer, and hold it captive till its owner came up. Akbar was so delighted with this feat of strength and skill that he wished to marry her, but her father declined the honour, without the consent of his caste. He assembled a committee of seventy one lambardars and chowdris; thirty five Jats and thirty six Rajputs, to decide the question. The Rajputs considered the alliance disgraceful; but the Jats, with Changa at their head, approved of it, and the marriage took place accordingly. Akbar rewarded the thirty five with lands and honours; and these were the ancestors of all the Jat families in the Panjab, of any consideration; so much so, that the chief Jat families are called 'painti,' i. e. thirty five; and the chief Rajput families 'chhati,' i. e. thirty six, at the present day. Changa, who from his antecedents might be expected to have been among the 'chhati,' was on the contrary found in the ranks of the Jats. His family had been so long Jat cultivators, that their Rajput prejudices had died away. He was a man of considerable influence and his son succeeded to his power; but his grandson Dibba was, during the reign of Jahangir, degraded from the office of chowdri for murder.

When the Sikhs rose to power, *Sukha Singh*, who was then the representative of the family, with his two sons *Mit Singh* and *Sahib Singh*, joined the popular faith. *Mit Singh* entered the service of Sirdar Mahan Singh Sukarchakia, and *Sahib Singh* that of Sirdar Gujar Singh of

Lahore. From the Sukarchakia leader *Mit Singh* received an estate worth 12,000 Rs., and on Mahan Singh's death he followed the fortunes of the young Ranjit Singh, and was with him at the capture of Lahore, in 1799. He later accompanied the Kassur expedition and rose high in favour with his master, who gave him many valuable estates. In 1814, he was in command of the rear guard of the army during its retreat from Kashmir. The tribes came down in force and handled *Mit Singh's* division very severely, and wounded the Sirdar himself mortally. Ranjit Singh was much grieved at his loss, and swore to befriend his son *Joala Singh*, to whom, accordingly, all his father's possessions were confirmed; and in addition he received a new jagir, worth 1,25,000 Rs., at Haripur Golehr in Kangra.

Sirdar *Joala Singh* was a brave and an able man. He was present at the capture of Multan, in 1818, and distinguished himself at Mankera, Tirah, Kotkapura and Kashmir; and on one occasion, being in charge of the Attock fort, he gallantly held out, with a few hundred horsemen, against the whole Afghan army.

In 1829, he was struck by paralysis, and though he lived till 1835, he was no longer able to serve in the field or to attend at darbar. His illness is said to have been brought on in the following manner. The troops occupying the Kangra fort had mutinied; and the Maharaja sent *Joala Singh*, who was very popular with the army, to induce them to return to their duty. The fort was too strong to reduce, and *Joala Singh* was compelled to confine himself to arguments; and, at length, on solemn promises of full pardon, persuaded the mutineers to submit. But the Maharaja cared nothing for the pledged word of *Joala Singh*. He put the ringleaders to death, and fined and degraded the other mutineers. This conduct so mortified *Joala Singh*, who considered his honor lost, that it brought on the illness from which he never recovered.

There is no one of the Sikh Sirdars whose name is more renowned for generosity and munificence than *Joala Singh*. The young daughter of his cousin *Kahn Singh,* who had died in very embarrassed circumstances, *Joala Singh* adopted as his own. He gave her a large dowry, and is said to have spent upwards of a lakh of rupees upon her marriage. At the commencement of his last illness, he distributed an equally large sum of money among the fakirs and Brahmans.

Nor was he less liberal to strangers than to his own family as the following story will show.

When Prince Sher Singh had failed so signally in his administration of Kashmir, the Maharaja looked about for victims upon whom to avenge the failure. Among others, the principal agent of the Prince, Diwan Baisakha Singh Chamyariwala, was ordered to Lahore; his accounts were declared fraudulent, and he was fined 1,25,000 Rs. Without enquiry into the proofs against him, there is no doubt the fine was deserved, for at that time Kashmir was considered by the Sikh officials as a sheep fold under the protection of the wolves. But the Diwan proclaimed that he was unable to pay the fine. The Maharaja ordered him to be flogged until he should discover where his wealth was concealed. The unhappy wretch was dragged out of the presence, past the 'deorhi,' or antechamber, where were seated Raja Dhian Singh, *Joala Singh* and many other chiefs. When Diwan Baisakha Singh saw them, he implored their intercession with the Maharaja, and threw himself before them, crying out "I am your cow. Save me!" But no one took the slightest notice of him, except Sirdar *Joala Singh.* He listened to the whole story, and then had the courage to go before the Maharaja, and beg for the remission of the punishment, offering himself to pay the whole fine. Ranjit Singh consented, and being utterly without the power of appreciating a noble and magnanimous action, recovered the fine, to the last rupee, from *Joala Singh,* whom, as might have been supposed, the Diwan forgot ever to pay.

As another instance of his generosity, it may be mentioned that in his ancestral village of Padhana, he never took rent or revenue from any of his own, the Sindhu tribe.

On the death of *Joala Singh*, the Maharaja resumed the larger portion of his jagir, for *Hardit Singh*, the Sirdar's only son, was of weak intellect, and although he used to attend at court, yet he was unable to hold any independent command. He, however, retained estates worth 27,425 Rs., subject to the service of one hundred horsemen.

In 1848, this contingent was in Hazara, with Sirdar Chattar Singh Attariwala, when he rebelled. Most of the men remained true to Government, and on the annexation of the Panjab, *Hardit Singh* and his mother were allowed to retain an estate worth 9,000 Rs., per annum.

In 1860, *Hardit Singh* died, leaving one son, *Sadho Singh*, a boy of thirteen years, now a student in the Government College at Lahore. He holds Padhana, worth 2,000 Rs., in perpetuity, and represents one of the best of the Jat families, a family wealthy and respected more than three hundred years ago.

SIRDAR JASSA SINGH, NAOSHEHRA NANGALI.

CHUHAR SINGH.

S. Mirza Singh.

- S. Jit Singh. B. 1845.
  - Wasawa Singh. B. 1847.
    - One daughter. infant,
- S. Kahn Singh.
  - S. Jassa Singh. B. 1793.
    - Harnam Singh. B. 1835.

HISTORY OF THE FAMILY.

Like the Majithia chiefs, Sirdar *Jassa Singh* is of the Shergil Jat tribe. Chowdhri *Sarwani*, the fifteenth in descent from Sher, the founder of the tribe, built the village of Naoshehra, otherwise known as Raipur Sarwani, during the reign of the Emperor Shahjahan, and was permitted to hold it, rent-free, as remuneration for collecting the revenue of the surrounding districts. For several generations the family held the office of Chowdhri, paying the revenue into the imperial treasury, until *Mirza Singh* joined the confederacy of Sirdars Jai Singh and Hakikat Singh, Kanheya, about 1752, and obtained, as his share of the conquered territory, the villages of Rattangarh ; Uchak ; Bhori ; Bhikuchak ; Rahmpur ; Saluwal ; Malkanah and several others, worth 15,000 Rs. per annum.

Mirza Singh died in 1787, and Sirdar Jaimal Singh, son of Hakikat Singh, unmindful of the many and great services of the deceased, resumed the larger portion of his estates, and Sirdar Fatah Singh Kanheya still further reduced them. When however the sons of *Mirza Singh* grew up, Sirdar Nidhan Singh Kanheya granted them Madhapur and Salowal in the Hoshiarpur district, worth 1,500 Rs. and Mai Sadda Kour, the mother-in-law of Ranjit Singh, gave to *Kahn Singh* the villages of Bhoghar, Barialah and Kohalah, worth 2,000 Rs. When Ranjit Singh seized the possessions of the Kanheya misl, *Kahn Singh* lost the last named villages, but he was made an officer in the Irregular Cavalry, and fought with his regiment at Kassur and in the Kangra expedition of 1809.

When Sirdar Desa Singh Majithia was made Governor of all the hill districts between the Beas and the Satlej, *Kahn Singh* was placed under his orders, and from that time both he and his son *Jassa Singh* remained in the service of the Majithia chiefs. They accompanied them in the field; filled civil offices under them; and their history differs in no important respect from that of their feudal lords.

Sirdar *Jassa Singh* had for two years charge of the Sikh Temple at Amritsar, under Sirdar Lehna Singh Majithia. After Lehna Singh's departure for Benares, *Jassa Singh* remained in the employ of the Lahore Darbar; but on the annexation of the Panjab was thrown out of employ and his cash pension of 770 Rs. was resumed.

He now holds jagirs to the value of 2,800 Rs. chiefly in the Gurdaspur district, at Malkanah; Hyati, Salowal; Behrumpur, Malkahwalah; Rattangarh and Sherghar, besides two wells at Naoshehra Nangal, where he usually resides. These jagirs are upheld in perpetuity, *Jassa Singh* paying one quarter and his heirs half revenue rates.

Harnam Singh, the only son of Sirdar *Jassa Singh,* is a Deputy Inspector of Police.

Jit Singh, the brother of *Kahn Singh,* was never under the Majithia chiefs. He was, soon after the death of his father, made a commandant of cavalry in Raja Hira Singh's brigade, inheriting a half share of his father's estate. He served at Multan, Bannu, Peshawar and elsewhere, but was not a man of any note.

He was killed in 1846, leaving one son *Wasawa Singh,* then a child six months old.

DIWAN RATTAN CHAND DARHIWALA.

LALA JOALA NATH.

Lala Karam Chand.

- Diwan Tara Chand. D. 1858.
- Lala Mangalsen D. 1864
  - Lala Budha Mal. B. 1858.
- Diwan Rattan Chand B. 1808.
  - Palwan Das B. 1838.
    - Raj Kour. B. 1858.
  - Rup Chand B. 1844.
  - Barkat Ram. B. 1855.
- Lala Har Nam Das. B. 1836.

HISTORY OF THE FAMILY.

The family of *Rattan Chand Darhiwala,* came originally from Payal, a village situated between Ludhianah and Pattialah, and held various revenue appointments under the Muhammadan Emperors. When the Sikhs rose to power *Joala Nath* entered the service of Sirdar Charrat Singh Sukarchakia, as a munshi, and remained with him and his son Mahan Singh till his death. *Karam Chand* was first employed by Sirdar Bishan Singh Kalal, the confidential agent of Maharaja Ranjit Singh, who retired, in the year 1813, to Benares, where he died. *Karam Chand* in course of time was promoted to offices of trust under the Maharaja. He accompanied him, in 1805, on his secret visit to Hardwar, and the following year was employed as an agent in the arrangements concluded between the Lahore State and the Sikh chiefs south of the Satlej. He also assisted in drawing up the Treaty the 25th April 1809, with the British Government. Sometime before he had been placed at the head of the Lahore office, if that can be called an office where no accounts were regularly kept. Pawani Dass first introduced a system of accounts, in 1809, from which time *Karam Chand* worked under him, and remained in the office till his death in 1836.

His eldest son *Tara Chand* had entered the service of Government when very young, and his first employment was in Peshawar, under Diwan Kirpa Ram, in 1822. He was sent, in the following year, to Kangra, with civil and military authority, to collect the revenue, and, in 1832, was posted at Firozpur to reduce the turbulent inhabitants of that district to order, and to suppress dacoity, which had become very common. *Tara Chand* was afterwards made Diwan and placed in charge of Bannu, Tank, and Derah Ismail Khan. His administration here was not very successful. Of all the frontier chiefs, no one was more hostile to the Sikhs than Dilassah Khan of Bannu. Diwan *Tara Chand*, who had with him the flower of the Sikh chivalry; the chiefs of Attari, Majitha, Nakka and Botala, led his force of eight thousand men and twelve guns against the little fort of Dilassah Khan, but was ignominiously repulsed with a loss of three hundred killed, including the younger Jai Singh Attariwala, and five hundred wounded. When the Maharaja heard of this repulse, he was very indignant, and fined the Diwan 7000 Rs. *Tara Chand* had also quarreled with Raja Suchet Singh, who was in authority in the Derajat, and who could not endure the Diwan's independent spirit; so *TaraChand*, making a virtue of necessity, and pleading ill health and his desire to make his peace with heaven, left the Panjab, in 1838, for Benares, where he died in 1858.

Mangalsen, the second son of *Karam Chand*, was commandant in a cavalry regiment under the Darbar. After annexation he received a pension of 480 Rs. a year. He died in November, 1864, leaving one son *Lala Budha Mal.*

Rattan Chand was a great favourite of Maharaja Ranjit Singh, and when quite a boy used to be in constant attendance at court. When the first down began to grow upon his lip and chin, Ranjit Singh gave him the nickname* of *Darhiwala* or '*the bearded*,' to distinguish him from

* Diwan *Rattan Chand* being now the fortunate possessor of a long white beard, many have erroneously supposed that his nickname of *Darhiwala* arose from the length of his beard, which was not the case.

Rattan Chand Dogal, who was four years younger and who had consequently no beard at all. He was, in 1829, appointed to the postal Department, on 200 Rs. a month, with certain assignments from the revenue of Peshawar and Hazara. He remained in this department, during the reign of Ranjit Singh and his successors, and under the Darbar was in the enjoyment of cash allowances to the amount of 2,610 Rs. and jagirs, in Dinanagar, Khanowal, Yuhianagar, Tiwan, Bhindan, Hazara and Peshawar, worth 13,600 Rs. *Rattan Chand* happened to be in the Lahore fort when the Sindhanwalia chiefs seized it, and Raja Hira Singh believing him their accomplice fined him 30,000 Rs. This money was given back by Sirdar Jowahir Singh, after Hira Singh's death. After the Satlej campaign *Rattan Chand* was appointed Post Master General in the Panjab, and did excellent service throughout the rebellion of 1848-49. His department had, at this time, to contend with great difficulties, but the Post Master General's energy and ability enabled him to surmount them. On the annexation of the Panjab, certain of his jagirs, amounting to 6,800 Rs. were released to him for life, free of all service, and a garden worth 200 Rs. near the Shahalami gate of Lahore, was released to his male heirs in perpetuity. *Rattan Chand* was appointed an Honorary Magistrate of the city of Lahore in 1862 and member of the Municipal Committee.

He is one of the most active and intelligent of the Honorary Magistrates, and through his liberality the city of Lahore has been much embellished. The most striking of the public works constructed by him is the fine Sarai and tank near the Shahalami gate. He also had a large share in the formation of the Public Gardens round the city, and whenever money has been required for any work of public utility, *Rattan Chand* has shown himself liberal in the extreme.

He was created a Diwan by the Supreme Government in January 1865.

FAKIR AZIZUDDIN, BUKHARI.

- GHULAM SHAH.
  - Ghulam Muhiuddin.
    - Fakir Azizuddin. D. 1845.
      - Nadiruddin. D. 1814.
      - Fazluddin. D. 1842.
      - Shahdin. D. 1842.
      - Chiraghuddin. D. 1851.
        - Sirajuddin. D. 1850.
          - Ferozuddin. B. 1842.
            - Sultanuddin. B. 1862.
        - Shahswaruddin. D. 1848.
        - Shah Nawazuddin. D. 1858.
        - Najibuddin. D. 1849.
        - Hussainuddin. D. 1850.
      - Jamaluddin. B. 1833.
      - Ruknuddin. B. 1840.
    - Fakir Imamuddin. D. 1844.
      - Fakir Tajuddin. D. 1846.
        - Marajuddin. B. 1842.
          - Muhammad Jamaluddin. B. 1863.
    - Fakir Nuruddin. D. 1852.
      - Zahuruddin. B. 1824.
        - Nobaharuddin.
      - Shamshuddin. B. 1825.
        - Burhanuddin. B. 1842.
        - Zeinalabuddin. B. 1845.
        - Shahabuddin. B. 1850.
      - Kamruddin. B. 1827.
        - Muzaffaruddin. B. 1851.
      - Hafizuddin. B. 1829.
        - Muhammad Ikbaluddin. B. 1860.

HISTORY OF THE FAMILY.

Syad Ghulam Mohiuddin, the father of *Azizuddin, Imamuddin* and *Nuruddin*, was the son of *Ghulam Shah*, who held a subordinate office under Nawab Abdusamad Khan and Zakria Khan governors of Lahore. The family of *Ghulam Shah* was respectable, and had from about the year 1550 resided at Chunian in the Lahore district, and before that time at Uchh in the Bahawalpur territory. The founder of it was Jalaluddin, a native of Arabia, who, at the close of the 7th century of the Muhammadan era, came to the court of Halaku Khan of Bukhara. He had served for some years as a priest at Mecca, Medina, and the shrine at Najib Sharif; and had made pilgrimages to the tomb of Sulaiman, and Ghosal Azam at Baghdad, and had gained a great reputation for sanctity. In Bukhara he gained many disciples, but incurred the hatred of Halaku Khan, who was an idolater and a tyrant, by bold denunciation of his cruelty and oppression, and was seized by the royal order and thrown into a blazing furnace. But like the three Jewish saints, his body was proof against fire, and he came forth unscorched and unharmed; and Halaku Khan, not proof against such arguments, became a convert to Muhammadanism with many of his subjects, and gave his own daughter in marriage to Jalaluddin, who lived for some years in Bukhara, where there are still many of his descendants. From the residence of Jalaluddin at Bukhara, the family has obtained the name of Bukhari. At length he again set out upon his travels, taking with him his little grandson Bahauddin. On the journey when the child was thirsty, does came and fed him with their milk, and after enduring many hardships they reached the Panjab. There Jalaluddin made many converts, and finally settled at Uchh, formerly known as Deoghar. He died in 1293, in the reign of Jalaluddin Feroze Khiji.*

* This account of the family, claiming descent from the Bukhari Syads, is possibly true. There are, however, many who assert that it was only when Fakir *Azizuddin* became rich and powerful that he discovered himself to be a Syad, and an amusing story is told of the manner in which the genealogy was manufactured and promulgated. Certain it is that until the time of Maharaja Sher Singh the Fakirs styled themselves and were styled in all official documents, 'Ansari,' after 1840, they styled themselves 'Bukhari.' But on the other hand, Fakir *Azizuddin* was so truthful a man, that it is impossible to believe that he would become a principal to such a fraud; and he was too careless of nominal distinctions to value the title of Syad, 'Ansari' or 'Bukhari.' He knew that the dress and style of Fákir were his greatest protection in the intriguing and unscrupulous court of Lahore, and he would never accept the titles and honours which the Maharaja desired to confer on him.

Ghulam Mohiuddin was born at Rahila on the river Beas. When he was three months old his father *Ghulam Shah* died, and his widowed mother, left in great poverty, came to Lahore to seek help from her husband's friends. Abdullah Ansari, a well known physician of Lahore, who had been judge in Kashmir early in the reign of Ahmad Shah, and whose father had written a medical work, 'Tazkira ishakiya,' which is still an authority, took pity upon her and supported both her and her son. He gave to *Ghulam Mohiuddin* a good education, and when the boy had grown up, married him to his niece, the daughter of his brother Khuda Baksh.

Ghulam Mohiuddin became a physician and a bookseller, and in pursuit of his trade, travelled over a large portion of the Panjab. He became a disciple of Fakir Imanat Shah Kadri, and himself assumed the title of Fakir, and his 'murids' or disciples are still to be found in Lahore and Bahawalpur.

Ghulam Mohiuddin left three sons, *Azizuddin*, *Imamuddin* and *Nuruddin*; of these *Azizuddin* the eldest was a pupil of Lala Hakim Rai, the chief Lahore physician, who placed him in attendance on Ranjit Singh, when that chief, soon after his capture of Lahore in 1799, was suffering from a severe affection of the eyes. The skill and attention of the young doctor won the chief's regard, and *Azizuddin* received a grant of the villages of Baddu and Sharakpur, and a cash assignment on Diwan Hukman Singh Pathban, who at that time farmed the customs of Lahore as Ramanand did those of Amritsar. Ranjit Singh made him his own physician, and as he extended his territories the jagirs of *Azizuddin* were also increased.

In the year 1808, when Mr. Metcalfe was sent to Lahore to draw up an agreement by which Ranjit Singh should be confined to the north of the Satlej, and in 1809, when the British troops were moved up to that river, the Sikh chief, supported by his Sirdars, had almost determined on war with the English; but *Azizuddin* strongly dissuaded him from such a course, and his wiser counsels at last prevailed. Ranjit Singh, appreciating the far-sightedness and wisdom of *Azizuddin*, consulted him on all occasions, and from this time to the end of his reign never undertook any important operation against his advice. In all matters connected with Europeans and the English Government, *Azizuddin* was specially employed; and to the Fakir's enlightened and liberal counsels it may be attributed that throughout his long reign the Maharaja maintained such close friendship with the English Government. Trusting implicitly to its good faith he would set out with his whole army on distant expeditions, leaving only the Fakir with a few orderlies for the protection of Lahore.

Azizuddin was employed on several occasions on military service. In 1810 he was sent to annex the Gujrat country of Sahib Singh Bhangi, and, in 1813, when Jahan Dad Khan had given up Attock to the Maharaja he was sent with Diwan Din Das, Sukhdyal and Sirdar Mohta Singh to reinforce the garrison and to settle the district. In 1819, he was sent as envoy to the Bahawalpur court, and was received there with great honour. He accompanied the expedition against Kangra; and, in 1826, when Diwan Kirpa Ram fell into disgrace, *Fakir Azizuddin* was sent to receive from him the fort of Philor, of which he took charge till it was placed under Sirdar Desa Singh Majithia; and shortly before this he had assumed charge of Kapurthalla, Jandiala, Hoshiarpur, and the Trans Satlej estates of Fatah Singh Ahluwalia, who had fled across the Satlej, for British protection. In April, 1831, *Azizuddin*, in company with Sirdar Hari Singh Nalwa, and Diwan Moti Ram, was sent to Simla, on a complimentary visit to Lord William Bentinck.* The envoys were received with great honour and arrangements were made for a meeting between the Maharaja and the Governor General, which took place at Rupar, in October of the same year.

In May, 1835, he was present in the Peshawar valley, when Amir Dost Muhammad Khan, with a large army arrived from Kabul with the

* It was during this visit to Simla that an English Officer asked Fakir *Azizuddin*, of which eye the Maharaja was blind? He replied, "The splendour of his face is such that I have never been able to look close enough to discover."

intention of recovering Peshawar from the Sikhs. *Azizuddin* was sent as the principal envoy to the Afghan camp, and contrived to delude the Amir so completely that the Afghan army was almost surrounded by the Sikhs, during the progress of the negotiations, and had to retire to Kabul, with all speed. The Maharaja was so pleased with the adroitness of the Fakir on this occasion that on his return to camp, a general salute was ordered in his honour.

In November, 1838, when the British forces were being assembled for the Kabul campaign, the Maharaja visited Lord Auckland, the Governor General, at Firozpur, where the splendour of the scene even surpassed that of the meeting at Rupar in 1831, which had been called the 'Meeting of the field of cloth of gold.' Shortly afterwards Lord Auckland paid the Maharaja a return visit at Lahore and Amritsar, and on both these occasions the Fakir had been foremost in his attentions, doing the honours in the most graceful manner for his master, whose health was fast giving way.

On the 27th June, 1839, Ranjit Singh died. To the last *Azizuddin*, the most faithful of his servants, the most devoted of his friends, had remained by him ; administering the medicine with his own hand, and telling him news from various quarters, which the Maharaja was anxious to hear. On the accession of Maharaja Kharrak Singh, *Azizuddin* and Sirdar Lehna Singh Majithia were sent to Simla to renew the engagements which had been entered into by Ranjit Singh with the British Government. While at Simla, news arrived of the murder of Sirdar Chet Singh, the minister and favourite of Kharrak Singh, and the assumption of power by Prince Nao Nihal Singh. This news caused some hesitation at Simla, but the treaty was eventually renewed and the envoys returned to Lahore.

The influence of the Fakir at court did not perceptibly decline during the reign of Kharrak Singh. In May, 1840, he was deputed by the Darbar to visit Mr. Clerk at Firozpur, and he made the arrangements for the visit which that officer paid the Maharaja at Lahore, in the same month. In September of the same year in company with Rai Govind Jas he was again sent on a confidential mission to Mr. Clerk, to discuss the treatment of the Ghilzi and Barakzai chiefs, and the interpretation of the first article of the Tripartite Treaty of 1838, which had been somewhat infringed by the action taken by the Sikhs in Yusafzai and Swat.

In the intrigues which succeeded the deaths of Kharrak Singh and Nao Nihal Singh, the Fakir did not take an active part. Raja Dhyan Singh indeed used always to consult him, and they both were parties to the arrangement by which Mai Chand Kour was appointed Regent during the pregnancy of Sahib Kour, widow of Prince Nao Nihal Singh. *Azizuddin* was well aware that this arrangement could not be a successful one, and his sympathies were all with Prince Sher Singh, but his great influence was in the foreign department, and regarding home politics, he at this time rarely ventured an opinion in Darbar.

When Sher Singh obtained the throne he treated *Azizuddin* with the greatest kindness, and in March, 1841, sent him to Ludhiana, to sound Mr. Clerk the agent of the Governor General as to the willingness of the British Government to aid him in reducing his troops to obedience. Mr. Clerk was not averse to the idea. The Sikhs, before the experience of the Satlej campaign, were not considered formidable in the field, and Mr. Clerk thought that with 12,000 troops, it was possible to reduce the Khalsa army to obedience throughout the plain country of the Panjab ; in case of resistance to disperse it, and to establish Sher Singh firmly on the throne. The terms on which such assistance would be rendered were the cession to the British Government of the Lahore Territory south of the Satlej, and the payment of forty lakhs of rupees, for the expenses of the expedition. The Fakir, with his colleague, Munshi Din Muhammad, had no authority to conclude so important a transaction as this ; and asked permission, as the matter could not be trusted to paper, to go to Lahore to consult the Maharaja, promising to return in eight days. He never returned and perhaps never intended to do so. The Maharaja was more afraid of the British Army than of his own, and in spite of the revolt of the troops in Mandi, wrote to the Agent to say that he had suppressed all mutiny, and that the Sikh Army, obedient and loyal, was ready to march against the enemies of the English.*

Sher Singh feared that the British Army, once having occupied Lahore would never again leave it. Fakir *Azizuddin,* who knew better the policy of the English Government, professed himself still anxious for its interference, and directed his son *Shahdin,* the Lahore agent at Ludhiana, to urge Mr. Clerk to renew the overtures made, and to send for Baba Mahan Singh, a confidential servant of the Maharaja, to conduct the negotiations. But Mr. Clerk did not find it politic again to take the initiative, and the scheme was wisely abandoned.

About this time an accident befel *Azizuddin,* which it was feared would end fatally. He was seated in Darbar, at Shah Bilawal, next to Diwan Bishan Singh whose sword, as he rose from his seat, wounded the Fakir severely in the leg. He fainted from loss of blood, and it was thought that lock-jaw would come on. Gradually, however, he recovered, and this accident afforded him an excuse to attend the Darbar less frequently, for he, with the other ministers, feared the abuse and excesses of the soldiery.

In February, 1842, *Azizuddin* was sent by the Maharaja to Makhu, on the south side of the Satlej, to meet Mr. Clerk who was proceeding to Lahore on a mission of congratulation on the Maharaja's accession, and condolence on the death of Kharrak Singh.

In December, 1842, Sirdar Lehna Singh Majithia, was deputed by the Lahore Court to wait on Lord Ellenborough, who was present with the British Army at Firozpur. Through some misunderstanding, the Sirdar, expecting the Agent of the Governor General to conduct him to the British

* The Supreme Government did not adopt the extreme views of Mr. Clerk, and deprecated armed interference, unless the course of events in the Panjab should render it absolutely necessary.

camp, remained in his tent, and the interview failed altogether to come off. Lord Ellenborough, thinking the slight intentional, demanded explanations. *Fakir Azizuddin*, accordingly, with Prince Partab Singh, Raja Hira Singh and other Sirdars proceeded to Firozpur, where a grand darbar and review of both the Sikh and British armies were held. *Azizuddin* explained away the apparent discourtesy, and so pleased the Governor General that he called him, in full darbar, "the protector of the friendship of both states," and taking from his pocket a gold watch, presented it to him. This gift, valued beyond other khillats, is now in the possession of Fakir *Jamaluddin*.

During the last year of Sher Singh's reign, Fakir *Azizuddin* fell out of favour. He was suspected of attachment to the Jammu Rajas, whom Sher Singh hated, though he was unable to resist them. The truth was that Raja Dhyan Singh found the abilities of *Azizuddin* necessary to him; and indeed no ministry at Lahore could have dispensed with the services of the Fakir. It was not without difficulty that *Azizuddin* forgave Raja Dhyan Singh for the murder of Sirdar Chet Singh, his particular friend; but at length he seemed to believe that the Dogra Rajas alone could save the state from disruption, and it was this belief which induced him to join their party.

After the death of Maharaja Sher Singh, the Fakir took little part in politics. His health was bad, his eyesight failing, and his influence day by day grew less, as the army became more powerful and reckless. He saw well whither the evil passions of the troops were hurrying them, and he raised his voice, unfortunately in vain, against the suicidal policy of Jowahir Singh and Lal Singh. His last act was to urge the recall of the invading army which had marched to the Satlej against the British, and he died, on the 3rd December, 1845, before ruin had fallen on the state he had served so long and so faithfully.

Fakir *Azizuddin* was one of the ablest and certainly the most honest of all Ranjit Singh's advisers. That monarch knew how to choose his ministers, and throughout his long reign his confidence in and affection for *Azizuddin* never lessened, as they were never betrayed or abused. There were few questions, either in home or foreign politics, on which the Maharaja did not ask his advice, while the conduct of negotiations with the English Government was left almost entirely in his hands, and it was undoubtedly owing in no small degree to the tact and wisdom of the Fakir that the two states remained till the close of Ranjit Singh's reign on terms of the most cordial friendship.

Fakir *Azizuddin* was of so engaging a disposition, and so perfect a courtier in his manners, that he made few declared enemies, though many were doubtless jealous of his influence. One reason of his popularity, as a Muhammadan minister at a Hindu court, was the liberality of his belief. He was a Sufi,* a sect held, indeed, as infidel, by orthodox Muhammadans, but to which the best thinkers and poets of the East have belonged. He had no attachment for the barren dogmata of the Kuran, but looked on all religions as equally to be respected and disregarded. On one occasion Ranjit Singh asked him whether he preferred the Hindu or the Muhammadan religion. "I am," he replied, "a man floating in the midst of a mighty river. I turn my eyes towards the land, but can distinguish no difference in either bank."

Fakir *Azizuddin* was celebrated as the most eloquent man of his day, and he was as able with his pen as with his tongue. The state papers drawn up by him and his brother *Nuruddin* are models of elegance and good taste, according to the oriental standard. He was himself a ripe scholar in all branches of Eastern learning, and also was a generous and discriminating patron of learning. At Lahore, he founded, at his own expense, a college for the study of Persian and Arabic, and to this

* *Note.*—The Sufi sect represents the mystical asceticism of Muhammadanism. All over the East its members are more or less numerous; Persia has for many centuries been its head quarters, while in the Panjab, a declared Sufi is rarely to be found. Yet the mystical doctrines of the Sufi are common every where. The Hindu Vedanti school of deistical philosophy hardly differs from Sufism except in name; and the principles upon which Guru Nanak founded the Sikh faith, are almost identical with those which may be found in the purely Sufi writings of Mahmud, Hafiz or Fakir *Azizuddin* himself.

institution very many of the Arabic scholars of the Panjab owe their education.

As a poet, *Azizuddin* must be allowed a high place. His Persian poems, of the mystical character which the Sufis affect, are often very beautiful, and are distinguished by simplicity and great elegance of style. A few stanzas, literally translated, are inserted here, to show, in some measure, the character of Sufi religious poetry :—

If you attentively regard the world
You will find it fugitive as a shadow :
Why should you vex yourself with vain desires
When you have no power to perform ?
Forget yourself, and leave your work with God,
Trust yourself with all confidence to Him ;
Wait with patience until He shall bless you,
And thank Him for what He has already given.
Stop your ears from the sound of earthly care ;
Rejoice in God, and be hopeful of His mercy.

The wise would consider me as an idolater
Should I thoughtlessly speak of myself as '*I*';
To the wise and to those who most nearly know,
It is a folly for any mortal to assert '*I am.*'
Although able to vanquish Sahrab, Zal and Rustam.
Yet at the last your stability is but as water :
It is a vain thought that your reason may spin
Her imaginings, as a spider spins her web.
It is well that I should breathe the air of freedom,
For I know that every thing is dependent upon God.

Only two of Fakir *Azizuddin's* six sons are now living. *Shahdin,* who died in 1842, was, in 1836, appointed agent with the British political officer at Ludhiana ; and two years later was appointed wakil at Firozpur. Fakir *Chiraghuddin* was, in 1838, made governor of Jasrota, and shortly afterwards was placed in attendance on Prince Kharrak Singh. He succeeded his brother as wakil, at Firozpur, in 1842, and was afterwards attached to the Council of Regency in the same capacity.

Jamaluddin, entered the service of the English Government as Tehsildar of Hafizabad. He was then transferred to Gujranwala, and, in 1864, was appointed Mir Munshi of the Panjab Secretariat. He and his brother *Ruknuddin* receive each a pension of 1000 Rs. per annum, for life.

Nasiruddin the eldest son of Fakir *Azizuddin* was murdered when quite a youth, in 1814. A Purbeah sepoy who had been dismissed by Fakir *Imamuddin* for some fault, determined upon revenge and came to Lahore to the shop of *Ghulam Mohiuddin*, and asked to be treated for some alleged disorder. Young *Naziruddin*, who used to assist his grandfather, took the sepoy into an inner room, wher. he drew his sword and cut the boy down. *Ghulam Mohiuddin* ran up, hearing the cries of his grandson, but the room was locked. He, however, broke the door down with an axe, and rushed upon the murderer, whom he disarmed, not without receiving severe wounds himself, and threw from the window into the street, where he was torn to pieces by the infuriated mob. *Nasiruddin* lingered a few days and then died.

Chiraghuddin was the only one of *Azizuddin's* sons to leave any family, and the fate of *Sirajuddin*, his eldest son, was as tragical as that of *Nasiruddin*.

This young man was in the employ of Bahawal Khan, the Nawab of Bahawalpur, who was succeeded by his favorite son Sadik Muhammad Khan. The new prince wished to put to death his brother Haji Khan, whom he found in prison, but *Sirajuddin* and the Daudputras took his part, and raising an insurrection in his favour placed him upon the throne. In gratitude for this, Haji Khan made *Sirajuddin* his minister, and his brother *Shah Nawaz Khan*, commander-in-chief. No long time afterwards, however, *Sirajuddin* quarreled with Azad Khan, the maternal uncle of the Nawab, who took his relative's part, and *Sirajuddin* prepared to leave Bahawalpur. But the Nawab sent several Syads to him, who swore on the Kuran that no injury was intended him, and he then resolved to remain. But two or three days later the house was surrounded by troops, and *Sirajuddin* was informed that he was a prisoner and must consent to be placed in irons. He refused to submit except to force, and the house was at last stormed. The brothers defended themselves gallantly, but they were almost unarmed. The principal officer *Sirajuddin* killed with his own hand and was then shot dead himself. *Shah Nawaz Khan* was captured, severely wounded, and was thrown into prison, where he remained eight months, until ransomed by his father for 80,000 Rs.

During the life of Fakir *Azizuddin*, his brothers played subordinate parts, but some account must be given of them here, as both were men of some importance. Fakir *Imamuddin* was, during a great portion of Ranjit Singh's reign, custodian of the celebrated fort of Govindghar* at Amritsar, and governor of the country immediately surrounding it. With this he had charge of the magazine, arsenals and royal stables. His occupations at Amritsar did not allow him to perform much service in the field, but he was one of the force sent to reduce the forts of Mai Sadda Kour and the Kanheyas, and also served in one or two other minor campaigns. He died in 1844, leaving one son *Tajuddin*, who had shared with him the charge of Govindghar, and who survived him only two years. *Murajuddin*, the only son of *Tajuddin*, enjoys a cash pension of 500 Rs. per annum.

Fakir *Nuruddin* neither possessed the ability or the courage of his brother *Azizuddin*, whom in many points he much resembled. His early life was passed in devotion, till, in 1810, Ranjit Singh, who had taken a great fancy to *Azizuddin* sent for *Nuruddin* to his darbar, and gave him the district of Dhanni to superintend. He acquitted himself

* The first Thannadar or Governor of Govindghar was Sirdar Shamir Singh of Thethar, Lahore. He rebuilt the fort, in a great measure, under Ranjit Singh's orders. After Shamir Singh, Fakir *Imamuddin* was appointed, who with his son *Tajuddin* held the fort till the reign of Maharaja Sher Singh. Subha Singh of Baghrian was then nominated, and remained governor till 1842, when Sarmukh Singh a Brahman of Botala was appointed. This man allowed Dheria Khan, a state prisoner, to escape, and he was consequently superseded by *Shamshuddin* son of Fakir *Nuruddin*, in 1847.

well, and was then sent to Gujrat, where he had some difficulty in reducing the Chibs to obedience. In 1812, Jalandhar was placed under him, and the next year Sialkot, Daska, Halowal and Wazirabad. In 1818 he was summoned to Lahore, and henceforward his duties were generally about court. These duties were multifarious and responsible. He was in charge of the arsenal at the fort, of the royal gardens and palaces. He was almoner to the Maharaja, and dispensed the royal bounty to deserving applicants. He kept one key of the royal treasury, the Moti Mandar; the two other keys being in charge of Misr Beli Ram and Diwan Hukman Singh.

In 1826, *Nuruddin* was sent to reduce the country around Pind Dadan Khan, and in 1831, he proceeded to Syadpur and Makhad to assist Raja Gulab Singh in his administration of that part of the country.

Nuruddin was closely associated with his brother *Azizuddin* in the conduct of negotiations with the British Government. Both were lovers of the English and earnestly desirous that the two states of India and Lahore should always remain on the most friendly terms.

On the 19th September, 1846, when the Khalsa army had mutinied, and required the Rani to give up her brother and the murderers of Prince Peshora Singh to their vengeance, Fakir *Nuruddin* was sent with Diwan Dina Nath and Sirdar Attar Singh Kalianwala to endeavour to soothe them. The mission was without result, and *Nuruddin* alone of the envoys was allowed to return to Lahore without insults and threats. After the Satlej war, *Nuruddin* was one of the subscribing witnesses to the treaty of the 9th March, on the part of the Lahore State; and in December, 1846, when Raja Lal Singh, the wazir, was deposed for treason, *Nuruddin* was appointed one of the Council of Regency to carry on the Government until Maharaja Dalip Singh should arrive at his majority.

Nuruddin was not an active member of the Council, but he was one of the most disinterested, and his advice was generally sound and well considered. He at all times was ready to facilitate matters for the British Resident, while remaining faithful to the interests of his own Government. In 1850, the Supreme Government confirmed to him for life all his jagirs and allowances, amounting to Rs. 20,885 per annum. To his two elder sons, *Zahuruddin* and *Shamshuddin*, were granted cash pensions of 1000 Rs. and 720 Rs. respectively; to the younger 540 Rs. each. On the death of their father *Nuruddin*, in 1852, these allowances were increased to 1,200 Rs., 2,400 Rs., and 1,080 Rs. respectively.

Fakir *Zahuruddin* was placed with the young Maharaja Dalip Singh as a tutor. He accompanied the prince to Fatahghar, and the way in which he fulfilled the duties of the office gave every satisfaction. At the end of 1851, he returned to the Panjab, and was, in 1855, appointed Tehsildar of Chunian, and was subsequently transferred to Moga and Lahore. In 1863, he was promoted to the rank of Extra Assistant Commissioner, at Sialkot, where he is still stationed.

Fakir *Shamshuddin*, second son of *Nuruddin*, was Thannadar of the Govindghar Fort during the second Sikh war. In this position he behaved with great fidelity, and made over the fort to European troops at a time when any hesitation on his part might have produced serious results. In 1850, he was appointed Tehsildar of Shahdera, but was compelled to resign the next year through ill health. In 1862, *Shamshuddin* was appointed an Honorary Magistrate of the city of Lahore, and a member of the Municipal Committee. He is a man of great energy and liberality. A finished scholar himself he is ever foremost in any schemes for the advancement of learning generally among his countrymen. It is very much owing to his exertions that Female Education has been so generally taken up in Lahore. He has also taken an active part in the establishment of a literary Society, the 'Anjaman-i-Panjab,' which is still young, but which promises most interesting and valuable results.

SIRDAR RICHPAL SINGH SINDHU OF SIRANWALI.

DARGAH SINGH.

Lal Singh. | Tegh Chand.

Tegh Chand. — Ghazita. — Hukm Singh.

Lal Singh:

- B. Isar Kour, M. M. R. Kharrak Singh. D. 1840.
- Sirdar Mangal Singh. D. 1864.
- B. Desan, M. Jamiyat Singh, Randhawa.

Sirdar Mangal Singh:

- Richpal Singh. B. 1850.
- B. Attar Kour, M. 1835.
- B. Prem Kour, M. 1864.

HISTORY OF THE FAMILY.

The ancestor of this family is said to have been one *Hassan* a Sindhu Jat, who, about the year 1500 A. D., founded the village of Hassanwala in the Gujranwala district. The village of Siranwali, (the place of heads) in the Pasrur pergannah of the Sialkot district, is also said to have been founded by him at the place where he overcame the powerful Karayah tribe, and having cut off the heads of the slain, collected them in a heap, and took his bath over them. But this blood-thirsty exploit was probably invented later to account for the name of the village. Siranwali at any rate passed out of the hands of the family, and *Dargah*, who first became a Sikh, had through poverty to leave the Sialkot district for Gurdaspur, where he became a sowar in the troop of Jaimal Singh Fatahgharia. His son *Lal Singh* succeeded him, but being a man of some ability he rose to the command of 100 horsemen.

The beauty of *Isar Kour*, the daughter of *Lal Singh*, was celebrated in the Sialkot district, and, in 1815, when Maharaja Ranjit Singh was travelling in that direction, *Lal Singh* brought the girl to him, and she was sent to the royal zanana at Lahore. Two months later, however, Ranjit Singh sent her to his son Prince Kharrak Singh, who married her by chaddar-dola, at Amritsar. *Lal Singh* died soon after this, but the young *Mangal Singh,* his son, profited by the royal connection. When he first came to court he was but a rude Jat peasant, and it is said that the Maharaja told the attendants to change his country garments for those fashionable at court. *Mangal Singh* had never worn paejamas (the tight Sikh trousers) and to the great amusement of the courtiers attempted to put both legs into that portion of the garment which nature and the tailor had intended for but one. But *Mangal Singh,* though no courtier, was a clever young man, and rapidly rose to favour at court. Prince Kharrak Singh gave to him the jagirs of Thallur and Khita, worth 5,000 Rs. and the charge of the Ilaka of Chunian, in the Lahore district. The Prince was so pleased with the adroitness of *Mangal Singh* in this appointment that in 1820, with the Maharaja's approbation, he made him manager of all his affairs, civil and military, and conferred upon him a jagir of 19,000 Rs. with the title of Sirdar. *Mangal Singh* recovered the old family village of Siranwali which had till this time been in possession of Sirdar Sham Singh Attariwala. For some years *Mangal Singh* remained in high favour, receiving large additions to his jagirs and attending Prince Kharrak Singh in all his expeditions and campaigns. But in the year 1834, Sirdar Chet Singh Bajwa, who had married *Chand Kour,* the niece of Sirdar *Mangal Singh,* and whom he himself had introduced to the notice of Kharrak Singh, was appointed to the management of the Prince's affairs in the room of *Mangal Singh.* The latter, however, did not suffer in fortune by the change, as Kharrak Singh gave him new jagirs, which with those already in his possession, amounted in value to 2,61,250 Rs. of which 62,750 Rs. were personal and the balance for service of 780 sowars, 30 zamburahs and 2 guns.

Chet Singh's elevation was the cause of his destruction. During Ranjit Singh's reign he remained chief favourite of the Prince, and his power was very great, for Kharrak Singh was a weak man and a favourite could influence him as he chose; but after the death of Ranjit Singh, and the accession of Kharrak Singh, the Sirdars whose jealousy Chet Singh had aroused determined to destroy him. Raja Dhyan Singh and Prince Nao Nihal Singh were the leaders of the conspiracy; and the unfortunate favourite was murdered openly in the palace and almost in the presence of his royal master.

In 1834, when Chet Singh was first taken into favour, Sirdar *Mangal Singh* was sent to the Multan district to keep the wild Muzari tribe in order; but although he was as energetic as any of his predecessors, he was unable to restore the frontier to any degree of quiet.

In November, 1840, Maharaja Kharrak Singh died, and Rani *Isar Kour* was burnt as a 'Sati' upon the funeral pile. It was asserted at the time, and there is every reason to believe truly, that this lady was not a voluntary victim. That she was urged and indeed compelled to burn, and that it was Raja Dhyan Singh who was the contriver of the tragedy. Great jealousy had always existed between *Isar Kour* and Chand Kour the principal wife of Kharrak Singh, and the influence of this Rani was also used to induce her rival to become a 'Sati.'

Mangal Singh hoped that he might obtain some share of power at this time. His position as brother-in-law of the late Maharaja and the great wealth which he had amassed during many years of service, gave him some reason to believe that he might, with Prince Sher Singh, be able to form some stable government; but Raja Dhyan Singh, having got rid of Sirdar Chet Singh, had no intention of permitting another rival to obtain power, and *Mangal Singh* fell gradually into the back ground. Some time later Maharaja Sher Singh resumed all *Mangal Singh's* original jagirs, except 37,000 Rs., but granted him new ones to the value of 1,24,500 Rs. at Sahiwal and Bankal Chimi. He held these up to 1846, when Raja Lal Singh seized them leaving the Sirdar only 86,000 Rs. of the old jagirs, and granting 36,000 Rs. new, subject to the service of 120 sowars. This reduction was the more unjust as Sirdar *Mangal*

Singh, after the death of Kharrak Singh, had not meddled with politics; and the reason of the confiscation was evident as the jagirs were given by Lal Singh to his brother Misr Amir Chand. In some measure to make up for his loss, Major Lawrence the Resident caused him to be appointed 'Adalati' or chief justice of the Rechna Doab. In this appointment he gave little satisfaction. He was a plain soldier and judicial work in no way suited him. When the rebellion broke out, in 1848, he was at Wazirabad, and was placed in charge of the ferries. According to his own account he was taken prisoner by Raja Sher Singh, when opposing the passage of the rebel force, and kept under restraint until just before the battle of Ramnagar, when he effected his escape and joined Major Nicholson, under whose orders he remained till the close of the campaign. The conduct of Sirdar *Mangal Singh* appeared suspicious to the authorities, and, after annexation, only a cash pension of 12,000 Rs. was allowed to him for life. But it must in fairness be remembered that no treason was ever proved against the Sirdar; that he joined the British at a critical time: and that he was employed in procuring supplies, and on other service for the British army, up to the very end of the war. Sirdar *Mangal Singh* died in June, 1864.

His only son, *Richpal Singh*, holds a life pension of 2,000 Rs., and resides at Siranwali, Sialkot district.

DIWAN SHANKAR NATH.

PANDIT RAGNATH KOUL.
|
Pandit Hari Ram.
|
Diwan Shankar Nath.
B. 1805.

- Prem Nath.
  - Dwarka Nath. B. 1847.
  - Kashi Nath. B. 1856.
  - Washeshar Nath. B. 1859.
  - Gopi Nath. B. 1862.
- Shiv Nath.

HISTORY OF THE FAMILY.

The ancestors of Diwan *Shankar Nath* were inhabitants of Kashmir. The first to leave his native country was *Lal Chand Koul* who emigrated to Dehli during the reign of the Emperor Shah Jahan, and entered the service of Ali Mardan Khan, the accomplished minister of the Mogal prince. There he acquired considerable wealth, and after some years returned to Kashmir. His success induced several others of the family to follow his example, and among the emigrants was *Ragnath Koul*, who settled at Faizabad, where a son *Hari Ram* was born to him. He then took service with the Maharaja of Gwalior, and became Mir Munshi of Colonel Louis Burqien, one of the French officers in the Mahratta army. His son *Hari Ram* worked under him till the overthrow of the Mahratta power threw both father and son on the world. *Hari Ram* soon after this was invited to Lahore by a relative, Diwan Ganga Ram, who had taken service with Ranjit Singh, in 1813, and had risen to offices of trust and profit. He accepted the invitation, and being a ready writer, was placed in charge of the Diwan's office. In 1817, he was attached as munshi to the person of the Maharaja, and in 1818, held the same office with Kharrak Singh the heir-apparent, whose jagir accounts he kept.

Shankar Nath, born at Dehli in 1805, was brought to Lahore by his father in 1820, and placed in Prince Kharrak Singh's treasury office. He was afterwards transferred to the Central Record office, in which he remained till the annexation of the Panjab. His connection with Raja Dina Nath, whose sister he had married, gave Pandit *Shankar Nath* much influence, and he was besides known for ability and unimpeachable honesty. During the time of the residency from 1846 to 1849, *Shankar Nath* was largely and confidentially employed by British officers, Messrs Bowring, Cocks, Wedderburn, and Major Macgregor, and all have borne witness to the value of his services and to his high character. Being chief munshi of Raja Dina Nath's office, a large amount of revenue work was made over to him, and he himself disposed of upwards of eight thousand cases. Till 1849, *Shankar Nath* held jagirs to the value of 6,500 Rs., besides cash allowances 1,360 Rs. and 2,412 Rs. for his establishment. The jagirs, situated in Sheikhupura and Gujrat were resumed, and a pension of 2,620 Rs. was assigned to him for life. In 1862, *Shankar Nath* was appointed Honorary Magistrate of Lahore. In this office he has given great satisfaction by his impartiality and activity. He possesses great knowledge of Hindu law, and in intricate cases of custom, inheritance and religion his opinion is sought with confidence by the English magistrates of Lahore. In January, 1865, he was created a Diwan by the Supreme Government.

BAKSHI BHAGGAT RAM.

BAISAKHI RAM.

Mihr Chand, B. 1795.	Bhaggat Ram, D. 1865.	Har Dyal, D. 1853.
	Jamiyat Rai, B. 1830.	

HISTORY OF THE FAMILY.

Baisakhi Ram, father of Bakshi *Bhaggat Ram,* was a money-changer, in a very small way of business, in the city of Lahore. In 1818, *Bhaggat Ram,* then nineteen years of age, was taken into the Treasury Office, as a writer on 60 Rs. a month, by Misr Beli Ram, the Chief Toshakhania or Keeper of the State Treasury. In 1824, he received the post of assistant writer of the accounts of the Privy Purse, with 50 Rs. per mensem additional pay. He was, in 1831, deputed to accompany Prince Sher Singh to the hill country of the Jalandhar Doab, to collect the revenue from Tirah and Sujanpur, and the tribute from Mandi, Suket and Kulu. The next year *Bhaggat Ram* returned to Lahore and was appointed 'Bakshi' or Paymaster of 50 battalions of infantry, 8 regiments of cavalry, and 20 batteries of artillery, on a cash salary of 2,520 Rs. a year. He held this appointment throughout the reigns of Maharajas Ranjit Singh and Kharrak Singh, and, in 1841, Maharaja Sher Singh granted to him, in addition to his cash allowance, jagirs at Ajnala and Surapur, worth 3,000 Rs.

Bakshi *Bhaggat Ram* was exceedingly popular with the army, and after the assassination of Sher Singh his influence became very great. He was at the head of one division of the 'Mutsaddi' or Munshi party, while Diwan Dina Nath was all powerful in another, composed of the clever and unscrupulous Kashmiri Brahmans. After the murder of Raja Hira Singh, and Pandit Jella on the 21st December, 1844, it was decided in Darbar that the government should be carried on by a council composed of Sirdar Jowahir Singh; Raja Lal Singh; Diwan Dina Nath; Sirdars Attar Singh, Kalianwala, Sham Singh, Attariwala, and Bakshi *Bhaggat Ram*, but it was not long before the chief power fell into the hands of Jowahir Singh and Lal Singh alone.

The Bakshi went to Jammu with the expedition against Raja Gulab Singh, in March, 1845, and his great influence with the troops induced the Raja to bestow upon him enormous presents; but these *Bhaggat Ram* was very near losing, for when the army had brought Gulab Singh to Lahore, that prince professed his willingness to guarantee to the troops a higher rate of pay, provided that all the chiefs contributed according to their means, and the Bakshi he put down for a donation of five lakhs of rupees, which was in reality less than he had received at Jammu.

In June, 1845, the army, weary of the incapacity of the Minister Jowahir Singh, demanded that he should be dismissed from office, and that in his stead Diwan Dina Nath, *Bhaggat Ram* or Raja Lal Singh, or the three conjointly, should be appointed to the Wazirship. The Rani, however, contrived to bring about a reconciliation between her brother Jowahir Singh and her lover Lal Singh, and the incompetent Wazir remained at the head of affairs until his assassination three months later.

A new jagir worth 8,000 Rs., at Datarpur in the Jalandhar Doab, was granted to the Bakshi by Maharaja Dalip Singh.

When this Doab was ceded to the British Government, by the treaty of the 9th March, 1846, *Bhaggat Ram* lost his jagir; but another of the same value was granted to him in the Talwandi Pargannah of the Amritsar district. His cash allowance was reduced to 1,300 Rs., and the next year, he received an additional jagir at Dharamkot worth 2,000 Rs. His emoluments at this time amounted in cash and land to 14,300 Rs.

When at the close of 1847, Mr. John Lawrence the Officiating Resident was attempting to introduce some order and system into the

Sikh administration, Bakshi *Bhaggat Ram* was directed to render the army accounts, which he had not done for several years. When he would do this by no inducement whatever, he was suspended from office, and four paymasters were appointed in his room, and a regular system of audit and account was introduced.

Still failing to render the accounts, the jagirs of Bakshi *Bhaggat Ram* were resumed. At length the accounts were produced. About five and a half lakhs of rupees appeared against him; but a large portion of this was allowed to be written off; part was due from various officers of the army; and on payment of the balance, the accounts were passed by the Darbar. Several months later Sir F. Currie refused to accede to the wish of the Darbar, and restore to the Bakshi his resumed jagirs, and accordingly, at the annexation of the Panjab, he had no claims on the new Government. A pension of 1,200 Rs. per annum was, however, granted to him, in 1853, on the recommendation of the Chief Commissioner.

Bhaggat Ram was never accused of embezzlement of the public money, and his poverty, when he possessed such ample opportunities of enriching himself at the expense of the state, is the proof of his personal honesty. But although he did not himself plunder the state, he was in no way careful to check the depredations of others. His subordinates in the Military Pay Department were the most greedy and unscrupulous of men. They grew rich on the plunder of the army and were the objects of universal hatred. If *Bhaggat Ram* had been less amiable and more energetic he would have been a valuable public servant.

He died at Lahore in March, 1865, leaving one son Jamiyat Rai, employed in the Revenue Department of the Jalandhar District.

MALIK KHAIRUDDIN KHAN, KASSURIA.

MANSUR KHAN.

- Khewa Khan, D. 1856.
  - Maujuddin Khan, B. 1806.
    - Kamaluddin Khan, B. 1836.
      - Sahib Khan, B. 1861.
  - Khairuddin Khan, B. 1810.
- Jiwa Khan,
  - Jalaluddin Khan, B. 1804.
    - Pir Baksh, B. 1828.
  - Shadi Khan, D. 1848.
    - Fatah Din.
  - Kaku Khan, B. 1807.
  - Buland Khan, B. 1829.
    - Fatah Din Khan, B. 1844.
    - Ismail Khan, B. 1851.
- Nasera Khan,
  - Amira,
  - Wazira.
  - Bela Khan.
- Jahangira Khan,
- Daughter M. Kutbuddin Khan of Mamdot.

HISTORY OF THE FAMILY.

The ancestors of Malik *Khairuddin Khan* were Bhatti Rajputs, resident in the Sirsa District. About the year 1520, *Gagau* and *Nolu,* two members of the family, obtained from Ibrahim, the last of the Lodi dynasty, a grant of thirty thousand acres of waste land in the Kassur District. Thither the brothers proceeded with their families, and founded several villages, Hariki, Beytu and the two Nowls. About this time also, whether from conviction or influenced by the grant of land, they became converts to Muhammadanism. When the Sikhs became powerful, about the middle of the 18th century, Kassur, with its large Muhammadan population, consisting partly of Pathan colonists and partly of Hindu converts, fell into the hands of the Bhangi chiefs, who held it till 1794, when Nizamuddin Khan, the Pathan leader, drove out the Sikhs, and contrived for some years to hold his own against all opposition. Nizamuddin Khan was assassinated by some of his relations, in 1802, and his brother Kutbuddin Khan became chief in Kassur. He married a daughter of *Khewa Khan*, and bestowed upon his father-in-law an estate worth 10,000 Rs. in addition to his ancestral villages. In 1807 Kassur was conquered by Ranjit Singh, and Kutbuddin Khan was permitted to retain Mamdot, to the south of the Satlej, whither he retired, accompanied by *Khewa Khan*, who received a jagir, in Mamdot, of the same value as that he had lost in Kassur, subject to the service of a contingent of horse. For many years, under Kutbuddin Khan and his successor Jamaluddin Khan, Malik *Khewa* performed military service, and when he grew old his son *Khairuddin* headed the contingent, on active service. *Khairuddin Khan* during the first Afghan war was stationed at Peshawar with the 100 horsemen of the Mamdot contingent; and after its disastrous termination he accompanied the second army under General Pollock to Kabul, with the Mamdot horse and 100 men from the Mokal and Attariwala contingents. His services, at a time when the Sikh Brigade was notoriously hostile and refused to advance, were very valuable, and on his return to the Panjab both General Pollock and Major Mackeson recommended him to the kindness of Maharaja Sher Singh, who promised to increase his jagir, but was assassinated before he was able to carry out his intention. At this time Jamaluddin Khan, chief of Mamdot, confiscated the jagir of *Khewa Khan*, who retired to the village of Beytu, an ancestral possession, where he died, at a very advanced age, in 1856. Maharaja Dalip Singh, in compensation for this loss of the Mamdot jagir, gave to *Khairuddin Khan*, in 1844, six villages near Kassur, worth 6,000 Rs. During the latter part of the Satlej war he fought on the side of the British, crossing the river with his whole family and joining the camp, soon after the battle of Firushahr. During the retrenchments that followed the deposition of Raja Lal Singh his jagir was reduced to 4,000 Rs., and shortly afterwards two more villages were taken away, the Kardars affirming that the revenue of the two remaining ones, Beytu and Matran, was fully 4,000 Rs. At the time of the Multan outbreak *Khairuddin* was at Dera Ismail Khan, under the orders of Captain Taylor. He was sent to Bannu to relieve

Fatah Khan Tiwana, who was besieged in Dalipghar; but Fatah Khan was slain and the fort reduced before he reached it. He was afterwards sent from Isakhel with 200 horse and 500 foot into the Pindi Gheb country to harrass Gohar Singh, the rebel Kardar of Sirdar Chattar Singh, and to encourage the Attock garrison. He performed the duty most satisfactorily. Gohar Singh was routed in two or three encounters, and was forced to fly the country, and while the Sikh army remained on the left bank of the Jhelam *Khairuddin* held his ground to the north of the Salt range. In 1857, at the requisition of the Chief Commissioner, he raised 100 horsemen, and with his nephews proceeded to Hissar under General Van-Cortlandt.

In this expedition *Kamaluddin Khan*, his nephew and adopted son, was made risaldar, and distinguished himself highly. *Khairuddin Khan* also did good service at Gogaira, against the rebel Ahmad Khan chief of the Kharrals.

He has served the British Government well in five campaigns, and is a man upon whom reliance may be confidently placed. He holds a jagir worth 2,500 Rs. for life, which descends, after his death, to *Kamaluddin Khan* and his heirs male for one generation.

PANDIT RADHA KISHAN.

SRI BRIJRAJ,
D. 1833.

Pandit Madhosudan,
D. 1863.

- Pandit Radha Kishan, B. 1805.
  - Rishi Kesh.
    - Kishori Lal.
- Bal Kishan, B. 1808.
  - Mohan Lal.
    - Sohan Lal.
    - Ram Lal.
- Har Kishan, D. 1861.
  - Amar Nath.
- Devdatt Parshad, B. 1840.
  - Durga Datt.

HISTORY OF THE FAMILY.

The traditions of this Brahman family go back to the year 1244 when Allah-ud-din Musaud was king of Delhi. In this year, on account of the persecutions suffered at the hands of the Muhammadans, the whole family emigrated, with other Hindus, from the sacred city of Mattra, to Uch near Multan. This new home was singularly chosen, and could hardly have been a pleasanter residence than Mattra, as at this very time, according to Ferishta, it was overrun by an army of Mogals from Kandahar. Some time afterwards the family settled at Lahore, but when happier times came round, returned to its old home at Mattra. One ancestor of *Radha Kishan*, by name *Narayan Das*, was celebrated for his learning and piety, and is mentioned in the 'Bhagatmal' or 'Fakir's Necklace' of Nabhaji. A firman of the Emperor Jahangir, granting to *Kishan Lal*, great grandson of *Narayan Das*, 24 bigahs of land at Mattra for the purpose of growing the flowers used in Hindu worship, is still extant. This document has every mark of being genuine and bears the date 1610 A. D.

Brij Bhukan, son of *Kishori Lal*, was the very Diogenes of Brahmans. The Emperor Shahjahan, hearing of his piety, paid him a visit, and was so pleased at his derivation of the word Hindu from '*hin*,' an abbreviation of 'Hinsa' Sansc. *sin,* and '*du*' abbreviation of 'dur,' Sansc. and Pers. *far*, 'far from sin,' that he desired the Brahman to ask any favour of him and it should he granted. "Do me then the favour," said *Brij Bhukan*, "of never paying me another visit."

During the reign of Aurangzeb, *Kawa Nain*, the youngest son of *Brij Bhukan*, went to Jaipur, at the invitation of Raja Jai Singh I. Here he obtained the charge of a temple, with a jagir for its support, which is still held by his descendants. *Bansidhar*, his grandson was a man of great piety, and numbered among his disciples Suraj Mal the famous Raja of Bhartpur.

Brijraj, or as he was generally called *Brijlal*, settled in Lahore about the middle of the last century. He was very much respected by the Bhangi chiefs, who were then rulers of the city, and when Ranjit Singh rose to power he was made Pandit, and appointed to read and explain the sacred Sanscrit books. He held this office, remaining in high favour with the Maharaja, till his death, in 1833. Like his father, Pandit *Madhosudan* was a great scholar, and there was no other Pandit in Lahore who had so extensive an acquaintance with Sanscrit literature. In 1808, he was appointed 'Dana Dhaksh,' or Almoner to the Maharaja, and chief Darbar Pandit, both which offices he held till the annexation. *Madhosudan* married the daughter of Misr Battalia, the great Amritsar banker. He was a great favourite of the Maharaja, who, in 1824, appointed his son *Radha Kishan* tutor to the young Raja Hira Singh, whose after-life, mean, sensual and untrue, did not certainly say much for his education.

Radha Kishan, who was like his father a Darbar Pandit, was, in 1846, appointed to superintend the education of the young Maharaja Dalip Singh.

Pandit *Madhosudan* held, under the Sikh Government, jagirs of the value of 9,935 Rs. One village, Kila Gujar Singh, had been granted by Ranjit Singh, as a 'Dharamarth' to *Brijlal* and his heirs for ever.

The other villages included in the estate were grants to Pandit *Madhosudan* himself. These were, in 1851, released for life, and two gardens, one at Lahore and another at Dinanagar granted in perpetuity.

Pandit *Madhosudan* died in 1863. With his three elder sons he had violently quarreled, and he consequently left his entire property, with the perpetual jagir, to *Devdatt Parshad,* his fourth son by a second wife. A law suit regarding the property is still pending in the courts.

Har Kishan died before his father, in 1861, leaving one son *Amar Nath.* His jagir of 900 Rs. lapsed at his death.

Of the jagir of Pandit *Radha Kishan,* amounting to 5,270 Rs., 4,700 Rs. were released for life, and a garden worth 100 Rs. in perpetuity.

*Radha Kisha n*resides at Lahore, where he is much respected. His exertions in the cause of education have been great. He was one of the first to advocate female education, and when the American Mission opened an English School at Lahore, the sons of Pandit *Radha Kishan* were among the first scholars. In the same way he sent one of his sons to study at the Lahore Medical College, when it was first opened, and when the prejudices of the Natives against it were very strong. The Pandit is a distinguished Sanscrit scholar, and is well versed in Hindu Law.

MISR RUP LAL.

- DIWAN CHAND.
  - Misr Rup Lal, D. 1864.
    - Kishan Das, D. 1856.
    - Mahash Das, B. 1825.
    - Sawan Mal, B. 1828.
      - Bishan Das.
        - Bishambar Das.
      - Kirpa Ram, D. 1861.
    - Govind Ram, B. 1838.
      - Muthra Das, B. 1856.
      - Har Narain, B. 1860.
      - A daughter, B. 1864.
  - Misr Beli Ram, D. 1843.
    - Misr Ram Das, B. 1814.
    - Thakar Das, B. 1834.
      - Lachman Das, B. 1854.
      - A daughter.
    - Karam Rai, D. 1855.
  - Misr Meghraj, D. 1864,
    - Sheo Das, B. 1826.
      - Daughter, B. 1861.
      - Daughter, B. 1864.
  - Ram Kishan, D. 1843.
    - Sundar Das, B. 1828.
      - Daughter, B. 1861.
  - Sukhraj, D. 1842.

HISTORY OF THE FAMILY.

The family of Misr *Rup Lal* is of the Brahman caste, and came originally from Mouza Dilwal, in the Jhelam District. *Diwan Chand* came with his sons to Lahore about the year 1809, and through the interest of his uncle *Basti Ram,* who was the Treasurer of Ranjit and held by him in great esteem, obtained a jagir of 1,000 Rs. for himself, at Kahun, Jhelam ; and places at court for his two eldest sons *Rup Lal* and *Beli Ram,* who were made assistants to their great uncle in the Treasury. *Beli Ram* soon became a great favourite with the Maharaja, and on the death of *Basti Ram,* in 1816, was appointed his successor in spite of the opposition and ill-will of the minister Raja Dhyan Singh, who wished Jessa Misr,* a protégé of his own, and father of Lal

* Jessa Misr was first employed by *Basti Ram* as a writer on five rupees a month in the Treasury. He gradually rose in the department, and the post of custodian of the Kashmir treasure, which Dhyan Singh procured for him, attached him to the Dogra party.

Singh (afterwards Raja) to obtain the vacant post of Toshakhania, or Treasurer. Misr *Meghraj* received about the same time charge of the treasure in the Govindghar Fort at Amritsar, and he held this office during the remainder of the Maharaja's reign. In 1826, *Ram Kishan* entered the Government Service, and was made chamberlain to Ranjit Singh, who always treated him with special kindness.

In 1832, Misr *Rup Lal* was appointed Nazim or Governor of the Jalandhar Doab. This rich district had been ever since its first conquest by Ranjit Singh, entrusted to Diwan Mokham Chand, Moti Ram his son, and Kirpa Ram his grandson. In 1831, when Diwan Moti Ram was recalled, Shaikh Ghulam Mohiuddin, a follower of Diwan Kirpa Ram, and a tyrannical and grasping man, was sent as Governor of Hoshiarpur and the neighbouring districts. The people of the Doab complained so bitterly of his oppression that, in 1832, he was recalled, and Misr *Rup Lal* sent in his place. The new Governor was of a very different character from his predecessor. Possessing considerable wealth himself he had no inducement to oppress the people, and being connected with a Jalandhar family, he had an interest in the prosperity of the district. His assessment was so light and equitable, that even in the famine year of 1833, there were very few unpaid balances. He would never accecpt the smallest present, and kept a close watch upon the conduct of his subordinates. It is refreshing, among the many Sikh Governors who have considered the people under them as created for their private profit, to meet with a man like Misr *Rup Lal*, upright and just, whose name is remembered to this day by the people with respect and affection. *Rup Lal* held the Jalandhar Governorship till 1839, when, some months after the death of Maharaja Ranjit Singh, he was recalled, and the old oppressor of the Doab, Ghulam Mohiuddin, restored. Prince Nao Nihal Singh, indignant with Misr *Beli Ram* for having supported his father's favourite Chet Singh, threw him and his brothers into prison where they remained six months, till at the intercession of Maharaja Kharrak Singh, they were released. *Beli Ram* was a zealous supporter of Prince

Sher Singh, who, when he ascended the throne, restored the Misr to his old post of Toshakhania. *Rup Lal* he made Governor of Kalanur and the lands of the Lahore State south of the Satlej, with orders to resume the fort and domain of Bhatpur from Jamadar Khushhal Singh. Misr *Meghraj* returned to Govindghar as Treasurer. *Beli Ram* was much in the confidence of Maharaja Sher Singh, and in conjunction with his friend Bhai Gurmukh Singh tried to form a party at Lahore against Raja Dhyan Singh the obnoxious Dogra Minister. His intrigues cost him his life, for when Raja Hira Singh succeeded his murdered father as minister, one of his first acts was to arrest Bhai Gurmukh Singh, *Beli Ram,* and his brothers. Misr *Meghraj* and *Rup Lal* were placed in charge of Misr Lal Singh, their old enemy; and Bhai Gurmukh Singh, *Beli Ram* and *Ram Kishan* were made over to Shaikh Imamuddin Khan, who imprisoned them in the stables attached to his house. For a long time their fate was uncertain, but it at length transpired that all three were secretly murdered by the Shaikh, acting under Raja Hira Singh's orders. *Rup Lal* and *Meghraj*, more fortunate, remained in confinement till the fall of Raja Hira Singh in December, 1844, when they were released, and *Rup Lal* was made, by the Minister Jowahir Singh, Governor of Jasrota. The sons of *Beli Ram,* who escaped to Ludhiana at the time of their father's arrest, remained under British protection till 1845 when they returned to the Panjab.

Rup Lal was at Jasrota, in 1846, when that country was made over to Raja Gulab Singh by the treaty of the 16th March. The Raja vehemently accused him of treason in not yielding up the hill forts in accordance with the terms of the treaty. He was accordingly removed by the Darbar from Jasrota and placed in charge of Rhotas and Jhelam, and was there when the rebellion broke out. He joined Sirdar Chattar Singh's camp, through compulsion, he himself asserts; but his sympathies were certainly with the insurgents, and there is every reason to believe that he supplied them with money. His sons also left Lahore at this critical time and joined their father. For this conduct his jagirs and property in Lahore were confiscated. He died in September 1864, upwards of 80 years of age, at Dilwal, in the Jhelam district. His son *Sawan Mal* is Risaldar in the 1st Sikh Cavalry. He served with great credit in Oude and China, and, in 1861, received a jagir of 400 Rs., 200 Rs. of which descend to his heirs, for one generation.

Misr *Meghraj* was, after the Satlej campaign, appointed Treasurer to the Darbar, and on the occasion of the visit of the Governor General to Lahore he received the title of 'Rai Buhadar.' In 1849, he was appointed Treasurer of the Lahore Division, a post which he held till his death on the 1st August 1864. Misr *Meghraj* had been appointed an Honorary Magistrate, in 1862, and there were few in Lahore more deservedly respected by both the European and Native community. At the of his death he was in enjoyment of jagirs to the value of 3,825 Rs., of which 405 Rs. descend to his male heirs in perpetuity.

Sukhraj, the youngest of *Diwan Chand's* sons, died in 1842. He was made a General by Maharaja Ranjit Singh in 1836, with command of 4 infantry regiments, a cavalry regiment and 2 troops of artillery.

Thakar Das, second son of *Beli Ram*, is Treasurer of the Rawal Pindi Division. He holds a jagir of 1,387 Rs. which descends for one generation.

Ram Das, his elder brother, enjoys a cash pension of 2,000 Rs. *Gulab Devi* and *Begam* the widows of *Misr Beli Ram* each enjoy a pension of 1,387 Rs.

Misr Sundar Das, who was for two years Keeper of the Privy Purse to Maharaja Dalip Singh, received, after annexation, a donation of 1,000 Rs., his jagir of 1,500 Rs. which was a recent grant of Raja Lal Singh, being resumed.

RAI KISHAN CHAND.

RAI ANAND SINGH.

- Rai Govind Jas.
- Lala Rai Singh. D. 1858.
  - Lala Devi Ditta Mal.
- Rai Ram Dyal. D. 1863.
  - Lala Khasita Mall.
    - Bishamba Das.
    - Shiv Saran.
    - Pali Ram.
  - Bishamba Singh.
    - Rattan Lal.
- Rai Kishan Chand.
  - Sharranpat Rai.
    - Ram Narayan.
  - Rai Bhag Singh.

HISTORY OF THE FAMILY.

The Bhandhari caste and family, to the Chamyari Patni branch of which *Rai Kishan Chand* belongs, were founded by Rai Bhag Mal, an adventurer, who, in the year 1256, went from Multan to Ghazni to seek his fortune and having in course of time obtained every thing fortune had to bestow, except a son, returned to India, and hearing of a famous ascetic named Baba Farid at Pak Pattan, went there to obtain his blessing. When he arrived he found the saint hanging head downwards in a well, where he had already remained so long that his followers, who were dependent upon his miracles for their food, were reduced to great straits. Rai Bhag Mal, who was very rich, built them houses and fed them for nine years, till Baba Farid, growing tired of the well, returned to the upper air. He was surprized to see the new village, and asked by whose liberality it had been built. The people pointed out Rai Bhag Mal, who, they said, had fed them during the Baba's absence. The saint said that he must indeed be a good steward or '*bhandhari*' and this name has remained with the family ever since. Bhag Mal then begged the saint to pray for a son for him. Baba Farid told him that he should have three sons, and asked that one might be given to him, which Bhag Mal promised. When three sons had been born, the saint sent to Bhag Mal to remind him of his promise ; but the father did not like to part with his sons, and accordingly sent one of them to his sister's house ; another he hid in a cellar, and met the Baba with his youngest son in his arms, and told him that he had but one son, which he could take or leave as he liked. The saint replied "You have three sons, yet this, the youngest, shall be my follower," and accordingly he took the child with him to Pak Pattan, whence the branch of the 'Bhandharis' descended from him is named Patni. The other two branches, descended from the elder sons, are called 'Bhoriah,' from 'bhorah' a cellar, and 'Birpalia' meaning 'brought up by a sister.'

Little is known of the family of *Rai Kishan Chand* till 1809, when, through the interest of Diwan Mokham Chand, his father *Anand Singh* was appointed vakil or agent of the Lahore court at Ludhiana, which had recently been occupied as a military station. *Anand Singh* afterwards was sent as agent to Dehli, while his eldest son *Govind Jas* occupied his place at Ludhiana, and his youngest son *Kishan Chand* was agent at Karnal and Amballa. *Anand Singh* accompanied Sir Charles Metcalfe on the successful expedition against Bhartpur, undertaken by Lord Combermere, in December, 1825, and on his return received from the Maharaja the title of 'Rai' with a dress of honour. He died in 1827, and his jagirs were divided among his four sons. *Rai Govind Jas* obtained Lakhowal, Pawadat and Lagrian ; *Rai Singh* took Kotlah and Sunarah ; *Rai Kishan Chand,* Rehli, Rupowal, and Rajpurah ; and Lohghar fell to the share of *Ram Dyal. Rai Govind Jas* succeeded his father at Dehli, and *Ram Dyal* was sent to Ludhiana, but shortly afterwards he quarreled with Colonel Wade the Political Agent, and was recalled to Lahore. *Rai Kishan Chand* took his place, receiving a jagir of 15,000 Rs. in the Jalandhar District, and an allowance of 1 R. per annum, on each village belonging to the Lahore State on the left bank of the Satlej. *Ram Dyal* was, in 1832, sent to Anandpur to settle the disagreements that had arisen among the Sodhis of that place. He remained there five years, and on his return to Lahore received a jagir of 4,000 Rs. in the Ludhiana District. He was, later, when Raja Hira Singh recalled Fakir Chiraghuddin from Firozpur, appointed to that place as agent. *Rai Kishan Chand* was an able and an upright man. He saw that the interests of the Maharaja required peace with the British, and he did his best to maintain a good understanding between the Governments. At the beginning of 1839, he accompanied Colonel Wade on his political mission to Peshawar, and during his absence which lasted the greater part of the year, his son *Bhaj Singh* acted for him at Ludhiana. The title of 'Rai' was granted to *Kishan Chand* by Prince Nao Nihal Singh in 1840.

After the death of Maharaja Sher Singh the position of the agents of Lahore on the British frontier underwent a considerable charge. In the days of Mr. Clerk and his predecessors the wakils were little more than newswriters; they conducted all current business, but important affairs were arranged by the Agent of the Governor General with the Maharaja by deputation or letter. But the changes which took place on Sher Singh's death gave to *Rai Kishan Chand* and his brother and son, who held the agencies at Firozpur and Ludhiana, great influence and power, which the Lahore ministry was ever trying to reduce and the wakils to retain. *Rai Kishan Chand* exercised certain civil and criminal powers in the Lahore protected states, and drew from them considerable wealth. This jurisdiction the ministry of Hira Singh took away, and in November, 1844, the proportion to be paid to the state from the wakil's farm and jagirs was raised to that of neighbouring districts. *Rai Kishan Chand* and his family however retained considerable influence at Lahore. Jealous of Fakir Azizuddin and somewhat opposed to his policy, they were supported in Darbar by powerful friends, chief of whom were Bhai Ram Singh, and Diwan Dina Nath, the leader of the Mutsaddi party.

Although in 1844, *Rai Kishan Chand* had perhaps encouraged, in some measure, the belief at Lahore that the British were hostile to the

Sikh Government, yet when war became really imminent, he protested against it earnestly ; but it was then too late. When the Sikh army was preparing to cross the Satlej he was ordered by the Political Agent to leave the camp and retire into the Lahore territories, which he did. After the close of the campaign and the cession to the British Government of the Jalandhar Doab, the family lost its jagirs on the left bank of the Beas, but *Rai Kishan Chand* was directed to attend on the Agent of the Governor General at Lahore, and this appointment he held till 1844, when he received permission to retire to Battala.

Bhag Singh had, on the return of peace, been appointed agent of the Darbar with the Commissioner Trans-Satlej States, and, in 1848, he received the title of " Rai " and a dress of honour. *Rai Kishan Chand* also received the title of Buhadar and a grant of nine villages in the Dinanagar District, worth 8,000 Rs. and a cash pension of 4000 Rs. was assigned to him in recognition of his faithful services, and as compensation for the jagir he had lost in Ludhiana. *Ramdyal* received at the same time a jagir of 3,000 Rs. and a cash pension of the same value. *Rai Bhag Sinhg* obtained 2,500 Rs. in jagir, and 2,500 Rs. cash, and *Sharanpat* 1,800 Rs. jagir and 1,800 Rs. cash. The two latter did not hold their jagirs or pensions long. At the annexation of the Panjab they were resumed, as were the cash allowances of *Rai Kishan Chand* and *Rai Bhag Singh.* The jagirs of the two latter were confirmed to them, and at *Rai Kishan Chand's* death, his two sons will each receive a pension of 1000 Rs. *Ramdyal* died in 1863, and his jagir has been resumed. In 1855, *Rai Bhag Singh* was appointed Tehsildar and has been stationed at Pathankot and Zaffarwal. He resigned his appointment in 1861 in order to accompany his father to Benares, where *Rai Kishan Singh* still resides. *Rai Bhag Singh* returned to the Panjab, in 1864, and is now resident at Battala.

DIWAN MULRAJ.

- HOSHNAK RAI.
  - Nanak Chand, D. 1831.
    - Daughter M. Gurdit Singh, Hafizabad.
    - Rattan Chand, D. 1830.
      - Ram Chand, B. 1820.
  - Gurmukh Rai.
    - Devidyal, B. 1811.
    - Ram Sarup, B. 1827.
  - Diwan Sawan Mal, D. 1844.
    - Ram Das, D. 1831.
      - Wazir Chand, B. 1829.
    - Diwan Mulraj, D. 1850.
      - Hari Singh, B. 1848.
    - Karam Narayan, B. 1817.
      - Lachmi Narayan.
    - Sham Singh, B. 1837.
    - Ram Singh, B. 1840.
    - Narayan Singh, B. 1844.

HISTORY OF THE FAMILY.

Hoshnak Rai, a Khatri of the Chopra caste, was a servant of Sirdar Dal Singh of Akalghar, with whom he took service about the year 1768. He was not himself a man of any note, and his name is only remembered through the genius of *Sawan Mal* his third son, and the rebellion of *Mulraj* his grandson.

Nanak Chand, the eldest son of *Hoshnak Rai,* entered the service of Dal Singh in 1788, and there remained until the death of the chief in 1804, when Akalghar, which was held as a dependency of the Sukarchakia misl, fell, by escheat, into the hands of Ranjit Singh. He then left his native town, and entered the force of Diwan Mohkam Chand, under whom he rose to posts of considerable trust, and after the death of that General he was employed in collecting the revenues of Multan and Kashmir. His only son *Rattan Chand,* died one year before him, in 1830; and *Ram Chand,* his grandson, succeeded to his appointment. *Ram Chand* was at this time but twelve years of age, but Maharaja Ranjit Singh took a fancy to him, and made him chancellor, giving him charge of his private seal. Since the death of the Maharaja he has taken no part in the public life. He resides at Akalghar, and is in receipt of a pension of 2,400 Rs. The esteem in which *Ram Chand* is held for his liberality and integrity is very great. He has built large tanks at Ichhri, near Lahore, and at Nankana, a place of pilgrimage sacred to Guru Nanak. At Lahore he maintains a native doctor and a dispensary for the gratuitous distribution of medicine to the poor; he has founded a Sanskrit school at Amritsar, and a Sadabart or poor-house at Benares.

Gurmukh Rai, brother of *Nanak Chand,* was an officer of irregular cavalry under Diwan Mohkam Chand. He died in 1830, leaving two sons, of whom *Devi Dyal,* the elder, was Multan agent at Lahore during the rule of his uncle *Sawan Mal.* In 1849, he was appointed Magistrate of the whole of the Jech Doab, and held this appointment until annexation. In 1853, he was made Tehsildar of Ramnagar, but resigned the next year.* He was created Honorary Magistrate of Akalghar and Ramnagar in 1862, and is in the enjoyment of a pension of 2,300 Rs. *Ram Sarup* the second son has become a Muhammadan, and is disowned by his family. He has taken the name of Ghulam Mohiuddin, and lives in Lahore, where he supports himself by copying manuscripts.

The third son of *Hoshnak Rai* was the celebrated *Sawan Mal,* who was born in the year 1788. He commenced public life in the office of his brother *Nanak Chand,* and, in 1820, was sent to Multan on 250 Rs. a month, as head of the account office under Bhaiya Badan

* In 1857, some enemies of *Devi Dyal* gave information to the effect that he was in possession of a large portion of Diwan *Mulraj's* property, which had been forfeited to government on his conviction. The house of *Devi Dyal* was accordingly searched and property worth more than a lakh of rupees was attached. A few months later he proved the falseness of the accusation and the property was restored to him.

Hazari* the governor. The next year when Badan Hazari was degraded, *Sawan Mal,* whose abilities were well known to the Maharaja, was appointed governor or viceroy of half the province of Multan, and, in 1829, he was made governor of the whole. The tract of country which thus came under the rule of *Sawan Mal* was very extensive, and comprised the districts of Multan, Leia, Derah Ghazi Khan, Khanghar, and part of Jhang. It was at this time almost a desert. For many years it had been the scene of rapine and war. Life and property were insecure, and the population which had once been numerous and wealthy had become scanty and impoverished. But under the new administration a great change was wrought. Diwan *Sawan Mal,* by offers of land and protection, induced many of the inhabitants of neighbouring districts to settle in the province; he excavated canals (in the Multan district alone of the length of three hundred miles); he favoured commerce and acted in every way as a wise and beneficent ruler. It has been often asserted that he regarded the Pathans, the late rulers of Multan, with no favour. That, himself a trader, he had no sympathy with the old aristocracy of the country; himself a Hindu, he neither trusted nor loved the Muhammadan portion of his subjects, and that with these feelings he ousted most of the Pathan proprietors from their holdings and supplied their places with Jat zamindars.† But there is little truth in these statements. The sympathies of *Sawan Mal* were, it is true, with the Hindus, but he

* Bhaiya Badan Hazari, once the governor of the province of Multan, now lives at Lahore, at the shop of his son, a cotton spinner, on a pension of 20 Rs. a month. It is difficult to understand how the Maharaja selected for so difficult a post as Multan, a governor as imbecile as Badan Hazari. In a very short time he threw the Multan finances into almost inextricable confusion, and so irritated Ranjit Singh that on the Bhaiya's recall and first appearance at Darbar, it is said the Maharaja was about to kill him with his own hand, and was only prevented from so doing by the intercession of Fakir Azizuddin.

† It is true that a great number of Pathan proprietors lost their estates between the years 1818 and 1822, but the evictions were chiefly made by the predecessors of Diwan *Sawan Mal*; and it was hardly to be expected that the claims of the vanquished would be much regarded in the early days of the conquest. Many Pathans voluntarily left Multan on its capture by Ranjit Singh, and only returned where *Sawan Mal* became governor. These, no doubt, found difficulty in recovering their estates which had fallen into Jat hands.

appreciated the fine qualities of the Pathans, and these supplied his army with its most distinguished and dashing officers.

During the reign of the great Maharaja, *Sawan Mal* was little disturbed. Ranjit Singh saw the gradual increase of the Diwan's power, but he knew that during his reign he would not rebel; and as the tribute was paid with the greatest regularity, there was no cause of complaint. But no sooner was Ranjit Singh dead than the enemies of the Diwan attempted to destroy him. Chief of these were the Jammu Rajas, Gulab Singh and Dhyan Singh, between whom and the Diwan had always existed jealousy and the most bitter hatred. It was proposed to demand from the Diwan half a million sterling, and he was summoned to Lahore to render his accounts. Had he refused to obey, it was the intention of the Darbar to send troops to compel him; but *Sawan Mal* knowing his power, and believing that the Court would not dare to proceed to extremities, came to Lahore in September, 1840, when amicable arrangements were made, and he returned to Multan.

In March, 1841, when Maharaja Sher Singh had just obtained the supreme power, he directed both *Sawan Mal* and Raja Dhyan Singh to raise fresh troops, intending to replace with them some of the turbulent Khalsa regiments. In compliance with this order the Diwan began to raise Muhammadan troops, with the greatest activity, with the real object of defending himself against Dhyan Singh; while the Raja was not less energetic, hoping with his new troops not only to overwhelm *Sawan Mal*, but to defend Jammu both against the Sikhs and the British.

In January, 1842, the Mazari tribe, which had always given trouble to Sikh governors, rebelled, and made a descent upon Kojhan, hoping to plunder it before the arrival of help. But *Sawan Mal* marched against them, in force, and they were compelled to retire.

When Raja Dhyan Singh was assassinated by the Sindhanwalias, Diwan *Sawan Mal* was freed from the most able of his enemies. But all the members of the Dogra family hated him; Raja Gulab Singh as an able and influential rival, and a better servant of the state than himself, and Raja Hira Singh because Pandit Jella, his minister and master, hated him. The Pandit was a man of no limited ambition. He hoped to be able first to destroy Raja Gulab Singh, by inciting the Khalsa army to march against Jammu, and then to crush Diwan *Sawan Mal*. Were these rivals removed he would wield the whole power of the state. But the Pandit was unable to control the army from which he hoped so much, and was murdered by the troops in December, 1844.

Through these years Diwan *Sawan Mal* had been strengthening himself at Multan. There is every reason to believe that he intended, at some favourable opportunity, to throw off his allegiance to Lahore and declare his independence. It was with this intention that he expended so much money and labour upon his fort at Multan, that it was all but impregnable to a native force. It was against the Sikh army that the defences were prepared, and though *Sawan Mal* would have held them as a rebel, there will be found few to condemn him. The empire which the genius of one man had founded, was falling asunder; no efforts of the Diwan could avail to save it, and he had as much right as others to a share of the spoil. Loyalty was not in question. To Maharaja Ranjit Singh he had ever been a faithful servant; but an hereditary claim to devotion on the part of Maharaja Dalip Singh, was, to all who knew the history of the zanana, ridiculous.

But whatever were the intentions of the Diwan, he was not destined to see them realized. On the 16th September, 1844, at his morning Darbar, a soldier, who had been caught thieving, was brought before the Diwan for trial. After investigation the prisoner was remanded and placed in the 'deorhi' or ante-chamber with a guard over him. The Diwan transacted all his business, and towards evening went out through the 'deorhi' to take the air. The prisoner, who had hidden a pistol in his waist cloth, drew it, and fired at the Diwan at a distance of five paces. The ball struck *Sawan Mal* on the left breast, and passing round the ribs came out at his back and wounded an officer of the name of Didar Singh, who was standing near, on the right arm. Sahib Singh and Sarbuland Khan cut the assassin down, and the Diwan severely but not dangerously wounded, was carried into the palace. For some days all went on well, and to all appearance the wound was healing, when a change for the worse took place; the wound re-opened, and *Sawan Mal* gradually sank and died on the 29th of September, 1844. *

Diwan *Sawan Mal* † was the best of all the Sikh governors. During the latter years of Maharaja Ranjit Singh's life and during the reigns of his successors, the Diwan was practically irresponsible; yet his great power was in no way abused. He amassed great wealth, it is true, and upwards of a million sterling was divided by his family after his death; but this was not wrung from the people by cruelty and oppression. The Government demand, under both *Sawan Mal* and his son, never exceeded one-third of the gross produce of the land, and was generally only one-fifth or one-sixth. But it was his impartiality which caused the people to regard *Sawan Mal* with such love. It is said that one day a peasant complained to him that some chief had destroyed his crop, by turning his horses loose to graze in the field. *Sawan Mal* asked the man if he could point out the offender in Darbar. The peasant pointed to *Ram Das*, the Diwan's eldest son. He admitted the complaint to be just, and *Sawan Mal*

---

* Sir H. B. Edwardes in his 'Year on the Punjab Frontier,' has given a different account of the manner in which the Diwan met his death. He states that the assassin was a soldier, who had served *Sawan Mal* faithfully, and who came to Darbar to ask for his pay and discharge. That *Sawan Mal* refused to grant these just demands, and caused the petitioner to be stripped of sword and shield and turned out of Darbar. That in revenge for this grievous insult the soldier shot him.

This version is incorrect. Among the authorities for the account given in the text may be mentioned *Karam Narayan*, son of the Diwan, and Sukhdyal, sherishtadar in the office of the Judicial Commissioner, who was standing beside *Sawan Mal* when he was shot and who was present in Darbar while the investigation into the theft case was being conducted.

† The Sikh governors, whose names are most revered by the people, are Diwan *Sawan Mal* of Multan, Mihan Singh of Kashmir, and Misr Rup Lal of Jalandhar. Of these *Sawan Mal* was far the wisest and the best. Misr Rup Lal's assessments were light, and the country flourished under his rule; but the people fancied him too fond of their wives and their daughters. He carried to the grave with him a long scar on the left shoulder, where he was wounded by the sword of a jealous Khatri, who caught him in his house too late at night.

ordered him to be imprisoned. The injured man begged for his pardon, but for several days *Ram Das* remained in confinement, and his spirit was so broken by this punishment that he fell ill and died shortly after his release.

Diwan *Sawan Mal* was succeeded as governor of Multan by his son *Mulraj*. Raja Hira Singh and the Court of Lahore would have preferred some nominee of their own, but the Multan family was too strong, both in fact and reputation, to be put aside. *Mulraj* was at this time about 30 years of age. He had served under his father, first as Kardar or manager of Shujaabad, and then as Kardar of the district of Jhang. In both these places he was hated for his oppression and avarice,* and although when he succeeded to the governorship of Multan he much improved in disposition, yet he was always unpopular with the people. Scarcely had *Mulraj* established himself than the Lahore Darbar, having heard reports of the vast wealth left by *Sawan Mal*, demanded a 'nazrana' or tribute of one million sterling. The state of his army was also a source of great anxiety to *Mulraj*. Nominally part of the Lahore army, the force at Multan was raised by the governor, who promoted or discharged men and officers at his pleasure. He was only bound to keep up a certain force. At this time, of the ten battalions at Multan, eight were composed of Muhammadans and two of Sikhs. The latter, instigated, it was believed, by the Darbar, rose in mutiny on the 24th of November, 1844, demanding higher pay. They were jealous of the Lahore army, in which, at this time, the pay of an infantry soldier was eleven rupees, eight annas, a month, while they only obtained seven rupees, eight annas. Diwan *Mulraj* and his brother *Karam Narayan* immediately on the outbreak attacked the mutineers, and entirely dispersed them; and this victory so much baffled the Darbar and strengthened the Diwan

---

* It was a common saying in the country that Multan was blessed with Sawan, (the month of rain); Leia with Karam, (kindness); while Jhang was desolated by Mula, (an insect which destroys the corn.)

The allusion of course was to *Sawan Mal*, governor of Multan; *Karam Narayan*, his third son Kardar of Leia, and *Mulraj*, Kardar of Jhang.

that he sent to Lahore to offer a very much smaller 'nazrana' than that demanded. Negotiations, however, went on for some time longer; till *Mulraj*, believing that the Sikh army on its return from Jammu would be marched against him, agreed to pay eighteen lakhs of rupees. But in the very month that this arrangement was made, Sirdar Jowahir Singh the minister was murdered; the country became the scene of anarchy and confusion, and the Khalsa army marched to the Satlej against the British.

During the war, *Mulraj* made no effort to pay his tribute, and on the return of peace the Darbar determined to press its claims. The eighteen lakhs agreed upon were demanded, with seven lakhs of arrears. Raja Lal Singh, the old enemy of *Mulraj*, was now minister at Lahore. He eagerly desired the ruin of the governor, and hoped to install his own brother, Bhagwan Singh, in his place. With this object he insisted upon sending troops to enforce the claim of the Darbar. *Mulraj* had at this time no wish to oppose the Government, and withdrew most of his troops towards Multan, as the Lahore force, under Misr Rallia Ram, advanced. However, three miles from Leia a collision took place between some irregulars of the Diwan and the advanced body of the Lahore force. The latter, after a sharp skirmish, was worsted, and its leader Khazan Singh, Chabalia, taken prisoner.

But *Mulraj* was now anxious to make his peace with the Darbar, and knowing that no mercy was to be expected from Raja Lal Singh, he appealed to Major H. Lawrence, the English Resident at Lahore, through whose influence a safe conduct was granted to the governor, who arrived at Lahore on the 9th October, 1846, accompanied by Diwan Dina Nath, who had escorted him from Multan. *Mulraj* tried hard to obtain more easy terms than had been previously granted, and at the end of November, an agreement was concluded by which he was to pay eight lakhs of what was due, at once, and the remainder by instalments. The districts, including portions of Leia and Jhang, which had been recently occupied by the Sikh troops were to be retained by the Darbar, and for the remaining portion of the province he was to pay 19,68,000 Rs. per annum.

Both parties appeared satisfied with this arrangement, and in November, 1846, *Mulraj* returned to Multan, where for some months all went on well. The eighteen lakhs were paid up, and the Darbar had no just cause of complaint. But the governor was not long content. He had lost a portion of his province ; and the new custom duties, though not as yet enforced in Multan, were beginning to diminish his revenue. His power was also less absolute, for there was now a strong Government in Lahore, which held that justice was the first virtue of an administration ; —and petitioners, bankers, merchants and cultivators had discovered that the road to redress lay through Lahore. This was more than the Diwan could endure. His father had been a king in all but the name, and had bequeathed his pride and his ambition to his son. So the Diwan returned in November, 1847, to Lahore, to endeavour to obtain some modification of the terms of his agreement, and a promise that no complaints against him should be received. Should these requests not be granted, he had resolved to resign his charge. Mr J. Lawrence was then Acting Resident at Lahore. To him the Diwan unfolded his troubles and his wish to resign. Mr. Lawrence endeavoured to dissuade him from doing so, but told him he was at liberty to act as he thought fit, so long as his resignation was given in at a time convenient to the Government he served. The Diwan still insisted on resigning as he saw that the objects for which he had come to Lahore could never be attained ; and it was arranged, that he should resign at the end of April, 1848 ; that for the present, the Darbar should not be informed of his intentions, and that two or three months before his resignation two English officers should be sent to Multan to be instructed by the Diwan in the state of affairs, and ultimately to be placed in charge of the province.

A few days after this arrangement, the Diwan left for Multan. When Sir F. Currie, appointed Resident at Lahore, arrived there at the beginning of April, he considered it right that the Darbar should be informed of the intention of *Mulraj* to resign. This was accordingly done, and the Diwan was addressed on the subject both by the Darbar and the Resident. He was told that he was still at liberty to retain his charge; but he reiterated his desire to resign, on account of ill health and dissentions in his family and his resignation was accordingly accepted by the Darbar. The appointment of governor of Multan was offered to Sirdar Shamsher Singh, Sindhanwalia, but he was disinclined to accept it, and it was consequently given to Sirdar Khan Singh Man, an intelligent man, who was to act in concert with Mr. Vans Agnew, of the Bengal Civil Service, who was appointed Political Agent, with Lieutenant Anderson of the Bombay Army as his Assistant. These officers proceeded to Multan, which they reached on the 17th April, and the next day joined their escort, under Sirdar Khan Singh. They were received by the Diwan with great civility, and it was arranged that he should accompany them over the fort the next morning. Accordingly on the morning of the 19th, they proceeded, with the Diwan and two Companies of Goorkhas to make the inspection. Mr. Vans Agnew left the Goorkhas at one of the gates, and made the round of the fortress, with the Diwan, who gave over charge. As they passed out of the gate, a soldier of the Diwan struck Mr. Vans Agnew with his spear and knocked him off his horse, and then attacked him with his sword and wounded him severely. Lieutenant Anderson was also cut down, and left for dead on the ground, till found by some of the Goorkha troops, who carried him to the Idgah, a strong building near the fort in which the English officers had taken up their quarters and where Mr. Vans Agnew had arrived before him. When the assault on the officers took place, at the gate of the fort, the Diwan rode off to his own house; and although later in the day Mr. Vans Agnew sent to him, desiring him to attend and prove his innocence by his acts, he never came, alleging that his soldiers would not allow him to do so. On the morning of the 20th the fort opened fire upon the Idgah, which was returned by the Sikh artillery of the escort, but at night Colonel Esra Singh, commanding the artillery, went over to the enemy with all his men. The Idgah was then assaulted by the enemy. No resistance could be offered, for the unfortunate English officers were severely wounded and deserted by those who had sworn to defend them. They died like gallant men, and their heads, severed from the mutilated bodies, were taken in triumph to the rebel Diwan, who rewarded the murderers with praise and money. Almost the last words of Mr. Vans Agnew, spoken to Sirdar Khan Singh, who remained faithful to the end, may be recorded here, for they were words noble and prophetic, and neither England nor the Panjab should forget them. "They may kill us two," he said, wounded and hopeless of human aid, "they may kill us two, but we are not the last of the English. Thousands of Englishmen will come when we are gone, and will annihilate *Mulraj*, and his soldiers and his fort."

And so the die was cast. The Diwan knew that he could not now retrace his steps, and prepared with energy and determination for war. He strengthened his fort and laid in supplies in anticipation of a siege; he called to his side all the disaffected in the province, and addressed the chief Sirdars telling them that now was the opportunity they had so long desired of freeing their country from the hated yoke of the English.

It is impossible in a biographical sketch to follow the course of the war that ensued, resulting in the annexation of the Panjab.

For some time the rebels at Multan remained unpunished. The season was unusually hot, and Multan had a bad reputation for unhealthiness, and the English Commander in Chief did not feel justified in sending a European force against it till later in the year. The Resident was thus compelled to send a Sikh army, whose disaffection was admitted by the chiefs who commanded it, and whose subsequent desertion to the enemy, with its general Raja Sher Singh, Attariwala, did not occasion much surprise. But the rebel Diwan was not left unmolested. Through the summer months Lieutenant H. B. Edwardes, with a small native force had kept *Mulraj* in check and had gained important victories over him, aided by the force of Bahawal Khan, Nawab of Bahawalpur, which was directed and virtually commanded by Lieutenant E. Lake. Shaikh Imamuddin Khan, one of the Sikh generals, who had remained loyal in the midst of disaffection, did also admirable service; and when the British Army arrived before Multan in August, 1848, *Mulraj* had little upon which he could depend beyond the walls of his fort.

The siege train arrived before Multan on the 4th September, and on the 6th opened fire upon the fort. But *Sawan Mal* had not laboured in vain at the defences, and the reduction of the fort was a matter of no small difficulty. The besieging force was small, and a large proportion of it consisted of irregular troops, brave indeed in the field but almost useless for the operations of a siege. The defection of Raja Sher Singh with his whole force, on the 14th of September, compelled General Whish to raise the siege, and wait for reinforcements. The suspicious nature of *Mulraj* did not allow him to profit by the desertion of the Sikhs. He thoroughly distrusted the motives which induced them to join him; and was much relieved when the Raja, disgusted at the suspicions of which he was the object, marched from Multan to join his father, Sirdar Chattar Singh, who was in open rebellion in the North West of the Panjab.

The fate of *Mulraj* was not long delayed. Reinforcements at length reached the British army, and on the 27th of December the siege was resumed. During the interval *Mulraj* had sought for help and allies in all directions. Dost Muhammad Khan was ready enough with promises, but Multan was too distant for active aid. The Sikhs, whom the Diwan had distrusted and insulted, would now have nothing to do with him. They had too their own work before them. From every quarter the heroes of Sobraon and Aliwal, the men who had fought under the great Maharaja and under Hari Singh Nalwa, were assembling, to try once more the fortune of battle, to be present at the approaching struggle, in which, at Chillianwala and Gujrat, the Khalsa for ever fell and the empire of the Sikhs was lost.

After some severe fighting before Multan, the exertions of the British troops were successful. On the 2nd January, 1849, the city was carried by assault, and, on the 22nd, *Mulraj*, who had shut himself up in the citadel, seeing further resistance to be hopeless, surrendered at discretion.

He was conveyed to Lahore and brought to trial, in the month of June, for the murder of Mr. Vans Agnew and Lieutenant Anderson. He was ably defended by Captain Hamilton; but was found guilty and condemned to death. The Governor General, Lord Dalhousie, with whom the confirmation of the sentence rested, accepted the judges' recommendation to mercy and commuted the sentence to transportation for life. *Mulraj* was, accordingly, sent as a prisoner to Calcutta, where he died the following year.

It is not for history to praise an unsuccessful rebel, but a careful review of the Diwan's history will show him to have been more unfortunate than criminal. It is certain that when Mr. Vans Agnew first arrived at Multan, the Diwan had no intention of rebelling. Had such been his design, he would not have resigned his charge or have given over the fort. It is equally certain that the first attack on the British officers was without the Diwan's privity or consent. That attack was either an outburst of fanatical hatred on the part of the Muhammadan soldiery, who saw the fort in which they took so much pride passing into the hands of strangers, or it was instigated by some of the Diwan's officers, who wished to compromise him and compel him to rebel. It is probable that he was under restraint and unable to command the obedience of his soldiers when the Idgah was assaulted and the English officers slain. At no time, from that fatal day, till the arrival of the British army before Multan, could the Diwan, with any safety to himself, have proposed terms of submission or have sued for pardon. He was surrounded by relatives, friends and troops who depended upon him for place and wealth and power, and who saw in a new governor nothing but ruin to themselves. They determined to force *Mulraj* to rebel, for his victory would enrich them, and his defeat could not be more injurious to them than his resignation. Diwan *Mulraj* was not an amiable character. He was mean, grasping, suspicious and vacillating. But the crimes of cold-blooded murder and of premeditated rebellion cannot, with any justice, be laid to his charge.

The Diwan left one son *Hari Singh*, born in 1848 ; who is now a student in the Government College at Lahore, and is in receipt of a pension of 360 Rs.

Karam Narayan, the third son of *Sawan Mal*, served as his Lieutenant in the Leia district, carrying on its civil duties, and at the same time holding military command in the celebrated fort of Mankera. He was much beloved by the people for his kindness and impartiality. After *Sawan Mal's* death *Karam Narayan* did not get on at all well with his brother *Mulraj*, who, in 1847, imprisoned him in his own house. For two months he remained in confinement, and was then allowed to leave Multan with his share of the property left by *Sawan Mal*, amounting to more than ten lakhs of rupees. He settled at Akalghar, where he still resides, and was in no way party to his brother's rebellion. * He holds a pension of 400 Rs.

Ram Singh and *Narayan Singh* were children at the time of their father's death. They each enjoy a pension of 400 Rs. a year.

---

* It was said at the time that *Ram Narayan* spent a large sum in getting up cases against his brother and bribing parties to go to Lahore and appeal against him.

DIWAN HUKM CHAND.

- MIHR CHAND.
  - Diwan Gurbaksh Rai.
    - Diwan Thakar Das.
      - Diwan Devi Das, D. 1830.
        - Shanker Das, D. 1858.
      - Kishan Das, D. 1847.
        - Har Sahai, D. 1861.
          - Hakim Rai, B. 1834.
          - Sukha Nand.
      - Diwan Bhawani Das, D. 1824.
        - Diwan Hukm Chand, B. 1807.
          - Bishambar Das, B. 1824.
            - Badrinath, B. 1864.
        - Shankar Das, B. 1816.
          - Tara Chand, B. 1837.
            - Arjan Das.
        - Ganga Bishan, B. 18
          - Tikta Sahai, B. 1846.
      - Lala Narain Das, D. 1842.
        - Lala Ramji Das.
          - Gopal Das, B. 1834.
      - Rajkour.
        - Natha Mal, B. 1824.
        - Govind Sahai, B. 1839.
        - Tagga nath. B 1832.
      - Rankour.
      - Lala Ram Das, B. 1784.
        - Jowahir Mal, D. 1854.
          - Nanak Chand, B. 1834.
        - Hira Nand, B. 1804.
          - Mya Das, B. 1838.
          - Nand Lal, B. 1839.
          - Rattan Chand, B. 1844.
      - Mangal Sen.

HISTORY OF THE FAMILY.

Gurbuksh Rai was the first of this family to rise to any eminence. He was the Diwan or minister of Nawab Nasir Khan, the ruler of Kabul and Peshawar, and possessed great influence. His son *Thakar Das* was Diwan to Haji Atta Khan, son-in-law of Shah Wali Khan, chief minister of Ahmad Shah, the celebrated Durani chief. On the death of the Haji, *Thakar Das* entered the service of Ahmad Shah, who made him Diwan Khas or privy counsellor, and gave him charge of the seal of state. His wealth and power were considerable, and his style of living was princely. He accompanied Ahmad Shah on his first expedition to India, in 1747, and after the capture and sack of Mathra received the grant of a valuable jagir in the Jalandhar Doab. Timur Shah succeeded his father in 1773, and during his reign of twenty years *Thakar Das* continued to fill the office of Diwan. He served Shah Zaman during the first year of his troublous reign, and died at an advanced age, in 1794.

Bhawani Das, the second son of *Thakar Das,* was a revenue officer of high standing under Shah Shuja. He was chiefly employed in collecting the customs of Multan and the Derajat, and, in 1808, disgusted at the manner in which he was treated by the Kabul court, he determined to try and obtain service with Ranjit Singh, and accordingly set off for Lahore, forgetting, it is asserted, to pay into the treasury the revenue that he had collected. He was well received by the Lahore chief, who, surrounded by illiterate soldiers, was much in want of some able man with a reputation as a financier, to keep his accounts. At this time there was no state Treasury, or regular system of accounts at Lahore. The revenue, which amounted to about thirty lakhs of rupees, was managed by the Amritsar banker Ramanand, who held the octroi of Amritsar and farmed the salt mines of Pind Dadan Khan. *Bhawani Das* soon effected a great improvement. He established a pay office for the troops, and a finance office, of both of which he was made the head.

Devi Das, his elder brother, joined him at Lahore towards the end of 1809. He had been in the service of Wazir Sher Muhammad, the son of Wazir Shah Wali Khan, minister of Ahmad Shah. After the assassination of his master he remained for some time in concealment as he feared the same fate, but at length effecting his escape he set out for Lukhnow, where his family had been promised an asylum. But his route lay through Lahore, and on his arrival there the persuasions of Ranjit Singh and the high position of his brother induced him to remain. He was associated with *Bhawani Das* in the Finance Department, neither being subordinate to the other, and they always got on well together. *Devi Das* was a man of as great ability and of far greater integrity than his brother, but he never became so prominent, as he was of a retiring disposition.

After the cession of the fort of Kangra to Ranjit Singh by Sansar Chand, in 1810, and the reduction of the hill chiefs, *Bhawani Das* was sent to collect the tribute from the Rajas of Mandi and Suket. In 1816, he was made chief Diwan to prince Kharrak Singh, and was employed to reduce the country of the Ramgharia Sirdars about Amritsar and Gurdaspur. The next year he was sent to Jammu to bring the district into order and to make it over to Gulab Singh, who had just received the title of Raja. He was present at the siege of Multan and shared the Peshawar and Yusafzai campaigns. But although the appointments filled by *Bhawani Das* were many and lucrative, his chief work was as head of the Finance Department. On one occasion he fell into deep disgrace. He had quarreled with Misr Beli Ram, the treasurer, who accused him to the Maharaja of embezzlement. The charge was considered proved, and Ranjit Singh, in his passion, struck *Bhawani Das,* in open Darbar with his sheathed sword and fined him a lakh of rupees.* The Diwan was then banished to a hill appointment ; but his services were too valuable to be lost and he was recalled after a few months. He remained Minister of Finance till his death in 1834, when he was succeeded by Lala Dina Nath. *Devi Das* died four years earlier, in 1830.

Hukm Chand was appointed a 'Daftari,' or office keeper, on the establishment of prince Kharrak Singh in 1836, and the next year was made Kardar of Satgharrah, on 100 Rs. per mensem, and he managed his district with tolerable ability. In 1840, he was sent to Bannu, under the orders of Raja Suchet Singh, in one of the many expeditions to collect the revenue by force of arms. He received the title of Diwan from

---

* It is commonly believed that this fine was paid by the generous Sirdar Joala Singh, Padhania, who was a great friend of *Bhawani Das,* but Diwan *Hukm Chand* denies the story.

Maharaja Sher Singh. In 1847-48, he was ordered to accompany Lieut. Edwardes to Bannu. He remained under that officer till the Multan war broke out, and his assistance in the settlement of the Trans-Indus districts was most valuable. He accompanied the British army to Multan, where he behaved very well. Before annexation he was in receipt of 6,700 Rs. per annum, and in 1850 was allowed to retain a jagir of 2,300 Rs. in the Pak Pattan District, and a pension of 1,300 Rs. a year. In 1855, he was made Tehsildar of Pasrur, in the Sialkot district, but he did not give satisfaction to the authorities, and, in 1858, was permitted to resign.

Shankar Das, brother of Diwan *Hukm Chand*, was a munshi in his father's office. He and his brother *Ganga Bishan* each enjoy a pension of 240 Rs.

Lala Narain Das, fourth son of *Thakar Das*, was successively Kardar of Umritsar, Kangra, Jammu and Jaswan. In 1825, he was made office keeper of the Moti Mandar Treasury, under Misr Beli Ram, and later obtained the Kardarship of Lahore, which he held till 1833. In 1838, he retired to Kabul, where he obtained a military command, and soon after died. His son and grandson are still resident in Afghanistan; *Gopal Das* being munshi of the forces stationed at Kandahar.

Raj Kour came to Lahore with his brother *Devi Das*, and after the capture of Mankera was made Kardar of the district, Sirdar Fatah Singh Man holding the military command. He acted for his brother *Bhawani Das*, when that officer was on duty in Kashmir, in 1819.

SIRDAR JODH SINGH, UMRITSUR.

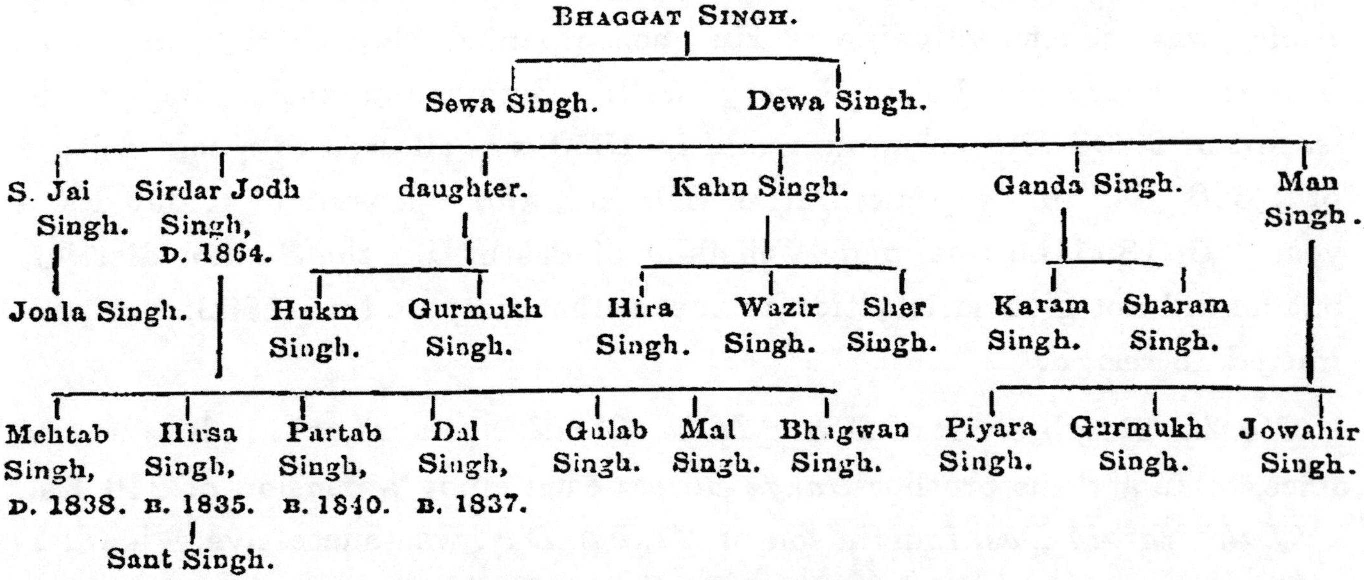

HISTORY OF THE FAMILY.

The village of Ruriala in the Gujranwala district is stated to have been founded by *Chowdri Taj* an ancestor of Sirdar *Jodh Singh.* It is certain that the family had long lived in the village and had for some time held the 'chowdrayat.' About the year 1759, *Bhaggat Singh* became a Sikh, and having married his daughter *Devi* to the powerful chief Gujur Singh Bhangi, obtained a grant of the village of Ruriala, free of service, from him. Gujar Singh also took the young *Sewa Singh* and *Dewa Singh* into his service, and gave them the jagir of Naoshera, in the Gujrat District, which was held by the brothers in joint possession till the death of *Sewa Singh,* who was killed in battle, and the jagir was resumed by Sahib Singh, son of Gujar Singh, who had succeeded his father in the command of the Bhangi misl. Two villages of the jagir were, however, left to *Dewa Singh,* and the ancestral village of Ruriala. *Jodh Singh* entered the force of Sirdar Jodh Singh, Sowrianwala, who had married his cousin, in the year 1813, when a boy of fifteen. He served with the Sirdar's Ghorcharahs till 1825, when, on the death of Sirdar Amir Singh, the jagir was resumed by the Maharaja and the irregular troops placed under the command of Prince Sher Singh.

In 1831, *Jodh Singh* accompanied the Prince in his successful campaign against Syud Ahmad Ali Khan. In 1834, he was placed as a trooper in Raja Hira Singh's Derah, in which he remained till 1848, having been, in 1836, promoted to the rank of commandant. The jagir of Ruriala, with 12,043 Rs., subject to the service of 2 sowars, had always remained in his possession, with the exception of the year 1835, when it had been temporarily resumed, and, in 1848, he received an additional grant of the village Kotli, in the Gujranwala district. During these years Sirdar *Jodh Singh* had performed good service to the state. He had served under Diwan Hakim Rai, who was in charge of Mamdot and Mokatsar, and was afterwards sent to the Manjha, where he was most energetic, and speedily cleared the country of robbers. During the reign of Sher Singh he was again sent to the Manjha, in command of 300 sowars, and remained there for six months, restoring order and administering justice. After the Satlej campaign *Jodh Singh* was appointed 'adalati,' or Judicial officer at Amritsar, on 3,000 Rs. inclusive of his jagir, and in 1849, after annexation, he was appointed Extra Assistant Commissioner at the same place, where he remained till his retirement from the Government service in December, 1862.

During the disturbances of 1848-49, Sirdar *Jodh Singh* remained faithful and did excellent service in preserving the peace of the city of Amritsar and in furnishing supplies to the British forces. In 1857, he accompanied Mr. F. Cooper, C. B., in pursuit of the Meean Meer mutineers, and rendered such zealous and prompt assistance that he received from Government a present of 1000 Rs. and a valuable watch. From annexation up to the beginning of 1862 he was in charge of the Darbar Sahib, the great Sikh temple at Amritsar, chosen by the Sikh aristocracy and priests themselves. This was an important duty, requiring great tact, honesty and powers of conciliation. These qualities the Sirdar possessed in an eminent degree. There have been special circumstances gravely affecting the good management of the temple of late years, but *Jodh Singh's* influence there was only for good. He guided its counsels through the difficult early years of the administration and through the critical period of 1857, when his loyalty and devotion to the Government were many times noticed ; while as a Judicial officer, he secured by his justice and unswerving honesty the respect of the inhabitants of Amritsar, without regard to caste or creed.

In recognition of Jodh Singh's services, the Government, on his retirement in 1862, allowed him to draw his full pay of 4,300 Rs. for life. Ruriala and Kotli were released rent-free for life, and the latter village, with two wells at Ruriala, was to descend to his heirs for two generations. He also received a grant of 50 acres of land in Rakh Shakarghar. Sirdar *Jodh Singh* died at Amritsar in August, 1864.

Sirdar *Mán Singh*, youngest brother of *Jodh Singh*, is one of the most distinguished native officers in the army. He entered Raja Suchet Singh's force when about twenty-five years of age, and was present at the capture of Peshawar and in the Trans-Indus campaign. He then entered Raja Hira Singh's brigade, where he was made an adjutant of cavalry. He fought against the British at Mudki, Firushahr and Sobraon ; and after the compaign was stationed at Lahore in command of a troop of 50 horse. In 1848, he was sent to Amritsar and remained with his brother during the war, doing excellent service ; and on the return of peace his troop was disbanded and he retired on a pension. But *Mán Singh* had no love for a quiet life at home. In 1852, he entered the Police under Colonel R. Lawrence, and remained in the force till 1857. At the first outbreak of the mutiny he was despatched to Dehli to join Major Hodson, with three troops of cavalry ; one raised by Nawab Imamuddin Khan, one by Raja Tej Singh, and the third in a great measure by *Mán Singh* himself. This force, first known as 'Montgomery Sahib ka Risala' became the nucleus of the famous 'Hodson's Horse.' *Mán Singh* served throughout the siege and capture of Dehli. He assisted in the capture of the king of Dehli and the capture and execution of the three Princes, and on that day the coolness and gallantry of *Mán Singh* were as conspicuous as those of his dashing commander. He then was sent with Col. Showers' column into the Reywari district, and returning to Dehli, about the end of October, was despatched to Lahore by Major Hodson to raise 500 recruits. This he effected in about four months, using the utmost exertions, and borrowing a considerable amount of the necessary funds on his personal security. He then hurried to Lukhnow. He arrived just in time to take part in the capture of the city, but too late to receive the thanks of his commandant, Major Hodson, who was killed the day before his arrival.

Mán Singh fought throughout the hot weather campaign of 1858, and was honorably mentioned in despatches for his gallantry at the battle of Nawabganj, on the 13th June, in dashing to the rescue of Lieut. Buller of his regiment, who was surrounded by the enemy. *Mán Singh* was, on this occasion, severely wounded in two places and his horse covered with sword cuts. He received for his conduct in this action the 2nd class order of Merit. He served throughout the Oude campaign of 1858-59, and was present at most of the important actions. At Nandganj, after capturing 3 guns, he was very badly injured by the blowing up of the tumbrils by a desperado from the enemy's ranks. From the injuries he received there he suffered for several months. The Government have rewarded the services of *Mán Singh* by the grant of jagirs in Oude and in Panjab of the value of 600 Rs., and 400 Rs., per annum, respectively. He still commands the same troop to which he was originally posted at Lahore, in 1857, and which has been incorporated with the 9th Regiment Bengal Cavalry.

Mehtab Singh, the eldest son of Sirdar *Jodh Singh,* was killed in suppressing a disturbance at Chakowal, in 1838.

Hirsa Singh, the second son, like his uncle *Mán Singh,* is a Risaldar in the 9th Bengal Cavalry. He was appointed to command one of the troops of cavalry raised by *Mán Singh,* in November, 1857. In the middle of 1858 he went with his detachment to Oude, and joined the head-quarters of 'Hodson's Horse' then commanded by Col. Daly, C. B. He fought with distinction in all the chief battles of the latter Oude campaign ; Sultanpur, Fyzabad, &c.

Partab Singh, in April, 1861, joined the Police Force as Subhadar. He is now Deputy Inspector in the Municipal Police of Amritsar.

Many others of the family have done good service under the British Government.

Dal Singh is Jamadar in the 18th Bengal Cavalry : *Joala Singh*, son of *Jai Singh*, is Subhabar of the 21st Native Infantry. *Hira Singh*, son of Khan *Singh*, is Subhadar of the 24th Native Infantry.

In the Police are *Karam Singh*, stationed at Fatahghar ; *Gurmukh* Singh, son of *Mán Singh*, Deputy Inspector at Sitapur, and *Gurmukh Singh*, son of a sister of *Mán Singh*, who is Inspector at Roy Bareilly.

Hukm Singh, brother of the *Gurmukh Singh* last named, is Naib Risaldar in the 9th Bengal Cavalry.

Most of these officers served throughout the mutiny with credit.

DIWAN HAKIM RAI.

MAHAN SINGH.
Kabuli Mal.

- Diwan Dhanpat Rai.
  - Matra Das.
- Har Baj Rai.
  - Kashi Ram.
    - Musaddi Mal.
      - Surjan Mal.
    - Diwan Hakim Rai, B. 1803.
      - Diwan Kishan Kour, B. 1825.
      - Arjan Singh, B. 1831.
        - Partab Singh, B. 1865.
      - Tara Chand, B. 1837.
    - Nand Gopal.

HISTORY OF THE FAMILY.

The ancestors of Diwan *Hakim Rai* were in the service of the Kanheya chiefs. *Mahan Singh* and *Kabuli Mal* undertook whatever civil administration was attempted by so rude and warlike a Sirdar as Hakikat Singh; collecting his revenue and keeping his accounts: and Diwan *Dhanpat Rai* and *Har Baj Rai* served Jaimal Singh, son of Hakikat Singh, in the same capacity. *Dhanpat Rai* was a man of considerable ability, and held the office and title of Diwan, and was engaged exclusively in civil work, while the duties of *Har Baj Rai* were of a very varied description. When in 1812, on the death of Jaimal Singh, his estates were seized by Ranjit Singh, *Har Baj Rai*, with his nephew *Matra Das*, entered the service of the Maharaja. He obtained a good appointment in the Judicial office, and his son *Kashi Ram* was placed under him. In 1824, *Hakim Rai* received an appointment in the Charyari Corps. He was an able man, and rose so rapidly to favour, that, in 1826, he was put in charge of the estates and person of the young Prince Nao Nihal Singh, and received an allowance of 1 per cent on all collections from the districts under him. At the same time he was honoured with the title of Diwan. In 1834, he accompanied the Prince and Hari Singh Nalwa across the Indus, and at the close of the successful Peshawar campaign, against Sultân Muhammad Khan, he was made governor of the conquered district, with Bannu and Yusafzai. The Maharaja also granted him a jagir of 5,000 Rs. in Pothiar. The Prince then proceeded down the frontier, which he found in a fearful state of misgovernment, and the Diwan was made governor of Dera Ismail Khan, Tak, Bannu and Isakheyl.

When Nao Nihal Singh, on the death of Ranjit Singh, obtained supreme power, he gave to the Diwan who had served him so well, a jagir worth 10,000 Rs. in the Sialkot district, and Hakim Rai relinquished his uncomfortable frontier duties for attendance at Court. During the reign of Maharaja Sher Singh he retained his honours ; and in the next reign was appointed Chief Justice of the city of Lahore. He was averse to the war with the English in 1845, but more from his knowledge of its certain danger than from any love to the British Government, for in 1844-45, he was the man, who at the head of 200 sowars, under the orders first of Raja Hira Singh and then of Sirdar Jowahir Singh, crossed the Satlej, and violated the provisions of the treaty, with the excuse of suppressing dacoity and punishing refractory zamindars. In 1846, he was sent, on the part of the Darbar, to Kashmir, to endeavour to bring to reason Shaikh Imamuddin Khan, then in active rebellion. He went there slowly enough, by the long road of Bhimbar, and although there is no certain evidence of treasonable acts on his part, yet it seems probable from his own statement at the time, and those of Wazir Ratnu and Colonel Matra Das, that his sympathies were with the traitor Lal Singh, though he did not venture to render any active assistance.

In April, 1847, the Diwan was sent, at the recommendation of the Resident, to Peshawar, as Chief Justice and Civil Governor in the room of Sirdar Chattar Singh, Attariwala. The entire administration of justice and collection of the revenue was made over to him, subject to the advice of Major G. Lawrence, Political Agent ; but the command of the troops was left with General Gulab Singh, Povindia. This appointment he did not hold for long. He had many enemies in Darbar, who were anxious to ruin him, and chief of them Sirdar Tej Singh, President of the Council. *Hakim Rai* was a nominee of Diwan Dina Nath, and this was in itself sufficient to make the Raja hostile. In a month and a half the administration of Peshawar was made over to Gulab Singh; while *Hakim Rai* was to remain content with the judicial portion of the work alone. This loss of power very much irritated the Diwan; he began to neglect his judicial duties,* and the Resident recommended his recall, in August, 1847.

On his return to Lahore, *Hakim Rai* obtained no other appointment, and the next year saw him one of the most conspicuous among the rebels. The reasons for his disaffection may be briefly related.

It has before been stated that Sirdar Tej Singh was an enemy of the Diwan. In the same month that *Hakim Rai* was recalled from Peshawar Tej Singh was created a Raja and given a jagir of 28,000 Rs. at Sialkot. At this town Diwan *Hakim Rai* resided, and here was the jagir of 10,000 Rs. granted to him, in perpetuity, by Nao Nihal Singh.† Tej Singh first confiscated two gardens and five wells which had been in the family for many years. The gardens were released on the representation of Diwan Dina Nath; and then the Raja caused the jagir to be resumed. The pensions of the Diwan and of his second son were also stopped, and the rebellion found him, not unnaturally, a disappointed and imbittered man. Some believe that Raja Tej Singh, who had certain knowledge of the storm which was preparing to break on the Panjab, desired to drive *Hakim Rai* into rebellion, that he might add the Diwan's

---

* Major G. Lawrence, who was the best judge of the Diwan's work, had a high opinion of him. In an Urdu letter to Raja Tej Singh, dated 12th August, 1847, he writes " a parwana regarding the recall of Diwan *Hakim Rai* was received some time ago, but owing to the good management of the Diwan, I considered it more for the interests of the Darbar to detain him. A second parwana to the same effect has now arrived. Since the Diwan's arrival at Peshawar he has paid constant attention to his duties and has given me every satisfaction by his good management."

† At the time of Prince Nao Nihal's death, Diwan *Hakim Rai* held jagirs and cash allowances amounting to 73,000 Rs. a year: *Kishan Kour* was in receipt of 39,000 Rs. jagirs and cash.

Sialkot jagirs to his own. If this was his intention it was eminently successful. In September, 1848, two regiments of the rebels were sent by Sirdar Utar Singh, Attariwala, to attack the fort of Bhopalwala, a few miles from Sialkot, belonging to Raja Tej Singh. They loudly proclaimed that when they had taken it they would destroy the houses of Diwan *Hakim Rai,* whose son *Kishan Kour* had destroyed and confiscated their houses in Gurdaspur. *Hakim Rai* sent to the Sialkot fort, asking for protection ; but the officers of the Raja would not give admittance to him or his family. Shortly after this he wrote to *Kishan Kour* to throw up his appointment and join him ; and father and son went over to Raja Sher Singh, Attariwala.

Diwan *Hakim Rai* was a great addition to the rebel strength. Though he brought with him neither men nor money, yet he was an exceedingly able man, and the document sent to the Resident, detailing the grievances felt by the Sirdars and the reasons for their rebellion, was drawn up by his hand.

But his cleverness could not avert the fate which fell upon him at the close of the war, when his jagirs, allowances and personal property were all confiscated, and he, with his sons, was sent a prisoner to the fort of Chunar. His ability made him dangerous and his removal necessary ; and he had also been detected in treasonable correspondence with some of the rebel leaders after the close of the war, but many, more criminal than Diwan *Hakim Rai,* remained in the Panjab.

Kishan Kour had been, from his childhood, the play-fellow and associate of Prince Nao Nihal Singh who entertained for him the greatest regard and affection. He received the title of Diwan, and favours of all kinds were heaped upon him. In 1837, when the Prince was at Peshawar, he gave to *Kishan Kour* command of four infantry and one cavalry regiments, with the customary proportion of artillery, on a salary of 1,500 Rs. a month.

In 1841, he was appointed Kardar of Rawalpindi, which office he held till after the Firozpur campaign. He rendered all assistance in his power to the British officers and troops in the way of procuring supplies at the time of the Afghan war. When, in 1848, Sirdar Lehna Singh Majithia, who had been the administrator of the country between the Ravi and the Satlej, left for Benares, *Kishan Kour* was appointed to the charge of the Battala, Dinanagar, and Kalanour Districts. He gave satisfaction by the manner in which he discharged his duties, and when the disturbances broke out, was at first very zealous in attaching and confiscating the property of rebels. He was not, however, able to resist his father's persuasions, and, as before related, they rebelled together.

Arjan Singh, the second son, was too young to be deeply implicated in the rebellion. He was, however, sent to Chunar with his father; but was released in 1853, and allowed to return to the Panjab, where a portion of the Sialkot property, owned by the family before the rebellion, was restored to him.

Diwan *Hakim Rai*, with his sons, was for four years confined in the Fort of Chunar, where Lal Singh Moraria and Mehtab Singh were also prisoners. In July, 1853, he was released, and permitted to retire to Benares. His pension was raised to 1,200 Rs. a year, and that of *Kishan Kour* to 600 Rs. In 1857, he did good service, and received a grant of some Zamindari rights and a house at Lakhnow where he and his son *Kishan Kour* reside. Both father and son, by their amiable disposition and irreproachable conduct through sixteen years of exile, have won the good opinion and esteem of the authorities of the North West.

Tara Chand, the youngest son of Diwan *Hakim Rai*, has been for several years in Government employ. He was first Peshkar of Daska in the Sialkot district: he was then made Naib Sherishtadar at Sialkot; and, in 1862, Judicial Sherishtadar at Gurdaspur, where he is highly spoken of.

DIWAN KARAM CHAND OF IMANABAD.

KIRORI MAL.

Jiwan Mal.

Diwan Karam Chand. Gurmakh Rai. Dhnraj Mal. Harnam Das.

(Sons of Diwan Karam Chand:) Sant Ram. Mohan Lal. Ganga Bishan.

HISTORY OF THE FAMILY.

The Nanda Khatri family, of which Diwan *Karam Chand* is the present representative, is of some antiquity. *Ujjar Sain*, the first of whom any mention is made, lived in the reign of Babar Shah, and by a marriage with the daughter of a wealthy official of Imanabad in Gujranwala, whither he had gone in the train of the Emperor, established the fortunes of the family. His son *Lukhu* was adopted by his father-in-law Daviditta, and, on his death, succeeded to his office of Kanungo, and for several generations the office, which was, in those days, of some consideration, remained with the family. The Sikhs under Sirdar Charrat Singh overran this part of the country, and the family lost most of their wealth; but the conqueror gave them a share in three villages, Kotli Dyanat, Raipur and Raffipur; and on the accession of Ranjit Singh, several members of the family were taken in his service. The only one who became of any importance was *Karam Chand.* He first went to Gujranwala, where he took a small contract for the revenue of Imanabad, and later he was sent as Tehsildar to Sri Har Govindpur, which was then administered by Tek Chand. For his services here he received a grant of three villages, Sulaiman, Kotli Mazbian and Kot Karam Chand, in the Gujranwala district.

When Sher Singh ascended the throne Tek Chand, an official of Nao Nihal Singh, was turned adrift. His subordinate *Karam Chand* was dismissed with him, but Raja Dhyan Singh took him into his service, and sent him to Bhimbar to manage his estates. After Dhyan Singh's death, *Karam Chand* served Raja Gulab Singh in Hazara; and when that country was exchanged by the Raja for Manawar, he retired to Peshawar. Two of his villages, Mazbian and Sulaiman, had been resumed in 1846 on his refusal to come to Lahore, and in 1850, *Karam Chand* had only three wells at Imanabad, worth 200 Rs., which were released for his life.

Karam Chand did not get on well in Kashmir, as he had an enemy at court in the person of Joala Sahai,* the Maharaja's chief agent. The mothers of *Karam Chand* and Joala Sahai were sisters, and there was between them a quarrel of long standing. Joala Sahai adopted his mother's quarrel, and making out that *Karam Chand* had embezzled very largely, caused him to be thrown into prison. The rights of the question cannot at this lapse of time be ascertained, but it is certain that Raja Jowahir Singh, nephew of the Maharaja, indignant at such treatment of his father's faithful servant, procured, with much difficulty, his release, and took him into his own service, in spite of the Maharaja's opposition. When Raja Jowahir Singh proceeded to Lahore, the Maharaja attacked his fort of Mangla on the Jammu road. It was most gallantly defended for some months by *Sant Ram*, son of Diwan *Karam Chand*, but was at last taken. Gulab Singh tried, it is said, to induce *Sant Ram*, to enter his service, but he refused, and the Maharaja threw him into prison. When the mutiny of 1857 broke out *Karam Chand* was at Lahore, in command of some troops belonging to Raja Jowahir Singh. He was directed to join General Van-Cortlandt, which he did, and was present as commandant of Raja Jowahir Singh's contingent at all the actions fought by the General between Firozpur and Rohtak. He then remained at Hissar till the Raja's contingent was amalgamated with the Police, when he was appointed commandant of the 10th Police Battalion, on his former pay of 500 Rs. per mensem. In 1861, when the Police were reorganised, *Karam Chand's* services were no longer required, but for his

* Diwan Joala Sahai is Prime Minister of the present Maharaja of Jammu.

loyalty and gallantry, he received a jagir of 3,000 Rs. at and near Imanabad, 1,200 Rs. of which were to descend to his son.

The services of *Karam Chand* were such that the influence of the Government was used to obtain the release of *Sant Ram*, from prison. In 1858, he was appointed Risaldar in the Hissar Police, in which he remained for three years.

SIRDAR MIAN SINGH BHAGOWALA.

- DHYAN SINGH.
  - Ram Singh
    - Anokh Singh.
    - Sirdar Mian Singh.
      - Sirdar Gulab Singh.
        - Kirpal Singh.
        - Richpal Singh.
          - Kaka Singh.
        - Bishan Singh.
      - Jai Singh.
      - Hira Singh.
    - Khazan Singh.
    - Kahn Singh.

HISTORY OF THE FAMILY.

The family of Bhagowala, of the Kahilon Jat caste, claims to have descended from the Powar Rajputs of Ujain. An ancestor of the name of Kahilon was the founder of the Jat family of that name, and Bhago the eleventh from Kahilon emigrated to the Panjab and built the village of Bhagowala, in the Batala Pargannah of the Amritsar District, from which the present family takes its name. *Ram Singh,* the father of Sirdar *Mian Singh,* was a follower of Sirdar Bhag Singh Bhagga, who, in 1795, gave him the two villages Bhugadh and Khattab. After the death of Bhag Singh, Ram Singh served with his brother Sirdar Budh Singh Bhagga. In 1809, Ranjit Singh took possession of the greater part of the Bhagga territory, and, among other places, of Bhagowala, which he granted to Sirdar Desa Singh Majithia. *Ram Singh* accompanied the Maharaja to Kangra in 1809, in the force of Sirdar Desa Singh, and in the first battle with the Goorkhas he was killed. His son *Mian Singh* was then a minor, but Desa Singh did not forget him, and, when he was able to bear arms, released in his favour some wells at Bhagowala, and placed him under his son Sirdar Lehna Singh. When this chief was made Governor of the hill districts, an assignment of 2,200 Rs. per annum was made to *Mian Singh* from the tribute of Mandi, Kulu, Suket, Kangra, Bilaspur, and Nadon. He accompanied Lehna Singh and Jamadar

Khushhal Singh on the expedition against Chowki Kotlehr, in 1825, and his old friendship with the Raja of that state had its effect in inducing him to surrender the fort, which was a strong one, and to accept a jagir, which the Jamadar pledged himself to obtain for him. After the death of Desa Singh Majithia, in 1832, his son confirmed *Mian Singh* in his jagir, and left him as Thannadar at Amritsar during his own absence in the Peshawar campaign. He also granted him an additional cash pension of 1,200 Rs. and jagirs of 1,550 Rs.

Gulab Singh, son of *Mian Singh*, entered the force of Lehna Singh Majithia, as a gunner in 1828, and was made a commandant in 1835. Up to the death of Maharaja Ranjit Singh, the Bhagowala chiefs had been merely feudal retainers of the Majithia Sirdars, but on the accession of Maharaja Sher Singh, *Gulab Singh* entered the regular army, and was made a Colonel of Artillery, with command of 11 guns, with a cash salary and jagirs of 2,116, Rs. Under Raja Hira Singh he was made a General, and his pay was raised to 3,458 Rs., being 1,000 Rs. in cash and the villages of Kharabad and Luhaika yielding 2,458, Rs., per annum. Under Jowahir Singh, his pay remained the same; but he was in command of 12 guns. When Sirdar Lehna Singh Majithia retired from the Panjab before the second Sikh war, *Gulab Singh* wished to accompany him, but he was not permitted, and was appointed Magistrate of Gogaira where he was stationed when the Multan war broke out. At that crisis he remained faithful to Government.

In 1853 *Gulab Singh* left the Panjab with Sirdar Lehna Majithia, to make a pilgrimage to Benares and other holy cities. He returned home the next year, and now holds a jagir of 2,500 Rs. per annum. Sirdar *Mian Singh* holds a jagir of 3,000 Rs.

SIRDAR BHUP SINGH BHAGGA.

AKAL.

- Sirdar Amar Singh, D. 1805.
  - Sirdar Bhag Singh, D. 1808.
    - Hari Singh, D. 1852.
      - Bhup Singh, B. 1836.
        - Daughter, M. son of Nihal Singh, Bhakowal.
      - Isar Singh, B. 1844.
        - Karam Singh.
      - Jiwan Singh.
        - Sant Singh.
    - Daughter.
    - Daughter.
  - Sirdar Budh Singh, D. 1846.
    - Partab Singh, D. 1847.
    - Gurmukh Singh.
    - Kaka Singh.
    - Daughter, M. Sirdar Thakar Singh, Attariwala
- Daughter, M. Nodh Singh, Majithia.

HISTORY OF THE FAMILY.

The Bhagga family, though at the present time of small consideration, formerly possessed both wealth and power. Its founder was *Amar Singh*, son of a Man Jat zamindar of the village of Bhagga in the Amritsar district, who, about the year 1759, left his village to seek his fortune. He adopted the Sikh faith, joined the Kanheya misl and set up as a robber. He was so successful in his new profession that he was joined by a considerable number of followers, the chief of whom was a man named Karam Singh. He overran and took possession of a large part of the Gurdaspur District, including Sujanpur, Sukalghar, Dharmkot, and Behrampur. He built a fort at Sukalghar, where he chiefly resided and where, in 1805, after a life spent in fighting, he quietly died in his bed, leaving his possessions, which he held intact till his death, to his eldest son *Bhag Singh*. This chief was not, like his father, of a warlike disposition, and made no attempts to extend his territory, but he was not the less a remarkable man. Few of the Sikh barons could spell out a page of the Granth or sign their names to a deed, but *Bhag Singh* was an accomplished scholar. He was master of both Persian and Sanskrit, he was a skilful painter and understood the art of casting guns. He only survived his father three years, and on his death a dispute arose about the succession. Desa Singh Majithia, son of *Amar Singh's* sister, had always been warmly attached to *Bhag Singh*, and now favoured the succession of *Hari Singh*, his son. The majority, however, supported *Budh Singh*, the brother, and declared that *Hari Singh* was illegitimate ; and *Budh Singh* took possession of the estates. But he did not hold them long. In 1809, Ranjit Singh demanded supplies from him for the Kangra expedition. The Bhagga Sirdar thought himself as good and as as strong as the Lahore Sirdar, and refused to give a man or a rupee. Ranjit Singh accordingly marched against him, and after a severe struggle defeated him and seized all the Bhagga territory. This result was much aided by the defection of Desa Singh Majithia. He had not forgiven *Budh Singh* for his triumph over *Hari Singh* and went over to the enemy, where his knowledge of the Bhagga position and resources were so valuable, that, after the affair was over, Ranjit Singh rewarded them by the grant of the Bhagga estates of Bhagowal and Sukalghar, the latter of which remained with the Majithia family till 1859, when, on the death of Sirdar Lehna Singh, it lapsed to Government.

Ranjit Singh left to *Budh Singh* a jagir at Dharamkot worth 22,000 Rs., which he held till his death, in 1846. Raja Lal Singh then resumed it, but, on the representations of Sirdar Lehna Singh, a jagir of 5,000 Rs. was released as a maintenance to *Partab Singh*, the only surviving son of *Budh Singh*, and his three widows. But before the grant could be issued *Partab Singh* died without issue; and the Darbar then assigned 3,800 Rs. to *Hari Singh* and the ladies of the family.

The three grandsons of *Bhag Singh* are now the only living representatives of the family. Their father *Hari Singh* died in 1852.

SIRDAR FATAH SINGH MAN OF MOGALCHAK.

- **Sarja Singh**, d. 1763.
  - Jai Singh.
    - Diwan Singh.
      - Wazir Singh.
        - Wasawa Singh.
      - Fatah Singh.
        - Joala Singh, d. 1858.
        - Sant Singh.
        - Hira Singh.
        - Richpal Singh.
      - Sher Singh.
        - Gurdit Singh.
        - Ganda Singh.
      - Jamiyat Singh, b. 1830.
        - Kirpal Singh.
        - Gopal Singh.
        - Sham Singh.
    - B. Mai Kour, m. Sirdar Mahan Singh, Sukarchakia.
    - Mihr Singh, d. 1814.
      - Kahn Singh.
    - Jodh Singh.
      - Anup Singh.
      - Gurbaksh Singh.
  - Mana Singh, d. 1807.
    - Sadda Singh.
    - Amir Singh, d. 1840.
    - Sham Singh, d. 1843.
      - Lehna Singh.
    - Hukm Singh.
    - Budh Singh, d. 1856.
      - Hira Sing,
      - Man Singh.
      - Ram Singh.
  - Nar Singh.
    - Attar Singh.
    - Rattan Singh.
      - Sant Singh.
        - Bhaggat Singh, b. 1863.
      - Nihal Singh.
      - Gulab Singh, b. 1838.
    - Bhaghel Singh, d. 1857.
      - Ganda Singh.
        - Richpal Singh. b. 1863.
      - Chanda Singh.
  - Pahar Singh, d. 1813.
    - Hari Singh, d. 1821.
      - Col. Jaggat Singh, d. 1860.
        - Nihal Singh, b. 1840, m. daughter of S. Kahn Singh, Nakai.
        - A daughter, m. S. Kesra Singh, Kanheya.
        - Narain Singh, b. 1847.
      - Partab Singh
        - Natha Singh, m daughter of S. Kahn Singh, Attariwala.

HISTORY OF THE FAMILY.

The Jats of the Panjab are divided into some ninety tribes with numberless subdivisions. Of these, the three oldest and from whom many of the others have descended are the tribes * Man, Her and Bhullar. It is not known, with any certainty, when the ancestors of the Man Jats emigrated to the Panjab. They were originally Rajputs, and inhabited the country about Delhi ; and to this day, near Jaipur, Thakur Man Rajputs are to be found.

Of this tribe and caste are many families distinguished in Panjab history. There is the Amritsar family of Mananwala ; the Gujranwala family of Mogalchak ; while to another branch Khan Singh Man, of Multan celebrity, and his gallant cousin Bhag Singh, belonged. Chief of the Ramnagar branch was Sirdar Desa Singh Man, Kardar of the Ramnagar Parganna, whose great grandson Ganda Singh, the only representative of the family, is living, in great poverty, at Amritsur. Of the Manblood, also, are the once powerful houses of Bhagga and Malwa, now represented by Sirdar Bhup Singh Dabbanwala and Sirdar Sarup Singh Malwai.

Ladda, the founder of the Mogalchak family, left Delhi in the year of a great drought and famine, and settled in the waste country near Gujranwala, where he founded the little village of Man, and was made headman over a circle of 22 villages. This office of chowdhri remained in the family for many generations till the decline of the Muhammadan power. *Nikka,* the fourth in descent from *Ladda,* founded the village of Nikka Man, but this soon passed out of his hands on account of a failure to meet the Government demand, and Mir Hamza, Governor of Imanabad, gave it to his brother Mirza Kilah, who destroyed it and built hard by a new village which he called Mogalchak. This village the Man family purchased later from the descendants of Mirza Kilah, and here they now reside. *Sarja Singh* is said to have been a follower of Sirdar Charrat Singh Sukarchakia, but little is known about him. He

* The 'mirasis' or bards state that 2½ Rajput tribes came first to the Panjab : the entire Man and Her tribes and half the Bhullar. The last named is not numerous at the present day. Its villages are found chiefly about Amritsar and Ajnala. The Man tribe is numerous about Kassur, Amritsar, Gujranwala, and indeed throughout the Manjha ; while the chief settlement of the Her Jats is in the Firozpur district.

died in1763, leaving four sons *Jai Singh, Manu Singh, Nar Singh* and *Pahar Singh.*

I. *Pahar Singh,* though the youngest of the brothers, will be more conveniently treated of first; as he was the most distinguished, and it was in a great measure through his assistance that his brothers rose in the world. He entered Charrat Singh's service as a trooper; but soon distinguished himself for energy and courage; obtained a grant of the four villages Jokian, Kalerh, Sal and Takuan, worth 3,277 Rs. and assumed the title of Sirdar. Under Sirdar Mahan Singh Sukarchakia his influence steadily increased, and he obtained 11,000 Rs. of additional jagirs near Ramnagar. He showed great gallantry in the many campaigns against the Chattahs; and under Ranjit Singh he served at Attock, Baisa and elsewhere. At the time of his death, in 1813, his jagirs amounted to upwards of two lakhs of rupees, subject to the service of 500 horse, 2 guns and 7 zamburahs or camel swivels.

Pahar Singh left one son *Hari Singh* a minor, and Sirdar Hukma Singh Chimmi was appointed his guardian. 47,000 Rs. of his father's jagirs were released to him, subject to the service of 125 horse; and when he become old enough to enter the army he was placed under Misr Diwan Chand, with whom he served at Bannu and Multan. He died of paralysis in 1821, being only twenty-two years of age. His two sons *Jaggat Singh* and *Partab Singh* were, at their father's death, infants, and the jagirs were consequently resumed; with the exception of 5,200 Rs. subject to the service of 13 horsemen. In 1843, *Jaggat Singh* was appointed orderly officer of Raja Hira Singh, and *Partab Singh* was made commandant in the Miwiwala regiment. Under the Darbar, *Jaggat Singh* was colonel of a cavalry regiment which formed part of Maharaja Dalip Singh's body-guard, and during the disturbances of 1848-49, he, with his troops, remained faithful to Government.

Jaggat Singh died in 1860, leaving two sons, *Nihal Singh* and *Narain Singh* aged respectively twenty-two and thirteen years at the time of his death. *Jaggat Singh* was in the enjoyment of jagirs worth 4,000 Rs. Of these a portion have been resumed, and his sons hold, in perpetuity, 1,637, Rs. being the mouza of Kalerh, and a share of Moghal Chak in the Gujranwala district.

II. *Nar Singh* was a misldar of the Sukarchakia confederacy, and fought under Mahan Singh at Manchar and Akalghar. He died young, and his three sons received allowances to the amount of 3,500 Rs. out of his jagirs. When *Rattan Singh* grew up, he was made adjutant in the Miwiwala regiment, and received estates in Gujranwala and Gurdaspur to the value of 1,200 Rs. He accompanied Sirdar Hari Singh Nalwa to Kashmir, and was, in 1820, very severely wounded at Mangli in the Kashmir hills where Hari Singh was reducing a strong fort defended by the mountaineers. For his services on this occasion he received a grant of Kharak in Gujranwala and the command of a regiment. His brother *Baghal Singh*, about this time, was made adjutant in Dhonkal Singh's regiment. Under Maharaja Kharrak Singh, *Rattan Singh* was sent in the force of Sirdar Sham Singh to Kulu and Mandi, where he was engaged for nearly two years in reducing the hill tribes to obedience. He was created a General by Sirdar Jowahir Singh, and Kila Desa Singh and Naoshera were given him in jagir. *Baghel Singh* was, in 1845, made commandant in his old regiment. *Rattan Singh* fought throughout the Satlej campaign, and soon after its close he was reduced to the rank of Colonel, and his jagirs were reduced to 5,000 Rs. with 1,000 Rs. free of service. He was serving at Peshawar in October, 1848, when the troops there mutinied. Major G. Lawrence spoke well of him, and he appears to have done his best to bring the mutineers to a sense of their duty, till the tide of rebellion became so strong that he was himself carried away by it. His son *Sant Singh*, then thirty years old, also joined the rebels and fought throughout the campaign of 1848-49. *Baghel Singh*, who accompanied Major H. B. Edwardes to Multan, stood firm; but died early in 1849 at Hanad in the Dera Ismail Khan district. After annexation, the jagirs of *Rattan Singh* were resumed; but he received a pension of 1,080 Rs, which lapsed at his death in 1857. *Sant Singh* is in receipt of a pension of 72 Rs., and also holds a share in Mouza Moghalchak. *Gulab Singh,* third son of *Rattan Singh,* is a convert to Muhammadanism, and is not acknowledged by his family.

III. *Jai Singh* married his daughter *Mai Man* to Mahan Singh Sukarchakia, and although this lady bore no children, yet the alliance very materially helped to build up the family fortunes. Under Ranjit Singh the family was very powerful, and at one time there were no less than twenty two members of it holding military appointments of trust and honour. Sirdar *Jai Singh* died young, but his sons were confirmed in possession of their father's estates. *Diwan Singh* did not long survive his father, and *Mihr Singh* the second son was killed in Kashmir in 1814. *Jodh Singh* accompanied the Maharaja on many of his campaigns. At the rebellion of 1848-49 *Jodh Singh,* who was a Colonel with jagirs worth 7,550 Rs. joined the rebels with his nephew *Jamiyat Singh,* but returned to Lahore before the end of the campaign. The jagirs of this branch of the family were resumed after annexation. *Jodh Singh* was allowed a pension of 720 Rs. which he still holds.

Fatah Singh, son of Sirdar *Diwan Singh,* was originally one of Ranjit Singh's orderlies. He was made adjutant of artillery, and under Sirdar Jowahir Singh commandant. After the Satlej campaign, Raja Lal Singh appointed him commandant in his cousin *Budh Singh's* regiment on 1,800 Rs. a month. He was with his cousin during the disturbances of 1848, and joined Captain Nicholson at the same time with him. One third of his salary of 1,800 Rs. was granted to him for life. In 1862, he was appointed Honorary Magistrate at Gujranwala.

Anup Singh the eldest son of *Jodh Singh* entered the 1st Sikh Irregular cavalry, afterwards better known as 'Probyn's Horse,' when it was first raised in August 1857, under the orders of Sir John Lawrence. After the fall of Delhi, *Anup Singh* accompanied the regiment to Oude and was present at the capture of Lukhnow in March, 1858. He served through the whole of the Baiswarra campaign, in the hot weather of 1858; and in the spring of 1859 in the Trans Gogra campaign. Where the fighting was the sharpest the 1st Sikhs were always to be found; and among many brave men *Anup Singh* distinguished himself for his cool and determined courage. During the Hindostan campaign he was four times wounded, and had three horses wounded under him.

In January 1860, he volunteered for China with his regiment and served with great credit throughout the campaign. He was again wounded, and his horse was again wounded under him.

The regiment was present with the force, during the late disturbances on the North West frontier; and, on one occasion, when it was engaged with the Bonairs, at Ambeyla, *Anup Singh* particularly distinguished himself and was very severely wounded in single combat with one of the enemy. He has twice received the Order of Valour for bravery in the field and has been granted a jagir of 500 Rs. per annum. The services of *Anup Singh* deserve especial notice. He is one of the finest native officers in the army; of undoubted loyalty, of conspicuous bravery, and a worthy representative of the old and gallant family to which he belongs. *Gurbaksh Singh,* his younger brother, was allowed by the Commander-in-Chief, in compliment to *Anup Singh,* to enter his brother's regiment, when a child only ten years of age. *Ganda Singh,* son of *Sher Singh,* also enlisted in the regiment in 1857, and served with the corps till its return from China in 1861. He then took his discharge, and is at present in civil employ at Gujranwala. *Joala Singh,* son of *Fatah Singh* entered the regiment with *Anup Singh.* He was a very promising soldier, and was killed in action at Nawabganj.

IV. *Mana Singh,* like his other brothers, was a subordinate chief in the following of Sirdar Mahan Singh Sukarchakia, from whom he received the estates of Pindori Kalan, Pindori Khurd and others. On his death in 1807 his elder son *Sadda Singh* succeeded to all his jagirs, and to the command of the contingent. This young man distinguished himself in the

Kashmir campaign where he was four times wounded, and received for his services a share in the Manawar Ilaka worth 12,000, Rs. *Sadda Singh* died childless, and Manawar, with other of his jagirs, was resumed ; but his brother *Amir Singh*, the handsomest man in the Khalsa army, was made a General and large estates were granted to him. The third son *Sham Singh* was created a colonel, on 5,000 Rs. per annum, and *Hukm Singh* a commandant. In 1840, *Amir Singh* died without issue ; and his jagir of 11,000 Rs. was assigned to his brother *Budh Singh* with the rank of General. *Amir Singh's* battalion, consisting of four infantry regiments, one cavalry regiment and two troops of artillery, was also placed under his command. *Budh Singh* had at this time been twenty-four years in the Sikh army. He had first entered it in 1816, as an orderly of the Maharaja, on 3,800 Rs. per annum, and this post he had held for five years. He had then, on his brother *Sadda Singh's* death, received command of thirty horsemen, with a jagir of 17,000 Rs. and after this had been commandant and colonel, in General Court's brigade, on 4,015 Rs. Under Maharaja Sher Singh his emoluments were reduced, for he was brother-in-law of Sirdar Attar Singh Sidhanwalia and Sher Singh's policy, at the commencement of his reign, was to destroy the power of the Sindhanwalia house.

Budh Singh served throughout the Satlej campaign, and shortly after its close he was reduced to the rank of a colonel in the Man battalion and sent with the Sher Singh brigade to assist Maharaja Gulab Singh in subduing the rebellion in that province. He behaved admirably on this occasion, and, in 1847, was of great service to Major Nicholson at Gandghar, and later in the year to Major Abbott, in the Dhoond mountains, where he and his men encamped in the snow for many days without a murmur. When the Multan rebellion broke out, *Budh Singh* was stationed at Hassan Abdal with his corps. Every effort was made by the insurgents to seduce him, by false accounts of the confiscation of his jagirs, by promises and by threats; but he stood firm, and when his men, in spite of all efforts, went over to Sirdar Chattar Singh, he left them and joined Major Nicholson with only his horse and his sword. He fought gallantly, under that officer, against the rebels in the Margalla Pass, where he was severely wounded in the head, and it was found necessary to send him to Peshawar, where he was afterwards captured by the Sikhs and kept under arrest until the battle of Gujrat, when he regained his freedom. *Budh Singh* was almost the only Sikh leader who remained sincerely on the side of the British at that critical time. There were some able men who stood by the British because they saw that they would eventually win; there were others who were faithful through hatred to the house of Attari. But *Budh Singh's* honesty did not depend upon political calculations. The Panjab proverb says, "The Man Sirdars are gallant, handsome and true;" and *Budh Singh* upheld the fame of his house. He was idolized by the army, and the estimation in which he was held is seen by the efforts made by the rebels to induce him to join them. But though his friends and relations were in the rebel ranks; though by loyalty he risked his life, his fortune and his reputation; yet he remained faithful to the end.

On the return of peace, his jagirs, amounting to 6,340 Rs. were confirmed to him for life, and 1,040 Rs. were released to his male heirs in perpetuity. This gallant officer died in October, 1856, leaving three sons, who reside at Mananwala in the Amritsar district, where a portion of their jagir lies.

Sham Singh, brother of *Budh Singh*, died in 1843, leaving one son *Lehna Singh*, who succeeded to the command of his father's regiment. He joined the rebels in 1848, and his jagirs were consequently resumed. He receives from Government a pension of 60 Rs. a month.

THE KANHEYA FAMILY.

I.—JIT SINGH.

- KUSHALI.
  - Jai Singh, D. 1789.
    - Gurbaksh Singh, D. 1785.
      - B. Mehtab Kour, M. M. R. Ranjit Singh, D. 1813.
    - Bhaggat Singh.
    - Nidhan Singh.
    - Bhag Singh.
  - Jhanda Singh. D. 1759.
  - Singha.
    - Hem Singh,
      - Mohr Singh,
        - Anup Singh.
        - Sarup Singh.
          - Jit Singh, B. 1814.
            - Jaggat Singh, B. 1838.
            - Sham Singh, B. 1845.
            - Ram Singh, B. 1846.
            - Narain Singh, B. 1847.
          - Gurdit Singh, B. 1827.
        - Attar Singh,
          - Mehtab Singh.
          - Megh Singh,

HISTORY OF THE FAMILY.

The Kanheya misl was at one time the most powerful of the Sikh confederacies, north of the Satlej. Its first leader was *Jai Singh*, the son of a Sindhu Jat cultivator named Kushali who lived at the village of Kanah, which had been founded by one of his tribe, some fifteen miles from Lahore. From the native village of its leader the confederacy took its name.*

---

* Some of the country bards tell a romantic story, to the effect that when the young *Jai Singh* went to Amritsar to be baptized as a Sikh, the assembled chiefs were so struck with his beauty that they asked him from what village he had come. "I am of Kanah" he said. "Well is your village named Kanah" was the reply "for you resemble Kanheya himself."

Kanheya, or Kanhia, is one of the names of the beautiful Krishan, an incarnation of Vishnu.

Jai Singh and his brother *Jhanda Singh* joined the confederacy of Kapur Singh, known as the Faizullapuria, Faizasadpuria or Singpuria, about the year 1749. On the death of this chief the brothers retired to Sohian, the villege of *Jai Singh's* father-in-law, about nine miles from Amritsar; collected a troop of about 400 horse, and took possession of the surrounding country. *Jhanda Singh* was killed five years later in a fight with Nidhan Singh Randhawa, at Rawalkotli, and his brother succeeded to his share in the estate, marrying the widow by the rite of 'chaddar dalna.' *Jai Singh* soon became a powerful chief, and seized Nag; Mokerian; Haji; Kerrot; Uthian and other Awan villages, while his subordinates and associates all won jagirs for themselves. Among the following of *Jai Singh* were many well known names: Amar Singh and Jhanda Singh Bhagga; Lakha Singh Kanhowala; Amar Singh Kankra; Budh Singh of Dharamkot; Jhanda Singh Keroh and others.

In 1759, *Desan*, the widow of *Jhanda Singh* and wife of *Jai Singh* gave birth to a son, *Gurbaksh Singh*, who was married, when nine years of age, to *Sada Kour*, daughter of Dasonda Singh of Alkolwala.

The leader of one great section of the Kanheya misl was Hakikat Singh Sangatpuria; a rival of *Jai Singh*, but nevertheless his friend and associate in many expeditions. In 1763, after Ahmed Shah had retired from the Panjab, having totally defeated the Sikhs near Ludhiana and destroyed the holy temples at Amritsar, these chiefs, allied with Jassa Singh Ahluwalia, Hari Singh Bhangi, and Jassa Singh Ramgharia, attacked the Pathan town of Kassur which they captured and sacked after a month's siege. Soon after this *Jai Singh* quarreled with Hari Singh Bhangi, and fought him near Imanabad. Neither party could claim the victory, and *Jai Singh* then marched to Sirhind, ravaging the country as he passed and was present in the great battle where Zein Khan was defeated and slain, and from which the Sikhs date their existence as a nation.

In 1773, Raja Ranjit Deo of Jammu, a tributary of Sirdar Jhanda Singh Bhangi, quarreled with his eldest son Brij Raj Deo, whom he desired to exclude from the succession in favour of his youngest son Mian Dalil Singh. Brij Raj Deo called to his assistance *Jai Singh* and Hakikat Singh Kanheya and Charrat Singh Sukarchakia; while the Raja summoned Jhanda Singh and all the Bhangi chiefs. The rival forces took up their position on either side of the Basanti, and for some months fought with varying success. The death of Charrat Singh from the bursting of his gun gave the advantage at length to the Bhangis, and the Kanheya chiefs then determined to assassinate Jhanda Singh. They heavily bribed a Masbi sweeper, who shot him dead as he was riding, attended by only three horsemen, through the camp. The death of Jhanda Singh ended the quarrel. The rival forces retired from Jammu, which became tributary to Hakikat Singh.

The next year *Jai Singh* and Hakikat Singh built the quarter at Amritsar, still known as the Kanheya Katrah; and soon after this *Jai Singh*, with a large force, escorted the young Mahan Singh, son of Charrat Singh, to Badrukh, where he was married to the daughter of Gajpat Singh of Jheend.

On the death of Nawab Sef Ali Khan, the Muhammadan governor of Kangra, in 1774, Raja Sansar Chand of Katoch laid siege to the celebrated fort, but was unable to reduce it. He then invited Sirdar *Jai Singh* to assist him; and *Gurbaksh Singh* was accordingly sent, with Sirdar Baghel Singh and a considerable force. It was not long, however, before *Gurbaksh Singh* saw that he who possessed the Kangra fort must be master of all the hill country, and determined to win it for himself. He persuaded the Raja to offer the garrison very favourable terms; free pardon, money and lands; and by hints of the Raja's treacherous intentions he induced the besieged to allow his troops to take possession, that their obtaining what was promised might be assured. Both parties were thus duped; *Gurbaksh Singh* occupied and held the fort, and Sansar Chand had to retire. Previous to this some of the hill states had been tributary to Sirdar Hakikat Singh, but *Jai Singh* now became paramount and all the hill chiefs sought his alliance.

The Ramgharias and Kanheyas had been fast friends in old days, but *Jai Singh* and Jassa Singh had quarreled about the Kassur prize money, and the former joined the Ahluwalia and Bhangi chiefs in expelling Jassa Singh from the Panjab.* Raja Ranjit Deo died in 1780, and his son Brij Raj Deo succeeded him. The new prince wished to win back some of his territory from the Bhangis, and asked Hakikat Singh to assist him. Neither *Jai Singh* nor Hakikat Singh much liked the business, for the Bhangis were their friends, and *Jai Singh* had recently married the daughter of Bhag Singh Hallowalia a Bhangi chief, but they marched to Karianwala, which after some fighting was taken possession of by the Raja. The Kanheya chiefs soon left their new ally, and went over to the Bhangis, and Hakikat Singh, with Gujar Singh and Bhag Singh Hallowalia, retook Karianwala and invaded Jammu. Sirdar Mahan Singh Sukarchakia, who professed the greatest affection for Brij Raj Deo, with whom he had exchanged turbans, hurried up from Ramnagar, where he had been engaged with the Chattahs, and attacked the camp of Hakikat Singh, but was repulsed with loss. He then, with the Raja, called *Jai Singh* and Jassa Singh Ahluwalia to his help. These chiefs came and tried to arrange terms, but finding this hopeless, returned to Amritsar. Mahan Singh was now obliged to submit; and the Raja agreed to pay a tribute of 30,000 Rs. to Hakikat Singh; who, six months later, finding that the payment of the tribute was evaded, proposed to Mahan Singh to join him in an attack on Jammu, dividing the booty between them. To this the Sukarchakia chief, forgetting his friendship with the Raja and the exchanged turbans, readily consented. He marched to Chapral, while Hakikat Singh took the road to Zaffarwal. But Mahan Singh kept faith with none of his allies. Finding that the Raja had fled and that he was strong enough to act alone, he plundered and burnt the city and palace of Jammu, and retired to the plains with great spoil. Hakikat Singh thought of revenge for this treachery, but was taken ill and died shortly afterwards.

---

* Vide Sirdar Mangal Singh Ramgharia.

When *Jai Singh* heard of the sack of Jammu and the death of Hakikat Singh he was very indignant. He prevented Jaimal Singh, son of Hakikat Singh, from going to Gujranwala, whither Mahan Singh had invited him, and threatened the Sukarchakia chief with his vengeance, and in 1783, he marched against Jandiala, and plundered Rassulpur and Mandiala, and then attached the possessions of Wazir Singh and Bhagwan Singh the Nakkai chiefs, connections of Mahan Singh, and compelled them to submit. At the Diwali of 1784 Mahan Singh went to Amritsar and tried hard to make peace with *Jai Singh*, but in vain. He was threatened with imprisonment if he did not restore the Jammu spoil, and was treated with so much rudeness that he fled from Amritsar, determined on revenge. There were many ready to join him in an attack on the Kanheya chief. Chief of these were Sansar Chand of Katoch and Jassa Singh Ramgharia who had been wandering for years an exile in the wastes of Harriana. The allies marched to Battala and about eight miles from that town were met by *Gurbaksh Singh* who offered them battle. For six hours the fight was continued, till an arrow, shot by one of Guru Sundar Das' men, struck *Gurbaksh Singh* in the breast and wounded him mortally, and the Kanheya troops, having lost their leader, were completely routed.

Jai Singh was so distressed at the loss of his son that he made no further resistance. Kangra he gave up to Sansar Chand, and restored to Jassa Singh Ramgharia his old possessions; while to cement friendship with Mahan Singh he betrothed *Mehtab Kour*, daughter of his dead son, to the youthful Ranjit Singh afterwards Maharaja of the Panjab. The betrothal took place in 1785, and the marriage at the close of the next year.

Jai Singh never recovered his former power, and died in 1789, when his daughter-in-law *Sada Kour* became head of the Kanheya misl. Mention has been made elsewhere of the ability, the uuscrupulousness and the intrigues of this woman. It was through her assistance mainly that Ranjit Singh became master of the Panjab, and she retained a large portion of the Kanheya estates till 1820, when her greedy son-in-law made an excuse for seizing them all.

Hem Singh, the nephew of Sirdar *Jai Singh*, had received the grant of the Ilaka of Rukhanwala, worth 40,000 Rs. after the capture of Kassur, and this he retained under Ranjit Singh. He fought, with that chief, against Kassur, during the last campaign of 1807, and received another estate at Khodian, worth 10,000 Rs. He died in 1820. His son *Mohr Singh* fought at Multan and in Kashmir, and in 1821, he was stationed at Pul Kanjri and Waniki to watch the ferries. He died at the last named place in 1823. To his sons, who were employed on the same service, 30,000 Rs. of their father's estate was assigned. *Sarup Singh* died in 1832, and the jagir was given by the Maharaja to Kahn Singh Banka. The village of Rukhanwala alone was left to the family, but the next year the village of Kali was granted to *Attar Singh's* seven widows, and this they still hold. The sons of *Attar Singh* made many applications to Maharaja Sher Singh for the release of the estate, but in vain. Both, with their cousin *Megh Singh,* served in the Ghorcharahs till 1846, when the general reductions were made after the Satlej campaign.

The village of Rukhanwala is confirmed to the family in perpetuity ; and here they now reside. The village of Kali will be resumed as the shares fall in.

THE KANHEYA FAMILY.

II. Sirdar Kesra Singh.

- **Baghel Singh.**
  - Hakikat Singh, D. 1782.
    - Jaimal Singh, D. 1812.
      - Chanda Singh, D. 1861.
        - Kesra Singh, B. 1836.
          - Jamal Singh, B. 1856.
        - Isra Singh, B. 1850. M. D. of Amar Singh, Bhagga.
        - Daughter, M. Kahn Singh, Behlolpur.
        - Daughter, M. Hatraj Singh, Bandala.
      - Ranjit Singh, D. 1808.
      - B. Chand Kour, M. M. R. Kharak Singh, D. 1842.
  - Mehtab Singh.
    - Fatah Singh.
  - Musada Singh.

HISTORY OF THE FAMILY.

A considerable portion of the history both of the Kanheya misl and of Sirdar *Hakikat Singh* has been given at some length in the preceding statement, (Jit Singh Kanheya), and does not require repetition here. *Hakikat Singh* was the son of a Sindhu Jat cultivator of the village of Julka, only a few miles from Kanah where Jai Singh Kanheya was born. Both Jai Singh and *Hakikat Singh* were in the service of Kapur Singh Singpuria, and both, on his death, set up as independent chiefs. To the latter fell Kalanur, Burah, Dalboh, Kahnghar, Adalatghar, Pathankot, Mattu and many other villages. Under him fought the Sangatpuria Sirdars; Sahib Singh Naniki; Dial Singh and Sant Singh Dadupuria; Desa Singh Mohal; Chet Singh Bannod; Sahib Singh Taragharia, and many others. In 1760, *Hakikat Singh*, having destroyed Churianwala, built on the ruins the village of Sangatpuria and the fort of Fatahghar, which he named after his nephew. *Mehtab Singh*, who possessed a large share of his brother's estates, built a fort hard by, which he named Chittorghar.

Sirdar *Hakikat Singh* died in 1782, and his only son *Jaimal Singh*, a boy eleven years of age, succeeded to his estates. This chief did not do much to extend the Kanheya possessions, but he held his own and did not lose any of them. In 1812 he died, leaving no son, and Ranjit Singh determined to seize the wealth supposed to be stored in Fatahghur. He sent thither one Ram Singh on a pretended mission of condolence to the widow, but no sooner was the officer admitted than he took possession in the name of the Maharaja.

Three months later the widow of *Jaimal Singh* gave birth to a son, and in favour of this infant, named *Chanda Singh*, the Maharaja released a portion of the estate, of the value of 15,000 Rs.

A few months before his death *Jaimal Singh* had married his only daughter *Chand Kour*, a girl of ten years of age, to Kharrak Singh, son of the Maharaja, and heir to the throne of the Panjab. The marriage was celebrated with the greatest splendour, at Fatahghar, on the 6th February, 1812. It was attended by the chiefs of Kythal, Nabha and Jheend, and by Colonel Ochterlony, Agent of the Governor General.

In February, 1821, *Chand Kour* gave birth to a son, who was named Nao Nihal Singh; and on the death of the great Maharaja, in June, 1839, her husband Kharrak Singh ascended the throne.

Kharrak Singh was a man of strong passions and weak intellect. Superstitious and regular in the discharge of his religious duties, he was yet addicted to many degrading vices; unforgiving and vindictive, he was entirely in the hands of the favourite of the hour. His peaceful succession was in a great measure owing to Raja Dhyan Singh, who gave out that Ranjit Singh, on his death-bed, had named Kharrak Singh to succeed him, and had chosen him, Dhyan Singh, as Minister.

Dhyan Singh had been almost absolute during the last years of Ranjit Singh's life, and he was determined that his power should not now decline. It was thus essential for him to have on the throne a prince who would consent to be led by his minister and who would not himself aspire to rule. Dhyan Singh had a still dearer ambition than this. His eldest son Hira Singh had been the darling of the old Maharaja. He was allowed a chair in the presence, when all others, except two or three of the most holy Bhais, were compelled to stand; without him the Maharaja could not go to sleep; without him he never went out to take the air. Hira Singh had thus been brought up like the Maharaja's own child, and as such he was regarded by the Khalsa army. Was it then too bold an ambition to hope that some day he might rule the Panjab as king; with Dhyan Singh, his father, as his chief adviser, holding all real power in the state; with one uncle, the gallant and debauched Raja Suchet Singh, commander-in-chief, and the other, Gulab Singh, ruling all the hill country. Then, in firm alliance with the Kabul Amir and the court of Nepal, the Dogra family of Jammu might become the most powerful in all India, and found a dynasty for itself.

Maharaja Kharrak Singh was found more difficult to lead than the minister had imagined. He hated Dhyan Singh and gave to Sirdar Chet Singh Bajwa all his confidence. This favourite well knew that so long as Dhyan Singh lived his position was an unsafe one, and conspired with the French Generals, who were bitterly opposed to the Dogra family, against his life. But Dhyan Singh was not to be defeated on his own ground of intrigue. He induced Rani *Chand Kour* and Nao Nihal Singh to admit the necessity for Chet Singh's removal, by urging upon them that should his conspiracy succeed all power would fall into the hands of Chet Singh and the French; and it was determined to assassinate the obnoxious favourite that very night. The Raja won the palace guards over to his side, and entering the fort by the Bhaiya Dyalwala gate, one hour before dawn, with Prince Nao Nihal Singh, Gulab Singh, Suchet Singh, Attar Singh, Sindhanwalia, Fatah Singh Man and some others, slew Chet Singh in the sleeping apartments of the Maharaja himself.

After this murder, committed on the 9th October, 1839, Kharrak Singh's reign was virtually over. It continued the fashion for his son to ask his directions and orders, which were carried out if the minister and the Prince concurred; and if not, they were disregarded: he was allowed to retain the form and pomp of kingship, and received Mr. Clerk Agent Governor General, in May, 1840, with great state, covered with jewels and wearing the famous Koh-i-nur diamond, but all power was gone from him, and during the last four months of his life he was never consulted on any matter of state and remained in the fort a prisoner in all but the name.

Raja Dhyan Singh now found a new danger to his power in Prince Nao Nihal Singh. This young man was high spirited and bold, and though disliked by the Sirdars was loved by the army, which hoped to see him rival the military exploits of his grandfather. This too was the Prince's own ambition. He does not appear to have shown any particular ability, but he was headstrong and impatient of control, and Dhyan Singh's influence over him decreased day by day; and the Raja began to fear that when he succeeded to the throne he might choose some new minister, whose removal might prove more difficult than that of Chet Singh had been. From the beginning of September the life of Kharrak Singh, who had always been of a weakly constitution, had been despaired of by the physicians. During October he rapidly sank, and on the 4th November, he died, aged thirty-eight. His end was accelerated, according to the general belief, by poison administered by the orders of Dhyan Singh and with the knowledge of his son. But even if Nao Nihal Singh had no such share as this in his father's death, he had certainly hastened it by his undutiful and cruel conduct. To the last the dying monarch had thought of his son with love, and had sent message after message calling him to his side. But Nao Nihal Singh never went. He was eager for the time when the death of the father he despised would leave him uncontrolled master of the state, and when the news reached him, when hunting at Shahbilor, that the Maharaja was dead, he had not the decency to conceal his satisfaction.

The next day, the 5th November, the body of Kharrak Singh was burnt on the plain beyond the Roshnai gate of the Fort. With it were also burnt the beautiful Rani Isar Kour, sister of Sirdar Mangal Singh Sindhu and three slave girls. Nao Nihal Singh attended the ceremony, but before the body was entirely consumed, faint with the heat of the sun, retired to perform his ablutions in the branch of the river Ravi that flowed by the fort. He returned on foot towards the palace, followed by the whole court, holding the hand of Mian Udham Singh his inseparable companion, eldest son of Raja Gulab Singh. As he approached the gateway he called for water to drink. None was at hand, and all the bottles of sacred Ganges water which had been brought to sprinkle on the funeral pile were empty. The superstitious Sirdars whispered that this was an evil omen, but the Prince laughed and passed on. As he stepped beneath the archway, down fell the battlements, beams, stone and brick work, with a tremendous crash. It was all over in a moment. Mian Udham Singh was extricated from the rubbish with his neck broken, quite dead; Nao Nihal Singh's left arm was broken and his skull fractured. He breathed heavily, but neither moved nor spoke. Raja Dhyan Singh who had been close behind when the catastrophe occurred, and who was himself grazed by the falling mass, called up a palanquin, of which there were many waiting, and placing the Prince in it had him carried into the marble garden-house where Ranjit Singh had been used to hold his morning darbar, and the great gates of the Hazuri Bagh were shut and locked. No one but Fakirs Azizuddin and Nuruddin, and Bhais Ram Singh and Govind Ram were allowed to enter, and within an hour Nao Nihal Singh had breathed his last.

Raja Dhyan Singh was not, however, at a loss. He sent a message to summon Prince Sher Singh who was shooting at Kanhwan, some eighty miles from Lahore; and placed relays of blood horses along the road to bring him in with all possible speed. He sent information to Multan, Peshawar, Mandi and elsewhere, that the Prince was but slightly hurt; and he wrote a letter to the Agent of the Governor General in the name of the Prince and as if dictated by him, saying that he was much hurt but hoped that he might recover, and on the 6th the Raja sent a chief to Amritsar to spread the report that the Prince was much better. For some time the corpse lay in a tent of shawls within the garden house, but was removed into the fort at night, and placed in one of the inner apartments. Dhyan Singh made all arrangements for securing the forts of Lahore and Govindgarh, till, at noon on the 7th, Prince Sher Singh arrived; concealment was no longer necessary, and the death of Nao Nihal Singh was proclaimed.

The death of the Prince* left two claimants for the vacant throne. The first of these was Prince Sher Singh, reputed son of Maharaja Ranjit

---

* The account of the death of Nao Nihal Singh given in the text has been taken from the statements of Rai Mul Singh, Col. Chet Singh, Bhai Fatah Singh, Diwan Rattan Chand and other eyewitnesses, and from the official reports submitted to Government. Colonel Chet Singh was on guard at the spot where the accident occurred; Bhai Fatah Singh, the chief priest of Maharaja Ranjit Singh's tomb, was seated with Fakir Nuruddin on the roof immediately overlooking the gateway. He saw the parapet fall; the Prince and the Mian struck down; and he also saw Raja Dhyan Singh, who was only two paces behind, struck by the falling bricks on the arm. Diwan Rattan Chand Darhiwala was walking in the procession but a few yards behind the Prince. He came up immediately the accident had happened, and saw the Prince's head smashed in and the brain oozing from the wound and from his ear. He was then insensible and dying.

There are some well informed and able men, intimately acquainted with the intrigues of the time, who have openly accused Raja Dhyan Singh as the murderer of the Prince. It is asserted by them that the parapet was thrown down by his orders; that Udham Singh, his nephew, was sacrificed to give a greater appearance of accident to the catastrophe; that the palanquin was in waiting to carry away the wounded or dead Prince, and even that Raja Hira Singh, seated on the top of the opposite gateway, must have given the signal for the parapet to be thrown down. It is also said that the Prince was only slightly wounded by the fall of the parapet and that he was afterwards heard to ask for water; that he was hurried

Singh, but in reality the son of one Nihala, a chintz weaver of Mokerian, from whom he was purchased by Mai Sada Kour, to palm off upon Ranjit Singh as the son of her barren daughter Rani Mehtab Kour. Sher Singh had, however, been always acknowledged by the Maharaja as his son, and a large party were ready to support his claims to the throne. He was at this time a man of thirty-three years of age, handsome and well made, a brave and dashing leader in the field and popular with the army; but of debauched habits, irresolute and infirm of purpose, and without the ability and energy needed to govern a people excitable as the Sikhs.

The second candidate for power was *Mai Chand Kour,* widow of Maharaja Kharrak Singh.

---

into the palanquin, carried into the fort and locked up in an inner room, where only the physician and the Raja were admitted; and that here the Prince was really murdered.

This story is unsupported by a shadow of proof, and the more attentively it is considered the more impossible it will appear. It was natural of course to attribute so sudden a death of one so high in station to intrigue and conspiracy. Princes do not die often by accident in native states. But there is no evidence to convict Raja Dhyan Singh of the crime. He has enough blood on his hands without false accusations being added. It may be admitted that the Raja had few scruples when his ambitious schemes were in question; and the fact of his nephew sharing the fate of his victim would have given him but little concern. But it is incredible that so great a master of intrigue should have resorted to so clumsy and brutal an expedient as throwing a parapet wall upon the Prince, before the whole court, when the subordinate actors in the conspiracy must have been detected, (for search was instantly made) and the share of the Raja discovered. Were there not a thousand opportunities of making away with the Prince, by poison or dagger; when there would be no danger of detection, and when the Raja would not be compromised by the help and knowledge of others? These methods would be sure; the fall of a parapet was uncertain. The signal given a moment too soon or too late; a step of the Prince backwards or forwards and the plot would have failed. With reference to the presence of the palanquin, it may be mentioned that, in a royal procession, elephants, led horses, and palanquins were always in attendance; that it was one of these the Raja summoned, that the Prince called for water immediately before the accident and this may have given rise, in a time of excitement and distrust, to the story that he was heard to ask for water after he had been struck down.

Those who assert that the Prince was at first but slightly wounded and that he was murdered afterwards within the fort, must be aware that they thus accuse Fakir Nuruddin of being a sharer in the crime. He never left the Prince from the time that the wall fell till his death. But to those who know the Fakir's gentle and amiable disposition; his loyalty to the house of the great Maharaja; his devoted love to the young Prince, such a supposition appears

When the death of her son took place she was at her ancestral village of Fatahgarh. She returned to Lahore on the 6th November, only to find that Raja Dhyan Singh had outwitted her, and had won oversome of the chiefs to agree to the succession of Prince Sher Singh. *Chand Kour*, finding affairs thus unfavourable, attempted a compromise. The first plan that she and her counsellor Bhai Ram Singh proposed was that she should adopt Raja Hira Singh, son of Dhyan Singh, and place him on the throne.

---

monstrous. Fakir Nuruddin, too, at this time was on bad terms with the Raja. Chet Singh, whom the Raja had murdered, was the friend of Fakirs Nuruddin and Azizuddin, and they never forgave Dhyan Singh or trusted him afterwards. Why then should Nuruddin murder the Prince he loved, to gratify the Raja he hated ? The only others who were admitted into the Hazuri Bagh were Bhai Ram Singh, Bhai Govind Ram and Fakir Azizuddin. The two former were brothers, and Ram Singh was the confidential minister of the Prince with whose life his power would cease. He was entirely opposed in policy to Dhyan Singh as was his brother Govind Ram. Yet if the Prince was murdered in the fort these must have been the murderers, these the accomplices of the Raja.

The only reason for the mystery which shrouded the death-bed of the Prince was the necessity which Dhyan Singh felt for keeping the fatal news from being generally known until the arrival of Sher Singh. If there had been an organized plot the Raja would have taken care that Sher Singh should have been present in Lahore at the time of the catastrophe. The absence of Sher Singh proves the innocence of the Raja.

The story of the conspiracy has originated in a belief that the death of Nao Nihal Singh was necessary to the development of the Dogra policy. But, although Hira Singh could never hope for the throne while Nao Nihal Singh was alive, yet the death of the Prince, at this time, was in no way desired by the Raja. The time for Hira Singh to be brought forward had not arrived ; and during the intrigues of the three succeeding months, his name was only mentioned by the party opposed to the Raja as a possible candidate for the throne. The Raja had some influence over Nao Nihal Singh ; but at this time he had none with Sher Singh, who was a military leader, popular with the troops, and who might be expected to be able to stand without his aid. Besides it was an equal chance whether the party of Rani *Chand Kour* might not obtain power, in which case the Raja would have been ruined. To say that the Raja raised Sher Singh to the throne in order to destroy him later is a mere assertion. Dhyan Singh did not create difficulties to have the pleasure of conquering them, and Sher Singh was eventually assassinated by the Sindhanwalias, the deadly enemies of Dhyan Singh. The death of Nao Nihal Singh was the greatest calamity that could have befallen the Raja. He extricated himself by the strength of his genius, but it was nevertheless a calamity.

There are some who believe that a Nemesis pursues and punishes great crime. These will not forget that it was when returning from the funeral pile of the father he had treated with so much unkindness, and whose death he had hastened and longed for, that Nao Nihal Singh was struck down, when wealth, power and the sovereignty of the Panjab were within his very grasp.

This was declined by the opposite party who proposed instead that she should marry Sher Singh. This she rejected with disdain and offered to acknowledge Sirdar Attar Singh Sindhanwalia as her heir. This proposal was received, as might have been imagined, with greater coldness than even the former ones ; and the Rani then declared that Sahib Kour, Gilwali, widow of her son Nao Nihal Singh, was three months gone with child. This announcement changed the aspect of affairs. The question was now not of a sovereign but a regent, and it was doubtful whether the Rani or the Prince would win the day.

On the side of the Mai (as Rani *Chand Kour* was called) were Bhais Ram Singh and Govind Ram ; Sirdars Attar Singh, Lehna Singh and Ajit Singh Sindhanwalia ; Fatah Singh Man ; General Golab Singh Povindia ; Shaikh Ghulam Mohiuddin ; Jamadar Khushhal Singh and General Tej Singh. With the Prince were Sirdars Fatah Singh Ahluwalia ; Dhanna Singh Malwai ; Sham Singh Attariwala ; the three Jammu Rajas, Dhyan Singh, Golab Singh, Suchet Singh ; Bhai Gurmukh Singh ; Fakir Azizuddin and the French Generals Ventura and Court. Among the neutrals were the crafty Dina Nath and the timid Sirdar Lehna Singh Majithia. Nor was the policy of the chiefs above named or their adherence to their party at all constant, or unwavering. The Jammu Rajas, though their policy and their interests were really the same, appeared now to adopt one side, now the other ; while Khushhal Singh and Tej Singh were ever ready to change to that party which seemed most able to enrich them. Few of the Sirdars had much interest in either candidate. Mai *Chand Kour* was not popular, as her chief adviser was Bhai Ram Singh, who in the days of Nao Nihal Singh had been so obnoxious to the chiefs by reducing their jagirs and increasing their contingents. Those who supported her did so in the hope that with a feeble zanana government they might retain that independence of authority, the love and boast of a Sikh, which they had enjoyed during the last year of Ranjit Singh's life. The Sindhanwalia chiefs who were her firmest allies, were, at the beginning of November, absent from Lahore : Ajit Singh, who was said to be her lover, being engaged in the Kulu and Mandi campaign and Attar Singh being at Hardwar. The latter, shortly followed by his nephew, arrived at Lahore about the 12th November, just after the Mai had proposed another scheme for uniting the parties. This was that she should adopt Partab Singh, eldest son of Sher Singh, thus attaching the Prince to her government, while it would remove the objection felt to him on account of his spurious birth; but this, like every other plan, failed, and the feeling in Lahore grew strong that a co-regency of the Prince and the Mai, during the pregnancy of the young widow, was the only way of obtaining union, the acts of the regents being controlled by a national council of chiefs.

This arrangement was in some measure modified, and on the 20th it was agreed that Mai *Chand Kour* should be the chief authority in the state; that Sher Singh should be President of the council of chiefs and have command of the army, while Dhyan Singh should be minister. This clumsy machinery could only break down; and every one expected that it would. But Dhyan Singh wanted to gain time, and made all swear to maintain this form of government. A week, however, saw its abandonment. It was found impossible to be carried out in practice, and every day brought with it the danger of a collision. Both parties occupied the fort; the Mai, the inner apartments; the Prince, the Hazuri Bagh and the outer portion. He occasionally went out in state, and *Chand Kour* more than once thought of closing the gates against his return. The mode of conducting business was equally anomalous. The early Darbar was held in Sher Singh's presence, in the marble garden house in the Hazuri Bagh; then the ministers retired to a conference in the Shish Mahal; and, lastly, waited on the Mai in the Samman Burj.

Raja Dhyan Singh now appeared to be won over to the side of *Chand Kour*, it was said through the advocacy of Raja Gulab Singh to whom the Mai had promised the restoration of Manawar, but the minister intended to show both parties how idle it was for them to hope to stand without his assistance. A final agreement was accordingly drawu up, on the 27th November, by which Sher Singh was to retire to his jagir at Battala for eight months, leaving his son Partab Singh a member of the council. Mai *Chand Kour* was to remain regent until the birth of Sahib Kour's child, when other arrangements were to be made. This agreement was signed by Rajas Dhyan Singh and Gulab Singh; Sirdar Lehna Singh Majithia; Attar Singh Sindhanwalia; Fatah Singh Man; Mangal Singh, Sindhu; Tej Singh; Sham Singh Attariwala; Dhanna Singh Malwai; Jamadar Khushhal Singh; Bhais Ram Singh and Gurmukh Singh; Fakir Azizuddin; Diwan Dina Nath, and Shaikh Ghulam Mohiuddin. Both parties, cajoled by Raja Dhyan Singh, were fully represented in the deed, and Prince Sher Singh, seeing resistance hopeless, and not understanding the policy of the Raja, retired to Battala, where he waited his opportunity for action.

The counsellors of the Mai were not long in discovering their weakness. The Raja scarcely ever attended Darbar, but spent his time in hunting and shooting; while day by day the country grew more unquiet; the roads became insecure, crime largely increased and the outlying frontier districts were preparing to rebel. Dhyan Singh had now convinced himself that the Government could not be carried on without him, but he wished to convince the counsellors of the Mai of the same fact, and accordingly on the 2nd January, 1841, he left for Jammu. Ruin now fast came on the Government. The army began to mutiny; the generals would not obey orders, and one week after the Raja's departure, expresses were sent off by Mai *Chand Kour* and Bhai Ram Singh, by the hand of Misr Lal Singh, Fatah Singh Man and others, urging him to return without delay. On the 13th January, Ajit Singh Sindhanwalia left Lahore under pretence of retiring to his village of Raja Sansi before the arrival of Dhyan Singh, but he instead travelled to Ludhiana with a message from *Chand Kour* to the Agent of the Governor General, but failed to obtain an interview.

On the 14th, Lahore was taken by surprise by the arrival of Sher Singh at Shalimar, six miles from the city. The Prince had been sounding the army, and found it generally well disposed towards him; the French Generals had promised him their support, and he accordingly prepared to try his fortune during the absence of Raja Dhyan Singh in Jammu. On his arrival at Shalimar an officer belonging to one of General Gulab Singh's battalions waited upon him, and begged him to proceed to their lines. The Prince accepted the invitation and marched to the Begampur lines, where he encamped amid Gulab Singh Povindia's battalions, under a general salute.

The garrison of the fort had not been idle. With the Mai in the fort were Rajas Gulab Singh and Hira Singh, and Sirdars Attar Singh Sindhanwalia, Mangal Singh Sindhu and Ghulam Mohiuddin. Re-inforcements were called in; three battalions of Amir Singh Man, and the artillery of Lehna Singh Majithia. Guns were posted at all the city gates, and the troops of Raja Suchet Singh and the Charyari horse were marched from Shahdera and drawn up in front of the fort. Camel messengers were also sent off to summon Raja Dhyan Singh with all speed.

During the 15th a large proportion of the army went over to the Prince, and on the morning of the 16th he had with him 26,000 foot, 8,000 horse and 45 guns. He then marched in great state, accompanied by Generals Ventura, Court, and many Sikh Sirdars to Lahore, and entered by the Taxali gate without opposition. At the Padshahi Mosque, Colonel Dhonkal Singh delivered up to him the magazine stored there, and in a short time he was in possession of the whole city. He then summoned the fort to surrender. But Gulab Singh had resolved to defend it. The garrison now consisted of about 3,000 men, principally hill troops of the Raja, and upon them the treasure of *Chand Kour* was lavishly spent. Gulab Singh went round to every post and inspected the defences, encouraging the men by presents and promises. The attack began by the discharge of fourteen double shotted guns against the Hazuri Bagh gate of the fort. The gate was blown in, and the besiegers, headed by a mob of fanatical Akalis, charged through the opening with shouts of triumph. But the besieged had two guns loaded with grape just behind the gate, and these were now fired with such terrible effect that the enemy were driven back in confusion and with great loss. The gate was then barricaded, and the fort opened fire upon the Hazuri Bagh. The Dogra soldiers were first-rate marksmen, and Sher Singh lost so many men that, on the morning of the 17th, he withdrew from the Hazuri Bagh to the Padshahi Mosque. During the night of the 16th, the assailants had kept up a heavy fire from 50 pieces of cannon and howitzers, and had brought down a considerable portion of the southern wall. The party of the Mai now began to think of their own safety. Bhai Ram Singh waited on the Prince and was well received; and the next day, Jamadar Khushhal Singh and his nephew Tej Singh, who had been most profuse in their professions of devotion to the Mai, tendered their allegiance to Sher Singh.

Raja Gulab Singh was again summoned to surrender. He asked for a truce till the arrival of his brother, who was hastening back to Lahore. This was refused, and he then swore that, as a Rajput, he would defend the fort to the last. Firing was then resumed, and was continued throughout the day. In the evening Raja Dhyan Singh and Suchet Singh arrived from Jammu and encamped outside the city. The latter visited Sher Singh and reported that Dhyan Singh would attend the next day. Accordingly on the morning of the 18th the Raja and the Prince met. The former expressed his regret at the hasty conduct of Sher Singh, and recommended immediate negotiation being opened with the defenders of the fort. Raja Gulab Singh was glad enough to treat and his brother obtained for him favourable terms. The garrison were allowed to retire with their arms and all the honours of war; Mai *Chand Kour* renouncing her pretentions to the regency and receiving the grant of a large jagir at Kadiali near Jammu. These terms being arranged, Raja Gulab Singh marched out of the fort at midnight on the 19th, and encamped on the plain in front of it : Sirdar Attar Singh Sindhanwalia followed and encamped at Shah Bilawal. The next morning the Prince with an immense procession went to review the artillery and thank them for their services, and then proceeded to the fort where he took his seat on the throne while all the artillery saluted. Mai *Chand Kour* was at this time in the Samman Burj, in charge of the high priest Bikrama Singh.

The city of Lahore now became a prey to an anarchy and license. The soldiery could not be restrained and plundered the houses of friends and foes alike. Jamadar Khushhal Singh very nearly fell a victim to their fury, and others peculiarly obnoxious were Raja Gulab Singh, General Court, Sirdar Muhammad Sultan Khan and Lehna Singh Majithia. The camp of the last named chief was plundered, and the army proposed to attack that of Gulab Singh, but he had been reinforced ; and set off for Jammu, with an immense amount of treasure, and accompanied by Jamadar Khushhal Singh, who found Lahore no longer safe. The house of General Court was attacked by three regiments of his own battalion, and he fled for protection to General Ventura who had to use his artillery to protect himself and his friend. The munshis and writers were hated by the army for their extortion and fraud, and were hunted down in all directions and killed. The life of no man was safe who admitted that he could write, or whose fingers showed that he was used to hold the pen. In these terrible days every man gratified his private revenge ; officers were killed by their men ; shopkeepers by their debtors ; and all the horrors of a storm had fallen upon the unhappy city. It was many days before the troops were pacified, and the license which they then enjoyed they never forgot ; from that time they grew more and more mutinous and reckless, till neither king nor minister could restrain them.

The state installation of Sher Singh as Maharaja did not take place till the 27th. The ' tika, ' or mark of Rajaship, was imprinted on his forehead by Baba Bikrama Singh, who also presented the khillats of investiture to the Maharaja, to Prince Partab Singh as heir-apparent, and to Raja Dhyan Singh as minister. All the Chiefs and Sirdars were present and tendered their allegiance to the new Sovereign, and for Rani *Chand Kour* the game was played out.

During these events Raja Dhyan Singh and Raja Gulab Singh appeared to take different sides, but there is every reason to believe that they always maintained the closest alliance between themselves. One brother adopted the cause of Sher Singh and the other that of the Rani, in order that whichever was successful their own power and wealth might be secured. Raja Dhyan Singh's conduct was such that his most devoted adherents were sometimes doubtful which party he really favoured, but, although prepared for any emergency, he had a definite policy. He left Lahore for Jammu, hoping that Prince Sher Singh would, in his absence, make an effort to win the throne. He desired his success, but wished to be absent from Lahore, as he should have been compromised by the failure of the Prince; and it would have been indecent to have openly joined him, while the minister of *Chand Kour*. But supposing Sher Singh too timid or too wanting in energy for the effort, Dhyan Singh's absence from Lahore would still be advantageous to him. It would finally convince the weak government of Rani *Chand Kour* that the Raja's help was necessary to their existence; and he would have been recalled with full powers, and would have been able to put Sher Singh aside, as no longer necessary to his personal ambition. The army was also devoted to the Raja, without whose aid Sher Singh could never hope to reign. But this project almost failed through the precipitance of Sher Singh. He knew Dhyan Singh sufficiently to fear and distrust him, and hoped to gain power without his assistance at all. For this reason he attacked the fort immediately the army had come over to his side. Raja Dhyan Singh at Jammu and Raja Gulab Singh in the fort had never anticipated this. Both knew that if the Prince should succeed without their help, their influence would be destroyed; and for this reason Gulab Singh tried to obtain a respite from hostilities till his brother should arrive; and when this was refused determined to defend the fort to the last. He was, too, in the presence of danger, brave as a lion; and though he always preferred intrigue to violence, yet, when intrigue had failed, there was no more skilful or gallant warrior than he; and he considered that in honour he could not yield the fort without a struggle. There was another reason which induced him to defend the fort. This was the immense wealth which it contained, and a great portion of which, in money and jewels,* he carried away with him to Jammu. But putting Gulab Singh, his policy, his bravery and his avarice aside, that the fort was defended in the interest of Dhyan Singh and not of *Chand Kour* is clear from Raja Hira Singh being present within it, and one of its ablest defenders being Sultan Muhammad Khan Barakzai, a devoted follower of the Raja.

There is little more to tell of Rani *Chand Kour*. Raja Gulab Singh proposed to take both her and Rani Sahib Kour with him to Jammu, but this Sher Singh would not allow. He did not wish to put weapons into the hands of his enemy. She was ordered to leave the Samman Burj and retire to her house in the city, and here she carried on her intrigues with the chiefs and the army. Sirdar Ajit Singh Sindhanwalia she sent to Calcutta to plead her cause with the Governor General, and her emissaries were busily employed all over the country. In October, 1841, Sirdar Attar Singh proceeded at her invitation from Thanesar to Firozpur, where he waited for a favourable opportunity to enter the Panjab. In the interest of the Mai were at this time about twelve thousand of the army and some powerful chiefs; but as Sher Singh grew unpopular from his inability to comply with the demands of the troops, the influence of the Mai increased, and in April, 1842, the army generally was favourable to her cause.

Maharaja Sher Singh now perceived that so long as this ambitious and scheming woman lived he could not be secure, and re-

* It has been stated that when Sher Singh entered the fort Gulab Singh presented to him the Koh-i-Nur diamond, which he asserted he had preserved. This is not correct. The Maharaja, on gaining the fort, was in great alarm at not finding the famous diamond, and both he and his ministers believed that Gulab Singh had carried it off, as no doubt he would have done had he been able. But about a fortnight later Misr Beli Ram discovered it at Fatahghar, the ancestral village of Rani *Chand Kour*, whither that lady had sent it with many other crown jewels.

solved on her destruction. Raja Dhyan Singh equally desired her death. It is true that she was at the head of a party which his countenance could at any time render formidable, should Sher Singh desire to get rid of him ; but he saw that this was an improbable contingency, and that the Maharaja was convinced that, however much he disliked his minister he was unable to carry on the Government without him. He thus agreed to the death of the Rani, which he believed would free him from the fear of the hated Sindhanwalias.

Early in June, 1842, Sher Singh, with most of the chiefs and a large force, marched to Wazirabad, Raja Dhyan Singh remaining behind in Lahore. *Chand Kour* had been ordered to take up her quarters again in the fort, of which Mian Singh was in charge ; and on the 12th of June, her slave girls, who had received their orders, attempted to kill her by mixing poison in a beverage which they offered her. She tasted it and threw it away ; and the girls, then, fearing their design was discovered, fell upon her with stones, fractured her skull and left her for dead. Raja Dhyan Singh attended his victim immediately and had her wounds dressed ; Fakir Nuruddin thought at one time there was some hope of her life, but she never recovered her senses and died within two days. The assassins were heavily ironed, and it is said that when threatened with mutilation they accused Dhyan Singh openly of having instigated the murder, and of having promised them great rewards for effecting it. Their fate is unknown, but it is supposed they were made away with by order of the Raja.

Chanda Singh, the brother of Rani *Chand Kour*, held the Kanheya estates until the accession of Sher Singh. They had been much improved by Nao Nihal Singh who had sent to Fatahghar much of his treasure, which, with that accumulated by *Chand Kour,* was seized by Sher Singh in February, 1841. *Kesra Singh* and his mother were taken to Lahore and were only released on the intercession of *Chand Kour,* whom Sher Singh at that time hoped to marry. Jagirs of the value of 60,000 Rs. were left to *Chanda Singh,* 45,000 Rs. of which were resumed after the murder of the Rani, when her large estates near Jammu fell into the hands of Raja Gulab Singh.

The misfortunes of the family were not yet ended. When Hira Singh rose to power he confiscated the whole of the remaining estates of *Chanda Singh*; the reason given being that he had illuminated his house on hearing of the death of Raja Dhyan Singh. Whether the story was true or false it is certain that in the Raja's death *Chanda Singh* had every reason for joy.

When Sirdar Jowahir Singh became Minister, he restored to the family a jagir worth 3,060 Rs., which is now enjoyed by *Kesra Singh* at Talwandi and Kotli.

Sirdar *Chanda Singh* died in 1861, leaving two sons, the elder of whom is now twenty-nine years of age.

THE KANHEYA FAMILY.

III. Arbel Singh Sangatpuriah.

- **Jassa Singh.**
  - Charrat Singh.
    - Sardul Singh.
      - Ran Singh, D. 1861.
        - Sahib Singh, B. 1851.
      - Gurmukh Singh.
        - Nihal Singh, B. 1824.
    - Nar Singh. M. D. of S. Sadho Singh, Kotli.
      - Ram Singh, D. 1850, M. D. of S. Sham Singh Man.
        - Arbel Singh.
          - Sant Singh, B. 1854.
          - Utam Singh, B. 1860.
          - Bulant Singh.
        - Isa Singh.
          - Apar Singh.
      - Sham Singh, B. 1809.
      - Kahn Singh, B. 1814.
    - Didar Singh, D. 1851.

HISTORY OF THE FAMILY.

The Sangatpuriah branch of the Kanheya family does not require much notice here. *Jassa Singh* was brother of Baghal Singh and uncle of Hakikat Singh. He and his son *Charrat Singh* fought with the Kanheya misl, and shared its good fortune and reverses. *Charrat Singh* obtained some twenty-eight villages in the Amritsar and Gurdaspur districts, valued at 40,000 Rs., which he held till his death and bequeathed to his three sons, who were not equally fortunate, for soon after Ranjit Singh's conquest of Amritsar, in 1802, their estates were seized. Ranjit Singh, however, gave them other jagirs; to *Sardul Singh,* Damudar; to *Nar Singh* Kotlah, Sheikhanwala and Kotla Majaka, with a cash allowance of 1000 Rs. per annum, while *Didar Singh* was placed in the orderly guard on 60 Rs. a month. The brothers fought in most of the Maharaja's campaigns, till 1816, when *Nar Singh* died, but his estates were confirmed to his sons, who were at the time of his death all minors, and three years later *Ram Singh* was taken into the Kanheya Ghorcharahs. Afterwards he was made commandant in the French Regiment. Both his younger brothers served in the Irregular Cavalry.

During the troublous times of Raja Hira Singh, when small Sirdars were in no way safe from spoliation, *Ram Singh* attached himself to the powerful Attari Chiof, Sham Singh, who looked after his fortunes, and gave him an estate in Laluchak. It was this perhaps that made *Ram Singh*, in 1848, think that he must cleave to the Attari family, for good or evil, for at that time he was commandant of a newly raised Muhammadan regiment, and deserted to the enemy. Before this he had been employed in the revenue work at Peshawar, under Golab Singh Povindia. After annexation, the jagirs of *Ram Singh*, to the value of 3,520 Rs. were confiscated, and a life pension was granted him of 360 Rs. per annum, but the very next year he died, and his sons were allowed 15 Rs. per mensem, which pension they still hold.

Sham Singh was made jamadar in 1857; but was discharged on the reduction of the corps, receiving a grant of 40 ghumaos of land at Karial.

THE ROSA FAMILY.

I. Attar Singh.

- **Thakar Singh.**
  - Lakhmir Singh, D. 1763.
  - Jodh Singh, D. 1819.
    - Dya Singh, D. 1845.
      - Attar Singh, B. 1796.
        - Lehna Singh, B. 1832.
          - Gurdit Singh, B. 1852.
          - Hardit Singh, D. 1862.
        - Lal Singh, B. 1834.
        - Khushhal Singh, 1838.
      - Sant Singh, D. 1834.
      - Amir Singh, B. 1844.
    - Diwan Singh, D. 1845.
      - Jowahir Singh.
    - Bhagwan Singh, D. 1846.
    - Megh Singh, D. 1821.
      - Sher Singh.
      - Baghel Singh, D. 1854.
    - Togh Singh, D. 1856.
      - Kesr Singh.
    - Khazan Singh, B. 1796.
      - Mehtab Singh.
    - Mardan Singh, D. 1845.

HISTORY OF THE FAMILY.

There is a tradition that Rosa or Rusah, a Sidhu Jat and an ancestor of this family, emigrated from Dehli, some hundred years ago, and founded, near Chunian in the Lahore district, a village, to which he gave his own name. *Thakar Singh* was a risaldar in the service of the famous Dina Beg Khan, Governor first of the Jalandhar Doab and then of the Panjab. On the death of his master, in 1758, he set up for himself, and contrived to possess himself of a large tract of country in the Gogaira and Gujranwala districts. In 1765, he joined Hari Singh Bhanghi and Jai Singh Kanheya in their expedition against Kassur, where he was killed by a musket shot. His eldest son *Lakhmir Singh* only survived him a year, and *Jodh Singh* succeeded to the entire estate. Some time after this *Jodh Singh* quarreled with Sirdar Sobha Singh of Lahore, and to avoid his enmity went to Gujranwala, where Sirdar Charrat Singh made him Thannadar. He rebuilt the old village of Rosa, in the Chunian Pargannah, and founded a second in Sheikhapurah, both of which are still held in proprietary right by the family. On the death of Charrat Singh, Sirdar Sobha Singh, who had claimed to be the heir of *Thakar Singh*, seized half the Rosa estates, without any resistance on the part of *Jodh Singh*, who retained his appointment at Gujranwala under Mahan Singh and Ranjit Singh, and, in 1799, he had the gratification of accompanying the latter to Lahore, when the city was taken and the son of his old enemy made prisoner.

Jodh Singh served under Ranjit Singh in the Kassur, Pindi Bhattian and Jhang campaigns, in the last of which he obtained, for his bravery, the jagir of Mohal and Draj in the Jhang district. He was shortly afterwards severely wounded at the siege of *Chandiot*. In the second Kashmir expedition, at Rajaori, he was killed in a skirmish. His three sons *Bhagwan Singh*, *Megh Singh* and *Tegh Singh* had some time before this entered the Maharaja's service, but the Kashmir campaign was the first in which *Dya Singh* had been engaged. He was confirmed in his father's estates, but after the Maharaja's return to Lahore, these were all resumed, and others were granted worth about 10,000 Rs., subject to the service of thirty horse ; *Bhagwan Singh* receiving a separate jagir. *Megh Singh* was killed at Mangli in 1821, when serving under Sirdar Hari Singh Nalwa. In 1832, *Attar Singh* was made adjutant in the Dhonkal Singh Brigade and afterwards in the Sher Singhwala, on its return from Kashmir. In 1834, the jagir of *Dya Singh* was resumed with that of his chief, Sirdar Attar Singh Kalianwala, who had incurred the Maharaja's displeasure by his refusal to proceed to Bannu. He was, however, left 4 villages, worth 3,000 Rs., but the family never recovered its former position.

Attar Singh accompanied Sirdar Ajit Singh Sindhanwalia to Kulu, in the Dasowala Derah under Buhadar Singh, and remained there through all the Lahore revolutions, in which his general Ajit Singh perished. The Satlej compaign was fatal to the family of Rosa, for, in one day, at Firushahar, *Dya Singh*, *Diwan Singh* and *Mardan Singh*, were killed. *Attar Singh* was placed under the orders of Sirdar Chattar Singh Attariwala, when that chief was sent as Governor to Hazara, and he joined him in rebellion in 1848. On crossing the Indus, on his march from Peshawar, Sirdar Chattar Singh made over Major G. Lawrence and family, whom he had taken prisoners, to *Attar Singh*, for safe custody, with directions to convey them to Pothiar. Thither they were escorted by *Attar Singh*, and subsequently to Mamhyala and Rawalpindi, where, after the battle of Gujrat, they were given up to the British authorities. *Attar Singh* treated the prisoners with all kindness and consideration, and on the annexation of the Panjab received a pension of 600 Rs. per annum, which he still enjoys. His half brothers *Sant Singh* and *Amir Singh*, with their mother, receive a pension of 300 Rs. The village of Rosa in the Sheikhapura Perganna is held by the family according to the ancestral shares. The present holders are *Jowahir Singh*, *Mehtab Singh*, *Attar Singh*, *Kesr Singh*, and *Sher Singh*.

THE ROSA FAMILY.

II. Hardit Singh.

- Tek Singh.
  - Sukha Singh.
    - Kahn Singh,
      - Sawal Singh.
      - Baisakha Singh.
      - Phulla Singh.
      - Hari Singh.
      - Musaddi Singh.
      - Hardit Singh.
      - Gurdit Singh.
        - Hira Singh.
  - Sahib Singh.

HISTORY OF THE FAMILY.

Tek Singh was in the service of the Bhangi Sirdars of Lahore, from whom he received a grant of the then deserted village of Nodhpur. In 1794, when Nizamuddin Khan drove the Sikhs out of Kassur, *Sukha Singh* became officer of 28 horse under him, and was killed, in 1806, in battle. *Sahib Singh* his brother was killed, about the same time, in a quarrel with the zamindars of Bablair.

In 1822, Monsieur Allard came to the Panjab and entered the service of the Maharaja. He was directed to raise a corps of Dragoons, and *Kahn Singh* Rosa was appointed Jamadar, on 30 Rs. a month, under him. The next year *Kahn Singh* was made Risaldar in the same regiment, in which he remained for seven years. He did such good service, in 1829, on the frontier, that at General Ventura's recommendation he was appointed Commandant in the Khas Paltan, or Life Guards, on 1000 Rs. a year ; being 280 Rs. cash, and the jagir of Bilandi, worth 720 Rs. He served with his regiment in Kulu, Mandi and elsewhere ; and Maharaja Sher Singh raised his cash allowance to 800. Rs. and gave him, in addition to Bilandi, the village of Jodhpur and some wells in Rampur, worth 1000 Rs. a year. *Kahn Singh* was severely wounded in the breast by a musket shot, in the attack on Raja Suchet Singh, in March 1844, and Hira Singh, who was then minister, made him a colonel and raised his emoluments to 6,120 Rs.

When Hira Singh was killed by the army, the colonel, who was considered a protégé of the Raja, was turned out of the regiment by his own men, and he then entered the force of Sirdar Sham Singh Attariwala. When the regiment was in front of the enemy at Sobraon, the men, finding that they could not fight without their old colonel, insisted upon his returning to command them; which he did, with distinguished gallantry, throughout the battle. After Firushahar he had been sent with a deputation from the Panchayats of the army to Raja Gulab Singh to implore him to join them without delay. But the Raja had other designs. He professed most earnestly to desire the success of the Sikhs; he pretended to send large convoys of provisions to the army; while he waited to see whether British or Sikhs would win. He longed, with his whole heart, for the destruction of the latter, and when he could no longer remain inactive, he moved from Jammu with the pretence of joining them; but at Shahdera, some three miles from Lahore, he waited for the news of the great battle; and when it arrived, he took possession of Lahore and the person of the Maharaja, and then marched to Kassur as the friend and ally of the British, to receive, as the reward for being the most astute man of his day, the kingdom of Kashmir. In 1846, Raja Lal Singh resumed the new jagirs of *Kahn Singh*; but, under the Regency, his pay was again raised to 2,880 Rs., at which it stood when the war of 1848 broke out.

At this time *Kahn Singh* was colonel of the Dragoons at Peshawar, and was one of the first to join the national party. He was a man of great bravery and an admirable cavalry officer, and his influence with the army was great. Through the whole campaign of 1848-49 he fought with the greatest gallantry, and he and Sirdar Jowahir Singh Nalwa were perhaps the most dashing officers among the Sikhs. After Chillianwala, a great council of chiefs was called and *Kahn Singh* proposed to attack the British Camp by night, with the entire Sikh force. This was negatived by the other chiefs, and *Kahn Singh* then advocated an attack early on the following morning. Sirdar Chattar Singh opposed this, and thought it better to march to Gujrat and from thence to Lahore, and the Colonel then told him that the only reason that he would not attack was that he was afraid. Swords were out in a moment, but other Sirdars interposed; and *Kahn Singh*, calling Chattar Singh a bastard and a coward, left the tent followed by Jowahir Singh Nalwa who alone had supported him.

After annexation the Colonel lost his jagirs but received a cash pension of 600 Rs. His eldest son entered the Guide Corps as a Jamadar, and was a young man of promise; but died, in 1856, of a fever contracted at Peshawar.

When the mutinies of 1857 broke out, *Kahn Singh* was one of the first chiefs selected by the Chief Commissioner for service before Dehli. At this time he was in very bad health, and the old wound which he had received in the days of Hira Singh had reopened, but he was eager to distinguish himself in fighting for the English against whom he had once fought so bravely. He started immediately for Dehli with fifteen horse and eighteen foot, and joined the Guides with whom he served till the fall of the city. In a sally of the enemy he received a severe wound in the shoulder and from the effects of this he never entirely recovered.

It was with his whole heart that *Kahn Singh* served in 1857. When disabled by his wound from actual fighting, he employed himself in procuring information, and on winning over to the side of the English such of his countrymen as were in the ranks of the enemy, and more than forty of them he induced to desert. In 1858, the Government conferred on him, in addition to his pension of 600 Rs., his old village of Balandi, worth 720 Rs. for his life; Todapur, worth 700, for his life and to descend for one generation, and the estate of Maloki-Prem in perpetuity. He also received a grant of the confiscated house of Mahbub Ali Khan, at Dehli, worth 4,000 Rs. Sirdar *Kahn Singh* died in June, 1864, leaving two sons *Hardit Singh* and *Gurdit Singh*, the eldest of whom is eighteen years of age.

THE ROSA FAMILY.

III. Tegh Singh.

Tegh Singh, son of *Karam Singh*, was for four years Risaldar in the second troop of the North Western Provinces Military Police. He did admirable service during the mutinies, and in April, 1859, was severely wounded in a fight with the rebels in the Mirzapur jungle. In October, 1861, when the new system of Police was introduced, *Tegh Singh* received his discharge. He was not only distinguished for gallantry in the field, but was also a first-rate officer, respected and obeyed by his men. Though of the Rosa family, he is very distantly connected with the branches of it represented by Hardit Singh and Attar Singh.

FATAH SINGH SIRDAR BUHADAR OF MARAKA.

- BUR SINGH.
  - Jassa Singh.
    - Nidhan Singh.
      - Gurbakhsh Singh, D. 1853.
        - Daughter M. Lal Singh, brother of S. Chet Singh, D. 1863.
      - Fatah Singh, B. 1804.
        - Gurdit Singh, B. 1836.
          - Sher Singh, B. 1862.
        - Hardit Singh, D. 1861.
      - Jodh Singh, D. 1855.
        - Sardul Singh.

HISTORY OF THE FAMILY.

The little village of Maraka, situated a few miles below Lahore on the Ravi, was founded by an ancestor of *Fatah Singh,* whose descendants resided there for many generations. When Ahmad Shah Durani invaded the Panjab for the third time, in 1752, *Bur Singh* was chowdhri of Maraka and the surrounding villages. But reports reached Lahore that Maraka was little better than a nest of robbers, and the monarch sent a force to destroy the village. The work was well done: Maraka was burned to the ground; men, women and children were put to the sword, and *Bur Singh* and his son *Jassa Singh,* who were absent from the village, were almost the only ones that escaped. Whether the reputation of *Bur Singh's* village was deserved or not, it is certain that, after its destruction, he joined a band of robbers, and in one of their marauding expeditions was killed. *Jassa Singh* followed his father's profession, and became of some importance at the head of an organized body of horse. He obtained possession of Daska in the Sialkot district, and took up his residence there. He was engaged in constant conflicts with Sirdar Charrat Singh, Sukarchakia, and with the residents of the neighbouring town of Iminabad. On one occasion the latter had assembled in force, and taking the town of Daska by surprise, carried off a large quantity of booty. *Jassa Singh* pursued them with his horsemen, and after a severe fight the booty was recovered, but the chief fell mortally wounded. His son *Nidhan Singh* was of a bold and enterprising disposition, and acquired a large increase of territory. The surrounding chiefs, Mahan Singh of Gujranwala, Sahib Singh of Gujrat, Panjab Singh of Sialkot, and Jodh Singh of Wazirabad, became jealous of his power, and were so continually engaged in hostilities with him that *Nidhan Singh* used to say that there was not a rood of ground in his territories on which men and horses had not fallen.

In 1797, when Shah Zaman invaded the Panjab, one of the few Sikh chiefs who welcomed him was Sirdar *Nidhan Singh,* who much felt the need of a powerful ally. He met the Kabul monarch on the banks of the Chenab, and was most graciously received, being confirmed in all his estates and appointed to keep open communications between Lahore and Wazirabad. Soon after this Ranjit Singh, rising to power, summoned *Nidhan Singh* to attend him, but the high spirited chief refused, and it was not till 1810 that he, with 250 horsemen, consented to accompany the Maharaja on his Multan expedition. At the close of the campaign, *Nidhan Singh* returned to Daska, contrary to the orders of Ranjit Singh, who determined to punish the contumacious chief. He laid siege to the fort of Daska, bringing against it the great Bhangi gun which was only used on important occasions. After a month's siege *Nidhan Singh* was forced to surrender, and on the promise of protection given to him by the Maharaja, through Baba Mulak Raj and Bedi Jamiyat Singh, he came into camp, where, in violation of the promise, he was arrested and put in irons. The priests were very indignant at this breach of faith, and, it is said, sat '*Dharna*' on Ranjit Singh until he released *Nidhan Singh,* who forthwith fled to Kashmir and took service with Atta Muhammad Khan. He was however soon recalled, and a great portion of his estate was restored to him, subject to the service of 100 horsemen. In

1822, after the fall of Mankera, he received the grant of Baharpur, near Dera Ismail Khan, worth 80,000 Rs., but this was shortly after restored to the Nawab, and *Nidhan Singh* received, in exchange, a large jagir in Hazara, where he remained for some time. After an engagement with Payinda Khan, in which he was severely wounded, he begged to be relieved of his troublesome charge, and was accordingly, in 1824, placed under the orders of Prince Kharrak Singh, and, in 1827, was transferred to the Ghorcharahs on 1,700 Rs. per mensem. He remained in this force till 1845, when he retired to Maraka where he died five years afterwards.

He was generally known as *Nidhan Singh* Hattu or Attu, and two derivations of the name are given. The first is that Hattu is derived from the Panjabi 'Hat' meaning 'courage.' The second derives Attu from the Panjabi 'Ath' eight, from a tradition regarding a lady of the family who was so fortunate as to secure eight husbands. But there does not appear any good authority for the latter derivation.

Sirdar Fattah Singh commenced his military career in his father's contingent in which he remained till 1827, when he was placed in the Ghorcharah Kalan Regiment, and two years later in the Dhanni Brigade under Misr Sukhraj, on 90 Rs. a month. In 1835, he accompanied the Maharaja to Peshawar when Dost Muhammad Khan was so cleverly out-manœuvred by Ranjit Singh, and in 1840 he was sent, under Arjan Singh Rangar Nanglia, to Kulu, which was in a disturbed state. He accompanied Imamuddin Khan to Kashmir, and after the death of Raja Hira Singh was ordered to Rajaori and Panch to put down an insurrection there. During the Satlej campaign *Fatah Singh* remained, under Sirdar Gulab Singh Povindia, to protect the Maharaja and the capital, and on the restoration of peace he was appointed commandant of the new corps Suraj Mukhi. In 1847, he accompanied Lieutenant (now Sir H. B.) Edwardes, to Bannu, and served throughout the Multan campaign. He was engaged with his corps at the battles of Kineri and Saddusam, and at both sieges of Multan his conduct and that of his men was exceedingly good. In 1857, he was in command of the Police Battalion at Ambala, and did admirable service both there and at Dehli. In 1862, he received his discharge, with a pension of 250 Rs. and a grant of 600 acres of waste land at Lakhuwal. He possesses, in addition, 300 Rs. of jagir at Maraka, where he resides, and has also proprietary rights in the village.

Gurdit Singh son of *Futah Singh* was first employed as jamadar in the Suraj Mukhi on 30 Rs. a month. He was successively promoted to the Subadarship, and adjutantcy in the 5th Police Battalion, on 150 Rs., but in 1862, at the time of the general police reductions, he was discharged, with a gratuity of 1,500 Rs. and is not at present in Government employ.

Jodh Singh, half brother of *Futah Singh,* changed his religion from inability to pay a bill. He took from a merchant at Rawalpindi a beautiful and valuable horse, the price of which he was unable to pay. He applied to his father, but *Nidhan Singh* had no money to spare. At length, seeing no way of paying for the horse which he could not bring himself to give up, he rode off to Kabul where he turned Muhammadan, and where he died in 1855, leaving one son, *Sardul Singh,* who is now a Subadar in the frontier force.

DEWA SINGH SIRDAR BUHADAR,

- SOMAN SINGH.
  - Sapha Singh.
    - Fatah Singh.
      - Dewa Singh, B. 1802.
        - Amar Singh, B. 1853. Betrothed to a grand daughter of Sirdar Kahn Singh Nakkai.
        - Isar Singh, B. 1862.
        - Daughter, B. 1860.
      - Sewa Singh, B. 1824.
      - Panjab Singh, B. 1834.
        - Sant Singh, B. 1848.
  - Dal Singh.
    - Vir Singh.
    - Wazir Singh.
      - Gurdit Singh, B. 1834.
      - Hardit Singh, B. 1838.

HISTORY OF THE FAMILY.

About 500 years ago there lived in the Firozpur district a Jat Zamindar named Gil, of Rajput Ragbansi descent. He must have been a man of some wealth, for he was the happy owner of two wives and seven concubines, but although of mature years, he had no children. At length one of his wives became pregnant, to the vexation of the other women who fancied the affection of their lord would be all given to her who should bring him a child, perhaps a son and heir. They, accordingly, when a son was born, stole it away and carried it far into the jungle where they left it to perish, placing in the mother's bed a large stone, of which they asserted she had been delivered. The next day the family bard, wandering in the jungle, saw, with astonishment, a lion, common in those days to the south of the Satlej, licking and fondling a new-born child. He ran home to tell the strange news, and returning with assistance, drove away the beast and brought the child to Gil, by whom the conspiracy was discovered, and the boy, to whom the name of Shergil (or Lion-Gil) was given, acknowledged to be the rightful heir. After this, by his slave girls, Gil had eleven other sons, whose descendants are still numerous in many parts of the Panjab. Shergil had four sons. The two youngest died without issue, but from the eldest Rana Dhar has descended the great house of Majitha, and from Jubal the second, *Dewa Singh,* in the twentieth generation, and the founders of the Nishanwala misl. Such is the traditional origin of the Jat tribes, Gil and Shergil.

Sawan Singh, the great grandfather of *Dewa Singh,* was third cousin of Sangat Singh the leader of the Nishanwala confederacy of which he himself was a member, although he does not seem to have been of a very warlike disposition. *Sapha Singh* was one of the Sirdars who held Sonti so gallantly against Jaswant Singh Raja of Nabha, and subsequently his own fort of Jhangir against Maharaja Ranjit Singh who had besieged it, in 1806. The fort would have fallen but for the remonstrances of Bedi Sahib Singh, to whom *Sapha Singh* had given a tenth of his jagir, and who persuaded Ranjit Singh to raise the siege. *Sapha Singh* would not enter the Maharaja's service, but his son *Fatah Singh* did so, and under Diwan Mohkam Chand became a very distinguished soldier. He received Jhangir Burj and Brampur in jagir, besides large cash allowances. He accompanied Diwan Kirparam to Kashmir, and remained high in his favour till his recall and disgrace, when the jagirs of Sirdar *Fatah Singh* north of the Satlej were resumed, and he retired to the Cis-Satlej estate of Sonti, where he remained till his death, although the Maharaja more than once tried to induce him to return to Lahore.

Dewa Singh entered the service of the Maharaja in 1816, at a very early age. He went to Kashmir with his father, and when the latter retired across the Satlej he received the command of 250 of his sowars, and the charge of the Ilaka of Durpanah. After a year and a half he was placed under the orders of Sirdar Lehna Singh Majithia, who made him commandant of the regiment of his brother Gujar Singh, the black sheep of the Majithia family. In 1834, he accompanied the young Sirdar to Calcutta on a mission half complimentary, half political. On his return he was transferred to the Dhonkalwala Regiment as Commandant. He did not however join his new corps, but remained with Sirdar Lehna Singh. In 1842, he was transferred to the Gurkha Regiment, with which he did service in Hazara. Under the Darbar he was posted at Dera Ismail Khan in command of the Suraj Mukhi Regiment, and when the outbreak at Multan took place, he proceeded with his regiment to join Lieutenant Edwardes and General Van Cortlandt, with whom he served throughout the campaign. He was present at the battle of Kineyri, on the 18th June, 1848; the battle of Sadosam on the 1st July, and during the first siege of Multan. When the Kattar Mukhi Regiment was disaffected and ready to join the rebels, *Dewa Singh* was transferred to it that he might repress its disposition to mutiny, and improve its discipline. After the fall of Multan, he marched with his regiment to Isakhel, and had there several skirmishes with the Waziris, in which he showed his known courage and energy.

When the Panjab Military Police was formed in 1853, *Dewa Singh* was selected to raise and command the 7th Police Battalion at Amritsar. After the native corps had been disarmed at Amritsar, on the outbreak of the mutinies of 1857, this Battalion was the only armed force at that important station, to watch the two disarmed regiments of Hindustanis; to preserve order in the city; to guard the treasury, and to uphold the Civil authority; and that this work was so well and successfully performed must be in a great measure attributed to the energy, ability and unswerving loyalty of *Dewa Singh.* He also rendered great assistance in raising levies for service at Dehli, and during 1857-58, a very large number of recruits were enlisted and sent down country by him. For his services, *Dewa Singh* was granted the Star of British India with the title of Sirdar Buhadar, and a personal allowance of 1,200 Rs. a year.

On the re-organization of the Panjab Police, and the disbandment of the old force, on the 1st January, 1861, *Dewa Singh* retired from Government service, after a long and honorable military career. He received a special retiring pension of 3,000 Rs. per annum, and a grant of 600 acres of waste land, the proprietary rights in which his family will hold in perpetuity.

COMMANDANT MOTA SINGH SIRDAR BUHADAR.

KANHEYA LAL,
D. 1802.
|
Lachman Das,
D. 1820.
|
Mulraj,
D. 1819.
|
Mota Singh,
B. 1814.

Sukh Dyal, B. 1855.	Har Dyal, B. 1858.	Sir Dyal, B. 1864.

HISTORY OF THE FAMILY.

Kanheya Lal, the great grandfather of *Mota Singh,* was in the service of Sirdar Sobha Singh Kanheya, one of the three Sikh chiefs who captured Lahore from the Muhammadan governor. He was in a humble position, and gave up active service after Ranjit Singh had obtained possession of the city, and soon afterwards died. His son *Lachman Das* finding no employment in the Panjab, retired to Kabul, where he set up as a schoolmaster; but three years before his death he returned to his native country, where, at Teja, he died of paralysis in 1820. His son *Mulraj* had died the preceding year.

Mota Singh entered the service of the Maharaja in 1832, and was placed in the battalion of Colonel Van Cortlandt. In 1837 he received a command in the Calcuttawala Battalion, but, in 1842, was replaced under Colonel Van Cortlandt. He was made Adjutant in 1844. After the Satlej campaign he was transferred to the Suraj Mukhi Regiment; and on the outbreak of Multan, he was Adjutant of that corps, stationed at Derah Ismail Khan. He served throughout the war and at the two sieges of Multan with credit, and on the annexation of the Panjab he was appointed Adjutant of the 7th Police Battalion, which he assisted to raise and organize.

On the death of the brave Colonel Subhan Khan, commanding the 1st Panjab Police Battalion, stationed at Lahore, *Mota Singh* was appointed to succeed him. This was in September, 1857, before the fall of Dehli, and the loyalty and influence of *Mota Singh* must have been highly estimated, as he was thus selected to command the only corps of armed native troops at the capital; while at the neighbouring cantonment of Mian Mir, there were four thousand disarmed and mutinous sepoys. *Mota Singh* performed his difficult duties to the entire satisfaction of the authorities and his regiment guarded the jails, treasuries and civil offices, and preserved the peace in the city of Lahore. A detachment from his corps did good service in the disturbed district of Gogaira. The Military Police were broken up on the 1st July, 1861, and the men of *Mota Singh's* force were transferred to the civil constabulary. The services of the Commandant were, accordingly, no longer required, and being an elderly man he wished to retire from active employ, and took his discharge.

Mota Singh has received the Star of British India, and the title of Sirdar Buhadar; and by an order of the Supreme Government of the 26th December, 1861, he was granted a life pension of 3,000 Rs. per annum, inclusive of the allowance of the order of British India, together with a grant of 600 acres of waste land in the Lahore district. The proprietary right of the land will continue, in perpetuity, in his family, subject to assessment after his death. He also owns a well outside the Masti gate of Lahore which had been previously granted to him by the British Government.

SHAMSHUDDIN KHAN KASSURIA.

- MUHAMMAD HAIYAT KHAN.
  - Osman Khan.
    - Madat Khan.
    - Abdul Rahman Khan.
      - Burhan Khan.
      - Subhan Khan.
      - Sultan Khan.
        - Shamshuddin Khan.
          - Daughter, M. Osman Khan.
        - Kadir Baksh.
          - Osman Khan.
            - Sirdar Khan.
    - Sulaiman Khan.

HISTORY OF THE FAMILY.

About 150 years ago *Muhammad Haiyat Khan,* of Bhatti Rajput descent, settled at Thathi Kotna, a now deserted village near Kassur, and set up in trade. Kassur some two hundred years before this had been settled by a colony of Pathans, and into the service of their chief Nizamuddin Khan the three sons of *Muhammad Haiyat* entered. They fought in many engagements under the chief, and at Chunian, in the great battle between the Imperial forces and the Kassur Pathans, who had refused to pay tribute, *Subhan Khan* was slain.

After the assassination of Nizamuddin Khan, *Sultan Khan* remained in the service of his brother Kutbuddin, and retired with him to Mamdot, when Kassur was conquered and taken possession of by Ranjit Singh in 1807. *Shamshuddin Khan* was also for many years a servant of the Mamdot chief and attended the Lahore court as his vakil, till, for some fault, he was summarily dismissed and became the confidential agent of Raja Lal Singh. This position he held at the time of the Satlej campaign, and was the medium of communication between the Raja and the British officers.

As the conduct of the Sikh leaders in 1845 has been variously represented, it may be interesting to state what amount of information was really given by Raja Lal Singh, and how far he was a traitor to the Sikh Government.

On the 12th December, 1845, when the Sikh army was crossing the Satlej, the Raja sent *Shamshuddin Khan* to Captain Nicholson at Firozpur to assure him that both he and the Maharani were the friends of the British, and desired nothing more than that the Sikh army might be destroyed. That he would keep his force back two days from joining the regulars; that he had marched that day back to Assal and the next day would march to Harriki. To this Captain Nicholson replied that he would report the matter, but that whether Lal Singh's horse joined the regular army or not was a matter of indifference, as the British could thrash one or both with equal ease. The next day Raja Lal Singh proposed delaying the army under pretence of making a bridge at Harriki and discovering fords.

On the 16th December, Captain Nicholson hearing that the Governor General and Commander in Chief were approaching by way of Mudki, sent for *Shamshuddin Khan,* who stated as before that his master was well disposed towards the British, that he had influence with certain Brigades which he would march, with all his own cavalry, to attack the Governor General, if the British force at Firozpur would attack the remainder. Captain Nicholson said that if the Raja had the influence he asserted he would act and not talk, and that his good intentions would be seen by his marching as he proposed.

On the 18th *Shamshuddin Khan* came and reported that the Raja had marched to Firushahr, and Captain Nicholson gave him a letter to Major Broadfoot, which it is believed was delivered to that officer as the troops were going into action at Firushahr on the afternoon of the

21st, as it was found in his pocket when his body was brought in on the 22nd.*

On the 19th of December, the day after the battle of Mudki, Raja Lal Singh sent a messenger to Major Broadfoot to express his desire to be of any service, but the Major considered that the only object of the Raja was to ascertain the effect of the action of the previous day and sent him with a guard beyond the pickets. Nothing more was heard of the Raja till two days before the battle of Sobraon. He had been hidden in a dry ditch during the battle of Firushahr, but gave out that he was wounded and retired to Amritsar ; where, according to popular report, he concealed himself in an oven from the fury of the soldiers who swore to murder

* The number of the Sikh troops engaged at Mudki has been variously estimated. Lord Gough, in his despatch of the 19th December, estimates them at from 15,000 to 20,000 infantry, about the same force of cavalry, and 40 guns. But the numbers engaged did not exceed, regulars and irregulars, 15,000 men. The force which marched from Firozpur with Lal Singh, a portion of which fought at Mudki and the whole at Firushahr, was thus composed :—

		Battalions.	*Cavalry.*	*Guns.*
Regular.	French Brigade.	4	2	26
	Buhadar Singh's Brigade,	4	1	16
	Mehtab Singh's Brigade,	4	1	18
	Total. ...	12	4	60
Irregular Cavalry,	Charyari, Naolakhas, &c., ...	...	...	4,500
	Orderlies, ...	...	...	3,500
	Raja Lal Singh, ...	...	...	1,800
	Raja Hira Singh, ...	...	...	3,350
	Pindiwala, ..	...	...	900
	Mulraj, ...	...	...	550
	Attar Singh, ...	...	...	1,700
	Bela Singh Mokal, ...	...	...	200
	Rattan Singh, ...	...	...	50
	Dogars, ...	...	...	100
	Nihangs, ...	...	...	1,000
	Ganda Singh, ...	...	...	162
				17,812
	Heavy guns, ...	...	...	28
	Zamburahs or Camel Swivels,	..	..	250

This is exclusive of the force of Sirdar Tej Singh who commanded the reserve. Raja Lal Singh left behind him at Firozpur 5,600 men, infantry and cavalry.

him. But through the remonstrances of the Maharani he joined the army about the middle of January; and on the 8th February he sent *Shamshuddin Khan* to Major H. Lawrence with a plan of the entrenchments and a detailed account of the number and disposition of the Sikh troops. This information was correct, though it came too late to be of any use beyond confirming the information which had been already acquired. It will thus be seen that Raja Lal Singh, though at heart a traitor, did little to serve the British. He may have prevented an attack by the Sikh army on Firozpur; but beyond this, which is not certain, he was of no service whatever.

When Major Lawrence was appointed Resident at Lahore, *Shamshuddin Khan* was made agent of the Darbar, to communicate its wishes and sentiments to the Resident. In 1848 he did good service, and was present at the battle of Gujranwala.

In July, 1846, a donation of 5,000 Rs. had been granted to him and after annexation, when his jagirs were resumed, he received a life pension of 2,500 Rs. He resides at Kassur, where also lives his great friend Malik Khairuddin Khan. Both had been servants of the Mamdot family; both had been deprived of their estates by Nawab Jamaluddin Khan, and they have ever since remained bitter enemies of the family. When Jamaluddin Khan was alive, they did all they could to injure him, and joined the party of his sons, who had openly quarreled with him.

Osman Khan, the nephew and son-in-law of *Shamshuddin Khan*, is a brave man and a good soldier. In 1857 he distinguished himself in command of a troop of cavalry which his uncle had raised. He subsequently served in the Police, as Risaldar under the old arrangements, and as Inspector under the new. He received his discharge, in 1863, on the reduction of the force, with the highest character for energy and integrity.

SIRDAR SURJAN SINGH MOKAL.

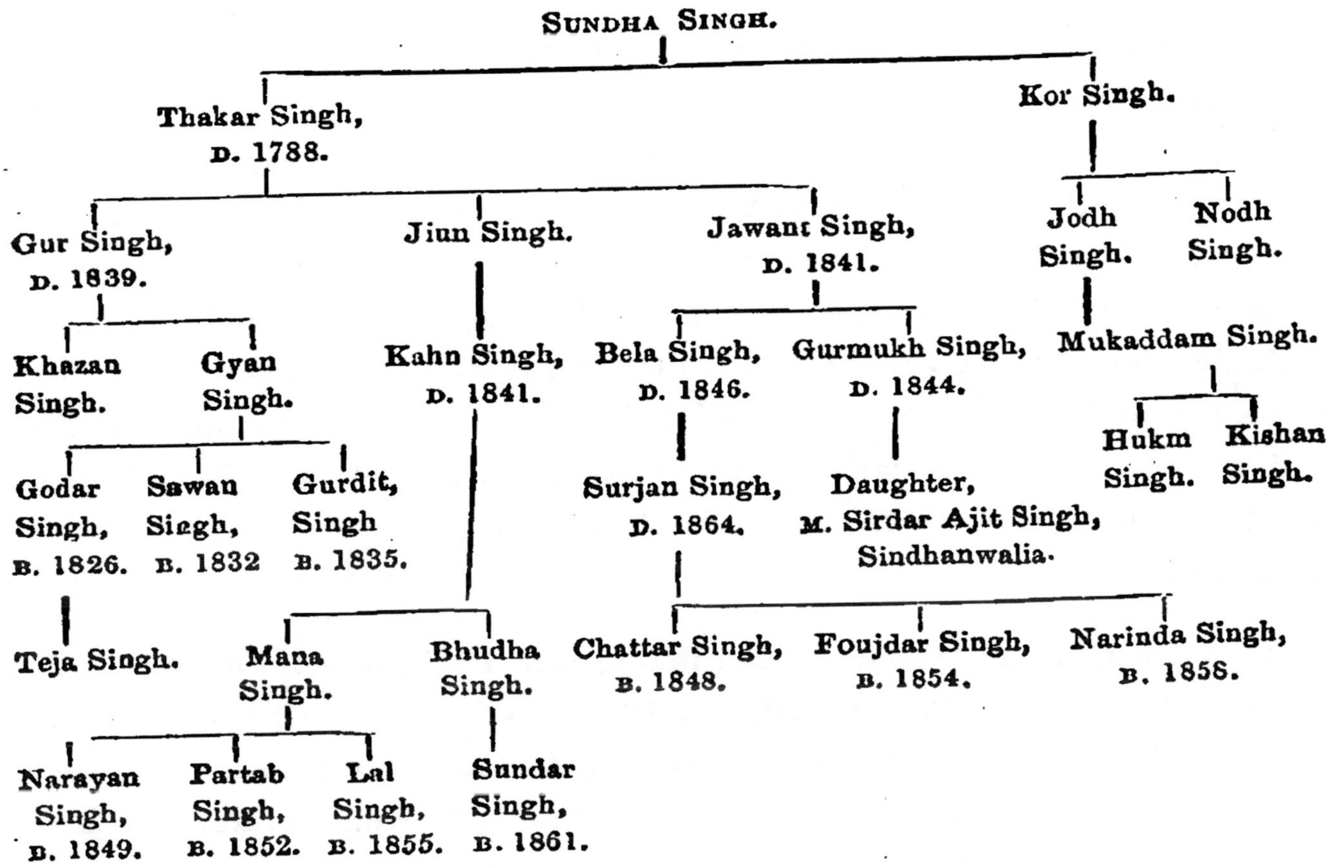

HISTORY OF THE FAMILY.

The Mokal family, of the Sindhu Jat caste, rose to considerable power during the reign of Maharaja Ranjit Singh. Even among the Sikh nobility the family is considered a new one, and it was more by their strength and prowess in battle than by their cleverness that its members gained lands and wealth.

Sundha Singh was a Jat villager, father of seven sons, of whom only the genealogy of two is here given as the descendants of these alone became distinguished. His only daughter *Kuran* he married to Sirdar Lal Singh, a jagirdar in the vicinity of Pak Pattan, who took his brothers-in-law into his service, and they rode behind him in all his marauding expeditions, till their sister, jealous for the influence of her husband, induced him to turn them adrift. *Jawant Singh* with his cousins came to Lahore and entered the service of Ranjit Singh. For some time they remained unnoticed, but at the bloody battle of Baisah, fought near Attock, in July 1813, by Diwan Mokham Chand against the Afghan Wazir, the cousins, six of whom were engaged in the fight, were so conspicuous for bravery and strength that the Maharaja gave them the jagir of Rangilpur, worth 2,500 Rs., and to *Jawant Singh,* who had specially distinguished himself, five villages in the Gujrat district, valued at 30,000 Rs. subject to the service of 150 Sowars, and his brothers were placed under his command. In 1818 he served at Multan, and the next year in Kashmir where he was severely wounded in the side by a spear. For this wound he received an assignment of 2,500 Rs. per annum, out of the Kashmir revenue. The family jagirs at one time reached 1,35,000 Rs. including 2,000 Rs. from the estate of their inhospitable connection Sirdar Lal Singh.

After the death of Maharaja Ranjit Singh in 1839, and of *Jawant Singh* in 1840, the jagirs of the Mokal family remained intact; those which had been specially assigned to *Jawant Singh* descending to his two sons *Bela Singh* and *Gurmukh Singh,* for the estate had been divided in 1836. Their contingent of 250 horsemen was, however, raised to 300, and the brothers were placed under the command of Prince Nao Nihal Singh. They did not get on well together; the elder suspecting the younger of a desire to obtain not only the larger portion of the jagir but the Sirdarship itself. Raja Hira Singh was minister at the time, and on a nazrana of 20,000 Rs. being paid by Sirdar *Bela Singh,* he confirmed him in the chiefship and jagir, which *Gurmukh Singh* took so much to heart that he died of vexation shortly afterwards, in 1845. When the first Panjab war broke out, Sirdars *Bela Singh* and *Surjan Singh* with 200 horsemen joined the army, and formed part of the detachment which advanced to Mudki and Firushahr. They were both present at Sobraon, and *Bela Singh,* severely wounded in the battle, was drowned in the Satlej in the vain attempt to ford the river after the bridge of boats had been broken down. For several days his servants searched for his body, but it was never found. When Raja Lal Singh was confirmed as minister at Lahore, nearly half of Sirdar *Bela Singh's* jagirs were resumed, but there was still left to *Surjan Singh* estates worth 63,800 Rs., of which 49,800 Rs. were subject to the service of 163 sowars. *Surjan Singh* enjoyed this estate up to 1849, when having with his cousin *Khazan Singh* joined the national party, it was resumed, with the exception of Rangilpur, worth 1000 Rs. which had been assigned on the death of Sirdar *Gurmukh Singh* as a provision for his widow and daughter. This was upheld to the widow *Ind Kour*. *Khazan Singh* received a pension of 450 Rs., and *Mukaddam Singh* one of 72 Rs. which they still hold. Sirdar *Surjan Singh's* pension of 1,200 Rs. lapsed at his death in March 1864. There is considerable ill will between the two branches of *Jawant Singh's* family, as it is believed that Sirdar *Gurmukh Singh* lost his life by the witchcraft and incantations of his elder brother.

In 1858, *Mana Singh* was made a Risaldar in the 5th Banda Military Police, in which he remained till 1861. In September, 1859, he distinguished himself by the manner in which he led his troop against very superior numbers of the enemy, and on this occasion he was wounded in the head, and his horse was wounded under him, but he mounted a fresh horse and was again foremost in the fight and the pursuit. In 1861, when he was discharged on the reduction of the Police force, he was made Zaildar or honorary Police Magistrate of twenty-eight villages in the neighbourhood of Mokal; and, in 1862, he received a grant of 720 acres of waste land in Rakh Modki, near Chunian. *Godar Singh* was Risaldar of the 4th troop of Hodson's Horse and served for more than two years in the regiment with credit. He was discharged when his troop was disbanded in March, 1860. When the Chinese war broke out *Godar Singh* volunteered his services, but there was no vacancy in Fane's Horse at the time, and they were declined. He received a grant of 50 acres of land in Rakh Modki at the same time as his cousin *Mana*

Singh. *Mukaddam Singh* was also Risaldar in the service of the British Government in 1858, and on his retirement received a grant of 100 acres of land. *Budha Singh,* the brother of *Mana Singh,* was Daffadar in the Banda Police, which he left in 1861, when the force was reduced. The family reside at Mokal in the Lahore district. They hold half the village in proprietary right, besides three shares (pattis) in Kila Jaswant Singh and 300 acres of land in Sulltanki.

SIRDAR NAR SINGH AIMAHWALA.

NATHA SINGH.

- Sujan Singh.
  - Nar Singh, M. daughter of S. Dharam Singh.
    - Sher Singh, B. 1814.
      - Lehna Singh, B. 1852.
    - Sant Singh, B. 1838.
      - Harnam Singh, B. 1854.
      - B. Raji, M. Sirdar Rajindar S. Katgharia.
  - Gulab Singh.
    - Asa Singh, D. 1850.
    - Hukm Singh.
  - Surmukh Singh.
    - Attar Singh.
    - B. Chand Kour, M. S. Chattar S., Attariwala.

HISTORY OF THE FAMILY.

About the year 1738, *Natha Singh*, an Upal Jat, left his home at Lakrki, in the Gurdaspur district, and coming to Amritsar, rebuilt a ruined village, to which, in defiance of the rights of the late inhabitants he gave the name of *Aimah*, signifying land held in proprietary right. His son *Sujan Singh* inherited not only this village but the jagirs of his uncle *Dal Singh*, who had been slain in a quarrel with Sirdar Sawa Singh Oulakhwala. These estates were of considerable size, comprising many villages in the Daska, Pasrur and Ajnala Pargannahs.

In the famine year of 1783,* *Sujan Singh* contrived to seize Chaharbajwa in the Sialkot district, from Brij Raj Deo son of Raja Ranjit Deo. He was associated with the Bhangi misl, and fought under Sirdar Karam Singh. He died in 1799, and his eldest son,

* The famine of 1783, was the most terrible of any remembered in the Panjab. It was the last of three bad years; many thousands died of starvation, and many emigrated to Kashmir and Hindostan. The year is known by the peeple as the 'San Chali,' being the Sambat year 1840.

Nar Singh, still a youth, joined Sirdar Gulab Singh Bhangi, who was chief of the confederacy formed against Ranjit Singh soon after his capture of Lahore. An expedition was fitted out against him, which *Nar Singh* joined, but it was broken up by the death of Sirdar Gulab Singh from the effects of a prolonged debauch at Kothani.

Soon after this, in 1803, *Nar Singh* joined Ranjit Singh, and accompanied him in the Pindi Bhattian campaign, and later in the expedition against the Bhangis and the fort of Kallar which was bravely defended by Jodh Singh Attariwala. In 1804 he went with Ranjit Singh against Raja Sansar Chand of Katoch, who had tried to possess himself of a portion of the Jalandhar Doab, but who was defeated near Hoshiarpur and driven back to the hills. The next expedition shared in by *Nar Singh* was that against Hafiz Ahmad Khan, of Jhang, resulting in the imprisonment of that chief, and the seizure of his estates. He served in the first unsuccessful campaign of Multan, and in both the Kashmir expeditions, under Diwan Ram Dyal in the Derah of Prince Kharrak Singh; and on the conquest of Kashmir received a jagir of 14,000 Rs. at Samba in the Jammu territory. He fought in the battle of Tehri, in 1823, and served under Sirdar Hari Singh Nalwa, in Narah. In 1835-36 he accompanied the Sikh force, under Prince Kharrak Singh, against the Mazaris of Mithankot.

When Jowahir Singh became minister, *Nar Singh* was treated with great favour, for he had married, as his second wife, an aunt of Maharani Jindan the sister of Jowahir Singh. He received the present of an elephant with gold housings, was placed in command of the Mulrajia Regiment, and was sent with the Samba Sirdar against the insurgents who had ravaged the country in the neighbourhood of Phalian, Gujrat, and had looted the shrine of Ker Sahib, a place of some sanctity where Guru Nanak had slept on the 'Ker' or heaps of earth thrown up by the rats. The insurgents were speedily reduced to order, and the plundered property, in a great measure, recovered.

During the Satlej campaign *Nar Singh* served under Sirdar Ranjodh Singh Majithia. He remained faithful to Government during the Multan rebellion, as did his contingent of sowars, and was sent to Pind Dadan Khan under the orders of Misr Rallia Ram, Superintendent of the salt mines. He returned to Lahore with Raja Dina Nath, after the latter's unsuccessful mission to Sirdar Chattar Singh. From the year 1825, when Sirdar *Nar Singh's* principal jagirs were resumed, he had only held jagirs worth 2,200 Rs. and cash allowances of 3,761. Total 5,961 Rs. His jagir was, in 1849, confirmed to him for life. He is now about 80 years of age, and resides at Aimah his ancestral village.

Gulab Singh, brother of *Nar Singh*, served in the Mulrajia Regiment on 500 Rs. per annum. His daughter married Sirdar Lehna Singh Majithia, but died within six months of her marriage. The third brother *Surmukh Singh* died young.

CHANDA SINGH KALALWALA.

- DIWAN SINGH.
  - Dhanna Singh.
    - Charrat Singh.
      - Amar Singh,
        - Gurdit Singh, D. 1852.
          - Bhagwan Singh, M. daughter of Sirdar Hardit Singh Padhania.
          - Daughter, M. Sirdar Tej Singh Attariwala.
        - Chanda Singh.
        - Aror Singh.
          - Kishan Singh.
        - Dhulla Singh.
    - Jodh Singh, D. 1824. M. daughter of Sirdar Sahib Singh, Gujratia.
      - Khem Kour, M. M. R. Kharrak Singh.
    - Nidhan Singh, D. 1863.
      - Wasawa Singh.

HISTORY OF THE FAMILY.

Hari Singh, the great leader of the Bhangi confederacy, having no son, adopted *Diwan Singh* and made him heir to half his large possessions, about the year 1760. The estates consisted of Kalalwala, Allar, Panwana, Chak Ram Das, Chobara, and others in the Sialkot and Amritsar districts. *Diwan Singh* also died without children, having enjoyed the Sirdarship some twenty-five years, and the Gurmata, the Supreme Council of the Khalsa, appointed *Dhanna Singh* a distant kinsman to succeed him. *Dhanna Singh* remained in possession until 1793, when, on his death, his son Sirdar *Jodh Singh* succeeded to the estate. *Jodh Singh* had married the daughter of Sahib Singh Gujratia, the rival and enemy of Ranjit Singh, and it was this connection, as much as the desire to increase his territories, that induced the Maharaja to make war upon him and to annex a portion of his estate, worth a lakh and a half of rupees, including Behrah, Chak Ram Das and Kila Rajo Singh. Sirdar Sahib Singh, to console his son-in-law for his losses, gave him the Ilaka of Karianwala in the Gujrat district, but in 1806-1807, Ranjit Singh again attacked Kalalwala, and after a short resistance on the part of *Jodh Singh*, compelled him to sue for terms and present a nazrana of 5,000 Rs. With this act of homage the Maharaja was satisfied, and left him jagirs to the value of 60,000 Rs.

In 1816, he married his son Prince Kharrak Singh to *Khem Kour, Jodh Singh's* only child, in spite of the remonstrance of Sahib Singh Gujratia who contended that the marriage would be contrary to Jat custom, as he, Sahib Singh, had married the sister of Mahan Singh, father of the Maharaja. *Jodh Singh* died the same year, and his widow tried to induce his brother *Nidhan Singh* to marry her by 'chaddar dalna,' a common Jat form of marriage; but he declined, and she, in pique, contrived by her influence at court, to get her husband's cousin, *Amar Singh*, appointed agent with full powers for managing the estate.

Amar Singh had been a Subadar in the Sham Sontah Regiment and was succeeded in the management of *Khem Kour's* jagirs by his son *Gurdit Singh*, who thus became the virtual jagirdar. When the rebellion of 1848 broke out, *Chanda Singh* was serving at Dera Ismail Khan, under General Van Cortlandt, as naib adalati, or deputy judge. He immediately left for Kalalwala, where, with his brother *Gurdit Singh*, he placed the fort, which was a very strong one, in a state of defence. It was necessary to move the Jalandhar field force, commanded by General Wheeler, against it, and on the 23rd November it was reduced, the rebels losing upwards of 300 men. No pension was granted to either *Gurdit Singh* or *Chanda Singh*. Rani *Khem Kour*, although deeply implicated in the rebellion, was entitled to consideration from her rank and sex. Her jagirs were resumed, but she received a pension of 2,400 Rs., which she still enjoys. Her establishment of women also received an allowance of 1,200 Rs. per annum, for their lives.

Gurdit Singh died in 1852; but *Chanda Singh* is still living at Kalalwala, four miles south of Pasrur in the Sialkot district.

SIRDAR GULAB SINGH POVINDIA.

KARAM SINGH.

Gulab Singh,
D. 1854.

Ala Singh,
D. 1854.

Lehna Singh,
D. 1856.

Kishan Singh. — Suchet Singh.

Hardit Singh.

Gopal Singh,
M. D. of S. Joala S. Man.

Isa Singh.

HISTORY OF THE FAMILY.

Karam Singh and his three brothers were among the Sikhs who overran and took possession of the Jalandhar Doab, in the latter half of the 18th century. They secured an estate at Saranpur, worth 8,000 Rs. which they held during their lifetime. All the brothers, with the exception of *Karam Singh,* died without issue, and, in 1806, soon after *Gulab Singh* had succeeded to the estate, Ranjit Singh conquered the plain country of the Doab, and *Gulab Singh* retired to his native village of Povind. He then entered Ranjit Singh's service, and received this village in jagir, with the rank of adjutant. He served with distinction under Misr Diwan Chand, at Nurpur and in Kashmir, and on the termination of the latter campaign was made commandant and received the village of Sidhu in jagir. After the capture of Multan in 1818, he was promoted to the rank of colonel, and did such good service the next year at Mankera that he received the grant of Akbarpur, near Gogaira, worth 500 Rs., with an elephant and valuable khillats. *Gulab Singh* was stationed at Peshawar for some years, and fought in most of the battles against Ali Akbar Khan and Dost Muhammad Khan. In the first Peshawar campaign he discovered a ford in the Indus, and led his troops over in the van of the army to Ranjit Singh's great satisfaction.

In 1826, he received command of 3 Infantry and 2 Cavalry regiments, with a troop of Horse Artillery, and the same year his son *Ala Singh* entered the service and was made commandant under his father, with an independent jagir. In 1839, when the regular army was first formed into brigades, *Gulab Singh* was made general, and held his rank and brigade throughout the following reign of Kharrak Singh.

In 1837, *Gulab Singh* was sent to Gujranwala with orders to confiscate the property of Sirdar Hari Singh Nalwa, who had been killed at Peshawar, and whose four sons were fighting about the succession. He drove Arjan Singh and Panjab Singh out of their fortified house; threatened to hang the former, and took possession of all the property and estates. Arjan Singh determined on revenge, and when Sher Singh became king, and every one had license to avenge his real or fancied wrongs, he attacked and burnt Povind where *Gulab Singh* resided. The General, fearing for his life, fled to Jammu, where he remained for some time under the protection of Raja Gulab Singh, till the Maharaja, by advice of Dhyan Singh, recalled him, and placed him in command of the contingent which was to support the British army during the Kabul campaign. He accompanied Colonel Lawrence to Kabul, and his services and knowledge of the country were of considerable value. Raja Hira Singh, whose family had always befriended *Gulab Singh*, gave him, on the death of Maharaja Sher Singh, new jagirs to the value of 7,625 Rs., and Colonel *Ala Singh* received new allowances, in jagirs and cash, to the value of 2,000 Rs.

Gulab Singh took no part in the Satlej campaign, his troops remaining in Lahore to protect the Maharaja; and in April, 1847, he was, at the recommendation of the Resident, appointed Governor of Peshawar, and being at this time the senior General he was placed in command of all the troops at that station. The elevation of *Gulab Singh* to this important post was a great source of gratification to the Khalsa army, for the brave old man was much loved and respected by the troops. He was created a Sirdar, and in a Darbar held at Lahore on the 26th November, 1847, received the honorary title of Buhadar. Sirdar *Gulab Singh* fulfilled the duties of his new appointment with ability and judgment, and when the Multan rebellion broke out he gave his most cordial assistance to Major G. Lawrence, then in charge at Peshawar, to preserve the peace of the district. For six months, while the insurrectionary movement was spreading more and more widely over the country, the influence of *Gulab Singh* and his son and Deputy, Colonel *Ala Singh,* kept the excited Sikh soldiery to their allegiance; but when Sirdar Chattar Singh approached Peshawar, the troops could no longer be restrained and broke into open mutiny. Major Lawrence held his post till all was hopelessly lost, and then retired to Kohat. *Gulab Singh* and *Ala Singh* would have accompanied him, but the General was too infirm to move quickly, and it was finally decided that he should retire to the fort of Shahmir Ghar, where he might make terms with the rebels. But this gallant officer refused any terms that would compromise his honour. Both he and his son remained loyal, and the Sikh army, finding that they could not be seduced by bribes or terrified by threats, kept them under restraint till the close of the campaign, when the victory of the British restored them to liberty.

On the annexation of the Panjab the whole of Sirdar *Gulab Singh's* personal jagirs to the value of 17,500 Rs. were confirmed to him for life, as were those of his two sons *Ala Singh* and *Lehna Singh* worth 3,000 and 1,050 Rs. respectively. The father and his sons are now all dead. *Gulab Singh* and *Ala Singh* died in 1854, and *Lehna Singh* in 1856. The sons of *Ala Singh,* three in number, do not hold either jagirs or pensions.

In 1857, Hari Singh, a servant of the late Sirdar, gave information to Government that 55,000 Rs. would be found buried in a house which had belonged to *Gulab Singh,* and, on search being made, the money was found and placed in the Treasury. It was claimed by *Nand Kour* the widow of *Gulab Singh* and the widows of *Lehna Singh,* who obtained a decree for the interest of the money in equal shares. This money will be inherited by *Kishan Singh* on the death of its present holders.

JAI SINGH CHINAH.

MILKHU.

- Hira Singh.
- Gurdit Singh.
- S. Karam Singh.
  - Sukh Singh.
    - Jai Singh.
      - Kirpal Singh.
      - Gopal Singh.
    - Hari Singh.
      - Natha Singh.
    - Badan Singh.
      - Kehr Singh.
    - Mahan Singh.
    - Amar Singh.
      - Sant Singh.
    - Hardit Singh.
      - Partab Singh.
  - Budh Singh, D. 1827.
- Uttam Singh.
- Bhup Singh.

HISTORY OF THE FAMILY.

An ancestor of this family, Miru, a Jat of the Gil tribe, founded the village of Chinah, some five miles from Raja Sansi in the Amritsar district, about the year 1600. His eldest son Dadu founded a second village of the same name near Jastarwal, and here his descendants have resided to the present day. The family were simple peasants till the time of *Milkhu,* who joined the confederacy of Tara Singh Shahid. Of *Milkhu's* five sons the most distinguished was *Karam Singh,* whom Tara Singh, who had no children of his own, adopted. After Tara Singh's death, *Karam Singh* joined the Bhangi misl and took possession of Firozki, Kaleki, Rurki and Bajra in the Sialkot district; besides holding Chinah and the neighbouring villages. All the Bhangi Sirdars fell, one by one, before Ranjit Singh, and *Jai Singh* shared the common fate and lost all his estates; but no long time afterwards he received back in jagir Chinah, Nagran and Firozki, worth 50,000 Rs. and subject to the service of 70 horsemen. With his two sons *Sukh Singh* and *Budh Singh,* he served in many campaigns; Multan, Kashmir, and Peshawar, and on his death, the jagir descended to his sons, in equal shares.

Through all the changes which ensued on the death of Ranjit Singh, the jagir remained undiminished, till, in 1846, Raja Lal Singh reduced it to 21,600 Rs. subject to the service of 25 horsemen. Two years later most of the members of the family joined the rebels under Sher Singh, and fought in their ranks throughout the war. Accordingly, on annexation, the shares of *Jai Singh, Mohr Singh, Hari Singh, Hardit Singh, Amar Singh, Attar Singh,* and *Fatah Singh,* were resumed; and an allowance of 240 Rs was granted to each of them for life. The confiscated shares amounted to 15,725 Rs. per mensem, and only *Badan Singh* and *Mahan Singh,* who had remained loyal, were allowed to retain their shares, amounting to 5,875 Rs., of which 1,750 Rs. were personal, and 4,125 Rs. subject to service.

During the mutiny of 1857, *Jai Singh, Hardit Singh* and *Amar Singh* entered Hodson's Horse; *Jai Singh* as Risaldar, *Hardit Singh* as Jamadar, and served with that distinguished corps till February 1859, when, on the general reduction, *Jai Singh* and *Amar Singh* obtained their discharge. The former received a grant of a life jagir of 300 Rs., and the latter forty ghumaos of land free of revenue. *Hardit Singh* is still in the same regiment, now the 10th Bengal Cavalry, as Risaldar.

DIDAR SINGH VEGLIA.

- SAHIB SINGH.
  - Jodh Singh.
    - Jowahir Singh.
      - Didar Singh.
        - Sundar Singh.
  - Vir Singh.
    - Ran Singh.
      - Sant Singh.
        - Harnam Singh.
      - Baksh Singh.
        - Hakim Singh.
    - (unnamed)
    - Dal Singh.
      - Partab Singh.
      - Ganda Singh.
        - Joala Singh.
  - Amir Singh.
  - Kahn Singh.
    - Jamiyat Singh.
      - Nihal Singh.
        - Kirpal Singh.
      - Isar Singh.
    - Sangat Singh.
      - Fatah Singh.
        - Mihr Singh.
        - Aror Singh.
          - Abtar Singh.
      - Asa Singh.
      - Ala Singh.
        - Jaggat Singh.
        - Ganesha Singh.
        - Jaimal Singh.

HISTORY OF THE FAMILY.

Sahib Singh joined the Kanheya confederacy about 1760, and fought under both Jai Singh and Hakikat Singh. He took possession of Taraghar, in the Pathankot parganna of the Gurdaspur district, and after Sirdar Mahan Singh's successful expedition against Jammu, *Sahib Singh*, who had accompanied it, received a grant of Syadghar, worth 30,000 Rs. He founded the village of Wachhoya, where he resided till his death in 1803. His estates in Taraghar, Syadghar and Wachhoya were of the value of 90,000 Rs. and were held intact by his four sons till 1812, when Maharaja Ranjit Singh marched against Taraghar, and after a short siege reduced the fort and confiscated a great portion of the estate. Twelve villages, including Wachhoya worth 10,000 Rs., were still left, free of service, but in the ten-years succeeding the confiscation, the four brothers all died, and Sirdar *Jowahir Singh* succeeded to the estate with his cousins *Jamiyat Singh*, *Sangat Singh* and *Ran Singh*. They fought in many of the Maharaja's campaigns, though their jagir was a subsistence one, and they had no obligation to supply a contingent, till *Desa Singh* Majithia, who was Governor of the Jalandhar Doab, told *Jowahir Singh*, that a Sirdar should give a contingent for the service of the state if he wished his name to endure, and fixed fifteen horsemen as the suitable number.

The Veglia jagirs were not interfered with till 1846, when Raja Lal Singh, who had no love for Sirdar Desa Singh, the family patron, took advantage of his departure to Benares to confiscate the whole estate; but a year afterwards the Darbar, with the sanction of the Resident, restored the jagir with an increased assessment of 21,000 Rs. and service of 30 sowars. During the disturbances of 1848-49, the Veglia family remained faithful. *Didar Singh* joined Captain Hodson, with his contingent, and did good service at Rangar Nangal, Parmanand and elsewhere. At annexation, the whole personal estate of the family, amounting to 8,608 Rs. was released, one-third of the share of each descending to the lineal male heirs in perpetuity. *Didar Singh* became a Risaldar in the Military Police, and took his discharge at the time of the general reductions.

Sant Singh, son of *Ran Singh*, was sent down to Dehli as Jamadar in the Risala raised by Major R. Lawrence, in July 1857, to serve with the Guide Cavalry at the siege. A portion of the Risala was permanently transferred to the Guide Corps, the remainder formed the nucleus of the Dehli mounted police, in which *Sant Singh* was promoted to be Risaldar. He served with zeal and ability till the reduction of the Military Police, when he received his discharge.

LEHNA SINGH CHIMNI.

- Ram Singh.
  - Hukma Singh.
    - Sher Singh, D. 1845.
      - Lehna Singh, B. 1835.
        - Jai Singh, B. 1856.
      - Thakar Singh, B. 1837.
    - Amar Singh, B. 1819.
      - Saudagar Singh.
      - Channa Singh.
      - Bahadar Singh.
    - Mihr Singh, D. 1858.
    - Kishan Singh, B. 1821.
    - Daughter, M. Sirdar Attar Singh, Pindi Lala.

HISTORY OF THE FAMILY.

Ram Singh, a Khatri of the Gandi Bonjai caste, was the first of the family to become a Sikh. He left Behrah in the Shahpur district for Gujranwala, where he entered the service of Sirdar Charrat Singh Sukarchakia as a trooper, and from whom he received the grant of a well at Gujranwala, which is still held by the family. He was killed at Bhulla Kariala, in a skirmish, and left one son *Hukma Singh*, a minor, who, when able to bear arms, entered Ranjit Singh's army. He soon afterwards distinguished himself in the Kassur expedition in 1807, in which he was severely wounded. He was created a Sirdar at the same time with Hari Singh Nalwa and received civil charge of the Ramnagar district and control of the customs and salt duties, on a salary of 24,000 Rs. with the military command of the contingents of the Darrap jagirdars. He accompanied the Lahore chief against Pathankot and Sialkot, and at the latter place showed himself so brave and energetic that Ranjit Singh embraced him and expressed his surprise that such a 'Chimna' of a man should be more courageous than men twice his size. '*Chimna*,' in the Panjab dialect, signifies both a man of small stature, and a little bird, swift and strong of wing; and *Hukma Singh*, who was somewhat undersized, found that the nickname 'Chimna' thus given, stuck to him till it became the agnomen of his family.

For his services *Hukma Singh* received jagirs worth 60,000 Rs. in Ugoki and Roras, and, on the marriage of Prince Kharrak Singh, in 1812, he received additional jagirs in Syadghar worth 40,000 Rs. and also a portion of the Sialkot jagir, alienated from Sirdar Ganda Singh, Safi, which he held for seven years. His force of irregular horse, which was under the command of his cousin Bhai *Gurdial Singh*, mutinied shortly afterwards, and the allowance of 24,000 Rs. which he had received for its maintenance from the Ramnagar customs, was discontinued. In 1814, Yar Muhammad, with the aid of the people of Khairabad, drove the Sikhs out of Attock. *Hukma Singh*, with Sham Singh Bhandari and 2,000 irregulars, attacked him and drove him with loss across the Indus, recovering the plunder which the Afghan army had collected. Khairabad was severely punished for its complicity in this affair.

In 1818, *Hukma Singh* was appointed governor of the districts of Attock and Hazara, and he named Bhai Makkan Singh as his deputy. The latter was of rather a peremptory disposition, and an insolent letter which he wrote to Muhammad Khan, the powerful Tarin chief, ordering him to pay the revenue without delay, set all Hazara in a blaze, for Muhammad Khan called out his tribe and attacked the Sikh force, which was overpowered and cut up, Makkan Singh being among the slain. The few who escaped brought the evil news to *Hukma Singh*, who marched out to avenge his friend. At Sultanpur he met Muhammad Khan, and a sharp fight ensued; neither party could fairly claim the victory, but it so far remained with the Tarin chief that *Hukma Singh* returned to Attock without seeking to bring on a second engagement. The Maharaja was much displeased by the conduct of *Hukma Singh* on this occasion, and there was besides another cause of offence in his having hung, to gratify his private revenge, one Syad Khan of Kot Hassan Ali, a wealthy and well disposed chief. He was fined 1,25,000 Rs., and removed from Hazara, where Diwan Ram Diyal was sent as his successor, in 1819.

Hukma Singh was a good soldier, and there were few of the Maharaja's campaigns in which he did not serve, and his skill and bravery were so well recompensed that at one time he held jagirs amounting to upwards of three lakhs of rupees. On his death, owing to disputes in the family the whole jagirs were resumed. His eldest son who had married the sister of Sirdar Jhanda Singh Botalia received command of 100 sowars on 500 Rs. per mensem. *Amar Singh* and *Mihr Singh* were made commandants, on 775 Rs. and 1,440 Rs. per annum respectively.

Sher Singh was killed at Sobraon and his son *Lehna Singh* received a situation about the person of the young Maharaja Dalip Singh, and received a jagir of 1,149 Rs. in the Sialkot district, which was afterwards resumed. *Lehna Singh*, with his uncles, was at Lahore during the Gujrat campaign and did not join the rebels. In 1857, *Amar Singh* was appointed to Colonel Voyle's Horse, and served with credit in Oude. He received a grant of a well worth 77 Rs. per annum. His son *Buhadur Singh* also served throughout the mutiny as Daffadar. He died on the voyage to China, whither he was proceeding with his regiment during the late war.

MIRZA GHULAM MURTAZA.

FAIZ MUHAMMAD.

Gul Muhammad,
D. 1800.

- Ata Muhammad.
  - Ghulam Haidar.
    - Ghulam Hussain.
  - Ghulam Muhammad.
    - Ghulam Kadir.
- Ghulam Mohiuddin.
  - Ghulam Mohiuddin.
  - Ghulam Murtaza.

HISTORY OF THE FAMILY.

In 1530, the last year of the Emperor Babar's reign, *Hadi Beg*, a Mogul of Samarkand, emigrated to the Panjab and settled in the Gurdaspur district. He was a man of some learning, and was appointed Kazi or Magistrate over seventy villages in the neighbourhood of Kadian, which town he is said to have founded, naming it Islampur Kazi, from which Kadian has by a natural change arisen.* For several generations the family held offices of respectability under the Imperial Government, and it was only when the Sikhs became powerful that it fell into poverty and insignificance. *Gul Muhammad* and his son *Ata Muhammad* were engaged in perpetual quarrels with the Ramgharia and Kanheya misls who held the country in the neighbourhood of Kadian and, at last, having lost all his estates, *Ata Muhammad* retired to Begowal, where, under the protection of Sirdar Fatah Singh Ahluwalia, he lived quietly for twelve years. On his death, Ranjit Singh, who had taken possession of all the lands of the Ramgharia misl, invited *Ghulam Murtaza* to return to Kadian and restored to him a large portion of his ancestral estates. He then, with his brothers, entered the army of the

---

* The Panjab dialect has no *z*. and the Arabic *z*. and *d*. are often interchanged; as *Gumbaz, Gumbad; Ustad, Ustaz.*

Maharaja and performed efficient service on the Kashmir frontier and at other places.

During the time of Nao Nihal Singh, Sher Singh and the Darbar, *Ghulam Murtaza* was continually employed on active service. In 1841, he was sent with General Ventura to Mandi and Kulu, and in 1843, to Peshawar, in command of an infantry regiment. He distinguished himself in Hazara at the time of the insurrection there, and when the rebellion of 1848 broke out, he remained faithful to his Government, and fought on its side. His brother, *Ghulam Mohiuddin,* also did good service at this time. When Bhai Maharaj Singh was marching with his force to Multan to the assistance of Diwan Mulraj, *Ghulam Mohiuddin,* with other jagirdars, Langar Khan Sahiwal and Sahib Khan Tiwana raised the Muhammadan population, and with the force of Misr Sahib Dyal, attacked the rebels and completely defeated them, driving them into the Chenab where upwards of six hundred perished. *Ghulam Kadir* son of *Ghulam Muhammad* was serving in the force under General Nicholson, when that officer destroyed the mutineers of the 46th N. I., who had fled from Sialkot, at Trimmu Ghat. *Mirza Ghulam Murtaza* resides at Kadian, District Gurdaspur. He possesses considerable local influence, although his family jagirs were resumed at annexation. He, with his brothers, enjoys a pension of 700 Rs., and proprietary rights in seven villages. He is also known as a skilful physician.

SIRDAR JODH SINGH CHHAPAWALA.

- SADDA SINGH.
  - Dyal Singh.
    - Kishan Singh.
      - Dewa Singh.
        - Mangal Singh, B. 1843.
        - B. Sohiah.
        - B. Kaku, M. son of Partab Singh Moran.
        - B. Tabu, M. son of Mia Singh.
        - B. Hukami, M. Nihal Singh, Bottala.
      - Kapur Singh.
    - Ram Singh, D. 1849.
      - Jodh Singh, B. 1823.
        - Hardit Singh, B. 1846.
        - Bhag Singh, B. 1855.
        - Nar Singh, B. 1860.
      - Hira Singh, B. 1834.
      - Sohan Singh, B. 1848.

HISTORY OF THE FAMILY.

Dyal Singh, son of a poor cultivator of Dadubajrah in the Sialkot district, entered the force of Tara Singh Kanheya as a trooper. He served his master in many expeditions and received from him a jagir worth 5,000 Rs. in the Pathankot district. On the death of Tara Singh great disputes regarding the succession arose between his sons, and in one of the fights which ensued *Dyal Singh* was killed and his jagir seized by the conqueror. His two sons *Kishan Singh* and *Ram Singh* were thus thrown upon the world as poor as their father when he commenced his career. They went into the Amritsar district to the village of Chhapa where, their father had first settled on leaving his home, and where, on a rising ground, he had built a 'chhapa' or wooden fence round his house, which gave its name to the family and the village.

Maharaja Ranjit Singh took the brothers into his service, and gave them the command of 500 sowars, under the orders of Prince Kharrak Singh. *Kishan Singh* was killed in battle in 1827, and his brother, who had distinguished himself on the same occasion, received a grant of seven villages in the Amritsar district. When Chet Singh, the favourite of Kharrak Singh, was murdered, the Prince, who had always been fond of *Ram Singh,* gave him charge of his private seal, and jagirs in the Amritsar and Shahpur district. Nao Nihal Singh, son of Kharrak Singh, had no love for his father's friends, and threatened to imprison *Ram Singh,* which he would probably have done, had he himself not been killed on the day of his father's incremation. Under Sher Singh, *Ram Singh* received various military commands, and his personal jagir was raised to 15,000 Rs. per annum, through the interest of Raja Dhyan Singh, whom he had been accustomed to supply with private information regarding Maharajah Kharrak Singh.

In 1847, Sirdar *Ram Singh* was sent in command of some irregular horse to Bannu, under Sirdar Shamsher Singh Sindhanwalia, who was in command of the Sikh force sent by the Darbar to assist Lieutenant H. B, Edwardes in the settlement and pacification of the district. He was the chief instigator of the rebellion of the Sikh force at Dalipghar, in 1848. Fatah Khan Tiwana, an enemy of *Ram Singh,* was in charge of the fort which the Sikhs besieged. It was gallantly defended, but the garrison had no water and were unable to hold out; Fatah Khan was killed and the fort captured. There was a Malik of one of the Tappas of Mudan, by name Mir Alim Khan, with whom *Ram Singh* had struck up a great friendship, and to whom he had advanced money to enable him to pay his arrears of revenue. Very much through the assistance of this man the fort was reduced, and it was left in his charge, when *Ram Singh,* with the Sikh force, marched to join Raja Sher Singh.

Sirdar *Ram Singh* was one of the bravest officers in the Sikh Army. He fought with great gallantry at Ramnagar and Chillianwala, and was one of the few men of note killed in the battle of Gujrat.

The whole jagirs of the family were confiscated for rebellion; but in 1857, *Dewa Singh* entered the service of Government as a Risaldar, and his houses and those of *Jodh Singh*, his cousin, were released.

THE BHANGI SIRDARS.

I. Gujar Singh Bhangi.

- **Natha.**
  - Garja Singh.
    - Chet Singh.
      - Ram Singh.
        - Partab Singh.
        - Mehtab Singh.
        - Hira Singh.
        - Jhanda Singh.
  - Gujar Singh, D. 1788.
    - Sukha Singh, M. D., S. Bhag Singh Hallowalia.
    - Sahib Singh, M. D., S. Charrat Singh Sukarchakia, D. 1811.
      - Gulab Singh, M. D. S. Bhag Singh Bhagga, D. 1832.
    - Fatah Singh, D. 1832.
      - Jaimal Singh.
        - Joala Singh.
          - Mian Singh.
          - Hira Singh.

II. Lehna Singh Bhangi.

- **Dargaha.**
  - Lehna Singh, D. 1797.
    - Chet Singh, D. 1815.
      - Attar Singh, B. 1815.
    - Bhagat Singh.

HISTORY OF THE CONFEDERACY.

Bhamma Singh, an inhabitant of Kassur, may be considered the founder of the powerful Bhangi confederacy. He was, however, little more than a robber, and his followers did not exceed three hundred. He was succeeded by his nephew Hari Singh, son of Bhup Singh, a Zamindar of Pattoh near Wadni, who was a man of great ability. He developed a band of robbers into an army and overran a large portion of the Panjab. It was his addiction to 'bhang' (an intoxicating preparation of hemp) that gave the name 'Bhangi' to the misl. Some indeed say that this name originated with Bhamma Singh, who was of so arrogant a disposition that he was called by the Sikhs Bala-bash (High-head.) This, being a Turkoman title, annoyed Bhamma Singh so much that he begged his comrades to change it for some other. Accordingly he was appointed, when in attendance at the Darbar Sahib of Amritsar, to pound bhang for the Khalsa, and was himself called Bhangi. The former account is the one commonly believed.

Hari Singh, whose head-quarters were at the village of Gilwali in the Amritsar district, seized much of the neighbouring country, Sialkot, Karial, Mirowal. He ravaged Chaniot and Jhang Sial, and attacked Jammu, which he rendered tributary, and Multan without success. In 1762, he attacked the village of Khwaja Syad ka Kot, two miles from Lahore, where Khwaja Abid the Afghan governor had his arsenal, and carried away with him much booty, arms and ammunition. In 1763 he joined the Kanheyas and Ramgharias in their attack on Kassur, and the next year was killed in a fight with Amar Singh Pattiala, and Jhanda Singh and Ganda Singh, two brothers who had served under him, succeeded to the command of one division of the Bhangi misl. They were Dhillon Jats of Panjwar near Taran Taran, and under them the confederacy became very powerful. Associated with them were many famous chiefs; Bhag Singh Hallowalia; Tara Singh, Sher Singh and Rai Singh Buriahwala; Sudh Singh Dodia; Sahib Singh Sialkotia; Nidhan Singh Attu, and with them too, though not inferior in rank, were the two Bhangi chiefs, Gujar Singh and Lehna Singh, whose history is given hereafter.

In 1766, Jhanda Singh and Ganda Singh with a large force invaded Multan. Shuja Khan the governor, and Mobarik Khan of Bahawalpur, gave them battle on the banks of the Satlej. Neither side could claim the victory, but a treaty was signed to the effect that Pakpattan should be the boundary between the Sikh and Afghan states. After this Jhanda Singh returned to Amritsar, where he employed himself in completing the Bhangi fort, which Hari Singh had begun, and the remains of which are still to be seen behind the Lunmandi Bazar. It was not long before Jhanda Singh broke the provisions of the treaty with the Multan chief, and invaded his country in 1771. He besieged the fort unsuccessfully for a month and a half, till the near approach of an Afghan force under Jahan Khan compelled him to raise the siege.

The next year, 1772, he was more successful. The successive governors of Multan, Shuja Khan, Sharif Khan Saddozai and Sharif Khan (or Sharif Beg) Taklu, had quarreled, and Sharif Khan Taklu invited Jhanda Singh and Ganda Singh to his assistance. They were ready enough to accept the invitation, and marching south with a large force, defeated Shuja Khan and his allies, the Daudputras of Bahawalpur, and seized Multan for themselves. Sharif Beg, thus fatally deceived, took refuge at Talamba and then at Khairpur Tanwain, where he soon after died.

Jhanda Singh then marched northwards, leaving in charge of Multan Diwan Singh Chhachowalia, with a strong garrison. He first went to Ramnagar where he recovered the Zamzama or Bhangi gun * from the Chattahs, and thence to Jammu, where his ally and tributary Raja Ranjit Deo was defending himself against his son Brij Raj Deo and the Kanheya and Sukarchakia chiefs.

---

* The history of this gun is somewhat remarkable. It was cast at Lahore, with another gun of the same size, in 1761, by Shah Nazir, under the directions of Shah Wali Khan, Prime minister of Ahmad Shah. The date of its founding (A. H. 1174) may be derived from the last of the twenty Persian verses engraved upon it, each letter having a numerical value.

Paikari Azhdakae Atishbar. پیکری اژدها ئی آتشبار

The material of which the guns were made was a mixture of copper and brass obtained by the '*Jizya*'; (a tribute levied by Muhammadans from the infidels) a metal vessel being taken from each house in Lahore. Ahmad Shah on his returning to Kabul after his victory over the Afghans at Panipat in 1761 left the *Zamzama* gun, the carriage of which was not ready, at Lahore, in the charge of Khwaja Abid whom he had appointed Governor. The other gun he took with him, and it was lost in the passage of the Chenab. The Zamzama had a longer life. Hari Singh Bhangi is said to have captured it when he plundered Khwaja Abid's arsenal and to have taken it to Amritsar, but this is not correct, for it is certain that during the whole Governorship of Khwaja Abid, 1761-1762, the gun was lying unmounted in the Shah Burj at Lahore. In 1764, when Lehna Singh and Gujar Singh Bhangi captured Lahore they obtained possession of it. Two days later Sirdar Charrat Singh Sukarchakia came to congratulate the Bhangis, and hinted that he should have some share of the spoil. The Bhangis,

From some time the rival forces engaged with varying success, till Sirdar Charrat Singh Sukarchakia was accidentally killed and the Bhangis seemed about to gain the victory. This the Kanheyas averted by the assassination of Jhanda Singh, causing him to be shot as he was riding through the camp.* This was in 1774.

Ganda Singh succeeded to the command of the misl, and, finding that no success could now be gained at Jammu, he retired to Amritsar where he engaged himself in enlarging and strengthening the Bhangi quarter and in plotting against the Kanheyas who had caused his brother's death. An opportunity for showing his enmity almost immediately occured. Jhanda Singh had bestowed Pathankot on one of his misldars, Nand Singh, otherwise known as Mansa Singh. This man died about the same time as his chief, and his widow gave her daughter and

---

who knew that Charrat Singh had come, not for congratulation, but only as a vulture who has scented a carcase, thought to outwit him, and unwilling to make so powerful a chief their enemy offered him, with the greatest politeness, the Zamzama gun ; they best part, they asserted, of the spoil, hoping and believing that he would be unable to carry it away. But Charrat Singh, seeing he could get nothing more, called his men together, and with great labour carried it off to his camp, and then to his fort at Gujranwala. Here it was captured by Ahmad Khan Chattah, who took it to his new fort of Ahmadnagar, much to the disgust of his brother Pir Muhammad who thought he had also a claim to it, and the two quarreled about its possession, and in the fights, which ensued a son of Pir Muhammad and two sons of Ahmad Khan were slain. Pir Muhammad at length called in Gujar Singh Bhangi to his assistance, who [illegible]pped Ahmad Khan and kept [illegible] a day and a night without water till he promised to give up the gun, which Gujar Singh, cheating his ally, carried to Gujrat and kept himself. Here it remained two years till, in an evil hour, the Bhangis took it with them on an expedition against Sirdar Charrat Singh Sukarchakia. The Bhangis were worsted, and the gun, too heavy to remove quickly, fell again into the hands of the Sukarchakia chief. In 1772, the Chattahs, who were always fighting with Charrat Singh, recovered the gun, and placed it in the fort of Manchar, and a short time afterwards removed it to Rasulnagar, now Ramnagar. Here, the next year, it was captured by Sirdar Jhanda Singh Bhangi on his return from Multan, and by him sent to Amritsar where it remained in the Bhangi fort, till 1802, when Ranjit Singh, who had the greatest desire to possess it, drove the Bhangis out of Amritsar and seized it. During the reign of Ranjit Singh, the gun was taken, with great pomp, on five different campaigns, viz., Daska, Kassur, Sujanpur, Wazirabad and Multan. At the siege of the last named place, in 1818, it was seriously injured, and being considerod unfit for further service it was brought to Lahore and placed at the Dehli gate of the city, where it remained till 1860, when it was placed in [illegible] of the La[illegible]ore museum, where it now stands.

* *Vide* Statement Jit Singh Kanheya.

the jagir of Pathankot to Tara Singh, a near relation of Hakikat Singh Kanheya. Ganda Singh was exceedingly indignant at this, and insisted that Tara Singh should give up the jagir; but the Kanheyas refused, and Ganda Singh, collecting a large force, taking with him the Bhangi gun, and with many of the Ramgharia chiefs as allies, marched against Pathankot. Hakikat Singh, Tara Singh and Gurbaksh Singh Kanheya and Amar Singh Bhagga marched to Dinanagar to oppose his progress, and here an indecisive engagement took place; but while encamped at Dinanagar Ganda Singh fell ill, and died after ten days. His son Desu Singh was a mere child, so Charrat Singh a nephew was selected by the troops to succeed him; but, in the very first fight with the Kanheyas, Charrat Singh was killed, and the Bhangi force, left without a leader, returned to Amritsar.

Desu Singh now became head of the confederacy, and one Gujar Singh acted as his minister. But the days of the great Bhangi misl were numbered, and the power and intellect of a boy were unable to control the many unruly chiefs who had been proud to fight under Hari Singh and Jhanda Singh. Bhag Singh Halluwalia first declared himself independent; then Jhang ceased to pay tribute, and in 1779, Multan was lost.

It will be remembered that Sirdar Jhanda Singh had left Diwan Singh in charge of Multan. He held his own for some years successfully, and in 1777, repulsed, though only with great loss, an attack of the Bahawalpur chief and Muzaffar Khan son of Shuja Khan. But in 1779, Timur Shah, son of Ahmad Shah, marched against Multan with a large army; and Diwan Singh, having held out for more than a month, was compelled to capitulate, and was allowed to retire unmolested. Desu Singh had also a great enemy in the person of Sirdar Mahan Singh, head of the Sukarchakia misl, which was now becoming very powerful, and in 1782, after holding the chiefship eight years he was killed in action, but whether before Chuniot, which he had marched to reduce, or in a skirmish with Mahan Singh, is uncertain. He was succeeded by his son Gulab Singh, and of this chief there is little to record. He was a debauched, weak man and had not energy sufficient to keep together the possessions which his father had left him. Year by year these diminished, till, at last, the town of Amritsar and some villages in the Manjha alone remained.

In 1800 a cabal was formed against Ranjit Singh, who had captured Lahore in July of the preceding year, and whose successes were beginning to fill all the Panjab chiefs with alarm. Chief in the cabal were Sirdars Jassa Singh Ramgharia, Sahib Singh and Gulab Singh Bhangi and Nizamuddin Khan of Kassur, and it was proposed to invite Ranjit Singh to a conference at Bhasin, and there assassinate him. But the young chief was too wily to attend without a force large enough to secure his safety, and after two months passed in festivities he returned to Lahore. But although Ranjit Singh escaped with his life, Gulab Singh was less fortunate. He had never missed an opportunity for drinking hard, and, on this occasion, when every night ended in a debauch, he drank so deep that he killed himself. Some have asserted that he was poisoned, but there is no shadow of foundation for the story, and he was so incapable a man that no one could possibly think it worth his while to destroy him. Gulab Singh left one son Gurdit Singh, a boy ten years of age, married to the daughters of Sirdars Sahib Singh Bhangi and Fatah Singh Kanheya. But no powerful alliances were of use against Ranjit Singh, who was determined to gain possession of Amritsar. He, in 1802, with the intention of picking a quarrel with the Bhangis, sent to demand from Gurdit Singh the famous Zamzama gun. But the glory and prestige of the confederacy was derived in great part from the possession of this, and although her chief advisers urged Sukhan, the mother of Gurdit Singh to give it up, she refused to part with it and prepared to fight. But such preparations were worse than useless. Ranjit Singh with Fatah Singh Ahluwalia marched to Amritsar, attacked the Bhangi fort, and in five hours reduced it. Sukhan and her son took refuge with Sirdar Jodh Singh Ramgharia, and Ranjit Singh seized all the Bhangi possessions. Little more is known of Gurdit Singh. He died at his ancestral village of Panjwar, in the Taran Taran Parganna of the Amritsar district, where his descendants are still living as simple peasants.

Notice must now be taken of two other powerful chiefs of the Bhangi misl, Sirdars Lehna Singh and Gujar Singh, who, though joining Jhanda Singh and Ganda Singh in some of their expeditions, have a history for the most part distinct. Lehna Singh's grandfather was a zamindar of the Kahilon Jat caste, who in a time of scarcity left his native village of Saddahwala in the Amritsar district for Mastapur near Kartarpur in the Jalandhar Doab. Here he was adopted by a man who joined the trades of carpentering and collecting taxes, and here his son Dargaha was born. Lehna Singh, the son of Dargaha, was a high spirited boy, and having been, on one occasion, beaten by his father for allowing cattle to stray into his field, ran away from home, and after wandering about for some time, at length reached the village of Roranwala, one mile from Attari, where Gurbaksh Singh Bhangi lived. This man was one of the best fighters under Sirdar Hari Singh. He owned about forty villages and used to scour the country with a band of horsemen and collect plunder from far and near. He took a fancy to young Lehna Singh and put him into his troop, and later, having no son of his own, adopted him. Gurbaksh Singh died in 1763, and dissentions straightway arose between Lehna Singh the adopted son and Gujar Singh the son of Gurbaksh Singh's daughter, each claiming the property. Jhanda Singh and Ganda Singh Bhangi came to Waniki to try and settle the dispute, but Gujar Singh would not listen to terms and set out with his followers for Roranwala. Lehna Singh pursued and came up with him, and a fight was the result, in which a few men were killed on either side. At length an arrangement was made, by which Lehna Singh and Gujar Singh divided the estate. The former kept Roranwala and the latter founded a new village between Bharwal and Ranni, which he called Ranghar, in remembrance of his fight with Lehna Singh, of whom he now became the fast friend.

The two Sirdars then planned the capture of Lahore, which Kabuli Mal held in the interest of Ahmad Shah. The Governor was a timid and at the same time a tyrannical man, and as the Sikh horse, becoming every day more bold, plundered the country up to the very walls of the city, he grew alarmed for his safety and, when he obtained secret intelligence of the Bhangi plot, he fled from Lahore leaving it in charge of his nephew Amir Singh. He took the road to Jammu, but some of the refugees, who had left Lahore through his tyranny, handled him so roughly that he would probably have been killed had not some troops, sent by Raja Ranjit Deo as his escort, rescued him. The Raja sent him to Rawal Pindi, where the rearguard of Ahmad Shah's army had halted and here he died shortly afterwards.

One dark night Lehna Singh and Gujur Singh with two hundred men determined to surprise Lahore. They found all the gates closed, but one Dyal Singh showed them a drain by which it was possible to enter with some squeezing. Gujur Singh led the way, Lehna Singh followed and the other Sikhs. The fort was taken by surprise ; Amir Singh the Deputy Governor captured at a nautch, and put in irons ; and before morning the whole city was in possession of the confederates. Early the next day Sobha Singh Kanheya, nephew of Jai Singh, arrived. He had, since the last Afghan invasion, been in hiding at his native village of Kanah. He was one of the confederates, and although too late to aid in the capture, was allowed a share of the prize. Then came the other Bhangi and Kanheya Sirdars, and lastly Charrat Singh Sukarchakia, who was very hard to please, and would not go away till the Bhangis had given him the Zamzama gun, which he carried to Gujranwala. The three Sirdars then divided Lahore among them ; Lehna Singh taking the citadel, with the Masti, Khizri, Kashmiri and Roshani gates. Gujur Singh built for himself a fort without the walls, which he called Kila Gujar Singh, and, in 1765, marched northwards to conquer new territory.

Lehna Singh and Sobha Singh remained in Lahore, in peace, till Ahmad Shah made his final descent upon the Panjab in 1767, when they retired to Panjwar. But the great Durani leader felt age and infirmity creeping upon him, and having no man of genius like Adina Beg Khan to leave in charge of the province, he resolved to conciliate the Sikh chiefs. To Lehna Singh he sent a present of fruit, but he returned it saying that grain was the food for peasants like him, not fruit which was a luxury for kings. Pleased with this humble reply, Ahmad Shah confirmed Lehna Singh in his possession of Lahore, and returned to Kabul, where he died in 1773. For thirty years after this the Lahore Sirdars ruled in tolerable quiet, till 1797, when Shah Zaman who had succeeded to the throne of Kabul, invaded the Panjab, and Lehna Singh again retired from Lahore, and returned after the departure of the Shah, but died the same year. Sobha Singh died about the same time, and was succeeded by his son Mohr Singh, while Chet Singh succeeded Lehna Singh.

Shah Zaman again appeared in 1798, but only remained a few months in Lahore, as news from Persia rendered his return necessary. Sirdar Ranjit Singh Sukarchakia obtained from the Shah a grant of the city in return for services which he rendered, the principal of which was the raising and forwarding to the Shah eight guns which had sunk in the river Ravi. But the gift was only nominal, and Ranjit Singh was left to gain possession for himself. This was not difficult. The only man of any energy among the joint rulers of Lahore was Sahib Singh, son of Gujar Singh, and he was absent at Gujrat. Chet Singh was an imbecile, and Mohr Singh possessed neither character nor influence. Their rule was hated by the people, and their own adherents Bhai Gurbaksh Singh, Hakîm Hâkim Rai and Mian Ashak Muhammad were in favour of Ranjit Singh and wrote him word that he could easily make himself master of the place. Ranjit Singh with a large force entered Anarkalli, and Chet Singh, who thought of marching to oppose him, was dissuaded from so doing by his agent Mokham Din Chowdhri of Kotnao, who was in charge of the Lohari gate, which he opened to the enemy. Ranjit Singh took possession without difficulty, and Chet Singh and Mohr Singh fled.

Some time later Ranjit Singh granted to Chet Singh a jagir of 60,000 Rs. in Waniki, which he held till his death in 1815. He left no son by any of his eight wives, but four months after his death, Bibi Hukm Kour gave birth to a son, named Attar Singh, in favour of whom Ranjit Singh released an estate of 6,000 Rs. at Waniaki. This was afterwards much reduced and exchanged for Laddi, which again, in 1819, was exchanged for Chak Didu, part of Lehna Singh's old estate. On annexation this village was released to Attar Singh and his mother for their lives. On the death of the latter, half will lapse to Government, and the remainder will descend to the legitimate male issue of Attar Singh in perpetuity. Attar Singh resides at Chak Didu. He is fifty years of age, and though he has three daughters, all of whom are married, has, as yet, no son.

Sirdar Gujar Singh's expedition to conquer the country to the north of Lahore was successful enough, and he soon became a far more powerful chief than Lehna Singh or Sobha Singh. He first attached Gujrat, which was then held by Sultan Mukarrab, a Ghakkar chief, and defeating him in an engagement just beyond the walls, took possession of both the city and the neighbouring country. Gujrat he now made his head-quarters, and the next year, 1766, marched to Jammu, which he overran and held tributary with Jhanda Singh Bhangi: and then successively reduced Punchh, Islamghar and Dewa Botala. In 1767, Ahmad Shah made his last invasion of India, driving before him all the new Sikh chiefs, for in those days the dread of an Afghan army was such that there was no thought of opposing it in the open field, and leaving behind him the proverb, "*Khada pida lada rahnda Ahmad Shahda*." Meaning that Ahmad Shah left nothing that men could call their own but what they had actually in their mouths.

Among those who fled was Gujar Singh. He went to Lahore, and thence, as Ahmad Shah advanced, to Firozpur; and when the Durani chief had finally turned his back on the Panjab, he recovered his share of the city of Lahore and left it in charge of Takht Singh, a near relation. He then went to Amritsar, and for the defence of the holy city laid the foundations of fort Gujar Singh, where now stands the newer fort of Govindghar. Charrat Singh Sukarchakia also built a fort to the north of the Darbar Sahib; (the Golden Temple), while that of Jassa Singh Ramgharia lay to the east, and that of the Bhangis to the south. Then, at his village of Ranghar, he married his eldest son to the daughter of Bhag Singh Hallowalia; and as soon as the festivities were over marched with his whole force to Gujrat, recovering all his old conquests with but with little trouble. Then, in conjunction with Sirdar Charrat Singh Sukarchakia, he besieged the famous fort of Rhotas, held by the Ghakkars. After a siege of several months it was reduced and the whole of the neighbouring country as far as Rawal Pindi, with its splendid fighting tribes, Janjoahs, Ghakkars, Awans, submitted to the allies. He then married his second son Sahib Singh to a daughter of Sirdar Charrat Singh, and some time later to a daughter of Hamir Singh of Jheend.

Gujar Singh had divided his territories between his two eldest sons, Sukha Singh and Sahib Singh. These quarreled, and the younger, at the instigation of Sirdar Mahan Singh Sukarchakia, who was always seeking to benefit by the mistakes of others, attacked his brother who was killed during the action. Gujar Singh was very indignant when he heard of this, and determined to dispossess Sahib Singh of all the country under his charge. He marched upon Gujrat, and was admitted without question, and Sahib Singh, now in open revolt, shut himself up in Islamghar. But Gujar Singh did not wish to proceed to extremities, and forgave his son the moment he showed a disposition to sue for pardon; and, confirming him in his old possessions, made over those which had been held by Sukha Singh to his youngest son Fatah Singh. But another cause of disunion soon arose. Sirdar Mahan Singh was besieging Rasulnagar, the capital of his enemies the Chattas, and a principal officer, escaping from the town, took refuge in Sirdar Gujar Singh's camp. Mahan Singh demanded his surrender, which was refused. Sahib Singh, however, willing to oblige his brother-in-law, made the refugee over to him, and he was put to death. Gujar Singh was indignant at this disobedience of his son: he cursed him, and prayed that as he had insulted and dishonoured his father, so his son might insult and dishonour him. This conduct of Sahib Singh so preyed upon the old Sirdar's mind that he fell ill, and leaving all his possessions to his youngest son Fatah Singh, he retired to Lahore, where he died in 1788. His tomb is situated near the Samman Burj.

However much Gujar Singh may have wished to exclude his eldest son from the succession, the Sirdars of the Khalsa would not admit his right to do so, and Sahib Singh took possession of his father's estates without active opposition from Fatah Singh, who went to live with Mahan Singh at Gujranwala. For some time there was peace between the brothers-in-law, Mahan Singh and Sahib Singh, but in 1789 they openly quarreled and for two years remained in constant hostility. At length in 1791, Mahan Singh shut up Sahib Singh in the fort of Sodhra and reduced him to great straits. The Bhangi chief called to his assistance Lehna Singh of Lahore and Karam Singh Dulu. The former would not move, but Karam Singh came with a large force to raise the siege, and an engagement took place between him and Mahan Singh. The Sukarchakia chief was at this time very ill, and during the fight fainted away on his elephant, the mahaut of which turned and carried his master from the field. His forces, missing their leader, fled: the siege was raised, and Mahan Singh retired to Gujranwala where he died three days afterwards, the desertion of his old friend Jodh Singh Wazirabadia * hastening his death. In 1797 Shah Zaman invaded the Panjab, and Sahib Singh retired to the hills. The Shah only remained a few days in Lahore and then returned to Afghanistan. He left behind him, at Pind Dadan Khan, an officer known as the Shahanchi, with 7000 Afghan troops, who, on Sahib Singh's return to Gujrat, marched against him with allies from among the Muhammadan tribes of the Jhelam district. Sahib Singh, with Nihal Singh and

* *Vide* Hira Singh Wazirabadia.

Wazir Singh Attariwala, Jodh Singh Wazirabadia, and Karam Singh Dulu, gave him battle and completely defeated him. This was in 1798, and was the first time that the Sikhs had fairly beaten the Afghans in the open field. A few months after this defeat of the Shahanchi, Shah Zaman again invaded the Panjab, but his stay was short and he retired making Ranjit Singh a grant of Lahore, which he captured as has been already related. Fatah Singh Bhangi now joined Ranjit Singh who promised to give him half of his brother's possessions, and with this assistance he seized Fatahghar, now called Kot Bari Khan, and Sodhra. When Sahib Singh heard of the fall of Lahore, he moved with a large force against Ranjit Singh; the Ramgharia and Kassur troops marching from the east and south to the same point; but the meeting at Bhasin passed off peaceably. Hostilities commenced later in the year, and continued for some time, Fatah Singh becoming reconciled to his brother; but this friendship did not last long, for on Fatah Singh favouring Mai Sahib Kour wife of Sahib Singh, who, disgusted at her husband's third marriage, held the fort of Jalalpur against him, his property and newly granted estates were all seized. Fatah Singh went back to Ranjit Singh, who, remembering that he had deserted him in the middle of the campaign, would do nothing for him, and after remaining in Lahore, in great poverty, for a year, he was compelled to return to his brother at Gujrat, who gave him Doulatnagar and other estates.

Sahib Singh now began to lose the energy which had so much distinguished him, and gave himself up to drunkenness and debauchery. He quarreled with Sirdar Nihal Singh Attariwala, and with Mokham Chand, his Diwan, afterwards so celebrated, who both went over to Ranjit Singh. In 1806, he accompanied the Lahore chief on the Pattiala campaign, and at its close returned to Gujrat. In 1810, Ranjit Singh determined to take possession of Sahib Singh's country, and sent for that purpose Hukm Singh Attariwala and Sewa Singh. Sahib Singh, seeing resistance hopeless, fled from Gujrat with 50 horsemen and took refuge in the fort of Dewa Botala, and his whole jagirs were seized, an estate of 25,000 Rs. being granted to Gulab Singh who had intrigued against his father. In 1810, when the Maharaja was engaged in the siege of Multan, Mai Lachmi, mother of Sahib Singh, proceeded thither and interceded for her son with such effect that the Ilaka of Bajwant, worth a lakh of rupees, was released in his favour. This he held till his death, which took place the next year, when Ranjit Singh took two of his widows, Dya Kour and Rattan Kour, into his Zanana, marrying them by chaddar dola. Dya Kour, daughter of Diwan Singh Wirk, was the reputed mother of Peshora Singh and Kashmira Singh ; Rattan Kour the reputed mother of Multana Singh.* Sirdar Fatah Singh Gujratia, on the death of his brother, and the resumption of the jagir, went to Kapurthalla, where he remained in the service of the Ahluwalia chief for two years, till, on the death of his mother Mai Lachmi, he received a grant of Ranghar and some other villages in the Amritsar district, and entered the service of Sirdar Sham Singh Attariwala, in whose contingent he served for many years. He was killed in Bannu, at the siege of the fort of Malik Dilasah Khan. About the same time, in 1832, Gulab Singh died and his jagirs were all resumed.

Jaimal Singh, only son of Fatah Singh, was for some time in Sirdar Sham Singh's force, and served on the frontier and at Peshawar. He however quarreled with his chief, and this brought on Jaimal Singh more troubles than there is space to record here. Through the enmity of Sham Singh his jagir was resumed, and when the British occupied the country he was in great poverty. He still resides at Ranghar, without pension or estate, the representative of the great Bhangi house which possessed more power and ruled over a larger territory than any other family between the Satlej and the Indus.

---

* *Ante*, *pp.* 4, 6, 7.

SIRDAR BALWANT SINGH RANGAR NANGLIA.

- RANDEO.
  - Natha Singh.
    - Karam Singh.
      - Jamiyat Singh.
        - Arjan Singh, D. 1859.
          - Balwant Singh.
          - Utar Singh.
        - Daughter, M. Dev Indra Singh, Raja of Nabha.
      - Wazir Singh.
        - Jowala Singh.
        - Chanda Singh.
    - Dharam Singh.
      - Ram Singh.
        - Sawan Singh.
      - Sardul Singh.
        - Bhuta Singh.
        - Sher Singh.
    - Charrat Singh.
      - Dal Singh.

HISTORY OF THE FAMILY.

This family came originally from Bikanir in Rajputana, and settled in the fertile district of Gurdaspur, where, near the city of Batala, they founded the village of Rangar Nangal. 'Rangar' is the name of the Rajput 'got' or clan to which Raja Jaggat, the founder of the family, belonged, and Nangal is a euphonic corruption of the Sanscrit word 'Mangal,' 'pleasing,' signifying that the emigrants were satisfied that after their many wanderings their lines had fallen in pleasant places.

Many years later *Natha*, the son of *Randeo*, became a Sikh, and joining the Kanheya confederacy, under Jai Singh, ravaged all the country around Rangar Nangal, where he built a strong fort. His son *Karam Singh* succeeded him, and very much increased both the power and possessions of the family. He rebuilt and strengthened the Rangar Nangal fort and took up his residence in Amritsar, where he built the 'Katra Karam Singh,' otherwise known as 'Katra Rangar Nangalia.' When

Ranjit Singh became powerful and seized Lahore and Amritsar, *Karam Singh* gave in his allegiance and ever after remained a faithful servant of the Maharaja. On one occasion, indeed, they quarreled. *Karam Singh* was captain of Ranjit Singh's irregulars, and as in these early days the chief had not much money to spare, the pay of the troops fell into arrears. *Karam Singh* took their side and demanded their pay of Ranjit Singh, who, fearing an outbreak, was compelled to pawn the jewels of his wife Mehtab Kour. The Maharaja afterwards punished *Karam Singh* for thus taking part against him by plundering and destroying his house in Amritsar. But a reconciliation took place, and the Sirdar accompanied Ranjit Singh on most of his expeditions, and in the Peshawar campaign, where he was severely wounded, he specially distinguished himself, and received for his services a new jagir in the Jalandhar Doab. He possessed, at one time, territory to the amount of several lakhs of rupees, principally situated in the Gurdaspur district. He was succeeded by his son *Jamiyat Singh*, who had been for long with the army and who was favourably known to Ranjit Singh for his bravery. His younger brother *Wazir Singh* received a jagir in Bhimbar, in 1821. *Jamiyat Singh* was, with his cousin *Ram Singh*, killed in Hazara, at the battle of Darband, in 1820, and on his death the jagirs were reduced by more than one half.

Arjan Singh was still, however, a powerful Sirdar, and remained in favour so long as Maharaja Ranjit Singh and Nao Nihal Singh were alive; but on the accession of Sher Singh, his jagirs were again reduced, and there was only left to him 28,000 Rs., of which 15,000 Rs. were personal and 13,000 Rs. subject to the service of 30 horsemen. *Arjan Singh's* mother was maternal aunt of Rani Chand Kour, the widow of Kharrak Singh and mother of Nao Nihal Singh, and in this relationship will be found the cause of Maharaja Sher Singh's enmity.

In 1845, previous to the Satlej campaign, *Arjan Singh* received from Raja Lal Singh command of 4 infantry regiments, one regiment of cavalry and a troop of horse artillery, and with this force he served at the battle of Sobraon. In 1846 he served with credit in the Kashmir expedition, and in August, 1847, received a Persian title of honour on the recommendation of Major Lawrence, the Resident at Lahore. In 1848, he accompanied Raja Sher Singh Attariwala to Multan and joined in his rebellion. His adherents, hearing of the Sirdar's disaffection, proceeded to follow his example, and defended the fort of Rangar Nangal successfully against two companies of the Darbar troops which had been sent to attach the property; but Brigadier Wheeler marched against it on the 15th October and speedily reduced it. On the termination of the war the whole estates of *Arjan Singh* were confiscated, and the Rangar Nangal jagir conferred on Sirdar *Mangal Singh* Ramgharia, who had displayed much energy in the capture of Hari Singh a notorious freebooter, who had, during the war, kept the neighbourhood of Battala in a state of alarm.

Arjan Singh received from Government a pension of 1,500 Rs.; but it was personal, and ceased at his death in 1859. At the request of the Raja of Nabha, the British Government gave a pension of 120 Rs. a year to each of the two widows of *Arjan Singh*, and the family also receives help from Nabha, but it is in very reduced circumstances.

The Raja of Nabha is second cousin of Sirdar *Balwant Singh*. The daughter of *Jamiyat Singh* married Raja Dev-Indra Singh, a match made up by Maharaja Ranjit Singh and never much liked by *Jamiyat Singh*. By this wife Dev-Indra Singh had two sons, Raja Bharpur Singh, who died in 1863, and Bhagwan Singh, the reigning chief.

Mehtab Kour, widow of *Arjan Singh*, was murdered in the courtyard of her own house at Rangar Nangal, early in 1864. One of the murderers, a resident of Nabha, has been convicted and sentenced to transportation for life, and Sirdar Gurbaksh Singh, prime minister of Nabha, is now under trial on suspicion of having been concerned in the crime.

THE CHATTAHS OF GUJRANWALA.

I. NUR MUHAMMAD.

- I. Nur Muhammad.
  - Pir Muhammad.
    - Fatah Muhammad.
    - Ghulam Muhammad.
      - Jan Muhammad.
        - Ghulam Kadar.
          - Ghulam Hassan.
          - Ghulam Hussain.
          - Ghulam Navi.
          - Ghulam Ali.
          - Ghulam Rasul.
            - Haiyat Khan.
            - Muhammad Khan.
  - Ahmad Khan.
    - Kadar Baksh.
    - Bahram Khan.

II. JAN BAKSH.

- II. Jan Baksh.
  - Khuda Baksh.
    - Sarbuland Khan.
      - Shamash Din.
    - Bakht Buland Khan.
      - Ghulam Haidar.
    - Ghulam Kadir.
      - Shahbaz Khan.
    - Syad Muhammad.
      - Fazl Dad Khan.
    - Dost Mahammad.
      - Rahmat Khan.
  - Sultan Muhammad.

HISTORY OF THE TRIBE.

I. The Chattahs are a numerous Muhammadan tribe chiefly inhabiting the Hafizabad and Wazirabad pargannahs of the Gujranwala district, where they hold seventy-eight villages. They claim to be by origin Chohan Rajputs and to have emigrated to the Panjab from the Dehli district. The date of the emigration is not exactly known, but it was probably about three hundred years ago. They rapidly increased in numbers, spreading along the banks of the Chenab, and founded Nadalab, Manchar, Bangali, Pandorian and other villages. One Gaggu seems to have been the first to adopt the Mahammadan faith, about the year 1600, and his example was followed by the remainder of the tribe. *Nur Muhammad* was born in 1704. When he grew up his friendship was sought by Raja Ranjit Deo of Jammu and by the chiefs of Multan, for the Chattahs had now grown powerful and *Nur Muhammad* was their acknowledged chief. When *Nur Muhammad* grew old, *Ahmad Khan*, his younger son, a brave and skilful soldier, led the Chattahs to battle. The great enemies of the tribe were the Sukarchakia chiefs of Gujranwala, who were ever striving to extend their possessions. In the time of Sirdar Charrat Singh the Chattahs held their own, and *Ahmad Khan*, in 1765, captured the celebrated Bhangi gun which Charrat Singh had placed in Gujranwala. Soon after this *Ahmad Khan* and his brother *Pir Muhammad* quarreled, and fought for some time with varying success, and among the killed were *Bahram Khan* and *Kadar Baksh*, sons of *Ahmad Khan*, and *Fatah Muhammad* his nephew. At last *Pir Muhammad* sought help from Gujar Singh and Sahib Singh Bhangi, who invited *Ahmad Khan* to a conference, captured him and shut him up without water till he agreed to resign the great gun which was carried to the fort of Gujrat.*

Mir Manu, the viceroy of Ahmad Shah Durani, laid siege to the fort of Manchar for some months without success, but when the Emperor himself invaded the Panjab, he seems to have treated the Chattah chiefs with consideration and to have confirmed them in their possessions. Sirdar Charrat Singh, the Chattah enemy, died in 1774, closely followed by *Nur Muhammad* and his son *Pir Muhammad*.

The towns founded in the Gujranwala district by these chiefs are neither few nor unimportant. Among those founded by *Nur Muhammad* were Ahmadnagar, Ghadhi Gul Muhammad and Rasulnagar, renamed by the Sikhs Ramnagar, while *Pir Muhammad* built three different forts called after his own name, also Kot Mian Khan, Alipur, renamed by the Sikhs Akalghar, Naiwala, Kot Salim, Kot Ali Muhammad and Fatahpur. *Ghulam Muhammad*, who succeeded to the estate succeeded also to the hatred of the Sukarchakias. Both Sirdar Mahan Singh son of Charrat Singh and *Ghulam Muhammad* were able and brave men, and it was clear that peace could only result from the

* *Vide* Note to Sirdar Gujar Singh Bhangi's statement.

death of one or the other. For a long time the advantage lay with the Chattahs and Mahan Singh was defeated on several occasions. Once he besieged Jhokian, held by *Mian Khan,* uncle of *Ghulam Muhammad,* who came down in haste to relieve it. After some hard fighting, peace was agreed upon, but in an unguarded moment the treacherous Sikh seized *Mian Khan* carried him off prisoner and blew him from a gun. At length, in 1790, Mahan Singh, having become very powerful, assembled his forces and besieged Manchar. The siege lasted for more than six months, and the Sikhs lost a large number of men. The young Ranjit Singh himself was in great danger, for *Hashmat Khan,* uncle of *Ghulam Muhammad,* charged his escort with a few sowars and climbing upon his elephant, was about to kill the child, when he was struck down by the attendants. *Ghulam Muhammad,* seeing that he could no longer hold the fort, offered to surrender if he were allowed to leave for Mecca in safety. This Mahan Singh promised solemnly, but he had hardly sworn his truth, than one of his men, by his orders or with his connivance, shot the brave Chattah chief through the head. Mahan Singh then gave up Manchar to plunder, and seized the greater part of the Chattah territory.

Jan Muhammad, son of *Ghulam Muhammad,* escaped to Kabul, from whence he returned in 1797, with Shah Zaman, and by the aid of the Afghans recovered his possessions on the Chenab ; but when his protector had returned to Afghanistan, Ranjit Singh attacked Rusulnagar, determined to destroy for ever the Chattah power. The besieged made a gallant resistance, but day by day their numbers and their strength diminished. Unlike the divine twin brothers who fought so well for Rome by Lake Regillus, the Muhammadan saints abandoned their followers, for the story is that the Chattahs asked a famous fakir who lived at Rasulnagar to aid them. "How can I help you," was his reply, "when I see the holy * Mahbub Subhani, dressed in green, fighting on the side of Ranjit Singh." At length *Jan Muhummad* was killed by a cannon shot and the fort surrendered.

---

* The saint alluded to is Abd-al-Kadar Gilani, whose shrine is situated in Baghdad.

The history of the family contains little worthy of notice after the fall of Rasulnagar. The sons of *Jan Muhammad* received a small jagir from Ranjit Singh and were employed by him in the irregular cavalry. Several members of the family have served under the English Government both in 1849 and 1857.

The only Chattah jagirdars, at the present time, are the descendants of *Jan Baksh*, a petty chief famous for his cattle lifting exploits. He was killed in 1791 in a fight with the enemy of his tribe, Sirdar Mahan Singh, who marched upon his village Gajar Golah and plundered it of considerable wealth, the family of *Jan Baksh* escaping to Pindi Bhattian. When Ranjit Singh had succeeded his father, *Khuda Baksh* and his brothers waited upon him, and were taken into the Ghorcharahs, receiving jagirs to the amount of 12,000 Rs. *Khuda Baksh* served, under the Maharaja, in all his chief campaigns, Kassur, Multan, Mankera, Kashmir and Peshawar, and was distinguished for his gallantry. He was several times wounded, and at the battle of Tehri, badly hurt himself, he cut off the head of an Afghan with a single blow. The family had a quarrel with Wasakha Singh, the Kardar of Kadianbad, and their jagirs with the exception of Kot Jan Baksh, Gajar Golah and two other villages, worth 2,500 Rs. were resumed. The cash pension of 2,500 Rs. was left to them.

During the disturbances of 1848-49, *Khuda Baksh* remained loyal. His two grandsons *Ghulam Haidar* and *Shamashdin* were made Thannadar and Deputy Thannadar at Kadianbad. On annexation, Gajar Golah, worth 1,500 Rs., was released for the life of *Khuda Baksh*. He died in 1856, and two-thirds of the jagir have been resumed. The remaining one-third descends to his heirs in perpetuity.

SHER SINGH KAMLA SIRDAR BUHADAR.

- **Bulaki.**
  - Utam Singh, D. 1803.
    - Saina Singh.
    - Mahma Singh.
    - Jai Singh Kamla, D. 1827.
      - Mangal Singh, D. 1821.
        - Wir Singh, D. 1838.
          - Buta Singh, B. 1825.
          - Ajaib Singh, B. 1835.
        - Chugatra Singh, D. 1830.
        - Khem Singh, B. 1812.
        - Sher Singh, B. 1816.
          - Suchet Singh, B. 1836.
          - Baj Singh. B. 1847.
          - Tara Singh, B. 1852.
      - Jaimal Singh, M. D. Mohr Singh, Mari, D. 1852.
        - Nihal Singh, B. 1847. M. D. Ram Singh, Chhapa.
        - Khushhal Singh.
        - Lal Singh.
      - Amar Singh.
        - Ranjodh Singh, B. 1836.
        - Ojaghar Singh, B. 1835.
  - Godh Singh.

HISTORY OF THE FAMILY.

Godh Singh, son of a chowdhri of Manihalah, became a follower of Sirdar Hari Singh Bhangi and became possessed of estates worth 40,000 Rs. On one occasion he and his brother *Utam Singh* were besieged in a small fort near Sialkot by some 300 irregulars of Raja Ranjit Deo of Jammu. The horses belonging to the besieged were stabled without the walls, and *Godh Singh*, fearing that they might fall into the hands of the enemy, made a sally and hamstringed them all. The Rajputs, thinking they were about to be attacked and frightened by the apparent audacity of the besieged, fled, and Sirdar Hari Singh when he heard of this needless destruction of the horses said, "This *Godh Singh* is a perfect ' Kamla" (idiot) ; and this uncomplimentary aguomen has since remained attached to him and the family.

Godh Singh and his brother fought under the Bhangi chiefs against Ranjit Deo, Sansar Chand of Katoch and the Sukarchakias, and on the death of *Godh Singh,* without issue, *Utam Singh* succeeded to the estate, but both he and his two elder sons died soon afterwards, and *Jai Singh* became the head of the family. His jagirs were increased by Sirdar Gulab Singh Bhangi to 50,000 Rs., and when that chief died in 1800, *Jai Singh* joined Ranjit Singh, then lately master of Lahore. He was a good soldier and fought bravely in many campaigns and received additional jagirs worth 40,000 Rs. in Shaikhopura, Sidhni and Bhaowal.

In 1817, becoming too old for active service, the Maharaja appointed him judge at Amritsar, resuming all but 16,000 Rs. of his jagir, and granting him a cash allowance of 8,000 Rs. *Jai Singh* died in 1827. Of his sons *Mangal Singh* had been killed at Mankera in 1821, and his jagirs of 9,000 Rs. had been continued to his son *Wir Singh. Jaimal Singh,* the second son, had also acquired a separate estate of 8,000 Rs., but on his father's death both this and the jagirs of his nephew were resumed, and in their stead the Maharaja granted *Jai Singh's* estate, less the village of Rasulpur in the Cis-Satlej States, which was worth 3,000 Rs. *Amar Singh* the third son of *Jai Singh,* received an annuity of 800 Rs.. while the three younger sons of *Mangal Singh* were provided for ; *Chugatra Singh* being made risaldar in General Ventura's brigade ; and *Khem Singh* and *Sher Singh* receiving the village of Patti in Sialkot, with a cash allowance. When *Wir Singh* died in 1839 half his estate was resumed and the remainder divided between his brother and his son *Buta Singh. Jaimal Singh* was commandant in the Charyari Horse, and served under Raja Suchet Singh on the frontier and elsewhere. At annexation 2,000 Rs. of his jagir were maintained for his life. *Sher Singh* and *Buta Singh* joined the rebels in 1848 and lost every thing ; and the 4,000 Rs. jagir of *Khem Singh,* whose conduct was suspicious, was reduced to

1,000 Rs. On the death of *Jaimal Singh* his sons received a pension of 666 Rs. which they still hold.

In 1857, *Sher Singh* entered the service of Government as naib risaldar under Colonel Voyle. He behaved with great gallantry throughout the disturbances in Oude, and was created risaldar and Sirdar Bahadar. He also received a jagir of 3,000 Rs. in the district of Bahraich. On the return of peace he resigned the service and paid a visit to England. He is now resident in the Amritsar district.

HIRA SINGH WAZIRABADIA.

- DYALA.
  - Gagna.
    - Himmat Singh.
    - Desa Singh.
      - Diwan Singh.
  - Ram Singh.
    - Gurbaksh Singh.
      - Wir Singh.
      - Jodh Singh.
        - Amrikh Singh.
        - Ganda Singh, D. 1855.
          - Hira Singh.
          - Prem Singh.
        - B. Gulab Kour, M. S. Nar Singh, Chamyari.
      - B. Desan, M. S. Charrat Singh, Sukarchakia.

HISTORY OF THE FAMILY.

Hira Singh Wazirabadia is the head of the Waraich tribe which is numerous in the Gujrat and Gujranwala districts. Originally Hindu, the Waraich Jats were converted to Muhammadanism about four hundred years ago, and there are now but few of the tribe of the ancient faith. The origin of the name Waraich is thus explained by the Gujrat portion of the tribe. Raja Jaipal of Lahore, when hunting in the neighbourhood of Thanesar saw a new born infant clinging to the dead body of its mother. On enquiry it was found that the husband of the woman had been killed in a skirmish, and that she had died of grief and hunger. The Raja, moved with pity, took the child and brought him up as his own, giving him the name of Barachh, as it was beneath the shade of a Bar tree that he had discovered him. When Barachh or Waraich grew up, he was married to his protector's daughter, and on the Raja's death without issue, Waraich succeeded to the throne, which his descendants filled for three generations. It was not for many years later that the clan of which Waraich was the founder emigrated to the Panjab, where it became Muhammadan and settled in the Gujrat district.*

The village bards (mirasis) of the Waraich Jats of Gujranwala give a different and a more probable account. They state that their ancestor was Barlas, a Hindu Jat who founded, near Ghazni, about the middle of the 10th century, the village of Bahowali. Shah, a descendant of Barlas, was a soldier in the army of Sultan Mahmud and came with that prince to India in 1001 A. D. Jypal the Raja of Lahore was defeated and the invading army withdrew ; but Shah, struck with the fertility of the country about Gujrat, remained there, and settled in Kalarchor, a Gujar village, where, till 1355, his family lived as husbandmen. Waraich, son of Matu, became wealthy and choudhri of the neighbouring villages. He turned the Gujars out of Kalarchor and was the father of five sons, Teju, Kela, Saijru, Leli and Wada, who, as the tribe became numerous and powerful, founded many villages in Gujrat and elsewhere. Teju founded Kala Katai and four other villages, still held by Waraich Jats, in Amritsar; Kela's descendants went as far south as Saharanpur where there are now five Waraich villages. Ladda was the first village founded in Gujranwala, where there are still 45 villages held by the tribe : while in Gujrat, out of 300 villages founded by Waraich Jats, there are still 192 inhabited by them.

The first member of the Wazirabad family about whom any thing is known was Gagna, who held a small office at Botala, under the Empire,

* This account of the origin of the tribe is purely fabulous. Raja Jypal was the ruler of the Panjab proper from the Satlej to Multan and the Indus, but Thanesar, where he is said to have found the infant, was under Raja Gulchanda Rai of Mahavan and Dehli. Raja Jypal reigned from A. D. 970 to A. D. 1001, when, having been defeated by Subakhtagin and Sultan Mahmud, he burst himself on a funeral pile, in accordance with a custom then prevailing among the Hindus that a prince twice defeated by a foreign army was incompetent to reign. He was succeeded, not by Waraich, but by his own son Anandpal.

Anandpal died in 1012 and was succeeded by his son Jypal the second. But this is not the Jypal to whom the Waraich tribe refers, nor did he found a dynasty, for he fled to the hills on the invasion of Mahmud, in 1013, and nine years later Lahore became a province subject to the Kings of Ghizni.

and is said to have been a man of some wealth. His son *Desa Singh* and his nephew *Gurbaksh Singh* joined the force of Sirdar Charrat Singh Sukarchakia who was then rising to power and were present at the attack on Amritsar, when the Bhangi tower between the Rambagh and Chatawind gates was captured and named Mahan Singhwala after the young son of Charrat Singh.

When Charrat Singh conquered the northern portion of the Gujranwala district, Wazirabad fell to the share of *Desa Singh* and *Gurbaksh Singh.* The jagir was soon afterwards divided; *Gurbaksh Singh* retaining Wazirabad, and *Desa Singh* taking Kunjah and Kalra Budha. *Gurbaksh Singh* gave his daughter *Desan* in marriage to his leader Charrat Singh, and by this connection his influence was much increased. During the invasions of Ahmad Shah Durani the Wazirabad chiefs were compelled to retire before the enemy, but when the storm had blown over they returned to their home.

Gurbaksh Singh died in 1776, and his son *Jodh Singh* succeeded to the estate which was worth about a lakh and a half. *Jodh Singh* and Sirdar Mahan Singh were great friends, and both were always fighting with Sahib Singh Bhangi of Gujrat, who had married the sister of the Sukarchakia chief. The peace which reigned, after the death of Sirdar Gujar Singh, between Gujrat and Gujranwala, was broken by Sahib Singh in the following manner. Mahan Singh and *Jodh Singh* paid a complimentary visit to Sirdar Sahib Singh, who received them with much politeness, but when he had got them safe inside his fort he arrested them both, and, rejoicing in his good luck, sat down to dinner. But the young Sirdars did not care to wait till Sahib Singh had dined, and, making a rush, cut down the guards and escaped to their own camp, after which the fighting went on briskly. Mahan Singh had the best of it on the whole, and took a large slice of his brother-in-law's territory.

At the siege of Sodhra it is said that *Jodh Singh* betrayed his friend. Sahib Singh, who was besieged in the fort, was short of powder, and his surrender was certain; but *Jodh Singh*, who feared that Mahan Singh would become too powerful were Sahib Singh destroyed, supplied the latter with ammunition. Mahan Singh had been dangerously ill throughout the siege, and this treachery hastened his death, which took place a few days after. This action of *Jodh Singh* is said to have been the cause of Ranjit Singh's hostility to him. But nothing is required to account for the Maharaja's conduct but his ambition. He found, for some years, that the Wazirabad chief was too strong to attack, and he endeavoured on one occasion to gain by strategem what he was unable to take by force. He invited *Jodh Singh* to Lahore, but he, suspecting the Maharaja's design, brought a large force with him from Wazirabad. This Ranjit Singh desired him to send back, which, too proud to show fear, he did, and arrived at Lahore with only 200 picked men. He attended Darbar the next day with 25 men, whom he left outside, and was received by the Maharaja with the greatest courtesy and kindness. Suddenly Ranjit Singh rose, and made a sign to his attendants to seize the Sirdar. *Jodh Singh* saw his danger and drawing his sword called on them to attack him as he did not know how to fly. Ranjit Singh loved a brave man, and *Jodh Singh's* gallantry proved his safety, for he was dismissed with honour and rich gifts, and a grant of the Mehdianbad Ilaka. After this Sirdar *Jodh Singh* lived at Wazirabad in great style, looked up to by all the neighbouring chiefs. There is a notice, in the annals of the family, of a European traveller, owning a silver leg, who visited *Jodh Singh* about the year 1807. The name of the gentleman who travelled with a limb so heavy and so likely to excite the curiosity of robbers is unfortunately not given.

Jodh Singh died in 1809, and as his sons were minors the Maharaja thought the time had come to seize the property. He marched to Wazirabad with a large force, but the young Sirdar presenting him with a very large sum of money, he deferred his plan for the time, and granted to *Ganda Singh* the customary khilats of investiture. Very shortly afterwards, however, he sent a force to Wazirabad and confiscated the estates.

He indeed promised that when *Amrik Singh* and *Ganda Singh* should come to manhood, Wazirabad should be restored, but this promise he never intended to perform. A jagir worth 10,000 Rs. was, however, left for the support of the brothers, in Thib. A few years afterwards *Amrik Singh* died, and his share of the jagir was resumed. *Ganda Singh* received an appointment in the Ghorcharah Kalan, but soon after lost the remainder of the Thib jagir, through the hostility of Raja Dhyan Singh. The Maharaja granted him soon afterwards Sangrian, Waddah Pind and six other villages, worth 5,000 Rs. This was afterwards still further reduced, and in the reign of Sher Singh the Sirdar only possessed Adamdaraz and Kathor worth 2,000 Rs.

At annexation this jagir was upheld for life, on payment of one-sixth nazrana, and on the death of Sirdar *Ganda Singh*, on the 22nd of August 1855, it was continued to *Hira Singh* and his lineal descendants in perpetuity at half revenue rates. The settlement however much reduced the value of the property, and *Hira Singh* does not at present enjoy more than 600 Rs. per annum.

SIRDAR NIDHAN SINGH, PANJHATHAH.

- **Dulchah Singh.**
  - Ramdatt Singh.
    - Sahib Singh.
    - Ran Singh.
      - Nidhan Singh.
        - Jowala Singh.
        - Alla Singh, B. 1824.
        - Foujdar Singh, B. 1818.
          - Udam Singh, B. 1857.
          - Sant Singh, B. 1859.
          - Gulab Singh, B. 1862.
      - Sujan Singh.
      - Mul Singh.
      - Mith Singh.
      - Jamel Singh.
        - Mehtab Singh.
        - Hira Singh.
          - Arjan Singh, B. 1852.
          - Sujan Singh, B. 1855.
        - Wazir Singh.

HISTORY OF THE FAMILY.

The Panjhathah family, of Tour Rajput origin, claim to have descended from Raja Dalip or Dehlu, the wise and just prince who, before Alexander had invaded India or Vikramajit had ascended the throne of Malwa, founded and ruled over the city of Dehli.* In the reign of Aurangzib, Rai Sehjran, an ancestor of Sirdar *Nidhan Singh,* emigrated to the Panjab and settled at Chawah Chhadah in the Jhelam district, where he lived for some 15 years and then removed to Amritsar, where his son Rai Than Wada founded the village which is still known by his name.

Dulchah Singh was the first of the family to become a Sikh, and entered the service of Raja Ranjit Deo of Jammu, who gave him a jagir, and posted him with some troops to guard the frontier, where he was

---

* Indraprasta, which is supposed to have stood on the site of the present city of Dehli, was the capital of the Pandus, made over, according to the Mahabharat, to Yudishtira by his Kuru cousin Dhuryodhan. Dehlu, who is said to have founded the modern Dehli and to have reigned there four years, from 344 B. C. to 340 B. C., was defeated and taken prisoner by Phur, Raja of Kumaon, whom Hindu tradition identifies with Porus the opponent of Alexander.

killed in an engagement with the Sikhs. His son *Ramdat Singh* joined the Sukarchakia confederacy under Sirdar Mahan Singh, who gave him the command of 200 horsemen. He was killed in the battle of Manchar near Ramnagar, when Mahan Singh was defeated by the Chattahs under Ghulam Muhammad Khan. His eldest son *Sahib Singh* was killed a few years later fighting against the same tribe. *Ran Singh* joined Ranjit Singh about 1798, and received the jagir of Chapparwal in the Sialkot district. In 1807 he was one of the first in the storming of Narayanghar, and was wounded in four places. He shortly afterwards fell into disgrace, and his jagirs, with the exception of the hereditary possession of Than Wada, were resumed.

Sirdar *Nidhan Singh* entered the Ghorcharahs on 4 Rs. a day, and served in several campaigns. In the fiercely contested battle of Tehri, 1823, he greatly distinguished himself; he was several times wounded and his horse was killed under him, and the Maharaja rewarded him with a grant of fourteen villages in the Gurdaspur district, worth about 14,000 Rs. *Gujar Singh* and *Mul Singh* also received appointments in General Court's brigade. *Nidhan Singh* accompanied the mission sent by the Lahore Government to Lord William Bentinck at Simla, in 1831, and three years later he joined Sirdar Hari Singh Nalwa and Prince Nao Nihal Singh in the Peshawar expedition. He served throughout the campaign till 1837, when the death of Hari Singh and retreat of the Afghan army brought it to a close, and two years later he himself died, worn out before his time. *Nidhan Singh* won the name 'Panjhathah' meaning 'five handed' by his valour. In every battle he was among the first to advance and the last to retreat, and his body was so covered with the marks of his courage that it was said that there was left no place which the hand could cover without a wound.

Maharaja Ranjit Singh died the same year as *Nidhan Singh*, and the estates were confirmed to his son *Jowala Singh* by the new monarch Kharrak Singh; *Ala Singh* being made commandant in the artillery.

Jowala Singh was killed at Sóbraon in 1846, and was succeeded in his jagirs by *Foujdar Singh,* but one year later Raja Lal Singh confiscated the whole estate, with the exception of three villages in the Gurdaspur district worth 2,500 Rs. Both *Foujdar Singh* and his brother joined the rebels in 1848, and the remaining jagirs were consequently resumed.

Foujdar Singh was in 1858 appointed Thannadar of Kahnwan, but was discharged at the time of the general reductions in the police force. He has lately been invested with the Zaildarship of 28 villages in the Gurdaspur district. In 1859 he gave certain information to the Commissioner of Amritsar, which led to the discovery of a criminal correspondence between Maharani Jindan, then resident in Nepal, and some disappointed persons in Lahore and Amritsar, and for this act of loyalty he received a present of 500 Rs. from Government.

Sujan Singh died in 1860. During the detention of Major George Lawrence and family by Sirdar Chattar Singh in 1849 he did his best to assist them, and on the return of peace received a small pension of 144 Rs. as an acknowledgment of his service. The widow of *Jowala Singh* receives a pension from Government of 120 Rs. and the family hold the village of Panju Chohan in proprietary right.

THE SINDHU TRIBE.

I. JOALA SINGH OF SINDHU WADALAH.

Diwan Singh.
|
Mehtab Singh.
|
Sham Singh.
|
Teg Singh.

Joala Singh. — Nihal Singh.

HISTORY OF THE FAMILY.

The Sindhu tribe, of which the Kanheya Sirdars and the family of Sirdar Sadho Singh Padhania are the chief representatives, is of Rajput origin, and although there is a tradition that Sindhu its founder came from Ghazni in Afghanistan, the original home of the tribe was undoubtedly in the north west of Rajputana. Their chief settlements at the present day are in the Manjha. Lahore and Amritsar have numerous Sindhu villages. There are many in Gurdaspur ; 90 in Gujranwala ; 50 in Sialkot ; and a few in Gujrat. Further north the tribe is not found.* Sindhu first settled in the Taran Taran parganna of the Amritsar district. Many years after his death, his descendant Mokal emigrated to Sialkot, where, ten miles south of Daska, he founded a village to which he gave his own name. Several generations later Gajju founded, three miles to the east of Mokal, another village, which, as he was the eldest of the family, he named

* The speculations of Colonel Tod, De Guignes and others regarding the Getic origin of the Jats are well known. The traditions of the Panjab Jats in almost all cases refer to a Rajput descent and emigration to the Panjab from Central India. Even the Sindhu and Waraich Jats who claim a trans-Indus origin are by no means unanimous, and portions of both tribes refer to Rajputana as their ancient home. And in no instance is there a record of any tribe emigration from the west of the Indus : the founders of both Sindhus and Waraichs being spoken of as solitary emigrants. There seems, too, nothing in the language of the Panjab Jats to favour the theory of Getic descent.

Wadalah (Panjabi; *Wada*, great). *Diwan Singh* in the latter days of the empire was made choudhri over the neighbouring villages and held three, Kotli Kewal Ram, Chakri and Paharipur, in proprietary right. His son *Mehtab Singh* was a follower of the Bhangi chiefs and obtained from them several villages about Daska. After the death of Sirdar Gujar Singh Bhangi in 1788, *Mehtab Singh* was invited to Gujranwala by Sirdar Mahan Singh Sukarchakia. On his arrival there he was arrested, and a body of troops sent to seize the fort of Wadalah. The sons of *Mehtab Singh* contrived to beat off the assailants and their father was eventually released, promising to pay a heavy fine, for the performance of which promise *Sultan Singh* was kept as a hostage. Before it was paid, however, Mahan Singh died, and *Sultan Singh* escaped from Gujranwala. On *Mehtab Singh's* death his two eldest sons *Sham Singh* and *Nidhan Singh* quarreled about the estate which they eventually divided. The brothers had no need to fight among themselves for there were many neighbouring chiefs ready to fight them and eager to seize the estate. Of these Nidhan Singh Hattu of Daska, and Bhag Singh Hallowalia of Zaffarwal, who were always great allies, were the most determined. In 1810, Maharaja Ranjit Singh seized the greater part of the Sialkot district. Nidhan Singh Hattu, driven out of Daska, and *Teg Singh*, eldest son of *Sham Singh* took refuge in Kashmir and entered the service of the governor Atta Muhammad Khan, where they renewed their old quarrels. In 1813, when Wazir Fatah Khan and Diwan Mokham Chand drove Atta Muhammad out of Kashmir, *Teg Singh* joined the Sikhs, and returned with the Diwan to Lahore, where the Maharaja made him a commandant and gave him three villages in the Hoshiarpur district. At the battle of Attock, in July of the same year, *Teg Singh* fought under Mokham Chand and he accompanied the Kashmir expedition of 1819, when his local knowledge was of great value. He fought under Hari Singh Nalwa against Ghulam Ali Khakka and Zulfkar Ali Bamba; in Hazara; Peshawar and elsewhere, and died in 1843 at Dopatta in the Kashmir territory. *Joala Singh*, when still a boy was provided for by General

Mian Singh the governor of Kashmir, who was murdered in April, 1841, by his mutinous troops, and at this time *Joala Singh* had a narrow escape with his life. He joined Ghulam Mohiuddin when he arrived to restore order, and held a command in the battle, in August, 1844, when the insurgents were defeated and Raja Habibullah Khan of Pakhli slain. He retained the estate of his father till the second Panjab war, when it was confiscated for his rebellion.

THE SINDHU TRIBE.

II. Kirpal Singh Chichahwala.

- **Ladha.**
  - Sewa Singh.
  - Nodh Singh.
    - Bhag Singh.
    - Akha Singh.
    - Gurbaksh Singh.
      - Jhanda Singh.
        - Joala Singh, M. D. of Sirdar Attar Singh Sindhanwalia.
          - Kirpal Singh, M. D. of Sirdar Badan Singh Chinah, B. 1840.
        - Dewa Singh.
          - Sant Singh.
        - Bhagwan Singh.
  - Mali Singh.
    - Mohr Singh.
      - Amar Singh.
        - Attar Singh.
          - Narindar Singh.

HISTORY OF THE FAMILY.

Ladha was a lamberdar of the village of Chichah which had been founded by an ancestor of that name, a Sindhu Jat, many generations before. *Sewa*, son of *Ladha*, about the year 1720, adopted the Sikh faith. It was a time trying to the zeal of new converts. Banda the blood-thirsty follower of Guru Govind had been recently executed at Dehli, and a bitter persecution was raging against the Sikhs who were put to death where-ever they were found. *Sewa Singh* fled with some companions to the wild region of the upper Ravi, and it was not for many years afterwards that he was able to return to his native village. He turned robber, like most of the Sikhs at that time, and fell at length in a foray in the direction of Lahore. His brother *Nodh Singh* joined the force of Sirdar Gujar Singh Bhangi, and managed, in the year 1767, to take and hold six villages in the Daska pargannah, two named Balkawala ; Jalal, Sahibran, Gilwala, and Kalarwala. After Gujar Singh obtained possession of Gujrat, *Nodh Singh* received six other villages in the neighbourhood of that city, but was killed shortly afterwards in a skirmish with Sultan Mukarrab, an officer of Ahmad Shah Durani. His son *Akha Singh* succeeded to the estate, but was killed in the year 1780 attempting to recover some cattle, which Ghulam Muhammad the inveterate foe of the Bhangi misl had carried off.

Akha Singh left no son, and his brother *Bagh Singh*, who was a brave soldier, very largely increased the family possessions. He became a Sirdar, and held, under Gujar Singh, a jagir worth 40,000 Rs. After his death, without issue, his nephew *Jhanda Singh* remained in the service of Sahib Singh son of Gujar Singh, till Ranjit Singh having taken possession of Amritsar, and the power of the Bhangi misl being on the decline, he joined the young chief and obtained from him a grant of eleven villages in the Amritsar district, though he lost all the old jagirs in Gujrat and Sialkot. *Jhanda Singh* fought in many of Ranjit Singh's campaigns, including those of Kashmir and Kangra. In 1833, he was killed in a private quarrel with one Jit Singh commandant, who also died of the wounds he received. *Jhanda Singh* appears to have been the aggressor in this affair, for on Jit Singh's family complaining to the Maharaja, all the jagirs of *Jhanda Singh* were resumed, with the exception of Chichah. *Joala Singh* his son was two years afterwards taken into favour and received back a portion of the jagir, subject to the service of 10 horsemen. He served for some time on the frontier, at Bannu and Kohat.

Joala Singh had married the daughter of Sirdar Attar Singh Sindhanwalia and this alliance brought great trouble upon him, for all his jagirs were confiscated by Maharaja Sher Singh when he ascended the throne.

When the Sindhanwalias came into favour the jagirs were released, but were again resumed by Raja Hira Singh whose father the Sindhanwalias had assassinated.

Joala Singh died in 1844. His son *Kirpal Singh* was then only seven years old, and Maharaja Dalip Singh confirmed to him Harrah, worth 700 Rs., a share in Taju, 300 Rs., and five wells in Chichah worth 500 Rs. per annum. This jagir is still held by *Kirpal Singh* for life; the wells at Chichah being alone granted in perpetuity.

THE SINDHU TRIBE.

III. Wachan Singh of Tehtar.

- **Chur Singh.**
  - Prem Singh.
    - Lakha Singh, D. 1807.
      - Mohr Singh.
      - Surdul Singh.
        - Malkya Singh.
      - Tej Singh.
        - Kamar Singh, B. 1839.
    - Shamir Singh. D. 1822.
      - Kesr Singh, D. 1863.
      - Wachan Singh, B. 1804.
        - Hari Singh, B. 1852.
        - Jaswant Singh, B. 1853.
      - Balant Singh, D. 1842.
    - Amar Singh, D. 1807.
      - Gulab Singh.
        - Gurdit Singh, B. 1840.
    - Sahib Singh, D. 1807.
      - Sher Singh, D. 1861.
        - Jiun Singh, D. 1844.
        - Joala Singh, B. 1830.
        - Rajindar Singh, B. 1836.
          - Lal Singh, B. 1860.
          - Khushhal Singh, B. 1862.
        - Indar Singh, B. 1837.
          - Bakshish Singh, B. 1853.
          - Teja Singh, B. 1859.
        - Dalip Singh, B. 1844.

HISTORY OF THE FAMILY.

Chur Singh, a Sindhu Jat and choudhri of the village Tehtar near Lahore, was the first of the family to adopt the Sikh faith about 1740. His grandson *Lakha Singh* joined Sirdar Charrat Singh Sukarchakia as a Sowar, and obtained Ilaka Ranjitghar, in jagir, also four villages in the Gujranwala district. He with his three brothers, fought for his master in his long struggle with the Bhangi misl. He also distinguished himself against Dharam Singh, better known as Pritasha, who, on Charrat Singh's death, trusting to the youth and weakness of his successor attempted to seize the chief power in the misl. *Shamir Singh* first came into notice in a battle against the warlike Chattahs, who had been expelled from Ramnagar by Mahan Singh, and who nearly defeated Ranjit Singh at Manchar in the vicinity of the city. The Maharaja had a fancy that swords were more effective than fire-arms, and directed his soldiers only to use the former in the battle. *Shamir Singh* retained his musket, and at a critical time, when the Maharaja's troops were wavering, shot the leader of the Chattahs dead. *Shamir Singh* was a celebrated shot, but he preferred the bow to the musket, and in his hands the bow was a deadly weapon. In 1808, by direction of the Maharaja, he built the fort of Govindghar at Amritsar. There had before been a fort on the same spot, built by Sirdar Gujar Singh Bhangi, but it was of no great strength. *Shamir Singh* was appointed Thannadar of the new fort, and held the post some years. He was succeeded by Fakir Imamuddin. He served in many campaigns, and at Kot Budhi Khan, during the war against the Pathans of Kassur, was almost killed by a spearman of the enemy who rushed upon him from behind when he was engaged with his favourite bow, which he did not find of much use at close quarters. In this Kassur campaign *Lakka Singh* was killed, and in the same year too were killed the two other brothers *Amir Singh* and *Sahib Singh*, the former in the Kangra hills, the latter before Sujanpur. In 1819 *Shamir Singh* was transferred as Thannadar to Nurpur. He died in 1822 and was succeeded in his jagir by his eldest son. *Wachan Singh* served at Peshawar, Kashmir, Tehri, and at many other places with credit. In 1848 he was sent, with his sowars, to Multan, under the command of Sirdar Lal Singh Kalianwala, but joined the rebels and fought against the British, at Ramnagar and Gujrat. After annexation his jagir was resumed, and he received a cash pension of 100 Rs. which he still holds. He is also proprietor of half the village of Tehtar, in the Lahore district. His brother *Kesr Singh,* who enjoyed a pension of 120 Rs., died in

1863. Several members of the family took service in 1857. *Rajindar Singh* as duffadar in Hodson's Horse, and *Indar Singh* his brother, now orderly to the Lieutenant Governor. *Kamar Singh* and *Malkya Singh* entered the Guide corps, the former as jamadar and the latter as daffadar. *Bishan Singh,* son of *Gurdit Singh,* a member of the family not included in this statement, served with credit in China. A younger brother of *Gurdit Singh,* by name *Ram Singh,* has lately entered the same regiment (10th Bengal Cavalry) as his cousin *Rajindar Singh.*

THE SINDHU TRIBE.

IV. Bhag Singh Kontal.

Desa Singh, the grandfather of *Bhag Singh* of Kontal, was a relative of Sirdar Jai Singh the great Kanheya chief. His history is that of Jai Singh, for he was his subordinate and accompanied him in his many expeditions. He built the fort known as Desa Singhwala in the Amritsar district, and Kontalpur near Pathankot. His son *Tek Singh* succeeded to the estate and fought under Mai Sada Kour, the head of the Kanheya misl, against the Ramgharias. The estate, on the death of *Tek Singh*, was reduced to 10,000 Rs., and on the death of *Sher Singh*, his eldest son, to 2,000 Rs., at Kontal, Ban, Kandarwari and Mangalian. Thus it remained till annexation, when the village of Kontalpur worth 1,100 Rs. was released to the three brothers *Bhag Singh*, *Budh Singh* and *Nihal Singh*, on payment of quarter revenue. Their respective shares in this village descend to their male heirs in perpetuity.

THE SINDHU TRIBE.

V. Rattan Singh of Kot Diwan Singh.

Diwan Singh was a follower of Sirdar Charrat Singh Sukarchakia, and fought under him against the Chattahs. He built the village Kila Diwan Singh in the Gurdaspur district, and his holding consisted of the villages Badangil, Chak Chattah and Kotghar, worth about 3,000 Rs. He was killed in a fight with Nur Muhammad Chattah at Akalghar. His only son *Hukm Singh* entered the force of Sirdar Mahan Singh and on his death that of Ranjit Singh, and served in the Kassur, Kangra, Jach, Multan and Yusafzai campaigns. He was killed on the banks of the Lunda or Landai River in an affair with the Yusafzais. On the death of *Hukm Singh*, the village of Kila Diwan Singh and Kotghar were confirmed to his son *Sobah Singh* who had served under Misr Diwan Chand and Bhawani Sahai in Kashmir. He was engaged in all the battles on the North West frontier ; Khakka, Bamba, Saidu, Tehri and Peshawar. In 1848 he remained loyal, and, with Sirdar Bur Singh Mokerian, furnished the British army with supplies. After annexation his two villages were maintained to him on payment of one quarter revenue. His eldest son *Rattan Singh* holds Kotjodh worth 100 Rs. *Sarup Singh,* his second son, was killed in the battle of Sobraon.

THE SINDHU TRIBE.

VI. JHANDA SINGH PHILUWASIAH.

This Sindhu family does not require any particular notice. *Amir Singh,* a good soldier, was killed at Manchar, and his brother *Karam Singh* at Daska, in 1810. The four sons of *Karam Singh* served in the Orderlies, and in Raja Hira Singh's brigade. Three of the family, *Amir Singh, Dal Singh* and *Ganda Singh* joined the rebels at Peshawar in 1848, and their jagirs were confiscated. The sons of *Hari Singh,* who died in 1857-58 and whose jagir was maintained for his loyalty in 1848, hold a jagir nominally worth 500 Rs. though its value has been reduced in the late settlement.

THE SIDHU TRIBE.

I. Karam Singh, Uthianwala.

- Kapur Singh.
  - Lakka Singh.
  - Sukka Singh.
    - Ditta Singh.
    - Bagh Singh.
    - Dyal Singh.
      - Karam Singh.
    - Dal Singh.
    - Fatah Singh.
      - Budha Singh.
  - Jodh Singh.
    - Amir Singh.

HISTORY OF THE FAMILY.

Ghumman, the founder of the Sidhu Jat tribe, came originally from Bhata in Malwah, about 300 years ago, during the reign of the Emperor Akbar, at the invitation of the famous chowdhri Changa, whose daughter he married, and settled near Taran Taran in the Amritsar district, where he founded a village named Sidhu which is still the residence of one part of the family. The four branches of the family now of any importance, will be treated of in order, but although once very powerful and in possession of large jagirs, the Sidhus have now fallen into decay and have little or no political importance.

Kapur Singh, the seventh in descent from Ghumman, the founder of Sidhu, lived during the reign of Muhammad Shah, and first became distinguished as the successful plunderer of an imperial caravan proceeding, with rich gifts, from Dehli to Mecca. The caravan was, however, robbed on strictly religious principles, and the silver doors of the Darshani of the Amritsar Temple, bear witness, to this day, to the piety of the robbers. *Kapur Singh* obtained both wealth and reputation by this exploit, and his wife and the wife of the powerful Sirdar Gujar Singh happening to be both pregnant at the time, it was agreed that if a boy and a girl were born, they should be at once betrothed. The wife of *Kapur Singh* soon after gave birth to a son, the famous *Jodh Singh*, and Sirdar Gujar Singh's wife giving birth to a girl, the children were betrothed, and when they grew up were married. The three sons of *Kapur Singh* acquired separate estates. *Sukka Singh* took possession of Uthian; *Lakka Singh* of Awan, and *Jodh Singh* seized, at different times, a great part of the Sowrian pargannah, inclusive of the Ilakas of Jagdeo, Ghuniwala, Karial and Sowrian, worth about 1,50,000 Rs. The estates of *Sukka Singh* and *Lakka Singh* may have been each worth 20,000 Rs. The reputation of *Jodh Singh* for bravery was great. He joined Ranjit Singh just before the attempt on Lahore in 1799, and that chief is reported to have said that *Jodh Singh's* adhesion to his cause outweighed the hostility of all the other Bhangis. It is certain that his influence with Chet Singh of Lahore had much to do with Ranjit Singh's peaceful occupation of the city.

Sirdar *Jodh Singh* held his possessions intact through a long life of war and commotion, and his son *Amir Singh* was equally fortunate and was treated with great consideration by Maharaja Ranjit Singh. But soon after the death of *Amir Singh* in 1825, the whole estate was confiscated, with other jagirs belonging to the different members of this family, and the irregular force of the Sirdar was placed under the command of Prince Sher Singh. The five sons of *Sukka Singh* received 5,000 Rs. a year, in addition to the pay of the military appointments they held.

Karam Singh, the present representative of the family, served in many campaigns, including those of Tehri, Peshawar and Hazara. He received, under the Darbar, 1,800 Rs. per annum, subject to the service of three sowars. He joined, with other members of his family, the rebel army in 1848, and his jagir and allowances were consequently resumed; but he received a pension of 240 Rs. and also had proprietary rights over half the village of Uthian, where he resides. His cousin *Budha Singh* entered the service of Government in 1857, and is now Daffadar in a native regiment.

THE SIDHU TRIBE.

II. Dewa Singh of Sidhu.

Dyal Singh.
- Bhagwan Singh.
  - Arbel Singh.
    - Chattar Singh.
    - Bhup Singh.
    - Budh Singh.
      - Kahn Singh.
        - Dewa Singh, B. 1812.
          - Bishan Singh.
      - Fatah Singh.
        - Mehtab Singh.
          - Chuhar Singh.
            - Lehna Singh.
          - Gurdit Singh.
            - Wasawa Singh.
    - Jamiyat Singh.

HISTORY OF THE FAMILY.

Dyal Singh was the first of this branch of the Sidhu family to become a Sikh, and was killed in battle near Anandpur, in 1698. His son *Bhagwan Singh* supported himself as much by plunder as by agriculture, and his grandson *Arbel Singh*, having built a fort at Sidhu, and having collected some 200 horsemen, contrived to make himself master of forty surrounding villages. He had connected himself with several of the powerful neighbouring chiefs, marrying one son to a daughter of Sirdar Gujar Singh of Lahore, and another to a daughter of Sirdar Sudh Singh Dodia ; so that he was not disturbed in his modest possessions. His son *Budh Singh*, who succeeded him, was less fortunate, for Sirdar Amir Singh of Sowrian, his kinsman, having invaded the estate and carried off a large quantity of plunder, *Budh Singh* pursued him, and was killed in an ambuscade laid by the enemy. Shortly afterwards Ranjit Singh seized most of the Sidhu territory, leaving in the possession of *Kahn Singh* about fifteen villages subject to the service of 25 sowars. He also made *Kahn Singh* commandant in a cavalry regiment, and gave *Fatah Singh* a subordinate appointment. *Fatah Singh* was killed in the Kangra campaign, in 1809, and his jagir was given to his brother *Kahn Singh,* who, however, did not enjoy it long, as he fell, with *Jamiyat Singh* and other members of his family, in the unsuccessful Kashmir expedition of 1814.

Dewa Singh, who was an infant at the time of his father's death, received a grant of four villages worth 3,000 Rs. for his maintenance, subject to the service of four sowars, and in 1838 was placed in Prince Kharrak Singh's force. In 1848 he remained faithful to Government and did good service against the rebel Dhara Singh of Gogaira. His villages, Bhudan, Bhattianwala, Dhar and Dilloki, worth 2,500 Rs., were released to him for life, on payment of two-fifths as nazarana, and on his death Bhudan and Bhattianwala will be maintained in perpetuity to his heirs, on payment of one-third nazarana.

Dewa Singh resides at Sidhoan or Sidhu in the Lahore district, the village founded by his ancestor Ghumman.

THE SIDHU TRIBE.

III. Kishan Singh of Bhilowal.

- Mohr Singh.
  - Budha Singh.
  - Ram Singh.
    - Jai Singh.
      - Dassonda Singh.
        - Kishan Singh.
          - Asa Singh.
        - Bhagwan Singh.
          - Lehna Singh.
          - Mangal Singh.
      - Chanda Singh.
  - Teg Chand.
    - Mahi Singh.

HISTORY OF THE FAMILY.

The Bhilowal branch of the Sidhu family includes no chief of any importance. *Budha Singh* made himself master of a good many villages in the Amritsar district, and was killed in one of Ahmad Shah's invasions. His brother *Ram Singh* succeeded to the estate, but in the early days of Sikh history few chiefs died in their beds, and after some years he also was killed in battle. His son *Jai Singh* was a mere child, at the time of his father's death, and *Mahi Singh* took possession of the estate, which he considerably increased and managed with much vigour and wisdom, till *Jai Singh* grew up and demanded his rightful inheritance. He was satisfied with obtaining from his cousin the two villages of Bhilowal and Khochakwal and died two years after the arrangement, leaving an infant son *Dassonda Singh*, from whom *Mahi Singh* took back Khochakwal, which he had only given to *Jai Singh* with great reluctance. But Maharaja Ranjit Singh seized the possessions of both, with the greatest impartiality, allowing *Dassonda Singh* 3,000 Rs. per annum, with which he was to supply five sowars to the Sowrian Derah, which was first under Prince Sher

Singh, and latterly under Jamadar Khushhal Singh. After his father's death *Kishan Singh* took his place in this regiment, but the contingent was raised to nine sowars, which he had to furnish till the annexation of the Panjab, when his jagir was confiscated, as he had joined Raja Sher Singh.

Kishan Singh resides at Bhilowal, in the Amritsar district and holds a pension of 240 Rs. per annum.

THE SIDHU TRIBE.

IV. Isar Singh Sowrianwala.

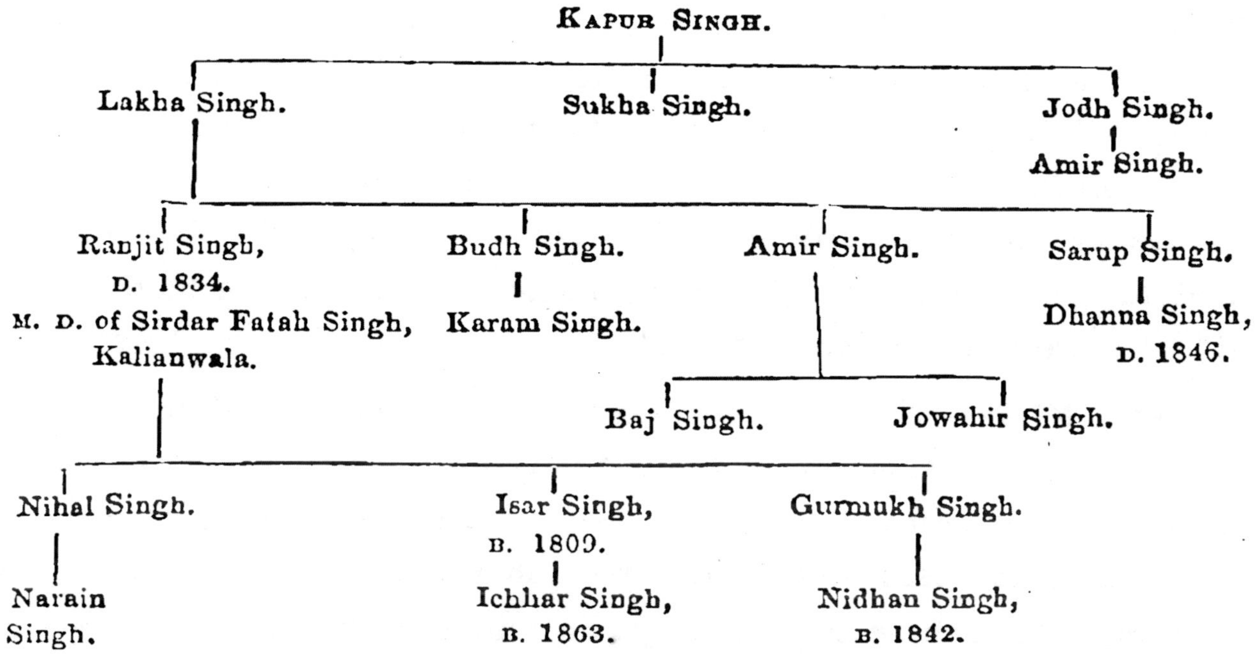

HISTORY OF THE FAMILY.

The history of *Kapur Singh* and his famous son *Jodh Singh* is given in the statement of Karam Singh Uthianwala; a short account of another branch of the family may here be given. *Lakka Singh* held the large estate of Awan to which, on his death, his eldest son *Ranjit Singh* succeeded. He had married the daughter of the celebrated Fatah Singh Kalianwala, and when that chief was killed in 1807 at the storming of the fort of Narayanghar, *Ranjit Singh* Sidhu succeeded to a large portion of his jagirs; the remainder going to Dal Singh Naharnah. Also on the death of *Amir Singh*, son of Sirdar *Jodh Singh*, without issue, he received the jagir of Sowrian, worth 1,50,000 Rs. subject to the service of 300 sowars. He only held this jagir for two years, after which it was conferred on Prince Sher Singh. He served at Multan, Theri and Kachhi, and was killed in action at Gheb Kamrial, in 1836. On his death all his jagirs were resumed with the exception of 15,000 Rs. principally from the estate of Sirdar Fatah Singh, which was confirmed to *Isar Singh* and *Gurmukh Singh*.

Isar Singh served with credit at Derah Ismail Khan and Peshawar, and in 1834 went with Prince Kharrak Singh on his expedition to Tank and Mittankot. In 1837 he contrived to offend the authorities at Lahore, and all his jagirs were taken from him, with the exception of the village of Salimpurah. He was, however, made a commandant of 42 sowars, on 800 Rs. per annum, and placed under the command of Sirdar Lehna Singh Sindhanwalia. *Sarup Singh*, uncle of *Isar Singh*, retained his jagirs; but at his death, his son *Dhanna Singh* having been killed at Sobraon, they were resumed.

In 1847 *Kishan Singh's* contingent was reduced to fifteen horse, and leaving these at Lahore, he went to Bannu with Lieut. Edwardes and afterwards to Multan. He returned to Lahore with Sirdar Attar Singh Kalianwala, escaping from the rebel army with difficulty, and only bringing back three of the fifty horsemen he had taken with him. He was then sent to Dinanagar under Sirdar Shamsher Singh Sindhanwalia and afterwards to Pind Dadan Khan. At annexation he received a pension of 360 Rs. which he still enjoys.

ARJAN SINGH CHAHAL.

NIHALA SINGH.

Amar Singh. | Katha Singh. | Kamar Singh.

Katha Singh: Karam Singh, D. 1823. | Nodh Singh,

Karam Singh, D. 1823.
Gurmukh Singh, D. 1836.
Joala Singh, D. 1846.
Arjan Singh, B. 1845.
Ikbal Singh, B. 1863.

HISTORY OF THE FAMILY.

Katha Singh, a Chahal Jat, was, with his brothers, in the service of the Bhangi Sirdars Lehna Singh and Gujar Singh, who, in 1764, had taken possession of Lahore. No one of them rose to any importance, but held small service jagirs. *Katha Singh* was killed in a skirmish on the borders of Bahawalpur and his son *Karam Singh* succeeded to the jagirs worth 5,000 Rs. For some years *Karam Singh* fought with the Bhangi misl, and he became known for gallantry and ability, till in 1799 Ranjit Singh took Lahore from Chet Singh son of Sirdar Lehna Singh. Karam Singh at first followed the fortunes of his old master to whom Ranjit Singh had given a jagir of 60,000 Rs., but seeing at last that it was useless to remain with one who could not advance his interests in any way, he took service with the Maharaja, who gave him several villages in Ajnala. He rapidly rose to favour and became a very powerful Sirdar. After the Pindi Bhattian and Jhang expeditions he received several new villages in jagir, and after the Kassur campaign, where he had especially distinguished himself, Ranjit Singh gave him the Ilakas of Dodah and Khanowal. His jagirs at length reached the value of 1,50,000 Rs. subject to the service of 250 horsemen ; and included the villages held by *Arjan Singh* at the present day. Sirdar *Karam Singh* fell mortally wounded by a musket ball, in the battle of Theri, in 1823, when the wild Yusafzai Ghazis so nearly defeated the best Sikh troops. He was carried to his tent but died the following day, and his loss was much felt both by the Maharaja and the army, in which he held command of the Ghurkha battalion. His only surviving son *Gurmukh Singh* succeeded to the whole jagir. This young man had already for some years served under his father and had fought in the battle of Theri. When Diwan Chuni Lal was appointed governor of Kashmir after Diwan Moti Ram had been for the second time recalled, *Gurmukh Singh* was sent to support him, and he remained there two years. In 1836 he was ordered to Kohat where he did good and gallant service, but was carried off by cholera in September of that year. *Joala Singh* was at the time of his father's death only four years old, and the Maharaja resumed all the estates, with the exception of one worth Rs. 3,000 which was placed under the superintendence of Raja Hira Singh. *Joala Singh* himself died in 1846, at the age of twenty four, leaving one son *Arjan Singh* aged seven. For his support and in consideration of his family, Maharaja Dalip Singh released two villages Ghari and Lahian, together worth 1000 Rs., which on the annexation of the Panjab were confirmed to him for life, with $2\frac{1}{2}$ wells at Chahal, in the Taran Taran parganna of the Amritsar district, which have been released in perpetuity.

SAHIB SINGH OF KARIAL.

LAL SINGH.
|
Bagh Singh.
|
Jodh Singh.
|
Sahib Singh,
B. 1809.
|
Jowahir Singh,
B. 1834.

HISTORY OF THE FAMILY.

The southern portion of the Gujranwala district is to so great an extent peopled by Jats of the Wirk tribe that the country from Shaikhopura to Miraliwala has long been known as the 'Wirkayat Tappa.' Over this tract *Lal Singh,* a Wirk Rajput emigrant from Jammu, held sway in the early days of the Sikh confederacies. His son Sirdar *Bagh Singh*, under Charrat Singh and Mahan Singh, acquired great power, and held a large portion of the Gujranwala and Shaikhopura pargannahs. When Ranjit Singh obtained possession of Lahore *Bagh Singh* was one of the most powerful chiefs in the neighbourhood of that city, but it was not long before he was compelled to become a feudatory and was placed in command of the Wirkayat Horse, with a jagir worth one lakh and a half of rupees, consisting of eighty-four villages in the vicinity of Karial Kalan, and Miraliwala. *Bagh Singh* died in 1806, and his only son *Jodh Singh* succeeded to his jagirs, and to the command of the Wirk force. He served in most of the Maharaja's campaigns, till 1814, when he was killed in the first unsuccessful Kashmir expedition. His son *Sahib Singh* was then but six years of age, and the family estates, with the exception of three villages, worth 1,700, Rs., were resumed. When *Sahib Singh* grew up he received command of his father's regiment, and a jagir worth 3,500 Rs., and subsequently was made commandant in the Rattan Singh Man Regiment. His estate at this time only consisted of Budha Guraiah in the Gujranwala district, and he also received a cash allowance of 300 Rs. He was implicated to some extent in the rebellion of 1848, and his jagir was confiscated. At present he holds a pension of 240 Rs. His only son *Jowahir Singh* is Subhadar in a native regiment.

JIUN SINGH BIKHI.

- SAHIB SINGH.
  - Arbel Singh.
    - Nidhan Singh, D. 1861.
      - B. Hukm Kour, M. S. Buhadar Singh, Gogaira.
      - B. Khem Kour, M. S. Dal Singh, Waraich.
    - Sujan Singh.
      - Wasawa Singh, B. 1842.
        - Jiun Singh, M. Daughter of S. Khazan Singh, Mokal.
          - Chattar Singh.
          - Sadho Singh.
        - Jaggat Singh.
          - Sher Beg Singh, M. Daughter of Badan Singh, Chini.
          - Partab Singh, M. Daughter of S. Rattan Singh, Mokal.
          - Didar Singh.
    - Foujdar Singh.
      - Mehtab Singh.
      - Sarapa Singh.
  - Dal Singh.
    - Amar Singh.
      - Mola Singh.
      - Sant Singh.
      - Jaswant Singh.

HISTORY OF THE FAMILY.

This family was of some respectability in the reign of the Emperor Akbar, when one of its members, Rai Lalu, was made chowdhri of thirty villages. This post the family retained for four generations till *Sahib Singh* and his brother Sahai went to Amritsar where they took the 'pahal' and became Sikhs. Being already possessed of some wealth they had no difficulty in following the prevailing fashion of collecting a band of horsemen, and ravaging the neighbouring country. Their most successful expedition was against Shaikhopura which they captured, and having ejected the Lobanah tribe from its holdings, made it their head-quarters. Their great rivals and enemies were the Kharrals, and in one of the fights with this tribe, *Sahai Singh* was slain, and no long time afterwards, *Sahib Singh* also fell, fighting with the very same

Lobanahs whom he had driven from Shaikhopura and whose new settlement at Mian Mir he was endeavouring to seize. The sons of *Sahib Singh* and *Sahai Singh* succeeded conjointly to their father's estate, and held it in peace till 1808, when Maharaja Ranjit Singh turned his arms against them. For some time the cousins defended the fort of Shaikhopura successfully, and were at length induced to surrender by Mit Singh Padhania and Nihal Singh Attariwala who promised to procure estates for them. The Maharaja gave them jagirs worth 40,000 Rs., in the Lahore and Gogaira districts. *Amir Singh* was made commandant in Amar Singh Majithia's force, and was sent to Attock where he was soon after killed near Burj Raja Hodi, in a skirmish with the mountain tribes. His jagirs were, however, distributed among the surviving members of the family. *Shamir Singh* and *Bagh Singh* received appointments in the Charyari * and the Ghorcharahs respectively. During the reign of Ranjit Singh the family were continually engaged in active service, and till his death retained their jagirs intact. *Bhagel Singh* died a few years before the Maharaja, and *Dal Singh, Hira Singh* and *Hari Singh* shortly after, in 1839. *Kishan Singh* and *Foujdar Singh* both fought in the Satlej campaign, while *Jiun Singh* and his cousin *Nidhan Singh* remained at Lahore, with the force in charge of the city. Almost all the members of the family joined the national party in 1849, and were among the troops who gave up their arms at Rawalpindi. Their jagirs, which amounted to 8,000 Rs., were confiscated. Pensions of 200 Rs. were given to the widows of *Hira Singh* and *Hari Singh*, and to *Arbel Singh* a pension of 300 Rs., which he still enjoys. *Nidhan Singh*, who received a pension of 60 Rs., died in 1861. The family is of the Wirak Jat tribe, and originally came from Jammu.

---

* The Charyari Horse obtained its name from the four friends *(Char-Yar)*, Sirdars Bhup Singh Saidhu, Chet Singh and Ram Singh Soddozai and Hardas Singh Bannia. These young men handsome and well dressed were always together, and the Maharaja was so pleased with their style that he called a body of horse after them.

BAGH SINGH HASSANWALA.

- RAM SINGH.
  - Gurmukh Singh.
    - Sher Singh.
    - Gajja Singh.
      - Bishan Singh, B. 1834.
      - Fatah Singh, B. 1838.
        - Lehna Singh, B. 1860.
    - Dharam Singh.
  - Sukha Singh.
    - Pardhan Singh, B. 1816.
      - Ladha Singh, B. 1846.
  - Attar Singh.
    - Sardul Singh.
    - Bagh Singh. B. 1826.
      - Amrik Singh, B. 1851.
    - Nihal Singh.
      - Bhaggat Singh, B. 1858.
      - Jaggat Singh, B. 1865.
    - Khushhal Singh,
      - Ikbal Singh, B. 1861.
      - Nanak Singh, B. 1864.
  - Partab Singh.

HISTORY OF THE FAMILY.

When *Ram Singh*, who was the son of a Khatri of Hassanwala in the Gujranwala district, was quite a boy, he was taken into the household of Sirdar Charrat Singh Sukarchakia, and when he grew up he rode in the chief's troop. Mahan Singh, son of Charrat Singh, was his 'potrela,'* having been by him initiated into the Sikh faith, and during his short life he treated *Ram Singh* with great consideration and gave him large jagirs. In 1813 he introduced his two elder sons into Maharaja Ranjit Singh's service, and a few years later the two younger, *Attar Singh* and *Partab Singh*, received appointments in the Ghorcharah Kalan. Sirdar *Ram Singh* was a fine old soldier, and with his sons served in the campaigns of Kashmir, Multan, Mankera, Peshawar and Bannu. In 1824, *Sher Singh*, eldest son of *Gurmukh Singh*, was made commandant,

* The term 'potrela' somewhat corresponds to the English word 'godson.' The derivation is 'putr' a son, and 'relah' another ; and expresses the relation which a man bears to the person who has initiated him into the Sikh faith by the rite of the 'pahal,' which resembles, in a great measure, the Christian rite of baptism.

and in 1829, his brother *Gajja Singh* entered the Ghorcharahs. *Ram Singh's* jagirs were worth about 20,000 Rs. He lived to the close of Ranjit Singh's reign, and then, having served grandfather, father and son faithfully and well, died in 1839, aged ninety-five years.

On the death of *Ram Singh*, the larger portion of his jagirs were resumed, but his three surviving sons *Gurmukh Singh*, *Sukha Singh* and *Attar Singh* received jagirs of 2,200 Rs., 1,500 Rs. and 1,000 Rs. respectively. On the outbreak of the rebellion of 1848, most of the family joined the rebels, and *Gajja Singh* and *Sardul Singh* fell at Chillianwala. The jagirs were consequently resumed. *Sukha Singh* does not appear to have joined the rebellion. He was at the time a cripple and unable to move from his bed, and his jagir would have been released had not his death occurred in 1850.

In 1857, *Bagh Singh*, son of *Attar Singh*, was taken into Government employ as Jamadar and was sent down country, where he did good service until the reduction of the army at the close of the campaign. He received a grant of two wells at Ramnagar, for life. The houses belonging to the family, which had been attached in 1849, were also released. *Bishan Singh* is a sowar in a cavalry regiment.

ISAR SINGH BHAKHA

CHARRAT SINGH.

Jodh Singh.	Subha Singh.	Soba Singh, D. 1824.	Godh Singh.

Soba Singh, D. 1824.
Hari Singh, D. 1857.
Isar Singh.

Attar Singh, B. 1844.	Chattar Singh, B. 1858.	Mehtab Singh, B. 1861.

HISTORY OF THE FAMILY.

The ancestors of *Isar Singh* came into the Panjab from Malwah about the beginning of the 17th century, and settled near Chunian in the Lahore district. In 1738 they made a second move to the village of Bhakha, in the Amritsar district, from which they derive their family name. Sirdar *Charrat Singh* was the son of a sister of Sirdar Sawal Singh Ulakhwala, a powerful Bhangi chief. On the death of Sawal Singh, without issue, the estate was divided by the Sikh Gurmata or national council between Nar Singh Chamyari, the 'potrela' of the deceased, and *Charrat Singh* the sister's son. The share of Nar Singh was the larger, but the jagirs of *Charrat Singh* were valuable and extensive, and he held them till his death. His son *Soba Singh* held jagirs worth 40,000 Rs. subject to the service of 150 horsemen, from Sirdar Hakikat Singh Kanheya, but Maharaja Ranjit Singh in the year 1802 seized all but 7,000 Rs. subject to the service of 5 horsemen, who with Soba Singh were employed in Ghorcharah Kalan. The estate was soon afterwards further reduced to 2,116 Rs. at Guraliah and Bhakka, *Soba Singh* having displeased the Maharaja by refusing to give him his daughter in marriage.

Soba Singh died in 1824, and the village of Guraliah was resumed, and the village of Bhakka worth 600 Rs. alone left to *Hari Singh*.

In 1848, *Hari Singh,* with his contingent, served under the orders of Captain Hodson at Rangal Nangal and elsewhere, and remained faithful throughout the disturbances. On the annexation of the country the jagir was upheld to him. He died in 1857, and to his son *Isar Singh* half the village of Bhakka, in the Sowrian parganna, where he resides, has been maintained in perpetuity.

RATTAN CHAND DOGAL.

SHIV DYAL.

- Shankar Das.
- Mya Das.
  - Ganesh Das.
    - Prem Das.
- Kanheya Lal.
  - Rattan Chand.
    - Manohar Lal.
    - Narinjan Das.
  - Thakar Das.
    - Karam Chand.
  - Nand Gopal.
    - Bhagwan Das.
- Jowahir Mal.
- Ram Narain.
  - Joti Ram.
- Sham Das.
- Trikta Sahai.
- Govind Sahai.

HISTORY OF THE FAMILY.

About the year 1635, during the reign of the Emperor Shah Jahan, Baba *Harya Ram* settled at Wazirabad, which had lately been rebuilt by Wazir Khan the imperial governor who gave it his own name. *Harya Ram* served the governor for many years, and when his sons grew up to manhood, abandoned worldly affairs and founded a sect of his own, still extant and known by the name of Harmilapi.*

The first of his descendants to take service with the Sikhs was *Kishan Kour*, who was a follower of Sirdar Gurbaksh Singh Wazirabadia, the friend and ally of Sirdar Charrat Singh; and *Shiv Dyal*, son of *Kishan Kour*, entered the employ of the Sukarchakia chief. The revenue

* This religious sect is better known on the frontier than in the Sikh part of the Panjab. Ram Kishan, chela or follower and adopted son of Swami Chetangir, came to Wazirabad at the beginning of the 18th century and took as his chela Harya Ram. Milawa Mal, a merchant of Dera Ismail Khan, visited Wazirabad and was so struck with the piety and wisdom of Harya that he became a disciple and brought his whole wealth into the concern, which took the name of both friends and is now known as Harmilapi. The head-quarters of the sect is at Dera Ismail Khan, and the present mohant is Ram Piyara. One Thakurdwara is at Chuniot, another at Chakowal. The disciples are of various castes; some have given up worldly affairs: others carry on business. The former wear clothes of a reddish brown color.

arrangements of the Sikhs were rude enough in these early days, and regarding *Shiv Dyal's* management of the Sukarchakia jagirs there is nothing to record. When Ranjit Singh conquered the Dhanni country he made *Shiv Dyal* the manager and gave him an estate at Nurpur, subject to service. When an old man he introduced his sons *Shankar Das* and *Kanheya Lal* at court, and retired to Wazirabad where he died. The brothers were placed under Prince Kharrak Singh ; *Shankar Das* for some time managing his jagirs ; while *Kanheya Lal* was made Tehsildar or Kardar of Sahiwal, part of the estate of the Prince. When Diwan Moti Ram was appointed governor of Kashmir, *Shankar Das* was sent as head of the Financial Office under him, and during Moti Ram's second tenure of office *Kanheya Lal* occupied the same post as his brother had done during the first.

Shankar Das died in 1832. When the salt mines of Pind Dadan Khan were made over to Raja Gulab Singh of Jammu, *Kanheya Lal* was appointed manager under him and held the post till 1834, and he and his eldest son *Rattan Chand* received a cash allowance of 2,000 Rs. from the salt revenue till annexation.

Rattan Chand was a Darbar munshi from 1831 to 1849. He was, with his brother *Shankar Das*, in favour at court, and received jagirs which in 1850 amounted to 10,302 Rs. He was, when quite a youth, appointed to the charge of the Maharaja's private seal,* and held the office with its emoluments for several years. He was afterwards made commandant in the Ghorcharah Khas and *Thakar Das* took his place, for a short time, as keeper of the seal. The latter, when Nao Nihal Singh was in power, was appointed manager of Dhanni, Kalar Kahar and Rupowal, on a salary of 4,320 Rs. per annum. During the reign

* The seal of which *Rattan Chand* had charge was the Maharaja's small private signet. Both this and the large seal were affixed to most documents. The keeper of the small seal received an allowance of 2 per cent on all khillats and money presents made by the Maharaja, and of 5 per cent on all new jagirs ; but of the income thus raised a certain proportion was taken by the Government. Besides *Rattan Chand* Dogal, the seal was kept at different times by Ram Chand, great nephew of Diwan Sawan Mal, by Harsukh Rai (afterwards General) by Rattan Chand Darhiwala and others.

of Maharaja Sher Singh the brothers held various offices at Lahore, and *Rattan Chand* became a man of considerable influence. He was fined 40,000 Rs. by Pandit Jalla in 1844, but this was remitted through the intercession of Bhai Ram Singh. He accompanied Raja Lal Singh to Jammu in February 1845, and was with the party of Sirdar Fatah Singh Man when that chief, with Wazir Bachna, was assassinated by Raja Gulab Singh at Jammu, and he was himself detained for some days as a hostage for the conduct of the army.

During 1848-49 the action of *Rattan Chand* was somewhat doubtful, and his jagirs were resumed with the exception of two gardens, one at Lahore and the other at Wazirabad, upon which he had expended much money. These were released in perpetuity, and he also received a life pension of 3,600 Rs. *Govind Sahai* his uncle, and *Joti Ram* and *Ganga Ram* his cousins, received each a pension of 100 Rs. and *Ganesh Das* 375 Rs. *Thakar Das* received a pension of 360 Rs.

Nand Gopal, the youngest brother of *Rattan Chand,* was taken into Government service as a darbar munshi in 1840, and in 1845 was made Paymaster of the force of Sirdar Kahn Singh Kohariah, brother-in-law of Raja Lal Singh, with the service jagirs of Pathanwali, Thattah, and Chakumbarik, worth 2,520 Rs. He accompanied the force under Raja Sher Singh Attariwala to Multan in 1848, and was believed to have joined the rebels, but he himself stated that his loyalty to his Government caused him to be seized and imprisoned by Sher Singh, and that he was only released though the influence of Diwan Hakim Rai, whose brother Mutsaddi Mal his sister had married. It is certain that *Nand Singh* came in before the final battle of Gujrat, and his excuses were accepted. Since annexation he has been in Government service, first as Kotwal at Gujranwala and Sialkot, then Tehsildar of Wazirabad and Moza successively. He was made Court Inspector of Police in 1861, and at the present time is 1st class Deputy Inspector of Police at Dehli. He is a zealous and efficient officer. *Rattan Chand* died in 1857, leaving two sons *Monohar Lal* and *Narinjan Das.*

FATAH SINGH OF GHARJAKH.

- SHAM SINGH.
  - Gulab Singh.
  - Panjab Singh.
    - Kahn Singh.
      - Fatah Singh.
        - Dharam Singh, B. 1853, betrothed to D. of S. Dyal Singh Botalia.
        - Sant Singh, B. 1847.
      - Jodh Singh.
        - Randhir Singh.
        - Harnam Singh, B. 1850.
        - Amar Singh, B. 1843.
        - Daughter M. to Diwan Hakim Rai Sialkotia.
      - Lehna Singh, M. daughter of S. Hari Singh Nalwa.
        - Isar Singh, B. 1850.

HISTORY OF THE FAMILY.

Sham Singh was a banker in the village of Gharjakh, near Gujranwala. Of his two sons the eldest *Gulab Singh* followed his father's profession, but *Panjab Singh* the younger enlisted in the force of Sirdar Fatah Singh Kalianwala, receiving 30 Rs. a month as a trooper. Like many other common soldiers in the Sikh army he rose to command by his courage, and after the death of his patron Sirdar Fatah Singh, not liking his successor Dal Singh, the nail-cutter, he went over to Ranjit Singh who placed him in a regiment and gave him in jagir the vilages of Aimah and Fatahpur in the Amritsar district, worth 2,500 Rs., and after the second Multan campaign, in 1818, he received jagirs to the value of 50,000 Rs., subject to the service of 125 sowars. On his death his jagirs were resumed by the State as his only son *Kahn Singh* was but 15 years old. However, when the boy grew up the Maharaja sent him to Makhad and Gheb, in command of 500 horsemen and conferred on him a jagir of 15,000 Rs. He remained here for nine years, when his payments having fallen into arrears and his accounts not successfully passing a rigid examination, he was recalled and dismissed from Government employ. He then became a follower of Sirdar Hari Singh Nalwa, and accompanied his new master in his numerous expeditions. He fought in the campaign against the Ghazis of Yusafzai, in 1831, and soon after, not getting on well with his brother officers, went over to Sirdar Attar Singh Sindhanwalia, who gave him a subordinate command, with a jagir of 7,000 Rs. He then went to Kashmir with the governor, General Mian Singh, and returned after three years to Lahore with a considerable fortune. His son *Lehna Singh* married the daughter of his old leader Sirdar Hari Singh, who took his son-in-law with him to Peshawar in the last and disastrous campaign of 1837, in which the great general was killed. During the life of Nao Nihal Singh, and the reign of Maharaja Sher Singh, Diwan *Kahn Singh* and his three sons were treated with favour and received military appointments; but when Raja Hira Singh rose to power, trouble came upon the family. *Lehna Singh* was in the service of Sirdar Ajit Singh Sindhanwalia, and the new minister, who hated the Sindhanwalias and their adherents, confiscated *Kahn Singh's* jagir, and threw him and *Fatah Singh* into prison. *Lehna Singh*, who contrived to escape, took refuge with Baba Bir Singh the great Sikh Guru. Not till Jowahir Singh became minister did the family regain their liberty and their former position. Diwan *Kahn Singh* was killed by a musket shot during the Satlej campaign in 1846, and the Darbar granted the family a jagir in Gharjakh and Dholanwala, worth 2,910 Rs., subject to service. On the annexation of the Panjab the jagir was resumed, and in lieu of it cash pensions of 600 Rs., and 360 Rs., were granted to *Fatah Singh* and *Lehna Singh* respectively. The widow of *Kahn Singh* also received a pension of 360 Rs. The family is of the Khatri tribe, and resides at Gharjakh, a village founded by the Wiraich Jats in the Gujranwala district.

SIRDAR SHAMSHER SINGH MARI.

MALLA SINGH.

Tara Singh — Kour Singh.

Jodh Singh. — Diwan Singh. — Sukha Singh. — Dal Singh. — Mohr Singh.

Gujar Singh. — Bhup Singh. — Kesra Singh. — Jaggat Singh. — Isar Singh.

Bijar Singh. — Partab Singh.

Shamsher Singh. — Janmejah Singh. M. B. Tej Kour Attariwala.

Sham Singh. — Narain Singh.

HISTORY OF THE FAMILY.

The Mari family is of the Shergil tribe, the origin of which has been elsewhere related.* By this tribe several villages were founded in the Lahore and Amritsar districts, and among others Mallanwala, Dewa, Dewa Masur and Mari. At the first named of these the family of *Shamsher Singh* resided till the Durani invasion when the village having been destroyed by the Afghans *Malla Singh* fled to Dewa Masur, which he made his head-quarters and from whence he conducted marauding expeditions, till he fell in a skirmish with the imperial troops, leaving two sons *Kour Singh* and *Tara Singh*, the former of whom became a powerful chief. He joined the Bhangi Sirdars and Khushhal Singh and Budh

* *Vide* Statement of Commandant Dewa Singh. The Gils, who have no chief of any importance in their ranks, inhabit the Lahore, Amritsar, Gujranwala and Firozpur districts. As romantic a story is told of Gil the founder of the tribe as that regarding his son Shergil. He was the son of a Rajput chief Prithipat or Pirthipal, by a Jat woman, and, like Shergil, he was exposed when an infant, in a swamp, 'gili,' from which his name Gil is derived.

Singh Faizulahpuria and took possession of territory in the Jalandhar Doab and to the south of the Satlej. Leaving his sons, *Jodh Singh, Diwan Singh* and *Sukha Singh* to hold these estates, *Kour Singh* returned to his ancestral village of Mari, half way between Amritsar and Firozpur, where he built a mud fort, traces of which still exist, and his name is perpetuated in the village which is known as Mari Kour Singhwala.

When Ranjit Singh seized the country south of Lahore, the fort of Mari, then held by *Mohr Singh* the youngest son of *Kour Singh,* was besieged by him. Resistance was useless, and *Mohr Singh* gave up the fort and territory, obtaining favourable terms and large estates at Piru Chak, Bujhara, Samrah and Manahpur.

Sirdar *Kour Singh* died shortly after this and the Cis-Satlej estates were seized by the Maharaja of Pattiala, Bhag Singh Ahluwalia and Jodh Singh Kalsia. The descendants of *Jodh Singh, Sukha Singh* and *Diwan Singh* are still resident in the Amballa district where they hold a few villages.

Mohr Singh, with his brother *Dal Singh,* held the jagir for some years exempt from service ; but it was later made subject to 100 horsemen. *Mohr Singh* served in the Kashmir campaign in which he was wounded. He distinguished himself at the battle of Tehri, in 1823, after which he was placed in command of 500 cavalry. He was engaged under General Ventura in 1831 in annexing the possessions of the Bahawalpur chief, north of the Satlej * and the next year he died, while half the estates in Sialkot, Dinanagar and Kassur were continued to his son *Isar Singh.* There is little to record of this chief who served with

* Soon after the death of Bahawal Khan II. in 1811, Ranjit Singh demanded tribute for the Bahawalpur territory north of the Satlej. Sadik Muhammad Khan sometimes refused payment altogether, and always resisted till he succeeded in gaining more favourable terms. First 50,000 Rs. a year was asked, then a lakh, and the demand was raised till at Sadik Muhammad's death, five lakhs, which was about as much as Bahawal Khan III. who succeeded Sadik Muhammad in 1826 could raise from the country, was demanded. The Khan neither could nor would pay, and in 1831 General Ventura occupied the territory pledging himself to pay eleven lakhs the first year to Government.

his contingent at Kulu, Suket, Hazara and Peshawar, at which latter place he died, in 1843, of fever.

Shamsher Singh held the jagirs throughout the administration of Hira Singh, Jowahir Singh and Lal Singh. He accompanied Raja Sher Singh Attariwala to Multan, in 1848, and rebelled with him. Although a very young man, he possessed ability and influence, and his whole jagirs, worth 27,000 Rs., were confiscated and in 1850, a pension of 720 Rs. was allowed him for life. To his younger brother *Janmejah Singh*, who had married Tej Kour, daughter of Sirdar Chattar Singh Attariwala, the young lady to whom Maharaja Dalip Singh had been betrothed, a life pension of 360 Rs. was granted. In 1860 a rent free holding was granted to *Shamsher Singh* worth 200 Rs. he also has proprietary rights in Mari Kour Singhwala and Kazi Chak.

Gujar Singh, Bhup Singh and *Kesra Singh*, sons of Sirdar *Dal Singh*, were fine cavalry officers under General Avitabile. They are all dead, and the widows of Colonel *Bhup Singh* draw an allowance of 720 Rs. from Government.

SIRDAR GANDA SINGH MATTU.

- GURYA SINGH.
  - B. Sehju.
  - Sehj Singh.
    - Fatah Singh.
      - Ganda Singh.
        - Basant Singh.
      - Nihal Singh.
        - Ranjodh Singh.
        - Basant Singh.
        - Kher Singh.
    - Jowahir Singh.
      - Karam Singh.
      - Dharam Singh.
        - Sher Singh.
        - Kher Singh.
      - Joala Singh.
    - Dasonda Singh.
    - Pardhan Singh.
      - Kharak Singh.
      - Dya Singh.
    - Lal Singh.

HISTORY OF THE FAMILY.

Gurya Singh, the founder of the family, was a misldar of Sirdar Charrat Singh Sukarchakia. The connection was strengthened by *Gurya Singh* marrying his daughter *Sehju* to Sirdar Dal Singh of Akalghar, the brother-in-law of Charrat Singh. When Ranjit Singh first succeeded his father he had great confidence in Dal Singh, and used to be guided in every thing by his advice, but they soon quarreled, and in the year 1800 Ranjit Singh imprisoned Dal Singh and marched against Akalghar, intending to take it by surprise. But *Sehju* was a brave woman, and with the assistance of her brother *Sehj Singh*, successfully held out for three months, till the siege was raised. Ranjit Singh obtained the fort later, in 1804, on the death of Dal Singh, and then attacked Ahmadabad, which was bravely defended by *Sehj Singh* for some time, but the garrison was at length compelled to capitulate. On the death of Dal Singh, *Sehj Singh* received in jagir the Ilakas of Jathu, Nangal and Bharial. Sirdar *Fatah Singh* his son served with credit against Fatah Khan Wazir of Kabul, and in the Kashmir and Multan expeditions. In 1834, the Maharaja made over the Bharial estate to Jamadar Khushhal Singh, giving another to Sirdar *Ganda Singh* in exchange. *Ganda Singh* was an officer under Hari Singh Nalwa, and fought in many frontier battles and skirmishes. In 1848, he and his cousins joined the rebels, and the family jagirs amounting to 19,000 Rs. were resumed. *Ganda Singh* receives a pension of 1,200 Rs. and *Dasonda Singh* and *Nihal Singh* each 120 Rs. per annum. The family is of the Mattu Jat caste, and resides at Mattu in the Gujranwala district.

KAHN CHAND.

RAM SINGH.
- Amir Chand.
  - Kanheya Lal.
  - Kahn Chand.
    - Hemraj.
      - Devi ki Nandan.
    - Chet Ram.
      - Radha Kishan.
  - Ganga Ram.
  - Atma Ram.

HISTORY OF THE FAMILY.

This family originally came from Multan, and several members of it served the Imperial Government at Lahore and elsewhere. Both *Amir Chand* the father and *Ram Singh* the grandfather of *Kahn Chand* were servants of Sirdar Sahib Singh Veglia. The former, after the establishment at the Sikh monarchy, became a revenue officer under Misr Diwan Chand, on whose death he received a military command under Sirdar Hari Singh Nalwa. He died at Wazirabad in 1835, at a very advanced age.

Kahn Chand entered Government service in 1823, soon after the battle of Tehri, as a secretary (hazuri-navis). He became known for honesty and ability, and in 1830 received a grant of two wells at Botala and the village of Kulla in Sialkot, together worth 600 Rs. a year ; and in 1834, he obtained Mangat, worth 500 Rs. In this year *Kahn Chand* was raised to the post of murasala-navis, or despatch writer. This was an office requiring some talent and would only be given to a munshi in whose honesty the fullest confidence could be reposed. This secret correspondence was conducted under the direct orders of the Maharaja, by Fakir Azizuddin, and later, associated with him, were Bhai Ram Singh and Bhai Govind Ram.

The Derah Khas, or body guards, a regiment containing many of the young Sikh Sirdars and the pick of the Khalsa army was first raised by

Kahn Chand. He had neither the health nor knowledge necessary for its command, which was held by his brother *Ganga Ram* for a short time till the regiment was placed under Raja Hira Singh. *Kahn Chand* was not one of those affected by the revolutions that followed the death of the great Maharaja. He held his office and his emoluments intact, and some Multan estates which had been granted to him at Nidhal were exchanged for others of equal value, 1,400 Rs., at Bankli, Lakra, Nangli Kalan and Nangli Gujran. After the Satlej campaign his Jalandhar estate, in the territory ceded to the British Government, was lost, and in lieu of it he received the estate of Kakka in Wazirabad, worth 3,000 Rs. On the annexation of the Panjab his jagirs were resumed and he received a life pension of 1,200 Rs., which he still holds.

Hemraj, eldest son of *Kahn Chand,* was appointed in 1841, as a Darbar munshi on 30 Rs. a month. He soon rose to be successively sanad writer, Sherishtadar to the Darbar under Lal Singh; and head munshi to the Residency. In 1849, he held jagirs and cash allowances to the amount of 7,438 Rs. per annum. These being new grants and *Hemraj* having only been in Government employ for eight years, were resumed, and a cash pension of 300 Rs. allowed him for life.

KEHR SINGH CHASMAHWALA.

GUJJA SINGH.

- Jodh Singh. D. 1252.
  - Kartar Singh, D. 1840.
    - Kharak Singh.
      - Kehr Singh, B. 1838.
        - Moti Singh.
      - Daughter M. Mokan Singh brother of Wazir Suchet Singh.
    - Sham Singh, D. 1841.
    - Prem Singh.
  - Sant Singh,

HISTORY OF THE FAMILY.

Gujja Singh joined the Kanheya confederacy under Sirdar Jai Singh about the year 1765, and having done good service received from his leader eight villages in jagir, worth 4,000 Rs. *Jodh Singh* was a child at the time of his father's death, but Sirdar Jai Singh treated him with liberality, and on his reaching maturity confirmed to him his father's possessions. When Sirdar Jai Singh died, his daughter-in-law Sada Kour succeeded to the command of the confederacy, and to her *Jodh Singh* transferred his allegiance, and until her imprisonment by Ranjit Singh in 1821, he remained in her service, assisting in the administration of her large and scattered estates. The blow struck by the Maharaja in the imprisonment of Sada Kour and the confiscation of her possessions was so sudden that little resistance was offered by the Kanheya chiefs. The fort of Atalghar, indeed, held out for some time, defended by a woman, one of the Rani's slaves, and *Jodh Singh* stung by a reproach of the Maharaja's, uttered in open Darbar, threw himself into the little fort of Nangah, near Jammu, which he defended for several days, but was at length compelled to surrender, and was heavily fined and thrown into prison, where he remained some months in charge of Hukma Singh Chimni. The next year, 1822, he was sent as Thannadar to Attock, and for four years held charge of the fort. He was then recalled to Lahore, and received a jagir in the Shakarghar district, with a third share in the village of Chashmah, subject to the service of thirty five sowars. He was placed under the orders of Sirdar Attar Singh Sindhanwalia, with whom he served, until the degradation of that powerful house. When Raja Hira Singh became minister, *Sirdar Jodh Singh* was posted to the Raja's own Regiment, the *Derah Khas.* In the many revolutions which took place between this time and the annexation of the Panjab, the modest estates of *Jodh Singh* were untouched. Although an old man he served with Sirdar Ranjodh Singh Majithia during the Satlej campaign, with his contingent, and at the close of the war retired to his estate at Chashmah, hoping to end his days in peace. But the Multan rebellion broke out, and his grandson *Kharrak Singh,* who had long served under Sirdar Sher Singh Attariwala, and who was with Sirdar Chattar Singh in Hazara when the insurrection began, joined the rebels, and marching to join the Sikh army under Sher Singh, with the family sowars, fought throughout the whole campaign. *Jodh Singh,* fearing the confiscation of his jagir and his probable confinement till the close of the war, fled to Jammu, where he remained till after the battle of Gujrat. In consequence of the rebellion of *Kharrak Singh* the jagirs of the family in the Gurdaspur district, to the value of 15,200 Rs., were confiscated; but *Jodh Singh,* who was in no way concerned in his grandson's rebellion, received a pension of 720 Rs. which he enjoyed till his death in 1859. The family have now resumed the occupation of agriculture which they gave up a hundred years ago. They possess neither jagirs nor pensions. *Jodh Singh* was a very aged man when he died. His life, embracing nearly a hundred years, had seen the rise of the Khalsa power; the glory and the fall of the Sikh empire.

The Chashmahwala family is of Harchand Rajput origin and emigrated to the Panjab from Oude.

PARTAB SINGH SADHUGURAYAHWALA.

- MUKTI CHAND.
  - Chanchal Das.
    - Har Singh.
    - Sarup Singh.
      - Dhana Singh.
        - Kahn Singh.
          - Partab Singh.
            - Prem Singh.
          - Kishan Singh.
            - Sardul Singh.
            - Ganda Singh.
          - Chattar Singh.
            - Tara Singh.
          - Sharm Singh.
            - Mul Singh.

HISTORY OF THE FAMILY.

Har Singh and *Sarup Singh,* sons of *Chanchal Das* of the Khatri tribe, joined the Sukarchakia misl, and fought under Sirdar Charrat Singh and Mahan Singh, as officers of irregular cavalry. *Har Singh* never married, but *Sarup Singh* left one son *Dhana Singh,* who followed his father's profession of arms. His son *Kahn Singh* became a distinguished leader of Ghorcharahs under Maharaja Ranjit Singh and received a jagir of 3,000 Rs., subject to the service of six horsemen. He was a dashing officer, and was at last killed in one of the numerous skirmishes on the Peshawar border. *Partab Singh* was taken into Government employ by his maternal uncle General Mian Singh, governor of Kashmir, who was murdered by his own troops in 1841. He first held a command under his father on a salary of 400 Rs., and on the death of Gurmukh Singh, brother of General Mian Singh, received his appointment of commandant on 800 Rs. In 1836, his salary was raised to 1,800 Rs., including the jagir of Miraliwala and an estate in the Lahore district. The revenue of these lands was raised by Raja *Hira Singh* to 2,300 Rs., and they remained in possession of *Partab Singh* until the annexation of the Panjab. During the rebellion of 1849 he was commandant of Maharaja Dalip Singh's guard and did not in any way join the insurgents, but his service jagir was resumed at the close of the war, and he received a pension of 600 Rs., for life. His brother *Kishan Singh* was an officer in General Avitabile's corps, and *Chattar Singh* served in Sultan Mahmud's brigade of artillery. *Tara Singh*, son of *Chattar Singh*, served with the China force but has now left the army.

CHARRAT SINGH OF KOT SYAD MAHMUD.

- **Dhir Singh.**
  - Jai Singh.
    - Sukha Singh, D. 1840.
    - Charrat Singh.
      - Nihal Singh.
        - Kishan Singh.
        - Kor Singh.
        - Isar Singh.
        - Mul Singh.
        - Ganda Singh.
        - Chanda Singh.
      - Dyal Singh.
    - Bhup Singh, D. 1818,
      - Khushhal Singh.
        - Guja Singh.
      - Kirpal Singh.
    - B. Rup Kour M. M. R. Ranjit Singh, 1809.
    - Jamiyat Singh.
    - Attar Singh.
    - Gulab Singh.
    - Panjab Singh.
    - Anup Singh.

HISTORY OF THE FAMILY.

Jai Singh, a Sindhu Jat of Kot Syad Mahmud, a small village two miles from the city of Amritsar, was a trooper in the employ of Sirdar Gulab Singh Bhangi. In the year 1809, Maharaja Ranjit Singh married *Jai Singh's* daughter *Rup Kour,* and this marriage made the fortune of the family, for the Illaka Akhnur worth 30,000 Rs. was assigned to *Charrat Singh* and *Bhup Singh,* subject to the service of 200 horsemen. They held it for 15 years when it was resumed, and *Charrat Singh* obtained instead the jagir of Dharuwal, worth 2,500 Rs., free of service, with the commandantship of an irregular regiment. In the year 1831 Charrat Singh was severely wounded at the battle of Syadki Serai, fought against Syad Ahmad Shah, by Prince Sher Singh. *Bhup Singh* was killed in the Khaibar in 1840, and his estate of 2,000 Rs. was assigned to his two sons. In 1848, the family, with but few exceptions, joined the rebels, and the jagirs they had enjoyed were confiscated. Charrat Singh received a pension of 100 Rs. per annum, and Rani *Rup Kour,* who is still living at Lahore, a pension of 1,980 Rs. The family also holds a fifth share in the village of Kot Syad Mahmud.

DIWAN DHANPAT RAI.

DYANAT RAI.

Gutu Mal.

Ram Kour.

Diwan Dhanpat Rai. | Diwan Ranpat Rai. | Narain Das.

Hukm Chand, B. 1838. | Kishan Chand, B. 1834. | Ganda Mal, B. 1837. | Janda Mal, B. 1845. | Bishan Das, B. 1842.

Mokham Chand. B. 1861. | Hari Chand B. 1852.

HISTORY OF THE FAMILY.

Dyanat Rai entered the service of Nadir Shah the conqueror of Kabul and Dehli in the year 1738. During the following reign of Ahmad Shah, his son *Gutu Mal*, not obtaining any employment in Kabul, determined to seek his fortune in the Panjab, where he settled in the village of Bherah in the Shahpore district. Sirdar Gujar Singh Bhangi was at that time owner of most of the neighbouring country and to him *Gutu Mal* offered his services. He remained with Gujar Singh and Sahib Singh till his death, acting as Diwan and regulating the civil affairs of the large tract over which these chiefs ruled. His son *Ram Kour* succeeded him in his office, which he held until Ranjit Singh, in 1810, took possession of Sahib Singh's estates. *Ram Kour* was growing too old for work but he obtained places at Lahore for his three sons. Diwan *Dhanpat Rai*, who was the eldest of the brothers received Majitha, Jagdeo and other villages in Jagir, which in 1814 were exchanged for the Ilaka of Sodhra, worth 21,000 Rs. from the territories of his old master Sahib Singh. He was then placed in charge of the Manjha where he remained some years. Later he received the Ilaka of Shuwala, worth 10,000 Rs. in jagir, and was made commander of Prince Kharrak Singh's force, which office he held for above a year, being succeeded by Bhaiya Ram Singh. The brothers did good service with their contingent at Multan, Mankera and Kashmir, and after each campaign received an enhancement of their jagirs. In 1831, at Diwan *Dhanpat Rai's* death, the jagirs of the family amounted to 43,500 Rs. These were resumed, with the exception of Sodhra, subject to the service of seventy eight horsemen. Diwan *Ranpat Rai* and *Narain Das* were then sent to Kangra and Nurpur to collect the revenue due from the Kardars of those districts. In 1842, Raja Gulab Singh, who had charge of Gujrat, took from the family lands about Beli to the value of 5,000 Rs., and on Sirdar Lehna Singh representing the case to Maharaja Sher Singh, the contingent was reduced by twenty men, and in 1846, Raja Lal Singh struck off eight more.

During the war of 1848-49, the contingent of Diwan *Ranpat Rai* was employed under Lala Gumani Lal, Adatali of the Manjha, in preserving the peace of the district. *Narain Das* died in 1848. On annexation the personal jagir of *Ranpat Rai*, 2,000 Rs. was maintained for his life, half descending to his sons. *Hukm Chand* and *Bishan Das* his two nephews also received pensions of 1000 Rs. for their lives, and *Dhanpat Rai's* widow, who soon afterwards died, the same amount. Diwan *Ranpat Rai* died in the year 1856. The family resides at Sodhra and is of the Brahman caste.

GURMUKH SINGH OF TUNG.

- SAHIB SINGH, D. 1804.
  - Fatah Singh, D. 1803.
    - Gurmukh Singh, B. 1799.
      - Narain Singh, B. 1839.
    - Sarmukh Singh. B. 1803.
      - Jodh Singh, B. 1824.
        - Ganda Singh. B. 1853.
    - Nidhan Singh, D. 1846.
      - Sant Singh, B. 1843.

HISTORY OF THE FAMILY.

The Sikhs of Tung near Amritsar, are of an old family of Tung Rajputs, who emigrated from Delhi about the beginning of the 18th century and founded the village which bears their name. In course of time from association and intermarriages they became Jats, and on the Sikhs rising to power joined the Ramgharia confederacy under Jassa Singh. *Sahib Singh* received Tung with some adjacent villages from his chief, in jagir, and died in 1804, his only son *Fatah Singh* having died the preceding year. *Fatah Singh's* three sons remained with Jodh Singh the Ramgharia Sirdar, till in 1816, the Maharaja seized the possessions of the confederacy, and they were glad to enter the service of the conqueror. *Gurmukh Singh* and *Nidhan Singh* each received command of 100 horsemen, and served under Misr Diwan Chand, and on his death, under Sirdar Desa Singh Majithia. After the capture of Multan in 1818, at which the brothers were present, they received a grant of their ancestral village of Tung, valued at 750 Rs. in three equal shares, subject to the service of three horsemen, and their salaries were considerably raised.

Gurmukh Singh, who was commandant in the Ramgharia brigade, served at Multan, Mankera, Tirah, Kashmir and Peshawar. He also fought in the Satlej campaign of 1845-46 when his brother *Nidhan Singh* was killed. Under the Darbar he was employed in the Manjah, as assistant to Gumani Lal and Lal Singh Talwandi, and afterwards was sent to Sowrian under Diwan Hakim Rai.

Sarmukh Singh and *Jodh Singh* still hold jagirs in Tung to the value of 660 Rs. and 400 Rs. respectively. *Gurmukh Singh* has neither jagir nor pension, though till 1855, when the revision of the settlement took place, he held his original share of the Tung village, but it was then resumed. The widow of *Narain Singh* receives a pension of 60 Rs.

SULTAN AHMAD ALI KHAN.

GHOSI KHAN.
|
Sultan Mahmud Khan.
|
Sultan Ahmad Ali Khan. — Muhammad Ali Khan.

HISTORY OF THE FAMILY.

This Muhammadan family claims to be of Rajput origin and to have emigrated to the Panjab from Nipal. Nothing certain is known about it, however, before the time of *Ghosi Khan* who was an artillery officer under Mahan Singh Sukarchakia, and after his death, under his son Ranjit Singh. He knew something of casting guns, and was skilful in his profession, and was rewarded by jagirs worth 5,000 Rs. at Wan and Bherowal, with a large house in Lahore now occupied by the Mission School.

On his death his son *Sultan Mahmud Khan,* who had served in the artillery under him, accompanied Maharaja Ranjit Singh in his expeditions against Multan and Kashmir. In the Tirah campaign in Kangra he so much distinguished himself that the Maharaja made him a general and placed him in command of 25 guns. He was of exceedingly intemperate habits, and his drunkenness brought him more than once into trouble with his master, but he was a useful officer and while Ranjit Singh lived was generally treated with favour. When Nao Nihal Singh obtained power *Sultan Mahmud* lost his command, and was sent in charge of a troop of artillery, under General Ventura, to Mandi, but on the death of the prince and the accession of Maharaja Sher Singh he was reinstated, and his son *Sultan Ahmad Khan* was made a colonel. In 1843, both father and son were engaged in the assault on the fort of Lahore, which had been taken possession of by the Sindhanwalias after the murder of Sher Singh, and for their services on this occasion they received additional jagirs from Raja Hira Singh. *Sultan Mahmud* was then sent in command of the artillery to Hazara, where he remained till, shortly before the outbreak of 1848, both he and his son were sent to the Derajat.

Sultan Ahmad Khan was in Bannu at the time of the outbreak, and assisted Ram Singh Chhapawala to reduce the fort of Dalipghar. This being accomplished he marched with the Sikh rebel force to Ram Nagar where he was joined by his father, and both fought against the English throughout the campaign. The service jagirs of *Sultan Mahmud*, which at the time of the rebellion amounted to 6,000 Rs. were resumed, but he received a life pension of 600 Rs. which he held till his death in 1859. His son *Sultan Ahmad* who resides at Bherowal in the Amritsar district, enjoys a pension of 120 Rs., and has also proprietary rights in the village.

COMMANDANT MUHAMMAD SHAH.

KAMR-UD-DIN.
|
Amir ud-Din.
|
Imam Shah. — Muhammad Hussain.
|
(sons of Imam Shah:) Inayat Shah. — Muhammad Shah. — Akbar Shah. — Hussain Shah. — Chiragh Shah.
|
(son of Muhammad Shah:) Sirdar Ali.

HISTORY OF THE FAMILY.

The family of *Muhammad Shah* is of Persian descent, *Kamr-ud-Din* was an officer in the army of Nadir Shah, and accompanied that chief to India, remaining behind as a settler in the neighbourhood of Dehli when the invading army retired. He afterwards went to live at Gungoh in Saharanpur, where he died in 1764. *Amiruddin* then left for Lukhnow, where Shujauddowlah was Nawab, and entered his service first as Thannadar and afterwards as a revenue collector. Failing to pay the government demand he was thrown into prison, and though released after a short time, did not obtain fresh employment till the accession of Asafuddowlah in 1775. He was murdered at Publi by some Gujars in 1798, and his son *Imam Shah* fearing the same fate, left for Lukhnow, where he lived for some time with an old retired officer of artillery, by name Buhadar Khan, who taught the lad all that he knew. As he could get no employment at the court of Oude, *Imam Shah* determined to seek his fortune elsewhere. Hearing that Hindostanis were in request in Kabul he proceeded thither, but at Wazirabad in the Panjab, he met Sirdar Jodh

Singh who easily induced him to enter his services as Jamadar of Artillery. The next year the Sirdar died, and *Imam Shah* then entered the army of Maharaja Ranjit Singh, and fought in many battles, as Colonel of Artillery. He served throughout the reign of Ranjit Singh and his successors, and was killed at Sobraon in 1846.

Muhammad Shah, his second son, was made a commandant of Artillery when eighteen years of age. He fought in the Satlej campaign, and under the Darbar was successively posted at Pind Dadan Khan, Hassan Abdal and Hazara. In 1849, when the 5th Panjab Cavalry was first raised, *Muhammad Shah* was appointed to it, and served in this regiment till 1859. On the frontier he was known as a first rate officer both for bravery and intelligence. As senior native officer of his squadron he served throughout the siege and capture of Delhi; the relief and capture of Lukhnow; the capture of Bareilly and the actions of Bolundshahr, Fatahghar, Agra and Allyghar. He received the order of British India for his gallantry at Agra, where, seeing a squadron of the 5th in danger of being cut up by a shower of grape, he galloped forward alone, and cut down the artilleryman who was about to fire the gun. When Lieut. Younghusband was killed near Fatahghar, *Muhammad Shah* cut down the sepoy who had fired the fatal ball. By the side of Major Sandford, who succeeded Lieut. Younghusband in command of the squadron, *Muhammad Shah* fought with conspicuous courage, and when that officer fell, he protected his body, buried it decently and built over it a tomb. The most valued of the many testimonials received by *Muhammad Shah* is a gold watch sent from England by the relatives of Major Sandford, in acknowledgment of his devotion.

In January 1859, *Muhammad Shah* was appointed commandant of the 3rd Oude Military Police under Captain C. Chamberlain. His services were specially asked for by this officer, who knew his worth, his energy and his thorough knowledge of his Military duties. When the Military Police were broken up in November 1859 he was made commandant in the new police and held the post with credit till February 1861, when, on reductions being made in the force, he took his discharge.

Muhammad Shah has received the title of Sirdar Buhadar. He holds a pension of 1,800 Rs. cash and a life jagir of 2,000 Rs. in the Beraich District. He is the author of a creditable work on cavalry tactics. His son, *Sirdar Ali* is eleven years of age. Of his four daughters, the eldest is married to Amjad Ali, son of Mir Muhammad Shah of Amritsar, and the second to Abbas Ali resident at Lahore.

MULTAN.

ABDUL MAJID KHAN SADDOZAI.
AHMAD ALI KHAN SADDOZAI.

- SADDO KHAN. B. 1558.
  - Khizar Khan, from whom descended Ahmed Shah Durani and the Khizar Khels.
    - Khudadad Khan.
  - Sultan Modud Khan.
    - Shah Hussain Khan.
    - Allah Dad Khan.
      - Inayat Khan.
        - Sher Muhammad Khan.
      - Abid Khan.
        - i. Nawab Zahid Khan, D. 1749.
          - ii. Nawab Shakar Khan.
            - Hassan Khan.
            - Hussain Khan.
          - iii. Nawab Shuja Khan, D. 1774.
            - iv. Nawab Muzaffar Khan, D. 1818.
              - v. Nawab Sarafraz Khan, D. 1851.
                - Firozdin Khan, D. 1855,
                  - Kasim Ali Khan, B. 1832.
                  - Hashan Ali Khan, B. 1834, lives at Bhawalpur.
                  - Sadik Ali Khan, B. 1838.
                  - Shamsher Khan, B. 1843.
                - Sham Ali Khan.
                - Mansur Ali Khan.
                - Ahmad Ali Khan, B. 1827.
                - Akbar Ali Khan, D. 1852.
              - Zu-l-fakar Khan, D 1847.
                - Abdul Khalik Khan, D. 1848.
                  - Abdul Majid Khan.
                - Jahangir Khan, B. 1822.
                - Muhammad Khan, D. 1850.
                - Gulzar Khan, B. 1837.
                - Ahmad Yar Khan, B. 1842.
              - Shah Nawaz Khan, D. 1818.
                - Abdul Majid Khan, B. 1817.
              - Mumtaz Khan, D. 1818.
              - Azaz Khan, D. 1818.
              - Hak Nawaz Khan, D. 1818.
                - Rob Nawaz Khan, lives at Bahawalpur.
              - Shah Baz Khan, D. 1818.
              - Amir Baz Khan, living at Bahawalpur.
      - Lashkar Khan.
  - Kamram Khan, from whom descended the tribe Kamram Khel.
  - Buhadar Khan, from whom descended the tribe Buhadar Khel.
  - Zafran Khan, from whom descended the tribe Zafran Khel.

HISTORY OF THE FAMILY.

Saddo Khan, the ancestor of the Saddozai tribe of Afghans, the Nawabs of Multan and Ahmad Shah Abdali, was a resident of Kandahar, where he was born in 1558. He succeeded his father as chief of the Habibzai tribe, but was a man of such bravery and ability that he was selected by the Abdali tribes, living between Kandahar and Hirat, to be their leader. This was in 1598.

Shadi Khan, the governor of the Emperor Akbar at Kandahar, was hostile to *Saddo Khan*, so he went over to the interests of Shah Abbas, King of Persia, who had lost Kandahar in 1594, and was intriguing for its recovery. This he effected in 1621, after Akbar's death, with the assistance of the Abdalis. *Saddo Khan* died in 1626, leaving five sons from whom have descended several well-known Afghan tribes. The descendants of *Saddo Khan* are known as Saddozai,* and one branch of the family to which Ahmad Shah,† Timur Shah, Zaman Shah and Shah Shuja belonged, reigned for many years in Kabul.

Khizar Khan, who succeeded his father in the chiefship, was of a mild disposition, unsuited to rule over a wild Afghan tribe. His authority was set at defiance, and at length seeing that he could not compel obedience to his orders, he made over the uneasy honour of chiefship to his brother *Modud Khan*, who was of a determined character and held the Abdalis in terror. *Khizar Khan* died in 1626, and *Modud Khan* held rule for seventeen years after his death. He resided at Saffa, some fifty miles north east of Kandahar, where Ali Mardan Khan was governor, and with this able and enlightened man *Modud Khan* always maintained friendship. In 1637, Ali Mardan Khan, who was no favourite of his

---

* A clan of the Niazi tribe, called Saddozai, inhabits the village of Dodah on the Indus. They are not, however, connected with the family of *Saddo Khan*.

† Ahmad Shah only adopted the name of Durani for his tribe in 1747. It had formerly been always called Abdali. Sherif Din had five sons, according to Afghan tradition, Osman, Drek, Tarin, Rawawak, and Abdal. The last received his name from a Saint, Khwaja Abdul Ahmad, whom he had for some time served as a disciple. (Pers. Abdal, a saint, hermit.)

master, the Shah of Persia, gave up Kandahar to Muhammad Said Khan, the Governor of Kabul for the Emperor Shah Jahan, and retired to Dehli, where he was received with great honour. *Modud Khan* was assassinated in a domestic brawl six years later. *Shah Hussain Khan* succeeded him, but was opposed by *Khudadad Khan* who claimed the chiefship in right of his father *Khizar Khan*. A battle was fought between the cousins, near Saffa, in which *Hussain Khan* was defeated, but he fled to Kandahar, and being aided by its governor Khas Khan, again took the field with aconsiderable force. *Khudadad Khan*, unable to oppose him, fled to Ispahan, where he was well received by Shah Abbas II., and he accompanied that monarch, in 1648, against Kandahar, which was taken before the army of Shah Jahan could arrive for its defence. The Shah then retired to Hirat leaving Mahrab Khan Kizilbash governor of Kandahar, and *Khudadad Khan* in command of the country without the walls.

The enemy of *Hussain Khan* was now in power, and it was with great joy that the latter saw, some months after the capture of the city, the Indian army, under Aurangzib and Said Ullah, approach. He joined the invaders, but Kandahar was so well and bravely defended by the Persian garrison, that, at the beginning of the cold weather of 1649, Aurangzib was compelled to raise the siege and to retire to Hindostan. With him went *Shah Hussain Khan* and all his family, for they could no longer remain in Afghanistan with safety.

Shah Hussain first obtained the Pargannah of Sialkot in jagir, and soon afterwards, in exchange for it, Rangpur, on the right bank of the Chenab, ten miles below the junction of that river with the Ravi. In 1653, he accompanied Prince Dara Sheko, eldest son of Shah Jahan, on his unsuccessful expedition against Kandahar, the last attempt on that city made by the Moguls. The next year he accompanied Prince Aurangzib to the Deccan of which he was viceroy, but in 1655 he returned to Dehli, and through the interest of Ali Mardan Khan obtained permission to raise seven hundred horse, and his brother two hundred.

When Aurangzib ascended the throne in 1658, *Hussain Khan* received an accession to his jagir, but his hot temper soon after brought him into disgrace. On one unlucky day, the Emperor was looking at some horses which had been presented to him, and, pointing to one of them he asked *Hussain Khan*, its breed. The chief hesitated, and a fine looking Pathan who stood by, answered the question. "Slave," said *Hussain Khan* in a fury, "when the Emperor addresses me, why do you speak?" "Slaves are known by their mean appearance," was the reply. *Hussain Khan*, who was short in stature and very swarthy in complexion, was so much irritated at this that he drew his dagger and stabbed the too bold speaker to the heart. For this offence, committed in the very presence of the Emperor, Hussain Khan was imprisoned, and though after a time released was banished for life from court. His services under the Emperor alone saved him from execution. Shortly after his return to Rangpur he died without issue. His brother *Allahdad Khan* had died a few months previously, leaving six sons, of whom *Inayat Khan* the eldest succeeded to his uncle's estate. When Muhammad Muazuddin Buhadar, son of Prince Muhammad Muazzam and grandson of Aurangzib, arrived at Multan, on his way to Shikarpur and Sind, *Inayat Khan* joined him and fought throughout the campaign. Bakhtiar Khan the chief Afghan rebel submitted, and was on the entreaty of *Inayat Khan*, forgiven.

This chief was succeeded by his eldest son *Sher Muhammad Khan*, who was almost an imbecile, and his uncle *Abid Khan* administered affairs and possessed all real power. On the death of *Abid Khan* great dissentions arose in the family. *Lashkar Khan*, brother of *Abid Khan*, claimed the chiefship from his seniority, while *Asghar Khan*, brother of *Sher Muhammad Khan*, claimed through his father and his brother. The Afghans ranged themselves, some on one side, some on the other, and it was only the influence of Hyat Khan the Governor that prevented bloodshed. Having induced all to promise to abide by his decision, he appointed *Zahid Khan* chief. His choice was a good one, and was unanimously approved.

Zahid Khan was an able man, of gentle manners and considerable learning. He was a great friend of Kamr-ud-din, Minister at Dehli, and when Nadir Shah invaded India and the Mogul power was becoming weak in the distant provinces, he was summoned to Dehli, and, through the interest of Kamr-ud-din, appointed Nawab of Multan. This was in 1738. *Zahid Khan*, immediately on his nomination, wrote to his son *Shakar Khan* to assume the Nawabship, but Ishak Khan, the Governor in possession, would not submit, and was only ousted after a severe struggle. In 1747, Ahmad Shah Durani invaded India, and after having put to flight Shah Nawaz Khan the Governor of Lahore, moved down to Multan, where he confirmed *Zahid Khan* in his appointment. This led the Dehli court to believe that *Zahid Khan* had betrayed them and gone over to the enemy, and Shahnawaz Khan was appointed to supersede him as Governor, while Mir Manu, son of Wazir Kamr-ud-din, was made Viceroy at Lahore. *Zahid Khan* did not at first oppose the new Governor, but during the Baisakhi festival a soldier in the service of Shah Nawaz Khan insulted an Afghan woman in a village near the city. This caused a general riot in which a relative of Diwan Lakhpat Rai lost his hand. *Zahid Khan* then assembled his Afghans, and attacked the forces of Shah Nawaz Khan, who was worsted and compelled to send to Lahore to beg assistance from Mir Manu. The Lahore Governor was the last man to give assistance to Shah Nawaz Khan, whom he hated as a rival, and sent instead a force against him under Kura Mal whom he appointed his deputy at Multan and created a Raja. Shah Nawaz Khan met the force about forty miles from Multan, but after an engagement, which is said to have lasted several days, he was defeated and slain.

Raja Kura Mal then entered Multan as Governor. He had before served in the province as Diwan, and *Zahid Khan*, thinking it beneath his dignity to render obedience to the new ruler, retired to Sitpur. Kura Mal was about to compel his submission by force of arms, but a new invasion of Ahmad Shah obliged him to proceed to Lahore, leaving Multan in the hands of *Shakar Khan*, son of *Zahid Khan*. Mir Manu and Kura Mal met the Abdali chief near Lahore on the 12th April 1752, and gave him battle, but were defeated, and Kura Mal was slain. Mir Manu made his peace and was confirmed in his viceroyalty, and under him Ali Muhammad Khan, an Afghan officer, was appointed Governor of Multan.

Zahid Khan had died in 1749, and his son *Shakar Khan* gave over charge and remained on good terms with the new Governor.

In 1757, the Mahrattas overran the Punjab. Ragoba, brother of the Peshwah, captured Lahore, and two Mahratta chiefs, Salah Beg and Sanjli Beg, were sent against Multan, which they captured almost without opposition, Ali Muhammad Khan taking to flight. The Mahrattas, whose rule was most oppressive, did not remain long; and the next Governor appointed by Ahmad Shah was Khwaja Yakut. Ali Muhammad Khan who had at first obeyed the royal order, after a little while finding the Khwaja a feeble Governor, expelled him and again took possession of the Nawabship.

Shakar Khan had died, and his eldest son was a man of no ability, so Ahmad Shah wrote to *Shuja Khan*, the second son of Zahid Khan, directing him to assume the Nawabship. *Shuja Khan* collected his Afghans, and Ali Muhammad having no force capable of opposing them submitted. *Shuja Khan* then became governor, and built the fortress of Shujaabad, twenty-three miles south of Multan. The turbulent Ali Muhammad Khan soon took up arms against him, and *Shuja Khan*, who had grown unpopular, was defeated and thrown into prison, while Ali Muhammad reassumed the government. This proceeding irritated the Durani Monarch in the highest degree, and when he reached Multan, in 1767, he ordered the arrest of Ali Muhammad who was bold enough to attend the Darbar. Both the offender and his son were, by order of Ahmad Shah, ripped up, and their bodies paraded on camels through the city, with a proclamation to the effect that this should be the fate of any one who should insult a Saddozai. *Shuja Khan* was then reinvested with the government of Multan, and Ahmad Shah left for Kabul.

In 1771, the Sikhs, who were becoming very powerful, and who had in 1766 overran the Multan country under Jhanda Singh, attacked Multan, and for a month and a half besieged the fort; but Jahan Khan marched to its relief, and compelled them to retire. After this, Haji Sharif Khan Saddozai was nominated governor by Timur Shah, and *Shuja Khan* again retired to his fort of Shujaabad, but when called upon to give up to government all the proceeds of his zamindari estates, he refused and came to an open rupture with the Governor. On this another Haji Sharif Khan, Taklu, otherwise known as Mirza Sharif Beg, was appointed, in conjunction with a merchant named Dharam Das, and contrived to keep on good terms with *Shuja Khan*. But Abdul Karim Khan Bamazai invaded Multan, and the Mirza called in the Sikhs to his assistance. Timur Shah, hearing that the Mirza had chosen allies from among his bitter enemies, superseded him, and sent Maddat Khan to fill the post. Sharif Beg resisted the new governor, but *Shuja Khan* supported him; and they together besieged Sharif Beg in the citadel. They could not take it, however, and Maddat Khan was recalled to Kandahar. Timur Shah now directed the Bahawalpur chief to reduce the rebellious governor to obedience. He accordingly marched to Multan with his Daudputras, accompanied by *Muzaffar Khan* son of *Shuja Khan*. The fort was besieged and taken in eighteen days; but the triumph was a short one. Sharif Beg had called to his assistance Sirdars Jhanda Singh and Ganda Singh, the Bhangi Chiefs, and they now appeared with a large force. They defeated the Bahawalpur troops and stormed the fort, which they kept for themselves. The Mirza on this fled to Talamba and from thence to Khairpur Tanwein, where he died not long afterwards.

The Sikhs then attacked and captured Shujaabad, whither *Shuja Khan* had fled, and he only escaped with difficulty, and took refuge at Bahawalpur. Sirdar Jhanda Singh then left Multan in charge of Diwan Singh Chhachowalia, one of his misldars, and returned to Amritsar. This was in 1772. Some time after this *Shuja Khan* died, and in 1777 his son *Muzaffar Khan* persuaded Bahawal Khan, Chief of Bahawalpur, to make another effort to recover the city. He accordingly attacked the fort and was at first successful, but after a siege of twenty-three days was repulsed with loss, and *Muzaffar Khan* then applied for aid to Kabul. Sirdar Maddat Khan was again despatched with a considerable force, but he did not reach Multan till early in the following year. Kabul politics had then changed, and his services were required at home, and he was recalled without having effected anything. *Muzaffar Khan* then retired to Uchh, where he lived under the protection of the famous Makhdum Sahib Shaikh Hamed till 1779, when Timur Shah, king of Kabul, marched to Multan with a large army, and recovered it from the Sikhs after a siege of forty days. The Sikhs were allowed to retire unmolested, and *Muzaffar Khan* was appointed governor with the title of Nawab 'Rukn-ud-doulah' (pillar of the State).

The new governor was an energetic and able man, and very much improved the province during his long rule. He had not, however, much time to bestow on works of peace for, from 1779 till his death in 1818, he was engaged in constant war. The Sikhs of the Bhangi Misl attacked him first, and then Sahib Khan Sial and Sirdar Karam Singh Bhangi made a joint attack, which was only repulsed with difficulty.

In 1790 *Muzaffar Khan*, leaving Multan in charge of Muhammad Khan Buhadarkhel, journeyed to Kabul, and remained absent for two years. When Zaman Shah ascended the throne, *Muzaffar Khan* was confirmed in his governorship, and in 1797, when that prince invaded India, and the Sikhs lost for a time their ascendency, he drove them out of Kot Kumalia, which he made over to its hereditary Rais, Saadat Yar Khan Kharral.

The great enemy of *Muzaffar Khan* at Multan was Abd-ul-Samad Khan, * one of the Badozai chiefs, who did all he could to injure the Nawab at the Courts of Lahore and Kabul, and who was at one time appointed governor by Shah Zaman; but at last he was defeated, his fort taken, and his jagirs confiscated.

---

* Vide Statement of Sadik Muhammad Khan Badozai.

In 1802, *Muzaffar Khan* first saw the young chief Ranjit Singh, who had marched towards Multan to spy out the land. The Nawab came out to meet him, thirty miles from the city, and the chiefs, having interchanged valuable presents, separated very good friends. Again, in 1806, after having reduced Jhang, Ranjit Singh marched towards Multan, and reached Mahtam twenty miles north of the city, when the Nawab, who had no wish to fight with the Sikh Chief, gave him 70,000 Rs. to retire. Ranjit Singh bestowed valuable Khilats on the Nawab and took his departure. Ahmad Khan Sial, the Chief of Jhang, who had been just ousted by Ranjit Singh, took refuge at Multan, and *Muzaffar Khan* gave him men and money, with which he contrived to recover a considerable portion of his territory, though he was unable to oust entirely Fatah Singh Kalianwala, the Sirdar in possession. Abd-ul-Samad Khan, the defeated Badozai Chief, who had taken refuge at Lahore, persuaded Ranjit Singh, in 1807, to attack Multan in force. The town was in part captured, but the fort held out against all the Sikh efforts, and an agreement was concluded through Fatah Singh Kalianwala, by which the Maharaja retired on receiving a large sum of money.

In this year *Muzuffar Khan*, tired of constant war, made over the Nawabship to his son *Sarafraz Khan*, and set out on the pilgrimage to Mecca. He met with many difficulties on the journey. The Arabs, attracted by the splendour of his cavalcade, attacked it in great numbers, and were only bought off with great difficulty. *Muzaffar Khan* was absent fourteen months and at the close of 1808, soon after his return as a Haji, (one who has made the pilgrimage to Mecca) Mr. Elphinstone visited Multan on his way to the court of Shah Shuja-ul-Mulk at Peshawur. He was hospitably received, and the Nawab wished to place himself under British protection, but the British envoy had no authority to accept his allegiance, and *Muzaffar Khan* opened a correspondence with the Governor General in Calcutta, expressing his desire to be on good terms with the English.

At the beginning of 1810, Maharaja Ranjit Singh again marched against Multan. He had just met Shah Shuja at Khushab, and the exiled monarch wished the Sikhs to take Multan and make it over to him. *Muzaffar Khan* had, in 1803, repulsed an attack of the Shah's troops, and in the hope of conciliating him, had more than once offered him an asylum at Multan, but Shah Shuja wished to obtain the city and province as his own by conquest. The Maharaja treated the weak minded prince with great respect, but, failing to obtain any money from him, determined to take Multan on his own account. On the 24th February 1810, he arrived before the walls, and the next day took possession of the city.

The neighbouring chiefs were much alarmed at the proceedings of the Maharaja; Muhammad Khan, chief of Leia and Bhakkar, paid 1,20,000 Rs. as the ransom of his country, and Sadik Muhammad Khan of Bahawalpur offered a lakh, with the same object, but it was not accepted. He, however, though *Muzaffar Khan* was his friend, was compelled to send 500 horsemen as a reinforcement to the Sikhs.

For some time the fort was bombarded without effect, and mining was then resorted to; but the besieged countermined with success, and blew up the battery of Attar Singh Dhari, killing him, with twelve men, and seriously wounding others, among whom were Sirdar Nihal Singh Attariwala and the young Hari Sing Nalwa. The battery was so near the fort that the Sikhs were unable to carry off their dead, and these were sent in by the besieged, the body of Attar Singh being covered with a pair of shawls.

Diwan Mokham Chand was sent to reduce Shujaabad, but this fort was of considerable strength and could not be taken. On the 21st March a general assault was ordered, but the Sikhs were repulsed with great loss, and they now grew disheartened, for provisions had become very dear in the camp; Diwan Mokham Chand was dangerously ill, and several leaders had been slain, while scarcely any impression had been made on the citadel. On the 25th another assault was made with the same result. It was necessary to raise the siege; and Ranjit Singh to his intense mortification, had to accept from *Muzaffar Khan* the terms he had many times rejected, namely, two and a half lakhs of rupees, twenty war horses and a contingent in time of war. Having received 30,000 Rs. in earnest of the ransom, the Maharaja retired from Multan on the 14th of April.

Seeing that his own strength was insufficient for the capture of Multan, Ranjit Singh addressed the Governor General, requesting the co-operation of Britsh troops. His proposition was not well received, the more so as he proposed that the force, instead of marching through the Panjab, should pass through the sterile country south of the Sutlej. Shah Shuja even prepared for an independent attack on Multan, but he was wise enough to relinquish the idea which could have had no chance of success.

The Nawab now quarreled with Sadik Khan of Bahawalpur, who had assisted his enemies in the late war. There was a strong party in Bahawalpur, headed by Fatah Muhammad Ghori and Ahmad Khan, opposed to the Khan, and these, having failed in an attempt to assassinate their master, took refuge in Multan territory. The Khan remonstrated with the Nawab for allowing them an asylum, but *Muzaffar Khan*, whose wrath was by no means appeased, supported the rebels, and when he saw that they were about to be overpowered, declared war against the Khan. He proceeded to Shujaabad himself in person, and sent forward his army against Yakub Muhammad Khan, the Bahawalpur general. An action ensued in which the Daudputras, being the more numerous and better supplied with artillery, were the victors, and the Afghan force retreated to Shujaabad. In 1811, *Muzaffar Khan* was engaged in conflict with Mehr Rajjab, of the Rajbanah tribe, a rebellious dependent of his own. He defeated him and destroyed his fort, upon the site of which he built Firozghar.

In February 1816, an irregular attack was made upon Multan by the Sikhs. A strong force had been sent to Bahawalpur and Multan to collect the tribute, and there being some delay in *Muzaffar Khan's* payment, Phula Singh Akali, mad and drunk with bhang, led a storming party of fanatics like himself against the town, and with such impetuosity did they make the attack that they gained possession of some of the outworks of the citadel. But Fakir Aziz-ud-din made due apologies; the Nawab paid his tribute quicker than he would otherwise have done, and the Sikh army proceeded towards Mankera. In 1817, a Sikh army, under Diwan Chand marched against Multan, and attacked the fort, but was repulsed and retired on payment of ten thousand rupees. These attacks, however, were not made in earnest. The Maharaja was collecting his strength for a great effort and he had sworn that Multan, which had so often defied him should yet be his. During the cold weather of 1817 he was collecting supplies and men from all quarters, and in January 1818, an army of 25,000 men under the nominal command of Prince Kharrak Singh, but in reality commanded by Misr Diwan Chand, marched from Lahore. On the way to Multan the forts of Khanghar and Muzaffarghar were taken; the city was invested and captured early in February, and the bombardment of the fort commenced. The Nawab had a garrison of only 2,000 men, and the citadel was not provisioned for a siege, but he made a defence the like of which the Sikhs had never before seen. Till the second of June the bombardment went on, and two large breaches had been made in the walls, for the great Bhangi gun,. the 'Zam-Zam' of Ahmad Shah Durani, had been brought from Lahore and had been four times fired with effect. More than one assault was made by the Sikhs, but they were repulsed, on one occasion with the loss of 1,800 men. The gates were blown in, but the garrison raised behind them mounds of earth on which they fought hand to hand with the Sikhs. The defenders of the fort were at length reduced to two or three hundred fighting men, most of them of the tribe or family of *Muzaffar Khan.* The rest had either been killed or had gone over to the enemy, for they had been heavily bribed to desert their master, and many of them were unable to resist the temptation. At length, on the 2nd June, an Akali by name Sadhu Singh, determined to surpass what Phula Singh had done in 1816, rushed with a few desperate followers into an outwork of the fort, and taking the Afghans by surprise captured it. The Sikh forces, seeing this success, advanced to the assault, and mounted the breach at the Khizri gate. Here the old Nawab, with his eight sons and all that remained of the garrison, stood sword in hand, resolved to fight to the death. So many fell beneath the keen Afghan swords, that the Sikhs drew back and opened fire on the little party with their match locks. "Come on like men" shouted the Afghans, "and let us fall in fair fight," but this was an invitation the Sikhs did not care to accept. There died the white bearded *Muzaffar Khan*, scorning to accept quarter, and there died his five sons, *Shah Nawaz Khan*, *Mumtaz Khan*, *Azaz Khan*, *Hak Nawaz Khan*, and *Shah Baz Khan*. *Zu-l-fakar Khan*, his second son, was also wounded severely in the face, and the two others *Sarafraz Khan* and *Amir Beg Khan* accepted quarter and were saved. Diwan Ram Dyal took *Sarafraz Khan* upon his elephant and conducted him with all honour to his own tent. Few of the garrison escaped with their lives,* and the whole city was given up to plunder. The fort of Shujaabad was also reduced and five guns taken from it. After this the walls of Multan were repaired, and a garrison of six hundred men under command of Sirdars Jodh Singh Kalsia and Dal Singh Naharna being left in the fort, the Sikh army returned to Lahore.

Multan was supposed to be very wealthy, and the share of the Maharaja amounting to only two lakhs of rupees he issued an order that all officers and soldiers should restore their plunder, and that if any was found with them after a certain date the penalty would be certain death. This order brought in some five lakhs to the state treasury, but the plunder of Multan was estimated at two millions sterling.†

---

* Mr. Moorcroft was told by Maharaja Ranjit Singh that five hundred of the garrison survived and received quarter. This was false. At the time of the last assault there were not three hundred fighting men in the fort, and most of these fell at the breach.

† Many are the stories told about the loot of Multan. It never brought happiness or good fortune to its possessors who were killed in battle, or died childless or in poverty.

Nawab *Muzaffar Khan* was buried with honor by the shrine of Bahauddin with his son *Shah Nawaz*.

Saraffraz Khan his eldest son had been for some years Nawab, his father having procured the confirmation of his succession from the Kabul court. He was carried prisoner to Lahore by Diwan Chand, and was well received by the Maharaja who gave him a jagir at Sharakpur and Naolakha, afterwards commuted to a cash pension. *Zu-l-fakar Khan* also received a pension. *Saraffraz Khan* was at first rigorously guarded in Lahore, but when the Maharaja's power was secure in Multan, he was allowed perfect freedom and was always treated with respect and friendship by Ranjit Singh.

In 1848, his influence was useful to the British Government in inducing the Multani Pathans to abandon the cause of Mulraj, which, however, they did not want much pressing to do. At annexation the Nawab had a jagir of 1,100 Rs., the village of Chamusa and a cash pension of 14,720 Rs. The pension was maintained for his life, and the jagir was to descend to his son *Firozdin*. *Saraffraz Khan* died on the 12th March 1851 leaving eight sons and seven daughters, and *Firozdin* in 1855. The village has accordingly lapsed to Government. The emoluments enjoyed by the family at present, are as follows :—

			Rs.
Ahmad Ali Khan,	...	...	1,200
Kasim Ali Khan,	...	...	1,200
Haidar Khan,	...	...	720
Ahmad Yar Khan,	...	...	1,440
Jahangir Khan,	...	...	1,620
Abdul Majid Khan,	...	...	3,000
Abdul Hamid Khan,	...	...	720
Sadik Ali Khan,	...	...	360
Shamsher Ali Khan,	...	...	360

Abdul Majid Khan is the only son of *Shah Nawaz Khan*. His mother was a Bamazai lady, daughter of Abdul Karim Khan, some time governor of the Derajat, and brother of Wazir Shah Wali Khan, minister of Ahmad Shah Durani. *Abdul Majid Khan* is much respected in Lahore, where he is a Member of the Municipal Committee and an Honorary Magistrate. He has been active in all measures for the good of the city, and has given satisfaction, as a Magistrate, by the justice of his decisions.

He is a man of considerable learning and is well versed in medicine. In January 1865 he was created a Nawab by the Supreme Government.

MAKDUM SHAH MAHMUD KURESHI.

1. Makdum Baha-ud-din Zikriya.
2. Makdum Haidar Jahan Katal.
3. Makdum Shah Rukn-ul-alam Abul-fatah.
4. Shaikh Ismail Shahid.
5. Shaikh Muhammad Sadr-ud-din.
6. Shaikh Ismail Sirwari.
7. Shaikh Amal-ud-din.
8. Shaikh Yusaf.
9. Shaikh Shahrullah.
10. Shaikh Baha-ud-din.
11. Shaikh Kabir.
12. Shaikh Kaim Muhammad.
13. Shaikh Kabir Sadi.
14. Shaikh Baha-ud-din.
15. Shaikh Kaim-ud-din.
16. Shaikh Muhammad Zikriya.
17. Shaikh Muhammad Ghaus.
18. Shaikh Baha-ud-din.
19. Shaikh Muhammad Ghaus.
20. Shaikh Makdum Bahawan Shah.
21. Makdum Shaikh Kabir-ud-din.
22. Makdum Shah Mahmud.

HISTORY OF THE FAMILY.

In the Multan district, *Makdum Shah Mahmud,* descendant of the celebrated Muhammadan Saint *Baha-ud-din,* is the foremost man both in rank and influence. He is the hereditary guardian of the shrines of *Baha-ud-din,* and of *Rukn-ul-alam* his grandson. His disciples and followers are numerous both in the south of the Panjab and in Sind, and his great influence has always been exerted on the side of law and order. *Baha-ud-din* was born at Kot Kiror in the Leia district, in the year 1170. He was descended lineally from Asad the son of Hasham the grandfather of the prophet. His ancestor Sultan Hussain had come to India with Sultan Mahmud of Ghazni in one of his many Indian expeditions and had settled at Kot Kiror. *Baha-ud-din* soon left his home and went to Khorasan, where he became a pupil of Shahab-ud-din Sawardi and was soon distinguished for his learning. He then set out on his travels, and for many years wandered over Turkistan, Syria and Arabia. He returned to India in 1222 intending to settle at Multan. There was some opposition to this at first, but he was eventually permitted to do so, and the fame of his miracles and his piety spread over the country and gained for him numerous disciples. While *Baha-ud-din* was in the zenith of his fame and power, the saint Shamash Tabrez, with one disciple, a boy of some thirteen years of age, arrived at Multan from the west, miraculously crossing the Indus upon the small praying carpet (musalla) used by all Muhammadans. When *Baha-ud-din* heard of his arrival he sent to him a cup full of milk to signify that Multan was already as full of fakirs as it could hold, and that there was not room for one more. Shamash Tabrez returned the milk, having placed a flower on its surface signifying that not only was there room for him but that his fame would be above that of all the holy men who had honored Multan with their presence. On this *Baha-ud-din* was much enraged, and ordered that no one should feed or assist in any way the contumacious saint. He was independent himself of food, but his young disciple soon became hungry and cried for something to eat, and at the call of Shamash Tabrez the docs from the wilderness came and allowed themselves to be milked. In return for their confidence the saint killed one, according to orthodox Muhammadan procedure, and sent the boy into the city to beg fire with which to cook it. But *Baha-ud-din* was not to be disobeyed, and all refused, while one sweetmeat seller threw a vessel of milk in the face of the boy who returned to his master in tears. Then Shamash Tabrez cried aloud, "O sun! from whom I take my name (Persian *Shams*, the sun) come near, and grant me the heat to cook my food, which these unbelievers deny me." The sun descended, and cooked the venison; but it did not return, and to this day is one spear's length nearer Multan than any other part of the world. But, in spite of the irritation caused by interlopers like Shamash Tabrez, *Baha-ud-din* lived to be one hundred years of age, and, dying in 1270, was buried with great pomp, and his shrine is still visited by Muhammadan pilgrims from all parts of India and Afghanistan.

Rukn-ul-alam was little inferior in learning or sanctity to his grandfather *Baha-ud-din.* From what remains of his doctrines, scattered through the works of his disciples, it appears that he taught a modified form of metempsychosis. He asserted that at the day of judgment the wicked would rise in bestial forms suitable to the characters they had borne when on earth ; the cruel man would rise a leopard ; the licentious man, a goat ; the glutton, a pig ; and so on through the animal kingdom. *Rukn-ul-alam* was visited by the Emperors of Dehli more than once, and his name was known throughout Northern India. He died in 1372, and his tomb was built by the Emperor Firoz Toghlak in the fort of Multan.

After the death of *Rukn-ul-alam* Multan passed through many revolutions, but the family of the saint was always respected. It was not till 1443, in the reign of Syad Muhammad that Multan ceased to be a tributary of Dehli. The country, under the weak rule of the Princes who had succeeded the able Firoz Toghlak, had fallen into the greatest disorder, and Multan was specially exposed to attack from Ghor and Kabul. Under these circumstances the inhabitants determined to select a ruler from among themselves. The choice fell upon *Shaikh Yusaf*, who was famed for his learning and piety. His reign was a prosperous one. He restored peace to the country and increased the revenue by his wise administration. He was deposed by an Afghan chief of the Langa tribe whose daughter he had married. This man brought his whole tribe to Multan under pretence of paying homage to the governor, but before going himself into the city he drank a cup of duck's blood. He dined at the governor's table, and in the course of the evening feigned violent pains in his stomach, and called for an emetic, after drinking which he threw up the blood which he had drunk earlier in the evening. The Shaikh was much alarmed and sent for the friends of the chief from the camp who, when they had arrived, armed to the teeth, seized and imprisoned *Shaikh Yusaf*, and placed the traitor on the throne under the name of Kutb-ud-din Mahmud. The usurper sent his prisoner to Dehli, where he was received with consideration by Bheilol Lodi, who even gave his daughter in marriage to the Shaikh's son. In the Ain Akbari the reign of Shaikh Yusaf is stated to have lasted seventeen years; in Ferishta's history only two. The former is more probably correct as *Yusaf* commenced his rule in 1443, and on his deposition he is said to have been received at Dehli by Bheilol Lodi who did not ascend the throne till 1453.

No other member of the family ever ruled in Multan, but many were distinguished for their learning. *Baha-ud-din* grandson of *Shaikh Yusaf*, a follower of the celebrated Haji Abdul Wahab, was a famous scholar. He was sent in 1523, as ambassador to Husain Argun, governor of Tatta, the lieutenant of Babar Shah, who was marching against Multan. The embassy however failed, the town was besieged, taken and sacked, and four years later Multan became again a province of the Dehli empire.

During the Sikh rule the shrines at Multan lost most of the valuable jagirs that had been assigned for their support.

After Maharaja Ranjit Singh had taken Multan in 1818, he assigned cash allowances of 3,500 Rs. to the shrines. Diwan Sawan Mal reduced this to 1,600 Rs. Under the Darbar the revenue, in land and cash, amounted to 2,030 Rs., the Nazrana having been deducted. During the mutiny of 1848-49 *Makdum Shah Mahmud* remained faithful to the Government. He had, it is true, no reason to love the Sikhs, yet his influence and the information he furnished were very valuable, and on the annexation of the Panjab, the allowances of the shrines were confirmed, 700 Rs. in land in perpetuity, subject to good behaviour, and 1,300 Rs. cash, for the life of the then incumbent. One-fourth of the village of Sahinath, which the Makdum had planted in 1834, was released to him in perpetuity as a personal grant.

The shrines of *Baha-ud-din* and *Rukn-ul-alum* had seen many a siege, but that of 1848 was almost too much for them. Situated, as both were, within the fort, they were exposed to the full fire of the besiegers, and were almost reduced to ruins. In 1850 the Local Government proposed a grant of 10,000 Rs. to restore them. This, however, the Supreme Government did not sanction. *Makdum Shah* was, however, an energetic man, and with the help and money of his disciples he restored them, at a great expense, to their former glory.*

In 1857, *Makdum Shah Mahmud* rendered excellent service to Government. He afforded the Commissioner information of every important occurrence that came to his knowledge, provided 20 men and horses for Ghulam Mustafa Khan's risala and several for the new Police risala. He also supplied men for the Police and Infantry levies. With twenty five horsemen he accompanied Colonel Hamilton against the insurgents, took upon himself a portion of the camp duties, and protected the baggage on the line of march. His presence on that occasion had a great effect on the rebels, who saw that the most influential man of their own faith was against them. On the mutiny of the disarmed regiments at Multan, he joined the Commissioner with his followers for the defence of the bridge leading to the cantonments. None of his disciples joined the rebels, and his conduct presents a strong contrast to that of the Makdum of Pakpattan, whose followers were prominent in the Gogaira insurrection. For his services *Shah Mahmud* received a present of 3,000 Rs. The cash allowance to the shrine was exchanged for a jagir worth 1,780 Rs. in addition to the eight wells granted in perpetuity worth 550 Rs. In 1860, the Makdum, on the occasion of the Viceroy's visit to Lahore, received a personal grant of a garden worth 150 Rs. per annum, known as the Bhangiwala Bagh.

Makdum Mahmud Shah is the son of *Shaikh Hassan Shah*, who married *Bibi Raji Sahiba*, daughter of *Shaikh Muhammad Ghaus*, the 19th in descent from *Baha-ud-din*.

---

* Just opposite the shrine of Baha-ud-din is the tomb of the gallant Nawab Muzaffar Khan. At the distance of some fifty paces is the ancient Hindu temple, known as Narsinghpuria or Pailadpuria, the scene of that incarnation of Vishnu, when, taking a form half man half tiger, he came forth from the red-hot pillar and tore in pieces the tyrant Harnakas, who was about to kill his own son Pailad for refusing to acknowledge his divinity.

SADIK MUHAMMAD KHAN BADOZAI OF MULTAN.

- KALU.
  - Haji Zila.
    - Muhammad Khan.
      - Hussain Khan.
        - Sarbdal Khan.
          - Bai Khan.
            - Muhabat Khan.
              - Muhammad Haiyat Khan.
                - Wali Muhammad Khan.
                  - Shah Muhammad Khan.
                    - Muhammad Sarfraz Khan.
                    - Abd-ul-Samad Khan.
                      - Ghulam Kadir Khan, B. 1839.
                      - Ghulam Mohiud-din Khan, D. 1850.
                    - Hafiz Muhammad Sarbuland Khan.
                      - Sadik Muhammad Khan, B. 1814.
                        - Muhammad Sherdil Khan, B. 1829.
                        - Ashak Muhammad Khan, B. 1841.
                        - Dost Muhammad Khan, B. 1849.
                    - Khan Jahan Khan.
                      - Ghulam Hussain Khan, B. 1838.
                  - Haji Ghulam Muhammad Khan.
  - Haji Saffar.
    - Mian Khan.

HISTORY OF THE FAMILY..

The Badozai tribe, like other Afghans, call themselves Bani Israil, or 'Children of Israel' and claim to have emigrated from the Holy Land (Bait-ul-mukaddas) to Afghanistan, where they settled in the mountains of Ghor and Firozah. The question of the Jewish origin of the Afghans is one that has been much discussed, and is too lengthy to be more than noticed here. In physiognomy, in manners and in their religious rites the Afghans much resemble the Jews. Among them is found the custom of driving the 'scape goat,' laden with the sins of the people, into the wilderness; the rite of the passover, offerings for sin and thank-offerings for deliverance from danger. The 'Matla-al-anwar,' written about 1510, considers the Afghans originally Egyptians, who, after the overthrow of Pharaoh in the Red Sea, left their native country, refusing to accept the Jewish faith, which others of the Egyptians adopted. In the 'Tawarikh Sher Shahi' it is stated that many years after the death of Solomon and during the reign of Asaf Syria was invaded by Bukht Nasr (Nebuchadnezzar) who destroyed Jerusalem and expelled the Afghans who settled in Ghor and Ghazni. This is the belief of all the Afghans at the present day, who consider themselves descendants of the captive ten Jewish tribes. The first converted to Muhammadanism was Kais, son of Ais an Afghan chief, who fought under the prophet himself and received from him the title '*Malik Abdal Rashid.*' Whether this story be true or false, it is certain that the tribes inhabiting the Ghor mountains were converted to Muhammadanism very early; probably between the years 60 A. H. and 80 A. H.

The Bani Afghans overran Sistan, Kirman, and part of Khorasan, and attained to great power under Sultan Mahmud; Shahab-ud-din, and Timur Shah, all of whom they accompanied on their Indian expeditions. The family of *Sadik Muhammad Khan* is called Hajizai Badozai, from *Haji Zila* or *Zalla,* who made the pilgrimage to Mecca about the year 1600. When Shah Jahan, in 1637, obtained possession of Kandahar, *Muhammad Khan,* son of *Haji Zila,* retired to Herat, and did not return home till Kandahar was recovered by Shah Abbas II. of Persia, in 1648.

At the time of Shah Jahan's invasion, two Saddozai chiefs, Hussain Khan and Alladad Khan, who had joined the Emperor, retired with him to Hindostan, and obtained permission to settle near Multan, then a province of Dehli, whither many of their tribe followed them. About 1670 *Muhammad Khan,* resolved to emigrate to India. Hussain Khan, Saddozai, hearing of this intention, and fearing that his influence might suffer by the arrival of the new chief at Multan, wrote to Sherak, chief of the Tarin tribe, to assassinate him while passing through the Tarin country to Kohat. Sherak, accordingly invited *Muhammad Khan* to an entertainment and poisoned him. *Hussain Khan*, his son, was too young to avenge his father's death, but his cousin *Mian Khan* assembled the Badozais, and attacking Sherak and his tribe, defeated him and put his family to death; but that chief himself escaped and fled to Dehli where he entered the service of the Emperor. Here he was followed by *Mian Khan* who stabbed him in the very presence of Aurangzib. On the story of Sherak's treachery being told the Emperor, *Mian Khan* was pardoned for the murder; but for his insolence in killing his enemy in open Darbar, he was imprisoned at Dehli for twelve years. Both the son and grandson of *Muhammad Khan* remained at Kandahar, and it was not till 1738, when Nadir Shah had captured the city, that *Bai Khan* his great grandson, emigrated to Multan. He returned a few years afterwards to Kandahar, but his son *Muhabat Khan* remained at Multan.

The family, till the time of *Shah Muhammad Khan*, were entirely engaged in agriculture. He was a man of energy and took service in the army of Ahmad Shah Durani, in his several invasions of India. In 1772 he assisted Shuja Khan, governor of Multan, to defend the city against Jhanda Singh and Ganda Singh the Bhangi chiefs, who took it after a brave defence. Shuja Khan soon after died, and Muzaffar Khan applied for help to Timur Shah, son of Ahmad Shah Durani, who marched against Multan and recovered it, after a siege of forty days, from the Sikhs, in 1779. Muzaffar Khan was appointed governor, and for his services, *Shah Muhammad* received a jagir at Derah Dinpanah and one at Derah Ghazi Khan, worth 10,000 Rs. It was not long before Nawab Muzaffar Khan became jealous of the power and influence of *Khah Muhammad*, and the latter thought it prudent to retire from Multan. He joined the army of Timur Shah then advancing against Bahawalpur, and so much distinguished himself at the siege of Deirawar that he was made by the Prince governor of the Derah Ghazi Khan with its dependencies, and custodian of the Deirawar fort. Very soon after the departure of Timur Shah, the Khan of Bahawalpur recovered the fort, and a year later Shah Muhammad died. *Sarfraz Khan* succeeded to his father's jagirs, but made no effort to keep the governorship of Mankera and Derah Ghazi Khan to which Abd-un-nabi the ex-ruler of Sind was appointed. He however became obnoxious for his tyranny, and as he failed to pay the Government dues, he was superseded in favour of Muhammad Khan Saddozai, and the governor of Multan and *Sarfraz Khan* Badozai were directed to aid the new ruler. Abd-un-nabi made a vigorous resistance, but near Leia an action was fought in which he was defeated and his son Mian Araf slain. The fort and town of Leia surrendered to the victors, but *Sarfraz Khan* was shot as he was riding through the city. Muhammad Khan then obtained possession of the country. He was a wise and beneficent ruler, and his great grandson is at the present day Nawab of Derah Ismail Khan.

On the death of *Sarfraz Khan,* his brothers *Abd-al-Samad Khan* and *Hafiz Sarbuland Khan* straightway began to quarrel, and the former contrived to seize the whole estate. *Sarbuland Khan,* on this, went to Kabul to obtain redress from the Emperor and received an allowance of 6,500 Rs., of which 4,500 Rs. was to be paid from the revenues of Multan. An order was also passed that the estate should be equally divided between the brothers; but *Abd-ul-Samad Khan* would not hear of division, and it was only the jagir in Multan which the Nawab was able to obtain for *Sarbuland Khan.*

The elder brother *Abd-ul-Samad Khan* was engaged in constant hostilities with Muzaffar Khan, Nawab of Multan; and in 1801, after the fall of Zaman Shah, the influence of Fatah Khan Barakzai, the new minister at the Kabul Court, obtained the nomination of the Badozai chief as governor. Muzaffar Khan had no intention of submitting. He called in the Bahawalpur chief to his aid, who sent 5,000 troops under Jiun Ram and Din Muhammad Khan. These with the Multan troops under Gulam Murtwa, besieged *Abd-al-Samad* in his fort at Dinpanah. Here he was joined by 1,000 horsemen of Mir Alim the governor of Derah Ghazi Khan, but this reinforcement only enabled him to prolong his resistance: the fort was eventually stormed and taken, while *Abd al-Samad* fled to Lahore to induce Ranjit Singh, then rising to power, to espouse his cause. Influenced somewhat by his representations and more by his own ambition, the Lahore chief attacked Multan several times, and at length, in 1818, captured it; Muzaffar Khan and his five sons dying in the defence.

Hafiz Sarbuland Khan had always stood high in the favour of the Multan Nawabs; and when they fell, he received, notwithstanding his brave conduct at Multan against the Sikhs, a command of two hundred horse from Ranjit Singh, and was sent to watch the frontiers of Bahawalpur. After the capture of Mankera in 1821, he received a jagir of 2,000 Rs. in the Leia district, which he retained till 1829, when it was exchanged for one of the same value in Multan. He served faithfully throughout the whole Multan campaign of 1848-49 and died in 1853, half of his jagir descending to his son, *Sadik Muhammad Khan.*

The quarrelsome *Abd-al-Samad Khan* was not so fortunate. Asad Allah Khan Biloch of Sakkar, who farmed the customs of Leia, was his great enemy, and they fought so continually that the country became impoverished and Asad Allah Khan had to throw up the contract, as he could not collect the revenue. The Maharaja then told *Abd-al-Samad* that he must either accept a jagir in another part of the country, or take the contract himself. He accepted the latter alternative as the lesser evil of the two; though it proved to be the greater; for two years afterwards, from his own carelessness and the dishonesty of his agents, he fell two lakhs of rupees into arrears; and not being able to pay, his whole property was seized and his jagir sequestered. An allowance of 3,200 Rs. was, however, paid him, which he held till his death in 1850. The British Government gave his sons a pension of 1,400 Rs., but the younger *Ghulam Mohi-ud-din,* was thrown from his carriage and killed in 1860, and 700 Rs.

of the pension was resumed. The allowance was again increased to 1,000 Rs. in November 1860.

Sadik Muhammad Khan was born in 1814. When sixteen years of age he was placed in command of 10 sowars, on 1,200 Rs. per annum, by Diwan Sawan Mal, governor of Multan. He accompanied the Diwan on his expedition, in 1833, against the Gurchani, Nishari, Laghari and Khosa tribes, when they made their incursion into Dajal and Khanpur and fought in the skirmish at the Kala Pahar. After this he was thought worthy of an independent command, and was sent with forty horsemen to Harrappa, and later received charge of the Ilakas of Kamalia and Syadwala. In 1838, he again had to march against his first enemies the Gurchanis and Nisharis, who had descended upon the plains and were ravaging the country, and drove them back to the hills with considerable loss. In November, 1843, he attacked and defeated the Katah tribe, which had taken advantage of the anarchy succeeding the murder of Maharaja Sher Singh to plunder the Syadwala, Satgharrah and Haveli districts. In September, 1844, Diwan Sawan Mal was assassinated, and his son and successor Mulraj sent *Sadik Muhammad* back to Kamalia with full civil and military powers. In 1845, he was sent against Fatah Khan Tiwana who had murdered Payindah Khan, Khajakzai with his son Sikandar Khan, and Ashik Muhammad Khan Alizai, father of Ghulam Hassan Khan, ambassador at the court of Kabul, and had forcibly seized the government of the province of Derah Ismail Khan. He was soon, however, compelled to return to his own district, where, at the time of the Satlej campaign, the Muhammadan tribes, Kharrals and Fatianas, had risen in revolt. Karam Nayaran, brother of Diwan Mulraj, was with the force of *Sadik Muhammad,* and the tribes were dispersed, with the loss of many of their number, including Walidad, elder brother of Bahawal Fattiana, who was imprisoned for life for rebellion in 1857.

When the rebellion broke out, at Multan, in April 1848, and Mulraj had summoned all his officers to swear fidelity to him on their respective

Scriptures, *Sadik Muhammad Khan,* with his father, refused to take the oath, and at the first opportunity went over to Major H. B. Edwardes, with whom he served faithfully throughout the war. His local knowledge was invaluable to the Engineer and Quarter Master General's Departments, and Majors Napier and Becher, and Major General Whish bore the warmest testimony to his valuable and zealous services. But the loyalty of *Sadik Muhammad* did not spring so much from love to the Lahore Government or to the British as from dislike to Diwan Mulraj. This governor was of a very different character from his father, and though not without ability was avaricious and suspicious. His confidence he only gave to Hindus, and consequently the Pathans in his employ all forsook him when a convenient opportunity offered. *Sadik Muhammad Khan,* at the close of the war, received a pension of 2,000 Rs., besides khillats and valuable presents and a garden at Multan, and retired with his well won honours from active service.

On the first outbreak of the mutiny of 1857 he was at Lahore and offered his services to Government. An order had been already sent to Multan for him to raise 100 sowars for active service, but, owing to his absence, these men were raised by Haji Ghulam Mustafa Khan. On his return south he accompanied Colonel Hamilton in the expedition against the Gogaira insurgents. He was present in the action that ensued, and was useful in preparing rafts, by which the force crossed the Ravi at Thalli. In 1860 he was made assessor of Income Tax at Multan, and performed his duties with intelligence and honesty. In exchange for his pension he obtained the Muhammad Khan-wala garden in perpetuity and a life jagir at Lutfabad and Kot Malik and a well in Bahawalpur, worth together 2,937 Rs. When the Income Tax Assessment was completed he was appointed Tehsildar of Shujaabad and has since been successively transferred to Lodran, Mailsi and Sarai Sidhu. The only other member of the family in Government employ is *Ghulam Hussain Khan,* son of *Khan Jahan Khan,* who is Thanadar of Kolachi in the Derah Ismail Khan district.

MUHAMMAD ISMAIL KHAN SIAL.

- Ghazi Khan.
  - Sultan Mahmud.
  - Lal Khan.
  - Mahram Khan.
    - Walidad
      - Khan Khan.
    - Bahram Khan.
      - Inayatullah Khan.
        - Sultan Mahmud.
        - Sahib Khan.
    - Sher Khan.
      - Shahadat Khan.

- RASHID KHAN.
  - Sher Khan.
    - Jahan Khan.
      - Khair Khan.
        - Dargahi Khan.
          - Ismail Khan.
            - Kabir Khan.
              - Fatah Khan.
              - Ahmad Khan.
                - Inayat Khan.
                  - Amir Khan.
                    - Ahmad Khan.
                - Muhammad Ismail Khan.
                  - Kabir Khan.
              - Jahan Khan.
                - Jalal Khan.
                  - Walidad Khan.

HISTORY OF THE FAMILY.

The Sials of Jhang are a Muhammadan tribe of great antiquity, and until the time of Maharaja Ranjit Singh possessed great power in the country bordering on the Chenab. They were originally Rajputs, and their ancestor Rai Shankar was a resident of Dhara Nagar, between Allahabad and Fatahpur. He emigrated, about the year 1230, to Jaunpur, and on his death, great dissentions arose between the different branches of the family, and his son *Sial*, in 1243, during the reign of Sultan Alla-ud-din, left Jaunpur for the Panjab, which had been two years before overrun by the Mogals. It seems that owing to the unsettled state of the lower provinces many Rajput families about this time emigrated to the Panjab, where they sooner or later adopted the Muhammadan faith. Among them were ancestors of the tribes known as the

Kharrals, Tiwanas, Ghebas, Chiddars, and the Panwar Sials.* *Sial* in search of a good place for settlement visited Pak Pattan, then called Ajodhan, and the residence of the famous Muhammadan saint Baba Farid-ud-din Shakarganj. He, with all his family, converted by the eloquence of the Saint, turned Musalman, and renewing his wanderings, came to † Sialkot, a very ancient Rajput settlement, where he built a fort. He soon left, however, and at Sahiwal, in the Shahpur district, married Sohag, the daughter of Bhao Khan Maikan, who bore him three sons,‡ *Bharmi*, *Kohli* and *Mahani*, each the founder of a Sial clan. *Kohli* led his tribe into the unoccupied lands of Chohistan and Kachhi, where for several generations they lived wholly engaged in pastoral pursuits.

Mahpal sixth in descent from *Sial*, about the year 1380 founded the town of Mankera, afterwards so celebrated, and his great grandson *Mal Khan* founded Jhang Sial, on the Chenab, in 1462. He was four years afterwards summoned to Lahore, and granted the territory of Jhang in hereditary possession, paying revenue to the Mogal emperors. Both *Mal Khan* and his son *Dowlat Khan* were liberal and intelligent chiefs, and much improved the district. *Ghazi Khan*, son of *Dowlat Khan*, built the fort of Choutra, and his cousin *Khewa Khan* the fort of Khewa, ten miles to the north of Jhang.

Jalal Khan the fourth chief of Jhang, was murdered by his nephew *Pahar Khan*, who had founded Paharpur in Uchh. His grandson *Firoz Khan* avenged his death, capturing Paharpur, and putting to

---

* The Tiwana, Gheb and Sial tribes have a common origin. Rai Shankar had three sons, Saino, Tenu and Gheo. From the first have descended the Sials ; the Tiwanas from the second, and the Ghebas from Gheo the youngest.

† Vide ante. p. 12.

‡ The story goes that Bharmi, Kohli and Mahani were playing together, when children, with a clay cow for a toy. Bharmi personated the husbandman, the owner of the cow ; Mahani was the thief who stole it, while Kohli was the chief and sat in mock judgment on the offender. This boyish play was prophetic, and in later years the reigning house of Sial was from the descendants of Kohli ; Bharmi's sons were simple peasants, and if news of a strayed buffalo was required, something was generally to be heard about it in the Mahani clan.

death all the descendants of *Pahar Khan* whom he took prisoners. *Kabir Khan, Jahan Khan, Ghazi Khan, Sultan Mahmud Khan, Lal Khan* and *Mahram Khan* were the next successive chiefs. *Walidad Khan* the thirteenth chief was the most famous and most powerful. He disarmed the Rais of Mírak, Shorkot, Kot Kamalia, and Khewah, and assigned them service jagirs. He brought large tracts of waste land under cultivation, and by his strong and wise government cleared the 'Bâr' of robbers. The Lahore Government, to which he remained faithful, although he might, with safety, have thrown off its yoke, granted him the fort and Ilaka of Chuniot, and he thus became possessed of the greater part of the country between the Ravi and the Chenab, as far North as Pindi Bhattian, also holding the country to the west of the Chenab and Jhelam, as far as Mankera. He died in 1747, and was succeeded by his nephew *Inayat Ullah Khan*, who had for minister his first cousin *Shahadat Khan*. In two years the cousins remained warm friends, but at length quarreling, *Shahadat Khan* took up arms against *Inayat*, but was totally defeated and forced to fly to Kadarpur across the river. Not disheartened, he raised a fresh force and attacked his cousin, but was again defeated and slain. *Inayat Khan* was shortly after this carried off prisoner to Syadpur by forty picked sowars belonging to his kinsmen of that town, who had espoused the cause of *Shahadat Khan*, but after six months he was released. He was a brave and a successful General, and is said to have won 22 battles. The most important of these were against the chiefs of Multan, who were encroaching on the Jhang territory and the recovery of Chuniot from the Bhangi Sirdars.

Inayat Khan died in 1787, and the rule of his son *Sultan Mahmud* who was an imbecile, did not last long, for his half brother *Sahib Khan*, son of *Inayat Khan* by a concubine, who had sworn allegiance to him on the Koran, rose in arms, and imprisoned him in the fort of Choutra, where he was put to death. *Sahib Khan* was himself assassinated soon after, in the house of Amar Khan, where he had gone to celebrate his marriage. The next Rais of Jhang, *Kabir Khan*, son of *Ismail Khan* brought back the direct line which had gone out with *Jahan Khan.* He was of a mild and peaceful disposition, and was much loved by his tribe. After a rule of eleven years he abdicated in favour of his son *Ahmad Khan,* who was the last of the Sial chiefs. The Sikhs had by this time become very powerful, and Karram Singh Dulu a Bhangi chief, had conquered Chuniot. Ranjit Singh marched against this fort, which was held by Jassa Singh, son of Karram Singh, and captured it. He then turned towards Jhang, but *Ahmad Khan* agreed to pay 60,000 Rs. yearly, and the Sikh chief accordingly returned to Lahore. This took place in the year 1803. Three years later, however, the Maharaja again invaded Jhang, with a large army, and after some hard fighting took the fort; *Ahmad Khan* escaping to Multan. The district of Jhang was then farmed to Sirdar Fatah Singh, Kalianwala, for 60,000 Rs. per annum. Not long after, *Ahmad Khan* returned with a Pathan force, given him by Muzaffar Khan Nawab of Multan, and recovered a great part of his old territories, Ranjit Singh accepting the former tribute of 60,000 Rs. as he was too fully engaged with other expeditions to march against Jhang.

After the Maharaja had unsuccessfully attacked Multan in 1810, he visited his chagrin on *Ahmad Khan,* whom he suspected of favoring Muzaffar Khan, and having captured him at Serai Sidhu, took him to Lahore, while his son *Inayat Khan* fled to Haidarabad in Sind. Ranjit Singh feared that *Inayat Khan* would excite the Sind Amirs against him, and promised *Ahmad Khan* his release from prison, if he would recall his son and leave him at Lahore as security for his good behaviour. This was done, and *Ahmad Khan* received a jagir of 12,000 Rs. at Mirowal in the Amritsar district. After Ranjit Singh had taken Multan in 1818, he granted *Inayat Khan* a jagir of 3,000 Rs., and on the death of *Ahmad Khan* in 1820, the son succeeded to the jagir. This was in 1823 exchanged for one of the same value at Serai Sidhu, in the Multan district, and in 1830, this was again exchanged for a jagir at Mustanwali, in Leia. In 1838, *Inayat Khan* was killed near Rassulpur, fighting on the side of Diwan Sawan Mal, against Raja Gulab Singh. His brother *Ismail Khan* went to Lahore to endeavour to obtain the confirmation of the jagir in his favour, but the Maharaja was paralytic, and Gulab Singh his enemy in the ascendant, and he only obtained a pension of 100 Rs. a month. He remained at Lahore four years, till his pension was discontinued, and he then returned to Jhang, where he lived upon an allowance of Rs. 41 a month granted to the family by Sawan Mal. This was raised, in 1848, to 60 Rs.

In October, 1848, Major H. Edwardes wrote to *Ismail Khan*, directing him to raise troops in behalf of Government, and to collect the revenue of the district. The poor chief, hoping the time was come when loyalty might retrieve his fortunes, raised a force, and, descending the river, attacked and defeated a rebel chief, Atta Muhammad, at Nikokarah. Afterwards, when Sirdar Sher Singh Attariwala had passed through Jhang and had left Deoraj in command of 1,000 men there, *Ismail Khan* attacked this detachment several times, with varying results. His Jemadar Pir Kumal of Isa Shah, captured at the fort of Taruka another rebel chief named Kanh Das. Thus *Ismail Khan*, the representative of a long and illustrious line of chiefs, stood out bravely on the side of the Government. His influence, which was great in the district, was all used against the rebels, and his services were especially valuable at a time when it was inexpedient to detach a force against the petty rebel leaders. After annexation *Ismail Khan* was made Risaldar of the Jhang mounted Police, but his services were, through inadvertence, overlooked, and it was not till 1856 that he received a pension of 600 Rs. for life. Three wells were also released to him and his male heirs in perpetuity.

In 1857 the services of the chief were conspicuous. He aided in raising a force of cavalry and served in person against the insurgents. For his loyalty he received a khillat of 500 Rs. and the title of Khan Buhadar, and his yearly grant of 600 Rs. was raised to 1,000 Rs. with the addition of a jagir of 350 Rs. for life. In 1860 his pension was, at his own desire, exchanged for a life jagir. He has recovered many of his old Zemindari rights in different villages, and although his estate is only held on a life tenure, yet the Government, on his death, will take care that this illustrious family does not sink into poverty. *Kabir Khan*, the son of *Ismail Khan*, is an Honorary Police Officer in the Jhang district.

Jahan Khan, brother of *Ahmad Khan*, and uncle of *Ismail Khan*, holds a jagir at Chand Burwana and Budhi Thatti worth 887 Rs., an old grant of Ranjit Singh to his father and confirmed for life by the British Government.

COLONEL BADRINATH SIRDAR BUHADAR.

Colonel *Badrinath* is one of the Sikh officers who, on the annexation of the Panjab, transferred their services to the British Government. His father was a native of Cashmir and emigrated to the Panjab at the beginning of the present century. In 1821, *Badrinath* entered the Maharaja's army as a private soldier, and gradually rose through all the grades of the service till, in 1835, he was made Colonel which rank he held till the second Sikh war. He saw plenty of fighting during these years and was in the campaigns of Swat, Peshawar, Hazara, Yusafzai, Bannu, Tirah and numerous actions. For long he served on the frontier; six years in charge of the forts of Dera Ismail Khan and Tank. He was with Sirdar Hari Singh Nalwa in 1833, when that chief, in the most masterly manner, won Peshawar from the Barakzais. In 1844 he was stationed in Hazara under Diwan Moolraj Dilwalwala, with the Katar Mukhi Regiment and some Gurkhas.

In 1846 he accompanied Major H. Laurence to Cashmir where Shaikh Immamuddin Khan was in revolt, and the next year went with Lieutenant Edwardes to Bannu.

He served throughout the siege of Multan with the Katar Mukhi, and after the close of the war retained his command, till, on the introduction of the new police, he took his discharge. Colonel *Badrinath* was known as a brave and able officer, and the force under him was always in good discipline. In 1857, the fort of Multan, the magazine and the treasury were intrusted to his corps, and the regiment also furnished detachments which fought against the mutineers and insurgents with gallantry and credit.

In 1861, the Government in sanctioning his retirement granted him a life pension of 3,600 Rs., inclusive of the allowance attached to the order of British India, which he obtained in 1857 in recognition of his loyalty and gallantry.

MUHAMMAD SARAFRAZ KHAN KHARRAL.

KAMAL KHAN.
- Said Khan.
  - Kamal-ud-din Khan.
    - Muhammad Khan.
      - Sakhi Saadat Yar Khan.
        - Ahmad Yar Khan.
          - Abdullah Khan.
        - Muhammad Yar Khan.
          - Ghulam Muhammad Khan.
            - Saadat Yar Khan.
              - Muhammad Muzaffar Khan.
              - Muhammd Sarafraz Khan
                - Muhammad Amir Ali Khan
              - Khan Kahan Khan.
                - Muhammad Khan.

HISTORY OF THE FAMILY.

The Kharral tribe, of which the late *Sarafraz Khan* was the acknowledged head, claims to be of Rajput descent, and traces its genealogy up to Raja Karam of the Lunar dynasty, a famous king of Hastinapur, The Kharrals have their chief settlements in the swampy jungles of the Gogaira district. There are many of them in Jhang, and they hold some forty villages in Lahore, chiefly about Shaikhopura. Through all historic times the Kharrals have been a turbulent, savage and thievish tribe, ever impatient of control and delighting in strife and plunder. More fanatic than other Muhammadan tribes they submitted with the greatest reluctance to Hindu rule, and it was as much Diwan Sawan Mal and the Sikhs could do to restrain them, for whenever an organized force was sent against them they retired into the marshes and thick jungle where it was almost impossible to follow them. Once they rebelled under British rule, during the disturbances of 1857, and the lesson taught them at that time will be sufficient for this generation at least.

Kamal Khan is the first of the tribe whose identity is very clear. He founded Kot Kamalia, in the 16th century, some forty miles to the south of Jhang, where lived the Sials, whom the Kharrals claimed as kinsmen but with whom they were always fighting. This claim of kinship was not liked by the Sials, and some of the most bitter quarrels between the tribes arose out of it. Once on a time, a Dehli prince, whose name is now forgotten, came to Kumalia, where *Saadat Yar Khan* was ruling, and was so much pleased with his handsome face and gallant bearing that he thought to patch up the disputes between the Kharrals and the Sials by an alliance ; and proposed that Ghazi Khan the eighth chief of Jhang should betroth his daughter to *Saadat Khan*. The Jhang chief was irritated beyond measure, and killed the unfortunate bearer of the proposal ; while he was himself murdered some time later by the prince's followers in retaliation.

There was yet another betrothal which brought great troubles upon the Kharrals. One Mirza, belonging to the Sahi branch of the tribe, fell desperately in love with his first cousin Sahiba, who was as fond of him though for long betrothed to a young man named Khanzad, and on the very night of the marriage, when all the friends were assembled, her lover put her on his thoroughbred mare and galloped off to Dhanabad. The clan mounted and pursued in hot haste ; and they caught the gallant before he reached home, and killed him though he fought hard for his life. Sahiba they carried home with them, and though her betrothed wished to spare her life, her parents strangled her. These murders were the cause of such bloody feuds between the clans that it at length was thought inauspicious to have daughters, and as soon as they were born they were strangled as Sahiba had been. This custom of female infanticide was common among the Kharrals till Colonel Hamilton, Commissioner of Multan, persuaded them to discontinue it.

Lal Khan the son and successor of Ghazi Khan of Jhang was not fonder of *Saadat Yar Khan* than his father had been. The Kamalia chief had called him the son of a dancing girl, and he gathered his Sials, and marched against Kamalia where he shut *Saadat Khan* up in the fort. "Come out," said Lal Khan, "come out and see what entertainment the son of the dancing girl can give you." But *Saadat Khan* was not to be tempted, and Lal Khan returned to Jhang, having plundered the whole of the Kharral country.

Walidad Khan the thirteenth chief of Jhang was in favour in court. He took possession of Kamalia; assigned the chief a service jagir, and held his conquest during his whole rule. His successor Inayat Khan, was either more generous or more foolish, for he restored Kamalia to *Muhammad Yar Khan* and *Ahmad Yar Khan* the sons of *Saadat Khan*. But in the next generation it was again lost. Sirdar Kamar Singh Nakkai conquered it, and on his death, it fell into the hands of Sirdar Ram Singh, head of the rival Nakkai house, whose father Nar Singh had been killed in a fight with the Kharrals.

Ghulam Muhammad Khan can scarcely be said to have had any power whatever; and his son *Saadat Yar Khan* the Second was not much more fortunate. For a short time he recovered his patrimony, for when in 1798, Shah Zaman invaded the Panjab, and the Sikhs took to flight in all directions, Muzaffar Khan governor of Multan thinking the opportunity not to be lost, marched to Kamalia, and drove out the Sikhs after a severe fight. *Saadat Yar Khan* was reinstated, but he did not hold his own very long for in 1803 he was compelled, after a fruitless struggle, to submit to Ranjit Singh who annexed Kamalia to Lahore. *Saadat Yar Khan* fled to the protection of Nawab Muzaffar Khan of Multan. Ranjit Singh, however, recalled him, and gave him proprietary rights over forty villages, in which he was succeeded by his son *Muzaffar Khan*. In 1810, the Maharaja gave him the village of Muhammad Shah which he held through Sawan Mal's administration.

Muzaffar Khan was succeeded by his brother *Muhammad Sarfaraz Khan*, who was an able man and a brave soldier. He held the family jagirs throughout the reign of Ranjit Singh, but Raja Hira Singh reduced them 300 Rs. This chief rendered excellent service at various times to the British Government. In 1831 he gave ready assistance to Lieutenant Burnes' embassy, when proceeding up the Ravi to Lahore. In the second Sikh war of 1848-49, he remained faithful to Government. Acting on the orders of the Resident, he raised his clan and attacked the Sikhs, whom, it must be confessed, he had good private reasons for hating. He captured from the rebels the fort of Talamba, and garrisoned it with his own men, and at the close of the war he was rewarded with a life pension of 500 Rs. a year. An assignment of 275 Rs. a year from the town dues of Kamalia was also allowed him. In September 1857, when a large portion of his tribe, under Ahmad Khan, rebelled, *Sarfaraz Khan* remained loyal. It was he who first gave to Captain Elphinstone information of the intended insurrection, coming to his house at night, half an hour after the Kharral chiefs had fled, and thus enabling that officer to obtain assistance from Lahore. He was afterwards most useful in procuring information of the movements of the rebels and after their dispersion in recovering the plunder. For these services, he received the title of Khan Buhadar; a khillat of 500 Rs. and a jagir of 525 Rs. for life.

Sarfaraz Khan died in October 1863, and his jagirs and pensions, amounting 1,775 Rs., lapsed to Government, with the exception of eleven wells worth 157 Rs. released in perpetuity. He left one son *Muhammad Amir Ali Khan*, who is now about seventeen years of age.

UTTAM SINGH NAKKAI.

- CHOWDRI MITTA.
  - Dewa Singh.
  - Kamar Singh.
  - Wazir Singh.
    - Mihr Singh.
      - Jaimal Singh.
      - Dhara Singh.
        - Uttam Singh, B. 1848.
        - Sher Singh, B. 1856.
      - Fatah Singh.
        - Chama Singh. B. 1846.
    - Mohr Singh.
      - Hira Singh.
  - Chanda Singh.
  - Mukair Singh.
  - Malka Singh.

HISTORY OF THE FAMILY.

The Nakka country, between Lahore and Gogaira, has given its name to two families, that of Sirdar Khan Singh of Bahrwal and that of *Dhara Singh* of Gogaira. Between the families there was no relationship, but they were near neighbours and were engaged in perpetual quarrels.

Kamar Singh, son of Chowdhri *Mitta,* was a bold and successful chief, and took possession of Kot Kamalia, Syadwala and the surrounding country. He generally contrived to hold his own against Sirdar Ran Singh of Bahrwal, but shortly before his death, in 1780, Syadwala fell into the hands of the enemy. *Wazir Singh,* who succeeded his brother, recovered the town from Bhagwan Singh, son of Ran Singh, and the fighting between the rival chiefs went on as fiercely and with as little result as ever. To strengthen himself Bhagwan Singh married his sister to the infant son of Mahan Singh Sukarchakia, but this alliance did him little good, as in 1783, Sirdar Jai Singh Kanheya, who was angry with Mahan Singh for sacking Jammu and deceiving Hakikat Singh Kanheya, marched into the Nakka country, and seized the territory of both *Wazir Singh* and

Bhagwan Singh with the greatest impartiality. The chiefs had however their revenge, for two years later they joined the Sukarchakias and Ramgharias in the attack on the Kanheyas, when the power of that great confederacy was broken and Sirdar Gurbaksh Singh slain.

Sirdar *Wazir Singh* was murdered in 1790 by Dal Singh, son of Hira Singh of Bahrwal, but his death was avenged on the assassin by a devoted servant, who slew Dal Singh in his own house and surrounded by his family and clan. *Mihr Singh* succeeded to the estate and held it till 1804, when his brother *Mohr Singh* excited the indignation of Ranjit Singh by secretly betrothing his daughter to Ishar Singh, the reputed son of Rani Mehtab Kour. Ranjit Singh knew that he was not the father of the child, but *Mohr Singh's* presumption gave him a good excuse for seizing all the estates of the family. This he did, only leaving a jagir worth 4,000 Rs.

Sirdar *Mihr Singh* died in 1843. His son *Dhara Singh* succeeded him, and during the Firozpur campaign rendered himself conspicuous by raising a band of horsemen, and plundering the country in every direction. For this conduct, on the return of peace, his jagirs were confiscated by the Darbar. In 1848 he joined Raja Sher Singh, with his sowars, at Multan. He soon, however, returned to his home, but was induced by Ahmad Khan, the celebrated leader of the Kharral tribe, to fortify Satgharah, and make a stand against the British. *Dhara Singh* consented, but his treacherous friend betrayed him to the Government and brought a force against him, which defeated him with considerable loss. He then fled to the Sikh army, and fought in the battles of Ramnagar and Gujrat. Some time after annexation the Board of Administration, finding him in great poverty, procured for him a pension of 300 Rs.

During the disturbances of 1857, *Dhara Singh* had an opportunity of avenging himself upon his old enemy, Ahmad Khan. This chief, who had great influence with the Kharrals and who had headed many successful insurrections in his day, thought the mutiny of 1857 an opportunity for disturbance and plunder which it would be criminal to miss, so he called the tribe to arms and invited *Dhara Singh* to join him. But the Sirdar thought of his ruined homestead and his plundered harvest, and gave information to the Government of Ahmad Khan's intentions. He joined the force under Major Marsden and marched against the rebels. He was present in several engagements and claims to have shot Ahmad Khan with his own hand. When the outbreak was crushed he gave important information which insured the conviction of many of the rebels. Whether *Dhara Singh* was influenced by loyalty or by revenge his services were equally valuable, and he received as a reward for them an additional grant of 300 Rs. per annum, with 2 villages Gasgorian and Mihr Singhwala, worth 200 Rs. which had belonged to his old jagir, in perpetuity.

Dhara Singh died in 1860, leaving two sons *Uttam Singh* and *Sher Singh*.

RAWALPINDI.

THE TIWANA MALIKS.

- AMIR ALI KHAN.
  - Mir Ahmad Khan.
    - Dadu Khan.
    - Mir Khan.
      - Sher Khan.
      - Alam Sher Khan.
        - Khan Muhammad Khan.
          - Chiragh Khan.
            - Ghulam Hassan Khan.
              - Mir Baz Khan.
              - Sher Khan.
            - Ghulam Ali Khan.
          - Ahmad Yar Khan.
            - Kadir Baksh Khan.
              - Sher Muhammad Khan.
            - Alim Khan.
            - Sahib Khan.
            - Jahan Khan.
            - Fatah Khan.
          - Khuda Yar Khan.
            - Fatah Khan.
              - Fatah Sher Khan.
              - Alim Sher Khan.
              - Sher Buhadar Khan.
              - Ahmad Khan.
              - Sultan Khan.
          - Fatah Khan.
          - Alim Sher Khan.
        - Khan Beg Khan.

HISTORY OF THE FAMILY.

From a common ancestor have descended three remarkable tribes, the Sials of Jhang, the Ghebas of Pindi Gheb and the Tiwanas of Mitha Tiwana in Shahpur. The Ghebas know but little of their past history, but they are claimed as kin by both Sials and Tiwanas who till lately were agreed as to their respective descent from Gheo, Tenu or Teo and Seo, the three sons of Rai Shankar a Rajput of Dharanagar, the ancestor of the Ghebas being Gheo, of the Tiwanas Teo, and of the Sials Seo. The bards of the Tiwana tribe have lately been making further enquiries and have now a different story which will be more easily understood by an extract from the genealogy.

KAMADEO.

- Karam Chand.
  - Tiwana, fourth in descent from Karam Chand.
    - Mailu, sixth in descent from Tiwana.
      - Titu.
        - Mal, from whom have descended the Tiwanas.
        - Marukh, from whom have descended the Ghebas.
      - * Wattu, from whom have descended the Daudputras of Bahawalpur.
      - Lakhu, from whom have descended the Hindu Tiwanas of Pattiala.
- Bijdeo.
  - Rai Shankar, third in descent from Bijdeo. From Rai Shankar have descended the Sials.

Whether the amended genealogy is more truthful than before it is impossible to say. It certainly seems more probable than the regular descent from the three sons of Rai Shankar. If the Tiwanas did not come to the Panjab with the Sials, their emigration was no long time after, and must have been before the close of the fifteenth century. They soon embraced Muhammadanism and settled at Jahangir on the Indus where they remained till the time of *Mir Ali Khan*, who by the advice of his spiritual guide, Fakir Sultan Haji, moved eastward with his tribe and many of the Shaikhs, Shahlolis, Mundials and others. He arrived at the country then called Danda, and founded the

* More will be said in the history of Bahawalpur regarding the alleged Hindu origin of the Daudputras. They themselves trace back to Abbas the uncle of the prophet Muhammad, and make Daud Khan, their ancestor, the great grandson of Chini Khan Amir of Sind, while, in truth, he was a weaver of Shikarpur, neither related to the Amir or the Prophet and only remarkable as a successful freebooter. Almost every Muhammadan family considers it a point of honour to trace its genealogy up to Abbas or Asad or some near relative of the Prophet, and many only stop at Noah or Adam.

village of Oukhli Moula, in the Shahpur district. His son *Mir Ahmad Khan,* about the year 1680, built Mitha Tiwana, seven miles east of Oukhli, where he had found sweet water, from which the town was named. (*mitha* ; sweet). This chief was engaged in constant hostilities with the Awans his neighbours to the north, and at Hadali, five miles from Mitha Tiwana, defeated them with great slaughter. *Dadu Khan* and *Sher Khan,* the third and fourth Maliks, improved and enlarged Mitha Tiwana, which soon became a flourishing town, and many settlers from other parts of the country took up their residence in it ; Awans from Jhelam ; Kurars from Mankera ; Chahals from the neighbourhood of Lahore, and Nuns from the upper Chenab.

Sher Khan became Malik in an irregular way. Discontented with the severe rule of his father, he rebelled with his brother *Alam Sher Khan,* and assassinating their uncle *Mir Khan,* killed their father in a skirmish outside the walls of the fort. The two brothers seem to have lived together without fighting between themselves, a circumstance remarkable enough among the Tiwanas, and they considerably enlarged their territory at the expense of the Awans, seizing Wurcha and other territory at the foot of the hills. It is related that *Alam Sher Khan,* thinking Awan shooting the finest sport in the world, would frequently go alone to the mountains with his gun, and after shooting two or three Awans, as other less ambitious men shoot partridges, would return to breakfast. *Sher Khan* now thought himself strong enough to refuse the tribute the Tiwanas had hitherto paid to the governors of Derah Ismail Khan. His brother accordingly attacked the troops which had been sent to collect it on their return march, and taking them by surprise, routed them with the loss of their leader. About the year 1745 *Sher Khan* founded Nurpur Tiwana, which soon became a large and thriving village. Some years later he contrived to quarrel with Inayat Khan the fighting chief of Jhang Sial. The latter had won Mari, on the right bank of the Jhelam, from the Nawab of Multan, and had placed it in charge of *Sher Khan* who was to receive a certain sum for its management. This was not paid with any regularity, and *Sher Khan* thinking to exact it by force, assembled his clan and driving the Sials out of Khai laid siege to Kot Langar Khan. Inayat Khan marched to relieve it, and defeated the Tiwanas in a battle before the walls. *Sher Khan* died in 1767, leaving two sons *Khan Muhammad Khan*, and *Khan Beg Khan*. His brother *Alam Sher Khan* had fallen some time before in an expedition against the Punchars. The first occupation of *Khan Muhammad* the new chief was the suppression of a revolt of the Hasnal and Mastial tribes who inhabited Butala,* Hadali and Hamokah. In this he was successful, and he then went to Jhang to visit his kinsman, leaving Mitha Tiwana in charge of his brother. On his return he found the gates closed against him and his brother the acknowledged chief. He then retired to Nurpur Tiwana, where he raised troops and marched against *Khan Beg Khan*, who was defeated and thrown into prison. He was however soon released, promising obedience for the future. *Khan Muhammad* was engaged in constant hostilities with his neighbours. Nurpur was attacked by the Nawab of Mankera, and only relieved after a siege of more than a month. With Lal Khan, the chief of Khushab, some fifteen miles from Mitha Tiwana, on the Jhelam, *Khan Muhammad* had always been friends, till Jaffir Khan, the son and heir of Lal Khan, suspecting the Tiwana chief's intentions were not quite honest, plotted against him while visiting Khushab. *Khan Muhammad* escaped to his own town and prepared for fight. Lal Khan, with his younger son Hakim Khan and his wife Nurphari, came to assure *Khan Muhammad* of their innocence, but he arrested them and marching to Khushab opened fire upon the town, tying his hapless prisoners to the guns to divert the fire of the enemy. Jaffir Khan called Mahan Singh Sukarchakia, an old friend of *Khan Muhammad*, to his aid. The Sikh came with a considerable force and compelled the Tiwana chief to retire. *Khan Muhammad*, however, had his revenge and like a bloodthirsty savage as he was killed in cold

* Called Butala from the number of idols (bût) found when digging the foundations of the village.

blood his wretched prisoners who had neither done nor wished him evil. Towards the end of his rule, his brother *Khan Beg Khan* again took up arms against him, being aided by Rajjab Khan, a Sial chief of Ghar Maharaja, Fatah Khan of Sahiwal and Jaffir Khan of Khushab. For some time *Khan Muhammad* defended himself, but his enemies were too powerful and in 1803 he applied to Ranjit Singh for succour. That Sirdar was by no means secure himself, but on the promise of a subsidy of one lakh of rupees he consented to trap *Khan Beg Khan.* It was arranged between the confederates that when Ranjit Singh marched into the country, *Khan Muhammad* should take to flight, seeing which, *Khan Beg Khan* would probably come to pay his respects, believing the Lahore chief his friend. All happened auspiciously: *Khan Beg Khan* was caught by Ranjit Singh, and made over to his brother by whom he was put to death. Ranjit Singh took his blood money, and with some small tribute from the Muhammadan Maliks of the neighbourhood returned to Lahore in 1804. *Khan Muhammad Khan* had outwitted his brother, but his second son *Ahmad Yar Khan* now rebelled against him, and having won over most of the tribe to his side, induced his father to make a virtue of necessity and yield the chiefship to him. He had no easy life and was always fighting with the chiefs of Mankera, Khushab, and Sahiwal, with varying success.

In 1817 Maharaja Ranjit Singh sent a force, under Misr Diwan Chand, against the Tiwana chief at Nurpur. After a short resistance the fort was taken, and *Ahmad Yar Khan* fled to Jhandhawala or Jandiala in the Mankera territory. When the Sikh army had retired, leaving a garrison under Jawant Singh Mokal in Nurpur, *Ahmad Yar Khan* returned and regained possession of the country; but he was a second time compelled to fly to Jandiala, from which he was driven by the Mankera Nawab who threw his sons into prison. He now submitted to the Maharaja, who granted him the Ilaka of Jhawarian, worth 10,000 Rs. in jagir, subject to the service of 60 horsemen. In 1821, Ranjit Singh marched against Hafiz Ahmad Khan, Nawab of Mankera, and the Tiwana Malik gladly joined the expedition as he had an old score to wipe out with the Nawab. Muhammad Khan, the predecessor of Hafiz Ahmad, had surrounded Mankera with a cordon of twelve forts, Haidarabad, Monjghar, Fatahpur, Pipal, Darya Khan, Khanpur, Jhandawala, Kalor, Dulehwala, Bhakkar, Dinganah and Choubara; while to make the central fortress inaccessible he had permitted no wells to be sunk within the cordon. But for all this the besieging army, with the invincible Ranjit Singh commanding in person, moved on, digging wells as it advanced, invested the fort and after a siege of 25 days, the Nawab capitulated, being allowed to retain the government of Derah Ismail Khan. The assistance rendered by the Tiwanas during this campaign was very great, and the Maharaja was so much struck with their handsome and manly appearance, their bold riding and their gallant fighting, that he insisted upon a troop of Tiwana horse returning with him to Lahore. Of this troop of 50 horsemen *Kadir Baksh* was the commander. He served at Multan some years, and in many campaigns, with distinction. In 1837 his cousin *Fatah Khan* shared with him the command of the sowars. *Khuda Yar Khan* found himself a person of very small importance at Lahore, where no one of the Sikh nobles cared a straw for his long genealogy or for his hereditary claim to rule over the Shahpur jungles. He was appointed on 1,000 Rs. a year, 'chabuk sowar' or rough rider to the Maharaja, whose hunting expeditions he superintended until his death in 1837. *Fatah Khan*, son of *Khuda Yar Khan*, had been, during these years, in the service of Sirdar Hari Singh Nalwa to whom the Mitha Tiwana country was given in jagir, in 1819, Jawant Singh Mokal having held it two years. He proved himself as impetuous and overbearing as his master, and quarreled and fought with Sirdars Fatah Singh Man and Amir Singh Sindhanwalia who successively held the adjacent district of Panjkotah. Till the death of Hari Singh in 1837, *Fatah Khan* held a command under him in his native country, and any jagir or estates he may have received were given by the Sirdar and not by the Lahore Government. In 1837 he came to Lahore, where Raja Dhyan Singh, who had heard of his courage and unscrupulousness, thought that he would make a useful employé and took him into favour; and, in 1838, procured for him the appointment of manager of the Mitha Tiwana country, with control of such of the salt mines, like Wurcha and Choha, as lay to the south of the range and close to the plain country. With him was associated Pras Ram a Khatri, but their joint administration was not very successful and in 1840 *Fatah Khan* was 20,000 Rs. in arrears, and Prince Nao Nihal Singh, glad of an opportunity to humble an adherent of Raja Dhyan Singh, placed him in arrest in the house of Misr Lal Singh Toshakhania until the arrears were paid off. On the death of Nao Nihal Singh the Raja regained his power and *Fatah Khan's* fortunes rose with those of his patron. He was sent as Manager of the Kachhi country and *Sahib Khan, Alam Khan* and other of his relations were made Kardars of Mianwali, Shaikhowal and Nurpur Tiwana. Soon after the accession of Sher Singh, *Fatah Khan* was sent on duty across the Indus. The country of Tank had been ruled for many years by a Kattekhel family, the last of whom Allahdad Khan had been ousted by the Sikhs. The country, however, brought little profit to its conquerors. Allahdad Khan, indolent when in power but active enough in opposition, ravaged the country, cut off Sikh convoys and foraging parties, and the revenue had fallen to next to nothing. In this state of things Raja Dhyan Singh proposed *Fatah Khan* as the only man who could restore order, and he was accordingly sent with a strong force and full powers. His mission was entirely successful. He proposed to reinstate Allahdad Khan as governor of Tank, but the chief died before it was possible to carry out the design. Then *Fatah Khan* proceeded to Marwat, the country to the North of Tank, to collect the government revenue, without fighting if possible but any how to collect it. The first thing that he did was to build a fort at Lakki, on the Gumbelah river, in the heart of the Marwat country. This was not opposed by the chiefs, for he had promised to reduce the revenue demand to one sixth of the produce, and had thus won their support, but no sooner was the fort completed then *Fatah Khan* begged for loans, in addition to the revenue charge, which loans could not be refused and which

Diwan Doulat Rai, his successor, made a perpetual poll tax odious to the last degree to the people. This accomplished, *Fatah Khan* returned in triumph to Lahore, taking with him Shah Niwaz Khan the young son of Allahdad Khan Kattekhel, who was well received at court. The fortunes of the Malik now seemed made, when, in one day, his friend and patron Raja Dhyan Singh and Maharaja Sher Singh fell by the hands of the Sindhanwalias. *Fatah Khan* was with the Raja just before his murder; but as the assassins and their victim passed into the Lahore fort, he fell behind and allowed himself to be shut out. No man was more versed in intrigue than he; he saw a catastrophe was impending, and had no such love for the Raja as to desire to share his fate.* Raja Hira Singh, the son of the murdered minister, openly accused *Fatah Khan* of being in the conspiracy, and put a price on his head. There was no reason to believe the charge true for by the Raja's death *Fatah Khan* could gain nothing and might lose all. He escaped in disguise from Lahore and fled to his native Tiwana, whither he was followed by a force sent to arrest him. But the Malik fled across the Indus to Bannu and took refuge with Swahn Khan, who was offered 3,000 Rs. to give up his guest, but this the Waziri chief was too honourable to do. *Kadir Baksh*, who would have been imprisoned had the Sikhs succeeded in capturing him, took refuge with his old master Sawan Mal at Multan. When the Lahore troops had retired, *Fatah Khan* re-crossed the Indus and called the Muhammadan tribes to arms. He was now well known along the Indus, and he soon had a large following at his back. He ravaged the country with fire and sword and defeated several bodies of irregular troops sent against him. When, however, a regular force under Sirdar Mangal Singh Siranwali marched against him he again escaped across the Indus, while Mitha Tiwana was sacked by the Sikhs. When at length Raja Hira Singh and Pandit Jalla fell from power *Fattah Khan* hurried to Lahore where he knew that he should be well received by Sirdar Jowahir Singh the new minister, whose battles he

---

* Vide pp. 23. 24.

had fought in fighting against the late administration. He was not disappointed. Jowahir Singh gave him valuable presents and made him governor of the Mitha Tiwana country, of portions of Jhelam and Rawalpindi and of the whole province of Derah Ismail Khan and Bannu, superseding Diwan Doulat Rai, son of Lakki Mal the governor first appointed by Maharaja Ranjit Singh when he resumed the country from Nawab Sher Muhammad Khan.* But Jowahir Singh had not given *Fatah Khan* this power and position for nothing. The minister had a dangerous rival in the person of Prince Peshora Singh, reputed son of Ranjit Singh, to whom the Sikhs now generally looked as the best man to seat on the throne. The Prince had, with the help of the Muhammadan tribes in the neighbourhood, gained possession of the fort of Attock, and *Fatah Khan* Tiwana and Sirdar Chattar Singh Attariwala, men upon whom the Minister knew he could rely, were directed to proceed against him. With some 8000 men they invested the fort, but the feeling in favour of the Prince was so strong that they would have been unable to reduce it by force. Strategem was accordingly resorted to, and on solemn promises of safety the Prince surrendered the fort to *Fatah Khan* and Chattar Singh. Having secured their victim the two chiefs began their march to Lahore, and in two days reached Hassan Abdal some 30 miles from Attock. At this place a letter from Lahore was received in which was written that it was unsafe in the present temper of the Sikhs to bring Peshora Singh to the capital and that he must be detained in the North country. The order was well understood. That very night *Fatah Khan* and his confederate entered the Prince's tent, with a guard; seized him, placed him in irons, and leaving the camp standing, marched back to Attock with all speed, accompanied by a few hundred horse, and carrying the Prince with them. As he drew near the gloomy walls of the fortress he saw his certain doom and begged for his sword and shield that he might die fighting like a man. But there was no mercy in the heart of *Fatah Khan*. The unfortunate Prince was hurried into the

* Commonly known as Shah Niwaz Khan.

fort and placed in the lower chamber of a tower past which rushed the black, swift Indus. When night came he was strangled and his body thrown into the river. Through all the evil history of the Panjab there is recorded no murder more cruel than this. Peshora Singh was a fine, high spirited and gallant youth, beloved by the troops and the people, and only hated by those who feared his rivalry. But the murder did not go unavenged. The weakminded, slavish Chattar Singh died in exile, many hundred miles from his native land. Jowahir Singh the instigator of the deed was killed by the enraged soldiery shortly afterwards, while upon Malik *Fatah Khan* came the troubles related here. After the murder he crossed the Indus at Kalabagh and took possession of his new province of Derah Ismail Khan. The governor Doulat Rai retired, not prepared to resist at this time, and the Malik then determined to get rid of some of his Tank enemies and thus render his own power the more secure. The three chief jagirdars in Tank were the famous Payinda Khan, Ashik Muhammad Khan and Haiyat Ullah Khan. These three chiefs were enticed to Derah Ismail Khan, and Payinda Khan visited the Darbar of the Malik to talk over his affairs and arrange them satisfactorily. The conversation grew somewhat excited, and at length *Fatah Khan* insulted the Afghan to his face. Payinda Khan saw his danger and sat still, but his young son, Sikandar Khan, unable to control himself, drew his sword and cut down the Malik's Jamadar Partaja, who was standing by him. *Fatah Khan* was ready for this. In a moment the room was full of armed men. Payinda Khan, his son and most of his retainers were cut to pieces. Then the Malik attacked the house of Hyat Ullah Khan where Ashik Muhammad Khan and Nasir Ullah Khan had taken refuge; stormed it and put the inmates to death. Hyat Ullah Khan himself escaped to the house of Nawab Sher Muhammad, who purchased safety for himself and the fugitives for 40,000 Rs. The indignation at this atrocity was great on the frontier and even the authorities at Lahore were compelled to appear shocked. *Fatah Khan* bribed high for immunity. Raja Lal

Singh, the Maharani, and Mangela the slave girl all took his money and promised him protection; but popular feeling was too strong against him, and Diwan Doulat Rai was again nominated governor of Derah Ismail Khan. The Malik determined on resistance, and when Doulat Rai arrived at Bhakkar, opposite Derah Ismail Khan on the left bank of the Indus, he crossed the river to attack him. The Diwan however had regular troops with him, and *Fatah Khan* was compelled to retire to Derah. Doulat Rai followed and marched upon the town, outside which the Malik met him with some 3,000 men. But these troops were undisciplined and did not care to wait the assault of the Diwan's Multanis whose prowess was well known, and they dispersed without fighting. *Fatah Khan*, deserted by his adherents, was compelled to retreat to the fort of Akalghar which he had left in charge of his son *Fatah Sher Khan*. There he murdered all his prisoners, and the same night crossing the Indus retired to Mitha Tiwana to wait for better days. The country was at this time in confusion after the Satlej campaign, and the English, to whom the Malik had offered his services during the war, were at Lahore. Raja Lal Singh was no friend of *Fatah Khan* and would have confiscated all his jagirs but for the intercession of Sirdar Sultan Muhammad Khan. In the hot weather of 1846, the Malik was sent to Kashmir, as he was an intimate friend of Shaikh Imam-uddin Khan the rebel governor, and it was thought that he might influence him favourably as he could gain nothing by playing the Government false. He went with Lieutenant Edwardes as far as Jammu, from thence to Kashmir with Puran Chand, and having performed his mission with ability and success returned to Jammu. He afterwards accompanied Major H. Lawrence to Kashmir.

On the return of *Fatah Khan* to Lahore he was called upon to explain the accounts of his late Government as Diwan Dinanath had brought him in a defaulter to the amount of seven lakhs of rupees. This *Fatah Khan* asserted was covered by the expenses of five thousand horse and foot engaged by orders of Sirdar Jowahir Singh, but the written orders which he produced as those of the Sirdar were without date, no particular service was specified nor any detail as to the number of men. After a long dispute and full allowance for these presumed levies having been granted, the demand against the Malik was reduced to four lakhs of rupees. *Fatah Khan* complained, and his son complains to this day, of the harshness of this demand, but in reality the Malik was treated with exceptional leniency; every rupee of the four lakhs was due, as the accounts still in Raja Dinanath's office show, and this was at the time admitted by himself and the admission signed and sealed with his own hand. *Fatah Khan* could have paid the four lakhs without the slightest inconvenience. He had not been a manager under the tyrannical Hari Singh, or irresponsible governor of the Derajat, for nothing; but he pretended that he could not pay and he was placed in restraint in the house of Khan Singh Man, with the approbation of Major H. Lawrence. For three and a half months he was thus kept under arrest; and then, as he resolutely asserted his inability to pay, he was removed to the fort of Govindghar. Directly the order for his imprisonment was issued he offered to pay two lakhs of rupees in eight days. The Darbar allowed him twenty days in addition to this, but when the time had elapsed *Fatah Khan* had changed his mind. He knew that a temporary imprisonment was all he had to fear, and he preferred this to paying what was due from him. But he had not done with his promises. His son *Fatah Sher Khan* was imprisoned with him, and after two months he petitioned that the young man might be released in order to raise the money. This was permitted; *Fatah Sher Khan* was liberated and declared in Darbar that Maharaja Gulab Singh would be answerable for one lakh, and that the rest should be paid on his father's release. After some delay 21,000 Rs. were paid into the Derah Ismail Khan treasury; and the Multan rebellion breaking out, Lieutenant Edwardes, thinking the Malik would be of use on the frontier, obtained his release, and in June 1848, when the state of the country made it advisable to recall Lieutenant Taylor from Bannu, *Fatah Khan* was sent as governor of that province with Marwat, Isakhel, Kachhi, and Mianwali. He would rather have fought Mulraj in the open field, but he was ready to work any where, and at the beginning of July took over charge from Lieutenant Taylor. The Sikh force of Bannu was thoroughly disaffected and the appointment of *Fatah Khan* increased its dissatisfaction. Early in August the troops broke into open mutiny, but the vigour of *Fatah Khan* suppressed it for the time. There were at this time in Bannu, four regiments of infantry, 500 cavalry and four heavy guns with a troop of horse artillery. The only European with them was Colonel John Holmes, an old servant of the Lahore State, and chief among the Sikhs was Sirdar Ram Singh Chhapawala. When the news of Raja Sher Singh's rebellion at Multan reached Bannu, about the 25th September, the Sikhs rose in mutiny. They murdered Colonel Holmes, seized four light guns which had been withdrawn from the bastions for the purpose of being sent to Multan, and besieged *Fatah Khan* in the inner fort of Dalipghar. He called the Muhammadan tribes to arms, and many answered to the call, but the Malik had even in Bannu as many enemies as friends. First came to his aid Muhammad Khan Isakhel whom the Malik had once reinstated in his chiefship : then Dilasah Khan, whose name was a terror to the Sikhs, and who had beaten from his mud fort Tara Chand and the bravest of the Sikh Sirdars. With these came Jaffir Khan of Tappi, Bazid Khan Shorani, Sher Khan and Muhammad Azaz Khan Isakhel. But the Sikhs found allies also : Mir Alim Khan of Mudan the intimate friend of Ram Singh Chhapawala, Musa Khan of Sikandarkhel, and on their side too were numbers, discipline and guns. But the gallant borderers at first got the best of the fight, and took possession of the town of Dalipghar, while the Sikhs had to stand on the defensive. But this was a temporary advantage, and the Sikhs attacked the Muhammadans in force, drove them out of the town with great loss and closely invested the fort. The Malik might have held the fort for ever against the besiegers had there been a supply of water ; but the well was then being sunk, and the defenders were soon reduced to the last extremity. They dug night and day, but they could reach no water and at last were compelled to surrender. *Fatah Khan*, to whom the Sikhs would never have given quarter even had he deigned to ask for it, was shot down at the gateway of the fort, and Muhammad Alim Khan and Sher Khan Isakhel and Lal Baz Khan of Bazar were carried away as prisoners and did not recover their liberty till after the final defeat of the Sikh army at Gujrat.

The more the character of Malik *Fatah Khan* is regarded, the less will he appear worthy of our admiration. He was brave indeed, but what is courage unless allied with generosity and honour? What was that courage worth which could murder in cold blood prince Peshora Singh; which could lure to their destruction the gallant Payinda Khan, and the chiefs of Bannu? It was only in times when might was right, and honesty was professed by none, that such men as *Fatah Khan* could become distinguished. Proud, treacherous and cruel, insolent to equals, tyrannical to inferiors, and a ready tool for the commission of any crime which a superior might assign to him, there is no virtue which can be claimed for him save a spurious liberality, which was generally indulged not at his own expense, but at that of the state. He died defending the fort entrusted to him, but this honourable end to a life of violence and blood should not induce men to forget or to extenuate his many crimes.

On the annexation of the Panjab it was not easy to discover the real position of the family with regard to estates and allowances. At the death of *Khudayar Khan* in 1837, the estate was divided between his son *Fatah Khan,* and his nephew *Kadir Baksh.* The former commanded 22 sowars and the latter 33; the allowance of *Fatah Khan* was 1,000 Rs., the same as his father had held as 'chabuk sowar;' that of *Kadir Baksh* was 720 Rs. Besides this there was 10,440 Rs. for the pay of the troopers. Total 12,160 Rs. When *Kadir Baksh* died the jagir was continued to his son *Sher Muhammad Khan.* In Jowahir Singh's time *Fatah Khan* was allowed one quarter of the revenue collections of Mitha Tiwana and Khushab, in consideration of the former position of his family in the district. This 'chaharam' or fourth amounted to 8,345 Rs. a year, but the Malik only held it one year. Under Lal Singh it was resumed, as were his other allowances, and his sowars were discharged. *Fatah Khan* seems also to have received from Raja Gulab Singh, the farmer of the salt revenue, some percentage on the collections at Fatahpur, where, in 1842, he had assisted to reopen and work a long disused mine. When sent by Jowahir Singh as governor of Derah Ismail Khan, his pay was fixed at 10,000 Rs., but this was nominal, and at so great a distance from Lahore a governor could make his pay what he liked. On the annexation of the Panjab the Tiwanas were not forgotten. Their services during the war had been valuable in the extreme. *Sher Muhammad Khan* expelled the rebel garrison from Khushab, and then took possession of Shahpur. The Mitha Tiwana fort, which had been seized by a body of the enemy, he besieged and reduced, as also Sahiwal and Ahmadabad. *Sahib Khan*, brother of *Kadir Baksh*, had his share of the fighting and he, with Langar Khan Sahiwal and some other chiefs, attacked and defeated the force of the rebel Bhai Maharaj Singh. *Fatah Sher Khan*, son of *Fatah Khan*, served as one of Major Edwardes' chief officers and fought with the greatest gallantry throughout the war of 1848-49. At the close of the war, the Government was anxious adequately to reward the services of the Tiwana chiefs, and allowed them the fourth of the revenue of the country from which they had been driven by Ranjit Singh. The whole revenue amounted to 50,105 Rs. including *Sher Muhammad's* jagir of 6,945 Rs., and this being resumed, a jagir of 6,000 Rs. in perpetuity was granted to *Sher Muhammad Khan*, and one of the same amount to *Fatah Sher Khan* and his four brothers: *Fatah Sher Khan* taking 2,000 Rs., and his brothers 1,000 Rs. each. In addition to these perpetual grants, *Sher Muhammad Khan's* personal jagir of 3,240 Rs. was continued to him as a pension for life, while *Fatah Sher Khan* received a cash pension of 5,000 Rs. *Sahib Khan* received a life pension of 480 Rs. a year.

During the mutiny of 1857, the three Tiwana Maliks rendered excellent service. *Fatah Sher Khan* left the Panjab with about 500 horse and joined General Van Cortlandt, and served with great distinction in Harriana, Hissar and Hansi, and fought at Jhajjar, Jamalpur, Narnoul,

Bengali and elsewhere. He and his men were always distinguished for their dash and gallantry.

The services of *Sher Muhammad Khan* were distinct from those of his cousin. He was first employed, from June to December 1857, in the Jalandhar Doab, and assisted in keeping that part of the country tranquil. He then, with his 300 men, volunteered for service down country and fought in Oude, Bareilly, and in several actions during 1858 with distinction.

Malik *Sahib Khan* was surpassed in loyalty by no other chief. Immediately the news of the Dehli mutiny reached him he asked and received permission to raise two hundred men of his clan, for the service of Government. He was present at the disarming of a mutinous regiment at Jhelam, and was with Mr. Cooper, Deputy Commissioner of Amritsar, at the destruction of the 26th Native Infantry. Afterwards he marched to Hindostan where his contingent did good service before Calpi and at other places. A portion of the troop served at Gwalior under General Napier, and in Oude under the Commander-in-Chief. At the close of the disturbances *Sahib Khan* received jagir of 1,200 Rs. with the title of Khan Buhadur. *Fatah Sher Khan* and *Sher Muhammad Khan* received the same title, and the former an additional jagir of 1,200 Rs. the latter an additional jagir of 600 Rs.

Fatah Sher Khan and his cousin Sher Muhammad are at bitter feud. One considers himself the head of the family being the descendant of the eldest son of *Malik Khan*, the other as being the son of *Fatah Khan* the most distinguished Tiwana chief. With a great name for gallantry, loyalty and ability, with large estates capable of indefinite improvement, with every wish on the part of Government to see those who have served so well, prosperous and happy, the two Maliks quarrel like children about a point of precedence utterly unimportant in itself and impossible to decide. Malik *Sahib Khan* has wisely and resolutely kept himself aloof from these disputes, and lives quietly on his jagir, a fine specimen of a Muhammadan country gentleman.

RAI FATAH KHAN GHEBA OF KOT.

- RAI ALYAS.
  - Mehr Muhammad.
    - Khair Muhammad.
      - Karam Khan.
      - Rai Jalal.
      - Rai Sarafraz.
        - Ahmad Khan.
        - Muhammad Khan.
          - Ghulam Muhammad Khan.
          - Fatah Khan.
            - daughter M. Oulia Khan of Pindi Gheb.
          - Ahmad Khan, D. 1843.
            - Ghulam Muhammad Khan.
      - Allah Yar Khan.

HISTORY OF THE FAMILY.

An account of the origin of the Gheba tribe will be found in the history of the Tiwana family and there is no occasion to repeat it in this place. The Ghebas came to the Panjab some time after both Sials and Tiwanas and settled in the wild, hilly country between the Indus and the Sohan rivers, now known as the pargannas of Fatahjang and Pindi Gheb. Here they held their own against the neighbouring tribes, Awans, Ghakkars and Jodras, till the days of Sirdar Charrat Singh Sukarchakia, grandfather of Maharaja Ranjit Singh. They had not been subdued by the Afghan invaders of India, for they were just off the highway and their country was difficult of acess, nor did they ever invite attack by their demeanour, but presented a small tribute such as a horse or a few head of cattle as the invader passed, and thus secured his good-will. Sirdar Gujar Singh Bhangi of Gujrat, who for a time held the country as far north as Rawalpindi, made but little impression on the Gheba district. Chattar Singh, after he had seized Pind Dadan Khan, overran the southern part of Rawalpindi and made *Rai Jalal* tributary, leaving him one fourth of the revenue called the 'Chaharam,' in consideration of his proprietary right in the land. But neither Chattar Singh nor his son Mahan Singh were able to get much out of the sturdy Ghebas, and their supremacy was little more than nominal. *Rai Jalal* managed his old territory, and gave up a certain proportion to the Sikh chiefs when they were strong enough to ask for it. In 1806 Ranjit Singh sent Sirdar Fatah Singh Kalianwala as the governor of the Rawalpindi district, and he continued the farm of the Kot and Khunda Ilakas to *Rai Muhammad Khan* the nephew of *Rai Jalal*. The village of Sher Buhadar, worth 500 Rs., was conferred on *Rai Muhammad*, with a 'maafi' or revenue free grant worth 1,075 Rs. a year. The great rivals of the Rais of Kot were the Maliks of Pindi Gheb, who farmed the Sil Ilaka from the Sikhs. Their jealousy at length ended in bloodshed, for during a year of scarcity, when both had failed to pay the revenue, they were summoned to the Darbar at Amritsar. There they quarreled and *Rai Muhammad* cut down Malik Ghulam Muhammad almost in the presence of the Maharaja himself and then fled to his home. It was not thought politic to punish him at that time, as his services were urgently needed on the side of Government in a wild country where the Sikh Kardars never gained full power. In 1836, *Rai Muhammad* served against Syad Ahmad the fanatic leader, who, having been compelled to retire from Peshawar which he had for some time absolutely ruled, had made Balakot in Hazara his head-quarters. Here he was attacked by the Sikh army commanded by prince Sher Singh and General Ventura and utterly defeated. *Rai Muhammad* much distinguished himself in this battle, and for his services received the village of Giro, worth 200 Rs. Jodh Singh, Dhanna Singh Malwai, Attar Singh Kalianwala and prince Nao Nihal Singh successively governed the Gheba country and all found *Rai Muhammad Khan* difficult to control and ever ready to rebel. Sirdar Attar Singh during his second tenure of office determined for the sake of peace to get rid of him. He invited the Rai to his fort of Pagh, which overlooked Kot on the opposite side of the little river Sîl. *Muhammad Khan* did not suspect treachery, and went to Pagh attended by his nephew *Ghulam Muhammad Khan* and two followers. No sooner had he entered the fort than the little party was attacked by Budha Khan Malal, an old enemy of his family, and the retainers of Attar Singh and were all killed. *Fatah Khan* succeeded his father and avenged his death upon Budha Khan whose family he almost extirpated. In 1845-46, *Fatah Khan,* taking advantage of the weakness of the Lahore Government, rose in revolt, but in August of the latter year he surrendered to Sirdar Chattar Singh Attariwala who thought of employing him to suppress future disturbances in the district. But two months later Misr Amir Chand, through folly or treachery, released him, and he again took up arms against the Government. Through the influence of Colonel Lawrence he was again induced to yield, and he soon had an opportunity of fighting against the Sikhs without being guilty of treason. During the war of 1848-49, he was of the greatest service to Captains Nicholson and Abbott. He kept open the communications, and raised as large a body of horse and foot as he was able, and on several occasions engaged parties of rebels with success. In 1857, the loyalty of *Fatah Khan* was equally conspicuous, and he has been rewarded by his jagirs being upheld, 4,381 Rs. for life and 2,574 Rs. in perpetuity. He owns Aruriah, Bujal, Giro, Pind Fatah, Sher Buhadar, Gagni, Galli and other villages, and has besides proprietary rights which bring him in 2,544 Rs. a year. Should *Rai Fatah Khan* have no son the perpetual estate descends to his nephew *Ghulam Muhammad Khan,* son of *Ahmad Khan* who was killed with Raja Dhyan Singh in 1843. *Fatah Khan* is a man of great influence in the Rawalpindi district, and this influence has, since annexation, been always used on the side of Government and in the cause of law and order.

MALIK OULIA KHAN OF PINDI GHEB.

- SHAHBAZ.
  - Fatah Khan.
    - Nur Khan.
      - Oulia Khan.
        - Amanat Khan.
          - Nawab.
          - Allah Yar.
          - Ghulam Muhammad Khan.
            - Allah Yar Khan.
              - Oulia Khan. M. D. of Rai Fatah Khan of Kot.
                - Ghulam Muhammad Khan.
              - Fatah Khan.
                - Nawab Khan.
                - Amanat Khan.

HISTORY OF THE FAMILY.

The Jodrahs are a Muhammadan tribe of Rajput descent, close neighbours of the Ghebas with whom they intermarry and with whom in old days they were perpetually fighting. They inhabit the parganna of Pindi Gheb in the Rawalpindi district, stretching along the river Indus from Mirzapur to within 12 miles of Attock. The tribe has its name from *Jodrah* who is said to have adopted Muhammadanism in the eleventh century, during the reign of Sultan Mahmud. He settled in Jammu where his descendants lived for some generations till the time of *Bhosi Khan* who removed to Dirahti, near where Pindi Gheb now stands. His grandson *Shahbaz Khan*, hunting near his home, was met by a devotee, Bhor Sultan, who addressed him in mysterious language and told him he would not be fortunate unless he moved his colony to the right bank of the Sîl, here a wide, sandy nullah. *Shahbaz* took the advice and built Pindi Gheb, and many villages were founded in its neighbourhood by him and his successors. The first Malik who became of any importance was *Oulia Khan,* who early in the eighteenth century overran the Ilakas of Nalah, Sohan, Sil and Tallagang in the Jhelam district, and held them throughout his life. His son *Amanat* was equally powerful. Nominally subject to the Sukarchakia chiefs, he paid but a small tribute, and with his own troops held the country his father had ruled. Not so fortunate was *Nawab* his son. This chief held in farm from Ranjit Singh the Ilakas of Sil and Bala Gheb. In 1813 he rebelled, but was not able to hold his own against the Sikhs, and fled to Kohat where he died in exile. His brother *Ghulam Muhammad Khan* succeeded him, being allowed one-fourth of the revenue of Sil. In the battle of Akora near Attock in 1827, *Ghulam Muhammad* fought under Attar Singh and Budh Singh Sindhanwalia against Syad Ahmad, and no long time afterwards he was assassinated by his rival and enemy Rai Muhammad Khan Gheba, at Amritsar, whither both had been summoned by the Maharaja. *Allah Yar Khan* succeeded to the estate, but of this chief there is little to record. He did good service in 1848-49, and with his five horsemen assisted in keeping open the communication between Captain Nicholson and Lieutenants Edwardes and Taylor. At annexation he was only in possession of Dholian worth 750 Rs. and a well at Pindi Gheb worth 80 Rs. He died shortly after annexation, leaving two minor sons. The Government treated them with liberality, and the position of the family is now much better than it was in Sikh days. The two brothers hold in jagir the four villages of Pindi Gheb, Iklas, Notha, and Ahmadal, worth 1,575 Rs. a year. They have also a large income from the 'Chaharam,' or one-fourth of the revenue, allowed to them by Government in many villages which formed part of the ancestral estate of the family. *Oulia Khan* and *Fatah Khan* showed themselves actively loyal in 1857, and received Khilats of 400 Rs. and 150 Rs. respectively. *Oulia Khan* has married the daughter of Rai Fatah Khan of Kot, and the long-standing feud between the families is now ended.

SIRDAR ATTAR SINGH LAMBA.

- CHARRAT RAM.
  - Basta Ram.
  - Hazari Mal.
  - Diwan Singh.
  - Pardhan Singh.
    - Gurmukh Singh.
      - Attar Singh.
        - Hari Singh.
        - Gyan Singh.
    - Ram Singh.
      - Amir Singh.

HISTORY OF THE FAMILY.

The founder of the Lamba family was *Gurmukh Singh*, one of the most famous of the Maharaja's generals. He was of humble origin, his father *Pardhan Singh* being a money-changer in the little town of Khewah situated on the right bank of the Jhelam opposite Jalalpur. In the summer of 1780 as Mahan Singh Sukarchakia was passing through the town on his return from an expedition in the neighbourhood of Pind Dadan Khan, *Gurmukh Singh*, then a boy of eight years, was presented by his uncle *Basta Ram* who was a petty officer in the service of the chief. Mahan Singh was pleased with the bright eyes and intelligent looks of the boy, and kept him with him. Later in the same year Ranjit Singh was born, and when he was two years old, *Gurmukh Singh* was appointed to be his play-fellow and companion. The children grew up together, and during the early years of Ranjit Singh's power, wealth and honours were showered on *Gurmukh Singh*. He was with Ranjit Singh at the capture of Lahore, in 1799, and was then made pay master of the forces, and put in charge of whatever treasure the Sukarchakia chief possessed. A detailed account of the military services of the Sirdar would be the history of all the wars of the Sikh empire. He fought at Kassur where he commanded 2,000 men, at

Jhang and Sialkot, and against the Gurkhas in 1809. The next year he was present at the siege of Multan and aided in the reduction of Sahiwal and Khushab. He commanded a division in the battle of Attock, in 1813, when the Afghans and the Kabul wazir were driven from the Panjab, and fought in Kashmir and all along the uorthern and north western borders of the province. Fifteen times he was wounded in battle ; eight times by musket balls, thrice by sword cuts, thrice by spear thrusts, once by an arrow. For his services he was munificently rewarded by his master. Before the capture of Lahore he received the jagir of Pindi Lalah and Shahdianwali and afterwards Dingah and Rhotas worth 15,000 Rs. and 35,000 Rs. respectively. After the Kassur campaign of 1807, where the Sirdar took the fort of Moradah and where he was wounded by a spear, he received jagirs in the Kassur Ilaka worth 82,000 Rs. When Nar Singh Chamyariwala died in 1806 his troops were placed under *Gurmukh Singh,* with a large portion of his estate worth 15,000 Rs. At one time his estates amounted to three lakhs and a half, but the enmity of the Jammu Rajas, Gulab Singh and Dhyan Singh, which he had incurred by attacking and defeating their father Mian Kissora Singh, destroyed both his wealth and power, for they opposed him on all occasions and procured, the resumption of the jagirs of Gamrolah, Dingah and Dhoutal. In 1832, he went with Tara Chand to Bannu, where the Sikh army was defeated by Dilasah Khan. The cowardly General had fled, leaving a gun in the hands of the enemy, but *Gurmukh Singh* charged at the head of his horsemen and recovered it. One by one the jagirs of the Sirdar were resumed, and in 1836 he lost Rhotas. This was through the hostile influence of Raja Dhyan Singh, who now ruled the failing monarch, but the reason given was the perpetual quarrels of the Sirdar with the Ghakkar chief Fazl Dad Khan, from whose father Nur Khan he had taken the famous Rhotas fort. On his death-bed the Maharaja feeling some remorse for his shameless ingratitude, directed his son Kharrak Singh to restore this jagir to the man who had fought so faithfully by his side throughout life, and this Kharrak Singh would have done had he lived lon-

enough. As it was *Gurmukh Singh* only recovered 5,500 Rs. of the estate. Maharaja Sher Singh, who hated the Dogra Rajas as much as the Sirdar did, promised to support him against them and gave him estates worth 25,000 Rs., and at annexation he was in possession of 36,600 Rs. a year. He had, in August, 1847, been appointed, with Sirdar Bhur Singh Mokerian, to take charge of the Rani Jindan whom it was necessary to confine in the fort at Shaikhopura, and he discharged his difficult duties with fidelity and discretion, till, on the outbreak of the Multan disturbances, the Rani was sent down country. The Government, in 1850, released his personal jagirs, worth 12,600 Rs. and that of his son, worth 2,000 Rs. for their lives. One-third of the Sirdar's jagir was to descend to his male heirs in perpetuity. Sirdar *Attar Singh* holds Naoshera in Shahpur, worth 4,275 Rs., and in Gujrat the villages of Pindi Lala, Chak Basowa, Doburgi, Kila Attar Singh, Kot Sitar and two wells, worth 2,807 Rs. The title 'Lamba' or tall was not given to *Gurmukh Singh* on account of his height for he was of middle stature, but from his taking command of the contingent of Mohr Singh Lamba who was an exceedingly tall man.

KISHAN SINGH LAMBA.

- RAI MAHA SINGH.
  - Laja Singh.
    - Budh Singh.
    - Amar Singh.
      - Fatah Singh.
        - Ram Singh.
          - Sarab Singh.
            - Jagdeo Singh.
        - Karam Singh.
          - Gurmukh Singh.
        - Narayan Singh.
          - Hukm Singh.
      - Dyal Singh.
        - Kishan Singh, B. 1827.
          - Mohr Singh, B. 1860.
          - Teja Singh, B. 1858.
          - Kehr Singh.
        - Bishan Singh, D. 1834.
      - Mohr Singh.
        - Tara Singh.
          - Bhagel Singh.
            - Didar Singh.
          - Parkash Singh.
            - Udho Singh.
            - Sant Singh.
        - Nihal Singh.
        - Kirpal Singh.
          - Bissashar Singh.

HISTORY OF THE FAMILY.

Among the petty Sirdars who followed the fortunes of Charrat Singh Sukarchakia was *Rai Maha Singh* and his son *Laja Singh*. Both fell in the service of their chief, for during one of the frequent Afghan invasions they volunteered to visit the enemy's camp, in disguise, to discover his strength and position, but they were detected and killed as spies. Charrat Singh took *Amar Singh*, the son of *Laja Singh*, into his service and gave him a jagir of 7,000 Rs. in the Nakka territory. *Amar Singh* served well and faithfully three generations of Sukarchakia chiefs, Charrat Singh, Mahan Singh and Ranjit Singh and died soon after the last named had taken command of the misl, but not until he had introduced his three sons *Mohr Singh*, *Dyal Singh* and *Fatah Singh*, into the chief's service. They soon rose into favour, and *Mohr Singh* especially distinguished himself in an action with the Afghans, at Khewah in the Gujrat district. Ranjit Singh gave him, at his own request, a jagir at Mikrach in exchange for the estate he possessed in Nakka. The three brothers received, in all, jagirs to the value of three lakhs of rupees, which they held for twelve years, when *Mohr Singh* retired to Benares contrary to the wish and order of the Maharaja who confiscated the jagirs, and gave the command of the contingent of 700 horse to Gurmukh Singh, who took the name of Lamba, which properly belonged to *Mohr Singh,* an agnomen given to him on account of his great height. *Dyal Singh* retrieved, in some measure, the fortunes of the family. He fought in the battle of Attock in 1813, when he was severely wounded, and the next year joined in the first expedition against Kashmir, when he was wounded again. For these services he received jagirs of the value of 32,000 Rs. In the year 1826 he fell into disgrace, and lost his estates with the single exception of Mung, five miles north of Khewa, worth 4,000 Rs., but two years later, the Maharaja restored him to favour and gave him other jagirs worth 28,000 Rs. He died in 1832, leaving two sons, the elder *Bishan Singh* aged seven, and the younger an infant in arms. *Bishan Singh* died two years after his father, and as the surviving brother could render no military service, the jagirs were resumed. Ranjit Singh did not however forget the child, but made over the Gujrat jagir to his cousin, *Nihal Singh,* who was enjoined to act as his guardian. Baduwal in the Jhelam district was also assigned to *Kirpal Singh,* another cousin, on the same conditions. When the Multan rebellion broke out in 1848, *Kishan Singh* remained loyal, but two of his cousins *Nihal Singh* and *Bissashar Singh* joined the rebels, and lost jagirs worth 10,000 Rs. and 1,100 Rs. respectively. In 1857, *Kishan Singh* rendered assistance in arresting some fugitives of the 14th Regiment Native Infantry which had mutinied at Jhelam. For his services on this occasion he received a present of 400 Rs., and his followers were suitably rewarded. The Sirdar died in 1860, leaving three children, *Mohr Singh, Teja Singh* and *Kehr Singh,* all under age. They receive a pension of 460 Rs.

MALIK LANGAR KHAN SAHIWAL.

MALIK BAJJAR KHAN.
- Gul Bhalak Khan.
  - Hot Khan.
    - Mubarak Khan.
      - Budha Khan.
        - Sahib Khan.
        - Lodha Khan.
          - Langar Khan.
            - Lal Khan.
              - Fatah Khan.
            - Mubarak Khan.
              - Muhammad Khan.
                - Allah Yar Khan.
                - Fatah Khan, D. 1820.
                  - Langar Khan, D. 1853.
                    - Muhammad Haiyat Khan.
                    - Mubarak Khan.
                      - Chiragh Khan.
                    - Lashkar Khan.
                  - Lal Khan, D. 1842.
            - Baihram Khan.
            - Lashkar Khan.
              - Kanun Khan.

HISTORY OF THE FAMILY.

The Biloch family of Sahiwal came to India in 1527. Malik *Bajjar Khan* was a petty chief of Kach Mekran, the most westerly province of Bilochistan, who had the misfortune to have a handsome daughter. The fame of the young girl's beauty having reached the ears of the neighbouring Sistan chief, he asked her in marriage, but *Bajjar Khan* had no desire for the alliance, and having for sometime opposed his more powerful neighbour with indifferent success, he fled with his family and retainers to Dehli, the throne of which the Emperor Babar had lately won. He was well received by the monarch; his younger brother *Amir* obtained the jagir of Farakabad, where his descendants still reside, and *Bajjar Khan* received the chiefship of the Thal country, about Shahpur in the Panjab, which was then in a most unsettled state. He took up his quarters near Khushab and soon succeeded in reducing the troublesome tribes of the neighbourhood to something like order. In 1530, at age of twenty, he died, and was succeeded by his son Gul Bhalak Khan, who founded several new villages in the Shahpur district, and defeated the Khatkian tribes with great slaughter at a spot named after the battle, Haddanwala (*Haddi* a bone) from the immense number of the slain whose bones for long after whitened the plain. The village is now known as Hadali.* He obtained from the Emperor the tract of country around Sahiwal, which he peopled and brought into cultivation. He died in 1547, having some time before his death resigned the chiefship in favour of his son *Hot Khan*. Little is known of this man or of his two immediate successors, but *Sahib Khan* the sixth chief of Sahiwal, was a man of so cruel and oppressive a disposition that the people rebelled against his authority, and having deposed him, made his nephew *Langar Khan*, chief in his stead. *Langar Khan* was of an easy disposition, and much improved his territory, paying great attention to agriculture. Fearing that his four sons by different wives might quarrel, he built for each a separate fort in the neighbourhood of Sahiwal, one of which is still standing. This remarkable method of ensuring the preservation of peace was not successful, and on the death of *Langar Khan* in 1735, his sons began to quarrel fiercely among themselves. *Lal Khan* the eldest held his own, and having put to death his brother *Bahram Khan*and *Lashkar Khan*, and his nephew *Kanun Khan* felt himself secure. When Ahmad Shah Durani first invaded India, *Lal Khan* gave him every assistance in the way of supplies and carriage. The Durani Prince treated him with such consideration that *Mubarak Khan* his only remaining brother became jealous of his fame, and conspiring with Fatah Khan of Bucharianwala, brought a large force against him. In the battle that ensued, *Lal Khan* was defeated and slain.

---

* The Tiwanas defeated the Awans at the same place.

Fatah Khan was but twelve years old when he succeeded his father. He was a clever boy, and soon avenged his father's death, forcing *Mubarak Khan* and his family to take refuge at Bahawalpur. Great severity must have been shown to the adherents of *Mubarak*, for a large emigration took place from the district, the Biloches of Khai, Kot Isa Shah and Kadarpur, going over the Sials of Jhang. *Fatah Khan's* reign was a short one. He was taken prisoner in an Afghan invasion, carried to Derah Ismail Khan and there put to death. He left no son, and his two brothers were so young that their mother *Bhandi* took the direction of affairs. She possessed courage and ability and was obeyed by the clan, and her only fault was that she was a woman. In 1750, Raja Kura Mal, the lieutenant of Ahmad Shah, arrived at Sahiwal and summoned the infant chiefs to his presence. *Bhandi* suspected treachery, and refusing compliance called the troops to arms and attacked the Raja, but was totally defeated. The children were taken prisoners, and, it is believed, put to death.

Mubarak now thought his turn was come, and, returning from Bahawalpur, assumed the chiefship without much opposition, and held it till his death, in 1770. His son *Muhammad Khan* found it difficult to make head against the Sikhs who were at this time overruning the country. Sirdar Jhanda Singh Bhangi attacked Sahiwal but was repulsed though he took possession of a portion of the territory. *Muhammad Khan* at length succeeded in recovering this with some loss, but was assassinated soon afterwards by some Sikhs and Biloches, who had come to Sahiwal on pretence of paying him a complimentary visit. Allahyar Khan having punished his father's murderers turned his attention to the improvement of the country, and was engaged in cutting a canal from the Jhelam, when he was killed by a fall from his horse. *Fatah Khan* the fourteenth chief was a minor at the time of his brother's death, and for some time his mother *Allah Jowahi* acted as regent, in conjunction with Diwan Dya Ram. When the boy grew up he determined to seize the power which his mother and the Diwan seemed to wish to retain, and his bold policy was completely successful. He then turned his arms against the Sikhs and recovered from them the forts of Nihang and Shaikh Jalil. From Mit Singh Bhangi he took Derah Jarah, and soon became dreaded for his energy and courage. On all sides he recovered ancestral possessions and acquired new ones, till he at length ruled over a larger tract of country than any of his predecessors, and his revenue amounted to about 1,50,000 Rs. When Mahan Singh rose to power *Fatah Khan* thought it politic to pay him a small tribute ; and in 1804 he agreed to give Ranjit Singh yearly, 25 horses and 25 camels. This tribute was, in 1809, commuted to 12,000 Rs. per annum.

It is not likely that *Fatah Khan* paid the tribute with any great regularity, but this point is immaterial, for an excuse was never wanting when Ranjit Singh desired to rob a weaker neighbour ; so in the spring of 1810, having collected his forces, Ranjit Singh marched to Sahiwal and summoned *Fatah Khan*, to his presence. The Biloch fox had noticed many foot-points going into the den of the lion, but no sign of a returning step, and hesitated to comply ; but Ranjit Singh expressed such devoted friendship for him, that at length he sent his son *Langar Khan*, a child of four years of age, with rich presents. The Maharaja received the boy with great cordiality, and having again expressed his friendship for *Fatah Khan*, marched against Zaffar Khan chief of Khushab, which place he reduced after several days' siege. *Fatah Khan* now thought himself secure, but Ranjit Singh returned at night to Sahiwal, took the fort by surprise and carried the chief prisoner to Lahore. After a year he was released, and a jagir of 14,400 Rs. was given to him at Jhang, with which he was to furnish fifty horsemen. In 1812 he returned to Lahore, and for three years remained about court, but this life was not to his taste. During these three years he saw Sultan Khan the Bhimbar Raja betrayed by Ranjit, as he himself had been betrayed ; he saw the miserable Shah Shuja tricked and robbed by the prince who had sworn to protect him ; and at last, he turned his back on the accursed court and fled to Mankera, to the protection of Muhammad Khan, the great and wise Biloch governor. He remained here for nine months, but Muhammad Khan could not do much to assist him, and he then left for Multan, where he lived for two more years, supported by Muzaffar Khan. But when his old enemy marched on Multan, in 1818, the poor outcast retired to Bahawalpur, where, in the town of Ahmadpur, he died, in 1820.

Langar Khan, his eldest son, was at his father's death, but 14 years' old, and Sadik Khan, the chief of Bahawalpur, took him and his horsemen into his own service. After three years, Ranjit Singh, who had heard of *Fatah Khan's* death, invited *Langar Khan* to Lahore and gave him a jagir of 1,200 Rs. in Jhang and Sahiwal, with allowances for 50 horsemen, and stationed him at Multan, where he remained, under the orders of Diwan Sawan Mal for ten years. Shortly before the Maharaja's death he granted a new jagir to *Langar Khan* at Moglanwala, Nun and Jhok Manjur, worth, with the old Sahiwal jagir, 3,000 Rs. and still in possession of the family. Besides this *Langar Khan* was allowed in cash 11,236 Rs., for the services of himself, his two sons and forty-two troopers. Maharaja Sher Singh ordered him with 200 horsemen to accompany the camp of General M'Caskill through the Panjab during the Afghan war, and in July 1841, commanding the same force, he went with Major H. Lawrence as far as Charbagh in Lughman. After the assassination of Sher Singh, *Langar Khan* was sent by Raja Hira Singh against Fatah Khan Tiwana, who was ravaging the country between the Chenab and the Indus, but the expedition had not much success, and it was not till the death of Hira Singh, that Fatah Khan submitted and came to Lahore, where he offered his services to Jowahir Singh the new wazir. Under this minister *Langar Khan* was stationed at Pind Dadan Khan, and at the close of 1847 was sent under Lieutenant Edwardes to Bannu. In June 1848, he did good service against the insurgent Bhai Maharaj Siug. For three days and nights, from Jhandiala to Jhang did *Langar Khan* with other Muhammadan chiefs hang on his tracks till, being joined by the fresh troops of Misr Sahib Dyal, they drove the rebel force into the swollen Chenab. Two months afterwards *Langar Khan* joined General Whish's camp at Sirdarpur, and served during the whole siege of Multan with great credit. On annexation, his personal jagirs, worth 3,000 Rs. were released in perpetuity, and a pension of 1,200 Rs. granted him which was resumed at his death on the 17th March, 1853. His eldest son *Muhammad Haiyat Khan* succeeded him. This young man had served at Kabul and Bannu and through the Multan siege, and was both loyal and brave. He died on the 7th February 1862, aged thirty-five years.

Mubarak Khan, a young man of 25, at present holds the jagir, being the twelfth in descent from *Bajjar Khan*, the first chief of Sahiwal.

DIWAN MOKHAM CHAND.
COLONEL DHUNRAJ.

- BAISAKHI MAL.
  - Mohkam Chand.
    - Moti Ram.
      - Ram Dyal.
      - Shiv Dyal.
        - Mya Lal, B. 1816.
          - Ram Chand, B. 1838.
            - Nihal Chand, B. 1860.
          - Hari Chand, B. 1844.
        - Kanheya Lal.
          - Radha Kishan.
          - Jagarnath.
      - Kirpa Ram.
        - Dhunraj, adopted.
  - Soba Ram.
    - Kishan Dyal.
    - Dittu Mal.
    - Ganpat Rai.
      - Baghwan Das.
      - Tara Chand.

HISTORY OF THE FAMILY.

The most distinguished of the generals by whose skill and courage Ranjit Singh rose from a subordinate chiefship to the Empire of the Panjab was Diwan *Mokham Chand.* The sagacity with which the Maharaja selected his officers was the reason of his uniform success. *Mokham Chand* was no soldier by birth; his father was a trader, and according to Hindu custom the son would have been a trader too, had he not, when quite young, been offered a post as munshi by Sirdar Dal Singh Gil of Akalghar. He is said indeed to have been served with Mahan Singh, father of Ranjit Singh, at the siege and capture of Rasulnagar, and to have gained there his first military experience, but this does not seem true. He remained with Dal Sing till 1804, when that chief died and his estates were seized by Ranjit Singh. Sehju, the widow of the Sirdar, disliked *Mokham Chand* and demanded his accounts, as for many years he had held the entire management of the Akalghar property, but the Diwan did not care to expose them to a close and unfriendly scrutiny, and left for Gujrat, where Sirdar Sahib Singh Bhangi gave him employment. But with this chief he soon quarreled, and in 1806, left Gujrat for Lahore, where Ranjit Singh, appreciating his talents, made him chief of the army, much to the annoyance of the Sikh Sirdars. The same year he led the army across the Satlej; and first seized Zira, which was for some time defended by the widow of Sirdar Mohr Singh Nishanwala. He then reduced the possessions of Jaggat Singh Buria, Mokatsar and Kot Kapura, being aided by a traitor in the camp, Sodhi Jowahir Singh, father of Guru Gulab Singh of Manawar; then Dharamkot, and he then marched to Faridkot from the chief of which he obtained tribute, on the way seizing Mari from Hari Singh and Arbel Singh brothers-in-law of Tara Singh Ghaiba. In October 1806, he accompanied Ranjit Singh in his expedition against Pattiala, in alliance with Raja Bhag Singh of Jheend, when Ludhiana, Jhandiala, Baddowal, Jagraon, Kot, Talwandi, Saniwal and other districts were seized, some being made over to the Raja of Jheend, some to Jaswant Singh of Nabha, and the remainder in jagir to the Lahore Sirdars, Gurdit Singh, Fatah Singh Ahluwalia and *Mokham Chand*.

In 1807, Tara Singh Ghaiba died, and his large possessions in the Jalandhar Doab were seized and divided between Ghurba Singh and *Mokham Chand*. The latter, in the three years 1806, 1807, 1808, received in jagir portions of the Ilakas of Gilla, Kot, Jagraon, Talwandi, Dharamkot, Kot Kapura, Zira, Faridkot, Saniwal, Jandbar, Bharampur, Dhari and Chandpur, comprising 268 villages and worth 1,54,255 Rs. a year. He was also made governor of the Jalandhar Doab, and at Philor, on the right bank of the Satlej, he built for the Maharaja the fort which still commands the passage of the river, on the site of an imperial Serai. The Rahon and Nakodar country worth 6,42,611 Rs. was also made over to him in jagir. The British had in 1809 made Ludhiana a military cantonment, and General Ochterlony the Resident stationed there did not find *Mokham Chand* a pleasant neighbour, for he hated the English who had made the Satlej the bound of his master's ambition. Early in 1810 he accompanied Ranjit Singh to Multan, the attack upon which was unsuccessful, and afterwards reduced the country held by Kahn Singh Nakkai. In 1811, he was sent against Bhimbar and returned to Lahore having extracted 40,000 Rs. from the Rajput chiefs in the hills above Gujrat. Some of the Jalandhar chiefs now showing a disposition to rise, he returned to Philor and quickly restored order, much to the Maharaja's satisfaction, who created him Diwan, bestowing on him at the same time valuable khilats. It was at this time that the Diwan annexed the territories of Sirdar Budh Singh Faizullapuria, valued at upwards of three lakhs of rupees. For long the Maharaja had desired his overthrow, and his refusal to attend at court gave a colourable excuse for attacking him. His forts of Jalandhar and Patti were reduced and the Sirdar fled to Ludhiana for safety. Strangely enough the two chiefs who brought their forces to aid the Diwan in this expedition were Fatah Singh Ahluwalia and Jodh Singh Ramgharia, although they were said to have formed an alliance with Budh Singh Faizullapuria to resist Ranjit Singh should he attack either of them. But it was perhaps to postpone an attack on themselves, which they saw was imminent, that they joined the Diwan in his attack on Jalandhar. They were now the only independent chiefs of importance between the Satlej and the Indus, and *Mokham Chand* urged his master to abolish, in a great measure if not altogether, the feudal tenure, and to take the whole country under his direct authority. But the time for so radical a change as this had not arrived.

In 1812, the Diwan reduced Kulu, and was then despatched to Kashmir, ostensibly to explain away the hostile movements of Prince Kharrak Singh and Bhaiya Ram Singh, but in reality to spy out the land and ascertain whether it was ripe for conquest. But another man, whose ambition was not less than that of Ranjit Singh, was preparing to attack Kashmir. This was Fatah Khan, the minister of Shah Mahmud of Kabul, who, seeing an alliance with the Sikhs was necessary to his success, invited the Maharaja to join forces and with him invade Kashmir. This was agreed to and Diwan *Mokham Chand* and Fatah Khan marched from Jhelam together. But the Afghan had no intention of allowing the Sikhs any large share either in the conquest or in its results and had only carried on negotiations to secure the Maharaja's neutrality. No sooner had the force reached the Pir Panjal than he, without consulting *Mokham Chand* or informing him of his intention, pressed on by double marches with his hardy mountain troops, while the Sikhs, never of much use in the hills, were unable to move owing to a heavy fall of snow. The Diwan saw the design of Fatah Khan but he was not disconcerted. He promised the Rajaori chief a jagir of 25,000 Rs. if he would show him a pass by which he might reach the valley at the same time as Fatah Khan, which he contrived to do with a handful of troops under Jodh Singh Kalsia and Nihal Singh Attari. The Diwan was thus present at the capture of Sher Ghar and Hari Parbat and the reduction of the valley, which was a work of no difficulty, for Atta Muhammad the Governor had fled and little resistance was offered, but his force was too weak to be of much assistance, and Fatah Khan declared that the Sikhs were not entitled to a third share of the plunder as had been agreed upon. Shah Shuja the ex-prince of Kabul was made over to the Diwan who brought him to Lahore where he was received with every appearance of respect, but Ranjit Singh, savage at his disappointment in Kashmir, and thinking hospitality to one in misfortune superfluous, robbed him of the famous Koh-i-Nur diamond and his other jewels, and detained him, under surveillance, till April 1815, when he made his escape. The Maharaja, when he heard that Fatah Khan would not divide the spoil of Kashmir, was very wrath and determined on revenge. He opened negotiations with Jahandad Khan, brother of Atta Muhammad the late Governor of Kashmir, who held the fort of Attock which commanded the passage of the Indus, and induced him to surrender it to a

Sikh force. It was now Fatah Khan's turn to be angry and he demanded the restoration of the fort, but Ranjit Singh refused until he should receive his share of the Kashmir plunder. The Wazir, in April 1813, set out from Kashmir, and invested Attock. Forces were hurried up from Lahore, first under Karam Singh Chahal and then under Diwan *Mokham Chand*. For long the armies lay opposite each other, the Sikhs suffering somewhat in the frequent skirmishes and not liking to force on a general engagement, till the garrison of the fort had exhausted its supplies and it was necessary to relieve it or abandon it altogether. The Diwan then determined on fighting, and at Haidaru, a few miles from Attock he drew up his force in order of battle. The ball was opened by a brilliant cavalry charge led by Dost Muhammad Khan, afterwards the celebrated ruler of Kabul, which broke the Sikh line. One wing was thrown into complete disorder and some guns captured. The Afghans, thinking the victory won, dispersed to plunder, when the Diwan led up his reserves in person and drove back the enemy at all points with great loss. Fatah Khan had already fled, believing Dost Muhammad to be slain, and the Afghan army, driven out of Khairabad, retired upon Kabul, from whence the Wazir led an expedition against Herat to endeavour to recover the reputation he had lost before Attock. The battle of Haidaru was fought on the 13th July 1813.

While *Mokham Chand* was engaged on active service his son *Moti Ram* managed the Jalandhar Doab. His grandson *Ramdyal*, though at this time only twenty-two years of age, was already distinguished for ability and bravery, and in May 1814, when the Maharaja determined to again invade Kashmir, he was appointed to command one division of the army. Against this expedition the Diwan remonstrated in vain. He urged that the season was not propitious; that no supplies had been collected on the road; that the hill Rajas were hostile; but when he saw that Ranjit Singh was determined to try his fortune he asked leave to accompany the army. But *Mokham Chand* was now very old and his health was failing, and the Maharaja desired him to remain at Lahore and preserve order during his absence. The Sikh army was massed at Sialkot, and from there marched to Rajaori, the Raja of which place recommended that the force should be divided, one portion, under the Maharaja in person, marching by way of Punch, the second, under *Ramdyal*, Dal Singh Naharnah, Jamadar Khushhal Singh and other Sirdars, marching through the Bahramgalla Pass. This advice was unfortunately followed, and *Ramdyal* with his division crossed the Pir Panjal and descended into the valley where Azim Khan with his whole force gave them battle. The Sikhs fought well but they were outnumbered and driven back with great loss. A repulse was in their case as disastrous as a total defeat; they had no reinforcements at hand and no supplies. Bhaiya Ram Singh was sent by Ranjit Singh to the assistance of the detachment, but he was a timid man, and when he heard of *Ramdyal's* repulse, he halted for a day or two at Bahramgalla, and then retired. The Maharaja now found that he must retreat himself, leaving *Ramdyal* to his fate. The retreat soon became a flight. The hill tribes disputed the passage of the army, and heavy rain came on making the road all but impracticable. But at length, with great loss of men and officers, among the latter the brave Mit Singh Padhania, the Maharaja fought his way out of the hills and retired to Lahore. Although the disasters which had befallen the expedition were in a great measure owing to the rashness and precipitancy of *Ramdyal*, yet he retrieved matters as far as was possible. He held his own in the Kashmir valley with such determination that Azim Khan was compelled to come to terms, allowing him a safe conduct and even admitting in a written document the supremacy of Lahore.

In October of the same year Diwan *Mokham Chand* died at Philor, to the grief of the Maharaja and the whole Sikh nation. As a general he had been almost always successful; his administrative talents were as great as his military ones, and in his death, Ranjit Singh lost his most loyal and devoted servant. But there were other good men left in the family. *Moti Ram* was created Diwan in his father's room and the Jalandhar Doab was entrusted to him, with the charge of the fort at Philor.

Ramdyal with Dal Singh Naharna was sent against the Kharals of Gogaira and to take tribute from Multan and Bahawalpur; and the next year against Rajaori to punish the treachery of Raja Agar Khan during the expedition of 1814. Agar Khan tried to buy forgiveness, but *Ramdyal* would not listen to terms, and sacked and burnt both the town of Rajaori and the palace of the Raja. The next year he was sent northwards to watch the movement of Fatah Khan, who had joined his brother Azim Khan in Kashmir, returning to Kabul the next year. Hukma Singh Chimni was at this time in charge of the Attock fort, and it was as much Ramdyal and he could do to keep in order the Muhammadans of Hazara and Yusafzai, who were instigated to revolt by Fatah Khan, and on one occasion *Ramdyal* was all but defeated by them.

In the spring of 1819, the Maharája, taking advantage of the absence from Kashmir of the Governor Azim Khan, determined again to attempt its reduction. The leader of the Sikh army was Misr Diwan Chand, the conqueror of Multan, while *Ramdyal* commanded the rear division. The latter was prevented from marching by the heavy rain and had no share in the fighting. Little resistance was, however, made; Zabar Khan took to flight, and the province of Kashmir was annexed by Ranjit Singh to his dominions, *Moti Ram* being appointed the first Governor.

Ramdyal was then sent against the Raja of Punch, and when Bhai Makkan Singh was killed in Hazara and Hukma Singh Chimni the governor recalled, he was sent there to restore order. This was no easy matter. The tribes had been thoroughly exasperated by the conduct of Hukma Singh, and their successes had given them confidence, and when *Ramdyal* had penetrated as far as the fort of Gandghar, he was surrounded by numbers of the enemy, the Afghans of Miswari, Srikot, Torbela, Yusafzai and Swat, and compelled to fight. Through the whole day, from sunrise to sunset, the battle was fought against enormous odds by the Sikhs, and at night, completely worn out, they retired to their entrenchments. Last to leave the field was *Ramdyal*, and the enemy perceiving that he was separated from the main body of the army, made a sudden dash and cut off and surrounded his party. The Sikhs fought desperately but in vain; and *Ramdyal* was killed and all his escort. The Sikhs in dismay at the death of their General struck their camp and retreated in all haste from Hazara.

The death of Ramdyal was a great grief to his father who desired to give up the Kashmir government and retire to Benares. The Maharaja was not unwilling to permit the Diwan's resignation, and appointed as his successor Sirdar Hari Singh Nalwa, the most dashing soldier in the Khalsa army, now that *Ramdyal* was dead. But the Kashmiris and hill tribes could not endure the tyranny of the Sirdar, and after one year, *Moti Ram* was re-appointed Governor, and held the post till 1826. The Diwan was a man of some ability and was liked by the people, but he was indolent and apathetic and his administration was not marked by any event of importance, except the advent of the cholera, which then visited Kashmir for the first time and decimated the population. While *Moti Ram* was in Kashmir his son *Kirpa Ram* managed the Jalandhar Doab, and *Shiv Dyal* lived on his jagir in the Gujrat district. Raja Dhyan Singh was jealous of the wealth and power of the family and persuaded the Maharaja to grant the estate of Siba near Philor to his brother-in-law Ram Singh. *Kirpa Ram* was so much irritated at this slight that when he was directed to join the Peshawar expedition with his whole contingent, he only brought 50 horsemen. The Maharaja was furious; he imprisoned *Kirpa Ram*; recalled *Moti Ram* from Kashmir, and sent there as the new governor Diwan Chuni Lal, while the fort of Philor he made over to Fakir Azizuddin and later to Sirdar Desa Singh Majithia. It was not for a year and a half that the family was again taken into favour, and then only on payment of a heavy fine. *Kirpa Ram* was now sent to Kashmir as governor, superseding Chuni Lal. His administration was tolerably successful. He was an extravagant man and fond of display, but at the same time of a gentle disposition. The Rambagh garden at Srinagar, in which Maharaja Gulab Singh's monument stands, was laid out by him, as were also many other gardens in the neighbourhood of the capital. In 1828, the valley suffered very much from earthquakes. Private and public buildings were destroyed, and the inhabitants forsook the towns for the greater security of the mountains. After the earthquakes came the cholera even worse than in the days of *Moti Ram*. The cholera was followed by the rebellion of the Raja of Muzaffarabad, but *Kirpa Ram* marched against him and completely defeated him. These were the only events of the administration. In 1831, *Kirpa Ram* again suffered from the enmity of Raja Dhyan Singh. He had given protection to Raja Faiz Talab Khan of Bhimbar, whom both the Dogra brothers hated and wished to capture, while *Kirpa Ram* resolutely refused to give him up. Dhyan Singh accused *Kirpa Ram* of contumacy and embezzlement, and had so much influence with the Maharaja that the Diwan was recalled from Kashmir and again imprisoned, while the Jalandhar Doab was taken from *Moti Ram* and given to Misr Rup Lal, after Shaikh Ghulam Mohiuddin had been tried in Hoshiarpur and found wanting. At this time *Moti Ram* was absent at Simla, where he had been sent with Hari Singh Nalwa and Fakir Azizuddin on a mission to the Governor General. On his return he tried to make peace between Raja Dhyan Singh and his son, who had been released on payment of a nazrana of nine lakhs of rupees, but seeing this impracticable and weary of public life, he retired to Benares where he died in 1839. *Kirpa Ram* served in Bannu in 1832, and then finding the enmity of Dhyan Singh as great as ever while his influence at court increased day by day, he asked permission to join his father at Benares. The permission was refused, and *Kirpa Ram* determined to go without it. He went on an assumed pilgrimage to Joala Mukhi, and from there, crossing the Satlej into British territory, he journeyed to Benares, where he remained till his death in 1842. He left no son of his own, but he had adopted *Dhunraj*, whom he left the sole agent of his still large jagirs, worth four lakhs of rupees. *Dhunraj* was made a colonel under Sirdar Jowahir Singh, and in 1848 did good service with Colonel Lawrence at Peshawar, where he is now Extra Assistant Commissioner. He holds in jagir the half of Kunjah, worth 1,300 Rs.

When *Kirpa Ram* left the Panjab his brother *Shiv Dyal,* who had been appointed governor of Gujrat, and his sons kept their appointments, *Kanheya Lal* acting as Deputy to his father, and *Mya Lal* holding an office at court. The latter accompanied Shaikh Ghulam Mohiuddin to Kashmir as treasurer, in 1841, but on his father's death, three years later, returned to Kunjah, where he succeeded to the estate worth 12,000 Rs. He did good service during the rebellion of 1848, and has since the annexation of the Panjab acted as Thannadar of Jalandhar and Gujrat. In 1858 he was appointed Tehsildar of Harappa in the Gogaira district, but did not hold the appointment for any length of time. He resides at Kunjah, and is not now in Government employ. *Kanheya Lal* filled the office of Kardar in several districts during Sikh rule. His eldest son *Radha Kishan* was Thanadar of Peshawar until the reorganization of the Police, when he received his discharge.

Regarding the other branch of the family a few words will be sufficient. *Soba Ram,* brother of *Mohkam Chand,* was for some years in the Maharaja's service, and left to his three sons, *Kishan Dyal, Ditta Mal* and *Ganpat Rai,* a jagir of 5,000 Rs. in the neighbourhood of Kunjah with the village of Gidarkot. Both *Ditta Mal* and *Ganpat Rai* accompanied Shaikh Mohiuddin to Kashmir, and remained in his service and that of his son Imamuddin Khan for three years as Kardars. During the rebellion of 1848, the brothers served under Major Edwardes and behaved well, and on the annexation of the Panjab were taken into Government employ. *Ditta Mal* was first made a Tehsildar, and subsequently Extra Assistant Commissioner. He died without issue. *Ganpat Rai* was employed in the Gogaira settlement, on the completion of which he received his discharge. He resides at Kunjah in Gujrat.

FATAH KHAN DREK.

- GHAIRAT ALI KHAN.
  - Moazam Khan.
    - Zulf-kar Khan.
      - Salabat Khan.
        - Abdullah Khan.
          - Khairuddin Khan.
            - Fatah Khan.
              - Kalai Khan.
              - Muhammad Khan, Dead.
              - Khudadad Khan.
            - Sher Khan.
              - Lal Khan.
          - Ghulam Khan.
          - Shahanchi Khan.
          - Fazl Khan.
            - Nawab Khan.
            - Karam Khan.

HISTORY OF THE FAMILY.

Malik Fatah Khan Drek is the head of one branch of the large and important Khattar tribe. It is not easy to determine with certainty the origin of the Khattars, but it seems probable that they were originally natives of Khorasan and came to India with the first Muhammadan invaders. They trace their genealogy up to Kutb Shah or Kutb-ud-din nicknamed 'Aibak' from his broken finger and 'Lakh baksh' from his liberality, who was for many years the Viceroy of Shahab-ud-din Ghori, in India, and who afterwards himself reigned, the first of the slave kings. But this story is certainly false. The Kutb Shah of Khattar genealog had nine sons, while Kutb Shah Aibak had no child of his own, A Shah who succeeded him being an adopted son. The Awans, the Kh and the Khattars seem to have had a common origin, all tracing their pedigree back to Kutb Shah, who may have lived about the beginning of the eleventh century and who probably came to India with one of the invading armies of Sultan Mahmud Ghaznivi. His nine sons were named Torai, Haji, Afik, Dusah, Gulgan, Khandan, Khokar, Ghora and Chohan. The two first remained in Afghanistan, and Afik and Dusah were killed in battle, leaving no issue. From Khokar have descended the Khokars of Hafizabad, in the Gujranwala district, in no way connected with the Kokhars of Pind Dadan Khan who are of Rajput descent. The Khattars have descended from Chohan the youngest son. From two of Chohan's sons, Hamir and Pasin, have descended some of the Awans of the Amritsar and Sialkot districts. To Ghora the Awans of Rawalpindi and Jhelam, Gujrat and Jalandhar trace their origin, while Gulgan also has Awan descendants in Sialkot and Rawalpindi. The Awans of the Sialkot villages Jandiala, Rawal, Milka and Saroba and those of Narowal in Amritsar trace from Durj, a brother of Kutb Shah. Chohan, the ancestor of the Khattar tribe, who is said to have been an officer of Sultan Mahmud, marched against Nilab then a large town on the Indus, fifteen miles below Attock, and after a short siege took it from the Hindu chief Raj Deo and made it his head-quarters. About the same time his brother Khokar had settled at Kosak in Jhelam later held by the Janjoahs, and famous for its almost impregnable fort, long besieged in vain by Ranjit Singh. To Ghora or Gholsa had been assigned Sukesar, and to Gulgan a strip of land along the river Jhelam. For many years the descendants of Chohan held Nilab without opposition till the days of *Khattar Khan* in the sixth generation from Chohan. The Hindus, growing powerful, drove the tribe out of Nilab, and compelled it to leave India for Afghanistan, where *Khattar Khan*, about the year 1175, entered the service of Muhammad Ghori who had just overrun the province of Ghazni and was preparing to attack India. With him *Khattar Khan* returned to the Panjab, and recovered Nilab by a strategem. He dressed his men as merchants and entered the town as if for trade, with large boxes filled with arms. No sooner had they got within the walls, than the disguise was thrown off, every man seized his arms, and the town, taken by surprise, was captured. The tribe now took the name of its leader Khattar. It was subordinate to the Imperial Governor of Attock, Langar Khan, who afterwards became Viceroy at Lahore. About this time the Khattars are said to have abandoned Muhammadanism. The tradition is that a jogi or ascetic came to Nilab, and by powerful enchantments induced the whole population to worship idols. He not only enchanted the people but also the cattle, which gave blood instead of milk, till news of these prodigies reached the ears of the saint Isa Abdul Wahab * at Uchh in the Leia district, who sent his son Shah Nuri Abdul Rahman to recall the people to the true faith. The apostle travelled to Nilab, and on the outskirts of the town he met an old woman from whom he asked a draught of milk. She told him of the calamity which had befallen the cattle, but Abdul Rahman insisted on her attempting to milk, and as a reward for her faith pure white milk flowed from the udder of the cow instead of blood. The jogi had heard of the saint's arrival, and, taking the form of a kite, came sailing down to watch his movements, but Abdul Rahman was not deceived. He threw his shoe at the bird which fell dead among the rocks, and the people, freed from enchantment, cast away their idols and returned to the faith of Muhammad. This curious legend seems to have been invented by the Khattars and Awans to account for the rise of a general belief in their Hindu origin, which they repudiate, asserting that if they were ever idol worshipers it was but a temporary lapse from Islamism. *Khattar Khan* had six sons, *Jand Khan*, *Isa Khan*, *Sarwar Khan*, *Firoz Khan*, *Sehra Khan* and *Pehru Khan*. About three generations after his death the tribe lost Nilab, but they took possession of the open country between Rawalpindi and the Indus, which became known by the name of Khatar. The descendants of *Jand Khan* took possession of the district called after them Jandal, between Khushhalghar and Nara, and

* Unfortunately for the legend, it is certain that Abdul Wahab did not come to Leia before 1580. Perhaps, however, the saint alluded to may be Abdul Kambir Bukhari who lived at Uchh in Bahawalpur at the end of the twelvth century and from whom the Leia saint was descended.

the other sons settled in the neighbouring Ilakas, driving out the Gujars and even their own kinsmen the Awans.

From *Firoz Khan*, the fourth son of *Khattar Khan*, has the Drek family descended. His great grandson was *Ratnah*, from whom have descended the clan known as Rattial. Two generations later were *Balu Khan* and *Isa Khan*, from the former of whom have sprung the Balwans who inhabit Barotah, where the river Haroh flows into the Indus. The offspring of the latter is the clan Isial, whose location is in Choi Gariala and Dher, to the South of Barota. *Ghor Khan*, the great nephew of *Balu Khan*, founded the Gharral clan who live at Akori. So, for many generations the tribe grew and prospered. They were not without good qualities, but were bad farmers, reckless and extravagant and never became rich or distinguished. The best of their chiefs was *Ghairat Khan* who left his home and went to seek his fortune at Dehli, where he entered the service of an officer of the court, and gradually rose in favour till he was able to return home with a portion of the Khatar country, as an imperial grant, in jagir. His second son, *Zul Kadar Khan*, rebuilt the village of Drek, which had been founded long before by the Awans and named Rashidpur, but which had fallen into ruins. *Salabat Khan*, grandson of *Ghairat Ali Khan*, founded Kot Salabat Khan and Zindai. *Khairuddin* and *Fazl Khan* were the fathers of the present chiefs.

Little can said of the history of the Khattars. Like their neighbours the Ghebas and Awans they resisted the Sikhs as long as they could, and, like them, resisted in vain. They assert that the Sikhs allowed them the fourth of the revenue as lords of the soil, and in the later Sikh revenue papers there is mention of such a grant, but it is not stated in favour of which chiefs the alienation was made. When the Sikh Kardar Diwan Mulraj was besieged in Hazara by the insurgents, Malik *Ghulam Khan* and *Fatah Khan* came to his aid, and rescued him. *Fatah Khan* possesses considerable influence in the Rawalpindi district, and his services have been always at the disposal of Government. In 1857, he furnished levies for guarding the ferries on the Indus, and testified his loyalty in other ways. He holds the villages of Bahtur Bhagowi, Kot Sundi and Lundi worth together 2,064 Rs. in jagir, of which 350 Rs. descend in perpetuity. He also, with his brother Sher Khan, holds proprietary rights in different villages to the value of 5,264 Rs. a year.

Nawab Khan and *Karam Khan*, are not on good terms with their cousins. They live separately and hold a jagir of 300 Rs. with proprietary rights in eight villages.

MUHAMMAD HAIYAT KHAN OF WAH.

SYAD AHMAD KHAN.
|
Ghazzar Khan.
|
Jamal Khan.
|
Jalal Khan.
|
Kamal Khan.
|
Karm Khan.

Buhadar Khan.	Muhammad Haiyat Khan.

HISTORY OF THE FAMILY.

This is a Khattar family and is like Fatah Khan Drek of the Firozal clan, being descended from Firoz Khan the fourth son of Khattar Khan. *Syad Ahmad Khan* seems to have gone to Dehli about the same time as Ghairat Khan, with his son *Ghazzar Khan*, and to have entered the imperial service. He was not however so fortunate, for a chief officer at court fell in love with the reputation of the beauty of *Gul Begam*, sister of *Ghazzar Khan*, and threw him into prison when he refused to give her up. *Syad Ahmad*, the father, fled by night with his pretty daughter, and returned to his native country where he founded a village which he named Ahmadabad, now in ruins. *Ghazzar Khan* died in prison, and his son *Jamal Khan*, quarreling with his relations, left Ahmadabad and founded a village for himself in the jungle, calling it Jalalsar after the name of his son. But the memory of *Jamal Khan's* humble village has been lost in the palace and serai built close at hand by the Emperor Shah Jahan, in 1645, when marching towards Kabul. Some traces of the buildings are still visible, as the Asaf Khani Mahal, and the name of the village Wah * is said to express the satisfaction of the Emperor as

* Wah ! an ejaculation commonly used in the Panjab, expressive of astonishment or satisfaction.

he looked on the beauty of the scene, with its running water and pleasant groves.

The present head of the family is *Muhammad Haiyat Khan.* His father *Karam Khan* was a brave soldier, and in 1848 he raised a force of horse and foot which Captain Nicholson employed in holding the Margalla Pass. His house at Wâh was burnt down by the rebel Sikh force, under the command of Utâr Singh Atariwala, and he was shortly afterwards killed by Fatah Khan, an old enemy of his house, who surprised him when taking his noonday siesta in a garden. *Muhammad Haiyat Khan* then joined Captain Abbott at Nara, with a few recruits, and remained with that officer till the close of the war. In 1857, General Nicholson was Deputy Commissioner of Peshawar, and when the mutiny first broke out he directed *Haiyat Khan* to raise a body of Afridis for service, and when he was appointed to command the Panjab moveable column he nominated the young man as his native aide-de-camp. *Haiyat Khan* was with the General when he so terribly punished the mutinous 55th Native Infantry at Hoti Murdan, and the 46th Native Infantry and the 9th Light Cavalry at Trimmu Ghat. He marched to Dehli with the force and fought gallantly throughout the siege. He was with the General when he was mortally wounded at the capture of the city, and remained with him to the last, attending him, for the few days that he survived, with the utmost devotion. After this, *Haiyat Khan* returned to Peshawar, where he was appointed Thannadar and a few months later he was transferred to Jhelam, and made Tehsildar of Tallagang. In May 1861 he was raised to the rank of Extra Assistant Commissioner and posted to Shahpur, whence he was transferred to Bannu where he is now stationed. He has proved himself as good in the office as gallant in the field. He has some literary ability, and is now preparing an account of the Afghan border tribes which will be valuable and interesting. *Buhadar Khan,* half brother of *Muhammad Haiyat Khan,* is a Deputy Inspector of Police in the Rawalpindi district.

KAZI FAZL AHMAD.

- MUHAMMAD SADIK.
  - Muhammad Sharif.
    - Haji Mustafa.
      - Muhammad Jaffir.
        - Shaikh Umr.
          - Kazi Gulam Muhammad.
            - Kazi Fazal Ahmad.
              - Kazi Fatah Muhammad.
                - Haji Ahmad.
              - Ali Ahmad.
              - Faiz Ahmad.
            - Nur Ahmad.
              - Ashraf Khan.
              - Ibrahim Khan.
            - Sultan Ahmad.
            - Ghazan Khan.
            - Mir Ahmad.
          - Gul Ahmad.
            - Syad Ahmad.

HISTORY OF THE FAMILY.

A little more than three centuries ago, in the reign of Humayun, *Muhammad Sadik* of the Khattar tribe, emigrated from the neighbourhood of Dehli to Chachh, where, about six miles from Attock, he founded the village of Fattuchak. He also built Gondal on the high road to Peshawar; Jattyal, Mirobasinal, and other villages which the Emperor granted him in jagir. *Muhammad Sadik* was a man of some learning, and as Chachh had few scholars, his acquirements procured him the office of Kazi or judge. This was held by him throughout life and descended to his son, but in the third generation it was taken away and given to a neighbouring chief Muhammad Hussain. *Muhammad Jaffir* recovered the title, which is still held by his descendants though without judicial powers. Little is known of the history of the family, which was at no time of much importance, and what papers were possessed by the Kazi were destroyed by the Sikhs when they gained possession of Attock in 1848. When Ranjit Singh took the fort in 1813, *Kazi Ghulam Muhammad,* fearing for his safety, fled across the Indus to Khattak, where he took refuge with Firoz Khan while his house was burnt and his property plundered by the Sikhs. Sirdar Amir Singh Sindhanwalia recalled him, and restored a portion of his old jagirs giving him a new one of 300 Rs. in Khattak. Soon after this Ranjit Singh made him 'wakil' or agent on the part of the Government in the Yusufzai and Khattak territories, and this office he held till 1824, when he was assassinated by a Nihang whom he had offended. His eldest son *Fazl Ahmad* succeeded to the wakilship, which he held, enjoying considerable authority and influence among the Pathans of the district, till the commencement of the British rule. The Kazi is a man of high character and possesses influence on both sides of the Indus. He has always been distinguished for loyalty and has rendered much assistance to the British officers in the management of the district. In 1848 he did good service, and his nephew and some of his men served with Captain Nicholson throughout the war. In 1857, he behaved loyally and well, and aided to provision the fort of Attock. He received for his services a khillat of 200 Rs., and 60 Rs., the share in the cash allowance of 600 Rs. held by his brother *Nur Ahmad* and which had lapsed at his death, was continued to the Kazi for his life. He holds the village of Gondal worth 839 Rs. in jagir, one quarter to descend in perpetuity. He has also proprietary rights in the district. He has permitted his brothers and his cousin *Syad Ahmad* to share the jagir with him, an act of kindness which he now regrets as their shares lapse on their death.

MALIK FIROZUDDIN KHAN OF SHAMSHABAD.

- MUHMAMAD MITH KHAN.
  - Sirafraz Khan.
  - Khudayar Khan.
  - Muhammad Allahyar Khan
    - Muhammad Nasim Khan.
      - Sultan Ahmad.
      - Haji Ahmad.
    - Firozuddin Khan.
      - Roshan-uddin.
      - Muhammad Shafi.
      - Ahmad Din.
      - Ghulam Jalani.
      - Wazl Ahmad.
      - Muham-mad Jaffir.
    - Hafiz Ghulam Ahmad Khan.
  - Muhammad Namdar Khan.

HISTORY OF THE FAMILY.

The origin of the Awan tribe, to which Malik Firoz-ud-din Khan belongs, has been the subject of much speculation. At one time the Awans have been considered of Hindu, at another of Afghan descent, and by some as the descendants of the so called Bactrian Greeks. But there is nothing in the traditions of the Awans themselves to favour the last supposition, and indeed it is very doubtful whether any Greeks settled in Bactria at all. The probability is that every Greek in Alexander's army turned his back with joy upon India and the East, while the detachment of the army which remained behind in Bactria was composed of barbarian auxiliaries, from whom no historian or philologist would care to derive any tribe whatever. The Awans are widely scattered throughout the Panjab. Thickest in Rawalpindi and Jhelam, they are numerous in Shahpur and Leia, and even stretch across the Indus into the Derajat, and some three thousand inhabit the Yusafzai plain. There are many Awan villages in Gujrat and Sialkot and a few in Amritsar and Jalandhar. But all branches of the tribe are unanimous in stating that they originally came from the neighbourhood of Ghazni to India, and all trace their genealogy to Hasrat Ali the son-in-law of the Prophet. Kutb Shah, who came from Ghazni with Sultan Mahmud, was the common ancestor of the Awans, the Khokars and the Khattars, and in the history of Fatah Khan Drek will be found some mention of the Awan connection with these tribes. The Awans seem first to have settled in Rawalpindi, where *Shamir Khan* built a town on the Indus which he called Shamirabad after his own name. They gradually spread over the country, fighting with the Gujars and their kinsmen the Khattars, driving before them the Janjoahs who in very old days had taken possession of the Jhelam district, and being in turn driven out of their holdings by the Ghakkars the most powerful tribe of all. It is not practicable to follow the history of the several branches of the Awan tribe. It was only in the Rawalpindi, Jhelam and Shahpur districts that they became of any political importance. In other parts of the Panjab they appear as quiet peasants, not such good agriculturists as the Jats, but still industrious and intelligent. In Rawalpindi they held in old days the Khatar country, and still inhabit it though not as proprietors, and in this district Mehndu Khan of Chihan, Samandar Khan of Sirwala and Sirafraz Khan of Jand Bugdial are their chief men. In the Shahpur district the Awans held the hilly country to the north west, Jalar, Naoshera and Sukesar, where the head of the tribe still resides; and in Jhelam, the west of the district known as the 'Awan Kari' between the Gabir River and Bannu. To the north of Rawalpindi live the Goleras, an Awan clan, famous in old days for their marauding propensities, but they are now few in number and have no chief of any note.

There is little to relate of the Shamshabad family. The head of it claims to have descended from *Shamir Khan* who founded the village and reclaimed the land between it and the Indus from the river which is said to have then been a wide shallow stream with swamps and marshes of great extent on the left bank. Shamshabad lies just off the high road, and the residents seem to have thought themselves too open to attack to meddle much in district or imperial politics, and lived quietly at their village while army after army marched past Dehli-wards, without molesting them. At last, in 1813, the Kabul army, part of which was investing Attock, chose Shamshabad for their camp, and after Diwan Mohkam Chand had defeated the Afghans he destroyed the village which he considered had favoured and assisted them. The Maharaja however restored the estate to the family and allowed *Muhammad Nasim Khan* to rebuild the village, which he did at considerable expense. ***Firoz-ud-din*** entered the Sikh service and on his brother's death succeeded to the jagir. In 1848-49 he did good service under Captain Nicholson at Ramnagar, Margalla, Pind Dadan Khan and elsewhere. In 1857, he again showed his loyalty and courage, and raising horse and foot guarded the ferries on the Indus. General Nicholson had a high opinion of the Malik, and desired to take him with his force to Dehli, but at that time he could not be spared from his own district. He was Tehsildar of Rawalpindi from 1850 to 1857 ; and from 1858 to 1863, Tehsildar of Gujar Khan. He holds a life pension of 400 Rs., and the village of Shamshabad worth 2,200 Rs. has been granted in perpetuity.

RAJA KARM DAD KHAN GHAKKAR.

- Sultan Kai Gohar Khan.
  - Sultan Rustam Khan.
    - Sultan Kabil Khan.
      - Sultan Ghakkar Shah.
        - Sultan Baj Khan.
          - Malik Machpal Khan.
            - Malik Rajar Khan.
              - Malik Sipher Khan.
                - Malik Nang Khan.
                  - Malik Lohar Khan.
                    - Malik Lakan Khan
                      - Malik Kadu Khan.
                        - Malik Gul Muhammad Khan.
                          - Malik Pir Khan.
                            - Malik Tatar Khan.
                              - Sultan Adam Khan.
                                - Lashkari Khan.
                                  - Moharir Khan.
                                - Sultan Ali Muhammad Khan.
                                  - Sultan Jalal Khan.
                                    - Sultan Akbar Kuli Khan.
                                      - Sultan Murad Kuli Khan.
                                        - Sultan Allahdad Khan.
                                          - Sultan Dulu Murad Khan.
                                            - Sultan Muazzam Khan.
                                              - Sultan Mukarrab Khan.
                                                - Sultan Sadulla Khan.
                                                - Sultan Nazir Ali Khan.
                                                - Mansur Khan.
                                                  - Raja Fatah Ali Khan.
                                                    - Bahadar Ali Khan.
                                                  - Maddat Khan.
                                                    - Fatah Khan.
                                                  - Faiz Talab Khan.
                                                  - Sher Khan.
                                                  - Ali Haidar Khan.
                                                    - Fatah Khan.
                                                    - Ali Gohar.
                                                    - Sharif Khan.
                                                    - Muhammad Ali.
                                                  - Jalal Khan.
                                                    - Bostan Khan.
                                                    - Jahan Khan.
                                                    - Faiz Talab Khan, dead,
                                                      - Dost Muhammad Khan.
                                                - Shadman Khan.
                                                  - Raja Haiyat Ullah Khan, D. 1865.
                                                    - Karmdad Khan, B. 1852.
                                                  - Muhammad Ali Khan.
                                                  - Kamal Khan.
                                                    - Allahdad Khan.
                                                    - Khudadad Khan.
                              - Sultan Sarang Khan.
                                - Alawal Khan.
                                - Kamal Khan.
                                  - Mubarik Khan.
                                    - Ajmir Khan.
                                      - Shadman Khan.
                                - Said Khan.
                            - Jastar Khan.
                            - Pilu Khan.
                              - Hati Khan.
                        - Joda Khan.
                          - Kayas Khan.
                    - Kulbeja Khan.
                      - Baja Khan.
                    - Wahid Khan.
                  - Salori Khan.
                  - San Khan.

HISTORY OF THE TRIBE.

No Panjab tribe is more frequently mentioned in Indian history than the Ghakkars, who for many hundred years were the possessors of great power and a wide extent of country. The reason of their strength was that they were united among themselves. Not that their history does not contain many feuds and long continued contests between rival chiefs, but they at all times acknowledged some one chief as head of the tribe, and under him all the clans marched to battle against any external foe. It was their organization which enabled them to defeat Awans, Gujars, Khattars and Janjoahs, tribes always divided among themselves, and never able to combine even against a common enemy. The Ghakkars trace their descent from Kaigohar, a native of Ispahan in Persia, whose son Sultan Kaid was a great and successful general, the conqueror of Badakshan and a part of Thibet which he held during his life and bequeathed to his son Sultan Teb. For seven generations the family ruled in Thibet, till Sultan Kab, the eighth in descent from Kaid, conquered Kashmir from Manowar Khan, whose daughter he married to his son Farukh. For thirteen generations the Ghakkars held Kashmir, Farukh Amir, Mir Dad, Khair-ud-din, Goharganj, Nur-ud-din, Murad, Bakhtyar, Alam, Sammand, Mehrab and Rustam ruling in succession. In this last reign the Kashmiris revolted and put Rustam to death, while his son Kabil fled to the court of Nasir-ud-din Sabaktugin who was then reigning in Kabul, 987 A. D. It is very difficult to ascertain how far this account of the Ghakkar occupation of Thibet and Kashmir is true. It is certain that they overran Kashmir in very early days, and traces of them are still found to the north and west of that country, but there is no proof whatever that they founded a dynasty there. Indeed the names of these chiefs are fabulous. Several are Muhammadan names, *e. g.* Khair-ud-din, Nur-ud-din, and at this time the Ghakkars were certainly not converted to Islamism. Those Muhammadan histories, like Haidar Doghlat, the Hajnama and Ferishta, in which mention is made of the Ghakkars, state that it was only in the 13th century that they embraced the true faith. Ferishta indeed speaks of them, in 1205 A. D., as savage barbarians, among whom prevailed female infanticide and polyandry, while they were bitter persecutors of Muhammadans, and were only converted at the close of the reign of Muhammad Ghori. Had there been a dynasty of Muhammadan rulers in Kashmir for thirteen generations, previous to 987 A. D. when Kabil fled to the court of Sabaktagin, it is probable that Kashmir would not require to be reconverted to Islamism, in 1327 A. D. as it certainly was during the reign of Shah Mir, otherwise known as Shamsh-ud-din. It may indeed be doubted whether the Ghakkars are of Persian origin at all. The chief point in its favour is that, as a rule, the Ghakkars are of the Shia sect, while all the other Muhammadan tribes of their part of the country are Sunis. It has again been thought that the Ghakkars are a branch of the Gujar tribe, but this theory which is supported by rather obscure philological argument, is not sufficiently interesting to be more than noticed here. As early as 682, according to Ferishta, the Ghakkars were resident in the Panjab, and about that year made an alliance offensive and defensive with the Afghans, who aided them against the Raja of Lahore. That the Ghakkars were then resident on the Indus seems probable, though their own history contradicts it; but it is not likely that the Afghans, then new converts to Muhammadanism, fierce and enthusiastic, would have formed an alliance with an idolatrous tribe.*

Kabil Khan obtained employ under Sabaktagin and his second son *Ghakkar Shah*, from whom the tribe derived its name, accompanied Mahmud of Ghuzni to India, at the beginning of the eleventh century, and

---

* The early history of the Ghakkars, as related by themselves, is necessarily given here. But it seems purely fabulous. The probability is they were emigrants from Khorasan or Afghanistan and settled in the Panjab not later than 300 A. D. Raja Hodi, a Ghakkar chief, is indeed said to have married the daughter of Risalu, the Rajput chief of Sialkot and one of Salvahan's sixteen sons, (vide pp. 12-209) who reigned about 120 A. D. This may be false, but it shows that the traditions of the country point to the Ghakkars as having been long resident in the Panjab. Again, where Ghakkar history makes the founder of the tribe to be an officer in Mahmud Shah's army, Ferishta records that this very Mahmud was in 1008 A. D. attacked in the neighbourhood of Peshawar by a force of 30,000 Ghakkars, who penetrated the Muhammadan camp and were only repulsed with the greatest difficulty, Mahmud losing 5,000 men.

obtained leave to settle with his tribe, then very numerous, at Chana Ponir, now Ram Kot, on the Jhelam. He soon became possessed of a wide extent of country known as Pothiar, between the Jhelam and the Indus, and inhabited by the Khak, Kalu and Khaire tribes. His son *Baj Khan* was a minor when his father died, and the widow ruled for some years with credit. *Seogi*, grandson of *Ghakkar Shah*, was the ancestor of the Sogial clan of Tehsil Gujar Khan. His nephew *Rajar Khan* founded the village of Dangalli which became the head-quarters of the tribe. Dan was a demon or jinn who harassed the neighbouring country, and *Rajar Khan* determined to get rid of him. He called to his assistance a holy fakir who stopped up every outlet of the haunted cave and then prepared to burn the demon. But he was not inclined to wait to be burnt, and making a hole, still visible, through the solid rock, he escaped. The name of the village which was built on the spot, was given in remembrance of the demon and of his passage (gali) through the rock. *Rajar Khan* died in 1160, and was succeeded by his son *Sipher Khan* of whom there is nothing to record. *Nang Khan*, the next chief, conspired with Fidai Khan Khokkar to assassinate the Emperor Muhammad Ghori, whose general Kutb-ud-din 'Aibak' had been sent against the Ghakkars who were ravaging the country up to the walls of Lahore itself. They were defeated by Kutb-ud-din with great slaughter, and *Nang Khan* thinking that the Emperor had determined on the annihilation of the tribe, planned his death. On the 14th of March, 1206, Muhammad Ghori, marching towards Ghazni, encamped on the banks of the Indus. The night being warm, the 'kanats' or screens which usually surrounded the royal tent had been raised, allowing the band of assassins to reach the tent door without detection. Here a sentry gave the alarm, but he was instantly stabbed to the heart and the Ghakkars entered the tent where the Emperor was lying asleep fanned by two slaves. They fell upon him and killed him, inflicting no fewer than twenty-two wounds. The guard hurried up hearing the cries of the slaves, but it was too late to save their master, though most of the murderers were caught and put to death with various tortures. *Lohar Khan* succeeded his father, and from the second son *Sahori*

Khan have descended the Satwal and Lori Ghakkars; while the Sanal clan is from *San Khan* the third son. *Lohar Khan* had no easy rule. In 1247, the Pothiar country was invaded by Nasir-ud-din Mahmud, and, as a punishment for the assistance which the tribe had rendered to the Mogals in their invasion of 1241, he carried away as slaves several thousand Ghakkars, men, women and children. *Boja Khan*, the nephew of *Lohar Khan*, rebelled against him, and set up an independent chiefship at Rotas, where he founded the Bogial clan, which still inhabits Rotas and Domeli. The invasion of Timur or Tamerlane took place during the chiefship of *Gul Muhammad*, who died in 1403 A. D. His two immediate successors were not men of any note, but *Jastar Khan*,* brother of *Pir Khan*, is often mentioned in Muhammadan history as a brave and successful general. He overran Kashmir and took prisoner Allah Shah king of that country. Then, uniting with Malik Toghan a Turki general, he seized Jalandhar and marched towards Dehli. At Ludhiana he was attacked by the king's troops and defeated, on the 8th October 1442, and retired to Rawalpindi, from whence he made attacks alternately on Lahore and Jammu, the Raja of which latter place, Rai Bhim, he defeated and killed, till 1453, when he died. *Tatar Khan's* rule was of short duration, for his nephew *Hati Khan* rebelled against him, captured and put him to death. His two sons were minors, and the Janjoah chief Darwesh Khan took the opportunity of recovering much of the country which the Ghakkars had taken from his tribe. *Hati Khan* opposed him, but was defeated and compelled to fly to Basal, while his cousins *Sarang Khan* and *Adam Khan* escaped to Dangalli where the Janjoah army followed them. *Hati Khan* now collected his tribe, and attacking the Janjoahs on their march, routed them with great slaughter. Babar Shah invaded India during the chiefship of *Hati Khan* and in the Emperor's interesting autobiography is a notice of his contest with the Ghakkar chief. He

* Jastar Khan or Jasrat is mentioned as being a brother of Shaikha who defended Tulamba against Timur Shah. But the Ghakkars never appear to have gone so far South as Tulamba, which was probably defended by the Khattias, an ancient Rajput tribe inhabiting the lower part of the Bari Doab.

marched against Pharwala, the capital of the Ghakkars, strongly situated in the hills, and captured it after a gallant resistance, *Hati Khan* making his escape from one gate of the town as the troops of Babar entered by another. *Sultan Sarang* was now of age, and finding that he could not oust his cousin by force of arms he procured his death by poison, and assumed the chiefship in 1525. He and his brother made their submission to Babar, and *Adam Khan*, with a Ghakkar force, attended him to Dehli, and for this service the Pothiar country was confirmed to them by the Emperor. In 1541, Sher Shah, having driven the Emperor Humayun from India, built the famous fort of Rotas, where he placed a garrison of 12,000 men under his general Khowas Khan, to hinder the exile's return. *Sarang Khan*, remembering the generous way in which he had been treated by Babar Shah, espoused the quarrel of his son, and kept the Rotas garrison in a perpetual state of disquiet, driving off convoys, and wasting the country around the fort. On the death of Sher Shah in 1545 his son Salim Shah determined to punish the Ghakkars, and moved against them in force. *Sarang Khan* sued for peace, but all terms were refused and his son *Kamal Khan*, sent to the imperial camp as an envoy, was thrown into chains. For two years, in the course of which Sultan Sarang and sixteen of his family fell in action, the Ghakkars fought with varying success, and in 1550, Prince Kamram, brother of Humayun with whom he was at feud and by whom he had just been expelled from Kabul, took refuge among them. The fort of Pharwala was often won and lost during these years of incessant war, but however many troops were sent against them, the Ghakkars, brave and united; held their own, and Salim Shah found it impossible to subdue them. In 1553 Prince Kamran who had again taken up arms against his brother and who had been defeated near the Khaibar, fled to India, and took refuge at the court of Dehli. Salim Shah did not receive him with any favour, and the Prince then returned northward to his former host *Adam Khan*, who had succeeded his brother *Sarang Khan*. This chief stained the Ghakkar reputation for hospitality, and gave up his guest to Humayun, who put out his eyes, and two years later re-entered Dehli in triumph, attended by the Ghakkar chief, who was richly rewarded for his treachery.

Sultan Sarang had left two sons *Kamal Khan* and *Alawal Khan*, and with the wife of the latter *Laskar Khan*, son of *Adam Khan*, fell in love, and in order to obtain her put her husband to death. *Kamal Khan* was at Dehli when he heard the news of his brother's murder, and he complained to the Emperor Akbar, who had succeeded Humayun in 1556, and obtained a grant of half the territory of *Adam Khan*. This chief would not yield and *Kamal Khan* attacked him, took him prisoner and hung him to satisfy his revenge. *Kamal Khan* did not long enjoy his triumph and died in 1559. The Ghakkar country now fell into a state of anarchy, and remained so for some years till the Emperor divided it between the rival chiefs.* To *Jalal Khan*, grandson of *Adam Khan*, he gave Dangalli, with 454 villages; to *Mubarik Khan*, son of *Kamal Khan*, Pharwala, with 333 villages; Akbarabad, with 242 villages, he assigned to *Shaikh Ganja*, one of *Adam Khan's* younger sons, and Rawalpindi to *Said Khan* the third son of *Sarang Khan*. *Mubarik Khan* died the year after this arrangement and his son did not long survive him. *Shadman Khan* was an imbecile, and Pharwala was granted by the Emperor to *Jalal Khan*. This chief was a great warrior and fought as an imperial general in Kohat, Bannu and Yusafzai, where he died at a great age in 1611. His son and grandson successively held rule, the latter dying in 1670. *Allahdad Khan* was like *Shadman* of weak intellect, but he had a clever wife, who carried on affairs with spirit and success, till her son *Dulu Murad Khan* grew up and assumed the chiefship. He was renowned for his liberality and on this account was named '*Lakhi*' *Dulu Khan*. He died in 1726. Then succeeded *Muazzam Khan*, who ruled 13 years, and *Sultan Mukarrab Khan* the last independent Ghakkar chief. In his days the Ghakkar power was greater

* About this time Fatah Khan, a near relative of Sarang Khan, emigrated to Hazara, where he founded the village of Khanpur. He was the ancestor of Rajas Firoz Khan and Haidar Baksh and the Hazara Ghakkars.

than it had perhaps ever been before. He defeated the Yusafzai Afghans and Jang Kuli Khan of Khattak, and captured Gujrat, overrunning the Chib country as far North as Bhimbar. He joined Ahmad Shah on his several Indian expeditions, and was treated by him with the greatest consideration being confirmed in the possession of his large territories which extended from the Chenab to the Indus. At length, in 1765, Sirdar Gujar Singh Bhangi, the powerful Sikh chief, marched from Lahore, with a large force, against him. *Mukarrab Khan* fought a battle outside the walls of Gujrat but was defeated, and compelled to retire across the Jhelam, giving up his possessions in the Jech Doab. His power being thus broken the rival chiefs of his own tribe declared against him, and *Himmat Khan* of Domeli took him prisoner by treachery and put him to death, himself assuming the headship of the tribe. The two elder sons of *Mukarrab Khan* took Pharwala the two younger Dangalli, but they quarreled among themselves and Sirdar Gujar Singh seized every thing, with the exception of Pharwala, which was divided among the brothers. *Sadullah Khan* and *Nazar Ali Khan* died without male issue and *Mansur Khan* and *Shadman Khan* succeeded to their shares, which they held till 1818, when Anand Singh Thepuria, grandson of the famous Milka Singh of Rawulpindi, seized their whole estates and reduced them to absolute poverty, though the family was, in 1826, allowed some proprietary rights in Pharwala. During Sikh days there is no history of the Ghakkars to record. They were ground down by the exactions of men like Budh Singh Sindhanwalia and Rajah Gulab Singh of Jammu, the latter of whom threw *Shadman Khan* and *Maddat Khan,* second son of *Mansur Khan,* into prison, where they miserably perished. *Karam Dad Khan* son of Raja *Hyat Ullah Khan* is now the head of the Pharwala family and the first among the Ghakkars of the Rawalpindi district. The father did excellent service under Captain Abbott in 1848-49, and also in 1857. He died in March 1865, and half his pension of 1,200 Rs. was resumed. The other half is granted in perpetuity. *Fatah Ali Khan* holds a life pension of 600 Rs.; his son, *Buhadar Ali Khan,* one of 100 Rs. and seven other members of the family hold 500 Rs. between them.

Other members of the tribe, though not of the Pharwala clan, deserving mention in the Rawalpindi and Jhelam districts, are Raja Roshan Khan of Domeli; Fazl Dad Khan of Manianda, a Deputy Inspector of Police; Mirza Khan of Sang and Shahwali Khan of Syadpur. Raja Roshan Khan of Domeli is the son of Raja Akbar Ali Khan who joined Captain Nicholson in 1848-49, and did good service under that officer. He now holds a jagir of 1,000 Rs. His cousin Fazl Dad Khan accompanied Raja Sher Singh to Multan in 1848, and rebelled with him. He had been released from prison by Major H. Lawrence, shortly before, but this did not prevent him from intriguing against the English. He was employed as the confidential agent between Raja Sher Singh and Maharaja Gulab Singh. His jagirs of 6,000 Rs. were resumed for his rebellion. He now holds the 'chaharam' or fourth of the revenue of Domeli, amounting to 425 Rs. a year.

However great may have been the reverses of the Ghakkars, they have lost neither their pride nor their courage. They have been crushed by the Sikhs, a people of yesterday, but there may still be seen in the chivalrous bearing of a Ghakkar gentleman some remembrance of the days when Pharwala was an asylum for all who were oppressed, and of the wars in which his ancestors fought, on equal terms, with the Emperors of Dehli.

BUDHA KHAN, MALAL.

AMANAT KHAN.
Sirdar Khan.
Sarafraz Khan.

- Budha Khan.
  - Allah Yar Khan.
    - Jahan Khan.
  - Karam Khan.
    - Ahmad Khan.
  - Dyanat Khan.
  - Fatah Khan.
  - Sahib Khan.
  - Sher Khan.
- Sher Khan.
- Fatah Khan.
- Haiyat Khan.
  - Jahan Khan.
    - Nur Khan.

HISTORY OF THE FAMILY.

There is little to relate of this family which calls itself Bhandial from Rai Bhandi Beg, an imaginary Mogal ancestor, but is, in reality, of Rajput descent like the Ghebas to which tribe it belongs. As was the case with most of the Muhammadan families of the Rawalpindi district, it was flourishing under the Empire, and, after fighting for some time, with more or less success, against the Sikhs, was at last reduced to obedience. The Malal Maliks were allowed, like the Rais of Kot and the Maliks of Pindi Gheb, a fourth share of the revenue of their villages, and when Prince Nao Nihal Singh held the Ilakas in 1836, *Budha Khan* received in jagir the village of Khadwal, worth 900 Rs. This Malik was one of the men who assassinated Rai Muhammad Khan of Kot in the fort of Pagh by order of Sirdar Attar Singh Kalianwala. The son of the murdered man well avenged his father, and killed all *Budha Khan's* family, with the exception of one or two who contrived to escape. There had been always a feud between the families and these murders did not tend to end it, and in 1848-49 it was partly by the representations of Fatah Khan of Kot that *Budha Khan* was found lukewarm in the service of the State and half his jagir resumed. However, in 1857, he proved his loyalty by performing all the service he could, and obtained a perpetual jagir of 500 Rs. at Khadwal, with a khillat of 500 Rs. He possesses, besides this, a 'chaharam' allowance, with proprietary rights in several villages, worth together 1030 Rs. a year.

RAJA SULTAN KAN.

RAJA FAZL DAD KHAN.

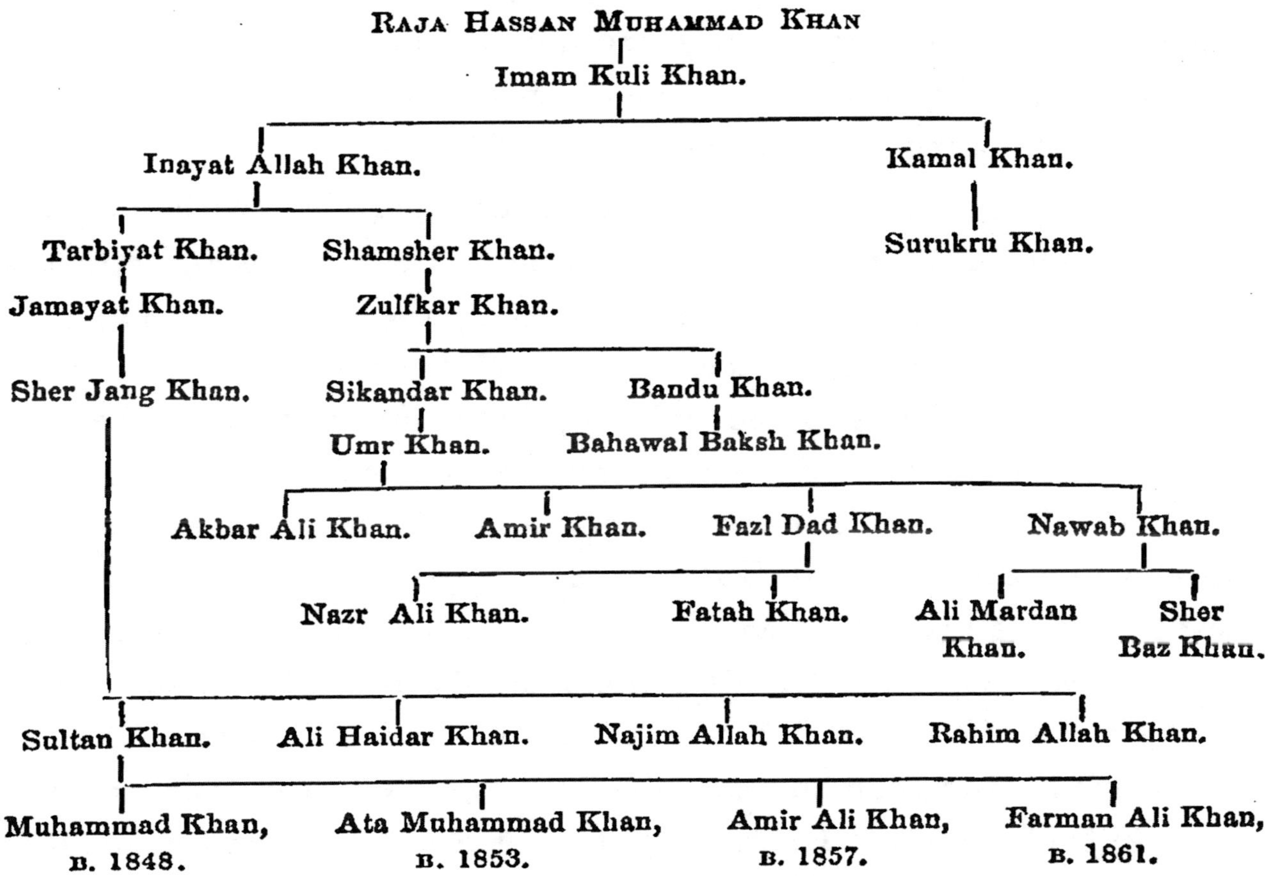

HISTORY OF THE TRIBE.

The Chibs are an ancient Rajput tribe scattered through the low range of hills between the rivers Beas and Jhelam. In the Gujrat district, where they are most numerous, they occupy 51 villages, and here they are mostly Muhammadans, while those of Kangra and Jammu retain the old Hindu faith. The Chibs are not descended from one of the royal Rajput houses; but they hold the second place and rank with Salaria, Harchandar and other honourable tribes. They themselves assert that they have some share of royal blood and that one of their ancestors, Hamir Chand, married the daughter of the Katoch Raja of Kangra and succeeded to the throne on the death of his father-in-law, his descendants ruling in Kangra for eight generations, until the time of Chib Chand and Odey Chand. But this story is probably false. No Mian belonging to a royal clan would give his daughter in marriage to an inferior in rank, nor in the long roll of 475 Katoch Kings are the ancestors of the Chibs to be found. The name of Hamir Chand, indeed, occurs twice, but the names, preceding and succeeding, are not those of Chib history. But it is possible that the accuracy of a genealogy which extends over a period of fourteen thousand years may be doubted.

Chib Chand the founder of the tribe quarreled with his brother Odey Chand, and leaving Kangra about the year 1400, settled near Bhimbar at the village of Malura or Muchalpura, where he married the daughter of Raja Sripat, the local ruler. Not content with the possession of the daughter he coveted the chiefship, and inviting his father-in-law with his whole family to a feast, he murdered them all, and became himself Raja. For several generations his descendants ruled in the neighbourhood of Bhimbar, till Sadi, in the reign of the Emperor Babar, went to pay his respects at court, and received an imperial confirmation of his possessions in return for his renouncing Hinduism and adopting the Muhammadan faith, taking the name of Shadab Khan. This chief accompanied Humayun on more than one of his expeditions, and was at length killed by one Pir Haibat, a native of Kandahar, with whom he had a quarrel. Apostacy is not always considered respectable, but the Chibs have made Shadab Khan a saint, and his tomb near Bhimbar is a sacred place of pilgrimage to which both Hindu and Muhammadan members of the tribe resort. The saint is generally known as 'Sur Sadi Shahid' and there is a custom in the tribe of leaving one lock of hair on the head of every infant until such time as the parents can visit the shrine when it is cut off with much ceremony, and the child is then and not till then considered a true Chib. This ceremony is as essential as the 'pahal' among the Sikhs or circumcision among Muhammadans. The

Chib chiefs held the district Khari Kariali, stretching along the Jhelam, below the fort of Mangla, and Naoshera, till the Sikhs rose to power. Then Sirdar Gujar Singh Bhangi, having captured Gujrat from the Ghakkars, turned his arms against them, but he was not able to make much impression upon them as their country was very difficult for an attacking force. Sahib Singh, son of Gujur Singh, and Mahan Singh Sukarchakia later attacked Mangla without success, and its reduction was left for the great Maharaja himself. In 1810, after Ranjit Singh had seized Gujrat from Sahib Singh, he marched northward and reduced the fort of Chunian held by Raja Umr Khan, who retired to his still stronger fort of Mangla. The Sikh Army then marched against Mangla, when Amr Khan thinking resistance useless sent his son Akbar Ali Khan to sue for peace. Before an answer could be received the chief died, and Ranjit Singh, not wishing to drive Akbar Ali Khan to extremities, left him half of his father's possessions, which he only lived six months to enjoy. All was then confiscated, but to *Amir Khan,* the second son, a pension of 4000 Rs. was assigned, and to his cousin Sher Jang Khan a pension of 3000 Rs. Some years later Amir Khan died, and the pension was continued to his younger brother Fazl Dad Khan. Prince Kharrak Singh to whom Khari Kariali was given in jagir, took Fazl Dad Khan into his service on 3 Rs. a day, and ten years later four sowars were also allowed him on 1,075 Rs. When Kashmir and Jammu were made over in independant possession to Maharaja Gulab Singh, the jagir of 4,000 Rs. was included in that territory, and the cash allowance of 1,075 Rs. was exchanged for a jagir of the same amount at Dal Kalu and Sithal. The Raja accompanied Sher Singh to Multan in 1848, but did not join in his rebellion and his jagir was continued to him. It was resumed on his death in 1864 and his sons Nazr Ali Khan and Fatah Khan hold a pension of 540 Rs.

Sultan Khan of Pothi is still living. His jagir of 3000 Rs. consisting of the villages of Pothi, Dak, Bhulwal and Phularwand was continued to him at annexation on payment of one quarter revenue. He did good service in 1857.

The only other man of note among the Chibs is Chowdhri Ghulam Ali Khan of Baisa, who possesses considerable influence. His father Bandu Khan was for many years Kardar under the Sikhs. On the death of his father, Ghulam Ali Khan succeeded to the office, and improved the district by his admirable management. Four villages, Sang, Baisa, Jaggu and Chang were released in his favour. In 1849 he showed himself hostile to the Government, and his jagir and his privileges were resumed; but he redeemed his character for loyalty in 1857, and received a pension of 300 Rs. for life. His son Murdan Ali Khan at this time entered the 2nd Sikh Cavalry and is still as jamadar in the same regiment, now known as the 12th Bengal Cavalry.

The Hindu Chibs have given far more trouble in Gujrat than their Muhammadan kinsmen. During the whole reign of Maharaja Ranjit Singh they were notorious for audacity and lawlessness. Inhabiting Dewa, Botala and other hill villages, a few miles beyond the Jammu frontier, they would descend upon the plains, burning and plundering, and even the larger towns were not safe from attack. Twice the Maharaja burnt their village, but this had only a temporary effect, and they are as evil minded at the present day as in old Sikh times. Twice since the annexation of the Panjab have they made raids upon British territory; in June 1849, when they attacked the village of Assar, and in August 1858, when they sacked Dokhoa. Maharaja Gulab Singh, on the strong representation of the British Government, sent a force against Dewa and burnt it to the ground, forbidding its reconstruction on the same site. Since then, fear of punishment has kept these marauders quiet, but they still have as great a love for a raid across the border, as when, in the old days, they could plunder without opposition up to the very walls of Gujrat.

HIMMAT SINGH MIRPURIA

- DATA RAM.
  - Mahan Singh, D. 1845.
    - Chattar Singh, D. 1846.
    - Himmat Singh, B. 1828.
      - Raghbir Singh, B. 1848.
    - Badawa Singh.
    - Sham Singh B. 1831.
      - Sundar Singh, B. 1855.
      - Sirdar Singh, B. 1857.

HISTORY OF THE FAMILY.

Data Ram was a confidential servant of Mukarrab Khan the Ghakkar chief of Gujrat. His son *Mahan Singh*, when quite young, went to Lahore to seek his fortune, and Maharaja Ranjit Singh, who was struck by his skill and courage on a hunting expedition when *Mahan Singh* unassisted killed a leopard with his sword, gave him an appointment in the army, under Sirdar Hari Singh Nalwa. The young man fought in several campaigns with great gallantry, and at the last siege of Multan was twice wounded. He also served in Kashmir and at Peshawar. He was a great favourite of Hari Singh, who advanced his fortunes and made him his confidant and lieutenant. *Mahan Singh* was in charge of the fort of Jamrud in April 1837, when the Afghan army, under Mirza Sami Khan, attacked it in force, and he held out bravely against enormous odds until Hari Singh himself arrived from Peshawar to fight the memorable battle in which he fell. On the death of his patron Sirdar *Mahan Singh* did not lose the favour of the Maharaja who, in 1839, gave him a jagir of 37,000 Rs., of which 12,000 Rs. were personal, and 25,000 Rs. for the service of 100 sowars. He retained this estate throughout the reigns of Maharajas Kharrak Singh and Sher Singh. In 1844, when the Sikh army was as brutal and licentious as it was possible for troops to be, *Mahan Singh* was murdered by his own men. *Chattar Singh* avenged his father's death, but was assassinated himself soon afterwards. Under the Darbar the jagir was reduced to 29,400 Rs., still subject to the service of 100 horsemen. These all joined the rebel army in 1848-49. *Himmat Singh* and his brother *Sham Singh* retired to Jammu, and when the rebellion was over, boasted that they had fought against the rebels with the Maharaja of Jammu's force, and in support of their statement produced a letter from Diwan Hari Chand to Joala Sahai, the confidential Agent of the Maharaja, but this letter from a man thoroughly distrusted himself did not do them much good. However admirable the intentions of *Himmat Singh* may have been, his conduct was certainly most suspicious. He was a large jagirdar, yet when his services were most required he did not come forward on the side of his Government ; indeed nothing was seen of him till the 17th May, 1849, three months after the battle of Gujrat had been fought. Under these circumstances the whole jagir was resumed. The widows of *Mahan Singh* and *Chattar Singh* were each allowed a pension of 360 Rs. per annum. *Himmat Singh* and *Sham Singh* 350 Rs. and 180 Rs. respectively, which they still hold. In 1857, *Himmat Singh* raised twelve horsemen for the service of Government. He resides at Mirpur, in the Jammu territory.

RAJA SULTAN AHMAD KHAN
RAJA SHAMSHER ALI KHAN.

RAJA DADAN KHAN.

- Shaffi Khan.
  - Waris Khan.
    - Ali Muhammad Khan.
      - Ahmad Khan.
        - Dalil Khan.
          - Agar Khan.
            - Ali Muhammad Khan.
              - Sher Dast Khan.
                - Sultan Ahmad Khan.
                  - Fatah Muhammad Khan, B. 1835.
- Fatah Muhammad Khan.
  - Lodha Khan.
    - Izzat Khan.
      - Sahib Khan.
        - Abdullah Khan.
          - Sarafraz Khan.
            - Fatah Khan.
              - Sher Dil Khan.
                - Sahib Khan, B. 1861.
              - Shamsher Ali Khan.
                - Sef Ali Khan, B. 1843.
              - Mihr Khan.
                - Dadan Khan, B. 1845.
- Firoz Khan.
  - Ahmad Khan.
    - Khuda Baksh Khan.
      - Sirdar Khan.
        - Zulfkar Khan.
          - Khuda Baksh, D. 1865.
            - Sirdar Khan, B. 1840.
            - Sher Khan.
          - Ahmad Khan.
            - Buhadar Khan.
          - Fatah Khan.
      - Buland Khan.
        - Mehdi Khan.
          - Gul Nawaz Khan, B. 1861.
    - Ruhallah Khan.
    - Faizullah Khan.
      - Nisari Khan.

HISTORY OF THE FAMILY.

The Kokhar Rajas of Pind Dadan Khan and Ahmadabad are of high Rajput origin and intermarry with the Ghakkars and Janjoahs. Nothing is known of them previous to 1623, when Dadan Khan a Kokhar Rajput in the service of the Emperor Jahangir, settled on the Jhelam at the foot of the Salt Range, then known as the hills of Jodh, and built a town, which he called after his own name, on the site of an ancient village of the name of Shamshabad Nimaksar. He was not permitted to settle without opposition. The country which he had chosen was first inhabited by the Janjoahs, who had been in part dispossessed by the Jalabs, a Rajput tribe that arrived in the Jhelam district no long time before the Kokhars. The country had become depopulated by the frequent wars of these rival tribes and the salt mines were no longer worked, for merchants could not visit them without being exposed to robbery and violence. The Kokhar chief held his own at Pind Dadan Khan which soon became a flourishing town and the centre of the salt trade. He left three sons, from whom have descended the families of Ahmadabad and Pind Dadan Khan. *Shaffi Khan*, the eldest, built a fort at Chak Shaffi, at the foot of the hills, six miles to the north east of Pind Dadan Khan to hinder the incursions of the Gujars and Janjoahs, while his brother *Fatah Muhammad* built Gujar, about two miles distant from Chak Shaffi, and a fort at Pind Dadan Khan. For several generations the tribe held the neighbouring district against all comers, founding many villages and fighting occasionally with their neighbours the Janjoahs and Ghakkars. *Agar Khan*, fifth in descent from *Shaffi Khan*, built Sultan Kot close to Pind Dadan Khan, and the great grandson of *Fatah Muhammad* built Kot Sahib Khan on the other side of the town.

Ahmad Khan, the grandson of *Firoz Khan*, quarreled with his cousins and, being worsted in an appeal to arms, left Pind Dadan Khan and founded the town of Ahmadabad, fifteen miles to the southward, on the river Jhelam, and here his descendants still reside. He seems to have been an able man, and to have ruled his little district with wisdom. He drove out the Awans of Nurpur, and obtained his recognition as a tributary chief from the Court of Dehli. Although *Khuda Baksh* succeeded him, the most distinguished of his sons was *Ruhallah Khan*. He, finding that his nephew Nisari Khan had plotted against him with the Kokhars of Pind Dadan Khan and the Jalabs of Harranpur, attacked the combination with so much vigour that he compelled them to sue for peace and to give their daughters in marriage to men of his clan. Raja *Khuda Baksh Khan* who died in April 1865, was great grandson of the founder of Ahmadabad. He fought against the Sikhs in 1848-49, joining the force of Malik Sher Khan Tiwana and received, in recognition of his loyalty, the village of Joran, worth 1,100 Rs. in jagir, subject to one quarter revenue, also a rent free grant in Ahmadabad worth 387 Rs. with proprietary rights in Kot Kachhah.

Of the Pind Dadan Khan Rajas, *Sarafraz Khan* was perhaps the most distinguished. He thought to make peace with the Janjoahs by giving his sister and his three daughters in marriage to their chief men. He accordingly betrothed them to Sultan Zulfkar Khan, Diwan Khuda Baksh of Garjakh, Nasir Ali Khan of Makialah and the Kureshi Pir of Mouza Pail. But before the marriages could come off, disputes had again broken out between the rival tribes, and Sultan Zulfkar Khan, who was on his way with the wedding procession to Makialah, was stopped at Pind Dadan Khan and had to fight for his life. Sirdar Charrat Singh, grandfather of Maharaja Ranjit Singh, conquered the Kokhar country, but he allowed the Ahmadabad Raja to hold his chiefship, with some rights still claimed by the family in the original colony. The Pind Dadan Khan Rajas were treated with equal leniency, till, early in Ranjit Singh's reign, *Sarafraz Khan* rose in revolt. A force was sent against him, and after a long fight he was utterly defeated and compelled to fly to Makialah. He later made his peace and received some villages in jagir, though Pind Dadan Khan was not restored. In 1848-49 these chiefs joined the national party, and all their jagirs and allowances were resumed. Sometime later a pension of 200 Rs. was granted to *Sherdil Khan*, and *Shamsher Ali Khan*, *Mihr Khan*, and their widowed mother each received a pension of 100 Rs. That of *Sherdil Khan* was raised to 350 Rs. for his loyalty in 1857, and at the recent settlement the pensions were consolidated into a perpetual grant of 1000 Rs. in favour of *Sultan Ahmad* and *Shamsher Ali Khan*, subject to life pensions to *Sherdil Khan*, *Mihr Khan*, and *Bibi Banu* the mother. The cousins have also recovered certain proprietary rights in Pind Dadan Khan and Ahmadabad.

THE DHOOND TRIBE

The Dhoonds inhabit a portion of the hills to the north of the Rawalpindi district, between Hazara and the Sanatarium of Murree. It is uncertain whether the tribe is of Hindu origin or whether, like their neighbours the Tarins, the Dilazaks or the Ghakkars, they emigrated to Hazara from the north west. But they have no doubt themselves upon the point, and trace their genealogy to Abbas the paternal uncle of the prophet Muhammad. From this ancestor the Daudputras of Bahawulpur also claim descent, and the pretensions of both tribes are equally ridiculous. One of the traditions of the Dhoonds seems to point to a Central Asian origin. It is stated that Takht Khan, one of the tribe, married the sister of Timur or Tamerlane, and accompanied him to Dehli. There Takht Khan remained, and his descendants after him, till the reign of Shah Jahan, when Zorab Khan, who had no children born to him in Dehli, thought that he might be more fortunate in his native country, and set out to return there. He reached the little village of Drankot, some three miles from Kahuta in Rawalpindi, where he met a holy fakir, whose prayers he earnestly entreated. The fakir promised a son, but on the condition that the child should be given to him. Zorab Khan promised, and when the child was born the fakir claimed him. Vainly the mother wept and protested, and begged that the boy might be left with her for a year, a month, a day. But the fakir said that if the child tasted milk he would be useless to him and carried him away, and placed him in a corner of his own hut, where he built him up with stones and then set off for Mecca. The 'Haji' was worshipping in the holy city, when he suddenly remembered the boy. Swiftly he hastened back, crossing seas and rivers dryshod by his miraculous power, and at last reached the house of Zorab Khan. He told the parents of what he feared was the fate of their child, and together they hurried to the hut, where they found the boy alive and laughing. The fakir cried aloud in joy "jai hojase! jai hojase!" (he will become many) and this word of good omen was given to the boy as his name, Jai Khan, who fulfilled the prophecy and had twenty-two sons, from four of whom have descended the Jadwal, Dhoond, Surara and Tanaoli tribes.

Khalura or Kulu Rai was the ancestor of the Dhoonds. He was directed by the Emperor to go to Kashmir, and bring to reason the Governor who was in open rebellion. He set off with Dhurmeh, the son of Manakrai, both armed with bows and arrows. It happened that at this time Kashmir was ravaged by a tiger, whose thirst for blood was only appeased by the daily offering of a man. As the travellers approached the valley, they met a widow who was making loud lamentation for her only son who was that day to be given to the tiger. Moved with pity Khalura and his friend determined to do what they could to aid her, and, lying in wait for the tiger, were so fortunate as to kill him with their arrows. Then cutting off his ears they went to sleep. While they slept a traveller passing by saw the carcase of the tiger and thought to gain the reward promised to the man who should kill it, and so, stripping off the skin, he carried it as the sign of his victory to the Nawab, who was about to reward him munificently. But at the critical moment Khalura and Dharmeh appeared. They produced the ears and claimed the prize. The Nawab was convinced, the pretender punished and the two friends left Kashmir with valuable presents, and each taking with him as his wife a daughter of the Nawab. By his Kashmir wife Khalura had two sons, Kund Khan and Kor Khan, from the former of whom have descended the Dhoonds. By another wife of the Khetwal tribe he had two sons, Baz Khan and Burcha Khan. The Dhoonds remained in Hazara for six generations and then spread over the hill country, occupying Kahuta, Murree and Dewal.

From an illegitimate son of Khalura the Sattis, inhabiting the same country, are said to have sprung, though they themselves deny any connection with the Dhoonds whose bitter enemies they are. The Dhoonds have ever been a lawless, untractable race, but their courage is not equal to their disposition to do evil.

Maharaja Gulab Singh, in 1837, almost exterminated them. They, the Sattis and several other mountain tribes had taken the opportunity of the repulse of the Sikhs at Jamrud and the death of Sirdar Hari Singh, to rise in revolt. Their country had been made over to Gulab Singh, and when he had reduced Yusufzai to something like order he marched with 20,000 men, regulars and irregulars, to crush revolt in the Murree and Hazara hills. At first the insurgents were successful. Under the leadership of Shamas Khan, a Sudhan, who had been a confidential follower of Raja Dhyan Singh, the whole country had risen, and all the hill forts of the Jammu Raja had fallen into their hands. But Gulab Singh bided his time. He made Kahuta his head quarters, and very soon his promises and his bribes brought disunion into the hostile camp. When he had so worked upon the chiefs that none know whom to trust, he marched into the hills, burning the crops and the villages as he advanced, and offering a reward of a rupee for the head of every man, woman or child connected with the insurgents. The wretched people, divided among themselves, and confounded by this display of ferocity in their enemy, made little resistance. They were hunted down like wild beasts in every direction and massacred without pity, men and women alike. At length Gulab Singh ordered the women to be spared, and kept as prisoners with the army, and there was soon to be seen, following each division, a troop of half-clothed starving females, driven like cattle by day, and at night, penned like cattle in a thorn enclosure, and exposed to the utmost brutality of the soldiery. Only a few hundred of these women, out of several thousand, reached Jammu. These, with the exception of a few of the handsomest reserved for Gulab Singh's Zanana, were sold as slaves. It is said, though the statement may be an exaggeration, that twelve thousand of the Dhoonds, Sattis and Sudhans perished in this hill campaign. Certain it is that some parts of the hills, before well peopled and fertile, became as a desert ;

men were not left sufficient to till the fields, and a famine the next year swept off many of the miserable survivors of Gulab Singh's revenge.

This terrible punishment was, however, soon forgotten by the Dhoonds. In September, 1857, thinking a time favourable for revolt had arrived, they conspired with the Khurals and their kinsmen of Hazara, and planned an attack on the hill station of Murree. But warning had been received in time of the proposed attack, and when the enemy 300 strong, advanced on the night of the 2nd expecting an easy victory and abundant spoil, they were surprised and driven back, and the next day, on the arrival of troops from Rawalpindi, the Dhoond country to the north west of Murree was entered and eleven villages of the rebels burnt; while fifteen of the ringleaders, who were subsequently captured, suffered death. The only chief of any consideration among the Dhoonds is Mansabdar Khan, who holds a jagir of 777 Rs.

MISR AMIR CHHND.
RAJA LAL SINGH.

DHANPAT.

- Ram Jas.
- Ram Kour.
  - Amir Chand.
    - Sukh Ram, B. 1832.
    - Raja Ram, B. 1840.
    - Karam Chand, B. 1854.
    - Kishan Chand, B. 1859.
  - Bhagwan Singh.
    - Lakhmir Chand, B. 1849.
    - Diwan Chand, B. 1858.
    - Kahn Chand, B. 1862.
- Jassa Mal.
  - Lal Singh.
    - Ranbir Singh.
    - Balbir Singh.
    - Infant.

HISTORY OF THE FAMILY.

The family of *Raja Lal Singh* is of no antiquity. Its rise was as sudden as its fall, and its fall was so complete, that only a brief outline of its history is given here. The history of *Lal Singh* himself was for three years the history of the Panjab, and will be found in some detail in former parts of this book. *Ram Jas*, the eldest of three brothers, sons of a petty Brahman shopkeeper, entered the service of Basti Ram the treasurer of Sirdar Mahan Singh Sukarchakia, as a munshi. He was killed in the hill country during a tax-collecting expedition in early part of the reign of Ranjit Singh, and was succeeded in his office by his brothers *Ram Kour* and *Jassa Mal*. Raja Dhyan Singh was the patron of the family, and on the death of Basti Ram his influence procured the appointment of *Jassa Mal* to the charge of the Bela Toshakhana, or small service treasury. In 1830, *Amir Chand* received an appointment under his uncle, and in 1832, *Lal Singh* and his cousin *Bhagwan Singh* were taken into the treasury. The next year *Bhagwan Singh* was sent as Kardar to Gujrat, and *Jassa Mal* was allowed to take the contracts for Rotas and Jhelam, which he held till his death in 1836. *Lal Singh* succeeded his father, and when Misr Beli Ram was imprisoned for several months by Nao Nihal Singh, on account of his connection with Sirdar Chet Singh, *Lal Singh* held his office of Treasurer; and when, four years later, Beli Ram was murdered by the orders of Raja Hira Singh, *Lal Singh* received the permanent appointment. He was a great favourite of Hira Singh, who created him Raja of Rotas. But *Lal Singh* was too greedy to be grateful, and he was deeply implicated in the successful conspiracy of December 1844 against Hira Singh's power and life. His influence increased under the next minister Jowahir Singh, for he was the lover of the Maharani, and on the death of Jowahir Singh, became himself minister; and he, with Raja Dinanath, induced the army, which he feared and hated, to cross the Satlej in 1845, and invade British territory. After the Satlej campaign he was confirmed as Minister, and this office he held till the close of 1846 when, being convicted of treason in opposing the occupation of Kashmir by Maharaja Gulab Singh under the treaty of the 16th March 1846, he was removed and banished to Hindostan, first to Agra, then to the Dehrah Dhoon where he still resides in receipt of a pension of 12,000 Rs. per annum.

Raja *Lal Singh* rose to power by the exercise of arts, which in a civilized community would have sent him to the scaffold. He was one of the chief instigators and chief actors in the murders of Raja *Hira Singh*, of *Misr Beli Ram* and of *Bhai Gurmukh Singh*. His intrigues with Maharani Jindan were so open and shameless that they even scandalized a people whose immorality was proverbial. By ingratitude, treachery and cunning he succeeded in acquiring the wealth and power for which better men are indebted to their virtue or their genius. He had great opportunities for serving his country, but he resolutely chose the evil in preference to the good. Had he possessed one spark of patriotism he might, after the Satlej campaign, have saved Kashmir to the Panjab. His ministry was supported by the whole strength of the British Government. Major Lawrence stood by him, with no petty interference, but offering wise and generous advice, which this greedy minister never cared to follow; and when, at length, his jealousy of Maharaja Gulab Singh led him into treason, his fall from power was hailed with joy by all; by the army, which hated him for the cowardice and imbecility that had been its ruin, and by the chiefs whose estates he had seized to enrich himself and his creatures.

Misr Amir Chand was, in 1838, sent to Kashmir to collect the revenue, and remained there six months. He, later, accompanied Nao Nihal Singh to Peshawar, in charge of the camp treasury. *Bhagwan Singh* was at this time employed in the treasury at Lahore. In 1844, *Amir Chand* was appointed governor of Gujrat and Pind Dadan Khan, on a salary of 12,000 Rs. per annum, and two years later his brother *Bhagwan Singh* was appointed Kardar of Jhang. Both lost their jagirs and appointments on the deposition of their cousin Raja *Lal Singh,* and it was some time before *Misr Amir Chand* cleared off the large outstanding balances against him. He resides at Sangoi in the Jhelam district. His eldest son *Sukh Ram* entered the service of the young Maharaja in 1845, and used to lay before him the daily report of the army. He was attached to the Darbar Toshakhana and received, during the last two years of his service, 4,300 Rs. per annum. *Raja Lal Singh* is the only member of the family who holds any pension or estate from the British Government. His cousins, having been employed as revenue officers under the Sikh government, are men of considerable private fortune.

THE SODHIS OF HARANPUR

- GURU RAM DAS.
  - Prithi Chand.
    - Mihrwan.
      - Harji.
        - Har Narayan.
          - Kol Sahib.
            - Sadanand.
              - Guru Gurbaksh Raj.
                - Baba Kiun Shah.
                  - Kishan Singh.
                    - Pahan Singh.
                      - Gurbattan Singh.
                    - Dhir Singh.
                    - Fatah Singh.
                  - Ram Singh.
                  - Harsa Singh.
                    - Sukha Singh.
                    - Prem Singh.
                    - Amar Singh.
                    - Bhagwan Singh.
                  - Megh Singh.
                    - Nihal Singh, D. 1859.
                      - Mul Singh.
                      - Sanpuran Singh.
                        - Nidhan Singh.
                    - Sham Singh, D. 1849.
                      - Sher Singh.
                    - Amrik Singh.
                      - Kartar Singh. B. 1849.
                      - Narinjan Singh, B. 1860.

HISTORY OF THE FAMILY.

A connected history of the great religious family of Sodhis, of their ancient establishments at Anandpur, Kartarpur, Manawah and Kot Har Sahai, of their wealth and large estates and of the manner in which they have influenced the politics of the Panjab, Cis and Trans Satlej, will be found in the Jalandhar division of this work. The little Sodhi colony in the Jhelam district was founded by *Baba Kiun Shah,* eighth in descent from Guru Ram Das, who settled at Haranpur in the year 1751, emigrating from Her, an estate that had been in the family ever since the days of the Guru. *Kiun Shah* had already in his former tours received charitable grants of villages in the Sind Sagar Doab, from Sirdars Ran Singh and Milka Singh Pindiwala, including the villages of Kotli, Chappar and Ramial. Sirdar Mahan Singh, father of Ranjit Singh, was one of his disciples, and in 1783 gave to him the Dharamarth worth 1,300 Rs. which is still in the possession of his descendants. His son *Ram Singh* entered the service of Ranjit Singh in 1796, and soon afterwards obtained a jagir of 7,000 Rs., consisting of Haranpur, Dharialah and two smaller villages. *Ram Singh* was a good soldier, and his fall, at the storming of Narayanghar, in 1807, was much regretted by his master. 4000 Rs. of the jagir were continued to his younger brother *Megh Singh*, who also received jagirs for his own services at Multan, Mankera and at the battle of Tehri in 1823, when he received a khillat worth 5000 Rs. *Sodhi Nihal Singh* entered the Maharaja's army in 1819, and five years later was made commandant of 100 horsemen in the Charyari corps. *Sham Singh* joined in 1826, receiving a separate jagir at Sagah. *Amrik Singh* served first in the Ghorcharahs under general Mian Singh, with a salary of 2000 Rs., but on the death of *Megh Singh*, in 1826, the cash allowances of the three brothers were stopped, though the personal jagir was divided between them. They fought for Maharaja Sher Singh at the siege of Lahore, in 1841, and shared in the rewards which the successful monarch presented to the army. Under Sher Singh's successor, *Nihal Singh* was sent, in command of 1000 horse, to administer the districts of Dhanni, Kachhi and Ahmadabad, which were in a state of insurrection. He shot the ambassador of the insurgents dead with his own hand, and by his vigour and severity soon reduced the country to submission. At the same time *Sham Singh* was sent, on duty, to Kangra. After Raja Hira Singh's death, *Nihal Singh* was sent to the Shahpur district to keep the tribes of the 'Bar,' in order, and in 1847, after the Satlej campaign, he was made 'adalati'; but a few months later was transferred to Jalandhar in the same capacity. He was a clever judge, but too severe to be popular. When the Multan rebellion broke out *Sham Singh* and *Amrik Singh* were summoned with their contingent by

Captain Nicholson to form the escort of his camp. By his direction they called their brother from Jalandhar who, with his horsemen, joined Capt. Nicholson, at Ramnagar. When the rebels, under Chattar Singh, found that the Sodhis had determined to remain faithful to Government, they plundered their house of every thing valuable, the women and children having barely time to escape, and fly to Jammu, where they remained until the return of peace. The Sodhis went through the whole campaign, fighting gallantly on the side of the British in every battle, and *Sham Singh* was unfortunately killed just before the battle of Gujrat. He had been sent to Kunjah to collect supplies, when the Commissariat officers were unable to go with safety, and he was surprised by the enemy, badly wounded and taken prisoner. He died a few days afterwards from his wounds. After the war *Nihal Singh* was employed in civil duties and in restoring order between Jhelam and Attock. At annexation the jagirs in possession of *Amrik Singh*, *Nihal Singh* and *Sher Singh* were confirmed to them for life, as also charitable grants to the value of 3,794 Rs., of which two-thirds were upheld in perpetuity. In 1862 the Supreme Government sanctioned the whole of these grants being continued in perpetuity, according to the ancestral shares. *Nihal Singh*'s share of the personal jagir, 2,200 Rs., lapsed at his death in 1859, and the shares of *Amrik Singh* and his nephew *Sher Singh* being 1,350 Rs. and 1,400 Rs. respectively, are only maintained for life. In 1857, *Sanpuran Singh* attended on the Commissioner of Rawalpindi with 10 sowars, and *Sher Singh* and *Amrik Singh* also supplied a contingent, which did good service during the disturbances, and in 1859, the Sodhis received a reward of 1,100 Rs. for their loyalty. The family of Sodhi *Megh Singh* has a deadly feud with the descendants of Sodhis *Kishan Singh* and *Harsa Singh*, their cousins. The two latter branches of the family joined the national party in 1848-49, and it was *Pahan Singh* who caused the house of his loyal kinsmen to be plundered. However when the Sikh army had been finally defeated at Gujrat, *Nihal Singh* plundered and destroyed the house of *Pahan Singh*, so that neither party has now cause of complaint.

THE JANJOAH TRIBE.

The most ancient tribes inhabiting the Panjab at the present day are of Rajput origin. It seems probable, and both history and the traditions of the country favour the supposition, that there have been in the Panjab three great Rajput immigrations. The first took place antecedent to all historic records, not later than 2,500 years before Christ, and the Princes of Katoch and Chamba and of the Jalandhar hills, whose ancestors ruled over the Bari and Rechna Doabs, are its living representatives. The second immigration was at least a thousand years later when Ujamida, the son of the founder of Hastinapur, led his Yadu Rajputs to the north of the Jhelam, and founded a dynasty which ruled the country from Rawalpindi to Multan. Lastly came the emigrations from the Deccan, extending over a long series of years, from the tenth to the fifteenth century of the Christian era, when Rajputs of many and various races came to the Panjab, the descendants of whom are the Jats, Tiwanas, Sials, Ghebas, Kokhars and many other well known tribes.

It is difficult to say with any approach to certainty how long the Janjoahs have been resident in the Panjab, but they are probably the descendants of the Yadu Rajputs, the companions of Ujamida. That this tribe has been identified with the Johyas and Jodhis of Rajputana history only increases the difficulties regarding it. It is true that the Salt Range, to the north of the river Jhelam, is recognized as the original settlement of Yadu Rajputs, and to this day retains its ancient name of the 'hills of Jodh.' But the Johyas of Bikanir, who, though now extinct, were numerous three hundred years ago about Bhuropal, seem to have had little in common with the Janjoahs of the Jhelam. As early as 740 A. D. the Johiyas and Jodhis are mentioned, with Kokhars, Dodis and Syads, as allies of Hussain Shah chief of the Langa Pathsan in his war with the Bhatti Rajputs. But the traditions of the Janjoahs themselves do not point to a very ancient occupancy of the Panjab. They all trace their descent from a Raja Mal, a descendant of the Pandus and of the Rahtore Rajput race, who, about the year 980 A. D., emigrated to the Panjab from Jodhpur or Kanouj, which latter country was then ruled by a Rahtore prince. Hearing that the Pandus had once taken shelter in the hills to the north of the Jhelam, he journeyed there with his followers and founded the village of Rajghar, now famous under the name of Mulot. There he ruled in peace till the invasion of India by Mahmud of Ghazi, when that monarch summoned him to his presence. Raja Mal refused to attend; so Mahmud sent a force against him, which defeated and took him prisoner, and to save his life and regain his liberty he was compelled to renounce his Hindu faith and adopt Islamism. The name of the tribe is said to have arisen from this conversion, when the 'janju' or thread worn by Raja Mal and all Hindus, and denoting his caste, was broken. The Janjoahs are unanimous in thus placing the advent of their great ancestor into the Panjab in the tenth century, which is the more remarkable as it is certainly erroneous. Their genealogies also confirm their story. The longest are those of the families of Natel, which gives 23 generations from Raja Mal; of Chuhar Saidan Shah and Baghanwala, which allow 22 and 21 respectively. There are families, as the Mulot and Dilwal, whose genealogical trees take only 17 and 18 generations to arrive at the same ancestor. Allowing 30 years for a generation, which is too liberal an average, the longest of these genealogies does not extend over more than seven hundred years. Raja Mal * is said to have built a temple and tank at Mulot, and also at Kutas which is a sacred place of pilgrimage, and is visited every year by many thousand Hindus.

* If Raja Mal built the temples of Mulot and Kutas, he must have lived at a very much earlier period than Janjoah history allows him, for both are very ancient, and were built long before the Muhammadan invasions of India. Kutas has always been a sacred spot, and is mentioned in the Mahabharat (300 B. C.) as the eye of the world. In a cave at Kutas is still shown a portion of the cow which supports the world.

He left five sons, Wir, Jodh, Kehla, Tarloni and Khakka. The descendants of Kehla are now to be found in the Kahar and Kahuta Ilakas of the Rawalpindi district, those of Tarloni live in Amb and the neighbourhood of Attock, while Khakka's offspring inhabit Muzaffarabad, Kot Khakka and other villages near the Jammu frontier.

But Jodh and Wir are the only sons of Raja Mal who require any special notice. On the death of their father they determined to divide the country called from Raja Mal, the Muloki Dhan * between them. Jodh took the salt mines about Makrach, and captured the town of Makshala from a colony of Brahmans who had settled there. He changed its name to Makhiala, and built there a fort and two tanks for rain water, on which the inhabitants still entirely depend as there is no spring of drinking water near the town. Wir Khan took possession of Khewra, near Pind Dadan Khan. He had one son, Raja Ahmad Khan, from whom have descended the families of Mulot, Badshapur and Dilwal. Jodh was the father of four sons, Rahpal, Sanspal, Jaspal and Jaipal. From the first of these have descended the families of Baghanwala, Kot Umr, Pindi Kokhar, Wagah, Chakri, Pir Chak, Nathial, Faridpur, Sherpur, Syadpur and Natel. Sanspal was the ancestor of the houses of Chuhar-Saidan-Shah, Dih-Chuhar, Kotli-Saidan, Katora, Salori, Kals, Chumi, Makdum-Sahan, Wali, Lahar, Dahali, Dariala and Khawala. The descendants of Jaspal are few and reside at Kulwala, while the lumberdars of Dhandot and Warand are of the family of Jaipal. Rahpal, the eldest son of Jodh, ruled at Mulot, and his son Naru built Nara on the Boonhan nalla; while his grandsons, Hast Khan and Tatar Khan founded Garjakh, which became a large and flourishing town, though now ruined and desolate. The Janjoahs soon became split up into many clans, divided among themselves and thus unable successively to oppose tribes in no way superior to them in courage or military skill. They joined Timur Shah when he invaded India, in 1398, and fought under him throughout

* The Dhanni country, so famous for its swift and enduring breed of horses, which is now almost extinct.

his campaign. In 1526, they readily submitted to Babar Shah, who has given a somewhat detailed account of the tribe in his memoirs. He mentions that its two divisions were then known by the names of Jodh and Janjoah, agreeing with the Jodhis and Johyas of Rajputana history, though at the present day both have the common name of Janjoah. The Ghakkars were the great enemies of the tribe and drove them out of many of their villages; the Awans also pressed them hard, and the Sikhs, last and worst of all, completed their overthrow. There is now no man of wealth or importance belonging to this ancient tribe.

The families of Kot-Sarang and Darapur may, among many of noble blood, be considered the first. Raja Sarang, the founder of the first named family, held fifty villages, and was a chief celebrated for his valour. He was killed in a fight with the Afghans near Makhad. Fatah Khan, sixth in descent from Sarang, was also a distinguished chief, and in his time the village was called Fatah Kot. The Awans dispossessed the family, though Dhanna Singh Malwai allowed them some small proprietary rights. Raja Muhammad Khan and Samand Khan, the latter of whom is lumberdar of Kot Sarang, are the present representatives of the family.

Rai Khair Mehdi Khan is the present Darapur chief. The town of Darapur was founded by his ancestor Malik Darwesh, a fighting chief who avenged many of the injuries his tribe had received from the Ghakkars. His great grandson, Shabt Khan, fought under Sirdar Mahan Singh Sukarchakia, and was left unmolested in his chiefship, but his son Ghulam Mohiuddin Khan was less fortunate, and was assassinated by Sirdar Attar Singh Dhari, who took possession of all his villages. His sons Haibat Khan and Ali Haidar Khan fled to Malikpur, a strong fort on the river, where they held out for some years, living by plunder. At last, to the joy of the brothers, Attar Singh Dhari was blown up in a mine at the siege of Multan in 1810, and they imagined that they might regain their rights. But Kour Singh, uncle of the deceased Sirdar, held Darapur against them, and so, through all the Sikh rule, the family became poorer and weaker year by year. Many were the changes in Kardars and Jagirdars; Sirdar Rattan Singh Garjakh, Khushi Mal, Soba Ram, Raja Gulab Singh, Raja Lal Singh, Misr Ram Chand, Misr Rup Lal, all came and went, but no one of them reinstated the Janjoah chiefs. Khair Mehdi Khan is in a far better position now than he was previous to annexation, and holds several of his twenty-six villages in jagir, Darapur, Chak Mouja, Malikpur, Miran and Shahghar, and he has also, in recognition of his proprietary rights, obtained a decree empowering him to levy one pice on every rupee paid as revenue by the villages which, in old days, belonged to his family.

SIKH SHRINES.

In the Panjab are numerous Shrines consecrated to the memory of the Sikh Gurus. These are known by the name of Gurdhwara, Darbar Sahib or Derah, and generally have been built at places associated in some way with the Guru, and commemorating some incident in his life. At all these shrines the several Granths or Sikh Scriptures are daily read aloud by the priests, or Granthis, and many of them support a large number of attendants, musicians and worshippers. Some of the shrines are of great beauty, like those of Katarpur, Nankana, Mokutsar and Amritsar, and have been richly endowed by the piety of various Sikh Chiefs. In the following list no mention has been made of the institutions, monasteries and Akharas of the Udasi Sadhs, Sodhis, Bedis or other Sikh sects, many of which possess great wealth and large estates.

NANAK THE FIRST GURU.

1. Nankanah is situated in the Sharakpur parganna of the Lahore district. In this village, formerly known as Talwandi Rai Bhullar, Nanak was born in 1469. A small gurdhwara was first built at Nankanah by Baba Dharam Chand Bedi. Sirdar Tej Singh, in 1832, built a fine masonry temple, and a short time later Ram Chand of Akalghar built the tank. There are four principal shrines in the neighbourhood of Nankanah, all richly endowed—I. The Nankanah Sahib; II. Bal Kurira Sahib, eight miles from Nankanah, where the Guru played when a child; III. Malastan, from the 'Mal' or 'Jal' tree under which the Guru slept; IV. Kiara Sahib, where in his youth the Guru tended cattle. Three times a year a gathering of votaries takes place; at the Baisakhi, the Nirjalla Ikadshi and the Guru Parb Dasmi, and at these festivals many thousand Sikhs and Hindus visit the shrines.

2. Nankanah Khurd in the Gujranwala district. The temple at this place was built to commemorate the following act of the Guru. When still a youth, his father Kalu gave him some money to invest in what might appear to him a profitable speculation. At this spot he gave the whole away in charity to fakirs, thinking that way of spending the money the best investment (sachha souda). The Mohant or head of the establishment is Prem Das.

3. Darbar Baoli Sahib, near Sialkot. Baba Nanak resided for some time in the suburbs of Sialkot, and on the spot where he used to sit Bhai Moti or Mula, a Khatri of Mianah, erected a Baoli or covered well. It was endowed by Maharaja Ranjit Singh, Joala Singh Padhania and Jamadar Khushhal Singh. The present Mohant is Dya Ram.

4. Ber Baba Nanak, at Sialkot, one mile and a half from the last named shrine. This takes its name from the 'Ber' tree, beneath which the Guru sat during his interview with the Muhammadan Saint Hamza Ghous. The Darbar Sahib was built by Natha Singh Shahid at a great cost, and no fewer than 53 grants of land were made in its favour. Here too is the tomb of Natha Singh, known as the Shahid Bungah.

5. Darbar Rori Sahib, near Imanabad in the Gujranwala district. Here the Guru for long remained in meditation, seated on the hard 'kankar' or 'rori.' Sewa Ram, a Khatri of Kabul, first built the shrine, which was improved by the Emperor Muhammad Shah, and his Lahore governor, Khan Buhadar Khan. The tanks and some of the houses connected with the shrine were built by Diwans Lakhpat Rai and Jaspat Rai; and Charrat Singh and Mahan Singh, the grandfather and father of Maharaja Ranjit Singh, endowed it richly.

6. Ker Baba Nanak, near Phalia in the Gujrat district. Here the Guru resided for some days. The sandy ground around his derah was full of rat holes, and from this circumstance has the name of the gurdhwara arisen, 'chûî ker' signifying a rat hole in the Panjabi dialect. It was not till the time of Maharaja Ranjit Singh that the present

buildings were erected, though some of its jagirs were granted upwards of 70 years age.

7. Panjah Sahib, at Hassan Abdal between Rawalpindi and Attock. Here is shown the print of the Guru's hand (panjah) upon a rock which was thrown at him by a Kandhari saint, jealous of the Guru's miraculous power.

8. Sultanpur, in Kapurthalla, contains the shop which was opened for Nanak, when he was first started in trade. He, however, gave all his goods to the poor. The weights that he used are here preserved as sacred relics.

9. Derah Baba Nanak. At this town, in the Gurdaspur district, the Guru died. This shrine is annually visited by great numbers of pilgrims. It supports a large establishment of Udasi Sadhs, and possessed at one time jagirs worth 12,192 Rs. a year, granted by many Sikh Chiefs. The most generous endower was Prince Kharrak Singh.

10. Derah Tali Sahib. This is an institution of Udasi fakirs founded in honor of Baba Sri Chand, son of Baba Nanak, who used to live under a 'Tali' (shisham) tree, on the spot where the derah now stands. Sri Chand was the founder of the Udasi sect. His father Guru Nanuk intended that the Sikh religion should be a practical one, suited not only for priests, but for real, every day life. The Udasi sect is so far schismatic that it ignores this principle, and its members give themselves up to meditation and profess no interest in worldly affairs. Their practice is not very different from that of the ascetic followers of Shiva and Vishnu, known in the Panjab as Sanyasis and Bairagis. They wear long hair and reddish yellow clothes. They are forbidden to marry and only a 'chela' or disciple can succeed to the headship of the institution. Marriage is not, however, uncommon among the Udasis, and although some adhere to the letter of the law and do not marry, yet it is not to be supposed that their chastity is anything remarkable. They are very numerous in the Panjab, and are generally respected by the Sikhs. They are found all over Northern India, and at Benares some

of the Udasis Sadhs are good Sanscrit scholars and well read in the Vedanta philosophy, which is the basis of the doctrines of Nanak. In the Panjab very few Udasis understand Sanscrit, but they are all expounders of the Granth and teach the doctrines both of Nanak and of Govind Singh.

ANGAD THE SECOND GURU.

1. There is only one shrine sacred to Angad. This is situated at Khaddor Sahib. The Guru was a native of Harriki, but it was at Khaddor that he first met with Nanak: at this place he always lived and here he died.

AMAR DAS THE THIRD GURU.

1. Govindwal or 'Gondwal, on the river Beas, where the Guru died. There is here a splendid Baoli or covered well with 84 steps leading to the water, built by Amar Das himself.

RAM DAS THE FOURTH GURU.

1. Amritsar. Guru Ram Das was the founder of the Darbar Sahib at Amritsar now the national temple of the Sikhs. The name of Darbar Sahib is given to the original temple of Ram Das and the numerous buildings connected with it, erected at different times and by various hands.

I. The Darbar Sahib, strictly so called, is the temple situated in the centre of the sacred tank 'Amritsar' (the pool of immortality.) It is a beautiful building, enriched with gold and precious stones.

II. The Akal Bungah. This is opposite the chief entrance to the Darbar Sahib, and is the favourite place for the administration of the 'pahal,' the Sikh baptism. This Bungah is sacred to Har Govind the 6th Sikh Guru, and here are carefully preserved his sword and mace.

III. The Jhanda Bungah. This Bungah receives its name from two lofty gilt standards raised in honour of Ram Das. ('Jhanda,' a standard.)

IV. The Shahid Bungah. Founded in remembrance of Dhip Singh, a celebrated disciple of Guru Ram Das, who was killed fighting with the Muhammadans, and is for this reason known as 'shahid' or the martyr. Besides these, there are many other Bungahs built around the tank and known by the names of their founders. The Darbar Sahib under the Sikh empire was very wealthy and possessed large estates in all parts of the Panjab. It supported a very large establishment of Granthis (readers of the Granth,) pujaris, (worshippers, secular priests,) rubâbis (musicians) Akalis, Udasis and attendants. The temple is still wealthy. A grant of 4000 Rs. per annum is allowed for repairs, and there are numerous other grants in favour of individuals connected with it. The votive offerings 'Charat' may be estimated at upwards of 6000 Rs. a year. This is however fluctuating, and a Sikh Raja or chief of importance will sometimes present to the shrine an offering of many thousand rupees. The late Maharaja of Pattiala was a very liberal donor both of money and jewels. Sirdar Mangal Singh, head of the noble Ramgharia house, is President of the Committee of Management and Bhai Pardhoman Singh, son of the celebrated Bhai Gurmukh Singh, has charge of the repairs.

2. A shrine of Guru Ram Das stood at Govindwal, where he had seen and loved and eventually married Bhani, the beautiful daughter of Guru Amar Das, and where he died in 1581, but it has been destroyed by the encroachments of the river Beas.

3. A Gurdhwara at Lahore known as Janamasthan, the place of his birth.

ARJAN THE FIFTH GURU.

1. Amritsar. Here Arjan lived for some time and built the sacred tanks Koulsar, Ramsar, Santoksar and Babeksar.

2. Taran Taran. Here the Guru built a temple and tank now held as little inferior in sanctity to those of Amritsar. The Emperor Aurangzeb took the bricks which the Guru had collected, to build a serai, and it was not till the time of Maharaja Ranjit Singh that the tank, which is one of the finest in upper India, was completed.

3. Chohla is a village near Taran Taran, where the Guru lived for some time, and where he built a 'Derah'. His shoes and staff are preserved as relics at the shrine.

4. Lahore. Here Guru Arjan built a 'baoli' or covered well. It was destroyed by the Muhammadans, but Ranjit Singh rebuilt it and assigned a jagir for its support. This jagir has been since given to Sodhi Sadhu Singh.

5. Wahila. There is at this village, where Guru Arjan arranged the marriage of his son Har Govind, a Gurdhwara built by Bhai Salu.

6. Kartarpur, ten miles north west of Jalandhar. In 1588, the Guru came to this place where he desired to build a derah. But a demon, who inhabited the trunk of a tree, would not permit any wood to be cut for beams, until the Guru promised that he should not be disturbed, but receive worship for ever at the shrine.

HAR GOVIND THE SIXTH GURU.

1. Wadali, a village four miles from Amritsar, where the Guru was born on the 5th of July 1595. An annual festival is held here.

2. The Akalbungah at Amritsar. *Vide* ante Ram Das.

3. Chabal in the Amritsar district. In this village the Guru gave his daughter in marriage.

4. Loghar. This is now the name of a gate of the city of Amritsar, where the Guru, fighting with Mehdi Khan, in 1610, turned sand into gunpowder of which his men had fallen short.

5. Mozang. This shrine is between Lahore and Mian Mir and marks the spot where Arjan met Chajju Bhaggat the Hindu saint and the Muhammadan Pir of Mian Mir.

6. Gurusar Sailani. This gurdhwara is erected where the Guru bathed when journeying from Lahore to Amritsar.

7. Sri Hargovindpur is situated on the Beas in the Gurdaspur district. Here lived Chandu Shah, the persecutor of Guru Arjan, and on the death of his father Har Govind purchased the village and built there a gurdhwara.

8. Nanak Matra. There was a shrine sacred to Nanak in this village, which Har Govind purchased. At the time of the sale a dispute arose regarding the right to a barren tree on the boundary of the village. Har Govind, to prove his claim, laid his hand on the tree, which was immediately covered with leaves.

9. Kirtpur, where the Guru died, in 1645, is sacred.

10. There are also gurdhwaras to his memory, at Jabrapur, Jandiali, Gurusar, Hafizabad and Kangur.

HAR RAI THE SEVENTH GURU.

1. Kirtpur is sacred to Har Rai. Here he was born in 1629, and here he died in 1661. The tomb of his elder brother Gurditta, who died in 1639, is also at Kirtpur and is visited by pilgrims as a shrine.

2. Phulmihraj, on the boundary of the three States of Pattiala, Nabha, and Jheend, has a gurdhwara to the memory of Guru Har Rai.

HAR KISHAN THE EIGHTH GURU.

1. Kirtpur, where Harkishan was born in 1655.

2. Panjukahra, where there is a gurdhwara.

3. Dehli, where a shrine has been raised on the banks of the Jamna where the Guru's body was burnt.

TEGH BUHADAR THE NINTH GURU.

1. Amritsar, where Tegh Buhadar was born in 1631, has a gurdhwara to his memory.

2. Walla Sahib, a village near Amritsar, where the Guru lived for some time.

3. Baba Bakala, the village where Tegh Buhadar was living when he was selected to succeed Har Kishan. There is a curious legend regarding his discovery as the chosen successor to the Guruship.

4. A gurdhwara at Anandpur, from which place he expelled a demon.

5. A gurdhwara at Hadiala, where he miraculously cured a great number of sick persons.

6. A famous shrine at Dehli, called the 'Shahidganj' where the Guru was beheaded by order of the Emperor Aurangzeb.

7. There are besides gurdhwaras at Muluwala, Sulisar, Dhamtal, Thanesar, Allahabad, Benares and Patna to the memory of Tegh Buhadar.

GOVIND SINGH THE TENTH GURU.

1. Patna has a shrine as being the birth-place of Guru Govind Singh. He was born on the 2nd January 1665.

2. At Naina Devi, twelve miles from Anandpur, there is a Gurdhwara attached to the famous temple of the goddess Devi, who in this place appeared to Govind and consecrated his sword by her touch.

3. Kesghar is also near Anandpur. Here the Guru administered the 'pahal' to his first five disciples, making them Singhs, Sikhs of the sword.

4. Nadown in the Kangra hills has a shrine on the spot where the Guru rested and restored a barren tree to freshness.

5. Lahore is a now ruined village between Anandpur and Naina Devi, where lived a girl to whom the Guru wished to be betrothed. Her father had vowed to betroth her in Lahore, (the capital) and by a miracle the Guru caused the tiny village to be transformed, in the eyes of the father, into a splendid city and the betrothal was allowed.

6. Amb Sahib, near Anandpur, where a gurdhwara was erected beneath a mango tree planted on the spot to which the Guru had shot an arrow.

7. At Kot Kapura, in the Firozpur district, and at Manji Sahib, which places Govind visited in his travels, are gurdhwaras.

8. Sirhind has a 'Shahidganj' or martyr's memorial, being the place, where Fatah Singh and Zowarar Singh, sons of the Guru, were buried alive by the Muhammadans. The very name of Sirhind is accursed ; and to this day no Sikhs and few Hindus, returning from the Ganges, pass the town without taking a brick from the old ruins and casting it into the Satlej.

9. Chamkour, in the Hoshiarpur district, has a 'Shahidganj' in memory of Ajit Singh and Johar Singh, the two remaining sons of Govind, who were there killed in battle with the Muhammadans.

10. Wanni, where Govind wrote a letter to the emperor Aurangzeb.

11. Mokutsar, or more properly Muktsar, in the Firozpur district. Here, after the deaths of his sons at Chamkour, the Guru fought a second battle with the imperial troops. He was utterly defeated, but he promised 'mukt' or exemption for transmigration to all his followers who should fall in action. The town of Muktsar was afterwards built on the site of the battle. Hari Singh Nalwa commenced a magnificent tank here, which has been since completed by the Maharaja of Pattiala and other assistance. There are several shrines and sacred places of pilgrimage in the immediate neighbourhood of the town. 'Tibbi Sahib,' a hillock from which Govind watched the action and shot his arrows;

the 'Shahidganj' where the bodies of the slain were buried ; the 'Tambu Sahib,' where the followers of the Guru dried their clothes after the rain.

12. Talwandi. After the defeat of Mokutsar, Govind Singh fled to Talwandi in Pattiala, since known as Damdama, or the breathing place. Here he wrote a charm in Gurmukhi for a barren woman who afterwards bore seven sons. The village was blessed, and to this day the best writers of Gurmukhi are found in Damdama.

13. A Gurdhwara has been built to the memory of the Guru at Bhatinda in Pattiala, where he expelled a demon.

14. At Hiraghat, on the Godavery in the Deccan, is a Gurdhwara, marking the spot where Govind dropped his signet into the river.

15. Abchalanagar. ('Ab, chala-am,' now I am departing) in the Deccan. Here the Guru was killed by his Pathan servant, who thought it a duty to avenge his father whom the Guru had accidentally shot while hunting. This is a sacred place of pilgrimage.

16. There are also Gurdhwaras in honor of Govind Singh at Jaipur, Narayanghar, Agra, Jandpur, Kapal Mochan and Machiwara.

INDEX I.

LAHORE AND AMRITSAR.

MULTAN.

RAWALPINDI.

INDEX II.

A.

K.

N.